MW00462214

NAZARETHGATE

To Alan and Marianne Zundel, with warm regards — R-J-SK

NAZARETHGATE

QUACK ARCHEOLOGY, HOLY HOAXES, AND THE INVENTED TOWN OF JESUS

René J. Salm

Edited and with a Foreword by Frank R. Zindler

2015
AMERICAN ATHEIST PRESS
Cranford, New Jersey

ISBN-10: 1-57884-038-4 (Paperback)
ISBN-13: 978-1-57884-038-0 (Paperback)
ISBN-10: 1-57884-040-6 (E-Book)
ISBN-13: 978-1-57884-040-3 (E-Book)

American Atheist Press
P. O. Box 5733
Parsippany, NJ 07054-6733
www.atheists.org

Copyright © 2015 by René J. Salm
All rights reserved. No part of this publication may be reproduced or transmitted in any form or by any means, electronic or mechanical, including photocopying, recording, or by any information storage or retrieval system, without permission in writing from the publisher.

Earlier versions of chapters 2, 3, 5, and 7 appeared originally in the journal *American Atheist* and are used with permission. Chapter 4 appeared originally in the *Bulletin of the Anglo-Israel Archaeological Society* vol. 26 (2008) and is used with permission. Chapter 9 appeared originally in the book *Bart Ehrman and the Quest of the Historical Jesus of Nazareth* (American Atheist Press, 2013) and is used with permission.

The beautiful cover photograph of the Roman Catholic Church of the Annunciation at dusk was taken by Evgeny Oserov and is used with permission.

Published October, 2015
in the United States of America

Library of Congress Cataloging-in-Publication Data

Salm, René J., 1952-
Nazarethgate : quack archeology, holy hoaxes, and the invented town of Jesus / René J. Salm ; with a foreword by Frank R. Zindler.
    pages cm
ISBN 978-1-57884-038-0 (pbk. : alk. paper) -- ISBN 1-57886-038-4 (pbk. : alk. paper) -- ISBN 978-1-57884-040-3 (e-book) -- ISBN 1-57884-040-6 (e-book)
1. Nazareth (Israel)--History. 2. Excavations (Archaeology)--Israel--Galilee. 3. Galilee (Israel)--Antiquities. 4. Jesus Christ--Historicity. 5. Christianity--Controversial literature. I. Title. II. Title: Nazareth gate.
DS110.N3S355 2015
933'.45--dc23

2015015246

Dedicated to

Frank Zindler,
indefatigable polymath
and generous colleague

and to

my dear mother
Marguerite ("Peggy") Salm—
that gracious yet tough,
elegant yet no-fuss woman from Maine
who taught me that gratefulness
overcomes adversity.

CONTENTS

List of Figures   XIV
Acknowledgments   XVII

Foreword by Frank Zindler   XVIII

1. INTRODUCTION (May 2006)   1
   Prelude: *The wild west of CrossTalk* 1
   The new Jesus mythicism 8
   Some implications 12
   Hitting the books 14
   Publication of The Myth of Nazareth 19
   Outward ripples and deeper currents 23
   NazarethGate *and the disintegrating consensus* 25

2. WHY THE TRUTH ABOUT NAZARETH IS IMPORTANT   30
   (*American Atheist* magazine, Nov.–Dec. 2006)
   The Bronze-Iron Age settlement 33
   The Catholic position 34
   The Hellenistic period 36
   The Roman period 39
   The tomb in Mary's bedroom 42

3. THE MYTH OF NAZARETH—DOES IT REALLY MATTER?   44
   (*American Atheist* magazine, March 2007)

4. A RESPONSE TO "SURVEYS AND EXCAVATIONS AT THE
   NAZARETH VILLAGE FARM (1997–2002): FINAL REPORT'" 48
   (*Bulletin of the Anglo-Israel Archaeological Society*, December 2008)
   Two surveys 51
   The NVF pottery 52
   Problems of double-attribution 53
   Non-Roman evidence 54
   Non-diagnostic artifacts 56
   Diagnostic artifacts 57
   Conclusions 57
   Postscript 58

5. NAZARETH, FAITH, AND THE DARK OPTION   62
   (*American Atheist* magazine, January 2009)

   A clever proposal? 64
   A Dark option 66
   Fact versus Faith 67
   Editor's Note 69

6. A CRITIQUE OF KEN DARK'S WRITINGS RELATIVE
   TO THE SISTERS OF NAZARETH CONVENT   71
   (December 2009)

   Dark's arguments 73
   Dr. Ken R. Dark 77
   Dark's Nazareth publications 79
The pottery and movable evidence 80
The date of the kokh tombs 84
   The terminus ante quem 84
   The terminus post quem 88
   Tomb typology 90
   "Rolling stones" 92
   Misrepresentation of sources 94
Phase 1–Phase 2 problems 97
   Archeology by vegetable matter 101
   Funereal and agricultural use 102
Was the above ground structure a dwelling? 107
   Not a model courtyard house 107
       The "Chambre Obscure"
       Wall 1
       Wall 2
       The southern wall
       The "courtyard"
       Discussion
The agricultural use of the structural remains 112
   No roof or upper storey 112
   The cistern 113
   The third option 114
   Conclusion 116
Postscript 118

7. CHRISTIANITY AT THE CROSSROADS—
   NAZARETH IN THE CROSSHAIRS   121
   (*American Atheist* magazine, July–August 2010)

   A Christmas announcement 122
   Alexandre's ragtime band 124
   A house from the time of Jesus? 126
   A time of change and challenge 128

8. THE ARCHEOLOGY OF NAZARETH:
   AN EXAMPLE OF PIOUS FRAUD?   130
   (*Society of Biblical Literature* convention, Chicago, November 2012)

   I. A survey of the most significant material finds 131
      From the Bronze Age to Roman times 131
      Nazareth could not have existed on the hill 135
   II. Nazareth archeology and "pious fraud" 137
      Lack of rigour in archeological training 137
      Hearsay replaces evidence 138
      The monopoly exercised by the Catholic Church 140
         Error
         Internal contradiction
         Outright fraud
   Conclusion 142

9. ARCHEOLOGY, BART EHRMAN,
   AND THE NAZARETH OF "JESUS"   144
   (*Bart Ehrman and the Quest of the Historical Jesus of Nazareth*, April 2013)

   I. DJE? and the new skepticism 144
   II. What's in a name? 150
      A little 'Jesus' skit 151
   III. The Nazareth controversy 154
      The lack of turn-of-the-era evidence 155
      The "house from the time of Jesus" 158
      Hellenistic coins? 160
      Shama's Roman bathhouse 166
      The oil lamps and tombs at Nazareth 168
      The burden of proof 169
   IV. The location of the ancient village 173

10. THE "HOUSE FROM THE TIME OF JESUS"   178
     A nexus of anomalies 183
     No professional report 185
     The short IAA report 188
     The timeline 191
   THE MATERIAL EVIDENCE 192
          The 2009 "house" plan
          The nonexistent 'wall' (L)
          Other house "walls"
          Changes made to the site
          The slope
   The winemaking installation....................... 207
          Area 1: a wine collecting vat
          Channel (k)
          Area 4: a grape treading floor
          Locus (j): a wine storage cellar
   The unauthorized excavation 217
          The 'large house' of the 2012 plan
          "Room 3" and the triple silo
   The "courtyard" 223
          Not a 'refuge pit'
          Area 6 and its features
   Pottery and dating 234
          Conclusion 237
   The IMC and the Church 238
          O. Bonnassies and the "New Evangelization" 238
          Christian-Jewish collaboration 242

11. QUACKERY AT MARY'S WELL   245
     The background 245
     The Salm-Alexandre correspondence 248
     The 2006 Mary's Well report 257
          Appearance and reaction
          "Hellenistic" in the 2006 report
     Jesus' bathhouse and the 'larger' Nazareth 260
   THE MATERIAL EVIDENCE 264
          Layout and chronology of the excavations
          The 2006 report and "Hellenistic" evidence
   The "Hellenistic" Pottery 266
          The late appearance of Hellenistic evidence 270
             "Hellenistic" pottery itemization
             from the Fountain Square area
          Hellenistic' pottery from the Church Square area 277
             "Hellenistic" pottery itemization
             from the Church Square area
          Summary of the pottery results 280

The "Hellenistic" Coins from Mary's Well 284
    The strange documentary trail 284
        (A) Alexandre's 2006 personal communication
        (B) The 2006 Mary's Well report
        (C) The Myth of Nazareth (2007–08)
        (D) The Nazareth Village Farm report (2007)
        (E) The BAIAS responses (2008)
        (F) The First International Conference, Nazareth (2010/12)
        (G) Bart Ehrman's Did Jesus Exist? (2012)
        (H) Alexandre's Mary's Well, Nazareth (2012)
The Berman coin chapter 295
    The coin catalog 296
    The "Hasmonean" coins 302
    The "Early Roman" coins 306
    Coin summary 307
The Water Channels at Mary's Well.................................... 308
    The Roman incipience of the water channels 310
    Conclusion. 313

12. THE FORGERY OF THE "CAESAREA INSCRIPTION"   314
    The CER 314
    The twenty-four priestly courses 316
    The SRA and FEA 318
    The professor and the kibbutznik 322
    Chaos in the field 323
    The push to find a synagogue 324
    Enter Jerry Vardaman 326
    The lost fragment of the priestly courses inscription . .327
    Vardaman and the Talmon fragment 332
    Vardaman and the 1962 excavation funding 334
    Chronology of the excavation 336
    The "chancel screen" fragment 339
The discovery of the "Nazareth" fragment 342
    The find 342
    The problems 345
The forgery of the "Nazareth" fragment 353
    No synagogue 353
    No "Caesarea Inscription". 359
The last week 360
    The "mem" fragment 360
    Reappearance of the "chancel screen" 368
    The choice 370
    Conclusion 371
Bibliography to Chapter 12 375

13. THE TOMBS UNDER THE HOUSE OF MARY   377

The enigma of the Nazareth tombs 377
The Greek Bishop's Residence 381
The tombs under the Church of the Annunciation . . . 386
Dark revisited 391
    Water, water everywhere
    The 'larger Nazareth' question
    The Synagogue Church site
Nazareth between two books 399

14. IN SEARCH OF THE REJECTED SEER   402

Controlling the story 402
An early gnostic prophet 406
Jesus of Nazareth was unknown to "Paul" 408
A human being 412
    The Epistle to the Hebrews
    The other New Testament epistles
Docetism 417
Clues to a lost teacher 419
Yeshu in Jewish writings 419
James the Just 428
A chronology corrected 434
    James and the beginning of the Jewish War
    Paul and "the brother of the Lord"
    Similar passion accounts
The invention of the Christian Jesus 444
Simon Magus 446
John the Baptist 448
John Mark 451
Dositheus 453
Qumran 461
    Two theologies
    Two hymns
    A revolt in the community
Bibliography to Chapter 14 476

COMPREHENSIVE NAZARETH BIBLIOGRAPHY 480
INDEX 500
INDEX OF ANCIENT PASSAGES 516

FIGURES

Figure		Page
1.1	Palestine and its principal trade routes	5
1.2	The Nazareth Range	11
1.3	Older view of Nazareth on the Nebi Sa'in hillside	16
1.4	Topography of the Nazareth basin	21
2.1	The Nazareth basin with Bronze and Iron Age loci	32
2.2	Typical Palestinian oil lamps.	35
2.3	Middle to Late Roman oil lamps found in a Nazareth tomb.	37
2.4	The earliest Nazareth oil lamps	40
2.5	Depiction of the Annunciation	42
4.1	[Non-Figure] A scene from the Nazareth Village Farm	50
5.1	The fifteen-acre Nazareth Village Farm during construction	64
5.2	Dr. Ken R. Dark	66
Table 1	Dark's publications relating to the Sisters of Nazareth Convent	79
6.1	Chronology of kokh tomb use in Palestine	86
6.2	The entrance to Tomb 1	93
6.3	The southern half of the Sisters of Nazareth Convent site	98
6.4	Tomb 1 under the Sisters of Nazareth Convent	100
6.5	General plan of the Sisters of Nazareth site	103
6.6	Dark's reconstruction of the alleged "courtyard house"	106
6.7	The rock cut Wall 1.	107
8.1	Chronology of the Bronze and Iron Age artifacts from Nazareth	132
8.2	A typical kokh tomb	133
8.3	The topography of the Nazareth basin	134
8.4	Section under the Church of St. Joseph	135
8.5	Middle and Late Roman tombs of Nazareth	136
10.1	Photo of the IMC excavation in early December, 2009	193
10.2	Comprehensive diagram of the IMC excavation in Dec. 2009	194
10.3	The 2009 plan of the 'house from the time of Jesus'	197
10.4	The northern portion of the IMC excavation	199
10.5	The eastern half of the IMC excavation site from the north	200
10.6	The eastern half of the IMC excavation from the SW	201
10.7	Another view of the excavation, from the South	205
10.8a	Photograph of Area 8	211
10.8b	Plan of Area 8	211
10.8c	Area 8 in section	211
10.9a	Reconstructed plan of cellar (j) with wine jars in situ	213
10.9b	Cellar (j) in section, with four wine jars depicted	213
10.10	The 2012 excavation plan as posted on the wall of the IMC	216

10.11   The 2012 excavation plan oriented north-south 217
10.12   The 2012 'house' plan superimposed on the physical remains 219
10.13   An artist's rendering of the 'house from the time of Jesus' 223
10.14a   Reconstructed plan of cellar (z) with wine jars *in situ*. 224
10.14b   Cellar (z) in section 224
10.15   Linear alignment of features in Area 6 229
10.16   A typical free-standing press bed 231
10.17   Two lever presses of antiquity 233

11.1   General plan of the Mary's Well excavations 247
11.2   Plan of the Church Square area with loci of Hellenistic pottery 269
11.3   Plan of the Fountain Square area with loci of Hellenistic pottery . . . 275
11.4   Diagrams of the alleged Hellenistic shards from Mary's Well 276
11.5   Plan of the Fountain Square area with loci of Hellenistic coins 301

Table 2. The alleged earliest 16 coins found at Mary's Well 303

11.6   The star symbol from the time of Janneus 306

12.1   Major features of ancient Caesarea 319
12.2   Areas within Field O excavated in 1956 and 1962 320
12.3   Photograph of "Fragment of a Table of Priestly Courses" 328
12.4   The reconstructed "Caesarea Inscription" with alleged fragments . . . 330
12.5   A notebook sketch of the "chancel screen" fragment from Area A . . . 341
12.6   The "Nazareth" fragment of the priestly courses inscription 343
12.7   Area D where the "Nazareth" fragment was found 344
12.8   Avi-Yonah's depiction of the "Caesarea Inscription" 354
12.9   Hebrew syntactical divisions of the "Caesarea Inscription" 355
12.10   The "*mem*" fragment of the "Caesarea Inscription" 363
12.11   Possibly the authentic state of the "*mem*" fragment 363
12.12   The three fragments of the alleged "Caesarea Inscription" 365

13.1   Roman-era tombs and agricultural installations under the CA 387

PLATES

Pl. 1   The "expanded" Venerated Area.
Pl. 2   Area 4 of the IMC site viewed from the northwest.
Pl. 3   The souvenir gift shop "Cactus" near Mary's Well.
Pl. 4   Computer printout of the short IAA report on the IMC excavation.
Pl. 5   Mislabeled coins From Mary's Well.
Pl. 6   Coin number eleven from Mary's Well.
Pl. 7   The large cave under the Greek Bishop's Residence.
Pl. 8.   Church of the Annunciation with associated buildings.

ACKNOWLEDGMENTS

My investigative skills were honed in researching *The Myth of Nazareth* (2008), and this book represents the advanced results of several further years' research into the sensitive heart of a much-guarded and very powerful religion. The generous—and sometimes unbidden—efforts of a number of people on three continents have been of critical value in this often difficult enterprise. Evgeny Oserov acted as my Man Friday in Israel, visiting sites, taking photos, interacting with the Israel Antiquities Authority, and knowing exactly whom to talk to and how to retrieve closely-held information. Chapters 10 and 12 particularly owe their results to his initiatives. Last but not least, Evgeny also contributed the beautiful cover photo.

Thanks go to Enrico Tuccinardi in Italy for first bringing to my attention problems associated with the so-called "Caesarea inscription," and then for his help in conclusively demonstrating that the inscription is a 1962 forgery (Chapter 12).

To Professor Heather Sweetser I owe thanks for photocopying (unrequested and practically before I could blink) the entire 1924 Arabic book by Assad Mansur, for translating numerous pages, and for ferreting out Mansur's sensitive information on one-time kokh tombs in and around the Venerated Area of Nazareth (Chapter 13).

This book would have been impossible without the constant reliable assistance of the professional staff at the University of Oregon library. It treated me like faculty and left no stone unturned in procuring hundreds of books and articles from several continents. In particular, the Religious Studies librarian Dr. Paul Frantz was never too busy to field my sometimes complex requests for arcane material, while Katy at the Interlibrary Loan Desk unfailingly ensured that those requests met with a successful outcome.

Dr. Robert Kool of the Israel Antiquities Authority was good enough to photograph at my request a number of coins recovered from Mary's Well, while Yael Barschak, Director of the IAA Photographic Archives, graciously made available a number of photographs for inclusion in this book. Other Israeli photographers who graciously helped in this endeavor are Gil Cohen-Magen and Assaf Peretz.

Last but not least, my thanks go to Frank Zindler, the dedicatee of this book. Frank has not only acted as capable publisher and editor, but has also lovingly shepherded this project along step by step from title to index, besides agreeing to write the Foreword and acting as patient colleague, friend, and the best possible resource of sane advice when that precious commodity was in short supply. Despite all of Frank's interventions, however, the errors remaining in this book are solely my own.   —René Salm

FOREWORD

*There is nothing more difficult to carry out, nor more doubt-
ful of success, nor more dangerous to handle, than to initiate a new
order of things. For the reformer has enemies in all those who profit
by the old order.*

— Niccolò Macchiavelli (1469–1527)

The future of a multibillion-dollar industry is teetering in the
balance—a balance so delicate that it is hoped by industry strategists that a
few broken shards, several ancient coins, and a bit of imaginative "archeology" can stabilize and secure it and deliver the enterprise from ruin. At its
foundational level of operation, that industry is the Israeli tourism business.
At the pinnacle from which this world-wide economic adventure is controlled, we find the Pope of Rome, the Orthodox Patriarchs, TV evangelists, and various other magnates who profit from a literalist understanding
of the Christian New Testament. If the weight of a few ancient (or not-so-
ancient!) coins, shards, and paper reconstructions of masonry walls is not
great enough to counterbalance the weight of the evidence presented in
this book, corporate headquarters for the religion trade all over the world
will collapse into ruin. Projected into the not-too-distant future, the cost to
supernaturalism could mount into the trillions of dollars.

The main purpose of the present book—René Salm's sequel to his
2008 *The Myth of Nazareth: The Invented Town of Jesus*—is to update his evidence showing, not only that there is no evidence to prove the existence of
an inhabited town called Nazareth at the turn of the era, there is actually
good evidence of its absence! That being the case, it seems useful briefly
to outline the evidence apart from archeology that tells against a historical
Nazareth at the turn of the era.

1. It is well to begin by noting that even many apologists and scholars who
argue in favor of present-day Nazareth having been inhabited since before
the turn of the era agree: it cannot be the site described in Luke 4:16–30, a
city (*polis*) built with a synagogue atop a hill with a cliff from which the congregation of the synagogue tried to cast Jesus down to his death. They pre-

fer to admit that "Luke" was incorrect in his description of the "city" (the New Testament scholar Bart Ehrman terms it "a one-dog town") rather than accept the fact that the present tourist Mecca was not inhabited when Jesus and the Holy Family should have been living in it.

2. Nazareth is unknown in the Old Testament, although the neighboring village of Japhia is mentioned [Josh. 19:12].

3. The two Talmuds, although mentioning 63 Galilean towns, know nothing of a place called Nazareth.

4. Josephus, although he waged war within two miles of present-day Nazareth and fortified the nearby town of Japhia, does not list Nazareth among the 45 cities and towns of Galilee in his experience.

5. No geographer/historian before the fourth century mentions Nazareth.

6. There is no *isnad*-like chain of attestation to support the Nazareth identity of the modern city. There are at least several centuries separating the gospel habitation from the first verifiable and datable attestations of its location at the present site. (With the exception of Jerusalem, Jericho, Tiberias, and several other places, this is true also for nearly all the gospel towns and places.)

7. Origen (*c.* 184–*c.* 254), although he lived at Caesarea, just thirty miles from Nazareth, did not know where it was located, even though he had made serious efforts to study the biblical sites: "We have visited the places to learn by inquiry of the footsteps of Jesus and of his disciples and of the prophets."

8. Origen could not decide if the place should be called *Nazareth* or *Nazara*, and the MSS of Luke show a stunning uncertainty as to the exact spelling of the name. Should we prefer *Nazara*, *Nazaret*, *Nazareth*, *Nazarat*, or *Nazared*—or possibly other variants found in other gospels and Church Fathers?

9. Scholars understandably disagree concerning the origin of the name Nazara/Nazaret/Nazareth. The hypothesis I favor (and here I do not claim to speak for René Salm) is the one advanced by the polymath William Benjamin Smith (1850–1934). Smith derived the name from the Hebrew *netser* [*nun-tsade-resh*], meaning "sprout, shoot," or "branch" as is found in Isaiah 11:1—"And there shall come forth a rod out of the stem of *Jesse*, and a *branch* shall grow out of his roots." This verse was popular at Qumran, and the connection with David's father Jesse resonates with Epiphanius' note that before Christians were called *Christianoi*, they were called *Iessaioi*—Jessaeans. (Interestingly, Jesus is called *Issa* in Arabic; this really equates to Jesse!)

According to this theory, *n-ts-r* (branch) would have become part of a title—"Jesus the Branch," in messianic reference to Isaiah 11:1. (The fact that the Hebrew word for Christian is *notsri* [*nun-vav-tsade-resh-yod*] is in perfect resonance with this verse.) When rendered into Greek, however, *n-ts-r* was not recognized as a title, but rather was thought to be a name. So, it was not *translated* into Greek, but rather *transliterated* with the addition of vowels. There was a problem, however, as Greek had no equivalent of the voiceless sibilant *tsade*. The closest sound in turn-of-the-era Greek was *zeta*. Pronounced *dzeta*, it was the voiced equivalent of *tsade*.

The common Greek epithets *nazoraios* or *nazarenos* (invariably mistranslated as *Nazareth* in the KJV) would easily be derived. Then, an expression such as *Iesus Nazoraios* would easily appear to be an epithet of the Jimmy-the-Greek sort. *Nazoraios* would be misunderstood as deriving from the name of a place (*Nazara*), just as *Parisian* can be derived from *Paris. Voilà!* We have invented an important town for the pilgrimage industry!

10. Nazareth is never mentioned in any of the epistles of the New Testament.

11. Nazareth is not mentioned in the Apocalypse, and is unknown to most of the apocryphal gospels and Gnostic works.

12. Nazareth is found only once in Mark (Mk. 1:9), the oldest of the canonical gospels. This seems clearly to be an interpolation, as the word *Iêsous* in that same verse is written without the definite article. In over 80 other places where it is grammatically possible for the word to take the definite article, Mark refers to "the Jesus"—as though the name were a title and should have its literal meaning, "the Savior." If one ignores the last twelve verses that were added some time in the fourth century, the Gospel of Mark has 666 verses. The probability that Mark's only mention of "Nazareth" would happen by accident to appear in the only verse in which "Jesus" occurs without a definite article is extremely low—about one in two hundred thousand.

13. If Mark's use of "Nazareth" in 1:9 were in fact original with whomever the author of that gospel may have been, it is extremely strange that he never uses the name again when describing events that later gospels say took place in Nazareth or use the name with relation to Jesus' origins! For example, in Matt. 4:12, right after the temptation, at the beginning of his ministry, we read: "Now when Jesus had heard that John was cast into prison, he departed into Galilee. 13 And leaving Nazara, he came and dwelt in Capernaum, which is upon the sea coast, in the borders of Zabulon and Nephthalim." But in Mark 1:14 we read merely, "Now after that John was put in prison, Jesus came into Galilee preaching the gospel of the kingdom

of God, 15 And saying, The time is fulfilled, and the kingdom of God is at hand: repent ye, and believe the gospel. 16 Now as he walked by the Sea of Galilee…" The author of Matthew's gospel clearly has added geographical details—not only Nazareth (*Nazara*), but Capernaum as well—to the text he took from Mark.

14. Nazareth is unknown in the Pauline epistles—generally thought to be the oldest parts of the New Testament—and appears as *Nazaret* in Mark 1:9, a provable interpolation (probably derived from Matt. 21:11). Absent from the oldest of the canonical gospels, Nazareth makes its first appearance (as *Nazara*) in Matt. 4:13 or (as *Nazareth*) in Matt. 21:11. The latest and only remaining Matthaean mention of the town (as *Nazaret*) is in Matt. 2:23—in the birth legend, the latest stratum in the compositional history of that gospel.

Nazaret makes two appearances in the late gospel of John (1:45, 46), but four out of the five appearances of the city's name (as *Nazareth*) in the very late gospel of Luke are found only in the very latest stratum of that gospel as well—in the nativity tale not found in Marcion's version of the gospel. Its only remaining appearance in Luke is in Luke 4:16—the verse that begins the story about the synagogue congregation trying to hurl Jesus off the Nazara cliff.

Tellingly, Acts of the Apostles records no apostolic activities occurring at Nazara/Nazaret/Nazareth. This is very strange if it actually was so important not only in the life of Jesus but of the lives of his disciples as well.

15. Eusebius (260/265–339/340 CE), like Origen, lived at Caesarea and had occasion to concern himself with Nazareth. Even so, he almost certainly never visited the site himself, even though he mentions it in his *Onomasticon*. When one reads the Greek text concerning Nazareth, it sort of makes sense—until one tries to map out Eusebius' directions onto a map of Roman-era Galilee. I claim it cannot be done. (It is just possible, however, that the present-day town received its name as a result of the work of Eusebius!)

16. Like many other holy places of the New Testament, Nazareth seems to have been "discovered" by Constantine's mother, with the aid of willing-to-please tour guides.

17. If Nazareth did not exist at the time in which the gospel stories are set, we must ask how and why it was invented. Although dating the various compositional strata of the New Testament books is hazardous and necessarily provisional, nevertheless it seems significant that the increase in gospel references to Nazara/Nazareth in later compositional strata appears to parallel the sequence of anti-Docetic interpolations in the gospels. In order

to thwart the Docetists, who claimed that Jesus only *seemed* (Greek *dokein*, 'to seem') to have a body and feel pain, it was necessary to invent Doubting Thomas and have Jesus eat fish. He had to have a human genealogy and at least a quasi-human birth. If he was "born of woman," he must have had a childhood. That would require a hometown, and would explain why most references to Nazareth relate to the nativity tales. Take *that*, Docetic swine!

18. Unlike other sites datable with certainty to the first centuries before and after the turn of the era, almost no coins datable to that period have ever been found before the several controversial claims examined in this volume. By contrast, *hundreds* to *thousands* of coins typically are recoverable from other sites independently established to have been inhabited at that time.

19. Similarly, the sparsity—indeed, nonexistence—of ceramic and architectural evidence found at the "venerated areas" of modern Nazareth resoundingly argue against its habitation at the turn of the era. But I stray into the territory René Salm has claimed for the substance of this book.

The research underlying this book is prodigious and, in my opinion, is a model to be followed when analyzing any of the various claims of "biblical archeology." It will be found that all but a very small part of such claims can be supported by the results of scientifically and impartially executed excavations. Probably none of the work pertaining to the Christian New Testament approaches the scientific quality of routine work in North American archeology. Worse yet, the preponderance of the "research" will be found to be nothing but apologetic exertions of the sort characteristic of "scientific creationists." This is actually a *necessary* fact. Truly scientific research in the arena of New Testament archeology would be lethal not only to the Israeli tourism industry, it would sound the knell for conservative Christianity itself.

—Frank R. Zindler, American Atheist Press

Chapter 1

INTRODUCTION

Prelude: The wild west of CrossTalk

Two years before publication of *The Myth of Nazareth: The Invented Town of Jesus* (American Atheist Press, March 2008), the view that Nazareth did not exist at the turn of the era had already been the subject of sporadic online discussion for a number of years. The view resurfaced regularly like a bad penny and was a convenient butt for ridicule, generally characterized as fringe lunacy and sometimes intentionally brought up when there was simply the desire for a good laugh. Regarding Nazareth, such was the attitude of mainstream New Testament scholarship at the beginning of this millennium.

June, 1998 witnessed the birth of an online forum called *CrossTalk* which—according to the welcome message—offered "anyone with an e-mail address the opportunity to discuss the JESUS 2000 e-mail debate that is taking place between Marcus Borg, John Dominic Crossan, and Luke Timothy Johnson. These three internationally acclaimed authors are discussing their views about the historical Jesus in a free electronic forum sponsored by Harper San Francisco."[1] Though dignified in intent, the forum quickly deteriorated into an irreverent and entirely unmoderated free-for-all involving about 120 participants, equally divided between scholars and laypeople. Anybody could join the discussions, anybody could say whatever he wanted (almost all the participants were male), and anybody could do so with impunity. While this represented far too much freedom for the predictably staid academics on the list, it was an unprecedented boon for impassioned laypeople to argue the most provocative (and, admittedly, sometimes outlandish) positions before scholars without the customary fear of ridicule.

---

1. As of this writing *CrossTalk* is still online at *https://groups.yahoo.com/neo/groups/cross-talk/info*.

For this reason *CrossTalk* was unique. By removing the advantages of prestige and reputation it leveled the playing field between academics and laypeople, allowing a fresh look at important issues which were traditionally off the table. A number of cutting-edge explorations took place on the list. These included an airing of Earl Doherty's mythicist position a full year before publication of *The Jesus Puzzle* (message 803). Doherty eventually defended himself ably on the list (beginning with message 5053). *CrossTalk* also witnessed the first detailed analysis of parallels between the Gospel of Thomas and the synoptics, considered whether Buddhism could have been a gnosticizing influence on Christianity, reconsidered the meaning of the word "Nazarene," and also discussed the non-existence of the town of Nazareth at the turn of the era—probably the most detailed exploration of this latter question in history.[2] I was not familiar at the time with Frank Zindler's prescient 1993 article "Where Jesus Never Walked," in which he argued that Nazareth and other Gospel towns were fictive places.[3]

I began reading *CrossTalk* soon after its creation and noted, among other topics, a swirl of confusing and half-formed opinions regarding the enigmatic but apparently related terms Nazarene and Nazorean on the one hand, and the place Nazareth on the other. The terms, of course, frequently occur in the New Testament in relation to the Jesus story, and they do so in a fundamental way: Jesus is a "Nazarene" or "Nazorean," he hails from "Nazareth," and his followers are called "Nazoreans" (Acts 24:5). To add to the confusion, the semitic traditions uniformly lack the voiced *z*-sound of the Greek cognates and have the (linguistically incompatible) unvoiced *tsade* (which I will render *ts*)—thus *Natsrath* (the town), *Notsri* (found in the Talmud), *Natsuraiia* (the Mandean name for those skilled in esoteric knowledge),[4] *Natsrani* (the modern Arabic name for "Christians"), *etc.*

Scholars have been scratching their heads for generations regarding the above enigmas but have produced, in my opinion, no overall nor convincing explanation. The *CrossTalk* messages were yet one more sign that after a century of discussion virtually no progress had been made in penetrating these mysteries which lie at the very heart of Christianity.

2. Parallels between the Gospel of Thomas and the synoptics: messages 3057, 3084, 3232, 3253, 3310. Whether Buddhism could have been a gnosticizing influence on Christianity: 3476, 3484, 3540, 3574. Reconsideration of the word "Nazarene": 3659, 3682, 3687, 3931. Non-existence of Nazareth: 5113, 5866, 6205, 6377, 6536, 6597 (most significant), *et multi.*
3. The article appeared in the Winter 1996-7 issue (Vol. 35, No. 1) of the hard-to-find journal *American Atheist.* This was the reprint of a lecture which Frank gave in April of 1993 at the American Atheists 30th Anniversary celebration in Sacramento, CA. See pp. 11–12.
4. Drower and Macuch, *A Mandaic Dictionary* 1963:285.

Great differences of opinion often reflect insufficient analysis of the primary data. To me, this seemed the key to progress. A clue to the way forward appeared in September, 1998, when the late Tom Simms (a very educated layperson on the *CrossTalk* list) asserted that there was only "tiny 'from the ground' evidence for a 1st c. Nazareth, that the place only took shape later..." (message 2455). A few days later he elaborated: "The evidence that I've seen (and right now can't pull out of thin air) gives some signs of occupation but not as it was later. From what I understand epigraphically there is no evidence for the identity Nazareth until into or past the 2nd Century. If I'm wrong, let me know, chapter and verse" (message 2530).

Some *CrossTalk* list members reacted. "I have long argued that the mention of Nazareth in Mark 1:9 was a gloss inserted once the Nazareth tradition had won out against Capernaum (village of Nahum or 'comfort'). It is not reflected in the parallel text in GMatt 3:13. Nazareth is not mentioned elsewhere in GMark, which sees Jesus's home town as Capernaum" (Ian Hutchesson, message 2579). "The gospel writers... were most interested in proving that Jesus' hometown was Nazareth, not Magdala. Because if Jesus was not from Nazareth, but from Magdala, why then was he called the Nazarene? That was too dangerous a question to entertain." (Jan Sammer, message 3306).

All this was entirely unexpected and at first I was shocked. The possibility that Nazareth did not exist at the turn of the era would powerfully change the discussion of Christian origins and would, in short, constitute a formidable assault on the historicity of "Jesus of Nazareth," if not of "Jesus" himself. The scholar Stevan Davies offered one theory to the *CrossTalk* list: "Jesus is a *netzer* or some darn thing and then this got translated into Nazarene which then presupposed some place called Nazareth and both Mt and Lk think there is such a place but there isn't until centuries later when, like Hometown USA in Disney World, somebody comes along and builds one for the tourists?" (message 3654). At the same time, Davies was able to broach vague mythicist ideas: "No Judeans born in Nazareth. Where does this leave Jesus the Jew (Jesus the Judean)? He's an early mythological creation..." (message 2533).

The Nazareth question was of far too great importance to casually ignore. So I determined to do a little research, enough to quickly dispose of the radical and most unlikely possibility that Nazareth did not yet exist at the turn of the era. For I was completely incredulous, convinced that scholarship could not be so wrong—and for so long!

I quickly learned, however, that investigating this question would take some time. Doubt regarding the historicity of Nazareth "at the time of Jesus" was not easy to find and quite old, buried in footnotes and tomes long out of date. Already in 1899, the editor of the once well-regarded *Encyclopedia Biblica*, T. K. Cheyne, wrote in his article "Nazareth": "It is very doubtful whether the beautiful mountain village of Nazareth was really the dwelling-place of Jesus." In that article Cheyne did not touch on the archeology of the place (for no such archeology yet existed) but discussed problems with the name and its cognates. His doubt regarding the historicity of Nazareth was not subsequently taken up by mainstream scholarship. But Cheyne was one of his generation's major figures in the field of biblical studies and his view—though very much a minority opinion—signaled that the question could not be answered by a cursory examination. It would require enough commitment to carry out an in-depth exploration. At the time, however, I had no idea that it would require an entire decade of work!

I first weighed in on the Nazareth issue on *CrossTalk* in November of 1998 and wondered why the town would have been invented. Sidestepping the archeological dimension, I asked a convoluted question: "If Jesus came from an 'invented' town, then why (and to whom) was it unacceptable that he come from wherever he really came from?" (message 3640). The question shows that I had no inkling Jesus may not have existed. Jesus mythicism was not yet even part of my intellectual universe. However, my researches into Nazareth altered that. They were largely responsible for my 'conversion' to mythicism in the early years of the new millennium.

Doubtless my most important contributions to *CrossTalk* were a score of investigative posts regarding Nazareth. I was not initially focussed on archeology but more concerned with general problems regarding "Nazareth" as word and place: it is not mentioned in Jewish scripture nor in the extensive writings of Josephus; Christian scripture has conflicting traditions regarding the provenance of Jesus (Bethlehem, Nazareth, Capernaum); and linguistic 'relatives' (*Nazirite, Nazorean, etc.*) had strong religious underpinnings (Jewish, Mandean), while *Nazarene* seemed to be used by the Markan evangelist not as a geographical referent but with theological intent ("the holy one of God," Mk 1:24). I was also aware that Paul is termed "a ringleader of the sect of the Nazoreans" (*Nazoraioi*) in Acts 24:5. Surely he was not the leader of inhabitants of Nazareth!

There were tantalizing links between the "Nazarenes" and other groups later denominated as "sects" or "heresies" by the Church (and, unfortunately, also by modern scholarship). In a post I ventured to identify the "Nasarenes" of Epiphanius (*Panarion*) with the Ebionites (message 3682), and noted that Epiphanius considered those Nasarenes to be "pre-Christian" (message 3687). It was becoming increasingly apparent to me that vital links existed just below the surface between the early Christian Nazarenes, the Ebionites, and the Mandeans—the latter considered by some

Figure 1.1. Palestine and its principal trade routes.

scholars (Lidzbarski, Bultmann) to be "pre-Christian" gnostic disciples of John the Baptist.

As I became more sensitized to the use of "Nazareth," "Nazarene," and their cognates in the New Testament, it became apparent that Luke in particular stresses Jesus' relationship to Nazareth (message 3857). The famous incident in the Nazareth synagogue described in Luke 4:16–30 was contrived largely to accomplish a subtle purpose: the replacement of Capernaum[5] with "Nazara" as the home of Jesus. Enduring traditions regarding the town (including that it was situated on a hill and possessed a steep precipice) also stem from that pericope.

I agreed with several CrossTalkers who noted that "Nazarene" does not linguistically derive from the semitic name of the town (*Natsrath*), despite the (now minority) opinion of some past authorities—including W.F. Albright. Increasingly, it appeared that "Nazareth" had nothing at all to do with "Nazarene."

This recognition was a major step forward. It now became clear that the link between "Nazareth" and "Nazarene" is artificial and apparently first effected by Matthew at the curious verse 2:23: "And he went and dwelt in a city called Nazaret, that what was spoken by the prophets might be fulfilled, 'He will be called a Nazorean.'" The lack of such a prophecy in Jewish scripture, coupled with the potential absence of any town of "Nazaret" at the turn of the era—these suggested to me that Matthew was engaged in nothing more than the writing of elaborate fiction.

In early 1999 I began to grapple with the archeology of Nazareth and submitted a series of exploratory posts to *CrossTalk* reviewing what is known regarding the material evidence for the settlement. Though expecting to encounter copious evidence of the town's existence at the turn of the era, in fact I encountered the opposite—no hard evidence at all of its Early Roman existence. Some evidence ("Hellenistic" oil lamps) was clearly misdated. Well known authorities had misrepresented and even mislabeled entire categories of evidence (*e.g.* "Herodian" tombs and "Herodian" oil lamps). Plentiful conclusions (both specific and general), when investigated, turned out to be either erroneous or completely without merit. Even the principal resource for the town's archeology—Father Belarmino Bagatti's 1969 tome, *Excavations in Nazareth*—revealed itself problematic in many of the above ways. Similarly, James Strange's influential article "Nazareth" in the *Anchor Bible Dictionary* (1992) was riddled with the above errors. I found all this astonishing and appalling, as if a few Christian scholars (both

---

5. In the Gospel of Mark, Capernaum appears to be Jesus' home (*cf.* Mk 6:1 *ff*). This becomes even more evident when "Nazareth" in Mk 1:9 (the only appearance of the town in the gospel) is recognized as a later interpolation.

Catholic and Protestant) shared a desire to produce the primary literature on the town in a certain way—that is, in a way calculated to defend the 'faith' and one in which the history of ancient Nazareth had hardly any factual 'history' at all. From then on my task was clear: the archeology of Nazareth needed to be re-evaluated and the history of the town rewritten from beginning to end.

By the Spring of 1999 I was confident that the scholarly literature presented no evidence of a settlement before *c.* 100 CE—unless one goes back to the Iron Age. There was evidently a hiatus in settlement between the late eighth century BCE and the early second century CE. This was the scenario, substantiated in prolix detail, which formed the backbone of *The Myth of Nazareth*, published almost a decade later.

My *CrossTalk* posts on Nazareth not only challenged the received tradition but also indicted it of moral turpitude. They were (predictably) met with vociferous opposition both from academics and from the more conservative lay people on the list. Typically, each new revelation of fact was treated as fiction, and each regression to tradition as fact. I was myself accused of grotesque invention and hence of moral turpitude. The message was unpalatable and the messenger attacked—my lack of formal training in archeology was repeatedly used as a pretext to discount the evidence. At the same time, former seminarians who studied Theology, General Bible History, or the New Testament were called "archeologists" if they could claim to have ever wielded a spade.

Thankfully, *CrossTalk* also contained a hardy mix of liberals and agnostics. Some supported my work while others were willing to take a wait-and-see attitude. Thus, I could not be shouted down. Quietly I presented damning evidence of one misdating after another—generally Late Roman evidence alleged to be Early Roman (or even Hellenistic). In a predictable and tiresome pattern, traditionalists would repeatedly cite a passage from Bagatti, Strange, or an encyclopedia article on Nazareth and metaphorically cry "Case closed!" I would then object that the oil lamps, pottery shards, or fragments of stone vessels in question actually dated to Middle or Late Roman times. This would be followed by the usual accusations of incompetence and dishonesty.[6] Finally, I would cite specialists in the applicable subfield—supported by exact parallels—whereupon the opposition would become curiously quiet.

It would be difficult to award a prize for the most egregious misrepresentation of Nazareth evidence. Perhaps Richmond's 1931 characterization of six later Roman oil lamps found in a Nazareth tomb as "Hellenistic"

---

6. One particularly belligerent *CrossTalk* scholar was responsible for the lion's share of opposition. See messages 5866, 6268, 6305, 6565, and 6587.

takes the cake (Salm 2008a:105 *f*).[7] On *CrossTalk* I was able to reveal other misdatings, including a Nazareth inscription claimed to be from the first century CE which actually dates between the fourth and sixth centuries of our era (message 6587).

In some ways, the forum revealed the best and the worst in participants. I was surprised to learn that collegiality was only skin deep and that academics could be just as snotty as the most uneducated country bumpkin. The difference was that academics were obsessively aloof in their snottiness—as if hanging onto a sheepskin will help when losing one's pants.

In all, *CrossTalk* was an equal opportunity shootout at the OK Corral, where skeptics, conservatives, atheists, and agnostics traded utterly frank opinions on the subject of Jesus of Nazareth. But Jesus is too important, too momentous, and too central to Western civilization not to enflame. Eventually, the forum suffered an ignominious death at the hands of what is, in the final analysis, an empty, enervating, and exalted conception: 'Jesus of Nazareth.'

The noise to signal ratio finally became intolerable. A proliferation of acrimonious and bizarre messages which (to put it charitably) were no longer "on topic" caused scholars to jump ship and signaled the imminent death of the forum. That demise was unworthy of the signal accomplishments of *CrossTalk*, whose archives can still provide instructive reading for those willing to select the wheat from the chaff. In all, *CrossTalk* was active for only one year (June 1998–May 1999) and was ultimately a casualty of its own freedom.

The new Jesus mythicism

At the time of my interactions on *CrossTalk* I entertained no suspicions at all that Jesus did not exist. I had heard the idea but it seemed absurd and simply unworthy of attention—on the same level as holocaust denial and Velikovsky's thesis that a cometary Venus caused the Exodus events. Yet (like so many New Testament scholars) I dismissed the grandiose biography of Jesus in the gospels as totally bogus—that somebody was born of a virgin two thousand years ago, walked on water, multiplied loaves and fishes for thousands of people, strutted around Galilee magically healing at will, and was bodily resurrected from the grave. Oh yes—I also didn't believe that such a person was *the* Son of God, forgave sins, and will come to judge all the rest of us in some mythical end times.

What was left of the gospels to believe? A few sayings and parables, that's all—and they could have been spoken by any wise man. Surprisingly,

7. In this book, references to *The Myth of Nazareth* use the bibliographical form "Salm 2008a" followed by the page number. General references to the book will use its title.

I was practically a Jesus mythicist already! When my research increasingly showed that the town of Nazareth 'in the time of Jesus' was a fiction, *then* my eyes really started to open on the colossal fakery of the gospels. I realized that they are fairy tales, like such beloved stories as *Hansel and Gretel, Cinderella,* or *The Wizard of Oz.* 'Jesus of Nazareth' was a fictional hero on the order of Hercules, Achilles, Paul Bunyan, and even Harry Potter, but combining all into one—wizardry, divinity, heroic adventure, and insight— to produce a fantastic mega-god-man who will save believers and damn all the rest of us.

Discarding the grand story of Jesus in the gospels was, however, only the beginning of my astonishment. I now discovered an entire body of scholarly literature which argues that Jesus of Nazareth never existed. This conception has been labeled 'Jesus mythicism' (or simply 'mythicism'). It is as old as biblical criticism itself, going back to Enlightenment thinkers.[8] Jesus mythicism has also been scrupulously ignored by Church and college from one generation to the next, so that—now two hundred years after the first scholarly exposition of the idea—it remains obscure and far from mainstream currents.

But—as Bob Dylan sang in 1964—*The Times They Are a-Changin'.* In this third Christian millennium Jesus mythicism is undergoing a resurgence and may have come into its own. There are signs that the mainstream is finally taking notice.[9] Five provocative books, all appearing in 1999, set the stage for the current view that Jesus of Nazareth never existed:

- Earl Doherty: *The Jesus Puzzle* (Age of Reason Publications)
- George A. Wells: *The Jesus Myth* (Open Court)
- Alvar Ellegård: Jesus—*One Hundred Years Before Christ* (Century)
- T. Freke and P. Gandy: *The Jesus Mysteries: Was the "Original Jesus" a Pagan God?* (Harmony)
- Gerd Lüdemann: *The Great Deception and What Jesus Really Said and Did* (Prometheus)

Lüdemann's book argues that only about 5% of the sayings attributed to Jesus are genuine. To the above we must add three important books which appeared in the first years of the new millennium: Frank Zindler's *The Jesus the Jews Never Knew* (showing that the ancient Jews never heard of Jesus of Nazareth), Robert M. Price's *The Incredible Shrinking Son of Man*

---

8. The list of Jesus mythicists of the past is impressive and includes C. F. Dupuis, Bruno Bauer, Allard Pierson, John Robertson, Wm. B. Smith, Arthur Drews, P.-L. Couchoud, G. van Eysinga, P. Alfaric, and G. Ory.

9. For more on the latter-day resurgence of Jesus mythicism, see the section beginning Chp. 9 in this volume, "*DJE?* and the New Skepticism."

(arguing that the early Christians adopted the model for the figure of Jesus from old Mediterranean dying-rising savior myths), and Robert Eisenman's *The New Testament Code* (maintaining that the Dead Sea Scrolls are the earliest Christian documents, that the 'Teacher of Righteousness' was James the Just, and that the 'Spouter of Lies' was Paul). My work on Nazareth archeology eventually hammered yet another nail into the coffin of the historical Jesus, with the 2008 publication of *The Myth of Nazareth*. Yet Jesus mythicism still remains very much on the fringe of biblical scholarship. This must continue until the 'fringe' is inexorably redefined, that is, until mainstream ('majority') opinion finally moves away from faith in the direction of science, reason—and Jesus mythicism.

The literary ferment summarized above signals more than a mere reassessment of old paradigms—it is an intellectual and cultural revolution, one in preparation for two centuries. Like all true and lasting revolutions, this one is messy and unfocused, drawing its energy from the overlap of numerous generally related initiatives. Within the current wave of Jesus mythicism there are disagreements, some heated. There are those who see 'Jesus' as primarily a mythological manifestation of Iron Age star lore ('astromythicists'), a symbolic reflection of the precession of equinoxes from Aries into Pisces about two thousand years ago. There are those who primarily see 'Jesus' as yet another dying-and-rising savior god, one familiar to the Levant since the Bronze Age. There are those who, while rejecting the existence of 'Jesus of Nazareth,' still maintain that a remarkable prophet with a very different biography walked in Palestine perhaps a hundred years before the turn of the era ('semi-mythicists'). And there are those who—recognizing ancient notions of the hierarchy of multiple heavens—see 'Jesus' as entirely spiritual entity whose sacrificial 'death,' while effective, took place entirely in a supramundane realm.

The above share an uncompromising rejection of the New Testament view of 'Jesus' and of the Christian theology which underpins it—that the only Son of God was born of a virgin, worked miracles, died for our sins, and will come at the end times in judgement. That conventional view, mixed with the theology which scholars sometimes refer to as the Pauline *kerygma* (Greek, 'proclamation'), is quickly eroding in the modern age. Like running water slowly dissolving a rock from multiple directions, two centuries of Jesus mythicism have been steadily dissolving the foundations of an increasingly rigid, infirm, and aged Christian tradition.

Christianity today is undergoing scientific scrutiny as never before and, in the process, is suffering death by a thousand cuts, as the modern world rejects what is increasingly seen as a fable unworthy of an evolving civilization. One cannot predict from which direction the next assault will come.

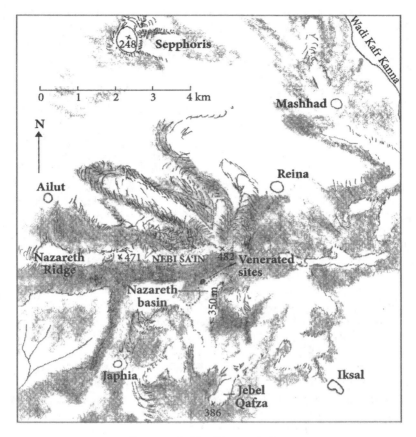

Figure. 1.2. The Nazareth Range.

Nazareth lies in the hills of Lower Galilee, 8 km south of Sepphoris and a scant 3 km northeast of ancient Japhia. It is nestled in a small upland valley about 2 km long and 1 km wide.

It may even emerge from within traditional Christianity itself, for the first mythicist priest has now come forward—Father Thomas Brodie. His astonishing book *Beyond the Quest for the Historical Jesus* appeared in 2012 and argues that the gospels are rewritings of Old Testament scriptures, and—incidentally—that Jesus never existed. Brodie's case is doubly damning of the tradition, for he is no fly-by-night crackpot but a soft-spoken cleric of standing and a well-published scholar. He founded and directed the Dominican Biblical Institute in Limerick, Ireland, and has authored numerous publications in the field of biblical studies spanning a career of forty years.

"He never existed" appears on p. 36 of Brodie's *Beyond*. With those three fateful words, written by a committed priest and an erudite bible scholar, a deep fissure appeared in the very foundation of Christendom. The needle of western man's compass, for millennia pointing towards Jesus of Nazareth, finally and irrevocably moved.

There are still penalties for speaking out. Immediately after the publication of his 2012 book, Brodie was relieved of his teaching duties. This echoes the case of Bruno Bauer, the German mythicist who argued that 'Jesus' was a second century CE fusion of Jewish, Greek, and Roman theologies. Bauer was relieved of his professorship in 1842, though he continued to write. Other mythicists of former generations published under pseudonyms. Going back even further, those who dared to espouse such ideas were tortured and burned at the stake. It is no surprise that today, even though western society is comparatively free, most mythicist authors are outside the guild of New Testament scholars. Some wait until retirement before writing their most controversial books.

A sure sign that Jesus mythicism is finally entering mainstream discourse occurred in 2012 with the appearance of *Did Jesus Exist?* by prominent New Testament scholar Bart D. Ehrman (University of North Carolina). *DJE?* is the first book-length attack on the notion that Jesus of Nazareth did not exist. Ehman's book has been criticized within mythicist circles for being poorly argued and not one of Ehrman's better efforts.[10] But *DJE?* brought the issue before a wide readership for the first time and showed that the tradition was no longer content (or able) to simply ignore the mythicist theory—as it had for well nigh two hundred years. Ehrman does not take Jesus mythicism seriously, sometimes engaging in ridicule and condescension. His book immediately was out of date, for—according to commentator Tom Dykstra—Ehrman "repeats over and over again the assertion that no reputable New Testament scholars deny the historicity of Jesus, but Brodie's book [also of 2012] certainly blows that assertion out of the water." Thus, in the fast changing currents of modern Jesus studies, the certainty of yesterday is the question of today and the falsehood of tomorrow.

Some implications

My research into the archeology of Nazareth removed any remaining vestige of belief that the figure of "Jesus of Nazareth," as described in the New Testament, could have existed. Even if a sage may have lived in late antiquity who uttered some of the sayings and parables enshrined in Christian scripture, that sage had nothing to do with the New Testament

---

10. My response to Ehrman's book is in Chapter 9.

prophet. Thus, in the first years of the new millennium, I joined the ranks of a small but growing number of Jesus mythicists.

The lack of a town of Nazareth at the turn of the era immediately highlighted one implication of critical significance: the word "Nazarene" originally must have carried a meaning independent of the (as yet unfounded) settlement. But what was that meaning? At Mk 1:24 Jesus is called a "Nazarene," and the evangelist apparently defines the term for the reader in that same verse—the "holy one of God." This definition appears to be a deliberate expansion on the part of the evangelist, implying that Mark's Greek readers were not familiar with the semitic word or its meaning. But did the evangelist supply the correct definition of the term? He appears to have provided a harmless, catch-all definition which does not reflect heretical dimensions of the term as found in non-traditional (heterodox) scriptures. For example, *The Gospel of Philip* (§62), a gnostic work, views the "Nazarene" as the possessor of hidden (secret) truth. This is precisely the term's use also in Mandean writings.

Once we remove "Nazareth" from the picture, then "Jesus" does not hail from a non-existent town but apparently from an obscure (and soon heretical) gnostic religious group. In fact, the ancient records bear witness to two similar sounding groups—both gnostic: Nasarenes[11] and *Natsuraiia* (the Mandean appellation for their priests).[12] These attestations make a search for the lost Nazarenes all the more intriguing, for they may have been the 'first Christians.'

Thus, quite early in my research I realized that the Nazareth issue was critically important on several levels. The preceding paragraph touched on one less obvious consequence—removing "Nazareth" from the picture focusses attention on obscure gnostic "Nazarenes" present at the origins of Christianity. More obviously, my research represented a direct assault on the inerrancy of scripture: if Nazareth did not exist at the turn of the era then the evangelists were engaged in nothing more (nor less) than the

---

11. The Nasarenes (with Gk. *sigma*) may bear important clues to the earliest tradition. Epiphanius (*Pan.* 18) even calls them "pre-Christian" and writes that they "did not know" Christ—showing how early and heretical he considered this group. From the descriptions, they are very similar to the Ebionites.

12. Syriac *Natsraiia*. Epiphanius also denominates a group of "Nazoreans" (*Pan.* 29.1.1). "He knows very little about them," comments one scholarly source, "except that they lived according to the Jewish Law and accepted some orthodox beliefs about Jesus" (Klijn and Reinink 1973:46). Epiphanius supposes that the Nazoreans took their name from the place Nazareth, "when they came to know that [Jesus] was conceived in Nazareth" (*Pan.* 29.1.6). If Epiphanius were correct, then the Nazoreans could not have existed before the second century CE. More likely, the Church Father's explanation is simply pious etymology—assuming such a group existed at all.

writing of *fiction*. The repercussions on the figure "Jesus of Nazareth" are similar—either he lived after *c.* 100 CE or he was not 'real.'

In the last few years my work has been characterized online and in print as primarily an assault on the historicity of Jesus. This is only partially correct for, astonishingly, the question is even broader than the debate between "mythicists" and "historicists." In other words, more is at stake than the mere historicity of Jesus—monumental though that may seem at the present time in history. The removal of "Nazareth" from earliest Christianity also leads to an exploration of the long lost Nazarenes and, further, undermines the inerrancy of scripture. The three levels of this question can be summarized as follows:

(1) "Nazarene" preceded "Nazareth" and had nothing to do with it ⇨ the focus of investigation must move to a consideration of pre-Christian gnosticism;

(2) The evangelists were writing fiction ⇨ the New Testament represents a tendentious and fabulous rewriting of history;

(3) "Jesus of Nazareth" was an invented figure ⇨ consideration must be given to the possibility that a prophet , one most unlike "Jesus," actually existed at the origins of Christianity.

At this point in time the above remain largely unexplored and only possibilities. But it must be granted that the current investigation into "Nazareth"—and that town's effective removal from the earliest stratum of Christianity—point to the above three avenues of investigation.

Obviously, these considerations go to the very heart of western civilization and involve both the essence of Christianity and the veracity of scripture. They invite questions of the most sensitive nature. Furthermore, the answers tell us a great deal about ourselves—our formative history, and why our forefathers may have fashioned a pseudo-religion around an invented savior.

Hitting the books

The preceding section alerts us that the Nazareth discussion involves far more than mere archeology. The veracity of scripture is implicated, as also the existence of a 'pre-Christian' religious group known to antiquity as the "Nasarenes." Last but not least, the historicity of "Jesus of Nazareth" hangs in the balance.

Realizing the potentially monumental importance of this investigation, beginning with the *CrossTalk* discussions I set about in earnest researching the archeological evidence. A modest inheritance from my late father enabled me to leave my day job as a mental health counselor and to devote all my energies to Nazareth research for several years.

From the start I left no stone unturned, did not hurry, skip any steps, nor overlook even minor reports. Lacking a relevant Ph.D, I knew that thoroughness would be my only credential—one that would have to be earned.

I began with the most accessible secondary material: encyclopedia articles and entries in secondary reference works. Scouring the footnotes and references, I slowly accumulated the obvious primary sources. Among these, the largest was B. Bagatti's long tome *Excavations in Nazareth* (vol. 1, 1969). Its 325 pages were laden with charts, diagrams, pottery, tombs, footnotes, *etc.* This book was the first (and often only) resource used by scholars who ventured to write about Nazareth's archeology. Much of its evidence was allegedly "from the time of Jesus"—but this central claim turned out to be very incorrect.

I live near the University of Oregon and over the decades have made use of its fine library which is surprisingly strong in the field of religious studies. The reference librarian taught for some years at the very high school in Beirut, Lebanon, which I attended as a teenager. This coincidence early cemented our friendship, and Paul has often been able to procure for me obscure books and hard-to-find articles which were otherwise unavailable. He also validated my status as a resident scholar so that the University of Oregon's critical interlibrary loan facilities would be made available to me as if I were a member of the faculty.

Accumulating the necessary research material also required trips to major libraries in Seattle and San Francisco, where I would feed the photocopy machines sometimes for hours on end only to return to Eugene each time with yet another suitcase full of papers.

Collecting the requisite material was of course only the first step. Each account, description, or excavation report had to be examined in a particularly careful way. It was not good enough simply to read the report, or even to collate all of its itemized artifacts in columns by type, date, and so on— things I learned to do early on. Incidentally, such collation could be quite revealing. For example, on one page Bagatti dates a certain pottery shard to the Roman period and on another page to the Iron Age.[13] Such errors are quickly detected through careful and complete bookkeeping.

All this was tedious, but the problem which required the most time, by far, was that each and every claim had to be *tested*. For example, in one place Bagatti claims that a fragment of pottery is "Hellenistic"—but the parallels he gives, when checked, date to the Iron Age. In another place, his alleged "Hellenistic" parallels actually date to Roman times.[14] Richmond,

---

13. Salm 2008a:176 and Chapter 4, below, where the same sort of sloppiness is evident in the Nazareth Village Farm report.
14. Salm 2008a:128, 129.

too, in 1931 claimed that six oil lamps found in a Nazareth tomb were "Hellenistic." Subsequent redating by specialists (as also inspection of the accompanying photo—see Chapter 2, *Fig. 3*) shows, however, that all the lamps in question are Roman.

Figure 1.3. Older view of Nazareth on the Nebi Sa'in hillside by Therond (as published in *Le Tour du Monde*, Paris, 1860).

There was also the problem of mislabeling. I learned that one scholar (J. Strange) termed the *kokh* type of tomb "Herodian" (*i.e.*, in the influential *Anchor Bible Dictionary* article, "Nazareth").[15] However, the important work of H.-P. Kuhnen shows that *kokh* tombs were not hewn in the Galilee before *c.* 50 CE. (They continued in use to *c.* 500 CE.) Thus, the term "Herodian" for these tombs is clearly erroneous and very misleading.

"Herodian" is also misapplied to a certain type of oil lamp, one which I have insisted on calling the "bow spouted oil lamp." This type only appeared in the Galilee *after* the reign of Herod the Great. It continued to be produced as late as *c.* 150 CE.[16] To label such an artifact—which may well

---

15. In Mishnaic Hebrew *kokh* (pl. *kokhim*) means "hole, hollow." In the archeological literature it refers to the horizontal receptacle hewn in the rock in which a single body was placed. Later, a wooden casket or stone ossuary was sometimes placed in a *kokh*.
16. Salm 2008a:167 *ff.*

date to the second century CE—"Herodian" is thus a cavalier misapplication of terminology. It is also clearly tendentious, for (in the cases both of tombs and oil lamps) the term "Herodian" *backdates* later Roman evidence into earlier Roman times.

Over two dozen *kokhim* tombs exist in the Nazareth basin. Unfortunately, Bagatti had the habit of repeatedly referring to the turn of the era as "the period of the *kokhim* tombs." This is a very convenient strategem for, via that single overused phrase, Bagatti erroneously assigned a great deal of Nazareth evidence to the time of Christ! Once again, however, Kuhnen's work furnishes the antidote: *kokhim* tombs did not yet exist in the Nazareth basin at the turn of the era.

In the above and other ways it soon became clear to me that serious flaws characterize the primary reports, not to mention the secondary reference articles based on them. As I wrote in my first book: "The tendentious nature of Bagatti's writings on Nazareth is clear, with the result that it is impossible to accord those writings the respect normally granted to scientific investigation... In fact, there is one and only one possible conclusion: in Bagatti's writings we are dealing primarily not with archaeology, but with faith."[17]

Yet Bagatti was only one author guilty of 'adapting' the evidence to the exigencies of faith. Virtually the entire body of scholarly literature dedicated to the archeology of Nazareth is replete with conclusions—general and specific—which are frankly incompatible with the material evidence. I call this *quack archeology.*

Though I could read, tabulate, compare, and analyze the reports which came under my gaze, I could not venture any opinion myself, for I am certainly not a professional archeologist nor have I excavated in Nazareth. As a result, any opinion which I produced that disagreed with Bagatti, Strange, Richmond, *etc.*, was necessarily the verifiable opinion of a leading specialist in the relevant field or subfield. This gave my writing 'teeth,' but it also required an enormous amount of time. In the process I could not help but become somewhat educated in Galilean archeology. That education extended to language classes at the university which afforded me the ability to also read excavation reports in Hebrew.

In December of 2005 I made contact with an archeologist employed by the Israel Antiquities Authority, one who would play a major role in subsequent Nazareth developments: Dr. Yardenna Alexandre. The reason for this initial contact was entirely mundane: I sought information on a small excavation in downtown Nazareth. Alexandre replied that there were "minimal finds" in that dig. However, in an ensuing email she directed my

---

17. Salm 2008a:177.

attention to a larger excavation she had conducted in 1997–98, at nearby Mary's Well. She wrote that a report on the Mary's Well findings would be forthcoming, but unfortunately too late for inclusion in my upcoming book. As it happens, her final report on Mary's Well did not appear in print until 2012—four years after publication of my book and a whopping fifteen years after her fieldwork at Mary's Well (see Chapter 11).

In what would prove to be a significant development, in May 2006 Alexandre emailed me a preliminary IAA report on her Mary's Well excavations. I had not requested it, but was grateful to her for sending the one-page report. It appeared similar in form and wording to those routinely published in the IAA's online journal, *Hadashot Arkheologiyot* ("Archeological News"). I replied that I could not use the Mary's Well report in my forthcoming book as it lacked itemizations, specificity, and was provisional (pending a projected 'Final Report').[18] Thus, I made no mention of the report in my book, consistent with my scrupulous policy of using only published evidence presented in such a way as to permit verification by others.

In the following year other scholars began to allege that Alexandre found Hellenistic coins at Mary's Well. However, I quickly verified that this remarkable claim was not at all reflected in Alexandre's own 2006 report now in my possession. Stephen Pfann was the first to make the coin claim. It occurs in his 2007 report dealing with the Nazareth Village Farm (NVF) at the other end of the valley. By introducing information on the unrelated Mary's Well excavation carried out a decade earlier, Pfann was apparently going out of his way to signal significant 'news' to the academic community—news, however, which had been unknown to the excavator herself.

Alexandre's book on Mary's Well finally appeared in 2012. It contradicted her 2006 report (which was never published) and now substantiated Pfann's claim regarding ten Hellenistic coins.[19] The book also claimed the discovery of a limited amount of Hellenistic pottery (also unmentioned in the 2006 report). However, in studying the book in the fall of 2013, I had little difficulty showing that the presentation of Hellenistic "evidence" was rife with internal contradictions and glaring errors—some of a fairly embarrassing nature. My overall conclusion (argued in Chapter 11) is that we are not dealing in this case with anything like a straightforward and candid account of the evidence, but with an 'evolving' account produced by multiple scholars in poor communication one with another.

---

18. The Final Report appeared in 2012 as a monograph entitled *Mary's Well, Nazareth: The Late Hellenistic to the Ottoman Periods* (IAA Reports, No. 49).

19. The full 2006 report is cited in Chapter 9. A detailed discussion of the genesis and denouement of the Hellenistic coin claim is in Chapter 11.

Publication of The Myth of Nazareth

It took eight years to complete the research for the book, and another two years to write it. It was necessary for me to address all eras, for the Church claimed that Nazareth has existed since the Bronze Age "down to our own days" (Bagatti 1969:319, Salm 2008a:85). The historical reality, however, proved to be very different. A substantial settlement—probably ancient Japhia—indeed existed in the Nazareth basin during the Bronze and Iron Ages. However, a long hiatus began in the late eighth century BCE—probably the result of Assyrian destruction. Settlement did not resume until the period between the two Jewish revolts, that is, about 100 CE. This is the essential core of *The Myth of Nazareth* which eventually contained six chapters, accompanied by a number of appendices in which the primary evidence is tabulated.

I was a lone researcher, without any institutional affiliation whatsoever. Furthermore, I lacked all pertinent (and expected) academic credentials. I knew these things before setting a single word to paper, however, so evidently they had little influence over my actions. Nor did I demand—or receive—much money for my work, whose primary motivation was a desire to understand Christian origins. That desire was unrealizable in the usual channels, for I have long known that a university education in biblical studies today is an exercise in learning what is permitted and what is politic. In all, then, my long Nazareth investigation was a hopelessly impractical task when measured in conventional ways. Yet it has proven of considerable value to others—so perhaps it was not so impractical after all.

I decided to self-publish *The Myth of Nazareth* in chapbooks. That is, each chapter would be issued to the public in hardcopy after it was written. This would be a 'pre-publication' way to get word out about the book and, since there were six chapters, the project would take about two years to complete. Hopefully, by the time the book was finished some publisher would have stepped forward.

In order to publicize the project I developed a website dedicated to the archeology of Nazareth: *www.nazarethmyth.info* (now called "The Truth About Nazareth" at the same URL). The first chapbook was entitled "The Myth of Nazareth: The Stone, Bronze, and Iron Ages," and encompassed fifty-four pages (including Index and Bibliography). In 2007, it sold via the website for $4 plus postage.[20]

This proved to be an effective strategy. Frank Zindler—now a colleague and friend, editor of this book, himself a redoubtable scholar, and

---

20. About fifty copies of each chapbook were issued in a yellow cover bearing the imprint "Kevalin Press." *Kevalin* is a Paali term meaning "accomplished one."

longtime editor of American Atheist press—ordered a copy of Chapter
One and evinced a lively interest in the project. We were soon in regular
contact. Frank promptly sent me his important article "Where Jesus Never
Walked." I later appraised it on my website in the following words:

> Zindler considers many places mentioned in the canonical gospels (in-
> cluding Nazareth and Capernaum), and finds that they are all without
> historical foundation at the turn of the era. As regards Nazareth, his 1996
> article presciently arrives at many conclusions detailed in my subsequent
> book, without the benefit of a close itemization and analysis of the mate-
> rial record. Zindler correctly places the town on the valley floor (not on
> the steep and rocky hillside, which is pockmarked by Late Roman-era
> tombs and agricultural installations), notes that the Venerated Area was
> itself full of tombs and quite uninhabitable by the ancient Jews, points to
> the lack of masonry remains dating to the first century, notes the vague
> (mis-)use of the phrase "Roman period" to backdate movable evidence,
> and concludes that the basin was settled long after the turn of the era.

Frank also noted that the oldest buildings found at Nazareth seem to
date to later Roman times, that "there is no information to indicate what
the inhabitants of those building *called* their village," that the second century church father Origen didn't know the location of the place, and that
tombs exist only a few yards from the holiest sites under the Church of the
Annunciation. He was correct in so many ways! My research merely modified Frank's views on one point which, though comparatively minor, has influenced many a discussion: that "Before the second or third century CE—
going back to the Middle Bronze Age—the site now occupied by Nazareth
was a necropolis, a city of the dead." (Zindler 2011:33). The proposition
follows that the Nazareth basin may have been an Early Roman necropolis
serving nearby Japhia. However, all the post-Iron Age tombs in the basin
are of the *kokh* type, a form of tomb design which Kuhnen has shown
postdates *c.* 50 CE in Lower Galilee (Salm 2008a:162). Thus, the tombs of
Nazareth—and hence their pottery and associated contents also—cannot
go back to the turn of the era or earlier times. The basin was evidently be-
reft of all human activity for approximately eight hundred years.

Long before the last chapbook appeared—or had even been written—Frank offered me a contract for publication of the complete work by
American Atheist Press. He took a vigorous interest in the book, which was
formatted by his late beloved wife, Ann, and which was splendidly edited
by Frank himself.

The Myth of Nazareth appeared in March, 2008. It contained over 800
footnotes, seven appendices, a complete Bibliography, and an exhaustive
index created by Frank—a feature which renders the book particularly useful for reference. In fact, it is the finest index I have seen anywhere.

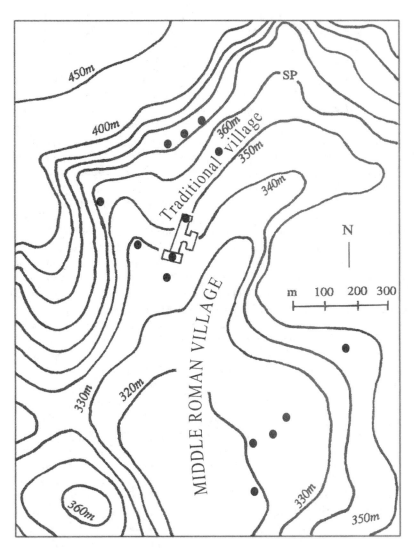

Figure 1.4. Topography of the Nazareth basin.

The Venerated Area is outlined at upper left of center. For centuries the "Traditional village" has been erroneously sited among known Middle-Late Roman *kokh* tombs (noted by black dots; *cf.* the fuller map at *Fig. 8.5*) and on the slope of the steep hill known as the Nebi Sa'in. On the other hand, the village (which began in Middle Roman times) could only have been located on the relatively flat basin floor between tombs to NW and SE. (*Cf.* Salm 2008a:*Fig. 5.2.*)

The book caused a notable stir in skeptical-mythicist circles, though my position is hardly new. After all, the non-existence of Nazareth at the turn of the era has been proposed by scholars for two centuries since the time of Bruno Bauer. However, archeology did not come into its own as a rigorous science until after the Second World War. Before then there were only claims, counterclaims, rumors, and innuendo.

The Myth of Nazareth blew the whistle on Christian archeology and communicated to academe as well as to the educated layperson that 'business as usual' is no longer good enough in this highly-charged discipline. Quack archeology can no longer be tolerated in Early Christian studies. We must return to the primary evidence. In a scientific endeavor this is, of course, self-explanatory—but "biblical archeology" is anything but scientific! A return to the primary evidence represents nothing less than a revolution against faith. In both Jewish and Christian archeology, dogma and faith have trumped evidentiary considerations with astonishing regularity in the past. Even today—at the beginning of the third Christian millennium—the facts of history hardly speak for themselves in biblical matters.

As a science, archeology has metaphorically progressed from the stone age to the space age in a single century. This phenomenal development has caught the tradition flat-footed. Excavation results are now being produced at such speed, and in such great quantity, that it can only be a matter of time before an empirically-based view obtains, at least in rational circles. What this means is that faith-based archeology—the norm fifty years ago—is on the defensive. The arc of history favors the scientist, not the believer who increasingly finds himself embattled and on loosening soil.

In a highly controlled excavation—one with carefully delimited parameters and accompanied by detailed publication—it is very difficult to contest what has and has not been found in the ground. In the contentious field of biblical studies, where hypothesizing and opinions so often pass for theological "research," modern archeology is for the first time increasingly able to inject hard evidence into the discussion. Unfortunately, such evidence is most unwelcome to those who proceed from a posture of faith.

The tradition often resorts to a shopworn mantra: "absence of evidence is not evidence of absence." Yet this is manifestly not true in a professional excavation, where absence of evidence is precisely that: *absence* of evidence! To a scientist such absence speaks volumes. It is tantamount to entering a small room at home, thoroughly searching under bed and in closet, and finding neither kangaroo, hippo, nor elephant. The only possible objective report is: "No kangaroo, hippo, or elephant is in the room." In every other discipline it would be ludicrous to contest such a conclusion. Why on earth then not in biblical archeology?

Outward ripples and deeper currents

It is clear that publication of *The Myth of Nazareth* caught many in the tradition by complete surprise. The years immediately following witnessed a veritable rush in Nazareth to find evidence dating to the turn of the era—a "house from the time of Jesus" (Alexandre at the International Marian Center, Dark at the Sisters of Nazareth Convent), coins and pottery similarly "from the time of Jesus" (Alexandre at Mary's Well), and even a village of Jesus' day (the Nazareth Village Farm, which pilgrims can visit today if they wish to experience what Jesus himself may have seen). Two of these venues are now major commercial enterprises: (1) the site of an alleged Early Roman house was incorporated into the ambitious International Marian Center (IMC—though the original excavation revealed no such Early Roman dwelling (Chapter 10); and (2) the NVF has mixed a *simulated* village from the time of Jesus with *actual claims* of (bogus) Jesus-era evidence (Chapter 4). Equally questionable Hellenistic coins and pottery have recently been imputed to the Mary's Well site (in contradiction to the afore-mentioned 2006 report by the archeologist herself—Chapter 11), and (perhaps most astonishing) the Sisters of Nazareth Convent has become the proposed site of a Jesus-era house, in a very unusual scenario proposed by Professor Dark (Chapter 6).

Thus, the years 2008–2014 have witnessed all sorts of novel claims in Nazareth regarding evidence dating to the time of Jesus, from multiple domestic dwellings to coins and pottery. I cannot say how much of this—if any—can be credited to the publication of *The Myth of Nazareth*. That book, however, appears to have altered the context of discussion and perhaps the actual situation on the ground. It has introduced new possibilities which only a few years ago were off the table—including a bolstering of the Jesus myth theory. "One of the most remarkable features of public discussion of Jesus of Nazareth in the twenty-first century," noted the late scholar Maurice Casey, "has been a massive upsurge in the view that this important historical figure did not even exist."[21] The Nazareth issue is a significant element in this upsurge—as witnessed, for example, by Bart Ehrman's (rather superficial) treatment of the issue in his 2013 *Did Jesus Exist?* (Chapter 9).

The word "mythicist" as applied to the nonexistence of Jesus did not even exist in English until about 2005 when it gained currency in a few online discussions. For a couple of years *mythist* existed side-by-side with *mythicist*. Eventually the small community of users settled on the latter term, though hostile debunkers still occasionally employ pejorative pseudo-terms such as *mythtic* (R. Joseph Hoffmann). As of this writing, "mythicist" (with

---

21. *Jesus: Evidence and Argument or Mythicist Myths?* (T & T. Clark, 2014). From the jacket cover.

the specific meaning of nonbelief in Jesus' historicity) is still not to be found in any standard English dictionary. There is, naturally, a huge ingrained resistance to the term in everyday life. There are also still very few openly professing Jesus mythicists, though the number of "closet" mythicists appears to be increasing, both inside and outside academe. At the same time, the number of scholars who today are willing to entertain the *possibility* that Jesus did not exist is much greater than it was a mere decade ago.

My research and writing on Nazareth did not end with publication of *The Myth of Nazareth* but continued as I grappled with the many new developments on the ground. Several written responses have been published in various places and are now included in this book. Six months after the book's appearance I penned an uncompromising critique of the "Final Report" from the Nazareth Village Farm—a fifteen acre plot northwest of the ancient settlement. The NVF report was authored by Dead Sea Scrolls epigrapher Stephen Pfann and two of his colleagues from the University of the Holy Land (which Pfann directs). No evidence of a controlled excavation was ever published from the NVF site. My response (Chapter 4) appeared in the 2008 issue of the *Bulletin of the Anglo-Israel Archaeological Society*, at the time under the capable editorship of Joan E. Taylor. I revealed critical flaws in the NVF report, including multiple cases of "double dating"—that is, dating the same shard of pottery to two widely differing periods from one page to another, and even describing it in impossibly contradictory ways. These revelations constituted a scholarly embarrassment for the authors of the NVF report and provoked a lengthy "Amendment," one which also appeared in the same issue of BAIAS. Yet the *Amendment* proved as problematic as the report it attempted to correct.

The same issue of BAIAS devotes no less than 47 pages to the archeology of Nazareth. Besides the *Amendment* just noted, it included a "Reply" (written by Stephen Pfann) to my "Response," another "Reply" by the British archeologist Ken Dark, and a hostile review of my book also by Dark. This flurry of activity (two responses, two replies, a review, and an amendment) show that—despite general shunning by the academic world—my Nazareth work had apparently struck a sore nerve in scholarly circles!

Beginning with the November-December 2006 issue of *American Atheist* magazine, that periodical has published four of my articles on Nazareth (reproduced in Chapters 2, 3, 5, 7). It can fairly be said that during the years 2006–2010 *American Atheist* unexpectedly emerged at the forefront of Nazareth research. Much of the credit goes, once again, to Frank Zindler who has been influential in seeing that my views are regularly published.

In the years since its inception, the *www.nazarethmyth.info* website has grown steadily to include a user-friendly quiz, a dozen "Scandal Sheets," articles, a video, and so on. It attempts to inform that large section of the population which does not read academic journals and scholarly books. In the seven years since its creation, the website has logged over half a million hits.

On December 21, 2009 news regarding the Nazareth discovery of a "house from the time of Jesus" was released simultaneously to multiple press agencies around the globe. Numerous articles in the global media immediately followed. Once again, the archeologist directing the excavation was Yardenna Alexandre. I deal with this bogus "Nazareth house" issue in Chapter 10. The brief official statement (soon taken offline) from the IAA made no mention of first-century remains, much less of evidence from the turn of the era ("time of Jesus"). Structural remains apparently date to "the Roman period," which lasted into the fourth century CE. The "small camouflaged grotto" was in fact probably a storage cellar for wine jugs. But the excavation site was soon an impressive new tourist venue ("The Mary of Nazareth International Center") under the auspices of the Catholic Church, replete with theater, restaurant, boutique, and botanical garden.

Between 2006 and 2009 Ken Dark worked in and around Nazareth. His activity took place in the open land between Nazareth and Sepphoris, and also at the Sisters of Nazareth Convent (located about 100m west of the Church of the Annunciation). As with the NVF team, there is no evidence that Dark has conducted controlled stratigraphic excavations at any site. His activities are explicitly (that is, by his own admission) restricted to surface surveys, as well as to reviewing prior excavation findings. This has not prevented Dark from radically reinterpreting those findings—often in contradiction to the opinion of the archeologists he is interpreting. A thorough study of Dark's Nazareth work shows that it involves (perhaps unwittingly) a wholesale reinterpretation of Galilean archeology. As a result, Dark's work misrepresents the work of others and he appears to lack the required specialist training. His arguments are poorly reasoned and he makes errors of a rudimentary nature, suggesting a lack of knowledge of the subfield. I discuss Dark's work in Chapters 5 and 6.

NazarethGate and the disintegrating consensus

In 2012 the Nazareth municipality published a monograph entitled *Nazareth: Archaeology, History and Cultural Heritage*. It's subtitle announced something new: *Proceedings of the 1st International Conference: Nazareth, November 22–24, 2010.* I had also been invited to the conference but tactfully declined, since I lacked institutional support and would have had to pay for the trip half way around the world. The book includes chapters by Stephen Pfann and Yardenna Alexandre (who both live in Israel) in addition to a number of chapters dealing with post-Roman times. Pfann reviews the NVF evidence and signals pottery "beginning with the Early Roman Period." He also characterizes the pottery at the NVF as "from the 1st to the 3rd centuries." That much is in conformity with my findings. Pfann also notes a "scholarly consensus that Nazareth [was] established in the 1st century BCE..." (p. 17), but this is wishful thinking, for Catholic scholars are chary of abandoning their pet theory of "continuous habitation" in favor of the increasingly fashionable thesis that the village was refounded in the first (or second) century BCE. In fact, I will show (Chapter 4) that the NVF findings are *themselves* too late to support a BCE emergence of the settlement.

At Frank's urging I temporarily joined the hopelessly stodgy Society of Biblical Literature (SBL). Soon thereafter I was invited by the noted Atheist author Hector Avalos (*The End of Biblical Studies*) to present a paper at the 2012 SBL convention in Chicago (Chapter 8). It was a long way to go for a 20-minute presentation in front of a few dozen people. True to form, however, I managed to ruffle a few feathers—including those of Bart Ehrman who later wrote on his blog that many scholars were outraged at my presence at the SBL. I was pretty outraged at my presence there too.

I recall introducing myself to Claire Pfann at a publisher's booth. She noticeably winced at the mention of my name and, for a moment, we stood awkwardly before one another. Claire and her husband Stephen live in Israel and are very much involved with the University of the Holy Land and with traditional "Christian archeology" (read: archeology seeking to validate the biblical accounts). Both scholars are often on TV (*National Geographic, CNN Presents, 60 Minutes*). In our short meeting I took the opportunity to mention Yardenna Alexandre, confident that Claire was familiar with Alexandre's recent astonishing claim of Hellenistic evidence at Nazareth. "Perhaps you would graciously convey to Ms. Alexandre," I asked sharply, "that she might talk less and publish more." This remark was in reference to Alexandre's extensive media exposure regarding the "house from the time of Jesus"—though no report on that site had appeared. It was also in reference to Alexandre's Mary's Well excavation carried out almost fifteen years earlier. That was the excavation which Stephen Pfann was claiming produced "Hellenistic" evidence—though, once again, no report from Alexandre had yet eventuated (Chapter 11).[22]

The most enjoyable part of my SBL experience was lunching with the legendary Robert Price (who also presented a paper). Unfortunately, Bob was ailing at the time and had to return home early from the convention.

---

22. Alexandre's book-length treatment of the 1997–98 Mary's Well excavation finally appeared at the end of 2012.

I took advantage of my SBL stay to visit the fabled Regenstein Library of the University of Chicago. This library was (in 2012) the only repository in the United States possessing a copy of Ken Dark's preliminary publications on the Sisters of Nazareth Convent, which is located a stone's throw from the Church of the Annunciation. Dark had been visiting Nazareth annually beginning in 2006 and authored four annual "interim" reports published by the "Research Centre for Late Antique and Byzantine Studies: University of Reading." These obscure reports focus on the Sisters of Nazareth Convent site and lead up to Dark's summary 2012 article in *The Antiquaries Journal*, an article which he also characterizes as "interim." Dark promises a definitive "final report" in book form. In Chapter 6 I critique Dark's publications to date on the Sisters of Nazareth site and argue that his conclusions (which are uniformly commensurate with the Church's positions) are as astonishing as they are indefensible. Dark does not seem familiar with standard chronologies of primary evidence (tombs, ossuaries) nor of Jewish praxis in late antiquity. His promised monograph will surely result in considerable embarrassment for the British archeologist, should it actually appear and should it conform to his published arguments to date.

In order to reach the Regenstein Library it was necessary for me to take the subway through several miles of South Chicago—about ten stops. I had no idea that I would be crossing what is tantamount to a war zone in which dozens of people are murdered each day. I was frankly unprepared for the level of racial tension and latent hostility in the poorer neighborhoods, and also didn't realize that the subway is largely considered a "police-free" zone and used for any number of illicit activities—especially at night.

On Friday evening about 7:00pm—after a long day of SBL lectures—I innocently boarded the train with a prepared list of books and articles to consult. I was the only caucasian in the graffiti-laden carriage and stood by the door. A few seats away a painfully thin man was dealing drugs out of a small suitcase. Teenagers arrived from neighboring carriages, handed the man with the suitcase a cigarette packet (no doubt full of money), and received a cigarette packet (presumably full of drugs) in return before they exited the carriage. This activity was pretty continual and everyone else in the carriage stared straight and apparently took no notice.

A teenager boarded with pants fallen to above his knees and his drawers barely covering his privates. I suppose it was the latest in fashion. I almost blurted out, "Hey, kid, you're losing your britches!" but thought the better of it, figuring that such a comment could send one to the morgue.

At the Regenstein Library I photocopied Dark's several interim reports on the Sisters of Nazareth Convent, and then took advantage of the library's rich holdings to consult books unavailable in Oregon. It was 11:00 pm when I ventured back into the subway for the return trip. Few people were in the carriage. A dazed-looking drunk sat opposite me and occasionally quaffed from a bottle in a brown paper bag. I tried not to make eye contact. After a couple of subway stops he rose and lurched in my direction, holding out his hand. "I'm Abdul Malik" he yelled, trying to keep his balance while practically falling backwards.

I declined to shake his hand. This was a mistake, for the next words out of Abdul Malik's mouth were, "I'm going to kill you!" I somehow managed to get the inebriated man to sit back down—after shaking his hand multiple times and giving him five dollars. My years of experience managing mental patients helped, and we eventually engaged in a fairly amicable though bizarre conversation in which I was "Santa." Abdul never produced a gun or a knife, but he did produce a yo-yo from his pocket and insisted on demonstrating its function. This took quite some time and it was hilarious watching the inebriated man trying to work a yo-yo as the subway carriage lurched back and forth. But I was scrupulously careful to always laugh *with* Abdul, never *at* him. I relate such vignettes to demonstrate that research entails more than boring bookwork!

2012 witnessed the birth of my website *Mythicist Papers*. The site is subtitled "Resources for the study of Christian origins." It provides numerous webpages (no fee or membership is required) dealing with the subject of Jesus mythicism. The site is a natural extension of my research on Nazareth. As of this writing, it is the only website of its kind.

The last four chapters of this book represent new material previously unpublished, with the exception that Chapter 12 includes a summary of a series of ground-breaking online entries relative to the so-called "Caesarea inscription" and posted to the *Mythicist Papers* website during the summer of 2013. Readers may be aware that three marble fragments of the claimed inscription were discovered in 1962. The Christian world (as well as the Israeli state) ignored suspicious circumstances attending the discovery and quickly touted the inscription as the first (and only) non-Christian epigraphic evidence for the settlement of Nazareth dating to Roman times. Conservative scholars even jumped to the conclusion that the inscription dates to the first century CE. However, recent research carried out by two overseas colleagues and myself shows that the the three fragments do not go together and that the "Caesarea inscription" as such never existed. Furthermore, the critical fragment A bearing the word "Nazareth" is in all likelihood a forgery perpetrated by the long discredited Jerry Vardaman, the pseudo-archeologist of microletter infamy.

The final chapter of this book, "The Tombs Under the House of Mary," summarizes where we now stand relative to the archeology of Nazareth. *Contra* Stephen Pfann (as noted above), there is hardly any "scholarly consensus that Nazareth [was] established in the 1st century BCE..." In fact, we are in a period of intense flux on this sensitive issue which is critical for an understanding of Christian origins. The tradition must come to grips with misrepresentations and falsehoods at the core of its message, as symbolized by the tombs under the 'house of Mary,' that is, under the Church of the Annunciation. The tombs postdate the turn of the era (perhaps by several centuries), and thus attest to habitation in the Nazareth basin long after the 'time of Mary.' Furthermore, the thesis that the ancient Jews of Nazareth hewed tombs under former dwellings (Dark's proposal) is as odd as it is unsubstantiated. Finally, it is not possible that Mary lived over or in the vicinity of existing or pre-existing tombs, as these were a prime source of ritual impurity.

This developing imbroglio—"NazarethGate"—represents a massive problem at the core of Christianity. Millions of pilgrims stream to Nazareth every year, and it is only a matter of time before the truths of the town's history reach their ears. As little as ten years ago the thesis that Nazareth did not exist at the turn of the era was hardly known even to Christian academics. Today, that thesis is well documented and familiar to a rapidly increasing number of scholars. It will not go away. On the contrary, the arc of history is bending in the direction of the new Jesus mythicism, one in which the 'invention' of Nazareth is forcing the tradition to produce increasingly absurd explanations regarding one of its most sacred, celebrated, and visited venues.

Chapter 2

WHY THE TRUTH ABOUT NAZARETH IS IMPORTANT

(*American Atheist*, November–December 2006, pp. 14–19)

Did Nazareth exist when Jesus was alive? Did Jesus even live at all? These unsettling questions remind me of the proverbial mad uncle in the cellar—he's there, but the household wants to keep it a secret, so when the guests come to dinner the hostess' smile covers a perpetual fear and an unvoiced prayer: "Please uncle Jack, please don't scream tonight!"

The trouble with a mad uncle in the cellar is that he can spoil the party upstairs. A similar problem exists with questions like "Did Nazareth exist when Jesus was alive?" and its bigger sibling, "Did Jesus even live at all?" (being seriously asked by scholars such as Frank Zindler and Earl Doherty). Such questions can spoil the party because if Jesus didn't exist, then the West's main excuse for feeling good ("I'm saved") is suddenly gone.

Now, we can argue until the Second Coming whether Jesus actually lived in the flesh—and I suspect he might appear on the clouds before we decide the matter—because there can be no proof for his terrestrial life. Even were someone to present a document they claimed was written by Jesus (say, from the Dead Sea Scrolls), or a garment he touched (like the Shroud of Turin), anybody could simply say: "No, I think that's someone else. That's not him." So, the believer is not likely to convince the skeptic. Nor is the skeptic likely to convince the believer, because the ability to disprove the gospel accounts of Jesus has generally been well beyond the capacity of science and scholarship.

Well, until now. Unlike aspects of the gospel story that are quite beyond verification—the miracles of Jesus, his bodily resurrection, his virgin birth, or even his human nature—the existence of Nazareth two thousand years ago can be proved or disproved by digging in the ground. After all, the archeology of a site is empirically demonstrable. And if no such town existed at the turn of the era, then Jesus "of Nazareth" is a pretty hard sell—even for a committed believer. This is what gives the Nazareth issue such great potency and places it in a category apart. It has the explosive potential to disprove the gospel accounts in a fundamental way. "Nazareth" is potentially a very loud scream from the cellar.

If the town didn't exist, that means the evangelists lied in a big way. The settlement is mentioned ten times in the canonical gospels and *Acts of the Apostles.* (The rest of the occurrences "Jesus of Nazareth" in the New Testament are better translated "Jesus the Nazarene" or "Nazorean"— whatever *that* was.) In other words, this is not a one-time error, but a calculated and recurrent invention shared by all four gospels. If the evangelists were spinning a yarn, then conservatives who have been touting scriptural inerrancy for so many years all suddenly have a great deal of egg on their faces.

No one likes to be duped. What hurts more is to be duped *and* shown a fool for telling a false story to one's children for two thousand years. And we should be clear on this—when it comes to the gospels, mega-bragging rights and total testosterone are involved. The New Testament documents are what drove Crusaders to kill Moslems, inquisitors to burn heretics, and the Church to stand on infallibility and hurl papal bulls at the world. We're talking about *being right, by God*, about metaphorically strutting down main street, and about having the blessing to shoot and ask questions later. Hmm... Sounds a lot like conservative Christianity.

Indeed, the conservative wing of Christianity has the most to lose from a scientific investigation of Christian origins. The archeologist's spade, at Nazareth as at other places in Palestine, has engendered the most fear in that quarter because it might show that things did not happen as the scriptures say, that the Bible is *not* the inerrant word of God.

No doubt partly for this reason, centuries ago the Roman Catholic Church resolved to buy the most sacred Christian places in the Holy Land. In this way the Church would be able to manage any investigation that took place on its property and thus shape the narrative. Not least, it would also be able to garner revenues from pilgrims...

The Custodia di Terra Santa, an arm of the Franciscan Order, was formed for the purpose of acquiring and controlling the venues deemed most sacred to Christians. In 1620 CE the Custodian of the Holy Land, Fr. Tommaso Obicini, acquired the present Venerated Area in Nazareth from the Druse emir, Fakr ed-Din. Today, that area is the premiere destination of Christian pilgrimage outside of Jerusalem. It's not very large—only about 100m by 60m, and includes three structures: (1) the Church of the

Annunciation (the largest Christian edifice in the Middle East), the Church
of St. Joseph to the north, and the Franciscan monastery between the two
churches.[1] The Venerated Area has been the venue of virtually all the Roman Catholic excavations in Nazareth, so we should not be surprised if
the history of the settlement is seen through thick Roman Catholic lenses.

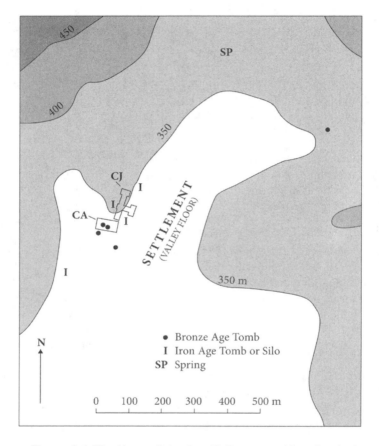

Figure. 2.1. The Nazareth basin with Bronze and Iron Age loci.

The present Venerated Area is marked by CA (Church of the Annunciation) and
CJ (Church of St. Joseph). Comparison with *Fig. 1.4* reveals that the Venerated
Area has been used for burial in many eras, beginning with the Bronze Age.
"SP" is the spring above Mary's Well. (*Cf.* Salm 2008a:*Fig. 1.3.*)

1. The Venerated Area has expanded since this article was written and now includes
the International Marian Center (Chapter 10), as well as the "tomb of the Just One"
under the Sisters of Nazareth Convent (Chapter 6).

The Bronze-Iron Age settlement

The Nazareth basin lies in southern Galilee roughly equidistant from the Mediterranean Sea and the Sea of Galilee – about an easy day's walk from either. It is surrounded by hills, and thus is both accessible and off the beaten path. The story of human habitation there begins at the dawn of history.

It became clear in the 1920s that a substantial settlement existed in the basin already in the Bronze and Iron Ages. My research has clarified prior proposals that the settlement started about 3000 BCE. In fact, it began a millennium later. But the name "Nazareth" does not appear in Jewish scripture, nor in any ancient records before the Christian gospels. This has always struck scholars as curious, but I am now able to offer one possible explanation.

There was an ancient settlement in the neighborhood of Nazareth called Japhia. It is mentioned in the Bible (Jos 19:12), as well as in the Egyptian Amarna letters of the fourteenth century BCE. Today, archeologists know of Japhia only from the Roman ruins of the town three kilometers southwest of Nazareth.[2] Japhia was destroyed in 67 CE, during the First Jewish Revolt. *Curiously, there are no Bronze-Iron Age remains of Japhia under the Roman ruins. So, the early town mentioned in the Bible must have been somewhere nearby.* There was indeed a considerable settlement in the Nazareth basin during those eras, one beginning about 2000 BCE and continuing for about thirteen centuries (from the Middle Bronze Age through the Middle Iron Age). Thus, by synoptically viewing the evidence from Japhia together with that from the neighboring Nazareth basin, one arrives at the very likely solution: *"Japhia" was located in the Nazareth basin in the Bronze and Iron Ages!* It moved in the course of centuries to its eventual Roman location three kilometers away. Such village movement over time was not unusual and could occur for a variety of reasons. In the case of Japhia we indeed have a good reason: Assyria conquered Israel in the late eighth century BCE and destroyed all the major towns in northern Palestine. It is likely that Japhia was also a casualty of the general destruction at that time. According to this scenario, *the earliest town of Nazareth was not "Nazareth" at all—it was Japhia.*

---

2. Since this article was first written (Fall, 2006) some Bronze-Iron Age remains have been discovered nearby. Y. Alexandre reports scattered Iron II potsherds (tenth–ninth centuries BCE)—but no structural remains—"in the vicinity" of Roman Japhia. She concludes: "This presumably was the Iron Age settlement of Yafiʻa in the tribal allotment of Zebulun in the Northern Kingdom of Israel." See *Hadashot Arkheologiyot* 124 (2012): "Yafiʻa."

The Catholic position

The first stage of "Nazareth" history comes to an end with the eighth century destruction of Japhia. Thereafter, according to surveys conducted by the Israeli archeologist Zvi Gal,[3] there was a general depopulation of Galilee. Japhia was abandoned along with many other sites, and the Nazareth basin lay empty of human settlement for many centuries. This is the beginning of what I call a "Great Hiatus" in habitation. There is no evidence at all in the ground at Nazareth from the ensuing Babylonian and Persian Periods (*c.* 612–*c.* 330 BCE), and the Church itself has never claimed any.

It's curious, then, that the Catholic Church maintains the doctrine of continuous habitation, namely, that Nazareth was inhabited from the Bronze Age all the way until the present. Thus Father B. Bagatti, the principal archeologist at the site: "...life did not begin in the place in a recent epoch, but already existed in the Bronze Period, to continue down to our own days."[4] This is tantamount to a denial of empirical fact, but the reason is clear: Christian doctrine requires that Nazareth existed in Jesus' time. This in turn requires that the settlement *already* existed for some time. Only two possibilities fulfill this requirement. Either (1) Nazareth has existed continuously since the Bronze Age; or (2) there was a hiatus in settlement, but the town was re-established before Jesus' time (for example, in the Hellenistic Age). The Church has officially embraced the simpler solution: Nazareth has existed continuously since 2000 BCE.

This is a truly remarkable position. According to the doctrine of continuous habitation, the hamlet of Nazareth has been settled uninterruptedly since the time of Abraham. Presumably, Nazareth joins Jerusalem and a select handful of the world's settlements to have enjoyed such outstanding longevity. Hardly any Canaanite towns can make a similar claim. Many ancient and venerable Biblical towns do not go back to patriarchal times (Gerasa, Hebron). Others ceased long ago (Gezer, Shechem). Yet others were abandoned or destroyed in the course of time, and then re-established at a different location (Gaza, Jericho, Japhia). In short, the tradition's shrill assertion that people continuously lived in the Nazareth basin for the last four thousand years would be, if true, quite amazing. Apart from any Christian considerations, it would raise the site inestimably in archeological value. The stratigraphy of the Venerated Area (for that is where habitation is claimed) would be of the greatest general interest. Archeologists would be able to systematically follow the levels of habitation downwards—as they can at the well-excavated site of Megiddo only seventeen kilometers

---

3. Gal 1988, 1992, 1994a, 1998.
4. Bagatti 1969:319.

away—beginning with the upper stratum and progressively exposing older and older settlements. Megiddo offers thirty strata encompassing approximately three millennia, a treasure trove for archeologists.

And Nazareth? No strata have been discovered there at all. In 1955 Bagatti had a special trench cut a few meters to the East of the Church of the Annunciation. Its purpose was to determine the stratigraphic profile of the Venerated Area, to once and for all find evidence of settlement in the various periods, and to provide some much-needed vindication of Church doctrine. The trench was dug 5.6 meters (18.4 ft.) down to solid bedrock, and was continued for a length of 12.9 meters (42.3 ft.). But the results disappointed the archeologist. He writes: "at least where excavated, there were no habitations." He found a few Byzantine sherds, similar to many others in the vicinity. Otherwise, no evidence of human presence was revealed. "All the fill," Bagatti admits simply, "follows normally the declivity of the hill." That is to say, no man-made strata were revealed at all—only virgin earth and rock.

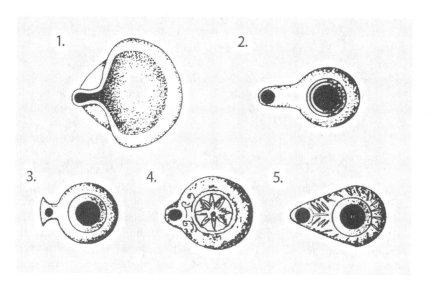

Figure 2.2. Typical Palestinian oil lamps.

(1) Bronze-Iron Age (2) Hellenistic
(3) Bow-spouted ("Herodian") (4) Roman (5) Byzantine
(*Cf.* Salm 2008a:*Illus. 3.3*)

The Hellenistic period

The mid-twentieth century witnessed the birth of the State of Israel and a great advance in technology, largely as a result of World War II. With the passing decades archeological data and methods became even more precise, and older theories regarding many Palestinian sites had to be discarded. As for Nazareth, some non-Catholic scholars realized that a hiatus in settlement could not be denied—there simply was no evidence for settlement there after the Assyrian conquest in 732 BCE. However, the doctrinal requirement for a village at and before the time of Jesus was as real for Protestant scholars as for Catholic. To solve the evidentiary dilemma, they proposed that Nazareth was resettled in Hellenistic times (330-63 BCE). I call this the "Hellenistic renaissance" hypothesis.

This hypothesis, however, is no more consistent with the evidence in the ground than is the doctrine of continuous habitation. *There is no Hellenistic evidence from Nazareth.* My careful examination of the literature shows that the tiny bit of evidence claimed as "Hellenistic" is bogus. For example, below is a photo of six oil lamps discovered in a Nazareth tomb and curtly labeled "Hellenistic" in the original 1931 report, signed by E. Richmond (*Fig. 2.3*). A few years later a Catholic writer, Father C. Kopp, wrote a series of articles on Nazareth in which he further characterizes the lamps: "R. classifies the era very generally as 'Hellenistic' based on 6 lamps; according to the accompanying photos of the finds [they] must surely go back at least as far as 200 BC."[5] In fact, the six lamps date from the Middle to Late Roman periods (70 CE–330 CE), long after the turn of the era. Incredibly, misdatings of the primary evidence, sometimes involving discrepancies of up to five hundred years (as in this case), are often encountered in the scholarly Nazareth literature.

Fr. Bagatti corrected the above misdating in his 1969 book, *Excavations in Nazareth* (p. 242) and accepted that these lamps were second–third century CE rather than second–third century BCE. A similar error is made in an influential article entitled "Nazareth" in the *Anchor Bible Dictionary* (1992), today the premiere American biblical encyclopedia. There, we read the astonishing statement that "The general archeological picture is of a small village, devoted wholly to agriculture, that came into being in the course of the 3d century B.C." I did a double-take when I first read this many years ago, assuming a misprint. *Surely*, I thought, *the author means "A.D." instead of "B.C."* But no, he is in earnest, and is simply describing the Hellenistic renaissance doctrine.

The word "Hellenistic" is peppered throughout Bagatti's 325-page book, occurring about a dozen times. But those claims are always tentative

---

5. Richmond 1931:plate xxxiv, no.2; Kopp 1938:194.

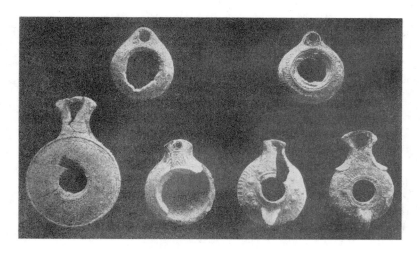

Figure. 2.3. Middle to Late Roman oil lamps found in a Nazareth tomb.
These lamps have *all* been falsely (and repeatedly) labeled "Hellenistic"
in the scholarly literature. (*Cf.* Salm 2008a:*Illus. 3.1.*)

and vague. The archeologist never shows us any complete Hellenistic artifacts, like an oil lamp or a pot, but a few ludicrously small shards each less
than one inch square. Such tiny pieces of pottery could be almost anything,
even to a specialist. Bagatti's ultimate summation (p. 319) is: "We have met
with only few traces of the Hellenistic period, but there are many elements
of the Roman period..." I set about finding those "few traces of the Hellenistic period," and came up against a brick wall—except for a few other
similar claims, such as "some sherds belong to the Hellenistic period" (p.
272), and the following gem of imprecision: "The black varnish given to
No. 8 reminds us of the custom in such products during Hellenistic-Roman
times" (p. 185). Now, Hellenistic-Roman times span a period of seven centuries, while black varnish is found on objects of many eras. So, Bagatti's
statement does not tell us much, but it does allow the author to use the word
"Hellenistic" once again.

On two pages of his book (*Exc*:136–37), Bagatti offers us the rare treat
of concrete evidence from "Hellenic times." Or does he? Again, these are
tiny pieces of pottery, less than an inch square. But Bagatti is not sure himself. He writes that one shard is from "Hellenic times *or earlier*" (my italics).
Indeed, both probably date to the Bronze or Iron Age. Another example:
"Well known as appertaining to the Hellenistic period is the foot of the little

vase, like a spindle (No. 15) *although these little vases remain in use until the 3rd cent. A.D., as we can see from Jerash"* (emphasis added). Well, the shard looks to me from the diagrams like the foot of a Roman-period vase, of which several similar examples survive from Nazareth.

The search for Hellenistic evidence enters a veritable quagmire of deception with Bagatti's following statement:

> The only pieces which seem to indicate the Hellenistic period is [*sic*] the nozzle No. 26 of fig. 233 and 2 of fig. 235, a bit short for the ordinary lamps, but not completely unusual. (*Exc*:309–310)

One would suppose that the archeologist is describing two specimens, for he uses the plural "pieces" and gives two examples. Crosschecking, however, shows that both examples refer to the identical nozzle: once in a photo (Fig. 233 no. 26), and once in a diagram *of the same artifact* (Fig. 235 no. 2). The caption to the diagram proclaims: "Pottery lamps of the Bronze, Hellenistic and Roman periods found in various places."

So, by eliminating all evidence that could be from other periods, it seems that *the sum total of Hellenistic evidence from Nazareth finally devolves upon a single broken oil lamp nozzle*, about one inch long and the same in width, that is, about the size of the extremity of an adult person's thumb. But is this nozzle really Hellenistic? We're speaking here of the protruding front part of all oil lamps, the part which is pierced at the end by the wick-hole. The typical Greek oil lamp had a long nozzle (*Fig. 2.2*, no. 2), considerably longer than Bagatti's example which the Italian, as we see in the above citation, freely admits is "a bit short for the ordinary lamps, but not completely unusual." Well, perhaps we are dealing with an *atypical* Hellenistic oil lamp. (Like the disappearing Cheshire cat in *Alice in Wonderland*, the Hellenistic evidence gets smaller and smaller...) In a footnote, Bagatti offers several "Hellenistic" parallels to this example. I dutifully looked them up, and with them we finally come to the end of this path leading into the brambles: the parallels do not resemble Bagatti's example at all. They are longer and exhibit an entirely different profile, with sloping as opposed to parallel sides. We have reached a dead end, and can be assured that there is no Hellenistic evidence at all from Nazareth.[6] We can also be assured that considerable effort has been expended to produce such evidence out of thin air.

---

6. Bagatti's 'Hellenistic' nozzle is probably the product of a local pottery tradition dating 50 CE–150 CE, similar to other oil lamps found in the Nazareth area. For discussion see Salm 2008a:111–120.

The Roman period

When the Hellenistic is added to the Assyrian, Babylonian, and Persian periods, then the hiatus in settlement at Nazareth extends from four to almost seven centuries (732 BCE-63 BCE). Yet we have still not reached the epoch when people reentered the basin. The first evidence of human presence begins in the first century CE, and consists of several oil lamps of the "Herodian" type. This name is a misnomer, for the type of lamp was made and used until the mid-second century CE,[7] long after the time of Herod the Great and even after the death of his last reigning descendant (c. 100 CE). Thus, like "Roman," "Herodian" is a word which has been misused by the tradition to characterize later evidence as earlier, namely, to the time of Herod the Great (37-4 BCE). In such subtle ways, the Nazareth literature is full of pitfalls for the unwary reader.

Oil lamps are particularly valuable for dating purposes because the many varieties have been on the whole well studied. An expert considers the composition, color, form, method of manufacture (by hand, wheel, or mold), decoration, and other features of the lamp. All these data can furnish a very good approximation of the date (and sometimes the place) of manufacture. In the case of Palestinian oil lamps of Greco-Roman times, a lamp can in certain instances be pinpointed to the quarter century.

"Herodian" oil lamps were characterized by a spatulate nozzle, as seen in the lamps at the lower left and lower right of *Figure 2.3*. Because such lamps were manufactured until the middle of the second century CE, I have not called them "Herodian" but "bow-spouted"—a description which actually matches their appearance.[8]

The large bow-spouted lamp at the lower left of *Figure 2.3* has very little decoration, no handle, and no volutes (collars at the neck). It is probably earlier than the smaller bow-spouted lamp on the lower right which possesses all these features.[9] These two oil lamps are included in the earliest Roman evidence we have from Nazareth. Though they can be as late as 135-150 CE, the more burning question is: how early can they be? That determination tells us how early people could have started coming into the Nazareth basin.

A number of bow-spouted oil lamps were found in a complex of tombs published by Nurit Feig in 1990. The tombs are 2.6 km east of the Church

---

7. Some specialists date the *terminus ante quem* for this lamp to the Bar Kokhba war (132–36 CE), others a few years later (c. 150 CE). For a detailed discussion of the dating for the bow-spouted lamp, see Salm 2008a:167–73.

8. The term "bow-spouted" for these lamps was first proposed by Paul Lapp in 1961.

9. The two subtypes of the bow-spouted oil lamp were proposed by R. Smith in 1961. For discussion, see Salm 2008a:171.

No.	Exc. fig.	Findspot	Description	Smith Type	Fernandez	Date
						[* = Found in kokhim tomb]
1-14		BOW-SPOUTED (Plain):				
1.	233:1	VA (L. 51c) 20m N of CA	Shard (nozzle and neck)	1	(3.1 or 3.2)	c. 25 CE–c. 135 CE
2.	233:2	VA (L. 51a) 20m N of CA	Shard (nozzle)	2	(3.4b)	c. 25 CE–c. 135 CE
3.	233:3	CA (L. 26) Byz. atrium	Shard (nozzle and neck)	2	3.4b	c. 25 CE–c. 135 CE
4.	233:4	CA (L. 46)	Shard (nozzle and neck)	2	(3.4b)	c. 25 CE–c. 135 CE
5.	233:5	VA (L. 48f) 20m N of CA	Shard (part of discus)	2	(3.4)	c. 25 CE–c. 135 CE
6.	235:3	VA (unspecified)	Shard (nozzle)	2	(3.4c)	c. 25 CE–c. 135 CE
7.	235:4	VA (unspecified)	Shard (nozzle and neck)	2	(Not included)	c. 25 CE–c. 135 CE
8.	235:5	VA (unspecified)	Shard (part of discus)	2	(3.4c)	c. 25 CE–c. 135 CE
9.	235:8	VA (unspecified)	Shard (part of discus)	2	(3.4c)	c. 25 CE–c. 135 CE
10.	192:6	T. 70 (30m S of CA)	Plain bow-spouted	2	3.2(b)	*c. 25 CE–c. 135 CE
11.	192:11	T. 70 (30m S of CA)	2 Lamps	2	(Not included)	*c. 25 CE–c. 135 CE
13.	—	T. 72 (350m SE of CA)	Richmond photo lower left	2	3.4	*c. 25 CE–c. 135 CE
14.	—	El Batris (500m NW of CA)	"Herodian" lamp	?	—	*c. 25 CE–c. 135 CE
15-19.		BOW-SPOUTED (Darom)	5 Lamps (see Chp. 5)	—	8	*c. 70 CE–c. 135 CE
20-22.		LOCAL TRADITION	3 Lamps (Exc. 192:15) Found in T. 70. Cf. Chp. 3:22f.			*c. 50 CE–c. 150 CE
23-29.		ROMAN	7 Lamps (Broneer XXV; Loeschke VIII)		9.1	*c. 50 CE– III CE

192:13-14 = 5 lamps from T. 70; Richmond photo upper left & rgt. = 2 lamps from T. 72

Figure. 2.4 The earliest Nazareth oil lamps.

The column at the right gives the first appearance of such lamps in the Galilee.

Those found in *kokhim* tombs must be dated *c.* 50 CE or later. (*Cf.* Salm 2008a:*Illus. 4.3*.)

of the Annunciation. The oil lamps are identical or similar to those discovered by Bagatti in the Venerated Area, which makes Feig's observations very pertinent to our study. Feig dates the bow-spouted lamps *c.* 50 CE–*c.* 150 CE and concludes: "From these facts and from the findings it is possible to relate the use of these tombs to a period of time between the middle of the first century [CE] to the third century CE. It is also possible to assume that the other tombs on the ridge are from the same time as well" (Feig 1990:79).

This dating is confirmed by F. Fernandez who has published a study on Roman Galilean pottery. He redates a good deal of evidence first reviewed by Bagatti and others. Regarding artifacts from the most important tomb, that which furnished the lion's share of Roman evidence at Nazareth (including a number of bow-spouted lamps), Fernandez concludes that the tomb is "certainly not before the second third of the first century after Christ" (Fernandez:63).

A survey of the published evidence shows that people started to come into the Nazareth basin in the generations between the First and Second Jewish Revolts (70 CE–130 CE). This stands to reason: Jerusalem was destroyed in 70 CE, and a number of Jews fled northwards. There are indications that Nazareth was Jewish (presence of stone vessels, complete absence of representational ornamentation on oil lamps). At the same time, no material evidence suggests that the settlement had anything to do with heretical Jewish-Christians (*minim* in Hebrew)—a favorite thesis of Bagatti, Testa, and other Roman Catholics who have attempted to demonstrate the continuous presence of Christians in the town from the time of Jesus onwards.[10]

Chronologically, then, it is evident that *the village of Nazareth did not yet exist in the time of Jesus, that is, at the turn of the era.* It came into existence about the time that the evangelists were writing their gospels. Perhaps they heard of the new village, and decided to make it the hometown of Jesus. I can't affirm this for sure, but note that scholars have long known that the Greek name for the village does not perfectly correspond with the Semitic name. The Greek name has a *zeta* (a voiced sibilant) while the Semitic name has a *tsade* (unvoiced). As scholars have long noted to their irritation, these letters are not compatible with the result that, on linguistic grounds, it is most unlikely that the the Greek *Nazareth* derived from the Semitic *Natsrath*. In short, it appears that the Greek name is artificial and not linked to any place known to geography before the fourth century of our era.

---

10. Joan Taylor decisively rebutted this thesis in her 1993 book, *Christians and the Holy Places*.

The tomb in Mary's bedroom

In a good year, over a million pilgrims come to Nazareth to visit where the archangel Gabriel announced to the Blessed Virgin, "Hail Mary, full of grace..." Supposedly, this occurred in the virgin's dwelling, which the Church claims was at the site of the present Church of the Annunciation. However, that church is located in the middle of an ancient Roman cemetery. This fact is quite overlooked in the scholarly Nazareth literature. For Jews, contact with the dead was a source of ritual impurity (Lev 21:11), and for this reason graves had to be located outside the town or village perimeter. The Talmud (m. *Bava Bathra* 2:9) specifies the required minimum distance ("fifty ells") from the nearest habitation. Of course, this is fatal to the traditional conception of the Venerated Area.

This Jewish prohibition was not generally appreciated until the 1950s, and so earlier Catholic archeologists innocently pointed out tombs in the Venerated Area, charted them, described them, and even opined that some of Jesus' family may have been buried in one or another of them. As a result, a careful review of the literature shows that Roman tombs once existed *directly under the Church of the Annunciation* as well as *close by in all directions*. In the 1950s it was realized that the Jewish prohibition against living in proximity to tombs could have a dire impact on the traditional view of the venerated sites, and thereafter we read no more of the presence of all these tombs.

Fotosearch.com

Figure 2.5 Depictions of the Annunciation have not noted the fact that it would have taken place in a cemetery.

But it was too late. The earlier data tell us that a number of tombs surround the Chapel of the Angel (the precise spot where the archangel spoke to Mary). One grave adjoins the northern edge of the Chapel—perhaps it was in her bedroom? This tomb is completely ignored in Bagatti's many writings on Nazareth. A few meters in another direction is a Roman tomb complex which contained four to twelve graves. The lame explanations for these interments are almost comical. Bagatti suggests (*Exc*:50) that these graves are from Crusader times. Were he correct, we should wonder at this sacrilegious (and otherwise unknown) Crusader custom of burying their dead under the house of the Virgin Mother. And who was important enough to be buried there yet, at the same time, escaping the gaze of history? In any case, the *kokh* design of the burials clearly dates them to later Roman times.

There are other reasons why the so-called Venerated Area in Nazareth could not have been what tradition claims. Located on the side of a steep and rocky hill called the Nebi Sa'in, it is inconceivable that the ancient peasantry would have wished (or would have had the engineering skills) to construct dwellings in that area. The grade of the slope is 14%, with the result that today one end of the Church of the Annunciation is about ten meters higher than the other. This fact is, of course, masked by the unusual architecture of the present mammoth structure, which includes internal stairs and two churches one on top of the other.

When the village of Nazareth became a reality in the second century CE, it must have been located on the valley floor, not on the steep and rocky hillside where the Church property lies. That slope was used as a necropolis and for agriculture—storage of grain, wine, and oil in silos and cisterns; the pressing of oil and wine; and the threshing of wheat, barley, *etc*.[11]

From this brief review of the data, we are now able to reconstruct the true history of settlement in the Nazareth basin:

c. 2000–*c.* 712 BCE	Bronze-Iron Age settlement of "Japhia"
c. 712 BCE–*c.* 70 CE	Great Hiatus (no settlement)
c. 100 CE	Founding of "Nazareth" (*Natsrath*)
To present	Continued existence of settlement

From these facts, we can now draw a conclusion that will be shocking to the orthodox faithful: "Jesus of Nazareth" and his family could not possibly have lived at the site now called Nazareth. Archeology shows quite plainly that the gospel accounts of Nazareth are fictive, not factual. This being the case, we may well ask: "Was Jesus of Nazareth himself a fiction?"

---

11. For the analysis of a nearby agricultural site, see Chapter 10.

Chapter 3

THE MYTH OF NAZARETH:
THE INVENTED TOWN OF JESUS
Does it really matter?

Adopting a partisan Atheist tone, this short article summarizes the conclusions contained in *The Myth of Nazareth*. It
appeared in the March 2007 issue of *American Atheist* magazine,
one year before the book's publication.[1]

* * *

A recent article in *American Atheist* contained surprising results of new
research into one of the most important venues of the Christian story: the
town of Nazareth.[2] This topic has been contentious for many years, and
it is no coincidence that significant research into the dubious origins of
Christianity should first appear in this magazine, given what I consider the
common sense and scientific acumen indigenous to Atheists. Of course,
damaging material such as this puts the very stiff Christian neck in a scientific noose, as it were, and the Christian press has no interest in kicking
the chair out from under itself. A nudge by well–intentioned Atheists at this
critical juncture won't hurt... With the knowledge that Nazareth did not
exist in the time of Jesus, we have our fingers wrapped around one of the
chair legs and are now poised to give it a decided heave.

The prior article was aptly titled "Why the Truth about Nazareth is
Important." It is indeed important, though perhaps not for the most obvi-
ous reason. After all, where Jesus really came from is hardly earthshaking.
What must matter to all Christians, however, is the inescapable fact that the

---

1.   The initial chapters of *The Myth of Nazareth* had begun circulating in the form of
chapbooks (see p. 19 *supra*).
2.   See Chapter 2.

evangelists invented this basic element in the story of cosmic redemption. The proof is now at hand that "Jesus of Nazareth," a long-standing icon of Western civilization, is bogus.

There can be no return to the comforting familiarity of the past, for with the proof that Nazareth did not exist at the turn of the era the gospels leave the realm of history and forever enter the realm of myth. It is a swift kick to the solar plexus of Christian inerrantism, the scholarly equivalent of a punch sending the opponent to the mat—perhaps even a knock-out.

The myth of Nazareth boots Christian certitude out the window, and the door is now wide open to ask, "What else did the evangelists invent?" As after the recent power shift in Congress, there will be questions...[3] Up until now the tradition has been able to fend off attacks from the intellectual left because those attacks lacked proof. Now, archeology has supplied the proof, and with it the balance finally shifts. The Church's position must fall like a house of cards. After all, Nazareth is mentioned in three of the four canonical gospels[4] and is neither an insignificant nor a passing element. If the tradition invented his hometown, then who can place faith in other aspects of the Jesus story, such as his virgin birth, miracles, crucifixion, or resurrection? Were these also invented? What, in other words, is left in the gospels of which the average Christian can be sure? What is left of his or her faith?

Scholars can now apply this radical new information to problems that have bedeviled them for three centuries, as they have fruitlessly tried to reconcile contradictions and make sense out of four narratives that obstinately refuse to agree. For example, it has long been known that the birth stories in Matthew and Luke are incompatible (in the Gospel of Matthew the Holy Family comes from Bethlehem, not Nazareth). Again, why is Jesus so often interacting with Pharisees in the Galilee, where they were hardly known before 70 CE? Why does Luke write about a preposterous Roman census in which everyone returned to his birthplace to register for taxation (2:1–7)? The Romans were far too practical to mandate such a recipe for instant social chaos. Besides, the evangelist was in error by several years (a different type of census took place in 6 CE). In any case, Galilee was not within the

---

3. The 2006 United States midterm elections were held on Tuesday, November 7, 2006. All United States House of Representatives seats and one third of the United States Senate seats were contested in this election, as well as 36 state governorships, many state legislatures, four territorial legislatures, and many state and local races. The election resulted in a sweeping victory for the Democratic Party which captured control of the House of Representatives, the Senate, and won a majority of governorships and state legislatures from the Republican Party. (Wikipedia)

4. I argue that the appearance of the word *Nazaret* in Mk 1:9 (the only appearance of the town in that gospel) is a later interpolation (Salm 2008a:299–302). When that verse is correctly amended, then "Nazareth" entirely disappears from the Gospel of Mark.

area of direct Roman jurisdiction (it was administered by the puppet ruler, Herod Antipas). To make a long story short, the invention of Nazareth now brings another alternative to the fore: these elements are not historical at all. They, too, were invented.

For readers who may wish to review the evidence, I would like to summarize the results of my research on Nazareth carried out over the last eight years. Chronologically, those results can be reduced to the following five points:

(1) The earliest settlement in the Nazareth basin was destroyed about 730 BCE during the Assyrian conquest of the Holy Land. Before that time, the Bronze-Iron Age settlement (which had been in existence for some 1300 years) was not known as Nazareth but as Japhia, a town mentioned in the Bible and in Egyptian records.

(2) The destruction of Japhia was followed by a hiatus in settlement lasting from late eighth century BCE until the late first century CE. During those eight centuries no one lived in the Nazareth basin.

(3) Nazareth came into being between the two Jewish revolts (70 CE–135 CE). That is, the town appeared when most scholars allege that the evangelists were writing their gospels. The appearance of Nazareth toward the end of the first century CE is confirmed most significantly by the 29 earliest oil lamps (of the bow-spouted type) which date from between c. 25 CE and the middle of the second century CE. In addition, the 20-odd Roman tombs in the basin all postdate 50 CE.

(4) It is not possible that Mary, Jesus, and Joseph lived where tradition says, namely, in the vicinity of the Church of the Annunciation. Not only was Nazareth not yet in existence during the time of the Holy Family, but Jewish law mandates that domiciles not be near tombs (corpses are a source of ritual impurity). This is significant because the Venerated Area was part of the village cemetery and agricultural district. For over fifteen hundred years, in fact, Christian pilgrims have been visiting and worshipping at a Late Roman cemetery and wine producing complex.

(5) Nazareth was at first a Jewish village (without the admixture of heretics or pagans). It has lasted continuously from about 100 CE to the present.

The invention of Nazareth is proof positive that the evangelists were spinning a yarn, that the Gospels are myth in a big way, and that the Christian faith is, well... (supply the appropriate word). No longer can conservatives tout "gospel truth," one of the three *solas* of the Reformation: *Sola gratia, sola fide, sola scriptura* ("Only grace, only faith, only scripture"). As the third leg of this triad dissolves before our very eyes, the other two must soon succumb as well.

Without Nazareth there can be no Christianity. After all, the village is more than the alleged hometown of Jesus. It is also the venue of the Annunciation. We all know the story: "In the sixth month the angel Gabriel was sent from God to a city of Galilee named Nazareth, to a virgin betrothed to a man whose name was Joseph, of the house of David; and the virgin's name was Mary" (Lk 1:26–27). The Church will now have to look for another venue where God united with the Blessed Virgin in the *mysterium verbi*, to produce a son both divine and human and to boggle the mind of man ever since. But we needn't hold our collective breath as twenty-first century priests and nuns scour the Galilee for the real site of the annunciation. If such bull-headed clerics and conservatives do embark on that misguided vision quest, we should wish them better luck than their first choice, *for the present Church of the Annunciation sits in a Roman cemetery dating a couple of hundred years after the time of Christ.* "The situation is hopeless..." runs a wry Austrian proverb, "but not serious." So also with Nazareth. The situation is hopeless for the tradition, but hopeful for freethinkers everywhere.

When one door closes another opens. If Nazareth did not exist in the time of Jesus, then the enigmatic term "Nazarene" (or "Nazorean")—frequently found in Mark and in the other gospels—cannot refer to a place at all but must refer to something else, something long forgotten. This makes sense, for in the Acts of the Apostles (24:5) Paul is accused of being a "ringleader of the sect of the Nazoreans"—which could not have referred to inhabitants of Nazareth. The Semitic root of *Nazarene* means "guard, preserve" (verb) and "branch, shoot" (noun). Thus, Paul was accused of being a leader of people who were trying to preserve something they considered precious. What that was has yet to be determined. In any case, the (probably pre-Pauline) religion of the Nazarenes must have been very different from the Christianity we know today.

Celebrate, freethinkers... Christianity as we know it may be finally coming to an end!

Chapter 4

A Response to 'Surveys and Excavations at the Nazareth Village Farm (1997–2002): Final Report'

This chapter was first published in the *Bulletin of the Anglo-Israel Archaeological Society* (BAIAS) Volume 26, 2008. It is a response to a long archeological report which appeared in BAIAS the preceding year. That article's authors attempted to provide archeological support for dating a new, robust commercial venture in Nazareth called the "Nazareth Village Farm" (NVF) to the turn of the era. My response below shows that the original report was seriously flawed, and that nothing from the NVF demonstrably (or even probably) dates to "the time of Jesus."

* * *

A 61-page report on Nazareth archeology was published in the 2007 issue of the *Bulletin of the Anglo-Israel Archaeological Society* (25; 16–79), too late for consideration in the recent book, *The Myth of Nazareth* (American Atheist Press, March 2008). The report, entitled 'Surveys and Excavations at the Nazareth Village Farm (1997–2002): Final Report', is authored by Stephen Pfann, Ross Voss, and Yehudah Rapuano. Arguably, this extended article constitutes the most significant contribution to the archeology of the basin since Fr. Bellarmino Bagatti's two volume *Excavations in Nazareth* (English edition 1969). It is referred to below as the NVFR (Nazareth Village Farm Report).

The Nazareth Village Farm (NVF) lies on approximately 15 acres to the south and west of the present Nazareth Hospital. The NVFR's authors locate the area "about 500 m from the site of ancient Nazareth," evidently measuring from the Latin Church of the Annunciation (in the so-called 'Venerated Area') to the nearest point of the NVF. *Contra* Luke 4:29 and longstanding Church tradition, however, the inhabited portion of the ancient village was not located on the hillside, as I have attempted to demonstrate in *The Myth of Nazareth*. The southern flank of the Nebi Sa'in, where the Franciscan Venerated Area is located, is honeycombed with tombs and agricultural installations (some immediately under the Church of the Annunciation itself),[1] and is quite steep (averaging a 14% grade). The Jewish village (of later Roman and early Byzantine times) surely existed on the relatively flat valley floor, between tombs to the east and the west.[2] Thus, the settlement was about 1 km from the NVF, still close enough for daily agricultural work by the ancient villagers.[3]

NVFR 19–68 amply demonstrates that the terraced area under examination was a locus of ancient agricultural activity. The steepness of the NVF (the average slope is 20%) and the discovery of a tomb[4] reveal that this area also was not the site of ancient habitations, despite the ambitious plan (known as 'Nazareth Village') presently underway in the NVF to create an impression of Jesus' hometown.[5]

The University of the Holy Land (UHL), as well as its subsidiary, the Center for the Study of Early Christianity (CSEC), seek to provide an "academic foundation" for the Nazareth Village Farm endeavor, as the opening sentence of the NVFR reveals:

> For nearly two decades, the University of the Holy Land (UHL) and its subsidiary, the Center for the Study of Early Christianity (CSEC), has labored to lay the academic foundation for the construction of a first-century Galilean village or town based upon archaeology and early Jewish and Christian sources. (NVFR:19)

Stephen Pfann, one of the NVFR authors, is President of the UHL, while Ross Voss chairs the institution's Department of Archaeology. Of the three NVFR authors, however, it is with Rapuano's work that we shall be

---

1. According to Torah, corpses were a source of impurity (Lev. 5:3; Num. 5:1–3). The Mishnah (*m. Bava Bathra* 2:9) mandates that tombs be outside village bounds.
2. For an older map of the tombs of the Roman era, see Kopp 1938: 193. An updated map is at Salm 2008a:224 (*Illus. 5.2*).
3. The location of the ancient settlement is discussed in Salm 2008a: Chapter 5.
4. The tomb, presumably Roman (as are 22 other tombs in the Nazareth basin), is mentioned only in passing at NVFR: 24. It is still unexcavated and lies in Area B (exact location unspecified).
5. On the NVF as an elaborate venue for tourists and pilgrims, see *Biblical Archaeology Review* 25 (May–June 1999):16.

most concerned, for he is responsible for the critical concluding section on pottery (NVFR: 68–77). As regards dating, the pottery is the most diagnostic element in the report for—with one brief exception (NVFR: 39–40, see below)—the remainder of the report concerns only very generally dateable structural remains such as terraces, watchtowers, and presses (if they are dateable at all).

Non-Figure 4.1. A scene from the Nazareth Village Farm

showing a male actor in peasant garb doing carpentry work, while a child watches, has unfortunately been deleted in compliance with strict NVF policy against the taking of unauthorized photographs and the unauthorized reproduction of all NVF material. According to publicity, however, Nazareth Village is "a carefully researched re-creation of Jesus hometown" which offers tours, a gift shop, "Biblical meals," and actors in "traditional garb."

The extended discussion of those structural features is illuminating and well written. It has apparently met the NVFR's own stated goal:

> It was concluded that excavation would be necessary in order to further define the nature of the ancient farm with the hope that the excavations would illuminate previously unknown aspects of terrace farming in the Galilee. Hitherto, little research had been undertaken on terracing and ancient methods of cultivation practised in the Galilee (Golomb and Kedar 1971). The remains of the farm were considered to be the most important, since they could potentially provide a key witness to the life and livelihood of the ancient villagers. (NVFR: 20)

The NVFR expands our knowledge of the character of the ancient Jewish settlement, and shows that the village of later Roman and Byzantine times tended both a "dry" and a "wet" farm (with a cistern and water channels, and possibly a spring house), producing a variety of crops on this hillside, principally vines, but also olive trees and possibly figs, almonds, wheat, barley, legumes, and leafy vegetables (NVFR: 23).

Two surveys

Until the NVFR, the only published report dealing with the Nazareth Village Farm area was a brief two-paragraph précis in *Hadashot Arkheologiyot* (1999; English p. 90, Hebrew p. 113) entitled "Nazerat (Nazareth) Area, Survey," authored by Mordechai Haiman.[6] The survey was conducted in April 1997, "on behalf of the [Israel] Antiquities Authority." At that time Haiman was director of the IAA's survey department, a post he held from 1994 to 2003. It is surprising that Haiman's Nazareth report is not mentioned in the NVFR bibliography. In the text of the NVFR, his survey work is delimited in the following ways: in duration (two days, NVFR: 25); in extent (only areas A and B were surveyed and, furthermore, features within them were only selectively plotted, NVFR: 25); and in scope (a "GPS survey," NVFR: 25, 77).

Another survey, conducted by UHL/CSEC in February of 1997, receives the following notice on the first page of the NVFR:

> [After the initial identification of an ancient winepress and agricultural terraces in 1996...] A survey of the area, which covered approximately 15 acres, was subsequently commissioned by UHL/CSEC and was conducted in February 1997 by the institution's archaeological staff, under the direction of Ross Voss.

This survey was "on behalf of UHL/CSEC," as a remark in the concluding "Acknowledgements" (*sic*) section makes clear:

> The survey of the site at Nazareth was conducted on behalf of the University of the Holy Land (UHL) and its subsidiary, the Center for the Study of Early Christianity (CSEC), in February 1997, under the direction of Ross Voss with Stephen Pfann, Yehudah Rapuano, and Jan Karnis. The GPS survey was undertaken by Mordechai Haiman. (NVFR: 77)

My principal purpose regarding these two surveys is to note that they make substantially different claims. The Haiman/IAA survey concludes that "[s]herds, mostly dating to the Late Roman period (second–fourth centuries CE), were scattered on the surface." It makes no mention of evidence from Hellenistic times or from Early Roman times. On the other hand, the UHL/CSEC survey (and subsequent excavations carried out under the auspices of UHL/CSEC)[7] claims that a substantial amount of pottery found at the NVF dates both to Hellenistic and to Early Roman times. These latter claims will be carefully examined below.

---

6.   Haiman received a Ph.D. in archeology from the Hebrew University in 1993.

7.   "In all, four successive seasons of excavation were carried out at the site between 1997 and 2000. The discoveries from this excavation and from the cleaning of the more eroded terrace areas in preparation for the construction of the Nazareth Village are the subject of the present report." (NVFR: 25.)

The NVF pottery

The NVFR repeatedly summarizes the dateable pottery evidence with a phrase whose meaning is quite equivocal:

> Potsherds were found on the surface of the terraces dating from various periods beginning with the early to late Roman period.

The phrase "beginning with the early to late Roman period" occurs at NVFR: 19, 24, 28, 32, and 56.[8] We shall determine the force of this phrase through a close consideration of the pottery itemizations at the end of the NVFR. In any case, the phrase is curiously at variance with the NVFR's own conclusions, which claim that a number of sherds date to Hellenistic times (see below). It also goes considerably beyond the Haiman survey report, as we noted above. Over 700 fragments were recovered at the NVF, and sometimes they are "tiny" or "very fragmentary" (NVFR: 74). In fact, the opening sentence of Rapuano's pottery report (under the rubric "Appendix 2," NVFR: 68–77) begins with a caveat:

> The ceramic finds from the Nazareth Village Farm excavations were for the most part quite fragmentary, as might be expected of pottery recovered from agricultural installations and terraces.

The accompanying NVFR pottery diagrams confirm the modest size of most of the sherds. We must keep this in mind when considering any emphatic claims regarding dating. As is well known, though observations can sometimes be made from small sherds regarding form and type, composition, colour, and even method of manufacture of the artifact, such modest sherds commonly offer a precarious basis indeed for determining those elements, as well as the artifact's date. It is no surprise that Rapuano's 75 itemizations are fairly peppered with tentative words such as *possibly, probably, evidently, appeared to be, etc.* Interestingly, the archeologist also appears to become increasingly tentative as his report proceeds, so that his final 15 itemizations (from 42: 5 onwards, NVFR: 76) have scarcely an entry without one of the above-noted equivocal words or phrases.

In my book, *The Myth of Nazareth*, I concluded that none of the post-Iron Age oil lamps dates before *c.* 25 CE, that none of the post-Iron Age tombs dates before *c.* 50 CE, and that "not a single post-Iron Age artifact,

---

8. I was subsequently upbraided by S. Pfann and R. Rapuano for this assertion. In their published "Response" (BAIAS 2008:106) they write that the actual quote "was never made." Technically, Pfann and Rapuano are correct. The NVF report used various wordings: potsherds from "the Early-to-late Roman Period" (NVFR 19); "Pottery from the first to the third centuries" (NVFR 24); "predominance of Early and Late Roman pottery" (NVFR 28 and 32); "The majority of the pottery was first to third centuries AD" (NVFR 56). See also footnote no. 15 below.

tomb or structure at Nazareth dates with certainty before 100 CE" (Salm 2008a: 205). My overall conclusion was that the settlement came into existence between the two Jewish revolts (*cf.* Salm 2008a: 206, 288*f.*). A post-70 CE emergence for Nazareth should be borne in mind when we note that in every case where Rapuano dates a sherd before c. 70 CE (*i.e.*, to the Hellenistic period, or to "Early Roman" times), he supplies a tentative word. The archeologist is, by his own admission, not certain of pre-70 CE evidence.

Problems of double-attribution

Additional problems confront the person who patiently itemizes all of Rapuano's findings. Readers of *The Myth of Nazareth* (pp. 176 *ff.*) will recall that, in an embarrassing but revealing lapse, Fr. Bagatti assigned the same sherd on one page to the Iron Age and on another page to Roman times. No printing error ("typo") could have been involved, due to the accompanying discussion by the Italian archeologist. Rapuano is capable of not one, but four similar contradictions.[9] Again, no mere printing errors obtain, for Rapuano's double datings are accompanied by incompatible descriptions as well as findspots. Though there is certainly an explanation (and I will not speculate how in these cases two apparently different sherds were assigned the same number), such internal contradictions must have a deleterious effect on our confidence in the entire NVF pottery report. The four double attributions require explanation as well as correction. They are as follows:

(1) On page 74 of the NVFR Rapuano assigns Fig. 41:32 to the Ottoman period, and on the next page dates it from "the third century to early fifth century AD." (The Ottoman period began in the fourteenth century, and hence the difference between the two attributions is a millennium or more.)

(2) On page 73 of the NVFR (6th line), Rapuano itemizes artifact 41:4. He describes it as the "plain rim" of a bowl of Adan-Bayewitz Type 1E ("mid-third to early fifth century AD"), and notes that the findspot was locus 31 of Area B2. On p. 75, however, the archeologist again itemizes artifact 41:4. The findspot is now Locus 7 of Area B2, and it is "evidently the rim of an everted-rim bowl, possibly Adan-Bayewitz Form 3B, dated from [the] early second century to the later fourth century AD."

(3) On page 77 of the NVFR (top line), Rapuano itemizes artifact 43:3. He describes it as "a small bowl with a cupped rim," and states that the findspot was Locus 2 of Area C3. No dating is offered for this shard, which from the diagram appears to be part of a rim. Later, on the same

---

9. The original article published in BAIAS itemized only three 'double-datings.' However, a fourth case has since come to my attention and is now also listed.

page, the archeologist again itemizes artifact 43:3. The findspot is now Locus 5 of Area C3, and Rapuano describes it as a "krater" dating "from the end of the first century to the mid-third century AD."

(4) On page 74 of the NVFR (tenth line), Rapuano itemizes artifact 41:8. He describes it as a "Tiny fragment of a rim, probably of a small bowl of the Roman period." The findspot is Locus 34 of area B2. Later, on the same page, the archeologist again itemizes artifact 41:8. The findspot is now Locus 43 of Area B2, and Rapuano describes it as "the edge of the rim of what was evidently a Galilean bowl with a plain rim (Adan-Bayewitz Type 1E)." He now dates it "from the mid-third century to earlier fifth century AD."

Incidentally, these anomalies do not impact a post-70 CE emergence of the settlement. In each case, at least one of the two furnished datings renders these artifacts compatible with the conclusions arrived at in *The Myth of Nazareth*: that the village was initially settled after the First Jewish War.

Non-Roman evidence

Before proceeding to a discussion of the Roman-Byzantine pottery from the NVF, we shall review the brief discussion at NVFR: 39–40, which presents extra-Roman evidence unearthed at the NVF, and which also offers a problematic review of coin evidence from the remainder of the basin.

An interesting shard from "Early Bronze III" is pictured at NVFR: 40. It measures about 3 x 4 inches and was found on the surface in an unstratified context. The photo is too small to make out much detail, but the discussion notes "indentation on the underside of the vessel, below the rim, [which] is typical of platters relatively late in the Early Bronze III." This description recalls a vessel found in nearby Tomb 7 with "incisions below the neck."[10] That bowl was among the earliest evidence from the basin, dating to 2200–2000 BCE. Those centuries are variously known as the Intermediate period, Middle Bronze I (Amiran), or Early Bronze III. The latter nomenclature is adopted by the authors of the NVFR, who note that the incision pattern "is typical of platters relatively late in the Early Bronze III." This shard can thus be added to the artifacts used by the very first settlers of the basin, those who established the Canaanite village which I have argued was known in the Bronze and Iron Ages as Japhia (Salm 2008a: 53–55).

For completeness, mention can be made of a Gaza Ware bowl (Ottoman period) pictured at NVFR: 40. On the previous page we also see the photo and description of a coin dating 578–582 CE. It was discovered in

---

10. Bagatti 1969: Fig. 211:18 and p. 263. *Cf.* Salm 2008a: 34 and *Illus.* 1:4. Tomb 7 is located under the Church of the Annunciation (Bagatti 1969; 35, Pl. XI).

Area A and "represents the latest Byzantine coin that has been found in the Nazareth area."

After discussing the preceding artifacts found at the NVF, the report launches into a review of coin evidence from the rest of the Nazareth basin, including a discussion of coins at Mary's Well (at the northern end of the basin) and of Bagatti's numismatic finds in the Venerated Area, from the latter's *Excavations in Nazareth* (*Exc.*). The appositeness of that discussion is not entirely clear, for the NVFR found only a single, and late, coin. The discussion is also problematic, for precisely in the review of these remote loci are several quite unsubstantiated claims made—claims which emphatically support the existence of a village at the turn of the era.

In chronological order, the data furnished by the NVFR résumé of Bagatti's coin finds is as follows:

- One coin of Gordian III (238–244 CE), found at the "Fright." This is the earliest coin from the general vicinity. [*Exc.* 251; Salm 2008a: 196, n.152]
- One coin of Constantius (337–351 CE) found in the plaster of L. 29.[11] [*Exc.* 209]
- Three unidentifiable Byzantine coins (probably late fourth–early fifth century CE), from L. 25. [*Exc.* 46]
- One coin of Anastasius (491–518 CE). [*Exc.* 234]
- More than 60 coins of the Islamic to Mamluk period. [*Exc.* II: 194–201]

The NVFR (40) then offers the following remarkable statement:

> In addition, 165 coins were uncovered by Yardenna Alexandre in the 1997–1998 excavations at Mary's Well, Nazareth. The coins were overwhelmingly Mamluk, but also included a few Hellenistic, Hasmonaean, Early Roman, Byzantine, Umayyad and Crusader coins (Alexandre, forthcoming).

The above statement is remarkable to me, because in 2006 Ms. Alexandre graciously shared with me a pre-publication copy of her official IAA report on the excavation at Mary's Well.[12] As I write these lines that short report is before me, and it contains no mention of "165 coins" nor of coins from Hellenistic or Hasmonaean times. What the Alexandre report states regarding coins is limited to the following brief statement:

> A clean-up including the dredging of many 14–15th century small denomination coins, may date [to] the Franciscan efforts in the early 17th century (known from the written records. . .)

---

11. Following an error at Bagatti 1969: 210 the NVFR attributes the coin to Constans, who ruled 337–350. See Taylor 1993: 255 and Salm 2008a: 147.
12. See Salm 2008a: 132 *ff.*

It may well be that the "many 14–15th century small denomination coins" cited above total 165, a fact perhaps subsequently shared by Ms. Alexandre with the authors of the NVFR. But, once again, her report makes no mention of coins belonging to eras other than the "14–15th century." Certainly, it is difficult to believe that such significant evidence as coins from the Hellenistic, Hasmonaean, and Early Roman periods (incidentally, not otherwise attested in the Nazareth basin) was subsequently divulged to the authors of the NVFR, but escaped the official IAA report.

Non-diagnostic artifacts

I have divided the pottery at the NVF, itemized by Yehudah Rapuano, into two categories: non-diagnostic and diagnostic. In this case, the difference between categories depends on the presence or absence of a cited parallel. The rationale behind such a categorization is that the NVFR's pottery drawings in section, and the short accompanying descriptions, are almost unanimously based on small sherds, not on complete (or virtually complete) vessels. It must be accepted that, given the modest pieces involved, the drawings and descriptions are largely reconstructions based upon the best supposition of the archeologist. Often, as we have seen, Rapuano's conclusions are qualified by a tentative word conveying uncertainty.

Though the presence of parallels to catalogued objects in the literature does not entirely validate Rapuano's reconstruction, it at least permits the reader to align the archeologist's reconstruction with standard typologies. On the other hand, the lack of typological parallels means that the reader is entirely reliant upon the opinion of the archeologist, both as regards the object's reconstructed form *and* its dating.

In sum, those itemizations not accompanied by a parallel (60 out of 75, or 80% of Rapuano's report) are 'non-diagnostic,' for they amount to no more than the unverifiable opinion of the archeologist himself.

It must be noted that the totality of the NVFR evidence for a pre-70 CE Nazareth rests on eleven small pottery sherds for which Rapuano provides no typological parallels.[13] Put more bluntly, the entire NVFR evidence for Nazareth in the time of Jesus rests upon this archeologist's unsupported (and perhaps unsupportable) opinion, both as regards the reconstruction of the vessels in question and as regards their dating. In other words, Rapuano can offer no substantiation to standard references for any of his pre-70 CE claims. It can, of course, also be noted that these early datings conflict with the panoply of evidence from the rest of the Nazareth basin, as determined in *The Myth of Nazareth*.

---

13.   The eleven pottery sherds at the NVF attributed by Rapuano to pre-70 CE are as follows: 37:5; 38:4–6; 40:2, 4, 5, 6, 7; 42:6, 8. "Uncertain" are also 38:3 and 40:3.

Diagnostic artifacts

We can repose more confidence in Rapuano's conclusions in those fifteen cases (20% of the itemized artifacts) where the archeologist offers a
typological reference, almost always to the same source: D. Adan-Bayewitz,
Common Pottery in Roman Galilee (1993, Bar Ilan—referred to henceforth as
'AB').[14] It can be immediately affirmed that the information of AB relative to all these critical and diagnostic artifacts is commensurate with a
post-70 CE beginning for the settlement. The dating range furnished by
Adan-Bayewitz in every case extends well beyond 70 CE, sometimes to the
second, third or even fifth century CE. In other words, all of these diagnostic artifacts fall comfortably into the scenario where Nazareth was settled
between the two Jewish Wars.

The inescapable result of the above discussion is the realization that,
despite many claims to the contrary made in the text,[15] NVFR support for
a pre-70 CE Nazareth does not extend beyond the unsupported opinion
of one of its authors. When the parallels furnished are examined, then
it becomes plain that no conflict exists between the NVFR data and the
emergence of the settlement after the First Jewish War. Conversely, there is
no evidence in the NVFR attesting to a settlement before 70 CE.

In two cases Rapuano struggles with his chosen reference. Adan-
Bayewitz dates two sherds (37:3, 4) "mid-first century BC to mid-second
century AD." Perhaps unsatisfied with this broad dating range, Rapuano
writes "evidently both of the earlier type" (emphasis added). We aver that
this additional step of the archeologist is *non-diagnostic*. It is Rapuano's opinion, entirely consistent with his early datings of the eleven non-diagnostic
sherds discussed above. We demur, and the affirmation holds that in every
case where Rapuano suggests a pre-70 CE dating, he offers no support.

Conclusions

We are now able to appreciate that the following over-arching conclusion (NVFR: 69) has no evidentiary basis:

> The earliest occupation seems to have occurred in the late Hellenistic pe-
> riod of the first and second centuries BC. Examples dating to this period
> were primarily the jar and jug sherds discovered in Area B-1. A single jug
> base of this period was also found in Area A-2 (Fig. 38:5). The horizontal

---

14.   The fifteen sherds furnished with a parallel are: 37:3–4; 38:1–2; 39:1–2; 41:2, 4
(double attribution), 5, 7, 8; 42:1–2; 43:1–2.

15.   *Cf.* the "Early-to-Late Roman" claim noted above; "Hellenistic to Early Roman"
pottery (NVFR: 52); "first to third centuries" (NVFR: 24, 52, 56); "first century BC to
first century AD" (NVFR: 69); "Early Roman" period (NVFR: 27, 34, 50); "Late Hellenistic to Islamic pottery" (NVFR: 28).

handle of the krater (Fig. 38:6) may derive from this period as well. A small amount of material dated to the Early Roman period of the first century BC to first century AD was found in Areas A-1, A-2, and C-1.

We read above that the evidence "from the late Hellenistic period of the first and second centuries BC" comes primarily from Area B-1. But not a single shard found in area B-1 (NVFR: 72) is accompanied by a diagnostic parallel. We see, then, that the NVFR's major claim to early evidence rests purely on Rapuano's opinion—an opinion which is, furthermore, often tentative (the word "probably" occurs with the datings of five artifacts from Area B-1). As for the other sherds cited above (38:5 and 6) they, too, are not accompanied by a typological parallel, and hence are also non-diagnostic.

There is no substantiation in the NVF pottery report for either Hellenistic or Early Roman evidence. The support which Rapuano offers (Adan-Bayewitz) is fully compatible with a Middle Roman emergence for Nazareth. As noted above, the panoply of evidence examined in *The Myth of Nazareth* leads to a post-50 CE dating for all the *kokhim* tombs in the basin, a post-25 CE dating for all the Roman oil lamps, and the summation that "not a single post-Iron Age artifact, tomb or structure at Nazareth dates with certainty before 100 CE" (Salm 2008a: 205). These conclusions are unaffected by the NVFR, whose pre-70 CE claims must be considered unsupported.

Postscript
(October 2014)

My above Response was delivered electronically to BAIAS in mid-2008—several months before publication. Rapuano, the archeologist responsible for the pottery analysis contained in the NVF's original 2007 "Final Report," hastily composed an "Amendment" (essentially a response to my response) which appeared side-by-side with my Response in the 2008 issue of BAIAS. Rapuano's Amendment extends to 23 pages—more than twice as long as his 2007 pottery report. In the Amendment the archeologist attempts to do what he should have done the first time: to provide an accurate and error-free itemization of the NVF pottery.

Alas, the Amendment is as flawed as Rapuano's first report. Though clear diagrams of the modest pottery pieces are now presented, he inexplicably abandons his only standard reference for pottery (Adan-Bayewitz) and adopts remote, out-of-the-way, and even unpublished comparisons to authenticate the few tiny, allegedly pre-70 CE artifacts which were apparently found lying right on the surface of the NVF. Of course, the inability of anyone to verify Rapuano's new (and much inferior) parallels renders his pottery Amendment undiagnostic and as problematic as the report it claims to correct.

It should be noted that Yehudah Rapuano is an archeologist working for the Israel Antiquities Authority. This reveals cooperation, at a fairly early stage, between the NVF and the IAA. We will witness a similar co-operation between the Israeli state and fundamentalist Christian interests when we come to consider the International Marian Center (Chapter 10), where Y. Alexandre is the appointed IAA archeologist who excavates (and reports on) a site which quickly becomes a major Christian pilgrim venue.

The 2008 issue of BAIAS devoted, in all, no less than 47 pages to the archeology of Nazareth. Besides my above "Response" and Rapuano's lengthy "Amendment," the issue also contained a four page "Reply to Salm" authored by S. Pfann and Y. Rapuano where the latter suggests that the embarrassing errors (see "Problems of double-attribution" above) were simply cases of "misnumbering." For two pages Rapuano explains how "the plates were reorganized... In the process, some of the connections between the drawings and the text were lost or changed... the original numbering scheme was admittedly somewhat complex... it was decided to leave out the Catalogue intended to accompany the text..." In the process, the archeologist includes an astonishing admission: what he means by the phrase "Early Roman period" actually extends "to the first half of the second century CE"![16] *Thus, in one single stroke, all the NVF evidence is summarily removed "from the time of Jesus" and potentially dated one century later...*[17]

As if the above "Reply to Salm" were not enough, for good measure the British archeologist Ken Dark entered the fray with yet another "Reply to Salm."[18] In his short article Dark accused me of "serious topographical misunderstanding of Nazareth"—though no reason was given. Dark then asserted "recent evidence for domestic structures terraced into hill-slopes," as if terracing in other settlements were automatically applicable to the Venerated Area of Nazareth—where no terracing has been detected or even claimed by anyone!

---

16. BAIAS 2008: 107.

17. *Editor's note:* If the NVF theme-park project had any scientific purposes at all, it would have carried out radiometric, dendrochronological, and palynological studies of the soils and archeological matrices of the NVF area in order to determine the types of crops being grown there (if any) and the agricultural microclimate at the turn of the era. The fact that such studies were not done belies the apologetic nature of the 'archeology' associated with the venture.—FRZ

18. BAIAS 2008: 109–111.

Dark also broaches a new thesis, one which I take up in Chapter 6: that "Jewish tombs could be sited [under] formerly inhabited areas." It is an astonishing idea, never proposed before. Dark expands on this thesis in his writings relative to the Sisters of Nazareth Convent site. In essence, he suggests that the ancient Nazarenes hewed multiple tombs under their former dwellings. Though no such practice is elsewhere attested, Dark proposes this as an explanation why (later) tombs are found today under highly venerated sites such as the Church of the Annunciation, *etc.*

Finally, the same 2008 issue of BAIAS contained a scathing review of my newly-published book, *The Myth of Nazareth*, also written by Ken Dark.[19] The archeologist acknowledges that it is "a long and wide-ranging book, apparently full of detail." Almost immediately, however, he asserts what has been the pet position of the tradition for a long time: that it is *impossible* to prove that Nazareth did *not* exist "in the Second Temple period (or at any other period)." Such double negatives are a sure sign of desperation, a last resort when no substantive argument is available. It claims correctness by mere fiat—and until proven wrong. But that claim has no empirical, much less compelling, basis. After all: *Why* should Nazareth exist until proven otherwise? And we may ask a further question: What else in the realm of human discourse exists by fiat until proven otherwise? (I should know: "God" answers the man of faith!)

If there were any evidence at all for the existence of Nazareth "in the time of Jesus," Dark would surely seize upon it as his central argument. Lacking such a solid basis, however, the double negative emerges as a convenient fall-back position in the form of the all-too-familiar and tiresome mantra: "absence of evidence is not evidence of absence." As noted in Chapter 1,[20] however, this mantra is simply not true in archeology, a discipline in which the absence of evidence speaks volumes and is often decisive.

Dark's specific reason for the futility of archeology where Nazareth is concerned is that "the focus of activity at any period may be outside the—still few—excavated and surveyed areas." In other words, we cannot know whether Nazareth did or did not exist at a certain period simply because we have not excavated, and cannot excavate, everywhere. In *The Myth of Nazareth* I address this fallacious argument by observing that various archeologists have thus far excavated over two dozen tombs from later Roman Nazareth, yet not one is dated to the turn of the era. "Is it possible to seriously maintain," I ask, "that not one tomb from Hellenistic or Early Roman times has been found, though a score of later Roman tombs have?" (Salm 2008a: 290.)

---

19. BAIAS 2008: 140–46.
20. Page 22 *supra.*

Dark falls into a particularly deep hole (BAIAS 2008:143) when he berates me for employing the tomb dating of Hans-Peter Kuhnen rather than that of Rachel Hachlili. I consider this problem in Chapter 6, where details are furnished why Hachlili's work (while entirely correct) is thoroughly inapplicable to the Galilee. Her dating applies—by her own careful parameters—only to Jerusalem and its immediate neighborhood. As Kuhnen's work has shown, applying a Jerusalem funeral chronology to the Galilee dates everything in the north far too early, for the *kokh* type of tomb arrived in the Galilee centuries after it appeared in Judea (Salm 2008a: 158–64). But Dark refuses to acknowledge Kuhnen's work. The German's writings are nowhere present in his bibliographies—a signal and astonishing omission.

Dark is the first archeologist in modern times to explicitly (and in print) question the presence of Roman period tombs under the Church of the Annunciation. Bagatti referred to them, Kopp detailed several, and Mansur and Viaud noted them. Dark simply writes: "the evidence is inconclusive."[21] One wonders what evidence, in this case, would be sufficient...

In all, I found Dark's review of *The Myth of Nazareth* weak and dealing in generalities, dismissing the book out of hand and not engaging with the fundamental issue: that no evidence of human habitation at Nazareth is extant from *c.* 730 BCE–*c.* 70 CE. In fact, Dark yields on this major point:

> Salm points to what he considers a lack of certain Late Hellenistic pottery from Nazareth... Adan-Bayewitz, Aviam, Frankel and others have shown that at least some Late Hellenistic and Roman period Jewish communities chose not to use ceramics made by non-Jews... Moreover, if Bagatti excavated an area used for agricultural storage and/or processing at the Church of the Annunciation, the lack of whole Late Hellenistic or Early Roman lamps at that site is unsurprising...

As I wrote on my *www.nazarethmyth.info* website some years ago, Dark insists upon Hellenistic and Early Roman presence at Nazareth while searching out reasons why such presence is not reflected in the material record. Not only is this argument from silence in conflict with the recovered evidence that we indeed have, but his stated reasons above are quite farfetched. The clearly Jewish nature of the village explains the lack of Gentile evidence but certainly not of Jewish evidence, and subsequent agricultural use may indeed have removed "whole" lamps, but we even lack any datable shards from the many centuries before Christ.

---

21. BAIAS 2008: 143. I reconsider the tombs "under the house of Mary" in the final chapter of this volume (pp. 385 *f*).

Chapter 5

NAZARETH, FAITH, AND THE DARK OPTION—
AN UPDATE

(*American Atheist*, January 2009, pp. 10–13)

American Atheist has always championed the no-nonsense view of religion, and readers may note with a certain pride that this magazine has
now emerged as a leading advocate for the wholesale revision of Christian
beginnings. Atheists have never shirked the challenge to take on the goliath
of establishment Christianity, and today that challenge must include the
controversial archeology of Nazareth, which Frank Zindler has called "the
Achilles' heel of a popular god." My recent book, *The Myth of Nazareth: The
Invented Town of Jesus*, has elicited the literary equivalent of a scream from
the opposition, and I'd like readers to know that the popular Christian god
is in a heap of trouble and may be teetering.

The organ of this brouhaha is an obscure journal with a small distribu-
tion but long name: *The Bulletin of the Anglo-Israel Archaeological Society*. Mer-
cifully, the annual publication has a catchy abbreviation: *BAIAS* (no pun
intended). Scholars who have dug at Nazareth and traditional apologists
must have been properly miffed at the various writings on Nazareth coming
from the Atheist camp, for the journal devotes no less than 47 pages (a third
of the issue) to five rebuttals. Wow. Apparently we have indeed struck the
Achilles' heel—or at least a very raw nerve.

Much of the *BAIAS* material deals with an ambitious commercial
enterprise presently underway in Nazareth to recreate Jesus' hometown.
The resort is known as Nazareth Village. When complete, the project will
contain streets and several dozen stone houses "inhabited by actors and
storytellers in authentic garb, [who] will illuminate the life and teachings
of Jesus. A Parable Walk, museum, study center and restaurant are also

planned..."[1] I don't have recent figures, but as of 1999 an international consortium of Christian groups (called the Miracle of Nazareth International Foundation) had raised a whopping $60 million for the project. Contributors in the U.S. include former President Jimmy Carter, Pat Boone, and Rev. Reggie White, the former Green Bay Packer football star. (*Gulp...*)

In the interests of full disclosure, perhaps I should say that I've got nothing against Pat Boone. I also greatly admire Jimmy Carter's advocating for free and fair elections, think his work with Habitat for Humanity is wonderful, and wish my teeth were half as shiny as his. The problem has to do with Nazareth, and specifically with the fact that certain scholars associated with the Nazareth Village project claim to have found evidence there for a town at the time of Jesus, that is, for a settlement before the First Jewish War (70 CE). One of the main thrusts of my book is to carefully show that the scholarly Nazareth literature is littered with previous claims of this ilk, and that they are all bogus, inevitably resulting from misdating, mislabeling, misinterpreting—or even from pure invention. Now, in the 11th hour, as it were, the world is being confronted with the possibility that a small group of scholars, intimately associated with a mega-resort, has 'found' all-important Jesus-evidence that has somehow eluded archeologists digging for the last hundred years. Furthermore, they claim this evidence was just lying around on the surface of the site. I, for one, am skeptical!

The Nazareth Village resort lies on a 15-acre plot of land called the Nazareth Village Farm (NVF). The scholars under discussion (Stephen Pfann, Ross Voss, and Yehudah Rapuano) surveyed the farm, dug on it, and published a lengthy report in the 2007 issue of *BAIAS* (pp. 19–79). The report appeared too late for inclusion in my book, but I had little difficulty showing that their Jesus-evidence does not exist. It consists of eleven small pieces of pottery—shards to which the NVF scholars assign an early date but which the standard textbook dates as late as the second century CE. In other words, the NVF scholars were choosing arbitrarily early dates for a few objects, and resting their Jesus-case on what amounts to mere preference. Significantly, in my book I show that the rest of the material from the Nazareth basin dates after the time of Jesus. So, an early dating for the NVF objects in question is not consistent with the evidentiary profile for the area.

Perhaps more embarrassing for the authors of the NVF report are a number of flagrant double-datings in their pottery report. Unbelievable as it may sound, they dated certain artifacts one way in certain passages, and

---

1. *Biblical Archeology Review*, vol. 25, May–June 1999, p. 16. At the time of this writing (December 2014) the website for the Nazareth Village was *http://www.nazarethvillage.com*.

another way in other passages. One can only conclude that either the NVF authors were very sloppy, or they were capable of looking at the same piece twice and coming up with different dates for it.[2]

Since *The Myth of Nazareth* had already appeared when this was published, I wrote a 15-page "Response" to the long NVF report and sent it to *BAIAS*, challenging them to publish it in their next (2008) issue. That issue has now appeared and is the subject of the rest of this article. In the Response I spell out the above confidence-sapping errors, with chapter and verse.[3] I also made sure that a few copies of the book got into their hands.

Well, all this confrontational material was too much, I guess, because the good scholars on the other end apparently went ballistic. Not only did they publish my Response in the next *BAIAS*, but they also published a wholesale correction of their previous pottery report—one now three times as long as the original, under the title "Amendment." The scholars in question averred that there was, in fact, no incompetent 'double-dating.' It was simply, they explained, a minor (!) difficulty of "misnumbering"—two numbering schemes that apparently were not harmonized. *Uh-huh.*

Figure 5.1. The fifteen-acre Nazareth Village Farm during construction.

A clever proposal?

Professor Ken Dark, a British archeologist not affiliated with the Nazareth Village Farm, has also been digging in and around Nazareth for the last several years. He wrote a review of *The Myth of Nazareth* which ap-

2. See above, pp. 53–54.
3. Above, Chapter 4.

peared in *BAIAS* along with the material mentioned above.[4] As expected, the review is hostile. It is also, in my opinion, fairly weak simply because it evades the main thesis of my book, which is that there is no demonstrable evidence from the Nazareth basin dating to the time of Jesus and to Hellenistic times. Prof. Dark's review does not acknowledge the shoddy history of scholarship relating to Nazareth, nor does it note the 800-year lacuna in evidence from the Nazareth basin (*c.* 730 BCE–*c.* 70 CE), nor even the post-Jesus dating for the all-important oil lamps. These are mainstays of my book's argument. It is as if evidence simply doesn't matter to the tradition. And, in fact, it doesn't (see below). At least, Prof. Dark admits that the earliest evidence from Nazareth is "ambiguous." That is a tacit admission that the case for Nazareth in the time of Jesus is not certain. Folks, an admission of uncertainty is probably the most we're going to get from the tradition!

For the standard scenario of Christian beginnings, the existence of tombs directly under the Church of the Annunciation at Nazareth is a particularly distressing issue, one emphasized in my book. That massive church (the largest Christian structure in the Middle East) is a prime destination of Christian pilgrims to the Holy Land. There, the Blessed Virgin allegedly received the annunciation from the Archangel Gabriel. For the faithful, tombs have no place under that structure because, according to Jewish religious law (Torah), Jews could not live in the vicinity of tombs, which are a prime source of ritual impurity. The Mishna (an ancient commentary on Jewish law) mandated that tombs must be located outside the village proper. Thus, tombs under the house of Mary have largely been denied by the tradition.

However, *The Myth of Nazareth* (Chapter Five) devotes many pages to various tombs under the Church of the Annunciation, and notes that several of them have not been denied by a number of archeologists. While Ken Dark writes that the evidence is "inconclusive" (above p. 61), he also seems to appreciate that a strong argument for their existence can be made. So, in the 2008 *BAIAS*, he offers a new twist on Nazareth history, one which cleverly accommodates both the tombs in the Venerated Area and the presence of the Holy Family. He suggests that early Nazareth was a two-stage affair. The first stage (Nazareth at the time of Jesus) was an agricultural village, apparently lacking tombs. Then, in the second century CE, the Nazarenes began to construct tombs on the hillside. Thus, the tombs detectable under the Church of the Annunciation do not affect the story of Mary—those tombs didn't yet exist when she lived.

At first it seems like a clever scenario, but a little thought shows that Prof. Dark is hardly doing the tradition a favor by advocating this line of

---

4. Other comments on Dark's review are above, pp. 60–61.

thinking. On the contrary, *by insisting that the Nazareth tombs came later, Dark also dates the wealth of artifacts found in those tombs to post-Jesus times.* If anything, his line supports the view argued in my book, for I demonstrate that the post-Iron Age tombs at Nazareth are indeed post-Jesus (*i.e.*, Middle Roman and later), and that the wealth of pottery found in them is also later. *Thus, Dark strongly supports a case for Nazareth in post-Jesus times, while impoverishing a case for Nazareth in the time of Jesus by excluding from consideration all the evidence found in the tombs.*

Figure 5.2. Dr. Ken R. Dark
(Associate Professor, Department of Economics, University of Reading, U.K.)

A dark option

There is, unfortunately, another option which is rather dark (pun intended). The tradition's case—and the British archeologist's scenario—can only be established by the verification of Hellenistic–I CE finds in the Nazareth basin. My book has pretty convincingly removed all prior claims of such evidence. Thus, the only chance for the tradition to exonerate itself is *if new evidence comes to light,* evidence which directly and incontrovertibly supports a settlement at the turn of the era. Presumably, such finds would be non-funerary, for both Dark and myself seem to agree that the tombs at Nazareth date to post-Jesus times.

Undoubtedly there is great pressure on the tradition now to discover such telling evidence from Nazareth. Continuing pilgrimage depends on it. The incipient Nazareth Village depends on it. Perhaps the entire Jesus-story depends on it. This is the time for stalwart defenders of the tradition to exercise their resourcefulness and acumen in defense of the Christian story, and to prevent a wound to the Achilles' heel from festering and becoming fatal. Let's not be too surprised if remarkable new 'finds' at Nazareth conveniently appear in the next few years—finds substantiating a settlement there at the time of Christ. To fit the demands of the tradition that are now in print, the forthcoming material will have to be early and non-funereal.

Well, guess what? According to the NVF report, a cache of Hellenistic and Early Roman coins has recently been 'found' at Mary's Well (at the Northern end of the Nazareth basin). Wow. Nothing remotely similar has ever been discovered in the Nazareth basin. The earliest coin found there dates to about 350 CE. A cache of Hellenistic and Early Roman coins is exactly the sort of evidence which the tradition needs in order to decide the matter in its favor.

My skepticism is increased by the fact that I possess a pre-publication report (dated 2006) from the Israel Antiquities Authority signed by the archeologist who dug at Mary's Well. In it she mentions no early coins at all. The only datable coins she signals were from the 14th–15th centuries CE. *Hmm...* What's going on here?

All of a sudden, claims of Jesus-era evidence are being made at Nazareth. Putative turn-of-the-era evidence is popping up all over the place— on the surface at the Nazareth Village Farm (see above), at Mary's Well... Where next?

It's all too late. Archeologists have been digging at Nazareth for over a hundred years and, as my book attempts to show, all the recovered finds include not a single artifact that can with certainty be dated before 100 CE. In other words, no demonstrable evidence dating either to the time of Jesus or to earlier Hellenistic times has been found. This is quite sufficient to decide the issue against the traditional view of Nazareth. The case is closed! No one, of course, is opposed to ongoing research at Nazareth, but that research will inform us about the nature of the Late Roman-Byzantine village, not about a mythical settlement at the turn of the era. That question has already been answered, and answered convincingly.

We should all look with great suspicion on new evidence 'coming to light' which conflicts with the evidentiary profile of the last hundred years, new evidence which astonishingly reopens the case for settlement in the time of Christ. Given the revelations documented in my book, and the lengthy history of duplicity associated with Nazareth archeology, we have every right to insist that any new evidence be rigorously documented as to findspot, circumstances of discovery, and description (preferably accompanied by photo or diagram). Any claim of new, pre-70 CE evidence should raise an alarum red flag. Such a claim tells us more about the persons making it than about Nazareth.

Fact versus Faith

When it comes to the archeology of Nazareth, there are now two camps, each capable of looking at the same evidence and reaching radically different conclusions. One camp I have called the tradition. It continues to claim the existence of Nazareth in the time of 'Jesus of Nazareth' (whose historicity is now increasingly questioned) and insists that the town was there, even as the gospels say, regardless of the facts in the ground.

For generations, the tradition has been defending itself by demanding, "Prove me wrong." So, empiricists come up with the required facts, only to discover that the facts don't seem to matter to some people. Unfortunately, there's simply no way to disprove a myth. After all, neither you nor I can prove that Santa Claus doesn't exist. We can go to the North Pole, can dig up there (under water and ice!) all we want, and can find absolutely no evidence for his gift-packing facility nor for his team of flying reindeer. But to a believer, we can't prove those don't exist. All the believer has to say is, "Well, you didn't look in the right places," "He's hiding," or even "He's invisible." Unfortunately, common myths involving Jesus are every bit as weird.

Empiricists need not waste their lives endlessly fact-checking, double-checking, and triple-checking, while faith-based refuseniks sit back and watch the comedy. In other words, we needn't waste our time trying to convince the unconvinceable. If people want to believe in Santa Claus and want to believe the Christian myth, that's their right. On the other hand, we also have every right not to partake of their mindless delusions, and to see the world as clearly as our senses and our reason permit.

Nazareth is a case in point, where facts are critical to one side and ir-relevant to the other. Empiricists are good at collecting and analyzing facts. They bring them to believers, perhaps thinking "This will convince them," and watch while the other side changes the rules or moves the goal posts. Theoretically, there's no end to the impossible demands of faith. People have been digging in Nazareth for generations, and no evidence from the time of Jesus has been forthcoming. That's good enough for empiricists, who sensibly conclude: a settlement at Nazareth didn't exist at the turn of the era. But the tradition can still stubbornly maintain that Nazareth existed in those parts of the basin where we haven't yet dug. That's like kicking the can down the road. Even a trained archaeologist like Ken Dark continues this false pattern, as demonstrated in his book review of *The Myth of Nazareth*:

> The initial question must be whether the stated aims of the book are archaeologically achievable. It would, hypothetically, be archaeologically possible to show that there was no Second Temple period [*i.e.* Hellenistic–I AD] settlement evidence on any of the sites so far excavated in Nazareth. But it is not possible to show archaeologically on the basis of available data that Nazareth did not exist in the Second Temple period (or at any other period), because the focus of activity at any period may be outside the still few excavated and surveyed areas. Hypothetically, it is possible

> that Late Roman pilgrims and church-builders were incorrect when they
> took the present site of Nazareth as its New Testament counterpart, and
> that New Testament period Nazareth was elsewhere.
>
> (*BAIAS* 2008:141–42)

Elsewhere? That's kicking the can down the road. After all, there's no way we can dig everywhere, and there's absolutely no reason why we should engage in the endless and futile effort of humoring the irrational wishes of theists. No. There comes a time when evidence (and its lack) must speak.

The two camps—rationalist and faith-based—are coalescing around many religious issues today, including the archeology of Nazareth. The traditional camp now has an extensive Nazareth literature upon which to draw for future citations and authority—the writings of generations of hidebound archeologists and scholars (Viaud, Kopp, Bagatti, Strange, now Dark). It is a self perpetuating culture which can (and probably will) go on *ad infinitum*, as the tradition cites false facts and skewed information, seeking only to appease the many who don't care to think anyway.

Then there's the rationalist camp, which on this issue is represented by a small but growing literature on Nazareth (Cheyne, Zindler, Salm). There may now exist the critical mass needed for this view to also become a self-perpetuating alternative to the traditional, bogus position. I certainly hope that's the case, and that we do not lose our initiative regarding this Achilles' heel of Christianity. It may be that the rationalist and faith-based camps are speaking past each other, and probably always will. But our side needs to assert itself when the opportunity presents, if only because none of us wants mankind to suffer through another Dark Ages ruled by faith and unreason.

Editor's Note

In all the disputation over coins and tombs and pottery shards—and now the claim that 'Nazareth' may have been located somewhere else—we must not lose sight of the fact that the so-called Venerated Sites at which the various Franciscan pseudoarcheologists have been digging for the last century or so were situated where they are out of a necessity to make them fit the requirements of the Gospels' descriptions as much as possible. Even so, the tradition has failed miserably in fitting the Venerated Sites into the picture painted by the Gospel accounts.

According to Luke 4:16–30, for example, there should be a synagogue at the top of Nazareth hill and a "brow of the hill" (cliff) over which the Jews once tried to cast Jesus down to his death. No such cliff exists, nor is there any reasonable place where such a cliff could have existed during the last hundred-thousand years. Of course, no synagogue remains have ever been found atop the Nazareth hill—or anywhere in the vicinity. In fact, no evidence of buildings of any kind dating to the turn of the era has ever been found at the Venerated Sites.

René Salm has presented exhaustive proof to show that the Gospel story cannot possibly be true if the Venerated Sites are, in fact, 'Nazareth.' Any archeologist who claims some other site is the true Nazareth must either show that it better fits the Gospel descriptions or state publicly, plainly, and loudly: "The Gospels are in error!"—FRZ

Chapter 6

A Critique of Dr. Ken Dark's Writings Relative to the Sisters of Nazareth Convent Site

Since 1881 the Sisters of Nazareth Convent has existed over the location of one or possibly two *kokh*-type tombs which over the years have been considerably disturbed and altered. The entryway to the southern tomb survives intact, as well as its large sealing stone ('rolling stone'). The tomb complex is fairly well documented in the literature[1] though Dark maintains that—until his recent arrival on the scene—"few of [the archeological features] have been accurately published by previous scholars."[2] Provocatively, Dark offers an interpretation of the site which varies considerably from previous views and which, I argue below, is poorly reasoned. Dark proposes that the site was first a dwelling and later a tomb. Not only does such a habitation-funerary sequence conflict with Jewish praxis in antiquity, but it is also undocumented elsewhere. Furthermore, Dark proposes that both domestic and funereal use of the site occurred during the first century CE. An analysis of the structural remains (walls, filtration basins, cisterns, forecourts), however, indicates a very different interpretation: agricultural use of the site above ground, and funereal use below ground, both beginning in Middle Roman times. The tombs at the site are Middle-Late Roman in date, and there is no evidence of prior domestic use.

---

1. Bagatti wrote in 1969: "The bibliography on these tombs is great" (1969:242 n. 21). Published literature on the site includes: Schumacher 1889:68–74; Hélène 1936; Bagatti 1937:253–58; Nazareth 1956:243–71; Bagatti 1969: 242–44; Livio 1980:26–34. Considerably more unpublished literature also exists.
2. Dark 2007:2.

Dark seems unaware of differing Judean and Galilean chronologies and has misrepresented the work of other scholars at significant junctures. His overall conclusions invariably support the
traditional view of Nazareth, namely, that the settlement existed
at the turn of the era and was situated on the hillside (Luke 4:29).

* * *

Beginning in 2006, the British archeologist Ken R. Dark (University of Reading) began a series of annual excavations under the Sisters of
Nazareth Convent, located on the western flank of the Nazareth basin (the
Jebel Nebi Saʻin) approximately one hundred meters west of the Church
of the Annunciation.[3] At the outset it should be made clear that Dark has
never excavated the site. In fact, to this writer's knowledge, he has never
obtained an official permit (from the IAA) to excavate anywhere in the
entire Nazareth area. According to his own writings, then, Dark's work at
the convent site has been limited to "investigation," "survey," "recording,"
and "re-analysis" in order to place "the features of the convent cellar in
context" (Dark 2008:iii). Though essentially an observer, recorder, and student of the visible features of the site and of its literature, Dark nevertheless
characterizes his activity as "fieldwork," claims "discoveries," and alleges
the use of "up-to-date archaeological techniques"—while at the same time
deprecating the techniques of his predecessors at the site (Dark 2007:2–3).

Dark's stated goal is to produce "a book-length report—fully illustrated with detailed scale drawings and photographs—covering all of the data"
(Dark 2007:1). As of this writing (Winter, 2014) that book has not material-
ized. The archeologist wishes "to bring the site and the existing material
(including the finds and all records of earlier work) to proper publication
according to current international professional archeological standards—
so ensuring that the evidence from this internationally important site will
receive the full publication, and scholarly attention, that it deserves" (Dark
2007:3–4). Laudable as these goals are, this chapter argues that Dark's
work at the Convent includes serious errors of methodology, reporting,
and logic. Those errors nullify his major conclusions regarding the site and
prompt one to question Dark's familiarity with the subspecialty of Israeli
(and particularly Galilean) archeology. The archeologist adopts false datings for *kokh*-type tombs in the Galilee, misapplies Judean chronologies to
the Galilee, and misrepresents the work of other scholars at critical points
(see below), resulting in a false chronology for the Sisters of Nazareth site
which is approximately two centuries too early.

---

3. New Israel Grid ref. 22811/73423. The elevation is 340 meters above sea level.

At the beginning of this third Christian millennium, the tradition is faced with a double conundrum at Nazareth: (1) to find evidence of human presence from the turn of the era; and (2) to find a satisfactory explanation for the presence of Roman-era tombs on the hillside. Prof. Dark's work at Nazareth appears intended to fulfill both these goals. Regarding the first point, evidence of human presence in the Nazareth basin dating to "the time of Jesus" has been surprisingly evasive, despite a century of archeological excavation. Dark claims to have now found evidence of a house "from the time of Jesus" for the *first* time (despite a similar claim of Y. Alexandre, see Chp. 10)—a house located under the Sisters of Nazareth Convent.

The evidence of tombs in the so-called Venerated Area has been studiously ignored since the Second World War, but my 2008 book brought this vexing matter to the forefront and to the attention of scholars interested in Nazareth archeology. *The Myth of Nazareth* also presented a detailed chronology of the *kokh*-type of tomb, showing that it did not appear in the Galilee until *after c. 50 CE*.

Dark meets these objections with a novel and complex theory: habitation occurred at multiple sites in the Venerated Area in the first century CE, they were abandoned during that century, and tombs were subsequently hewn under those sites—also in that century. In this way he proposes to explain how tombs and habitations could exist at the same site, and also how habitation occurred at the turn of the era (the "time of Jesus"). However, Dark's complex theory encounters several problems which we will explore in this chapter.

Dark's arguments

The British archeologist claims that a dwelling existed in Early Roman times at the southern portion of the Sisters of Nazareth site. He calls an alleged dwelling there "Structure 1" and interprets it as a "model courtyard house," based on the analysis of traditional courtyard houses by Y. Hirschfeld (1995:57-85). We note here that Hirshfeld's analysis concerns large urban dwellings of the upper-class—rendering it of little obvious relevance to Dark's alleged "low-status" inhabitants of Nazareth at the turn of the era.[4]

Prof. Dark has two principal arguments for ascertaining a dwelling: one from movable evidence, and the other from structural evidence. Both arguments converge on the same conclusion: there was human habitation at the Sisters of Nazareth site during the first century CE.

---

4. Dark 2012 :62. This is the British archeologist's 2012 *The Antiquaries Journal* article (see below, "Dark's Nazareth publications"), hereafter referred to as "AJ."

Dark's argument from the movable evidence is fairly straightforward: pottery shards found at the site indicate human presence there in the first century CE. We will find this conclusion untenable (see "The pottery and movable evidence" below), and Dark himself admits that the weak ceramic evidence necessitates reliance primarily on dating the structural features. His argument from the structural evidence contains three steps—all of which, however, are questionable:

(1) use of the *kokh*-type tomb ended in the Galilee about 100 CE;
(2) the *kokh* Tomb 1 under the Sisters of Nazareth convent site "cuts into" the pre-existing above-ground structure, thus showing the priority of the structure to the tomb;
(3) the above-ground structure was domestic in nature.

According to Dark's reasoning, then, a dwelling existed at the site prior to *c.* 100 CE. He specifically proposes the following:

- a dwelling existed at the Sisters of Nazareth site at the beginning of the first century CE (as indicated by the pottery *and* by the structural evidence)
- that dwelling was abandoned towards the middle of the first century CE (this would allow time for hewing the tomb during that century)
- a *kokh*-type tomb (Tomb 1) was hewn after the site had been abandoned, but before the end of the first century CE
- the *kokh* tomb was abandoned before the end of the first century CE.

The above is Prof. Dark's overall proposal, synthesized from his five articles on the site to date. He is suggesting that ancient Nazarenes lived on the steep and rocky hillside, vacated their home (at the Convent site) in the course of the first century, constructed a *kokh* tomb under their former dwelling (or perhaps under the dwelling of their parents) before the end of that century (Dark 2009:13), and finally that the newly-hewn tomb was not used after *c.* 100 CE. Thus Dark writes: "at least the main rooms of Structure 1 were built and disused during the first century AD" (AJ:52).

Unabashedly, Dark fits the physical evidence into a preconceived chronology. "One might suggest," he opines, "that a date in the later first century AD may better suit this tomb than one earlier in that century, to leave time for the Phase 1 structure to be built, used and disused, prior to the construction of the tomb" (Dark 2009:13). All this relies on a false *terminus ante quem* of 100 CE for the *kokh* tomb—leading not only to a false chronology but also to a very short life for the tomb. This *terminus* is a critical element in his reasoning, for it allows him to date the anteriority of the dwelling *by structural evidence* (and not merely by fairly weak ceramic evidence), according to his proposition that the dwelling is 'cut into' by the tomb (see below).

Dark thus proposes that Tomb 1 was hewn directly beneath the abandoned Structure 1 and, furthermore, that both the abandonment of the structure and the hewing of the tomb took place during the first century CE. We will investigate why so much activity is required within such a remarkably short period of time, and will conclude the intersection of several reasons: traditional Christian demands that habitation occurred at Nazareth at the turn of the era; exigencies of Jewish religious law precluding the co-existence of tombs and habitations in the same vicinity; and the material remains under the Sisters of Nazareth Convent, where both tomb and above-ground (though hardly domestic) structures existed in antiquity.

Ultimately, the critical element in Dark's chronology can be traced back to the false *terminus ante quem* for *kokh* tomb usage in the Galilee: *c.* 100 CE. In fact, such tombs were only just appearing in the province at that time. Yet, it is upon the pre-100 CE dating for the *kokh* tomb that the archeologist falsely concludes a similar pre-100 CE dating for the "domestic" structure. The end results are imaginary: a short span of time for habitation at the site, abandonment by the family dwelling there, construction of a tomb under their erstwhile house, a very short lifespan for the tomb, and disuse of that tomb after *c.* 100 CE. None of this is credible.

In sum, Dark's scenario admirably fulfills the requirements of Christian scripture, but it does so by adopting an increasingly complex and improbable series of steps compressed into very little time.

The archeologist also insists on claiming the palm for having discovered the first incontrovertible evidence of a first century Nazareth dwelling:

> As Tomb 1 probably dates to the first century AD, and Roman-period pottery—dating to the first century at earliest—was found in Structure 1, both of these phases may be dated to the first century AD. That is, Structure 1 was the first surface-built first century AD domestic building to be discovered in Nazareth. (Dark 2010:14; *cf.* Dark 2007:19)

Thus, Dark dates the construction, use, as well as abandonment of Structure 1 to the first century CE. However, the chronological complexity of his argument may not be the most curious aspect of this scenario. The custom of Jews hewing tombs under abandoned dwellings is undocumented elsewhere. My use of the words "custom" and the plural "dwellings" is apposite here because Dark also ventures to extend his thesis to other sites in the Nazareth basin—as if the dwelling-tomb sequence (his "Phase 1–Phase 2") were common practice (Dark 2008a:12). Remarkably, the archeologist appears aware that the proposition of Jews hewing a tomb under a former dwelling is unusual (Dark 2008a:11; *cf.* Dark 2009:11).

This is not all. The generalized abandonment of dwellings in the Venerated Area, and the subsequent hewing of tombs there, suggest to

Dark that the entire community of Nazareth underwent "settlement shift" (AJ:37; cf. Dark 2007:20; 2010:17) towards the end of the first century CE. He does this by extending the domestic-tomb sequence to several venues:

> ... A *similar* re-use of a former occupation area for burial might *also* be attested close to the Church of the Annunciation site, where a Roman-period tomb is sited close to the excavated Early Roman-period agricultural (and perhaps occupation) area... (Dark 2008a:11-12, emphasis added.)

In his 2012 article, the British archeologist is more explicit:

> ... However, it must be remembered that the relationship between occupation areas and burial zones might have been more fluid than often imagined. There is possible evidence for the *abandonment of settlement areas* at the Church of the Annunciation site, at the IMC [International Marian Center] site and, probably later, at 'St Mary's Well', as well as at the Sisters of Nazareth site. (AJ:61, emphasis added. *Cf.* Dark 2010:19.)

These speculations allow Dark to propose a larger "Early Roman" Nazareth, one conforming to the New Testament "town" (Gk. *polis*):

> ... [T]his has important implications for establishing the extent of the Early Roman settlement at Nazareth. If domestic occupation might occur at sites later used for burials, then the ring of tombs known from around Nazareth does not fix the limits of the Early Roman settlement. This is important in several ways, not least because it allows the possibility that Roman-period Nazareth was a larger settlement or perhaps what archeologists of the Roman Empire often call a 'small-town'—rather than a small village as usually argued. This, in turn, would relate to several widely discussed question concerning the New Testament description of Nazareth. (Dark 2008a:12)

Dark's solution would apparently solve the riddle of tombs occurring at some of the most sacred venues in Christendom, even under the Church of the Annunciation itself—those tombs are under former dwellings! Dark states that he consulted with several scholars regarding this novel idea and they assured him "that there was no prohibition against burial on a former house site in the relevant period" (Dark 2008a:11; 2009:11; 2010:15). He also found support from M. Henig, a scholar who speculates that the hewing of tombs by the "first-century Christians in Nazareth" might represent "the veneration of the [former dwelling] structure by those responsible for constructing the tombs." Henig proposes that this could be "an active process of very early Christian commemoration analogous to the widespread later practice of burial '*per sanctos*' or '*ad sanctos*' (Dark 2008a:12; 2009:14).

Of course, the difficulties with the above line of reasoning are considerable. Not only is such a domestic-funereal sequence unknown to ancient (or modern) Judaism, but history reveals that the ancient inhabitants of

Nazareth were hardly Christian-friendly. In the early seventh century the Jewish inhabitants of the town helped the invading Persians to massacre Christians in the land (Salm 2008a:333). Joan Taylor (Taylor 1993) has also extensively demonstrated that the Roman inhabitants of Nazareth were definitely not proto-Christians who venerated well-known sacred sites (a theory beloved by the tradition).

At least Prof. Dark candidly admits the presence of "a Roman-period tomb" under the nearby Church of the Annunciation (Dark 2010:18). This is noteworthy because the tradition has quietly, yet obstinately, refused to acknowledge this most embarrassing fact (see Chapter 13). On the same page Dark also acknowledges that the two tombs under the Sisters of Nazareth Convent are part of an "extensive cemetery"—something also rarely admitted by Christian archeologists. He finally states that many Roman tombs (known to be situated on both the western and eastern hillsides) encircled "the center of modern Nazareth." This is an oblique acknowledgment that the ancient city was, indeed, sited not at the Venerated Area but on the basin floor (where the center of the modern town is located).

Dr. Ken R. Dark

Prof. Dark is a Lecturer at the University of Reading, U.K. He received his Ph.D in Archaeology from the University of Cambridge. His areas of interest (as evidenced from his publications and the university Website) are the archeology and history of 1st millennium AD Europe (Roman and immediately post-Roman Britain); urban and landscape archeology; pre-modern societies and economies; archeology and history of religion (especially early Christianity); archeological method and theory; interdisciplinary relationships between archeological and historical research, and studies of contemporary economics and international relations.[5]

In this vast universe of interests, Dark cannot be expected to have gained a deep knowledge of Palestinian archeology—a unique discipline as removed from the archeology of ancient Britain as it is from that of ancient China. Dark makes elementary errors such as using the term "acrosolia" (his routine misspelling of *arcosolia* which may, however, be a typist's error), to more critical errors such as applying Judean chronologies to the Galilee and egregiously misdating the era of *kokh* tomb usage.

Research in the subfield of Israeli archeology makes special linguistic demands. The scholarly literature encompasses the usual modern Europe-

---

5. "[C]ontemporary economics and international relations" have little obvious relation to Dark's archeological interests. It may be noted, however, that Dark is not in a faculty of archeology, but is curiously an Associate Professor in the "Department of Economics" at the University of Reading.

an languages as well as modern Hebrew. Dark's familiarity with the literature is suspect. He has evidently come to the subfield at an advanced stage
in his professional career, shows unfamiliarity with the rudiments of Semitic linguistics, and ignores signal works in the field—including the works
in German of H.-P. Kuhnen. The latter may not be entirely coincidental,
for Kuhnen's writings immediately invalidate Dark's chronology relative to
the Sisters of Nazareth site.[6]

Works in Hebrew are absent from Dark's bibliographies. The archeologist's fairly obvious ignorance of that language has consequences more
grave than an inability to read the wealth of untranslated excavation reports
and articles in Hebrew (whether in journals, books, or online). For example,
he ignores the distinction between the semitic *tsade* and *zain*, thus confusing
the etymology of "Nazirite" (with *zain*) with that of the town (with *tsade*).
No one with even an elementary acquaintance of Hebrew would be capable of such an error. In the event, this seriously impacts Dark's theories, for
he erroneously concludes his interpretation of the Sisters of Nazareth site
by linking Middle Roman "Nazareth" (in Hebrew, *nun-tsade-resh-tav*) with a
population of "separatist religious" Christians (Dark 2010:3) inspired in the
"Nazirite" tradition (*nun-zain-resh*).

It can be observed that Dark's researches have clearly met the approval
of Christian interests in the area—if not their direct sponsorship—as witnessed by his unfettered access to the Sisters of Nazareth site, as well as
stored artifacts and documents in the possession of the Catholic Church.

It can also be pointed out that details of Dark's writing signal a confessional rather than a purely scholarly bent. One is his routine use of "AD"
and "BC." This convention went out of scholarly fashion a generation
ago. It persists primarily in Christian confessional literature and is particularly abrasive to Jews for whom *anno domini* and "before Christ" are hardly
appropriate. Similarly, Dark precedes many names with "St.," as in "St.
Paul," "St. Joseph," *etc*. While in other literature we read the customary
appellation "Mary's Well," Dark always refers to the venue as *St.* Mary's
Well—a markedly confessional locution found not even in standard tourist
literature.

Such conservative idiosyncrasies are not, in themselves, of any moment. However, they betray the tenor of the archeologist's views. Dark's
various bibliographies also reveal considerable reliance on certain Catholic researchers (Corbo, Fernandez, Loffreda, Testa) who, incidentally, were
mostly concerned not with Nazareth but with Capernaum. At the same

---

6.   A mildly irritating curiosity also exists in Dark's use of French. The archeologist
repeatedly uses the spelling "Souer" instead of "Soeur" (Sister), correcting this finally
in his 2012 article. Perhaps it is another typist error.

time, Dark surprisingly omits specialist secular literature directly pertinent to his archeological work, including not only Kuhnen (on *kokh* tombs) as noted above, but also Sussman (on oil lamps), Kloner (on round blocking stones), and Deines (on stone vessels).

Dark's Nazareth publications

Professor Dark is Director of the Late Antiquities Research Group, an entity affiliated with the University of Reading, U.K., where he teaches. Dark's Sisters of Nazareth writings fall into two main categories and include five writings: four annual Interim Reports (published 2007-10, all 32–36 pages long), followed by a comprehensive article in *The Antiquaries Journal* (vol. 92, September 2012, pp. 37-64) entitled "Early Roman Period Nazareth and the Sisters of Nazareth convent." The AJ article is also characterized as "interim" by the author.[7]

It can be noted that though Dark's first season of work at the Sisters of Nazareth convent was in 2006, that year is noted as the "third season" in his reports. The reason is that though the archeologist began working in the general Nazareth area in 2004, his work at the Sisters of Nazareth convent did not begin until 2006. The five Dark reports can be tabulated as follows:

Season number	Interim report	Year of work	Publication date	OCLC number
3	1	2006	2007*	227271052
4	2	2007	2008	262649469
5	3	2008	2009	551684061
6	4	2009	2010	670192089
—	AJ**	Cumulative	2012	—

Table 1: Dark's publications relating to the Sisters of Nazareth Convent

* Reference is to publication date. Thus, "Dark 2008:21" signals page 21 of the second interim report, recording work carried out in 2007.
** Dark, K., 2012. "Early roman-period Nazareth and the sisters of Nazareth convent," *The Antiquaries Journal* 92:37–64. (Online: http://centaur.reading.ac.uk/29782/, with different pagination.)

At the time of compiling the primary material for this chapter only one library in North America possessed the above reports: the University of

---

7. Dark has also penned several articles relative to other sites in and around Nazareth (Dark 2005, 2008b, 2012c), as well as a short précis in PEQ (Dark 2010b).

Chicago's Regenstein Library.[8] Of the five publications listed, *The Antiquaries Journal* article of 2012 (AJ) is the most important for our purposes, being (in Dark's words) "an interim report on the Early Roman-period phases of the site, summarizing data relevant only to these phases" (AJ:37). A footnote on the same page notifies the reader: "The final report, to be published as a research monograph following further analysis of the recorded data, will include much more detailed archeological documentation of the site and present all drawn plans and sections and the recorded finds."

As interim reports, then, we cannot fault Dark's writings on the Sisters of Nazareth site for their lack of descriptive detail nor of the precision promised in the final report. As of this writing (Winter, 2014), all of Prof. Dark's publications on the Sisters of Nazareth site must be viewed as primarily interpretive. As such, it is precisely the professor's interpretation of the evidence which is the focus of this critique—his reasoning, his assumptions, his chronology, and his methodology. These do not change from interim to final report. Hence, this critique itself is not to be viewed as "interim" but addresses unchanging and critical elements of Dark's work at the Sisters of Nazareth convent.

The pottery and movable evidence from "Early Roman" times

The first of Dark's two principal arguments deals with the movable evidence recovered at the Sisters of Nazareth site. He maintains that pottery shards found indicate human presence in the "Early Roman period," a period which includes the first century CE: "finds within Structure 1 strongly support a date in the Early Roman period" (AJ:51). Specifically, the alleged finds are the following:

(1) "A freshly broken body sherd of Early Roman-period cooking pottery was found on the original floor surface just south of the doorway of Structure 1"

(2) Another shard "was on the surface of what seems to be the original cave floor on the south-west edge of the twentieth-century cut."

---

8. I visited the Regenstein Library in Sept. 2012 and photocopied the reports (above, pp. 27 f). In the library's online catalog the last issue is mislabeled as the "fifth season 2009." 2009 was in fact the sixth season, according to the above method of reckoning. Perhaps reflecting this confusion, WorldCat offers an apparently non-existent title: "Nazareth archeological project: a preliminary report on the... season... LARG 2008-09. OCLC 721886083." I have not found any information on such a publication.

(3) A spindle whorl "can be confidently assigned" to the Early Roman period since it was found "in the earliest soil layer" (AJ:53)

In a box labeled long ago by Senès (*i.e.*, in an unstratified context, not *in situ*) and ostensibly deriving from under the Sisters of Nazareth Convent, Dark also alleges (AJ:52):

(4) "small Early Roman-period Kefar Hananya-type pottery sherds"
(5) "two fragments of what may be light greyish-white limestone vessels—also probably dating from the Early Roman period"
(6) "decayed yellowish-white wall plaster... and small shards of 'Roman-style' thin-walled green glass vessel" (*sic*).

In a footnote, Dark communicates that "Tony Grey has kindly provided his independent report on all stratified pottery from the convent" (AJ:53, n. 36). We must await Dark's promised monograph and "final report" for an itemization, photos/drawings, dimensions, and individual descriptions of the claimed movable artifacts.

It is clear that the items in the box of Senès (nos. 3-6 above—for the spindle whorl was also in the box), some presumably with labels, are unprovenanced and cannot be securely associated with any particular locus—nor even linked with certainly to the convent site. They could, in fact, have come from elsewhere (though I am not suggesting this is the case). In addition, once we incorporate the correct later chronology of the site (*cf.* the following sections), then it becomes clear that "the *earliest* soil layer" actually dates to Middle-Late Roman times. In other words, Dark has transposed items 1-3 above to an earlier period. He has similarly transposed the contents of the box of Senès—items 3–6—for they are also from "the earliest soil layer." In this way, we recognize that—when the correct chronology of the site is introduced—*all* the movable artifacts Dark notes above are Middle-Late Roman in date.

In a later Interim Report, the British archeologist astonishingly describes a much more robust repertoire of movable finds:

[The pottery preserved in the convent museum forms] an invaluable archaeological resource, but only a minority of the finds survive (many others are known from unpublished records) and the exact find-spots of most of those that survive are unknown. In 2006-8 we recorded all of the existing finds, drawing those—over 500 artifacts—that can be assigned to a find-spot by preserved labels or are intrinsically dateable. (Dark 2010:5)

It is difficult to tally the apparently contradictory statements contained in this passage: "the exact find-spots of most of those that survive are unknown" with "over 500 artifacts" that can be assigned a findspot "or are intrinsically dateable." A similar contrast exists between the earlier limited repertoire (basically the box of Senès) described in 2007 and this much vaster repertoire noted in 2010. Five hundred artifacts is an immense number and would furnish a thorough profile of the site, even if only a portion of them could be securely provenanced. The question, naturally, immediately arises: from where do all these 500 artifacts come? Dark does not say and, presumably, we must await his book/final report for the answer.

In 2007 Dark gloomily noted a bevy of problems relating to the movable evidence from the Sisters of Nazareth site:

> The majority of the finds seem to have been given away, or even discarded, without record but some have been kept in the small convent museum. Regrettably only a minority of these bear any sort of identifying labeling telling us where they were found. There is also useful information about the finds, structures and stratification at the site contained in the large quantity of unpublished notes, written descriptions and drawings, made available by the convent. The latter have not received any detailed published archeological analysis and many previous scholars have written as if these notes and drawings do not exist at all. (Dark 2007:3)

The above is damning as regards the usefulness of most of the movable artifacts which Dark has identified, at least prior to 2010. Certainly, those artifacts without labels must immediately be excluded as "evidence." This includes most of what is found in the convent museum. Dark's observation that most of the museum artifacts lack "any sort of" identifying label is chilling. Furthermore, the labels which survive may be incomplete, erroneous, and/or imperfect.

For now, the most reliable pottery evidence is the two shards in points 1 and 2 above—those found *in situ*. Dark characterizes the first as "Early Roman-period cooking pottery" and the second simply as "Another," implying close similarity. However, the two shards could come from cooking pots used in the second-fourth centuries CE—whether or not the pots were manufactured somewhat earlier. Thus, their "Early Roman" characterization is unsupported. There is also some question as to the findspot of the shard in point number 2. This appears to be a locus *outside* the alleged house in question. Finally, in all likelihood these are both Kfar Hananya ware, for the more proximate Sikhnin pottery industry did not produce ware for cooking—a specialty of Kfar Hananya (Adan-Bayewitz and Wieder 1992:194). Production of Kefar Hananya pottery *continued into the fifth century CE* (Adan-Bayewitz 1993:149; Adan-Bayewitz and Wieder 1992:194). It should be noted that the majority of shards in the pottery repertoire of the Sisters of Nazareth Convent are apparently Kfar Hananya ware.

Dark notes that the spindle whorl "may support a domestic interpretation" (AJ:53). This is hardly certain as the object could have been *buried* with a female and—with all the disturbance of the site—been found somewhat out of place.

A consideration of finds from the rest of the hillside is germane and sobering. Of the 100+ provenanced pieces of pottery from the Venerated Area itemized in *The Myth of Nazareth* (Appendix 6), it was concluded that "not a single post-Iron Age artifact, tomb or structure at Nazareth dates with certainty before 100 CE" (Salm 2008a:165, 205).

It is no fault of Prof. Dark that the movable evidence from under the Sisters of Nazareth convent is non-diagnostic. That evidence was found many decades after discovery, in a box with few labels, and in a museum. Only two shards were found *in situ.* They are described generally as "Early Roman"—a dating which arguably extends *into the second century CE.*

Because the pottery is non-diagnostic, conclusions drawn therefrom are suspect, as in the following passage:

> The lowest stratified deposits within Structure 1 are therefore, associated with pottery that was produced only in the Roman period *and include no material later than the Early Roman period.*   (AJ:52, emphasis added.)

This provocative statement cannot be sustained, for Dark bases it upon the material in the box of unprovenanced material collected by Senès. More specifically, Dark is alluding to "small Early Roman-period Kefar Hananya-type pottery sherds" found in that box (point 3 above). A categorical "Early Roman period" dating for Kfar Hanaya ware found at Nazareth is, however, immediately suspect. Such ware continued in use through Roman times.

In an unpublished description, Senès stated that the contents of the box came from a layer of earth beneath the Crusader layer (AJ:51-52). The Crusader period began in the eleventh century, one thousand years after the period Dark actually claims for the pottery in the box. However, Dark writes that the box's contents came from "The lowest stratified deposits within Structure 1." This is meaningful to him in a special way, for the lowest stratum of the "domestic" structure signals to him "before *c.* 100 CE," the *false terminus ante quem* for construction of the tomb. Thus, it would appear that the archeologist engages in a species of circular reasoning: (a) the pottery dates to the first century because it was found in the "lowest stratified deposits" (wrongly dated to the first century CE); and (b) the lowest stratified deposits (*i.e.*, the domestic Structure 1) date to the first century *because of the pottery allegedly found there.* When we introduce the correct *terminus ante quem* for construction of the tomb, however, we see that the "lowest stratified deposits" could date as late as Byzantine times! In other words, all the artifacts in the box of Senès are in all likelihood Middle-Late Roman (in conformity with the panoply of evidence reported in *The Myth of Nazareth*).

In one Interim Report (2010:13-14), Dark furnishes more information regarding the movable artifacts in the box of Senès. Those artifacts include "freshly broken, sherds of Early Roman-period domestic pottery," glass vessel shards, a spindle whorl, and what "may" be fragments of stone vessels. However, all such objects have been found in Nazareth tombs. They are not necessarily "domestic." In addition, the pottery Dark terms "Early Roman" does not *demand* a first century date at all. It could be second-third century—as is much of the pottery itemized in *The Myth of Nazareth*.

Because so much of the ceramic evidence (pottery) and small artifacts is unprovenanced and poorly labeled, we must conclude that *the movable evidence from the Sisters of Nazareth site is not determinative, for it is accompanied by too many imponderables*. Dark is entirely correct when he writes: "The main evidence for the date and interpretation of the site, therefore, is still the series of rock-cut and built features exposed by earlier work" (Dark 2008:3). We will now turn our attention to those *structural* features, for it is upon them that the site's chronology must principally reside.

The date of the *kokh* tombs

The terminus ante quem

The reader will recall Prof. Dark's overall conclusion (above): there was human habitation at the Sisters of Nazareth site in the first century CE. This conclusion is theoretically based on two elements: the *movable* and the *structural* evidence. However, we have seen that the former (primarily pottery) is insecure for a variety of reasons, including uncertain findspot, poor labeling, and equivocal dating. It is upon the structural evidence that Dark's conclusions must primarily be tested.

The nub of Dark's faulty reasoning is the following sentence:

> Given that Tomb 1 is a *kokhim* tomb, typologically dating to the first century AD (see below), then Structure 1 must date from the first century AD or earlier.   (AJ:51)

Here the archeologist begins with a very false premise: the *kokh*-type tomb typologically dates to the first century CE. In apparent support, his parenthesis "see below" refers to a passage several pages later where he signals the work of R. Hachlili on Jerusalem-area tombs:

> Hachlili's dating of the use of loculi to after the first century BC, and the use of a rolling stone to seal a burial of this type *to no later than the end of the first century AD*, [note 55] argue that Tomb 1 may be dated typologically to the first century AD.   (AJ:58; emphasis added)

We will have more to say regarding Dark's misuse of Jerusalem evidence (Hachlili) to date Nazareth tombs (see "The *terminus post quem*" below). For now, we simply follow the trail that Dark has left the reader, for he signals yet another passage via his "note 55" in the above citation. That passage, in the tome by Hachlili, reads as follows:

> A round rolling stone (*golel*), closing the entrance was found in several rock-cut tombs, dated to the end of the first century BCE and the first century CE... (Hachlili 2005:64)

These "several rock-cut tombs" were all in the Jerusalem area and aristocratic (see "Rolling stones" below). They are exceptionally early. As Hachlili notes, the rolling stone custom of tomb closure does indeed come to an end *in the Jerusalem area* in the first century CE. However, a very different chronology applies to the Galilee where, as we will see, round blocking stones actually become very frequent in later Roman times (Kloner). All of this escapes Dark, for he applies the Jerusalem dating to the round blocking stone found under the Sisters of Nazareth convent. With no further ado he then globally dates the Nazareth tombs "to the first century AD or earlier" (AJ:51, cited above). This is the genesis of Dark's "hard" *terminus ante quem* of *c.* 100 CE for *kokh* tombs in the Galilee.

It is also the loose sand upon which the entire edifice of Dark's reasoning founders. The first century CE is, in fact, the *terminus post quem* of the *kokh* tomb in the Galilee, not the *terminus ante quem*. His false chronology places Dark in the untenable position of having to ignore literally dozens of *kokh* tombs excavated in the Galilee dating after the first century—in fact, *all* the Jewish *kokh* tombs excavated to date do! M. Aviam has stated: "Few *first century* tombs have been found in Galilee and *none* in the Jewish area" (Aviam 2004a:20, emphasis added). Dark ignores this and similar crucial information—though it is readily accessible in the literature.

We know (though the work of Kuhnen and others) that the *kokh*-type of tomb was current in the Galilee (and Jerusalem) through Roman times. It did not come to an end in the first century CE, nor even in the second, as Catholic scholars of a past generation argued. Thus, Robert Smith in 1961:

> Various viewpoints on the use-span of the kok type of interment are brought together by H. Vincent in [*Revue Biblique*], XLIII (1934), pp. 564-67. Vincent expresses a preference for the round dates of 200 B.C.–A.D. 200... J. T. Milik informs me from his wide knowledge that kok burials definitely came to an end by A.D. 135. The late date formerly given probably arose from instances in which tombs cut prior to 135 were re-used after that date. (Smith 1961:59, n. 18.)

However, as I wrote in *The Myth of Nazareth* (p. 161): "The view of Father Milik is neither tenable nor universally held. We now know that the *kokh* type of burial endured in Northern Palestine through Roman and into Byzantine times. *Kokhim* have been found in Sepphoris dating to III CE, in the catacombs of Beth Shearim dating to III-IV CE, and in a burial cave at Kafr Kanna (7 km NE of Nazareth) dating to IV CE. In the hill country of Manasseh, a particularly late example was excavated with ten *kokhim* in a 'IV-VI CE' context." I went on to note that knowledge of *kokhim* use through Roman times has been known since the work of E. Goodenough, who wrote in 1953: "In the centuries which followed the fall of Jerusalem, however, the dominant Jewish convention of burial was that of the chamber tomb with kokim. This is the form stipulated in the Mishna, and the type most commonly found" (Goodenough 1:88).

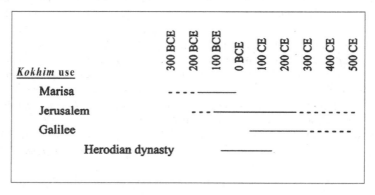

Figure 6.1. Chronology of *kokh* tomb use in Palestine

Critical to this issue is the more recent work of Hans-Peter Kuhnen. In various publications over several decades (see Bibliography), Kuhnen surveyed known Roman tombs in the Galilee. He found not a single example of the *kokh* type datable before the middle of the first century CE. Kuhnen also set forth a detailed chronology of the *kokh* tomb, from simple *kokhim* (single burial "tubes" dug horizontally into the rock), to shelf burials, to arcosolia, to trough graves. He articulated a chronology of *kokh* tomb dispersion from south to north, beginning at Marisa (southern Judea) in the third century BCE, reaching Jerusalem and its environs a century later, but not reaching the Galilee until the mid-first century CE. Kuhnen's work has been confirmed by other archeologists. To requote M. Aviam, for example: "Few first century tombs [including those of the *kokh* type] have been found in Galilee and none in the Jewish area" (Aviam 2004a:20).

Kuhnen's work was highlighted in my book, *The Myth of Nazareth* (pp. 158-62). Dark reviewed that book (*BAIAS* 2008:140-46), thus one can infer that he certainly is familiar with the modern view of *kokhim* chronology. Yet Dark ignores this vital information. None of Kuhnen's works appears in his writings nor in his bibliographies.

At issue is as much as four hundred years—a *terminus ante quem* of *c.* 500 CE rather than *c.* 100 CE. When we incorporate the correct chronology of *kokh* tomb use, we see that *even if the 'dwelling' at the Sisters of Nazareth Convent were earlier* than the tomb, as Dark alleges, *that 'dwelling' could date as late as the fourth century CE!*

Dark's cited sources include ample data showing that the *kokh* tomb existed in the Galilee through Roman times. (The issue of misrepresentation of sources will be taken up later.) One resource footnoted by Dark is a 2002 article by Aviam and Syon entitled "Jewish ossilegium in Galilee." That article presents a panoply of *kokh* tomb datings reaching into the second, third, and fourth centuries CE. This obviously nullifies Dark's *terminus ante quem* for *kokh* tomb use in the Galilee (above), for the ossuaries which Aviam and Syon consider were from *kokh* tombs dated by them as follows:

- Gush Halav: IV–V CE
- Nahariya: Two periods—*c.* 50–150 CE and III–IV CE
- Horvat 'Uza: 70-135 CE "or slightly later"
- Sajur: After 70 or 135 CE. Artifacts III–IV CE
- Kabul: II CE
- Ibellin: I-IV CE
- Horvat Ofrath: II–IV CE
- Sepphoris: End II–III CE
- Kafr Kanna: I–III CE
- Tivon: Late I–III CE
- Kfar Barukh: II CE
- Near Nazareth: II–III CE (lamps I–II CE)
- Dabburiye: I–III CE
- Huqoq: *c.* 70– *c.* 130 CE
- Kfar Hittin: *c.* 70– *c.* 130 CE

The above fully demonstrates the groundlessness of Prof. Dark's working assumption that the *kokh* tomb came to an end in the first century CE. On the contrary, Aviam and Syon pointedly affirm: "Not a single excavated Galilean tomb with ossuaries can be dated solely to the first century CE" (p. 183).

In his third Interim Report, Dark extrapolates his false early dating of the tombs to encompass the entire hillside (Dark 2009:12-15) under the rubric, "Phase 2: An Early Roman period cemetery." To justify this egregiously early dating he uses the aforementioned Jerusalem chronology which is approximately two centuries too early (see "The *terminus post quem,*" below). Thus, for Dark, all the Nazareth *kokhim* tombs are pre-100 CE—an amazing contrast with the work of specialists in the field (Aviam, Kuhnen) who have discovered *no* pre-50–100 CE Jewish *kokh* tombs in the Galilee at all.

If Prof. Dark's purpose is to support the existence of a turn-of-the-era settlement at Nazareth, then the (now well-established) chronology of *kokh* tomb use is most inconvenient. In fact, it completely overturns his scenario for the Sisters of Nazareth site. This is because a crucial link in Dark's reasoning involves a relative dating: the *anteriority* of the above ground structure ('dwelling') to the tomb. By falsely setting a "hard" *terminus ante quem* for the Galilean *kokh* tomb of *c.* 100 CE, Dark then attempts to date the above ground structure (on the basis of an alleged "cutting"—see below) *before* it, thus ostensibly showing (a) priority of the 'dwelling,' and (b) its necessary existence well before 100 CE. We consider this problematic reasoning below ("Phase 1 – Phase 2 problems"), but note here that all ultimately depends on Dark's false *terminus ante quem* for the *kokh* tomb: *c.* 100 CE.

When one acknowledges that *kokhim* use continued through Late Roman and even into Early Byzantine times, then Dark's argument simply loses all force. The structure under the Sisters of Nazareth convent could well be Late Roman (and the tomb even later if Dark's structure-tomb sequence is honored).

The presence of a rolling stone and a niche (probably for bone collection) in fact point to the second-third centuries CE, as does the movable evidence. A post-100 CE dating also agrees well with the archeological profile from the rest of the Nazareth basin (Salm 2008a:Appendices 5–6). In any case, the structure-tomb sequence is not necessarily correct nor even important once one acknowledges that the above ground structural features were dedicated to agricultural uses (*e.g*, viniculture, production of olive oil, *etc*). Both structure and tomb might then be roughly contemporaneous, and Dark has presented no evidence to the contrary.

The terminus post quem

Though the late abandonment of *kokh* tomb use is the principal impediment to Dark's artificial chronology, the beginning of *kokh* use in the Galilee is also significant. Kuhnen has shown that the *kokh* tomb appeared in the Galilee *much later* than in the Jerusalem area. *The difference is over two centuries*, as the above chart (Fig. 6.1) makes clear. It is fair to say that Kuhnen's work is indispensable for an understanding of Jewish burial customs in the Galilee in Roman times. His conclusions are sufficiently critical that they merit extended citation:

> *Kokhim* tombs [*Schiebestollengräber*], which under the Hasmoneans grad-
> ually replaced the older chamber tombs, also dominated the graveyards
> of [Jerusalem] almost with exclusivity after the accession of Herod...
> Under Herod and his heirs, the *kokhim* type of grave also appeared in
> the Jewish-populated surroundings of Jerusalem, for example, in Tell en-
> Nasbe and in el-'Ezriye (Bethany)... Apparently only later, from approxi-
> mately the middle of the first century after Christ, did people begin to
> build *kokhim* tombs in other upland regions of Palestine, as seen in Galilee
> at Huqoq, Meron, H. Sema and H. Usa...
> So it is evident that during the first century after Christ *kokhim* came
> into fashion in all parts of the land west and east of the Jordan...
>   (Kuhnen 1990:254-55)

From this we see that *kokh* tomb use begins *c.* 150 BCE in Jerusalem,
comes to prevail in that city after Herod's accession, and spreads to Galilee
only after *c.* 50 CE. The first century CE is a *terminus post quem* for the *kokh*
tomb in the Galilee, not a *terminus ante quem* as Dark supposes. Dr. Kuhnen's
work, elaborated in a number of publications, has now superseded the earlier Catholic tomb chronology which it has shown to be wide of the mark
by many centuries, for we now know that the *kokh* tomb continued in use in
northern Israel as late as the sixth century CE (Salm 2008:158–64).

As alluded to above, Prof. Dark also arbitrarily applies Judean chronologies to the Galilee—a faulty methodology that no specialist in Palestinian
archeology would adopt. The well known tome by R. Hachlili upon which
he relies deals explicitly with Jerusalem-area tombs: *Jewish Funerary Customs,
Practices and Rites in the Second Temple Period* (2005). The title is somewhat
unfortunate, in that the more geographically restrictive word "Judean"
would be far more appropriate to the contents of the book than the more
inclusive word "Jewish." Perhaps the oversight owes to a translator. In any
case, Hachlili's results—as she notes in her book's Foreword—relate to a
relatively small area around Jerusalem: "The study outlines the material
preserved in the ancient Jewish cemeteries of the Hellenistic and Roman
periods at Jerusalem, Jericho, 'En Gedi, and Qumran" (Hachlili 2005:xxxi).

When we incorporate recent work on burial customs in late antiquity,
including both Hachlili's work on the Jerusalem area and Kuhnen's work
on the Galilee, we arrive at the *kokh* tomb chronology diagrammed above.
There was a particularly early period of *kokh* tomb use—already in Hellenistic and Hasmonean times—exemplified by the tombs at Marisa in the
south of the land. The type came to Jerusalem in the second century BCE
and endured there for many centuries. Finally, in the middle of the first
century CE, *kokh* use spread to the northern part of the country. Thus, M.
Aviam noted the lack of Jewish tombs from the Hasmonean and Early Roman periods in the Galilee (Aviam 2004b:236). There is a 200-year delay

from the first appearance of the *kokh* tomb in Jerusalem to its appearance in the Galilee (Salm 2008a:159).

Dark's application of a Judean tomb chronology to the Galilee allows him to avoid what would otherwise be a ridiculous scenario: *kokh* tombs come to the Galilee *c.* 50 CE (Kuhnen) but disappear there fifty years later (the old Catholic position—see above). By adopting a Judean chronology, Dark effectively backdates the Nazareth tombs by as much as two centuries and allows for a substantial longevity of *kokh* tomb use in the north.

As an aside, it may be noted that the application of Judean datings to Galilean evidence is fairly common among conservative archeologists, for it quickly facilitates the backdating of a considerable amount of material. This is apparent, for example, in the recent treatment of pottery at the Nazareth Village Farm (*BAIAS* 2008:113–35, "Amendment"), where the archeologist Y. Rapuano adopts chronologies and typologies from Jerusalem and Gezer to arrive at egregiously early datings for a number of Nazareth shards. Using southern parallels effectively moves the *terminus post quem* back generations (as in the case of certain oil lamps) or even centuries (as in the case of *kokh* tombs). Besides his too-early dating of Galilean *kokh* tombs, Dark has similarly transposed the earlier dating of round blocking stones in Judea to their later use in the Galilee (below).

In his published review of *The Myth of Nazareth* (Dark 2008d), Prof. Dark has the temerity to berate me for not applying Hachlili's results to my Nazareth work. The shoe, however, is on the other foot. Erroneously applying Hachlili's chronology to Nazareth, Dark ignores not only the work of Kuhnen, Aviam, and others, but also four centuries of enduring *kokh* tomb use in the Galilee.

Tomb typology

Prof. Dark also fundamentally misunderstands Hachlili's tomb typology. In the first Interim Report, he makes the following observation regarding one of the two *kokh* tombs under the Sisters of Nazareth convent:

> According to Hachlili's typology, this is a Jerusalem Type I tomb. These are what she calls 'family tombs' dateable to the Hasmonean period in the Jerusalem area. However, as Hachlili has shown, Type I tombs were constructed into the Early Roman period in the Galilee because of the late introduction of ossuary burial in the region. (Dark 2007:7; *cf.* AJ:58)

This is certainly false for, as we have seen, Hachlili never intended that her chronology be applied to the Galilee. Secondly, Dark's assertion that Type I tombs were "constructed" demonstrates a fundamental misunderstanding. Hachlili's typology is independent of tomb constuction and design. She offers three categories of *Customs, Practices, and Rites* (words from the title of her book) regarding burial in the Jerusalem area. *Her distinguishing three types has primarily to do with the presence or absence of post-inhumation activity*—secondary bone collection and/or reburial:

> Type I — Primary burials placed on benches and in loculi, dated to the Hasmonean period [*in the Jerusalem area!*]...
>
> Type II — Primary burial and the transfer of bones to a communal charnel, side loculi or chambers, before the use of ossuaries, is evinced in Jerusalem; this custom is dated to Herodian times [*in Jerusalem!*].
>
> Type III — Reburial and bones collected into ossuaries...

Thus, Hachlili's three types are:

> I. *kokh*/loculus burial
> II. secondary bone collection (not in ossuaries)
> III. secondary reburial and bone collection (in ossuaries).

According to the above typology, the presence of ossuaries signals a Type III tomb. The presence of secondary bone collection without ossuaries is Type II. The presence of human remains still in *kokhim*/loculi, with no secondary bone collection, is Type I.

However, *Prof. Dark supposes that Hachlili's tomb typology refers to structural elements* and her "Type I" to ossuary use:

> Tomb I is a well-preserved example of a *kokhim* tomb with a rolling stone (33cm thick x 109cm in diameter) in a rock-cut track, probably a Hachlili '(Jerusalem) Type I tomb'...
>
> While dating Type I tombs in Jerusalem to the Hasmonean period, Hachlili has argued that they may be later in the Galilee, especially as ossuary burial—with which they are often associated, and which could be evidenced by the small niche—probably began in the Galilee only after *c.* AD 70.   (AJ:58, emphasis added)

Because the Sisters of Nazareth site has been extensively reworked over millennia, human remains would have been disturbed long ago. According to Hachlili's typology it is therefore not possible to affirm whether these tombs were Type I, Type II, or Type III in Roman times—or perhaps multiple types at different times. (An added complication is that there is also considerable evidence of burial at the site in post-Roman times.—Dark 2009:14–15, 20.)

Prof. Dark posits that the Nazareth tomb could be Early Roman "because of the late introduction of ossuary burial in the region." But in this case ossuary use is irrelevant to dating, for the various burial customs existed simultaneously in Middle-Late Roman times. The introduction of ossuaries and secondary burial did not bring to an end "Type I" tombs, *i.e.*, primary inhumation (without secondary bone collection or ossuary use. *Cf.* Salm 2008a:161 *f*). In any case, no evidence of ossuaries has been found at the Sisters of Nazareth site.

Dark persists in mischaracterizing Tomb 1 as Hachlili's "Type I," as we read in his last Interim Report:

> Tomb 1 is an excellent example of a Hachlili '(Jerusalem) Type I tomb' dateable to the first century AD, perhaps in this case to the later first century AD.   (Dark 2010:18)

This is embarrassingly wrong, as the reader is now aware—both as regards tomb type and tomb date.

"Rolling stones"

Prof. Dark writes:

> Hachlili has argued—on the grounds of much evidence from excavated tombs—that the use of rolling stones was characteristic of the first century BC to first century AD. So the Sisters of Nazareth tomb may belong to this period, but it probably postdates earlier occupation in the Early Roman period. This implies a date of the later first century BC to late first century AD at broadest.   (Dark 2007:7, n. 18)

This is a misrepresentation of Hachlili's writing, besides being patently false. The least of the above passage's problems is that it, once again, applies *Judean evidence* to Nazareth in Galilee. As with the false chronology for the *kokh* tomb, this leads Dark to an erroneous chronology for round blocking stones. Since the *kokh* tomb did not exist in the Galilee before *c.* 50 CE (above), we can be sure that neither did round blocking stones.

Amos Kloner has carefully studied the prevalence of round blocking stones and their dating (Kloner 1980, 1999). He concludes that they did not occur anywhere in Palestine before the First Jewish War—except in a very few aristocratic tombs of the Jerusalem area. Hachlili in fact refers to those few high class tombs in the following passage:

> A round rolling-stone *golel*, closing the entrance was found in several rock-cut tombs, dated to the end of the first century BCE and the first century CE... The following tombs in Jerusalem were sealed by means of rolling stones: The tomb of Helene, Herod's family tomb...
> (Hachlili 2005:64)

Regarding the Jerusalem area, Kloner observes further:

> [I]n Jesus' time, round blocking stones were extremely rare and appeared only in the tombs of the wealthiest Jews.

[M]ore than 98 percent of the Jewish tombs from this period, called the Second Temple period (*c.* first century B.C.E. to 70 C.E.), were closed with square blocking stones. Of the more than 900 burial caves from the Second Temple period found in and around Jerusalem, only four are known to have used round (disk-shaped) blocking stones.

In later periods the situation changed, and round blocking stones became much more common. Dozens of them have been found from the late Roman to Byzantine period...   (Kloner 1999:28, 23, 25)

We see, then, that the round blocking stones "became much more common" in later Roman times. *This refutes Dark's view "that the use of rolling stones was characteristic of the first century BC to first century AD."* His statement would apply to *square* blocking stones. He also mischaracterizes Hachlili, who simply describes a few *rare* aristocratic tombs in Jerusalem with round blocking stones from "the end of the first century BCE and the first century CE" (Hachlili 2005:64). Hachlili's dating of these early aristocratic examples in the Jerusalem area does not mean, of course, that round blocking stones were *not* used later and in other parts of the country, as Dark seems to think: "Hachlili's dating... of a rolling stone to seal a burial of this type *to no later than the end of the first century AD*, argue[s] that Tomb I may be dated typologically to the first century AD" (AJ:58, emphasis added).

Figure 6.2. The entrance to Tomb 1
under the Sisters of Nazareth Convent.

The rolling stone is *in situ*, and two *kokhim* are visible through the tomb doorway.
Cf. Figs. 6.3 and 6.4. (Public domain.)

When one understands that round blocking stones actually became quite common in Late Roman and Byzantine times (Kloner), then the presence of a rolling stone at the Sisters of Nazareth tomb is a powerful indication that this Galilean *kokh* tomb is post-100 CE, not pre-100 CE as Dark contends. In fact, it could well date to Late Roman times.

Dark writes: "[I]n Nazareth, rolling stones certainly closed 'ordinary' Early Roman-period *kokhim* burials: see, for example, Mansur 1923; Bagatti 1969, tomb no. 70, figs 4 and 192" (AJ:58, n. 51). Both references (Mansur/ Bagatti) are to one and the same Tomb 70. In my first book, I ascertained that tomb's material to range "from *c.* 50 CE–*c.* 150 CE (pot #18) into early Byzantine times (pan #19), which gives a good idea of the life span of this tomb" (Salm 2008a:273). Thus, the tomb's use is Middle-Late Roman, not Early Roman.

In short, Dark's supposition that the presence of a rolling stone in Nazareth "was characteristic of the first century BC to first century AD" is a gross misunderstanding of the history of round blocking stones. It fails to recognize that such blocking stones were used only rarely in the Jerusalem area pre-70 CE, and also that they did not appear in the Galilee before *c.* 70 CE. Dark's chronology of the rolling stone could scarcely be more misleading for (like his chronology of the *kokh* tomb) it ends where it should begin. 'Late I CE to late IV CE' is the correct timespan for the rolling stone under the Sisters of Nazareth Convent.

Misrepresentation of sources

We have noted, above, Dark's misrepresentation of Hachlili's position regarding rolling stones. Sadly, other instances of misrepresentation are not difficult to find in his writings. I mention a few further examples which, significantly, are critical to Dark's false chronology and hence to his argument.

(1) Dark writes:

> Aviam has noted that such *kokhim* tombs with rolling stones are rare in the Galilee in general. Nevertheless, *the same scholar has drawn attention to Early Roman-period examples from Migdal Ha'Emeq*[9] (grid ref: 1740/2708) near Nazareth, and others exist among the known *kokhim* burials surrounding the Roman-period village. Consequently, the Phase 2 *kokhim* tomb at the Sisters of Nazareth site may be dated to the Early Roman period and could belong to a sub-regional group of 'rolling stone' tombs in the Nazareth area.   (Dark 2007:7, emphasis added.)

---

9.   The name is variously spelled in English with and without a hyphen, as well as with and without the transliteration symbol for *ayin* (erroneously pointed to the left in Dark's writings). Except in citations, we will adopt the simplest spelling with accepted capitalizations: HaEmeq.

This is incorrect, both with respect to what Aviam has written and with respect to the tombs at Migdal HaEmeq. Aviam does not use the words "Early Roman" at all in his discussion (footnoted citation no. 19, "Aviam 2004B, pp. 296–7").[10] Regarding the large cemetery at Migdal HaEmeq, Aviam notes that some of the tombs had "round burial stones." As to elsewhere in the Galilee, he writes in one place of a "*Late Roman* tomb closed with a round burial stone," and also of (*later Roman*) tombs "of the arcosolia type and closed with a round burial stone"[11] (emphasis added). Thus, the inference of "Early Roman" evidence from Migdal HaEmeq is entirely Dark's creation and also clashes with what we have already cited multiple times from Aviam, namely, that "no Jewish tombs from the Hasmonaean or Early Roman periods have yet been excavated in the Galilee" (Aviam 2004b:306; *cf.* Aviam 2004a:20). It also clashes with what we have reviewed regarding the *later* appearance of "rolling stones" in the Galilee.

An article written in 2009 by A. Tatcher and Zvi Gal details the findings from Migdal HaEmeq.[12] One small tomb was Hellenistic (Tomb AH, Plan 1, p. 2) with a typical oil lamp. Chronologically next is the "Early Phase" of tombs M and L, as well as tomb Z.[13] The recovered movable finds from the site date between the two Jewish revolts (Fig. 3, p. 4) *and onwards*. It is certainly incorrect to conclude that the *kokhim* tombs at Migdal HaEmeq date before Kuhnen's *terminus a quo* of *c.* 50 CE. In sum, the published results from various archeologists do *not* support an "Early Roman" dating for this cemetery, as Dark asserts and (astonishingly) imputes to Aviam.

(2) Dark writes:

> While dating Type I tombs in Jerusalem to the Hasmonean period, Hachlili has argued that they may be later in the Galilee, especially as ossuary burial—with which they are often associated, and which could be evidenced by the small niche— probably began in the Galilee only after *c.* AD 70. *Aviam, Berlin and others have dated similar tombs in the Galilee to the first century AD, and Aviam has suggested that they may have been introduced from the south by Late Hellenistic farmers.* (AJ:58, emphasis added)

The first sentence of this passage has already been cited with regard to Dark's misinterpretation of Hachlili's tomb typology. Here I would like to focus on the italicized second sentence. In it, Dark alleges that "Aviam, Berlin and others have dated [Type I] tombs in the Galilee to the first century

---

10. Dark's reference is to Aviam's 2004 book, *Jews, Pagans and Christians in the Galilee.*

11. Aviam 2004b:296. The sites are El Makr and Kh. el Waziya.

12. "The Ancient Cemetery at Migdal Ha'Emeq."*Atiqot* 61 [2009]:1-47 (Hebrew) +131-32 (English summary).

13. From these results it seems possible that there was a break in settlement at Migdal HaEmeq between *c.* 100 BCE and *c.* 100 CE.

AD." This extraordinary assertion once again contradicts Aviam's dictum that that *no Jewish tombs have been excavated in the Galilee dating to the first century CE* (Aviam 2004b:306; 2004a:20). Furthermore, Dark's flight of fancy that "Aviam has suggested that [Type I *kokh* tombs] may have been introduced from the south by *Late Hellenistic* farmers" (emphasis added) is categorically precluded by Aviam's published writings. In all this, we should bear in mind that Prof. Dark has not grasped Hachlili's concept of the "Type I" tomb.

(3) In his 2012 *Antiquaries Journal* article—Dark's summation of his work at the Sisters of Nazareth Convent—the archeologist mischaracterizes statements by Kloner and Zissu regarding rolling stones:

> Kloner and Zissu agree that tombs sealed by rolling stones in rock-cut tracks, especially if, as here, the 'round stone' has a diameter of over 80cm, can be dated to the first century AD but they add that they see these are especially popular 'in the middle of the century.'
> (Dark 2012:58)

In the above citation, Prof. Dark simply ignores the fact that Kloner and Zissu are considering *Jerusalem* tombs. In fact, Kloner has specifically argued that the rolling stone did not appear in the Galilee before the First Jewish Revolt, as we have seen. *Even in Jerusalem it was very rare before that time.* On the other hand, the round blocking stone becomes quite common in the Galilee in Late Roman and Byzantine times (Salm 2008a:186). There is no scholarly foundation (claimed or falsely imputed to others) for Dark's view that rolling stones "can be dated to the first century AD."

A similar blindness to geography and chronology occurs in Dark's following 2012 AJ passage:

> Hachlili's dating of the use of loculi [*in Jerusalem!*] to after the first century BC, and the use of a rolling stone to seal a burial of this type [*in Jerusalem!*] to no later than the end of the first century AD, argue that Tomb I [*in Nazareth!*] may be dated typologically to the first century AD.
> (Dark AJ:58. Brackets added.)

Here we again witness the intemperate confounding of evidence from Jerusalem and Nazareth. No one versed in Palestinian archeology could make such a blunder, nor could approach the field with such crude unprofessionalism. In fact, the Jerusalem *kokh* tombs date as much as two centuries before their Nazareth descendants.

Phase 1 – Phase 2 problems

Dark's argument for the priority of 'dwelling' to tomb (thus supporting the existence of Nazareth at the 'time of Jesus') rests primarily on the structural evidence, given the inconclusive nature of the movable finds and their uncertain provenance (above). Unfortunately, the walls and other physical features which he considers have been much reworked over the centuries, are poorly attested, or in some cases are even nonexistent.

The nub of Dark's argument from structural evidence hinges on his claim that, at a certain locus ("F" in Fig. 6.3), an extension of the tomb "cuts into" an extension of the above-ground structure's Wall 1. This demonstrates, for him, that the above ground stucture was already in existence when the tomb cut into it—that is, when it was hewn. In turn, this recognition is Dark's entire basis for his "Phase 1–Phase 2" scenario whereby a domestic phase (the above-ground "Structure 1") was followed by a funereal phase ("Tomb 1").

Dark has described the locus in question as "south of a massive Crusader period masonry wall" labeled "M4" in various diagrams (Dark 2010:10; *cf.* Fig. 6.3). However, it is *several meters outside both the tomb and the above-ground structure*—thus having no obvious relation to either. Perhaps reacting to this fairly straightforward observation, Dark posits that both the Structure 1 and the tomb had extensions of considerable size which he terms "forecourts." It is the forecourts of each which impinge upon one another at F. In his conception, then, a "cutting into" the above ground (domestic) structure occurs at an *extremity* of a western *extension* of an alleged tomb *forecourt*.

In fact, both forecourts are doubtful. Bagatti knew nothing of a forecourt to Tomb 1. His plan from 1937 (Fig. 6.4) and a recent photograph (Fig. 6.2) depict a typical *kokh* tomb entryway, known as a *dromos*.[14] Because the tomb was underground, the floor of the *dromos* generally sloped downwards as one neared the tomb door (often sealed with a rolling stone). The left and right walls of the *dromos* were usually vertical, and they could be graced with ornamentation. In Fig. 6.2 we see that the left wall of the *dromos* to Tomb 1 has been augmented by what appears to be a low rock shelf, possibly a temporary place to lay the wrapped body while moving the rolling stone out of the way. This small area—about one meter wide—is the only structural "extension" to the west that can be detected.

Whether or not one terms the entryway leading to Tomb 1 a *dromos* or small "forecourt," the photograph Fig. 6.2 shows that it is bounded on the west (left) by a rock-cut wall reaching to the ceiling. At the same time, Fig.

---

14. See Aviam 2004:291–94 for further photographs and discussion.

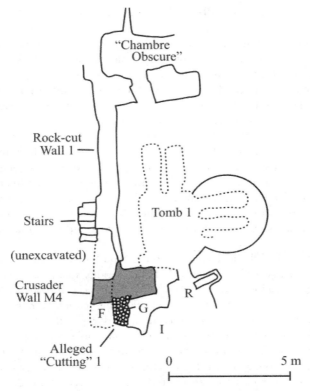

Figure 6.3. The southern half of the Sisters of Nazareth Convent site.

Key: Solid line = above ground features. Dotted lines of Tomb 1 = underground
features. Dotted lines at left and F = alleged extensions of Wall 1 to the south.
G = wall tumble. I = infill. R = round blocking stone. (Drawn by author.)

6.3 shows that the "Alleged Cutting" at locus F is well outside the *dromos* and
in a direct line with the rolling stone. One must, then, appreciate that locus
F is *on the other side* of the vertical rock wall depicted in the photograph. It
is a mystery how Dark envisages a tomb extension "of the forecourt to the
west" (AJ:58) which reaches to the required locus. His alleged tomb "extension" goes straight through a vertical rock wall!

Dark re-evaluates this locus F in each of his annual reports, finally
admitting that he experiences enormous problems interpreting it:

> These [features] are extremely hard to interpret and have been examined
> by us from the 2006 [report], but it is only in 2009 that we may be begin-
> ning to make sense of what they represent. (Dark 2010:10)

Astonishingly, *this difficult locus comprises the entirety of Dark's evidence for positing the priority of dwelling to tomb.* Undeterred by the weakness of the argument, the archeologist then uses it to date the alleged dwelling to "the first century AD or earlier":

> The deep rectilinear forecourt of Tomb 1 (fig 14) cuts away the south of Structure 1. Given that Tomb 1 is a *kokhim* tomb, typologically dating to the first century AD (see below), then Structure 1 must date from the first century AD or earlier.   (AJ:51)

The above argument is invalidated because the *kokh*-type tomb does not "date to the first century" but to later centuries (above). *Even granting* (for the sake of discussion) *the alleged priority of dwelling to tomb, the dwelling would then in all likelihood date to the third or fourth century CE*—consistent with the panoply of other evidence from Nazareth. However (owing to his false tomb chronology) this likelihood escapes Prof. Dark. It may also be noted that the tomb does not *typologically* date "to the first century AD." As we have seen, Dark has here misinterpreted Hachlili's Judean typology (as well as her dating).

There are yet further problems with this critical locus to the west of Tomb 1. In contrast to Dark's claim that the tomb "cuts into" the above ground structure at F, a careful reading of his prose reveals no "cutting" there at all: the alleged tomb extension does not directly impinge upon the above ground wall extension at F but into "wall tumble" at G (Fig. 6.3; cf. Dark 2010:11). This further complicates Dark's thesis, for not only is it unclear that the "tumble" is from the claimed wall F, but—even if it were—a cutting of the alleged tomb extension into wall tumble is hardly useful for positing that the tomb cut into the *above ground structure*. The tumble is not identical to the wall next to it, and *hence no "cutting" is in fact demonstrated.* To be minimally diagnostic, the cutting must be at F, not G.

One further complication is noted. Examination of Fig. 6.3[15] shows that the alleged tomb forecourt is separated from the wall tumble by two meters of "infill" (I), a word which appears to be Dark's euphemism for the *solid rock* separating the *dromos* from locus G. Regardless of what Dark means by "infill," it is clear that the tomb and the above ground structure are not and never were contiguous. Curiously, Dark claims that the infill is "later" and that it occludes the required evidence. This, however, appears to be little more than convenient rationalization, and he quickly passses over the point.

Thus, assumptions multiply and the actual physical features of the site, step-by-step, render the existence of Dark's (domestic) "Phase 1" increas-

---

15. Fig. 6.3 was redrawn based on Dark's 2012 Figs. 5 and 16 (AJ:44, 59).

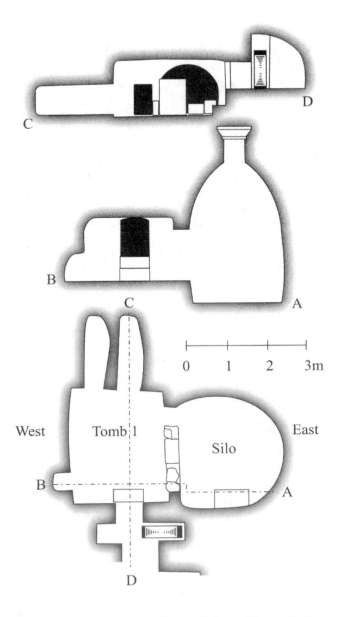

Figure 6.4. Tomb 1 under the Sisters of Nazareth Convent.
(Redrawn from Bagatti 1937:257 and 1969:242, fig. 194.)

ingly unlikely. While he argues for a domestic-funereal sequence at the Sisters of Nazareth site, the funereal phase is obvious. A pre-existing phase of any kind (whether domestic or not) is asserted only by him, however, on the basis of an untenable "cutting" of one structure into another.

Archeology by vegetable matter

In his final Interim Report, Dark struggles with an interpretation of the area F-G "south of wall M4." Lacking clear structural evidence for his overall thesis at this critical locus, he astonishingly resorts to a thin layer of soil and accompanying vegetable matter:

> Especially if it was once covered with a soil deposit, however thin, and vegetation, there would be no reason for anyone to notice or remove such a deposit in this location since its deposition at the end of Phase 1. *This deposit is very important to the interpretation of Phase 1*, as it strongly suggests that built walls of (perhaps roughly-constructed) masonry once stood on the top of at least some—although, as already observed above, probably not all—of the Phase 1 rock-cut walls.
>
> (Dark 2010:11-12, emphasis added.)

This is all quite forced. The present thinness of the soil layer implies, for Dark, a relatively short period of time. He concludes, therefore, that a second wall (since disappeared) once stood over "at least some" of the structural remains, including at locus F.[16] Dark arrives at this opinion by inferring that, had no subsequent walling been present, the soil deposit would today be *thicker*. In any case, this is an *argumentum e silencio*, for no masonry evidence survives of any built wall which "once stood on top of" the alleged Phase 1 wall at F. We will leave that telling absence aside, however, and simply note that out of scant vegetable matter Dark has created an invisible wall—one upon whose nonexistence he bases the priority of a wall we can all see. This 'earlier' wall was 'cut into' in a manner no one can verify, for it involves a remote tomb whose forecourt mysteriously extended to the required locus through a solid rock-cut wall (or under two meters of "infill"), and finally through wall tumble which has still not been removed. According to Dark's misinterpretation of Judean funereal typology and chronology (see above), the tomb ceased use before *c.* 100 CE (centuries too early) and thus—because it allegedly once cut into the wall at F—then the wall must date earlier than the tomb...

---

16. Even if two phases of walling could be deduced from the mere presence of a thin soil layer, the earlier wall would surely have dated to Middle Roman times and been dedicated to agricultural use (see below). In any case, Dark has not demonstrated a second phase of walling at this locus.

The foregoing lengthy series of steps ultimately devolves upon a thin layer of soil. On the basis of *all* those steps, however—vegetable matter, invisible wall, unverified cutting, tomb extension, and the false application of Jerusalem evidence—Dark concludes that the low wall at locus F is nothing less than the vestige of a domicile from the time of Christ—the first such "house" ever found at Nazareth! *Quod erat demonstrandum.*

All this is more than astonishing. If we suspect that Prof. Dark's logic is by turns tendentious, imaginative, and even false, we may remind ourselves that these very qualities are marks of distinction in the field of quack archeology.

Funereal and agricultural use

Dark's overall two-phase thesis—that a dwelling preceded a tomb in the southern half of the Sisters of Nazareth site—rests on an obviously tortured analysis of the locus F, as well as on the multiple errors of logic and interpretation described above. In general, his dwelling-tomb thesis is unprecedented—not only for this site but for any site in Palestine known to me. Nonetheless, the British archeologist boldly extends this poorly-argued sequence to nearby installations on the Nebi Sa'in hillside (below). The intention is clear. The priority of domesticity at numerous tomb sites would—if sustainable—reconcile the scriptural demand for dwellings (*i.e.*, for a village on the Nazareth hillside in the time of Jesus)[17] with the re-emergent reality of tombs under the very sites critical to the Christian tradition.[18] This reconciliation has recently become increasingly pressing, for my first book systematically revealed the considerable (though obscure) literature on numerous tombs in and around the Venerated Area, together with descriptions and discussion (Salm 2008a:243–59).

Like a knight in shining armor, Dark has attempted to meet the challenge posed by the undeniable, embarassing, and potentially threatening funereal evidence now brought to light not merely on the hillside but under some of the most venerated Christian sites themselves. With one venturesome idea, his novel two-phase thesis attempts to solve this problem known to cognoscenti of Christian archeology for almost a century, but successfully hidden until 2008.

Generally speaking, Dark's suggested domestic-funereal sequence must grapple with numerous difficulties, beginning with the hillside location. It

---

17. This would be the "Traditional village" (see Fig. 1.4).

18. Thus far, *kokh* tombs have been identified under the Church of the Annunciation, the Church of St. Joseph, the Sisters of Nazareth Convent, and the Bishop's Residence (midway between the Venerated Area and Mary's Well). For further information, see the Index: "Tombs" and the individual sites.

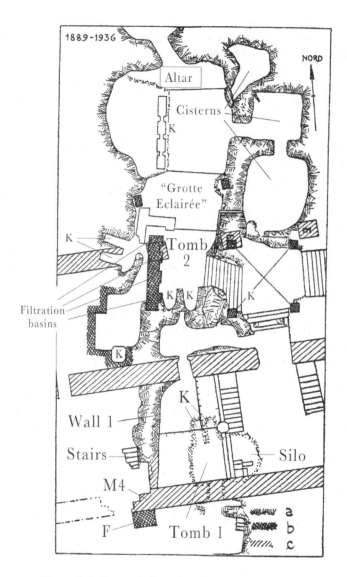

Figure 6.5. General plan of the Sisters of Nazareth site.

Adapted from Bagatti 1969:241 and based on drawings from the early 20th century.
K = receptacle for body (kokh).
Original key at lower right:
a = rock; b = medieval masonry; c = modern masonry.

is counterintuitive to suppose that the ancient Nazarenes spurned the flat valley floor readily available nearby, and chose rather to construct their dwellings on the steep, rocky, and pock-marked slope of the Nebi Sa'in. No evidence of terracing (which would permit the construction of dwellings) has been found in and around the Venerated Area, and thus it is unlikely that the hillside had habitations in any pre-modern era. On the other hand, no one any longer contests that the slope of the Nebi Sa'in was a cemetery in Roman times. The evidence for this is now undeniable.[19]

Quite overlooked in the literature is the third option—agricultural use. Jewish villages in antiquity often used the surrounding hillsides for dual funerary-agricultural purposes. After all, neither Torah nor Mishna forbid working in the vicinity of tombs. They only forbid habitation in their vicinity, as well as direct contact with the deceased. The co-existence of tombs and agricultural installations on hillslopes is so prevalent in antiquity as to be normative. It is also evident that some tombs were partially or wholly converted to agricultural use after they ceased to be used as funerary chambers. The conversion usually included removing the tomb roof—thus opening up the installation to the sky—and also making other modifications as necessary. In such cases, traces of the original tomb (*e.g.*, vestiges of one or more *kokhim*) can usually still be detected. This is the case with Tomb 2 (the northern tomb) under the Sisters of Nazareth Convent (below).

A funerary-agricultural sequence is also suggested from an analysis of the nearby Church of the Annunciation site, as described in *The Myth of Nazareth*:

> This discussion sheds some light on the history of Nazareth, in that at least some places on the hillside were first used for burial and then modified for agricultural purposes. When those modifications took place is not entirely clear. This funerary-agricultural sequence will be observed again when we consider the nearby graves o/p. (Salm 2008a:253)

The so-called "graves o/p" are two burials under the Church of the Annunciation which are a good two meters below "the old basilica." They probably preceded the agricultural installations which, significantly, are sometimes intrusive. "The tombs apparently were first, followed by the agricultural installations" (Salm 2008a:259).

Numerous elements at the Sisters of Nazareth site suggest a similar funerary-agricultural sequence. Dark himself admits that Wall 2 may date to Crusader times (AJ:52). We have also cited Kopp (above), who noted that the large silo on the eastern side of Tomb 1 was later than the tomb (see Fig. 6.4 above; *cf.* AJ:51). Large cisterns in the northern portion of the Sisters of

---

19. For a map of the many known Roman-era tombs in and around the Venerated Area, see Salm 2008a:Fig. 5.2.

Nazareth site appear to have been worked in the fourth and fifth centuries CE (Livio 1980:28). In fact, not one of the above ground structural features at the Sisters of Nazareth site demands an Early Roman ("Phase 1") dating at all!

Immediately north of the alleged "model courtyard house" are some revealing structural remains. This is the area of Tomb 2 (Fig. 6.5), from which signs of seven *kokhim* shafts remain. Between *kokhim* to the west and south is a series of four filtration basins in a line, each emptying into the next (Livio 1980:28). These basins are obviously related to agricultural work and are not funereal. Since both basins and burials would not have been in use at the same time, we should ask: which was first?

The answer is clear: the burials were first. Had the contrary been the case, the agricultural basins would surely have been destroyed by the ensuing *kokhim* hewn around them in all directions. It is equally unlikely that the agricultural basins would have been used in a dark underground cavity (as would have been the case if the *kokh* tomb installation were later). The locus is now called the "*Grotte Eclairée*" because it receives a good deal of light from a wide opening in the roof. Obviously, it was opened to light from above at a time subsequent to its use as a tomb. *These considerations point to funerary use preceding agricultural use.*

For similar reasons, the same funerary-agricultural sequence must also have taken place a few metres to the south (in the area of Tomb 1), as was long ago noted by Kopp. The eastern part of the installation is a large silo—one which clearly postdated a number of burials, for both Bagatti and Kopp noted signs of several *kokhim* in its floor and sides.[20] Thus, in both the northern and southern areas of the Sisters of Nazareth site, evidence clearly demonstrates a funerary-agricultural sequence of use. This being the case, *it is highly unlikely that a dwelling was ever at the site, since Jews would not live on a site previously used for burial.*

In sum, multiple lines of argument show that *no dwelling ever existed under the Sisters of Nazareth Convent. Kokh* burials at the site were followed by a variety of *agricultural* installations.

This conforms with what we have also learned from installations nearby on the hillside. For example, a tomb under the Church of the Annunciation was converted into a large cistern (Salm 2008a:Illus 5.4, no. 10). In its immediate vicinity, other agricultural installations similarly intrude upon tombs, indicating that the funerary installations were first.[21] Of course, all this argues against Dark's attempt to expand his questionable domestic-funerary sequence (discussed above) to multiple sites on the hillside.

---

20. Kopp 1938:198.
21. Salm 2008a:240, 244, 247, 253, 255, 259.

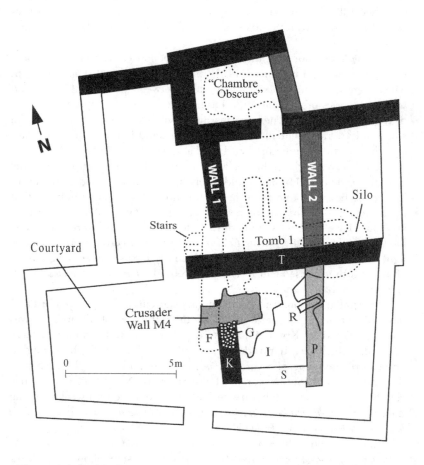

Figure 6.6. Dark's reconstruction of the alleged "model courtyard house."

Tomb 1, the silo, and the "*Chambre Obscure*" are noted for reference. All walls are hypothetical except Wall 1 and the fragmentary Crusader Wall M4. The shading is according to Dark who maintains that walls in black are "certainly partially or wholly present" (*sic*), those in medium gray "may be reasonably inferred," and those in light gray are walls which have been destroyed. Dark considers the walls in white hypothetical but presumably includes them for reference to the "model courtyard house" as proposed by other scholars.
(Redrawn from Dark 2012 [AJ]: Figs. 5, 15,16.)

It is clear that the Nazarenes of yore carried out agricultural work among tombs, and that they sometimes converted old and no longer used burial sites into agricultural installations. The latter is certainly what occurred under the Sisters of Nazareth Convent—as evidenced most dramatically by the filtration basins in Tomb 2 and by the large silo/cistern to the east of Tomb 1.

Was the above ground structure a dwelling?

Not a model courtyard house

Problems abound when matching the existing structural remains to Prof. Dark's proposed scenario of a "model courtyard house," an alleged structure which he summarizes as follows:

> A purely structural interpretation of the Phase 1 features, unconcerned for the moment with their date or function, is that they consisted of a rectilinear room built by cutting back a (probably low-roofed) natural cave at the base of an east-facing break-of-slope to form Wall 1, and another smaller room to its north, made by cutting into the south-facing rock-face of the hillside.   (AJ:48)

Figure 6.7. The rock cut Wall 1.

Looking north towards the doorway into the "Chambre Obscure."
The anonymous photo was taken in 1945.

The greatest problem with the above interpretation is that many of the requisite walls for such a house do not exist. Fig. 6.6 (above) is based on Dark's reconstruction of the house. The features in black are walls which the archeologist claims are "certainly partially or wholly present." Those in medium gray "may be reasonably inferred," while the southern wall in light gray "would have been destroyed by the construction of Tomb 1's forecourt" (AJ:54). Yet, we have seen that such an extensive forecourt is problematic if not entirely hypothetical. Furthermore, of all these walls (in black, dark, or light gray), *only the rock-cut Wall 1 is represented in the material remains*. The result is that the "rectilinear room" (between Walls 1 and 2)— the central feature of Dark's alleged model courtyard house—is especially poorly evidenced and is not even a "room." Its western rock-cut wall is hardly suited to a domestic structure, while the eastern Wall 2 is probably a Crusader-era construction and thus chronologically problematic. In addition, the southern wall of the "room" is not manifest for 80% of its alleged length. All this contrasts dramatically with Prof. Dark's remarkable assessment:

> Locating the model house relative to the cellar, one finds that of eleven walls, there is direct evidence for eight walls wholly or partially at the Sisters of Nazareth site, with two more being the stone-built eastern walls postulated on site-specific grounds above.　　　　　(AJ:53)

This view requires one to accept a number of conjectures—including that two Crusader walls are "largely obscuring Phase 1 rock-cut walling" (AJ:44) and that three further walls "may be reasonably inferred" (AJ:54). In contrast, *all* walls in Fig. 6.6—excepting the rough, rock-cut Wall 1 and the fragmentary Crusader Wall M4—are hypothetical.[22] In addition, the reconstructed 'house' in Fig. 6.6 shows two doorways in the western Wall 1. However, *no such 'doorways' exist, for Wall 1 is continuous and unbroken for a full seven meters* (Fig. 6.3). In sum, Dark's view that "the main surviving part of Structure 1 is a rectilinear room built against the hill slope" (2010:12) is not based on the empirical material evidence at all. His venturesome reconstruction is astonishing.

The evident disconnect between the underlying physical remains and Dark's reconstruction renders his long discussion "Interpreting Structure 1" (AJ:52-57) moot, for that discussion does not fulfill the primary requirement of the archeology, namely, basis in the material evidence.

Dark's claim that "Structure 1 finds many analogies among known Early Roman-period domestic structures from the Galilee" (AJ:52) also does not bear scrutiny. A footnote directs the reader's attention to works

---

22. See Fig. 6.3. We will briefly consider the individual structural features below.

by Edwards (2001, 2002) and Richardson (2004, 2006). Upon inspection, however, the "analogies" claimed are not readily apparent in those works (see "Misrepresentation of sources" above).

We will now briefly consider in order a few elements of Dark's reconstruction: the "Chambre Obscure," "Wall 1," "Wall 2," the "Southern wall," and the "Courtyard."

The "Chambre Obscure." This hypothetical northernmost room of the "model courtyard house" (Fig. 6.3) is poorly approximated by the structural remains. *The eastern wall of the "room" does not exist.* Dark writes: "it is most likely (on the basis of wall-tumble found in 2009) [that] stone-built walls would have completed a rectilinear floor plan" (2010:12). Here, however, the archeologist once again sees what he wishes rather than what the evidence presents. Furthermore, the *"Chambre Obscure"* is too small to have ever been an habitable room in a domestic dwelling. At best, it might have served as a storage area. We must conclude that the interpretation of this irregular, underground rock-cut space as a "room" in a domestic structure is quite unconvincing. More likely is that the space was originally a *kokh* (*loculus*) grave, subsequently enlarged. In fact, *kokhim* exist immediately to the north (Fig. 6.5) as well as to the south (Fig. 6.6).

Wall 1. This most unsatisfacory feature (from a domestic standpoint) is the principal surviving element of Prof. Dark's alleged Roman-era dwelling—a long rock-cut western wall which runs almost the entire length of the posited above-ground dwelling (as far south as "K" in Fig. 6.6). Was this even a "wall" in Roman times? A 1945 photo of the feature shows that it lacks masonry fill along its entire length near the ground (Fig. 6.7). Dark assumes that this considerable void was filled with masonry in ancient times, but the assumption is, once again, not reflected by the evidence.

Walls in domestic dwellings typically have flat surfaces. However, Wall 1 is rough and grossly uneven. Bagatti (1937:256) observed long ago that it is "hewn irregularly out of rock..." Remarkably, Dark affirms: "Wall 1 was well made and its sides and top smoothed. This employed rock-cutting technology resembling that used locally in the Roman period" (AJ:50). Given more than one marked indentation and an "overhang" in the rock cutting, this structural feature—which appears to begin 3–4 feet above the floor of the "dwelling"—would have made a most unusual domestic wall!

Wall 2. This wall, as presently constituted, is only one meter high—far too low for any dwelling. It also appears to be post-Roman.[23] Dark himself

---

23. A photograph of Wall 2 is at AJ:Fig. 11.

admits that "The date of this built wall (Wall 2), which will be discussed further below, is problematical." A few pages later he admits candidly: "It may be a wholly Crusader-period feature" (AJ:46, 52).

The British archeologist conveniently opines that a Roman wall is "reasonably inferred" at this location. "If this seems unlikely," he observes, "one should note that exactly this type of reuse was observed at the nearby excavated site at the International Marian Centre site." However, the Marian site (excavated by Y. Alexandre) was also not a dwelling as claimed but an agricultural installation (Chapter 10). In sum, "Wall 2" is another hypothetical addition to an equally hypothetical "model courtyard house."

Dark concludes: "Even if one accepts that Wall 2 merely follows the line of a no longer extant Phase 1 built wall, then this indicates the eastern wall of Structure 1." Unfortunately, even this is asking too much, for by assuming wall segment "P" (Fig. 6.6)—that is, the southern extension of the hypothetical Wall 2—*the archeologist is assuming what is precisely in doubt.*

The southern wall. Dark's treatment of this wall exposes a contradiction. On the one hand the archeologist diagrams east-west walls at "S" and "T" (Fig. 6.6; *cf.* Dark 2012: Fig. 15). On the other hand, his discussion places the wall at neither locus:

> A short stretch of east-west rock-cut wall runs across the south of Structure 1, below the substantial east-west Crusader-period wall called by earlier investigators 'M4'. This may have stretched as far as the line of Wall 2, as is suggested by a cut into the natural limestone parallel with the south of the Crusader-period paving immediately to its north, but this cut might have been made merely to accommodate that paving. Its original east-west length cannot, therefore, be determined definitively from visible evidence, but it certainly ran as far as is shown by its outline in medium grey tone on figure 5.   (AJ: 46)

Here Dark claims that an older wall once existed "under" the Crusader Wall M4. He (very) tentatively suggests that it "may have stretched" as far as "the line of Wall 2" (from "K" to "P" in Fig. 6.6). Yet we see that no wall of the alleged Structure 1 (bounded by walls T, P, S, and K) occurs at this locus at all—Crusader Wall M4 is situated *between* the reconstructed walls S and T of Structure 1. This is clear if one superimposes the plans to scale, as we have done in Fig. 6.6. Had Dark done this, he would immediately have appreciated that his argument does not fit *his own* reconstruction.

The "courtyard." Dark's argument for the existence of a courtyard (Fig. 6.6, west of "K" and south of "S") evaporates when we consider the data already presented. *Not one of its walls is attested in the material remains.*

The archeologist shades wall "P" light gray, signifying that it "would have been destroyed by the construction of Tomb 1's forecourt" (AJ: Fig. 15 with caption). This maneuver is unwarranted as there is no material evidence for the putative tomb forecourt itself (as we have seen).

In sum, an objective view of the material evidence as it presently survives shows Dark's assumed "courtyard" to be entirely hypothetical. All of its walls are dubious. *Only a short "extension" of Wall 1 to the south ("F") is extant, with some wall tumble at "G."* From these paltry remains, it is impossible to reproduce the southern "room" K-S-P-T or the courtyard. In the general and the specific, the material remains do not match anything like what Dark envisages. On the other hand, one can readily admit that the surviving low, rough-hewn structural remains are entirely compatible with agricultural activities in later Roman times.

Discussion. The careful reader of Dark's prose is left scratching his head, for one feature after another proves (upon comparison with the material remains) to be hypothetical—the "courtyard," the "forecourt," many "walls," and so on. These considerations, taken together, certainly invalidate Dark's Phase 1–Phase 2 sequence. This proves to be no more than one hypothetical feature impinging upon another: the *alleged* western extension of the tomb forecourt impinging on the *alleged* southern extension of Wall 1 (at locus F); the *alleged* eastern wall of the above-ground structure ("P") "destroyed by the construction of Tomb 1's [*alleged*] forecourt," *etc.* In all this, it is also not clear how a tomb *below* ground could impinge upon an *above* ground structure!

Given that his "model courtyard house" is not substantiated, Dark's long section (AJ:52–57) "Interpreting Structure I" is moot. He begins:

> Structure I finds many analogies among known Early Roman-period domestic structures from the Galilee. For example, the plan of the main room and its annexes may be paralleled in the western part of the first-century AD settlement at Capernaum. The hill-slope location resembles the Roman-period houses at Khirbet Kana and Yodefat, and the flight of steps to an upper floor is paralleled in the Galilee at several Early Roman-period domestic sites. Indeed, the similarities are striking if one maps the plan onto the model 'courtyard house' as first set out by Hirschfeld and accepted by the Nazareth Village Farm project (fig 15). Although Hirschfeld himself supposed 'courtyard houses' to be an urban phenomenon, Galor has shown that this is not the case in the Galilee.
>
> (AJ:52–53)

Each of the above sentences is problematic. We cannot find parallels in Capernaum to "the main room and its annexes" because such structures are not demonstrable under the Sisters of Nazareth convent. The analogy with the *inhabited* hill-slopes at Khirbet Kana and Yodefat also does not obtain since those hill-slopes are not *full of tombs* as is the Nazareth hillside—which, it may be added, is also pitted with hollows and cisterns—considerations which, when taken together, render the Nazareth hillside quite uninhabitable in antiquity. Finally, the "flight of steps" can be interpreted as a means of passing provisions from one agricultural area to another, not necessarily as access to a claimed second floor.

Dark invokes the "model courtyard house" as described by Hirschfeld. But such houses belonged to wealthy urban families:

> The "courtyard house" is more characteristic of private construction in the cities. Most courtyard houses in the country were of a traditional type: a house with an inner courtyard, simple, and without columns. These were relatively spacious houses (with an area of at least 200–300 m²) belonging to wealthy urban families. Some elaborate courtyard houses were also found in the agricultural areas of the country—presumably the estate houses of wealthy landowners. They may be considered the local version of the villa in the Roman architectural tradition.
>
> (Hirschfeld 1995:102)

This does not sound at all like the dwelling of poor villagers in an out-of-the-way hamlet—as the tradition is wont to describe the first century settlement of Nazareth. The end result of this discussion is that one must question the entire applicability of Dark's "model courtyard house" to the Sisters of Nazareth site.

In passing, the British archeologist also makes sweeping statements which he does not trouble himself to substantiate. An example is found in his Interim Report on the 2009 season (Dark 2010:7). He writes that movable artifacts in the box found by Senès "support a date in the Early Roman period for the structure and suggest a domestic interpretation." Yet no itemization of the pottery is provided. Thus, *there is no way to verify Dark's "support" for an Early Roman dating.* In addition, one can only wonder on what basis the archeologist is able, from mere pottery finds, to conclude "domestic" use—for pottery often is also found in funereal and agricultural contexts.

The agricultural use of the above ground structural remains

No roof or upper storey

Dark writes: "A stairway on the west side of the room gave access to a roof or upper storey, which was presumably of timber as no roofing tile was found anywhere on the convent site and the cave roof had been cut back." As has been hinted above, the staircase could be for the conveyance of provisions (either liquid or grain) in jugs, *etc.*, from one side of the wall to the other. It is also possible that a ladder was once positioned on the eastern side of the wall to facilitate the transfer of goods. As the ground apparently does not slope at this spot, a cart could also have been pulled up to the wall on the eastern side to receive provisions. The "retained rock overhang" at the top of the stairs (AJ: fig. 13) provided an ideal standing place for a workman receiving and transmitting such agricultural materials at the top of the wall, a spot from which he had access to both sides of Wall 1.

The cistern

Prof. Dark mentions a "squint... adjacent to Tomb 1... [showing] similar tool marks to those on Structure 1 and Tomb 1" (AJ:50). This "squint" (a small opening in a wall) would be contiguous with the silo (Figs. 6.4, 6.5, 6.6). In one report (Dark 2010:8) the archeologist supposes that it dates to "Phase 1 or Phase 2," but in the 2012 AJ article he admits: "Although a Crusader-period date for the whole feature is more likely... a Phase 1 date for the top of this feature could be just possible." Dark finally considers the feature to be something very different: an intake channel for a cistern collecting run-off water and associated with "roofs in domestic contexts in the Roman-period Galilee." A cistern is very possible, but (particularly given the aforementioned lack of requisite walls) its *non-domestic* use is readily postulated—either for the collection of run-off water or possibly as a wine collecting vat, as witnessed in nearby agricultural installations under the Church of the Annunciation and under the IMC (Chapter 10). Finally, Dark's suspicion of a late Crusader dating for this feature is also likely—rendering it entirely too late for his "Phase 1 or Phase 2."

In one passage Dark demonstrates how quickly his logic can move from speculation to certainty through a series of questionable steps. Concerning the cistern in question, he writes:

> [G]iven the function of silos to store crops and cisterns to store drinking water, then this feature probably predates the tomb (and, therefore, according to parsimony belongs to Phase 1). Thus, the presence of this feature is strong evidence that activities other than burial took place at the site during the Early Roman period probably during Phase 1. (2010:8)

It is not at all clear why silos and cisterns should *predate* tombs simply because they serve for food storage. (Could the Nazarenes of antiquity not have hewn such agricultural installations *after* the tombs were in existence, that is, near *pre-existing* tombs?) Once again, Dark forces the evidence into a preconceived "Phase 1–Phase 2" model, concluding "strong evidence" of the "Early Roman period"—where no such evidence actually exists.

The third option

Dark nowhere seriously entertains the possibility that the above ground structural remains at the Sisters of Nazareth site could have been *agricultural* in nature. The oversight is convenient but fatal. He argues at length how the structural remains could *not* have been funerary (Dark 2010:14–17) and summarily concludes that they must therefore have been "domestic"— quite overlooking the third (agricultural) option. Similarly, in his 2012 article, the archeologist enumerates five points against a funerary interpretation of the structural remains (AJ:55), summarily concluding that they must therefore have been domestic. Putting aside the fact that his five points are not entirely convincing, Dark studiously ignores the viable (and fairly compelling) option that the structural remains were dedicated to agricultural activities of various sorts.

Dark observes that the lack of a *miqveh* on site does not imply the lack of a dwelling. He hastens to observe that *some* "Jewish domestic structures in the Galilee" also lacked ritual baths (AJ:56). But this is a strawman. Of course, most simple dwellings lacked a *mikveh*—but so did agricultural installations! The latter possibility never enters Dark's discussion.

In another place the archeologist writes: "Other than being partly rock-cut, Structure 1 has almost no resemblance to either *kokhim* tombs of Second Temple date or to the large underground halls and acrosolia [*sic*] of later Roman-period Jewish catacombs, as at Beth She'arim [*sic*]" (AJ:54; *cf.* Dark 2010, 14–15). This unfortunate statement demonstrates Dark's unfamiliarity with the subject matter at hand. *Kokh* tombs in the Galilee were not "of Second Temple date." The catacombs of Beth Shearim were used for centuries as a mecca for Jews from throughout Israel to bury their dead. The comparison of those elaborate catacombs to the relatively few *kokhim* under the Sisters of Nazareth Convent is hardly apposite. Finally, Structure 1—being *above* ground—obviously bears no comparison to *underground* funereal structures.

Even in the (unlikely) case that Dark were correct in interpreting a remote extension of Tomb 1 as 'cutting into' the above-ground structure at F (see above), that cutting would merely suggest that the tomb intruded upon a pre-existing *agricultural* feature. But Dark ignores this inconvenient possibility. Similarly, he assumes that small chips of plaster found at the site must indicate a dwelling (AJ:57). Yet wine treading floors, collecting vats, cisterns, and other agricultural installations were normally plastered (rendering them watertight), *while plastering a humble dwelling would have served no obvious purpose*. It is also possible, in this case, that the tomb underwent later alteration (including the later use of plastering) when the site was converted to agricultural use. This appears to have been the case with Tomb 29 at the nearby Church of the Annunciation (Salm 2008a:253). That locus has no less than six layers of plaster, layers not associated with the pre-existing *kokh* but with a subsequent wine collecting vat.

In forcing a domestic interpretation onto the site, Dark also resorts to unsubstantiated claims. In one place he writes: "rock-cut components were commonly employed in domestic structures of Early Roman period date in the Galilee" (AJ:53). In this way he attempts to defend his interpretation of the rock-cut Wall 1 as a domestic feature. However, rock-cut walls were typical of *agricultural* installations, though they were not at all frequent in domestic contexts.

When one surveys Dark's writings on the Sisters of Nazareth Convent site, his insistent ignoring of the agricultural option can be seen as almost perverse. To review: walls—even if low and crudely chiseled (and well adapted to an agricultural installation)—become for him elements of a "model courtyard house" (above). Fragments of plaster (probably from a cistern) indicate "walls of the house" (AJ:57). Multiple cisterns on site (quite typical of an agricultural area) are to collect "run-off from roofs in domestic contexts" (AJ:51). A narrow staircase becomes evidence of a "roof or upper storey, which was presumably of timber as no roofing tile was found" (AJ :50)—though stairs were actually found nearby in an agricultural context (under the Church of the Annunciation "in front of a granary," Bagatti 1969:46).

Quite apart from the fairly clear agricultural elements present (multiple cisterns, rough and low walling, a series of four filtration basins in the area of Tomb 2, *etc.*), overarching considerations preclude Dark's domestic interpretation of the site—most obviously (1) the pronounced slope of the terrain (Dark 2010:16) with no evidence of terracing; and (2) the underground presence of *kokh* burials. *These two elephants in the room effectively render the archeologist's domestic interpretation a non-starter.*

The realization that above ground structural elements were devoted to agricultural use greatly simplifies an interpretation of the site. Thus, it is no longer necessary to discriminate phases of use, for agricultural work (pressing of grape and/or olive, processing and storage of grain and liquids) could have taken place at any time—before hewing of the tomb below ground, contemporary with the tomb's use, and/or after abandonment of the tomb—or in all three cases.

It should not be supposed that Dark is the first or only scholar to interpret agricultural installations as domestic. This is a familiar ploy, one that has characterized the tradition's approach to Nazareth archeology for decades, even generations. After all, the Venerated Area is replete with fairly unremarkable agricultural (and funereal) features, but (in order to conform with scripture) the Christian tradition has insisted on interpreting these in a domestic or 'congregational' context. Thus, Bagatti (followed by Finegan, Strange, and others) interpreted a wine collecting vat under the Church of the Annunciation as a basin for "baptisms" (Bagatti 1969:120; *cf.* Salm 2008a:195). Bagatti interpreted a vat under the Church of St. Joseph in the same way. However, Taylor has effectively demonstrated that both basins were integral features of wine making installations (Taylor 1993:249*ff*).

Walls, staircases, cisterns, silos, and occasionally doorways can occur in both domestic and agricultural contexts. At Nazareth, the tradition has insited upon interpreting these features as 'domestic.' Indeed, this penchant continues unabated, as we will see, in connection with the recent excavations under the International Marian Center (Chapter 10). There, low walls become evidence of the first *house* ever discovered "from the time of Jesus," and an underground hollow (in all likelihood a cellar for the storage of wine jars during fermentation) becomes a *domestic* 'hiding place.'

In sum, elements suggestive of agricultural use specifically at the Sisters of Nazareth site include a slope inimical to habitation, the underground presence of tombs (which, according to Jewish religious law obviate prior or contemporaneous habitation), and the above ground presence of certain clearly agricultural features (multiple cisterns [Dark 2009:16], a large silo, filtration basins), and low, roughly hewn rock-cut walling best interpreted in an agricultural context.

Of course, the general bias toward a domestic interpretation of hillside structures has its roots in the New Testament, for the evangelist Luke described Nazareth as sitting "on the brow of [a] hill" (Luke 4:29). Hence, from ancient times Christians have located the town of Jesus on the hillside. This view is proving increasingly untenable, however, as archeology continues to expose the emphatically non-domestic nature of the hillside structures, including the embarrassing presence of tombs and agricultural installations directly under the venerated religious sites themselves.

Conclusion

In this chapter we have systematically removed all the "Early Roman" evidence from Prof. Dark's calculus. We have seen that his thesis of a pre-tomb dwelling is both highly unlikely and unusual, involving as it does a short period of habitation on the steep hillside, abandonment, the construction of two tombs (Tomb 1 and Tomb 2) at the locus of the alleged former habitation, and finally a very short period of tomb use (perhaps as little as one generation). In contrast, the *kokh* tombs definitively date to Middle-Late Roman times (certainly not earlier) and, *contra* Dark, nothing in the movable evidence from the site is demonstrably "Early Roman."

Taken together, all these elements render the archeologist's conception of the site untenable.

Dark concludes a major section of his 2012 article with a paragraph amenable to ready citation:

> Together, this evidence allows us to reconstruct Structure 1 in some detail, identify what is probably an associated assemblage of artefacts, and date the structure to the first century AD. These attributes provide a basis for proposing a data-based interpretation for Structure 1 using conventional archaeological logic.   (AJ:52)

However, we can now appreciate that *the material remains do not corroborate the structure that Prof. Dark alleges*. Most importantly:

- The two "rooms" and courtyard of Structure 1 do not exist, because all the walls save Wall 1 are hypothetical;
- Wall 1 is rock-cut and hardly suitable for a dwelling;
- A contradiction obtains between Dark's reconstruction and the physical remains (*cf.* Wall M4, Fig. 6.6);
- The critical Phase 1–Phase 2 arguments are not borne out by the material evidence (primarily involving the locus F).

Dark's re-creation of the model courtyard house "in some detail" must be considered a result of speculation rather than archeology. The "assemblage of artefacts" he claims in the preceding citation is poorly provenanced and not determinative. An impartial view of the extant evidence—taking into account well-published chronologies—shows that Dark's dating of "first century AD" for the remains under the Sisters of Nazareth convent is too early by as much as three hundred years. His scenario ignores a good deal of critical data readily available in the scholarly literature and also suffers comparison when measured against a much more likely interpretation of the empirical remains. In sum, it must be concluded that his interpretation is not "data-based."

Dark insists upon applying a false chronology to the *kokh*-type tomb. Again, this is due to ignoring important available research. The British archeologist uses Judean datings to backdate the appearance of Galilean tombs at the Sisters of Nazareth site by two centuries or more, and he also bypasses a wealth of research which shows that the *kokh*-type of burial continued in the Galilee through Roman and even into Byzantine times.

As for the "domestic" character of the above ground remains, the archeologist never explores the possibility—and strong probability—of their having been dedicated to agricultural use.

Dark's "model courtyard house" under the Sisters of Nazareth Convent is a hypothetical structure with no basis in the extant remains. Those remains reflect Later Roman agricultural installations, some of which (*e.g.*, the filtration basins and silo) can definitely be dated subsequent to the hewing of underground *kokh* tombs. Dark's central thesis of a domestic phase followed by a funereal phase ("Phase 1–Phase 2") is certainly untenable. As a result, his argument for a first century CE date for the above ground structural elements must be rejected.

The material evidence shows that below ground are the remains of *kokh* tombs dating no earlier than the middle of the first century CE, and possibly as late as the fourth century. Above ground are Middle to Late Roman agricultural installations. In sum, the site under the present Sisters of Nazareth Convent was the locus of funereal and agricultural activity long after the time of Jesus.

Postscript
(December 2014)

Publication of *The Myth of Nazareth* in March, 2008, took place as Prof. Ken Dark was beginning his annual seasons of work at the Sisters of Nazareth Convent. The book made slight mention of the convent site beyond noting it as the location of one or possibly two *kokh* tombs not far from the Church of the Annunciation. In researching the book, I had no inkling that Dark would soon claim the existence of a first century CE habitation there, nor that the site would be a springboard for his astonishing thesis that multiple sites in Nazareth were habitations *before* they became the locations of *first century CE* tombs!

Dark soon learned of *The Myth of Nazareth* and penned a hostile review, published in the 2008 issue of the *Bulletin of the Anglo-Israel Archaeological Society* (see above, pp. 59–61). His review elicited reactions both positive and negative. One British scholar termed it "snotty" and humorously advised a colleague: "If you print it out, you may find reading it in one of the smaller rooms in your house will suggest another use for it..."

Evidently, the publication of my book had certain repercussions on the ground in Nazareth—in some ways, repercussions as humorous as the foregoing comment. A colleague of mine who lives in Israel and who has been of invaluable help in conducting onsite research, Evgeny Oserov, first visited the Sisters of Nazareth Convent in 2009. At that time, the nuns solemnly informed him that St. Joseph (the father of Jesus) was buried there. Evgeny was then given the standard tour of the underground installations.

Something evidently transpired in the ensuing years, for the good nuns radically changed their story. When Evgeny visited for a second time in 2012, the nuns reacted with great irritation at his mention of "St. Joseph," even became furious, and finally categorically refused to allow him to visit the underground ruins. I here take the liberty of including an email (lightly edited for punctuation and formatting) from Evgeny, reviewing the situation:

[Summer, 2012]

René, good day! Again writing you from Israel.

Yesterday, a friend of mine and I tried to visit the Sisters of Nazareth Convent. I visited the excavations under the nunnery during one of my first visits to the town in 2009. Then the guide (one of the sisters) told us that they found the tomb of St. Joseph, etc. It was a funny, but common story, upon which the sisters insisted.

Now, suddenly, everything has changed. The same (!) sister asked us why we came. I told her that I wanted to show my friend the excavations. She asked what I knew about the excavations. I said in short what I knew from the previous visit. She stammered something like "Which Joseph!?" Then she became furious and refused to take us on the underground tour.

While leaving, I purchased a small brochure in French from the hotel desk. Although I don't know French, it is clear to me that the sisters have changed their position. Now it is "1 century AD ruins and tomb of a saint, but they don't know which saint it is." The brochure is obviously very new (although no date of printing is available).

Maybe you know what forced them to change their position after so many years? Has the Vatican become more strict? Or (probably) is their financial situation so poor that they need help from the Franciscans?

With respect,

Evgeny

Well, I don't think that the change in the Sisters' story had anything to do with finances, nor that the Vatican was becoming more strict. It may, however, have had something to do with the on site activities of Professor Dark, who since 2007 had now spent five summers working at the convent. It would appear that Dark pointedly relayed to the Sisters that their beloved story of St. Joseph—told by them for generations and with the greatest pride and veneration—was simply not true.

In fact, that venerable story must now have been a great embarrassment to Professor Dark, for he was bringing something very new to the interpretation of the site: *a dwelling from the time of Jesus!* No one before him had claimed the existence of an habitation on the premises—much less one from the turn of the era. If the good Sisters continued to trumpet 'the tomb of St. Joseph' under their premises, then Dark's new thesis of a dwelling from that precise era was doomed—*for no Jew would have lived above a tomb!*

Hence, in all likelihood Dark severely disabused the now thoroughly confused nuns of their cherished story. The tomb under their premises was *not* that of St. Joseph... It was (according to Dark's Phase 1–Phase 2 scenario) from a generation or two later... Perhaps it was the burial place of a Jewish-Christian follower of Jesus...,[24] a follower now buried under the (alleged) recently abandoned dwelling... As we have seen, Dark supposes that all this activity took place in the first century CE (above, p. 74).

It is undeniable that—from the time Dark first cogitated the thesis of a Jesus-era habitation at the Sisters of Nazareth Convent—the presence of *kokh* tombs on site must have presented a frightful complication, as well as a considerable challenge to adequately explain. Dark's two-phase thesis is one possible (though hardly adequate) explanation: the tombs predate *c.* 100 CE (his false *terminus ante quem*); and (because the southern tomb 'cuts into' the dwelling) habitation had *already* taken place at the site. In addition, Dark claims that (because the dwelling dates to the time of Jesus—this in turn falsely surmised from the alleged 'Early Roman' pottery finds) the tomb must have had a very short period of use, entirely within the first century CE. However (because Jews living at the site could not have been living there when the tomb was hewn) the residents had *abandoned* their dwelling sometime during the first century CE. In a nutshell, this is Dark's complex scenario for the site, a scenario which, as Evgeny discovered, has apparently resulted in a new 'edition' of literature for visitors.

Today, tours continue under the Sisters of Nazareth Convent. Visitors can see the impressive rolling stone, as well as the lugubrious remains of several *kokhim*. But the nuns no longer mention St. Joseph, not even in whisper. Now, visitors are solemnly informed that under the premises simply lies the tomb of "the Just One."

> *NOTE:* A version of this chapter was submitted in 2013 for publication in the *Palestine Exploration Quarterly*. The article (independently revised by a well-respected scholar) was subsequently rejected by a single hostile referee who, apparently, did not accord the article a careful reading (as revealed by his returned comments).

---

24. This accords with false Catholic doctrine that the venerated sites in Nazareth have always been in Christian hands. See above p. 77 and Taylor 1993.

Chapter 7

CHRISTIANITY AT THE CROSSROADS— NAZARETH IN THE CROSSHAIRS

(*American Atheist*, July–August 2010, pp. 8–12)[1]

A few days ago I had lunch with my neighbors. Ben is a retired financial analyst, a practical, intelligent man with a dry wit and little patience for superstition. His wife Karen works as a psychiatric nurse and had the day off. As we ate, the TV was on in the background, tuned to CNN. This was Holy Week, the time of year when Christ's death and resurrection are celebrated, and when the Christian world is more than usually interested in topics religious. This year those topics were spicier than usual, for the breaking news was the Catholic Church's sex scandal. Perhaps catering to America's insatiable appetite for the salacious, the top story on CNN that day was pedophile priests. Our table talk was a commentary on the increasingly lurid revelations which now threatened to implicate even Pope Benedict. Over coffee and dessert, Ben (my neighbor, that is, not the pope) muttered in disgust, "Why does anyone still go to church?"

Karen shook her head in silence. "There are still a lot of believers," I answered with a sigh.

The three of us were raised Roman Catholic but, in a perhaps revealing statistic, not one of us remains a believer today.

"Does anybody," Ben continued, "really think that the wine turns into Jesus' blood, and the bread into his body? Isn't this the twenty-first century?"

"It is. But they're still teaching those things in catechism class," I offered.

---

1. This article was an initial public response to the much touted "house from the time of Jesus" announced by Y. Alexandre on Dec. 21, 2009 at a Nazareth news conference. For a more detailed and up-to-date treatment of the site see Chapter 10.—RS

"Cannibals!" Ben retorted, taking a bite of pie.

The TV droned on: "... molested two hundred children... difficult to prove the pope's direct involvement... Vatican very angry with the New York times... thousands of cases now surfacing in Germany... Bavarian Catholics leaving the Church in droves..."

I glanced at my watch and turned to Karen. "That was a wonderful lunch," I said, standing up to leave.

"More pie and ice cream?" she offered.

"Wish I could stay longer, Karen, but I need to write an article this afternoon. It's for *American Atheist* magazine."

"Maybe you can include something about these scandals," she said.

"That's a good idea. But the article is about the bogus archeology of Nazareth a long time ago. Is there a tie-in?"

"Yes," Ben interjected, rising from the table to get my jacket. "The latest sex scandals are just the most recent form of hypocrisy, aren't they? I mean, the Church didn't become this rotten overnight. It must have gone wrong some time ago. A long time ago. Maybe even at the very beginning... That's where Nazareth comes in."

I reflected on his words while walking home and realized that Ben was absolutely right. The hypocrisy now surfacing in the Catholic church has a long and sickening pedigree. Today's pedophile priest, yesterday's holier-than-thou inquisitor, and the grand dissemblers who led western civilization astray two thousand years ago with a cock-and-bull Jesus story all have one thing in common: a pathological betrayal of trust.

A Christmas announcement

On December 20, 2009, the Israel Antiquities Authority (IAA) notified major wire services as well as journalists from leading newspapers around the world of breaking news about to take place in Nazareth. That afternoon, I read the following notice on my computer in Eugene, Oregon:

> This morning the IAA spokesperson circulated a notice to journalists inviting them to a press conference to be held tomorrow morning, December 21, at which the IAA will reveal a new archaeological find in Nazareth. The meeting point will be behind the Church of the Annunciation, next to the upper entrance to the old school of Saint Joseph at 10:20 AM.

I found the timing predictable, even suspicious, as the Catholic Church has a penchant for announcing convenient 'news' on or about the winter solstice and just a few days before Christmas. That is peak piety season when the congregation is, presumably, at peak receptivity.

On winter solstice morning a veritable gaggle of international media representatives were assembled on Franciscan property in Nazareth,

Israel, for the promised news. They stood outside the Church of the Annunciation, a few yards from the fabled spot where the fourteen-year old Virgin Mary received the assignation from the archangel Gabriel that she would be bearing God, or the Son of God, or God with Us ("Emmanuel," Mt 1:23). Christian theologians have long debated the exact nature of this interruption in the young maiden's life by the LORD. The hardest information we have of this history-changing event remains the contradictory reports in the first chapters of *Matthew, Luke,* and (for more intrepid readers) the once popular *Protevangelium of James.*

> **Bill Hemmer** (*FOX NEWS* interviewer):
>
> It's such a wonderful time of the year to have such a great discovery...
>
> **James Hamilton Charlesworth** (noted academic at Princeton Theological Seminary, professor and Methodist minister):
>
> I almost said at the beginning, 'Let's be cynical.' You know, this is the time of year when nonsense hits because it's Christmas. But wait a minute... This is not nonsense! This is *real* stuff, from Jesus' Nazareth—from Jesus' time!
>
> **BH**: Wait a minute... You don't need to be *cynical*. You can be *SKEPTICAL!*
>
> **JHC**: [*Somewhat taken aback.*]
>
> That's a good correction... Yeah.
>
> (Excerpt from "Glimpse into Jesus' time," *FOX NEWS* video, Dec. 22, 2009.)

AP, UPI, Reuters, and Agence France Presse were all present—I mean, at last year's press conference, not at the fabled Annunciation (for which there were no witnesses). By nightfall the news had circled the globe: HOUSE FROM THE TIME OF JESUS FOUND IN NAZARETH screamed the FOX headline. A plethora of print, video, audio, and digital reports eventuated in succeeding weeks, all basically saying the same thing since they ultimately all go back to the same news conference.

Instantly the Internet was abuzz with the story. Google returns for 'nazareth archeology' soared from 50 to 1350 hits overnight. December 22nd, the day after the conference, papers from *The New York Times* to *The Jerusalem Post* featured this 'Jesus' announcement, which also made the evening news on all the major TV networks.

Personally, I was impressed not so much with the content of this story as with the awesome speed of its dissemination. Everything about the 'discovery' betrayed a coordinated, first-class media blitz—one which, in our day, only a mountain of money can buy. The first giveaway was that 'pre-announcement' which instantly reached the general public and people like myself. There was not merely a story here—there was evidently also massive preparation *for* the story...[2]

Secondly, there was implicit coordination between the Israeli government and the Christian establishment. After all, the announcement was by the IAA, a staid arm of the Israeli government and one which does not routinely hold press conferences. On the other hand, the venue (both of the excavation and of the press conference) was Franciscan church property, and the headliner was none other than "Jesus." The excavation had, evidently, enlisted the vast publicity efforts of both the Jewish and Christian mega-establishments—a breathtakingly broad base.

Thirdly, the post-conference publicity—at warp speed across all the world's major media—was a public relations *tour de force* which betrayed the work of Madison Avenue's finest. Similar excavations in Israel (which occur almost daily) routinely garner only a paragraph or two in a recondite archeological journal. They lack a scintilla of media attention and, from a publicity standpoint, die an instant death. Obviously, this excavation was very different.

Fourthly, big name Christian scholars instantly jumped on board. Within twenty-four hours James Charlesworth discussed the excavation on *FOX NEWS* in an extended interview (see above). In fact, the matter was important enough to find Charlesworth on a plane to Nazareth within days. Other prominent Christian scholars, such as James Tabor, also voiced their interest, support, and pleasure at the new "Nazareth house" finds which—finally!—offered "proof" of the town's existence in the time of Jesus. One could almost hear a collective sigh of relief from the entire Christian world.[3]

Alexandre's ragtime band

At the center of this story is a name suddenly catapulted from virtual obscurity onto the global stage: Yardenna Alexandre. Hers is the smiling face of a sixtyish woman that appeared on so many TV screens and computers, explaining almost apologetically: "I don't think I really appre-

---

2. See below, pp. 178 *f* for more information on the news conference and its aftermath.

3. See Chapter 10 for an in depth rebuttal of the "house from the time of Jesus" thesis and its ramifications.

ciated the extent of interest that [this excavation] would generate in the world..." Ms. Alexandre has been active for several decades as an archeologist for the IAA, either assisting or directing a number of smaller excavations in Israel, most in the vicinity of Nazareth. Some years ago, during the lengthy research for my book *The Myth of Nazareth*, she and I engaged in an email correspondence in the course of which Alexandre made the claim of having found "Hellenistic" evidence at Mary's Well in Nazareth, a small excavation she had directed some years before. Alexandre sent me an attached document which would later prove of considerable value: her one-page IAA report on the Mary's Well excavation. I was surprised to see that the document had only just been prepared—it was dated 2006 though the excavation had taken place eight years before. Alexandre's report only mentioned the word "Hellenistic" once, in the final line and in a vague context: "...some occupation here in the Hellenistic, Crusader and Mamluk periods."[4]

Hellenistic evidence, of course, was entirely inconsistent with the rest of the data that I'd been collecting from the Nazareth basin—and also, incidentally, inconsistent with the rest of Alexandre's IAA report which mentioned no evidence at all from the Hellenistic era.[5] If such evidence were true, it would effectively scuttle my case against Nazareth's existence at the time of Jesus. I pressed Alexandre on this provocative claim. However, she was either unwilling or unable to produce documentation—or even a description of the "Hellenistic" evidence involved. This greatly surprised me.

In a bizarre twist, a year or so later Christian excavators elsewhere in Nazareth independently alleged that Alexandre had discovered "Hellenistic coins" at Mary's Well.[6] When I heard of this, I again examined Alexandre's IAA report now in my possession and found nothing there at all regarding Hellenistic coins at Mary's Well. This was a red flag to me—a strong indication that something was amiss, for significant claims were now being made which were not present in the official report. I also wondered how these Christian excavators (working at the other end of the basin, at the Nazareth Village Farm resort) could know more about Alexandre's discoveries than she evidently did herself. Once again, such a "Hellenistic coins" claim could undermine my skeptic's case against Nazareth. To date, however, Ms. Alexandre has not substantiated this claim with any verifiable data, and she has even refused to address it.[7] All this was a second surprise.

---

4. A copy of the report is in Chp. 9.

5. Alexandre's 2006 report and its ramifications are discussed in detail in Chp. 11.

6. These were S. Pfann *et al.* working at the Nazareth Village Farm. *Cf.* Chp. 4 (pp. 54 *f*) and Chp. 11 (pp. 286 *f*).

7. A monograph on the Mary's Well excavation appeared in 2012 (two years after this

A house from the time of Jesus?

Thus, Ms. Alexandre has been at the center of several pro-tradition claims at Nazareth, yet her inability to support them with demonstrable evidence—telling silences which amount to a default in the science of archeology—alert us to the questionable character of those past claims which have invariably bolstered the traditional Christian view of Nazareth. Given this track record, I was not surprised to see Alexandre chosen by the Church to direct this latest dig which has allegedly uncovered a "house from the time of Jesus." The excavation is at the behest of the "Association Mary of Nazareth," a Catholic organization with plans to incorporate the ancient house into a tourist destination called the "International Mary of Nazareth Center" (*Centre Internationale Marie de Nazareth*, Chapter 10).

Alexandre describes the dig as "a rescue excavation in a very small area adjacent to the Church of the Annunciation." In her winter solstice press conference she concluded as follows:

> The discovery is of the utmost importance since it reveals for the very first time a house from the Jewish village of Nazareth and thereby sheds light on the way of life at the time of Jesus.[8]

Alexandre's claim is based on a few pieces of pottery dating (in her words) "from the Early Roman Period. We're talking about the first century BCE ('before the common era') and the first century CE, which is really the time of Jesus Christ."[9]

For the record, let me state that this claim is highly improbable. First of all, the presence of Nazareth pottery from "the time of Jesus" (the turn of the era) flies in the face of the rest of the evidence from the area, evidence gathered in over a century of digging which clearly shows the beginning of settlement several generations after Jesus' time (*The Myth of Nazareth*, Chapter Four).

Secondly, we have yet to "see" any such pottery in the published scholarly literature. As discussed above, Alexandre has a track record of making pro-tradition claims and not backing them up with evidence that can be properly itemized, drawn, and described, as is normal in academic literature dealing with archeology.

I'm not the only skeptic. An American archeologist (who at his request will remain nameless) has eloquently observed:

...What I find most notable is that to date the excavators [of the 'Nazareth

---

article was written). It includes a very problematic coin chapter (Chp. 11).

8. From "Residential building at the time of Jesus of Nazareth," Israel Ministry of Foreign Affairs release, Dec. 21, 2009.

9. *FOX NEWS* video, "A Christmas Discovery," Dec. 27, 2009.

house'] have yet to report even one shred of evidence that places this structure in the first century CE as opposed to the second century. People can "trust" all they wish, but it is precisely this type of trust that leads the gullible to pay no heed to the requirements of evidence. Instead, they buy into the spurious idea that the traces of farms, Roman bath houses, garrison works, vineyards, caravanseries, synagogues, *etc.*, have been discovered from a turn of the era Nazareth. These edifices do not exist in the factual record, but they widely populate apologists' fiction.

The same archeologist contacted a colleague in Israel and continues:

> ...After reading the MFA [Israel Ministry of Foreign Affairs] press release, which states that the ceramics found at the site were perhaps second century CE, I contacted a friend of mine who is a director at the Albright [W. F. Albright Institute of Archaeological Research]. He confirmed for me that the typology is first-second century CE, and presently the ceramic finds are so sparse and disjointed that it is still too early to rule out stratigraphic intrusion. So, judging from the finds themselves, the "Jesus era" is apparently first-second century CE or perhaps even later. Obviously, this dig adds little if anything to our previous body of knowledge at this time, as we already have scarce first-second century ceramic remains at Nazareth and an evidentiary profile that confirms occupation of the site in the second century CE.
>
> ...I find it highly revealing that an IAA representative would state that we have a "few written sources that [let us] know that Nazareth was a small, Jewish village in the first century CE." Anyone care to venture a guess as to what these written sources might be? Nazareth is a cash/political cow and professional/confessional bulwark that they will never allow to crumble, no matter what the evidence might be.

Thus, archeologists both in Israel and the U.S. exist who doubt Alexandre's early dating regarding this 'house from the time of Jesus.' Perhaps even more telling is that a short, official IAA statement of this "house" excavation (not to be confused with Alexandre's Mary's Well report noted above) also does not support the archeologist's claim. It took me only fifteen minutes online to track down that terse summary, one which gives a picture very different from Alexandre's words to the press, and which reads:

> The excavation in the Church of the Annunciation was expanded to include two squares. Remains of a building from the Roman period were exposed in which there were two rock-cuttings in the bedrock: one a silo and the other, in the excavator's opinion, a refuge pit. There were also the remains of a large building there that dates to the Mamluk period, of which a vault and a number of walls were exposed.
>
> The excavation has ended.[10]

---

10. Surprisingly, this short IAA report was soon taken offline. See pp. 188 *f*.

Remarkably, the above IAA report merely mentions structural remains from "the Roman period," which lasted into the fourth century CE. The only other dating divulged is the Mamluk period (13th–19th centuries). It makes no mention of first-century remains, much less of evidence from the turn of the era ("time of Jesus"). Once again, Ms. Alexandre appears to be making early claims that are not backed up by the evidence. As for the "refuge pit," this would point to a hiding place at the time of the Second Jewish Revolt (132–135 CE), consistent with much other material from Nazareth, not to the time of the First Revolt (c. 70 CE).[11]

In other words, the official statement from the Israel Antiquities Authority, though very brief, does not support Alexandre's stunning remarks about a "house from the time of Jesus" which have been trumpeted across the globe since Christmas. There really is no story here at all! This is the dirty little secret known to myself, to a few others—and now to you too.

This pattern of deception repeats over and over again in so-called "Christian archeology." Against the encroaching work of science, the church makes claims which support the fantastic gospel story of Jesus. Upon investigation, however, those claims invariably turn out to be bogus.

In the case of this recent Nazareth house excavation, an Israeli archaeologist is the mouthpiece for the church. Nevertheless, her interpretive remarks to the press (which go far beyond the official IAA report) must be supported by the presentation of verifiable evidence if they are to be taken seriously. Until the archeologist decides to do that, we have absolutely nothing to go on except her word. So it is in science—when someone makes a claim, s/he must support it with facts. Will Alexandre choose to publish a report with diagrams, description, and discussion, so that the rest of the world can verify what she says? Who knows.[12] But until she does, her statements which contradict the official IAA report must be viewed with skepticism. As the American archeologist cited above aptly concludes: "It really looks like our Israeli and Franciscan friends are merely up to their old tricks."

I could not agree more.

A time of change and challenge

Our generation is one of transformation and change, when the Catholic Church is embattled on several fronts, and when the axiomatic religious assumptions of the past two thousand years may be finally giving way. For an Atheist, this is an exciting time.

---

11.   In fact, my research for this book has shown that this was no refuge pit but a typical underground storage facility for wine jars (below, pp. 223 f).
12. As of Summer, 2015, Alexandre has published no report on the IMC "house" excavation site.

The Nazareth issue is a small but critical element in the multivalent demise of Christianity, in the dismemberment of an entitled, corrupt, and power-hungry religion which will probably endure continuing torture by a thousand stings. We must be patient, for the beast has been around for an awfully long time and is exceptionally well rooted in our culture. No one need look for the "death" of Christianity anytime soon. I would not be surprised if, five hundred years from now, there still are popes, the Vatican, priestly pedophilia, and belief in the resurrection of Jesus of Nazareth (if only among a bullheaded segment of the population). Nevertheless, that real possibility should not deter us. Given man's penchant for wishing, occasionally dissembling, and often dreaming, Atheists and reasoning people need not set their sights on utterly destroying Christianity in the near term. Rather, we need to make sure that religious unreason never again gains the ascendancy in human affairs, now or in the future.

Our generation is especially empowered in this regard. If we persevere in our mandate for reason at this critical juncture, we will finally succeed in giving a post-mortem voice to the myriad victims of Christianity's bloody past, and we will help ensure that future generations forever live free from mind-numbing religious tyranny.

Chapter 8

THE ARCHEOLOGY OF NAZARETH: AN EXAMPLE OF PIOUS FRAUD?

(Paper presented at the *Society of Biblical Literature convention,*
Chicago, November 2012)

Good morning. This presentation will be divided into two parts. The first part will consist of a brief survey of the most significant material finds from the Nazareth basin as they relate to the possible existence of a settlement there at the turn of the era. The second part will briefly discuss the question of "pious fraud" as this may relate to the history of Nazareth archeology.

First, however, I would like to preface these remarks with a little background on myself and on some false assumptions regarding my work.

You may be aware that I wrote a book called *The Myth of Nazareth: The Invented Town of Jesus.* It was published in 2008 by American Atheist Press. The book required eight years of research and has over 800 footnotes, seven appendices, and a bibliography that extends to hundreds of works. It's major thesis has since met violent and sustained opposition from scholars of virtually every stripe. The evidence in the book, however, has not yet been contradicted.

Not being an archeologist myself, I am often asked: "How can *you* date evidence, Mr. Salm?" or: "How can *you* presume to correct professional archeologists?" or: "How can *you* have any opinion on these matters?" However, there is a misunderstanding inherent in these questions, for I have never dated anything at all. I have simply identified the relevant archeological experts and quoted *their* published datings: Hans-Peter Kuhnen on *kokhim* tombs, Varda Sussman on bow-spouted oil lamps, Roland Deines on Jewish stone vessels, Amos Kloner on circular blocking stones, and so on. The case regarding Nazareth does not rest on my opinion at all. Anyone who disagrees with *The Myth of Nazareth* is not disagreeing with me but is taking issue with the leading archeological experts in the world. As we will see, this is fatal for traditional conclusions regarding Nazareth.

I.
A brief survey of the most significant material finds from the Nazareth basin

The demonstrable material record shows that the settlement that eventually came to be called Nazareth did not come into existence until after the First Jewish War, that is, after 70 CE. We should first agree on what constitutes the "demonstrable material record." All can agree that it is found in scholarly publications. Note my inclusion here of the word "scholarly." Many opinions are now current on the Internet and in the popular press which claim, for example, the existence of a house in Nazareth from the time of Jesus, the existence of coins dating to Hasmonaean times, and even that a bath-house in Nazareth existed at the turn of the era—one in which Jesus himself may have bathed.[1] However, these popular claims do not meet scholarly standards of publication, description, context, itemization, parallels, *etc.* That is, they do not allow other scholars to verify the nature of the evidence and hence to weigh the claims themselves. These non-academic press reports—quite frequent these days—are not what one can term "diagnostic." Until the evidence is itemized and described in a scientific way, such claims are the equivalent of unfounded opinion, hearsay, and innuendo.

From the Bronze Age to Roman times
The Myth of Nazareth surveys the material from the Stone Age to Later Roman times. It shows that there was indeed a settlement of considerable size in that locality in the Bronze and Iron ages. The material evidence is congruent with the thesis, presented in my book, that this settlement was in fact Biblical "Japhia" and, furthermore, that the Assyrians destroyed this important town in the later eighth century BCE. A complete and total lack of material evidence in the Nazareth basin for the ensuing 800 years (from roughly 700 BCE to 100 CE) is systematically demonstrated in *The Myth of Nazareth*. I term those eight centuries the "Great Hiatus."

---

1. See Chp. 10 ("house in Nazareth from the time of Jesus"); Chp. 11 ("coins dating to Hasmonaean times"); Salm 2008a:133 (bath-house in which Jesus may have bathed).

The traditional Catholic view is that Nazareth has existed continuously since the Bronze Age. However, this view has become increasingly untenable, partly as a result of the appearance of my first book. An alternate (but equally untenable) view, now gaining currency, is that Nazareth came into existence in Hellenistic times. The critical evidence to substantiate this view also cannot be found in the published scientific literature. In the third chapter of my book I showed that all the specific evidence relative to the Hellenistic era claimed by Bagatti and other archeologists simply does not exist. The ethical and scientific implications of that statement should not escape us. *Those Hellenistic claims reduce to eleven pieces of movable evidence, including pottery and some oil lamps.* In every case the evidence has been redated by specialists to later times, and in one case to the Iron Age. In short, there is no material Hellenistic evidence from the Nazareth basin at all.

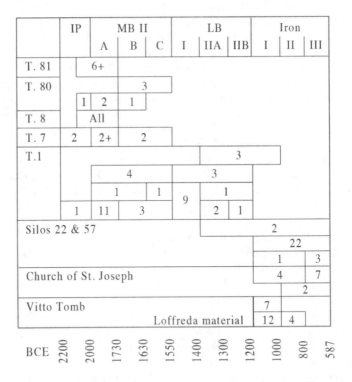

Figure 8.1. Chronology of the Bronze and Iron Age artifacts from Nazareth.
(From Salm 2008a:Illus. 1.5. By author.)

The evidence relative to the turn of the era ("Early Roman Period") is equally problematic and results from a compounding of errors both in dating and in nomenclature. *The Myth of Nazareth* attempted to set the record straight. Firstly, according to the work of Hans-Peter Kuhnen—a leading expert on *kokhim* tombs in the Galilee—those tombs first spread to the areas north of Jerusalem from the south, and they did so not before about the middle of the first century CE.[2] This means that not only do the approximately two dozen *kokhim* tombs in the Nazareth basin date well after the time of Christ, but the panoply of movable evidence found inside them must also be assigned to Middle and Later Roman times. *This fact alone dates the great preponderance of Nazareth evidence to well after the turn of the era*, for approximately 90% of the artifacts from the basin that have been published were found in *kokhim* tombs.

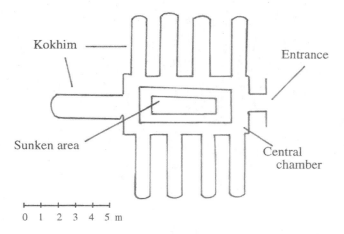

Figure 8.2. A typical *kokh* tomb (Nazareth Tomb 72).
(From *The Myth of Nazareth*, Illus. 3.2. Redrawn by author from QDAP 1931:54.)

Secondly, the so-called "Herodian" oil lamp is a critical component traditionally used to date the settlement to the time of Christ. This is the earliest post-Iron Age lamp type that has been found at Nazareth. However, a careful examination of the specialist literature shows that the name "Herodian" is a misnomer, and that these lamps first appeared in the Galilee

2.   Salm 2008a:158–59; Kuhnen 1990:253*ff. Kokh* (pl. *kokhim*) means "grave, cave for burial" in Mishnaic Hebrew. Each shaft is generally referred to as a *kokh* or, occasionally, by the Latin *loculus* (pl. *loculi*).

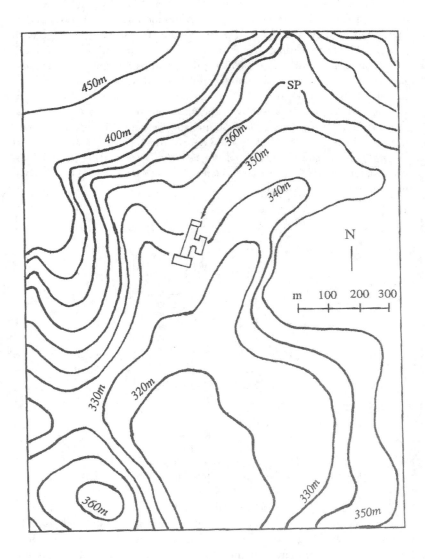

Figure 8.3. The topography of the Nazareth basin.
(From *The Myth of Nazareth*, Illus. 5.1. Drawn by author.)

in CE times—this according to the work of specialist Varda Sussman, corroborated by other scholars.[3] In my book I adopt the term "bow-spouted lamps" (first used by Paul Lapp in the 1960s). Until *The Myth of Nazareth* appeared such oil lamps were assumed to date to the time of Herod the Great or even before. However we can now say that, in the Galilee, they definitely postdate the time of Herod the Great and certainly do not constitute evidence for the existence of a settlement at the turn of the era. Simply put: like the *kokhim* tombs, *the earliest Nazareth oil lamps are powerful evidence for a post-Jesus founding of Nazareth.* In fact, my book reaches the remarkable conclusion (pp. 165, 205) that *not a single artifact, tomb or structure at Nazareth can be dated with certainty before 100 CE*—that is, unless one goes back to the Iron Age.

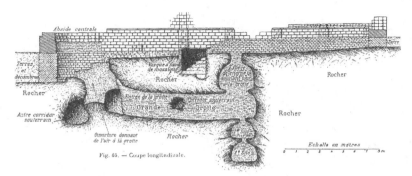

Figure 8.4. Section under the Church of St. Joseph.

The view is from the north (east is to the left). Note the marked slope of the hill with several meters of foundation infill under the church to the east. The large grotto with associated tunnels shows no signs of having ever been an habitation. *Contra* persistent Christian tradition, it is now identified as a hiding complex for Jews, probably at the time of the Bar Kochba Revolt. (*Cf.* Aviam 2004:130. From Salm 2008a:Illus. 5.5. Original at Viaud 1910:135. Public domain.)

Nazareth could not have existed on the hill

The Venerated Area with the Churches of the Annunciation and of St. Joseph are on the flank of the so-called Nebi Sa'in because the tradition has, since ancient times, insisted that Nazareth existed on the hillside—as we read in Luke 4:29: "And they led him to the brow of the hill on which their city was built, that they might throw [Jesus] down headlong."

---

3. For an extended discussion of the types and dating of "bow-spouted oil lamps" see Salm 2008a:167–72 (with relevant bibliography). Typical Palestinian oil lamps of late antiquity are diagrammed above in Chapter 2: Fig. 2.2.

However, the hillside location of Roman Nazareth is hardly tenable. Firstly, *the Nazareth basin lacks any satisfactory cliff which would accommodate the Lucan scene.* Secondly, the incline of the hill is steep and reaches a grade of 20% in places. This is not steep enough to throw someone off a cliff, but it is certainly too steep for ancient Galilean villagers to conveniently build homes—particularly when the flat valley floor is readily at hand. It is true that—with the use of terracing—some Galilean settlements existed on hillsides.[4] But there is no evidence of terracing in or around the Venerated Area of Nazareth, where the tradition has long claimed the existence of the ancient village.

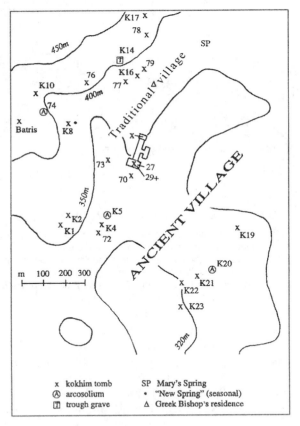

Figure 8.5. Middle and Late Roman tombs of Nazareth.
The "K" numbers conform to Kopp 1938.
(From Salm 2008a: Illus. 5.2. Drawn by author.)

---

4. Fiensy and Strange 222–23.

Then again, the hillside is pockmarked with hollows, caves, and silos—some extending to several superimposed chambers within the earth (see Fig. 8.4). The Franciscan area—where most of the excavations have taken place—is literally honeycombed with cavities with over 68 identified silos once used for the storage of grain. This could not have been an area of habitations. Rather, the material record emphatically demonstrates that it was an area used for agricultural activity and associated food storage.

Finally, the presence of literally dozens of *kokhim* tombs shows that the hillside was not the locus of settlement. It is well known that the Jews consider contact with the dead to be a grave source of ritual impurity. Jews buried their dead outside the village—as is explicitly stipulated in the Talmud (*m. Bava Bathra* 2:9). The inconvenient fact that the Venerated Area is located in the middle of a Roman-era cemetery is fatal to the traditional siting of Nazareth on the hillside. Indeed, up to five *kokhim* tombs under the Church of the Annunciation itself have, at one time or other, been documented in the scholarly literature (Chapter 13). The existence of three is proven, while two more may also have been hewn. Of course, the modern tourist to Nazareth does not read about these tombs in any guidebook. Yet their undeniable existence in Middle to Late Roman times seriously complicates the traditional view that this was a Jewish domicile when the Virgin Mary received the annunciation from the Archangel Gabriel.[5]

In summary, the following four major conclusions should be noted regarding the material evidence from Nazareth:

(1) No evidence in the published literature can be dated with certainty between c. 700 BCE and c. 100 CE;
(2) All oil lamps from the Nazareth excavations date after 25 CE;
(3) All (post-Iron Age) tombs at Nazareth date after 50 CE;
(4) A number of Middle Roman tombs exist under the Roman Catholic Church of the Annunciation.

II.
Nazareth archeology and "pious fraud"

Lack of rigor in archeological training

In biblical archeology, a considerable looseness of terminology exists (and has for several decades) as to what constitutes an "archeologist."

---

5.   The latest theory to deal the unwanted presence of tombs introduces even more complications. It is offered by Ken Dark, the British archeologist who proposes that that some ancient Nazarenes built houses on the steep hillside, then vacated those houses, and then subsequently hewed tombs under their old domiciles (Chapter 6).

Regarding those who have actually dug at Nazareth, we have a right to know: How extensive was their scientific training? How rigorous was that training? These are not idle questions for, over and over, we find that the excavators on Catholic property have failed to follow standard guidelines of stratigraphy, documentation, publication, and preservation.[6]

Amnon ben Tor, author of the well-known reference work, *The Archaeology of Ancient Israel*, notes the overriding goal of some "archeologists" to validate scripture, rather than to determine the facts of history. In such cases, archeological integrity suffers as science gives way to faith. Ben Tor observes that many archeologists active in the Land of Israel "received a large part of their education at various theological seminaries, while their archaeological training was often deficient." He adds disturbingly: "This is particularly evident among American archaeologists... This state of affairs has given biblical archeology a reputation for amateurism in some archeological circles. Modern scientific excavation is so complex that those who have not received adequate training (which is the case with most of those educated at theological seminaries) cannot conduct [an excavation] properly."[7]

The excavators digging in the ground at Nazareth have by and large been seminary-trained priests, pastors, and ministers intent on seeking out "evidence" that corroborates the gospel accounts. On this basis, their work must be characterized as tendentious. By "tendentious" I mean that such excavators present data and conclusions lacking adequate foundation in the material evidence and serving extra-scientific goals. I call this "pious fraud."

Hearsay replaces evidence

Accompanying a broadening in the definition of an "archeologist" in the field of biblical studies, there has also been a concomitant loosening in what constitutes "evidence." This is especially noticeable in Nazareth archeology, a sensitive subfield of biblical studies in which the demands of scripture are particularly high. Often, publication is nonexistent or much delayed. When publication exists, the literature shows that mere assertions can replace verifiability, that the itemization of finds is rare, and that the employment of rigorous methodology (such as controlled stratigraphy) is all but unknown. Is it any wonder that Ben Tor and others find the field of biblical archeology riddled with amateurism?

---

6.   In the last decade Dr. Ken Dark is the first fully trained archeologist to publish routinely on Nazareth (see the LARG bulletins). Ms. Y. Alexandre's recent excavations remain unpublished.

7.   Ben Tor 1992:9. Cited and discussed in Salm 2008a: xi *ff.*

It has gotten so bad that prestigious scholars can consider an archeo-logical claim valid merely because a reputable peer 'said it is so.' A good example occurred recently with regards to Hellenistic coins allegedly dis-covered at Mary's Well in Nazareth. If valid, the discovery would power-fully impact the question of Nazareth's existence at the turn of the era. I have found, however, strong reasons to consider this claim suspicious. Firstly, no coins from Nazareth have previously been found that date before the middle of the fourth century CE. Thus, a claim of Hellenistic coins conflicts with the panoply of evidence from the rest of the basin. Secondly, an official pre-publication report signed by the excavator herself (dated May, 2006) and in my possession makes no mention at all of such early coins. Are we to believe that the excavator (Ms. Yardenna Alexandre) later changed her mind? Thirdly, the scientific literature makes no mention of these coins, though fifteen years have now elapsed since the excavation.[8] For these reasons, this 'Hellenistic' coin claim lacks all verifiability—includ-ing the critical element of scholarly publication. We are entirely dependent on the *unsupported* assertion of one archeologist in the field.

In his recent book, *Did Jesus Exist?*, a scholar of the considerable stature of Bart D. Ehrman (University of North Carolina) writes that Alexandre's above claim constitutes "compelling" evidence for the existence and dat-ing of those allegedly Hellenistic coins. This is astonishing, for Ehrman's certainty resides entirely upon hearsay. He writes: "Alexandre has verbally confirmed that in fact it is the case: there were coins in the collection that date to the time prior to the Jewish uprising."[9] In this way, verbal confirma-tion has replaced the rigors of scientific publication. This illustrates how far the field of biblical studies can stray from the scientific method when deemed useful or politic.

In fact, it would appear that Ehrman did not himself interact directly with Alexandre. Her 'verbal confirmation' of this critical evidence was a *claim* made by two other scholars. Ehrman had read a passage authored by Stephen Pfann and Yehuda Rapuano of the University of the Holy Land, a passage in which these scholars, in turn, claim that Alexandre discov-ered those coins.[10] Thus, Ehrman's 'certainty' is based on what amounts to hearsay at third hand. In all this, nowhere are the alleged coins itemized,

---

8. Roughly contemporary with my presentation of this paper to the SBL (in Novem-ber 2012), the IAA in Jerusalem issued a monograph on the Mary's Well excavation. I read it in 2013 and offer an analysis in Chapter 11, with special consideration to a problematic chapter on the coins (authored by Ariel Berman).

9. Ehrman, *Did Jesus Exist?* pp. 195–96 and his note 15, p. 357.

10. The claim is at BAIAS 2008:106 (reflecting the Nazareth Village Farm Report, BAIAS 2007:40).

photographed, or even described. All we have is a general assertion that ten such coins exist, an assertion originating not from the primary archeologist but from Pfann *et al.* at the Nazareth Village Farm.

Thus, we witness a round-robin of hearsay, as one scholar alleges what another scholar claims, and so on—in contradiction to a report which I possess signed by the primary archeologist (Alexandre) herself.[11] In all this, the actual evidence in the ground (the only basis of an empirical argument) is nowhere to be seen.

The monopoly exercised by the Catholic Church

A further corrosive problem is that until very recently the Catholic Church has exercised a virtual monopoly on excavation, evaluation, and publication in the so-called "Venerated Area" of Nazareth—the area which has produced the lion's share of work in the basin. Over the decades, the Church has controlled Nazareth results by limiting access to both the terrain and the material evidence. This monopoly has been accompanied by a persistent history of (a) error, (b) internal contradiction, and (c) out-right fraud, each of which continues to mar critical claims from Nazareth. I will give one or two brief examples of each category.

Error. In 1930 six oil lamps were discovered in a Nazareth tomb, lamps which have been used in the scholarly literature as proof of a village in Hellenistic times (as early as the third century BCE). In fact, all six lamps date from the Middle Roman to the Late Roman periods, in some cases long after the time of Christ. The two lamps in the upper row of Fig. 2.3 have been specifically dated by Israeli specialists to Middle-Late Roman times. The lamps at lower left and lower right are of the bow-spouted type (mislabeled "Herodian"). They date in the Galilee from *c.* 25 CE to *c.* 135 CE. The remaining two lamps are typical Late Roman examples. The error, in other words, amounts to as much as 500 years in the case of these lamps.

Additionally, the six oil lamps cannot be lumped together into the same category—an elementary error that no archeologist would conscientiously make. Perhaps most egregiously, none of the lamps dates as far back as Hellenistic times.

Unfortunately, this brazen complex of errors has allowed the word "Hellenistic" to be falsely used—and repeatedly so—in connection with Nazareth evidence for many decades. My book shows, however, that such gross misdating is not unusual in the Nazareth literature.

Internal contradiction. The cases of internal contradiction in the Nazareth literature are many and varied. A notable example occurred, once again,

---

11. The circumstances and Alexandre's 2006 report are found in Chapters 9 and 11.

in relation to the Nazareth Village Farm excavation directed by Stephan Pfann under the auspices of the University of the Holy Land (Chapter 4). The "Final Report" of this excavation was published in the *Bulletin of the Anglo-Israel Archeological Society* (2007 issue). It claimed to find pottery at Nazareth dating to the time of Jesus and even to before that time. However, I discovered that the pottery in question was repeatedly misdated. *In at least four cases, the authors dated the same piece of pottery to one period on one page and to a different period on another page.* At best, such internal contradiction reflects outstandingly sloppy work—this despite the (unpersuasive) published *Response* by Pfann *et al.* in the next issue of BAIAS, in which Rapuano pleaded mere "misnumbering." At worst it intentionally misrepresents sensitive material evidence (see next section). Incidentally, Bagatti also was guilty of this type of error when he dated a cooking pot on one page to the Iron Age and on another page to Roman times.[12]

Outright fraud. As we approach the end of our unflattering review of the history of Nazareth archeology, we must ask: Are the above frequent and sometimes inexplicable irregularities merely the result of sloppiness, of information overlooked, and of imperfect knowledge? I have noted several errors, the most significant being: (1) the egregious misdating of Roman oil lamps to the Hellenistic era; (2) the overlooking of tombs situated immediately under the Church of the Annunciation; (3) "compelling evidence" based on hearsay; (4) the double-dating of Early Roman evidence; and (5) the recent claim of Hellenistic coins from Nazareth—contrary to the primary archeologist's own written communication to me.

In light of the foregoing, it is impossible to avoid a suspicion of fraud, for the archeology of Nazareth combines an undeniably powerful motive to validate scripture with an astoundingly high incidence of error. The misdatings of oil lamps and inscriptions by five centuries, the double dating of Early Roman evidence, the reliance on hearsay contrary to a written report—these are not comprehensible as professional 'mistakes.' And yet, *only on the basis of the above astonishing errors and oversights is it possible to demonstrate a settlement of Nazareth at the turn of the era.* This is the bottom line with Nazareth archeology: the traditional view of the settlement *requires* error.

The principal archeologist of Nazareth during the last century was Father Bellarmino Bagatti. In his 325 page book, *Excavations in Nazareth*, Bagatti repeatedly noted the all-important presence of Hellenistic evidence. When I carefully examined his tome, however, I discovered that *his alleged Hellenistic evidence boiled down to a single shard.* If this were not surprising enough, I then discovered that the shard in question is not Hellenistic at

---

12. Bagatti *Exc.* 269, 282, 285. For discussion see BAIAS 2008:107, Salm 2008a:176.

all—it is the nozzle of a Roman oil lamp (as verified by studies of Nurit Feig and others).[13] In other words, Bagatti's much-reiterated claim of Hellenistic evidence at Nazareth is fraudulent.

Fraud can be clearly imputed to published evidence from Nazareth as long ago as 1931. In that year E.T.A. Richmond, Director of the Department of Antiquities in Palestine, alleged that the six oil lamps mentioned above (p. 140) were Hellenistic when they were in fact Roman. No trained scholar would be capable of such an egregious misstep. The same lamps were similarly 'misdated' a few years later by another scholar, Father Clemens Kopp. Both Richmond and Kopp should have known better, and it is my opinion that they certainly did know better.

I don't wish here to rehearse the many scandals which ornament the history of Nazareth archeology like so many fake pearls—those who are interested may read *The Myth of Nazareth* and visit my website.[14] The purpose of this paper is to show that anyone who denies duplicity in this highly-charged field is denying what is patently demonstrable.

Conclusion

The archeology of Nazareth presents a persistent pattern of error, internal contradiction, and outright fraud ranging from the mischaracterization of evidence, to the misdating of structural and movable finds, to the possible "planting" of Hellenistic coins into an excavation at Mary's Well.[15] All this error and subterfuge has produced a false history of the site. It should be totally unacceptable to those who sincerely seek an understanding of Christian origins.

When one objectively reviews the archeological reports from Nazareth which have been published over the years, only one conclusion can be reasonably drawn, and it is very clear: *the settlement of Nazareth did not yet exist at the turn of the era!*

In closing, I would like to quote from one of my articles which appeared in the January 2009 issue of *American Atheist* magazine:[16]

> We should all look with great suspicion on new evidence 'coming to light' which conflicts with the evidentiary profile of the last hundred years, new evidence which astonishingly reopens the case for settlement in the time of Christ. Given the revelations documented in my book, and the lengthy history of duplicity associated with Nazareth archeology, we

---

13. Salm 2008a:111–19.
14. *http://www.nazarethmyth.info.*
15. It is now apparent that the alleged pre-Roman coins at Mary's Well were not "planted" so much as grossly misdated and mischaracterized (Chapter 11, pp. 284 *f*).
16. Above p. 67.

have every right to insist that any new evidence be rigorously documented as to findspot, circumstances of discovery, and description (preferably accompanied by photo or diagram). Any claim of new, pre-70 CE evidence, should raise an alarum red flag. Such a claim tells us more about the persons making it than about Nazareth...

Archeologists have been digging at Nazareth for over a hundred years and, as my book attempts to show, *all the recovered finds include not a single artifact that can with certainty be dated before 100 CE.* In other words, no demonstrable evidence dating either to the time of Jesus or to earlier Hellenistic times has been found. This is quite sufficient to decide the issue against the traditional view of Nazareth. The case is closed! No one, of course, is opposed to ongoing research at Nazareth, but that research will inform us about the nature of the Later Roman-Byzantine village, not about a mythical settlement at the turn of the era. That question has already been answered, and answered convincingly.

Chapter 9

ARCHEOLOGY, BART EHRMAN, AND THE NAZARETH OF "JESUS"

(An earlier version of this chapter was first published in
Bart Ehrman and the Quest of the Historical Jesus of Nazareth,
American Atheist Press 2013, pp. 327–68.)

I. *DJE?* [1] and the new skepticism

When I first learned that Dr. Ehrman was writing a book combating
the Mythicist position, I was elated and knew in advance that this was a
'win' for Mythicists, regardless of what the good doctor might write. After
all, his book would finally bring Jesus Mythicism before a general readership. Ehrman's book—slim though it may be in substance—has also
opened the door for other efforts attacking Mythicism.[2] This is all laudable from a Mythicist perspective, for Ehrman, Casey, Hoffmann and others are—through their generally vociferous, often emotional, and always
poorly argued denunciations—firmly placing Jesus Mythicism on the radar
screen of scholarship. It's about time.

A scant few years ago the word "Mythicist" was unknown to everyone,
including biblical scholars. We have now turned a page. Though mainstream scholars may by and large continue to ignore the Mythicist position—that Jesus of Nazareth was an invention—the position now demands
address. This is the fundamental significance of Ehrman's book, not what
he writes.

---

1. Bart D. Ehrman, *Did Jesus Exist? The Historical Argument for Jesus of Nazareth.* (New
York: HarperOne, 2012.)
2. One is planned by a consortium of scholars and edited by R. Joseph Hoffmann.
The late Maurice Casey also produced a recent book: *Jesus: Evidence and Argument or
Mythicist Myths?* (Bloomsbury T&T Clark, 2014.)

After all, *Did Jesus Exist?* has all the earmarks of being lightweight both in content and argument. It is a book to be read with the TV on or while cooking dinner. In fact, I think this was definitely Ehrman's (and/or his editor's) intention. The book is lightweight simply because its intended readership is lightweight. It does not have the scholar and the seminar room in mind, but the "millions of people [who] have acquired their knowledge about early Christianity—about Jesus, Mary Magdalene, the emperor Constantine, the Council of Nicaea—from Dan Brown," author of *The DaVinci Code* (*DJE?* 4). The great fear is that skeptical claims "are seeping into the popular consciousness at an alarming rate" (*DJE?* 6–7).

Thus *DJE?* properly locates itself not in academe but in America's increasingly hot culture wars. This explains the immediate and vociferous reactions from both traditional and skeptical sides of the issue. We can't suppose that those reactions constitute validation for Ehrman's opus, or that it in any way marks a signal advance in learning. The hundreds of Mythicist rebuttals to *DJE?* (mostly on the Internet) are something of a celebration—namely, that Jesus Mythicism has come of age.

But Ehrman is not writing for Jesus Mythicists—whom he caricatures from the start as "conspiracy theorists" resisting "a traditional view [which] is thoroughly persuasive" (*DJE?* 5). Rather, his goal is to inoculate the general reader against the dangerous new heresy of Jesus Mythicism. It is a pre-emptive strike, hopefully carried out before Mythicism has a chance to gain a firm foothold in the culture. Unfortunately for him, Ehrman is about a decade too late.

DJE? seeks to influence rather than to inform. It is at heart a book of 'propaganda'—the perfect word for what Ehrman does, which is to skew, ignore, caricature, and use all the tools of a publicist who cares far more for rhetoric than rigorous argument. But rhetoric is not the problem with *DJE?* After all, every good writer uses it, and—though Ehrman can be faulted for many things—he is a good writer. The main problem with his book is its astonishing *lack* of rigorous argument. Instead, the reader is time and time again regaled with cheap appeal to authority. Such an appeal is simply not good enough any longer. In our time every scintilla of data regarding Jesus of Nazareth has been subject to careful scrutiny and often to strident disagreement. Invested authority is hardly enough, even if it comes rolling down the mountain in the form of pronouncements from the 'James A. Gray Distinguished Professor of Religious Studies at the University of North Carolina at Chapel Hill.' (*Whew!*) And, after 339 breezy pages, we read the ultimate pronouncement in *DJE?*'s final sentence: "Jesus did exist, whether we like it or not." Ironically, like the entire book which preceded it, that affirmation rings hollow and carries absolutely no weight.

Mohandas Gandhi famously said, "First they ignore you, then they ridicule you, then they fight you, then you win." In the first reactions to *DJE?* one Mythicist pundit opined that "Ehrman's book presents the paradigm shift from Ignore to Ridicule. As such, it is an important milestone." A milestone, perhaps, but hardly important in itself. *DJE?* does demonstrate that Mythicists have progressed beyond the "ignore" stage and are entering that of "ridicule," however. Appeal to authority is a veiled form of ridicule, and Ehrman repeatedly invokes it against Mythicism:

> I agree with Schweitzer and *virtually all scholars* in the field since his day that Jesus existed, that he was ineluctably Jewish, that there is historical information about him in the Gospels, and that we can therefore know some things about what he said and did. (*DJE?* 14, emphasis added.)

For Mythicists there are three considerable errors in this citation: (1) that Jesus existed; (2) that he was "ineluctably Jewish"; and (3) that there is historical information about him in the Gospels. The first point is the thrust of *DJE?*. Yet Ehrman demonstrates that he is not well read in Mythicist literature—apparently he has merely scanned the most recent crop of books from Acharya S. to G. A. Wells. He indeed grapples with the thesis that 'Christ' was a spiritual entity (Doherty *et al.*), but seems woefully unaware of other issues important to Mythicists, such as the critical distinction between 'Jesus' and 'Christ' (Ehrman tiresomely equates these, *e.g.*, p. 52), the priority of Greek *Chrestos* (meaning 'good') over *Christos* (meaning 'anointed'), not to mention provocative theories that identify *Chrestos* with the 'prophet,' 'soothsayer' (*chrestes*) of the Delphic mysteries, and 'Jesus' with John the Baptist (Ory, Price) or with the Teacher of Righteousness (Eisenman, others). All of these, for Ehrman, are unknown, unexplored, or *off the table*. They are not within the purview of respectable discussion. But such details *are* important to Jesus Mythicism!

The result is that, for Ehrman, Mythicism is itself largely off the table. That sentence bears re-reading, because it means that the very subject of Ehrman's book is off limits! Thus, Ehrman can't *really* deal with Mythicism or he would accord it too much respect. His book is not a real appraisal but a sort of shadow-fencing, a virtual boxing match where the opponent is not flesh and blood but like a moving two-dimensional image trapped on some computer screen.

Though academics generally pride themselves in attention to detail, it may be said that Mythicism is the victim of nothing more than the lack of careful scrutiny. From *DJE?* one can say that Ehrman deals with a subject that he neither knows nor likes, and that he does so with an obvious cavalier dismissal. The predictable result is a superficial book which treats a serious subject with neither rigor nor skill.

Though the 'meat' of the Mythicist position may still be off the table for academic discussion, and though Ehrman treats Mythicism with a good dose of *hauteur*, I am optimistic that his book marks an even more advanced stage than Gandhi's second level, Ridicule. For if Ehrman were simply ridiculing Mythicism then he wouldn't have *bothered* to devote a whole book to it, for he wrote it without pleasure—as intimated on his page 6: "I need to admit that I write this book with some fear and trepidation."

The real reason Ehrman wrote *DJE?* has already been noted—it stems from alarm over the recent burgeoning progress of Jesus Mythicism. Yet Mythicism is not new. Albert Schweitzer dedicated a chapter to rationalism, skepticism, and Mythicism in his expanded (German) version of the *Quest* (*Geschichte der Leben-Jesu-Forschung*, 1913). However, the tradition—to which Schweitzer very much belonged—has always been able to marginalize Mythicist voices. Today—a century after Schweitzer's book appeared—the gathering forces of skepticism are demonstrating unparalleled vigor, numbers, and the remarkable and perhaps unprecedented ability to advance their agenda despite a most uneven playing field. With *DJE?*, if I am not mistaken, the tradition has blinked for the first time.

And the playing field—lest any one doubt—is still grossly tilted against the Mythicist position. While Ehrman is handsomely paid for the books he writes, has no trouble finding a publisher, and is a lauded luminary in the field of New Testament studies, Mythicists are underfunded (or even unfunded), may lose academic positions for their views, and must often carry out research in their spare time. There are no conferences on Jesus Mythicism, no prestigious 'series' and books to be edited in *that* domain. Not yet anyway. Pointing in accusation that Mythicists are not professionally engaged academics—as Ehrman does repeatedly in his book—is simply unfair, for academe has worked hard precisely to keep Mythicism *out*. A Mythicist may even possess all the customary credentials yet still be unable to find work in academe. A case in point is Dr. Robert Price, a scholar who possesses not one but two doctoral degrees in the field of religion. Hence, let no one think that their lack of credentials ultimately bars Mythicists from the guild—it is their views.

I long ago perceived this state of affairs and knew—given my independent views—that pursuit of a doctorate in religious studies was ultimately a waste of both time and money. Fellowships and grants would be difficult to obtain, I would be subjected to cant and narrow-minded indoctrination during long years of study, would have to take courses which did not appeal to me, and no job would await upon completion of all that labor. Rather than embark on such a stifling and counterproductive road, I determined to do the necessary learning on my own while availing myself of occasional offerings in language and history at the local university. To the academic who haughtily maintains that it is not possible to get the equivalent of a PhD in religious studies *outside* the classroom, I respond that it is not worthwhile getting such a PhD *inside* the classroom.

The credentialed often hurl the term 'amateur' at the Mythicist. This is no longer correct, as Robert Price, Richard Carrier, and Hermann Detering (all with Ph.D's), Fr. Thomas Brodie and Thomas Harpur (both having worked in academe), and other academics now champion the Mythicist case. While I personally happen to consider it an indiscretion to mingle religious truth with a paycheck, I am not ashamed of the term 'amateur.' Indeed, there may be no finer endorsement for a real devotee of religion.

Seething discontent within the field of Biblical Studies (including both Old and New Testaments) is now producing a flood of scholarly literature decidedly favoring skeptical views. Many academics are straining against the bit which the tradition has for so long placed in their mouths. The tenor of our age favors this New Skepticism in two important ways. Firstly, recent years have seen Christianity stumble repeatedly, as one ethical compromise after another diminishes its former reputation and drives away the faithful. Secondly, the uneducated public has shown itself finally willing to cast aside traditional views inculcated over millennia. Skepticism regarding Jesus is no longer the province of fringe would-be academics. It has infected the population at large, thanks to a steady stream of best-selling books and movies which not long ago would have been banned as sacrilegious.

All this demonstrates that Jesus Mythicism has arrived. It is a product of our age. This recognition, too, is causing alarm. Ridicule is no longer an appropriate or sufficient response. We are now entering Gandhi's third stage: Engagement ('fight'). The fact that a leading scholar like Bart Ehrman has written a book called *Did Jesus Exist?* witnesses to the new reality: Mythicism is finally being taken seriously.

Well—up to a point... Ehrman's book is not serious and it is certainly not scholarly. He plants one foot in the Ridicule stage and with the other tentatively seeks a foothold in unfamiliar territory that was, until his tome, *outside* polite discussion. The result of such ambivalence is that he does not satisfactorily engage with Mythicist issues. An immediate deluge of Mythicist rebuttals on the Internet (some extensive, such as those of Doherty and Carrier) revealed how shallow and wanting are many of his positions.

Now, I have little doubt that Ehrman could have written a more scholarly tome had he wished to address Mythicism in more depth—and, it should be said, with more respect. Had he done so, however, he would have lost his vast intended readership: the largely uneducated public. Mythicists may have been hoping for a serious treatment, one at least validating the seriousness of their proposition. Ehrman withholds such validation. He never intended that *DJE?* be part of any *serious* conversation, but merely that it be a prominent contribution to America's *cultural* conversation.

The upshot is that Ehrman's book could have been written equally poorly by just about any freelance writer. The fact that it was written by a scholar of Ehrman's stature is yet another indication that, as regards 'the historical Jesus,' academe has simply dropped the ball—as it did in its First Quest, its Second Quest, and its recent 'Third Quest.' The fundamental lesson learned from the last two hundred years of biblical scholarship is that scholarship has not been able to seriously grapple with the question of 'the historical Jesus.' Its repeated failure reflects an erroneous goal, and more success would surely attend the emerging quest for the *ahistorical* Jesus!

We cannot now rely upon scholarship for any Fourth Quest. Valuable and significant advances are being made by disenfranchised researchers *outside* the guild. At the same time, the most courageous within academe are trying to break out of the imposed straitjacket of tradition and of religious conservatism. These two camps—radical outsiders and rebellious insiders—are edging towards fragile cooperation. The coming years may not see a breakthrough so much as a realignment of forces *behind* the lines as it were. In fact, there is evidence such realignment is already taking place.

Centuries ago the Church burned heretics. When that was no longer possible it excommunicated them—a serious penalty which amounted to loss of livelihood and social ostracism. But today excommunication carries little weight. The Church has slowly been defanged.

Though the arc of history is clearly bending away from the tradition, Jesus Mythicists should not become complacent nor unduly optimistic. For we are speaking of a struggle centuries old and one that will not be resolved overnight. It is sobering to read old assessments of the imminent demise of Christianity, such as the following by the much maligned Theosophist and Jesus Mythicist Helena Blavatsky:

> I have no intention of repeating here stale arguments and logical exposés of the whole theological scheme; for all this has been done, over and over again, and in a most excellent way, by the ablest "Infidels" of England and America. But I may briefly repeat a prophecy which is a self-evident result of the present state of men's minds in Christendom. Belief in the Bible *literally*, and in a *carnalized* Christ, will not last a quarter of a century longer. The Churches will have to part with their cherished dogmas, or the 20th century will witness the downfall and ruin of all Christendom... The very name has now become obnoxious, and theological Christianity must die out, *never to resurrect* again in its present form.
> —"The Esoteric Character of the Gospels," II, *c.* 1890.
> (Emphasis in the original.)

Today, literal belief in the Bible is still widespread and belief in a "carnalized Christ" is well-nigh universal. We have not witnessed "the downfall and ruin of all Christendom." Yet the cracks in its walls are more pronounced than ever. I believe those cracks will ultimately prove lethal. But who can time the demise of this global institution now almost two thousand years old? In the near term the pendulum may swing yet again. Secularism may yield to the gathering forces of a reactionary fundamentalism, forces which, unfortunately, even today threaten America.

II. What's in a Name?

I mentioned above that Ehrman fails to make a critical distinction in *DJE?*—that between 'Jesus' and 'Christ.' The two names are not interchangeable, as Mythicists, skeptics, and even mainstream liberal scholars have long appreciated. The French Mythicist Georges Ory showed that Paul knew only the *Christ*, while the canonical gospels knew only *Jesus*. The union of the two names was relatively late and entailed the wholesale revision of both the Pauline corpus and of the gospels.[3]

The history of these names is more complex and revealing than most traditionalists suspect. 'Jesus' alone can produce considerable confusion when going from Semitic to Greek—it has manifestly different forms, histories, and allusions in each linguistic realm. Then we have the English name 'Jesus' which corresponds to the Semitic 'Joshua' (*Yehoshua* = 'Yah saves'). It is important to digest this critical fact which I shall now repeat: *The English name Jesus corresponds to the Semitic Joshua.*

If one asked a Hebrew at the turn of the era, "Who was Yehoshua?" he would have answered without hesitation: "He was the great prophet who came after Moses and who led the children of Israel into the Promised Land." For the Jews, Jehoshua/Joshua was *the* quintessentially successful conqueror and also the successor to Moses. He was very much a messianic figure. The Samaritan *Book of Joshua* (*Sepher Yehoshua*, quite different from the OT book of that name) even witnesses to a pre-Christian cult in which Yehoshua/Joshua/Jesus had twelve appointed disciples. Such, I submit, is eminently fertile ground for an investigation into Christian origins. But this line completely escapes Ehrman (and the tradition), for whom a pre-Christian Jesus is definitely *persona non grata*.[4]

---

3. Georges Ory, *Le Christ et Jésus*. Éditions du Cercle d'Éducation Populaire, Brussels, 1968, pp. 29–38.

4. For the pre-Christian Jesus see J. Bowman, *Samaritan Documents Relating to their History, Religion and Life*. Pittsburgh: The Pickwick Press, 1977:61 *ff*.; also Tom Harpur, *The*

A Little 'Jesus' Skit

Lest the reader suppose that the linguistic identity between 'Jesus' and 'Joshua' is only an irrelevant detail, I invite him or her to imagine an introductory History of Christianity class, one typical in every way except for a single detail—instead of using the name 'Jesus,' the college professor uses its Semitic equivalent 'Joshua.' After all, he knows that the two names are identical in Greek (*Iesous*). Of course, the professor wishes to make that point, and he watches as his class quickly descends into confusion. Somewhat maliciously, he has also warned the students that there will be a pop quiz at the end of the lecture:

Thus, let us imagine two co-ed's attending a conservative college in the Bible Belt. They are friends and like to sit in the back row during religion class, often whispering to one another. We will call them Co-ed A and Co-ed B.

Professor: When Joshua rises from the dead...
Co-ed A [*whispers to Co-Ed B sitting next to her*]: Did he say "Joshua"?
Co-ed B: I think so...
　　[*Both open their Bibles to the Book of Joshua looking for where he rises from the dead.*]
Professor: ...After three days Joshua rose from the dead, and he appeared to many, many people.
Co-ed A: [*Still frantically searching in the Book of Joshua.*] I can't find anything... It's all about him conquesting Israel.
Co-ed B: Oh, I think I know... It must be in the New Testament. Remember, at the Transfiguration Jesus goes up the mountain. The prophets from the Old Testament are there! That must be when Joshua rises from the dead.
Co-ed A: Oh, yeah... [*Both quickly turn to the New Testament and find the story of the Transfiguration in Mark 9.*]
Co-ed B: My Bible says Elijah and Moses were there. And Peter, too... "And they were exceedingly afraid." But I don't see Joshua.
Co-ed A: You're right... I see "Jesus" but not "Joshua"!
Co-ed B: Didn't the prof say there'll be a quiz at the end of class?
　　[*Blankly stare at one another.*]
Together: OH MY GOD!!

Now, if one asked the same question of a Greek-speaker at the turn of the era, the wording would be: "Who was *Iesous*?" *Iesous* is the Greek form of Yehoshua/Joshua as found, for example, in the Septuagint. So we see that in the Greek language *Iesous* has a pre-Christian history going back at least to *c*. 250 BCE when the Septuagint began to be translated. To make matters even more interesting, *Iesous* also closely corresponds to the Greek *Iaso, Iason* (Jason), and *iaomai*, "to heal." These aspects of the name Jesus have long been overlooked and are only recently receiving attention.[5]

Those in the Roman Empire who were not Jews would have had little familiarity with, and also little interest in, the Old Testament heroes such as Joshua/*Iesous*. Ehrman points out that linguistic proficiency in antiquity was far less than it is in the present developed world, and that only about 10% of ancients could read at all (*DJE?* 47). If one presented them—say, in Corinth, Ephesus or Antioch—with the Greek name *Iesous* then their most immediate association would be to the name 'Jason' (*Iêsôn* in Ionic) and the verb *iaomai*, 'heal.' The long history of the Semitic name Joshua, and its many associations in the Old Testament, would be entirely lost on those Hellenists—at least on the vast majority who were not Jews.

Figuratively speaking, then, when going from Semitic into Greek, the name Jesus passes from the semantic field of a *conqueror* to that of a *healer*.

Today we have quite forgotten these associations and have even ignored a most basic one—that *Yehoshua* yields both 'Joshua' *and* 'Jesus.' In ancient times—indeed, at the birth of Christianity—*Jesus* was separated from *Joshua* as the religion split along linguistic, cultural, and theological lines (*cf.* the friction between Hellenists and Hebrews, Acts 6:1*f*). Before that, however, these names were identical. Accompanying the split, I would suggest, was a linguistic sleight of hand which corresponds with the invention of the new *theios aner* Jesus. In other words the birth of Christianity had a lot to do with the splitting off of Hellenist followers in the first century CE—Hellenists whose *Iesous* now was *not* the same as the old 'Joshua.'

The *separation* of 'Jesus' and 'Joshua' is only one problem attending to the name of 'the prophet from Nazareth.' Scholars routinely confound *Jesus* and *Christ*, as if the two designations—in any language—were synonymous. Thus Bart Ehrman writes: "Moreover, Pliny informs the emperor, the Christians 'sing hymns to Christ as to a god'... That is all he says about Jesus" (*DJE?* 52). But Pliny, of course, doesn't mention *Jesus* at all—only *Christ* and *Christians*. Ehrman suggests that the reader take Pliny's letter as evidence for the man Jesus—but this argument is groundless. For a trained historian like Ehrman, such inattention to detail is appalling. In such ways,

---

Pagan Christ. Toronto: Thomas Allen 2005, p. 164.
5. J. Moles, "Jesus the Healer," *Histos* 5 [2011] 127*ff*.

only with a careful treatment of the primary evidence does the man 'Jesus of Nazareth' indeed evaporate from history.[6]

The Mythicist thesis relies on such care. But Ehrman chastises Mythicists for—of all things—*not being careful!* He begins his discussion by virtually destroying Acharya S and Freke and Gandy precisely on this account (*DJE?* 21 *f*). It is clear, however, that the pot calls the kettle black.

Like the name 'Jesus,' the name 'Christ' is also a complex issue, for we are dealing not only with the Hebrew *Meshiach* and Greek *Chrestos* and *Christos*, but also with Latin *Christus*—as well as with some evident tampering of the texts that has altered "*Chrestianos*" (Tacitus) and "*Chresto*" (Suetonius).[7] It is little appreciated by traditionalists that *Chrestos* in Greek was a common name in antiquity meaning 'good,' 'wholesome,' 'auspicious.' But that is all I will say on these important matters that impinge on the existence of 'Jesus Christ' and 'Jesus of Nazareth,' but which are entirely bypassed by Ehrman.

---

6.   *Editor's Note.* This oversight is far more appalling than readers might suppose if they are unfamiliar with Ehrman's scholarly books. Examination of his *The Orthodox Corruption of Scripture: The Effects of Early Christological Controversies on the Text of the New Testament* (Oxford, 1993) shows that he is actually an authority on the subject of "separationism"—indeed he seems to have invented the term "separationist" himself!

On p. 14 of *The Orthodox Corruption* Ehrman writes: "Other Christians agreed with the adoptionists that Jesus was a full flesh and blood human and that something significant had happened to him at his baptism. For them, however, it was not that he was adopted to be God's Son; instead, at his baptism Jesus came to be indwelt by God. It was then that an emissary from the divine realm, one of the deities of the Godhead, named 'Christ,' entered into Jesus to empower him for his ministry. Again, at some time prior to his crucifixion, the divine Christ departed from Jesus to return to the Pleroma, the divine realm, leaving him to suffer his fate alone. This is a Christology that I will label separationist, because it posits a division between the man Jesus and the divine Christ..."

The entirety of Ehrman's chapter 3 ("Anti-Separationist Corruptions of Scripture") is devoted to showing how the orthodox tradition has "corrupted" the passages by systematically conflating the Jesus and the Christ! So when Ehrman cites Pliny's mention of Christ to prove the existence of Jesus, he himself is trumpeting the orthodox "corrupted" view!

There is something sinister in Ehrman's repeated refusal to deal with the logical implications of the very stuff for which he is an acknowledged authority. Similarly, he is an authority on Docetism, yet he completely refuses to explain how the earliest Christian "heresy" could have developed so early if Jesus Christ had been historical. Repeatedly, he begs every question in favor of orthodox "corrupt" tradition!—FRZ

7.   Erik Zara, Th.D, "The Chrestianos Issue in Tacitus Reinvestigated" (2009) *http://www.textexcavation.com/documents/zaratacituschrestianos.pdf*; "A Minor Compilation of Readings of Suetonius-Nero 16.2," 2011; *http://www.textexcavation.com/documents/zarasuetoniuschristiani.pdf* (both online).

III. The Nazareth Controversy

Bart Ehrman devotes seven pages to the archeology of Nazareth and four pages (193–97) to my work. It is a cursory treatment which does not grapple with the seminal issues. For example, he makes no mention of oil lamps, a central element of my argument. Perhaps Ehrman doesn't do so because the earliest oil lamps from the Nazareth basin incontestably date to CE times (Salm 2008a:170). In any event, his offhand treatment of the Nazareth issue simply conforms to the general superficiality of *Did Jesus Exist?*

At his request, I personally mailed a copy of *The Myth of Nazareth* to Prof. Ehrman in August of 2010. Therefore he possessed a copy almost two years before the publication of *Did Jesus Exist?* Had he cared to do so, he had ample time to read my book and to study its contents.

Since Ehrman critiques my work, one would expect him to be familiar with the issues of Nazareth archeology and with the main points of my argument. However, given his cursory treatment, I am not so sure. For the reader, I here offer a summary of my book's argument:

A. The material finds reveal the following:
  (1) the lack of material evidence from *c.* 700 BCE to *c.* 100 CE;
  (2) the 25 CE+ dating of the earliest oil lamps at Nazareth;
  (3) the 50 CE+ dating of all the post-Iron Age tombs at Nazareth, which are of the *kokh* type;

B. The following points impinge upon the question of pious fraud:
  (4) the existence of Middle Roman tombs under the Church of the Annunciation.
  (5) the non-rigorous nature of 'Christian archeology' wherein priests train in seminaries and are unable to conduct a rigorous modern excavation;
  (6) the monopoly exercised in Nazareth by the Catholic Church, evident in Church ownership of the sites where most of the digging has taken place (thus limiting access, evaluation, and publication);
  (7) a persistent history of error, internal contradiction, and outright fraud which continues to mar critical findings from Nazareth.

Let me say at the outset that the case for or against Nazareth at the turn of the era rests entirely on part (A) above—that is, on the material finds in points 1–3. We may inveigh all we wish against shoddy digging, lack of access, and fraud, but once seen for what they are, these can and must be put aside so that we can focus on the verifiable material record regarding the turn of the era. And that material record is damning as regards the existence of a settlement in the Nazareth basin at 'the time of Jesus.'

In his book Ehrman does not address most of the seven points above. In fact, he does not directly deal with the Nazareth evidence at all but with conclusions that *others* have made regarding that evidence (Bagatti, Dark, Alexandre, Pfann). However, a primary thrust of my first book was to return to the material evidence and to show that those conclusions are generally inconsistent with the evidence itself. By accepting the conclusions of his colleagues on faith and without further ado, Ehrman entirely bypasses my arguments and, in fact, writes as if my book had never been written. After all, *The Myth of Nazareth* showed that the conclusions of biblical archeologists emphatically *cannot* be taken on faith—and this precisely for the reasons itemized in points 5–7 above.

Ehrman pulls rank. He impugns my right to make assessments, "since Salm himself is not an archaeologist" (*DJE?* 194). What he fails to appreciate, however, is that I have not made any archeological assessments at all. I have collected, read, and cited the published reports of eminent specialists in numerous subfields of biblical archeology. It is *their* verdicts regarding specific Nazareth finds that have decided the case. Moreover, I have not relied upon *unpublished* and quite *unverifiable* claims—as Ehrman is willing to do with Alexandre's claim of a "house from the time of Jesus," and with her claim that coins from Mary's Well date to Hellenistic times.[8]

Ehrman's appeal to authority, in this case, is doubly wrong. Firstly, as just mentioned, he misinterprets my role which is not that of an "archaeologist" but merely that of a careful compiler. Secondly, by appealing to credentials, he implicitly rejects my imputation of fraud against those who are credentialed in the field of Nazareth archeology (point 7 above). A reasonable person would decide the issue on the basis of the material finds— *not on the basis of authority.* Therein lies our fundamental difference.

The lack of turn-of-the-era evidence

I will systematically proceed to consider Ehrman's remarks according to the first three points above. In the next several pages I address point number one—whether Ehrman provides any "demonstrable material evidence from *c.* 700 BCE to *c.* 100 CE." This is perhaps the most critical aspect of any discussion regarding the archeology of Nazareth in 'the time of Jesus.'

To begin, Ehrman notes my claim that there was a hiatus in settlement. He writes:

> [*Citation #1*] Salm's basic argument is that Nazareth did exist in more ancient times and through the Bronze Age. But then there was a hiatus. It

---

8. The coin claim was published after this presentation was given. See Chp. 11.

ceased to exist and did not exist in Jesus's day. Based on archaeological evidence, especially the tombs found in the area, Salm claims that the town
came to be reinhabited sometime between the two Jewish revolts (between 70 CE and 132 CE), as Jews who resettled following the destruction
of Jerusalem by the Romans relocated in northern climes (*DJE?* 193–94).

This is a mischaracterization. "Bronze Age" should read "Iron Age"—
a difference of five hundred years. The error indicates remarkable sloppiness and is one clue that Ehrman probably did not, in fact, read my book.

Secondly, I don't claim that "the town came to be reinhabited" but
that the *site* came to be reinhabited. It may appear like a minor detail, but
the first chapter of *The Myth of Nazareth* showed that a settlement indeed
existed in the basin in the Bronze and Iron Ages. It was, however, not called
"Nazareth" but "Japhia" (Salm 2008a:53–55). Again, one wonders if Ehrman paid attention to the book.

Thirdly, my argument was not based "especially [on] the tombs found
in the area." Here Ehrman omits the two other mainstays of my reasoning:
the lack of demonstrable material evidence from *c.* 700 BCE to *c.* 100 CE;
and the 25 CE+ dating of the earliest oil lamps at Nazareth. *Ehrman does not
mention these two critical points at all.*

The "Great Hiatus," as I have called it, lasted 800 years: *c.* 700 BCE–*c.*
100 CE. Of course, if that hiatus in the Nazareth settlement existed then
the case for a village at the turn of the era is closed. If Ehrman wanted to
contest this, his task would be simple: to point to material evidence of human presence at Nazareth before the turn of the era—particularly in the
first century BCE, for that would establish the existence of a village when
Jesus was supposedly born (Salm 2008a:288).

Of course Ehrman does not do this—though he claims to. Here is
what he writes:

> [*Citation #2*] *Many compelling pieces* of archaeological evidence indicate that
> in fact Nazareth did exist *in Jesus's day.* (*DJE?* 195, emphasis added.)

My response is simple: Where are these "many compelling pieces"?
Certainly they are not in the literature of Nazareth published prior to 2008,
as examined in Chapter Four of *The Myth of Nazareth* (Salm 2008a: 153–
210). There I show that there is no evidence datable to the turn of the era
("Jesus's day"). I treat in turn: pottery, stone vessels, oil lamps, tombs, ossuaries, sarcophagi, inscriptions, graffiti, 'domestic installations,' basins, and
coins. All I could come up with that could *possibly* date to the turn of the era
were two stone vessels. Roland Deines, a specialist who studied these very
two Nazareth vessels, writes that such vessels continued to be manufactured
into the second century CE. Hence, their presence at Nazareth constitutes
no evidence at all of human presence at the turn of the era.

There is much pressure now on the tradition to produce evidence for Nazareth at the turn of the era. Several much-publicized but poorly validated feints have been made in this direction since publication of my first book. Ehrman swallows the bait each time—hook, line, and sinker. This will be clear as we continue to look for his "many compelling pieces" of evidence. Perhaps he means the following:

> [*Citation #3*] For one thing, archaeologists have excavated a farm connected with the village, and it dates to the time of Jesus (*DJE?* 195).

Ehrman is referring to the Nazareth Village Farm (NVF), whose 61-page report arguably brought "Christian archaeology" to a new low.[9] That report was published in the 2007 issue of the *Bulletin of the Anglo-Israel Archaeological Society* (BAIAS). My eight-page "Response," published in the next issue of that journal, showed that nothing in the NVF report reflects settlement at the turn of the era. The core issue is the report's characterization of eleven pieces of pottery as "early Roman" (*i.e.*, potentially dating to the time of Jesus) or even "Hellenistic." The archeologist responsible for the NVF pottery datings is a certain Yehuda Rapuano. I took him to task in my rebuttal, showing that in every case the shards in question could have been produced as much as a century after 'the time of Christ'—this according to the standard dating references that Rapuano himself used. My published conclusion as stated in BAIAS: "in every case where Rapuano suggests a pre-70 dating, he offers no support" (2008:102). In other words, he arbitrarily assumed the *earliest possible dating* for these shards. On that unsupportable basis, the entire NVF report claimed settlement contemporary with 'the time of Jesus.' In fact, however, the artifacts in question fit in very well with my overall thesis that Nazareth was first settled in the years between the two Jewish revolts. As with the two stone vessels mentioned above, they constitute no evidence at all for human presence at the turn of the era.

Incidentally, there were several other problems in the NVF report, *e.g.*, some of the artifacts were given different dates, findspots, and even descriptions from one page to another ('double dating'). In all, it was a very embarrassing report, which is why it had to be completely rewritten after my rebuttal appeared.

At the minimum, the NVF excavation is controversial and constitutes weak evidence indeed (much less the principal evidence) for a village "at the time of Jesus." Yet Ehrman claims that this evidence is "compelling," presumably solely on the basis of Rapuano's authority as an "archaeologist." But I will affirm here that authority alone is insufficient. After all, *authority does not replace evidence.*

---

9. See Chapter 4.

The Nazareth Village Farm is associated with a multimillion-dollar megaresort called the Nazareth Village. The resort's stated vision is to recreate streets and stone houses "inhabited by actors and storytellers in authentic garb, [who] will illuminate the life and teachings of Jesus. A Parable Walk, museum, study center and restaurant are also planned. . ."[10] It has been well funded by an international consortium of Christian groups called the Miracle of Nazareth International Foundation. Since the project's inception the consortium has raised over $60 million towards the venture. Contributors in the U.S. have included former President Jimmy Carter, Pat Boone, and Rev. Reggie White, the former Green Bay Packer football star.

Here the intimate connection between academia and commerce is patent, witnessed also by the fact that the Nazareth Village resort is associated with the evangelical University of the Holy Land (UHL) whose Director, not surprisingly, is none other than Stephen Pfann—the principal author of the NVF excavation report.

The "house from the time of Jesus"

To continue our review of "demonstrable material evidence from *c.* 700 BCE to *c.* 100 CE" (point #1), Ehrman notes the much-touted 2009 excavation of a "house from the time of Jesus" (*DJE?* 196–97)[11]—excavated by the now-familiar Yardenna Alexandre, an archeologist working for the Israel Antiquities Authority (IAA). News of this excavation broke just before Christmas 2009:

> On winter solstice morning a veritable gaggle of international media representatives were assembled on Franciscan property in Nazareth, Israel, for the promised news. They stood outside the Church of the Annunciation, a few yards from the fabled spot where the fourteen-year old Virgin Mary received the assignation from the archangel Gabriel that she would be bearing God, or the Son of God, or God with Us ("Emmanuel," Mt 1:23)...
>
> AP, UPI, Reuters, and Agence France Presse were all present—I mean, at last year's press conference, not at the fabled Annunciation (for which there were no witnesses). By nightfall the news had circled the globe: HOUSE FROM THE TIME OF JESUS FOUND IN NAZARETH screamed the FOX headline.[12]

The timing smacks of propaganda, not news, but a couple of other aspects of the excavation also aroused my suspicion. First of all, results of

---

10. *Biblical Archaeology Review,* May-June 1999, p. 16. At the time of this writing (January 2015) the website for the Nazareth Village is *http://nazarethvillage.com.*

11. *Cf.* Chapters 7 and 10.

12. Above, pp. 122–23.

this excavation have never been published in any scholarly way. (*Publication* here must be carefully distinguished from the plethora of *news articles* that quickly appeared in the general press.) A possible exception was a short one-paragraph statement from the IAA that was briefly on the Internet. However, it made no mention of first-century remains, much less of evidence from the turn of the era ("time of Jesus"), but only to "the Roman period"—which, of course, lasted into the fourth century CE.

Once again we see Ms. Alexandre not publishing her results so that the rest of the world can verify that what she claims is true. In the Nazareth house excavation she made shrill claims which immediately circled the world—but she has failed to document them in the standard scientific manner. We will again see a 'failure to document' in the coin imbroglio stemming from Alexandre's Mary's Well excavation.[13]

This is simply background to Ehrman's glibly confident affirmation that the house Alexandre excavated "dates to the days of Jesus" (*DJE?* 196). Ehrman writes that he had "personally written to the principal archaeologist, Yardena Alexandre," and she told him all kinds of things—which he believes *without any published evidence*. This is a significant problem in the archeology of Nazareth: scholars not only trust their peers as a matter of course—they do so *in lieu of* verifiable evidence!

Almost a year before the Christmas 'discoveries,' I wrote the following in an *American Atheist* article:[14]

> Archeologists have been digging at Nazareth for over a hundred years and, as my book attempts to show, all the recovered finds include not a single artefact that can with certainty be dated before 100 CE. In other words, no demonstrable evidence dating either to the time of Jesus or to earlier Hellenistic times has been found...
>
> We should all look with great suspicion on new evidence "coming to light" which conflicts with the evidentiary profile of the last hundred years, new evidence which astonishingly reopens the case for settlement in the time of Christ. Given the revelations documented in my book, and the lengthy history of duplicity associated with Nazareth archaeology, we have every right to insist that any new evidence be rigorously documented as to findspot, circumstances of discovery, and description (preferably accompanied by photo or diagram). Any claim of new, pre-70 CE evidence, should raise an alarum red flag. Such a claim tells us more about the persons making it than about Nazareth.

---

13.   Alexandre would eventually publish a final report on the Mary's Well site in 2012—almost fifteen years after the excavation (see Chp. 11 below).

14.   Also cited above, p. 67.

To show the vacuity of Ehrman's sources, he closes his Nazareth section by discussing an AP story. *Nota bene*: here we witness a premiere New Testament scholar arguing on the basis of information *from the Associated Press*. Ehrman's parting summation is vacuous: "Jesus really came from there, as attested in multiple sources."

Evidently, the sources this distinguished scholar finds so persuasive are AP, Reuters, and Agence France Presse!

Hellenistic coins?

Our search for Ehrman's "many compelling pieces" of evidence (Citation #2 above) continues. We now turn our attention to a revealing and rather curious story involving coins that he brings up (*DJE?* 195). The coins in question already enjoyed a rather sordid history in the Nazareth literature before the appearance of *DJE?* (see pp. 284 *f*, below), but Ehrman adds a new twist.

He writes that 165 coins were found in a Nazareth excavation, and that some of them dated as early as Hellenistic times. These coins—allegedly discovered by Y. Alexandre at Mary's Well—have been passed from scholar to scholar in the recent literature with apparently no concern for any *precise* information (*i.e.*, individual treatment of any coins). I will here attempt to recap the growth of this vaguely-based brouhaha, one which seems to have become a pet claim for those now arguing the traditional case for Nazareth's existence at the 'time of Jesus.'

It should first be noted that, prior to 2006, very few coins had been found in the Nazareth basin (see Citation #4 below). In 2008, the coin evidence required only two short paragraphs to be adquately addressed in *The Myth of Nazareth* (p.196). The earliest coin from the basin *that has been documented* dates to the time of Emperor Constantius II (r. 337–351 CE). In 1997–98 Ms. Alexandre excavated near Mary's Well at the northern end of the Nazareth basin. The first notice of this excavation appeared much later in the form of a "pre-publication notice" for the IAA dated "1st May 2006" which—curiously—has to my knowledge never been published. Alexandre shared that signed notice with me via an email attachment during the research for my first book. It is a standard single-page report and looks entirely official both in format and wording—similar to those routinely produced for the IAA and published in the Israeli journal *Atiqot*.

In this report (cited on the following pages), Ms. Alexandre notes remains from the excavation which date generally "from the Roman, the Crusader, the Mamluk and the Ottoman periods." She signals the presence of "Middle Roman pottery." She notes no material dating earlier than this. As regards coins, she mentions them three times—in Crusader, Mamluk, and

Ottoman contexts (11th century CE onwards). Alexandre notes "the dredging of many 14-15th century small denomination coins" and "coins from Feodalic France" (9th to 15th centuries CE). In the same paragraph she also signals the presence of "worn coins" unearthed around the Mamluk vaulted Fountain House, together with "considerable quantities of broken jars and other vessels, coloured glass bracelets, [and] wire earrings"—also dating to the Mamluk period. Nothing in her description suggests that any of the coins or other material go back to Roman times or to late antiquity. I did not even mention Alexandre's report in my book because it was "prepublication" and because it contained no *verifiable* material evidence dating to Early Roman times, that is, to the time of "Jesus" or to BCE times. Surprising to me was only the enigmatic word "Hellenistic" in the last line.

For the next several years, the Mary's Well excavation received no further scholarly attention. Then, in Dec. 2007, appeared the NVF "Final Report" in BAIAS authored, we recall, by Stephen Pfann, Ross Voss, and Yehudah Rapuano.[15] On its page 39 we encounter a section entitled, "Area A: finds made during the construction of the Nazareth Village." There we read:

> [*Citation #4*] Various finds were made during the construction of the Nazareth Village Project in 2000-2002 and were recorded by Mark Goodman. These conprise [*sic*] a number of unstratified finds including a coin and pottery vessel fragments from Area A (Figs. 19 and 20).[16] This represents the latest Byzantine coin that has been found in the Nazareth area.
>
> From Bagatti's excavations in Nazareth 4 coins were found, all Byzantine (mid-fourth to early fifth century) and 2 coins from the vicinity: one Late Roman (the earliest coin, mid-third century) and one Byzantine (late fifth to early sixth century). These were recorded as follows: Grotto no. 25: 3 unidentifiable Byzantine (one with head of Emperor; two very small, typical of late fourth to early fifth century AD) (Bagatti 1969:I: 46). Grotto No. 29 (embedded in the plaster): one with head of Emperor, apparently Constans (AD 337–350) (Bagatti 1969: I, 210, Fig. 172). In addition there were finds from the village: one coin of Anastasius (AD 491-518) (Bagatti 1969: I, 234). Surface find from ploughing the land around the village: one coin of Gordian III (AD 238–244) (Bagatti 1969: I, 251). More than 60 other coins from the Islamic to Mamluk Period were unearthed in the 1955 excavations (Bagatii 1969: II, 194–201). *In addition, 165 coins were uncovered by Yardenna Alexandre in the 1997–1998 excavations at*

---

15. The 61 page NVF report begins with the sections: "The Nazareth Farm site discovery and survey," "The Nazareth Village Farm: initial survey," "GPS mapping survey," a lengthy "Summary of excavated areas," and finally "The stone quarries."

16. Fig. 19 follows in the NVF report. It is a coin from the time of Tiberius II (578–82 CE). The authors add a few lines of description of the coin which, incidentally, includes the Chi-Rho staurogram. Fig. 20 is of a Gaza Ware bowl of Early Bronze III.

ARCHAEOLOGICAL EXCAVATIONS AT MARY'S WELL, NAZARETH

Yardenna Alexandre, Israel Antiquities Authority
1st May 2006

Archaeological excavations were carried out in the Fountain Square and in the adjacent St. Gabriel's Square in 1997-1998 by the Israel Antiquities Authority under the direction of Yardenna Alexandre on the initiative of the Government Tourist Ministry and the Nazareth Municipality in the context of the Nazareth 2000 development programme.

The main excavations were carried out under the modern 1960s concrete Fountain House, which was demolished with the aim of reconstructing the ruined Ottoman stone Fountain House. The archaeological remains exposed dated from the Roman, the Crusader, the Mamluk and the Ottoman periods. From the Roman period part of a covered dressed stone channel was exposed, as well as some wall stubs and Middle Roman pottery. Major construction works carried out in the Crusader period produced finely-dressed stone pools paved with marble slabs, a fine plastered arched reservoir and large and small stone channels, the major of which may have carried water from the spring the the Church of the Annunciation. The evidence indicates that [sic] a clear Crusader presence at the site, including a variety of local and imported glazed wares and coins from Feodalic France. In the early Mamluk period the Fountain House continued in use, without destruction and in the fourteenth century the Mamluks built a new vaulted Fountain House, whilst the old Crusader pools served as a 'shop', or small storeroom for a local potter's wares. The activity around the Fountain House is reflected in considerable quantities of broken jars and other vessels, coloured glass bracelets, wire earrings and worn coins. A fifteenth century destruction of the shop seems to have been followed by a period of delapidation. A clean-up including the dredging of many 14-15th century small denomination coins, may date the Franciscan efforts in the early 17th century (known from the written records), but David Roberts drawing from the 1840s indicates that the Fountain House was in a bad state of repair. The vaulted Fountain House was rebuilt in the 1860s and stood until it was replaced in the 1960s.

The limited excavations in the St. Gabriel's Church Square were carried out as some ancient walls were exposed when the infrastructures were being renewed. The excavations revealed a complete underground vaulted reservoir with four well openings in a row, overlain by a stone-paved courtyard. This plastered reservoir or cistern was in use in the 18th-early 19th centuries. Two large stone channels were exposed here, the ancient of which seems to have been part of the Crusader channel that originally transported the water from the source, under and past the St. Gabriel's church and down to the water house. The vaulted reservoir, however, captured these waters and cut off the connection with the Fountain House. The second channel was built after the vaulted reservoir, to bypass this reservoir and again allow the waters to reach the Fountain House. Some fragmentary stone walls and floors were cut by the vaulted reservoir, thus indicating that there was some occupation here in the Hellenistic, Crusader and Mamluk periods.

Mary's Well, Nazareth. The coins were over-whelmingly Mamluk, but also included a few Hellenistic, Hasmonaean, Early Roman, Byzantine, Umayyad and Crusader coins (Alexandre, forthcoming).

    The unstratified pottery vessels included a complete Gaza Ware bowl (Fig. 20), which was found during the clearance operations which preceded the construction of the Nazareth Village.   (Emphasis added.)

I was amazed to read the italicized words in this last citation. In her IAA report communicated to me (above), Alexandre mentioned nothing about coins from "Hellenistic, Hasmonaean, Early Roman" times. Had such critically important coin evidence been found in her excavation, she surely would have included such in her official report. It is also interesting that *the short official report printed above and dated "1st May 2006" has never been published*. Despite the regular dust-off "Alexandre, forthcoming," we are now almost fifteen years after the original excavation and her report has still not appeared![17]

My first response to this astonishing coin claim was in an article that appeared in *American Atheist* magazine in January, 2009 (see Chapter 5):

[*Citation #5*] Undoubtedly there is great pressure on the tradition now to discover such telling evidence from Nazareth. Continuing pilgrimage depends on it. The incipient Nazareth Village depends on it. Perhaps the entire Jesus-story depends on it. This is the time for stalwart defenders of the tradition to exercise their resourcefulness and acumen in defense of the Christian story and to prevent a wound to the Achilles' heel from festering and becoming fatal. Let's not be too surprised if remarkable new 'finds' at Nazareth conveniently appear in the next few years—finds substantiating a settlement there at the time of Christ. To fit the demands

---

17. The promised report (a complete monograph) finally appeared in print in late 2012. I did not see it until after this article was written (in early 2013) and consider Alexandre's problematic Mary's Well report in detail in Chapter 11.

of the tradition that are now in print, the forthcoming material will have to be early and non-funereal.

Well, guess what? According to the NVF report, a cache of Hellenistic and Early Roman coins has recently been 'found' at Mary's Well (at the Northern end of the Nazareth basin). Wow. Nothing remotely similar has ever been found in the Nazareth basin. The earliest coin found there dates to about 350 CE. A cache of Hellenistic and Early Roman coins is exactly the sort of evidence which the tradition needs in order to decide the matter in its favor.

My skepticism is increased by the fact that I possess a pre-publication report (dated 2006) from the Israel Antiquities Authority signed by the archaeologist who dug at Mary's Well. In it she mentions no early coins at all. The only datable coins she signals were from the 14th–15th centuries CE. Hmm... What's going on here?

All of a sudden, claims of Jesus-era evidence are being made at Nazareth. Putative turn-of-the-era evidence is popping up all over the place—on the surface at the Nazareth Village Farm (see above), at Mary's Well... Where next?

So far, then, we have no more than an imputation of turn of the era evidence: the NVFR authors (Citation #4) are *ascribing* such evidence to Y. Alexandre. It is curious that Pfann *et al.* had no obvious reason to bring up Alexandre's findings at all. After all, her excavation had nothing to do with the Nazareth Village Farm—*it was conducted two kilometers to the north.* Why, I wondered, were the NVFR authors discussing finds from an excavation that had taken place a decade earlier and far away, and why were they alleging new results that were not in Ms. Alexandre's *own* IAA report?

The next stage in this developing coin saga was a four page "Reply to Salm" published in the subsequent issue of BAIAS. In it, the Nazareth Village Farm proponents (once again) imputed early evidence to Alexandre. Now, however, they went a step farther and claimed to have received a *verbatim* confirmation from her regarding their *own* Early Roman coin claim:

> [*Citation #6.* Pfann and Rapuano write...] *Pace* Salm, Dr. Alexandre herself provided the following text to quote in our report: 'In addition, 165 coins were uncovered by Yardenna Alexandre in the 1997–1998 excavations at Mary's Well, Nazareth. The coins were overwhelmingly Mamluk, but also included a few Hellenistic, Hasmonaean, Early Roman, Byzantine, Umayyad and Crusader coins' [BAIAS 2008:106].

So, Pfann *et al.* are here alleging that the two critical sentences from their former 61-page report had actually been a verbatim quotation from "Dr. Alexandre herself." A glance above at Citation #4, however, shows that this is not the case—the sentences under examination lack quotation marks and are clearly part of *their* prose. If it were a quotation it would indeed be a curious one: (1) Dr. Alexandre would be referring to herself in the third person; (2) Pfann and Rapuano would have embedded two of her verbatim sentences into their prose without signaling such to the reader by conventional punctuation; and (3) they would have done so without any footnote of attribution (as is normal scholarly practice). Presumably, then, in this whole boondoggle regarding the Nazareth coins, we are to believe the following fairly incredible sequence of events:

— Alexandre excavated 165 coins at Mary's Well but *omitted* critical information about Hellenistic and Roman coins in her official IAA report, one which she shared with me in May 2006;

— While *withholding* such early coin information from myself (and presumably from the IAA), Alexandre subsequently selectively shared it with Pfann *et al.* working at the other end of the Nazareth basin;

— Pfann *et al.* revealed that astonishingly critical evidence for a 'Jesus-era Nazareth' in *their* 2007 report dealing with the NVF;

— After being critiqued by myself, Pfann *et al.* alleged that the two sentences under scrutiny were a *verbatim* quote from Alexandre, despite the fact that the original passage doesn't appear to be a quotation and that in substance their claim conflicts with Alexandre's own IAA report—one which I already had in my possession for two years.

In 2012 Ehrman entered the fray with the publication of *DJE?*. He decidedly aligned himself with the tradition and added a disturbing new twist. The following passage occurs directly after Ehrman's over-the-top statement regarding "Many compelling pieces" of Jesus-era evidence being found at Nazareth (*DJE?* 195). He writes:

[*Citation #7*] For one thing, archaeologists have excavated a farm connected with the village, and it dates to the time of Jesus. [Ehrman is speaking of the NVF, and he bases this assertion on Rapuano's eleven pieces of 'evidence' falsely dated to the time of Jesus—above pp. 56–57.] Salm disputes the finding of the archaeologists who did the excavation (remember that he himself is not an archaeologist but bases his views on what the real archaeologists—all of whom disagree with him—say). For one thing when archaeologist Yardena Alexandre indicated that 165 coins were found *in this excavation*, she specified in the report that some of them were late, from the fourteenth or fifteenth century. This suits Salm's purposes just fine. But as it turns out, among the coins were some that date to the Hellenistic, Hasmonean, and early Roman period, that is, the days of Jesus. Salm objected that this was not stated in Alexandre's report, but Alexandre has verbally confirmed that in fact it is the case: there were coins in the collection that date to the time prior to the Jewish uprising.

(*DJE?* 195. My comments in brackets and emphasis added.)

"In this excavation"? Ehrman apparently doesn't understand that *two different excavations* are involved: one at Mary's Well and one at the NVF! He seems to have conflated the two venues and to claim that the alleged Hellenistic, Hasmonean, and early Roman period coins were found at the NVF! I am carefully putting us on notice here because, given past shenanigans at Nazareth, *anything* and *everything* is possible. Who knows? Given the prominence of Ehrman's book, pretty soon the tradition may run with this novel and *very false* line that Jesus-era coins have been found at the Nazareth Village Farm (by Alexandre?). Desperation is known to produce strange results...

Let us be clear: when Ehrman writes that "Alexandre has verbally confirmed that in fact it is the case" he is reporting *hearsay*. Without published finds at Mary's Well from the pen of Alexandre herself as the primary archeologist,[18] any imputation of Hellenistic to Early Roman coins ascribed to her is just that: an imputation. It is not "evidence."

Regarding these coins, we can conclude the following: (a) In 1997–98 Alexandre excavated a large cache of 14th–15th century CE coins near Mary's Well at the northern end of the Nazareth basin. Her IAA report noted no coins dating prior to the fourteenth century CE. (b) In 2007 Pfann, Rapuano (and subsequently Ehman) imputed turn-of-the-era coin finds to Alexandre. (c) Poor scholarship mars the work of all the above academics, in that the NVF report was riddled with errors (as my "Response" in BA-IAS 2008 shows, requiring the publication of a wholesale "Amendment"). Furthermore, Ehrman conflates two excavations into one. (d) Finally, Alexandre has been reported to admit that her original IAA notice omitted critical Jesus-era evidence and was *not definitive*—and she has refused to set the record straight via publication.[19]

I leave the reader to decide whether these irregularities are merely coincidence, if they manifest atrocious sloppiness on the part of several scholars, or if perhaps they conceal a more suspect intent.

Shama's Roman bathhouse

In *DJE?* (p. 196) Ehrman defers on several issues to Ken Dark and mentions the latter's review of my book (BAIAS 2008:140–146) which Ehrman characterizes (correctly) as "thoroughly negative." I have dealt with Prof. Dark's comments elsewhere,[20] concluding that nothing in his review

---

18. See note 17 above.
19. See note 17 above.
20. Above pp. 24, 59–61, 64–65, 68–69, 86. *Editor's Note*: When Hellenistic, Hasmonean, Early Roman, and Byzantine coins were pulled like rabbits from a hat out of Alexandre's cache of 14th–15th-century coins, did anyone consider the implications of

actually impacts the material record from the Nazareth basin at the turn of the era. However, my observations would probably be too detailed for Ehrman who, it seems, is less interested in the data than in credentials and hearsay.

Echoing an element in Dark's review of my book, Ehrman raises the issue of "hydrology" (*DJE?* 196): "Salm has misunderstood both the hydrology (how the water systems worked) and the topography (the layout) of Nazareth." This is a strawman argument which, apparently, offers Ehrman an opportunity for criticism. I will deal with the topographical aspects of the Nazareth argument later in this chapter. As regards hydrology—though I may understand it better than Dark and Ehrman aver—it is entirely irrelevant to the existence or non-existence of a settlement *at the turn of the era*—my particular concern.

To my knowledge, only one person has attempted to link the hydrology of the Nazareth basin to the 'time of Jesus.' That person is not inclined to scholarship but, rather, is the owner of a particularly successful souvenir shop across the street from Mary's Well. This gifted entrepreneur, Elias Shama by name, makes it his business to entice as many pilgrims as possible into his shop, called *Cactus*. Of course, busloads of pilgrims already empty daily at his very doorstep, and Shama makes the most of such good fortune. To make a long story short, he claims that a Roman bath house exists directly under his shop, one which he—on entirely mysterious grounds—dates to the turn of the era. Shama even advertises that, in all likelihood, *Jesus himself* bathed there. For a fee, he (Shama, not Jesus) or an assistant will conduct pilgrims down a flight of stairs to a 'hypocaust'—an underground system used in former times to heat hot baths. Unfortunately for the entrepreneur, however, a number of archeologists (including Ms. Alexandre, incidentally) have dated the waterworks under the *Cactus* shop to at least

---

finding coins dating to a period 332–63 BCE *in the same cache with coins nearly two thousand years younger?* Does this mean that she had come upon the safety deposit pot of a rare-coin collector? Does this mean that the circulation half-life of Hellenistic coins was almost a millennium in magnitude? If Hellenistic coins had circulated so long, why weren't more than "a few" Byzantine coins found? Was their circulation half-life for some reason much shorter than that of the Hellenistic coins? If those Hellenistic coins should ever be proved to exist, what evidence is there that they had found their ways to 'Nazareth' before the fifteenth century? One might have hoped that when Ms. Alexandre—a scientist presumably proficient in mathematics—published her official report in 2012, she would have applied Bayesian analysis to these problems. Although such problems are ideal for Bayesian investigation, no such mathematical studies were done. In fact, the chapter on coins was not even written by her. Rather, it was assigned to another scholar who seems unaware of the need for mathematical methods.—FRZ [See Chapter 11.—RS]

one millennium after the turn of the era (Salm 2008a:133). This untoward scholarly verdict has apparently not deterred Shama or his steady stream of visitors. He continues to do excellent business and to garner a great deal of publicity on the Internet, in tourist literature directed at prospective pilgrims to the Holy Land, and in traditionalist print outlets—including a number of conservative Christian journals.

The oil lamps and tombs at Nazareth

The reader will recall that my 2008 book argued a number of central points regarding the non-existence of Nazareth at the turn of the era (see above p. 154 for a summary). Only the first three points are diagnostic, for they alone deal with the material evidence which must decide the case. The preceding several pages have discussed the first point—the lack of material evidence from *c.* 700 BCE to *c.* 100 CE. We now come to the second and third points—consideration of the oil lamps and the tombs, both of which decidedly date to CE times. Astonishingly, Ehrman does not once mention the oil lamp evidence—perhaps, one may suppose, because it is clearly damning to the tradition's case. After all, what possible rebuttal can there be to the *scholarly* verdict that the earliest oil lamps excavated in the Nazareth basin postdate 25 CE (Salm 2008a:170)? I say "scholarly verdict" because that dating is not mine—it is the conclusion of oil lamp specialists noted in *The Myth of Nazareth*. There is plenty of evidence in this regard. In a century of digging, scores of ceramic lamps have been found in the basin. Naturally many are fragmentary, but approximately two dozen have been recovered in complete, or virtually complete, condition. As my earlier book demonstrated, *no oil lamp* (nor oil lamp shard) *can be dated with certainty before c. 100 CE.*[21] Even without considering other factors, how then is it possible to envisage a village existing in Hellenistic times, and at the turn of the era, when *every* dated oil lamp shard recovered from the basin dates to the common era?

Bow-spouted in form (mislabeled "Herodian"), the earliest Nazareth oil lamps were *still* being produced as late as the Bar Kochba rebellion. Though I offer a *terminus post quem* of 25 CE for these lamps, that would be a charitably early date for any of them. In all likelihood the Nazareth bow-spouted lamps were manufactured between the two Jewish revolts—the period in which the settlement came into being (Salm 2008a:207).

While Ehrman conveniently ignores the oil lamp evidence, he devotes an entire page to the Nazareth tombs. Point three of the seven points summarized above noted that *all* the post-Iron Age tombs at Nazareth are later than 50 CE. These tombs are of the well-known *kokh* type (also called *locu-*

---

21. Salm 2008a:205, 165–75, and Appendix 5.

lus tombs) which consist of burial shafts radiating from a central chamber (Salm 2008a:158*ff*). Naturally, Ehrman does not contest the existence of these many *kokh* tombs. He merely notes that they were expensive to hew and speculates, therefore, that in the first century the poor Nazarenes used shallow burials which have simply not been found. Of course, *this is no more than a convenient argument from silence.* A similar argument could be applied to the oil lamps: even though none have been found clearly predating *c.* 100 CE, that doesn't *prove* earlier lamps didn't exist... Once again, then, we are inexorably led to the famous double negative beloved of a desperate tradition, one whose logic is approximately as follows: You have *not proven* that [something] did *not* exist—*therefore it existed!*

We can summarize the preceding Nazareth discussion as follows:

(1) **The lack of demonstrable material evidence from *c.* 700 BCE to *c.* 100 CE.** Ehrman rejects this but provides no evidence for settlement before 70 CE. He simply *asserts* the existence of "many compelling pieces of archaeological evidence" from the time of Jesus (Citation #2 above). This thoroughly unsubstantiated misstatement ranks with other egregious untruths documented in my first book.

(2) **The 25 CE+ dating of the earliest oil lamps at Nazareth.** Ehrman does not even mention oil lamps.

(3) **The 50 CE+ dating of all the post-Iron Age tombs at Nazareth.** Ehrman speculates that shallow, non-*kokh* type burials predating 50 CE have simply not been found.

Thus Ehrman's treatment amounts to very little. He rejects the first point while providing no evidence to support his cause. The second point he simply ignores, while the third he evades through an argument from silence. On all three major points regarding the material evidence Ehrman offers nothing substantive (much less compelling) to counter my argument that Nazareth began after 'the time of Jesus.'

The burden of proof

A defensive position is now coalescing several years after publication of *The Myth of Nazareth.* It is a posture which—while explicitly in rank denial—tacitly accepts, though grudgingly, that the material evidence at Nazareth indeed probably points to post-Jesus times. So, Ehrman challenges (*DJE?* 194): "just because later habitation can be established in Nazareth, how does that show that the town was not inhabited earlier?" Here the burden of proof is placed entirely upon the shoulders of the skeptic. The traditional view is *assumed* correct until *proven* wrong. The tradition, apparently, can say what it wishes (no matter how outlandish) without the need for evidence. Furthermore, it will apparently continue to do so *until that strategy is no longer possible.*

As mentioned above, Ehrman falls into the double negatives characteristic of a last-ditch argument: 'Well, even though the evidence is post-Jesus, that *doesn't* prove that Nazareth *didn't* exist in the time of Jesus!' In an American court of law, of course, the accused is innocent until proven guilty "beyond a shadow of a doubt." A similar standard of protection seems to be assumed by the tradition. It arrogates correctness to itself (that is, 'innocence')—even if the weight of evidence is otherwise. Indeed, the tradition assumes correctness though the substantial totality of evidence is to the contrary. It is correct until *proven* wrong!

Thus one side of the argument assumes a free pass as regards evidence. In effect, the tradition says to Mythicists: "You have not *proved* that Nazareth *wasn't* there." That is, Mythicists have not proven a negative. This same *modus operandi*, of course, is elsewhere extended to protect pious beliefs regarding the life of Jesus, his miracles, and his resurrection from the grave. In all these cases the tradition challenges nonbelievers to disprove what are essentially myths. For practical reasons, this is often impossible—as the tradition is well aware. In one of my articles for *American Atheist* magazine (p. 68 above) I explained how it is impossible to formally disprove a myth—especially when common sense is jettisoned:

> After all, neither you nor I can prove that Santa Claus doesn't exist. We can go to the North Pole, can dig up there (under water and ice!) all we want, and can find absolutely no evidence for his gift-packing facility nor for his team of flying reindeer. But to a believer, we can't prove those don't exist. All the believer has to say is, "Well, you didn't look in the right places," "He's hiding," or even "He's invisible." Unfortunately, common myths involving Jesus are every bit as weird.

I discussed such arguments from silence in *The Myth of Nazareth* (pp. 288–91), where I summed up the material evidence from Nazareth in two stark columns:

I BCE	**I CE**
Evidence of Nazareth at the Time of Jesus:	*Evidence of the birth of Nazareth in the common era:*
— None —	After 25 CE: All oil lamps After 50 CE: All post-Iron age tombs After 50 CE: All pottery

It is clear that we are dealing here with an extremely tilted playing field. The tradition arrogates correctness to its position. That, however, is purely speculative—*i.e.*, without any evidence! The proof of the pudding was revealed in my first book. It showed that the tradition has—*in over a century of digging*—not actually produced any Nazareth material from the time of Jesus. In this light, Ehrman's cavalier claim of "many compelling pieces of archeological evidence" (*DJE?* 195; Citation #2, p. 156 above) dating to the time of Jesus emerges as frankly absurd.

But *archeology is indeed now able to prove the negative*—simply by digging in the ground. With today's careful and advanced excavation techniques (where even pollen can be counted!) what is *not* found is as significant as what is found. As I wrote in the Introduction to *The Myth of Nazareth*:

> This is what gives the Nazareth issue such great potency. Unlike aspects of the gospel story that are quite beyond verification—the miracles of Jesus, his bodily resurrection, his virgin birth, or even his human nature—the existence of Nazareth two thousand years ago can be proved or disproved by digging in the ground. Because the archaeology of a site is empirically demonstrable, "Nazareth" is in a category apart. To this day, it preserves the explosive potential to either prove or disprove the gospel accounts (Salm 2008a:*xii*).

This is common sense. When one looks for something and doesn't find it, one does not say: "Well, I don't see it—but it's there!" We would term such illogic irrational, yet it is precisely the sort of logic that obtains with a turn-of-the-era Nazareth. Archeologists have been looking for over one hundred years, and not a shred of solid material evidence for human habitation at the "time of Jesus" has resulted. My exhaustive review of *all* the evidence shows that *only two artifacts*—both stone vessels—*could* date to the turn of the era. However, such vessels continued in production as late as the Bar Kokhba revolt (*c.* 135 CE)—their presence in the Nazareth assemblage is not at all diagnostic of human presence at the turn of the era (they could well date to the second century CE).

Thus, the tradition has apparently even lost the argument from silence. All that remains is empty rhetoric and bombast. Thankfully, the burden of proof lays on the shoulders of the one who takes a position contrary to evidence and common sense. In the case of Nazareth, it resides (or should reside) squarely on the shoulders of the tradition which insists on the existence of a village at the turn of the era—but does so without any evidence.

Now, even though excavations have taken place only in a relatively small area of the hillside, the evidentiary results of decades of work are by no means weak. They are considerable and—to use Ehrman's term—"compelling." But, as is well known, traditionalist Christians refuse to be convinced by evidence (especially when it turns against them) and ultimately resort to *faith*, which I define as 'a repository of infinite hope in impossible circumstances.' Faith is a curious blind spot in our human psychology, a mental drunkenness where jettisoning reason is altogether laudable—'for the glory of God.' Indeed, it is their willingness to abdicate their innate reasoning capacities that validates the commitment of Christians:

> For the word of the cross is folly to those who are perishing, but to us who are being saved it is the power of God. For it is written, "I will destroy the wisdom of the wise, and the cleverness of the clever I will thwart."
> Where is the wise man? Where is the scribe? Where is the debater of this age? Has not God made foolish the wisdom of the world? For since, in the wisdom of God, the world did not know God through wisdom, it pleased God through the folly of what we preach to save those who believe. For Jews demand signs and Greeks seek wisdom, but we preach Christ crucified, a stumbling block to Jews and folly to Gentiles, but to those who are called, both Jews and Greeks, Christ the power of God and the wisdom of God. For the foolishness of God is wiser than men, and the weakness of God is stronger than men.　(1 Cor. 1:18–25)

Here is the great divide in biblical studies: sufficient faith *vs.* sufficient reason. Each party labels the other "foolish" because the other lacks what it so greatly esteems. Skeptics and believers speak different languages and eternally talk past one another. One group provides evidence, while the other trumpets a message carefully crafted long ago:

> We believe in one Lord, Jesus Christ, the only Son of God, eternally begotten of the Father.... For us and for our salvation he came down from heaven: by the power of the Holy Spirit he became incarnate from the Virgin Mary, and was made man. For our sake he was crucified under Pontius Pilate; he suffered death and was buried. On the third day he rose again in accordance with the Scriptures; he ascended into heaven and is seated at the right hand of the Father. He will come again in glory to judge the living and the dead, and his kingdom will have no end.
> (Nicene Creed, 325 CE)

As the data of science accumulate in favor of skeptics, they will continue to show that the above has no rational basis and is thus foolishness. Psychiatrists also will eventually step in and diagnose the malaise of Christianity for what it is: wishful thinking carried to a delusional extreme. Historians, too, will show that the growth and resilience of the religion has had as much to do with the aggrandizement of power as with loving one's neighbor. Together, all these witnesses will demonstrate that the quest for global domination is hardly restricted to the Hitlers and Stalins of the world. 'Triumphalism' is also the central element of Christianity, a religion which is absolutely terrifying because it combines the complete abdication of reason with the *modus operandi* that the end justifies the means.

The location of the ancient village

Like the post-Jesus dating of the oil lamps and the Middle Roman tombs, the presence of many such tombs *precisely* in the Venerated Area at Nazareth is most inconvenient for the tradition. After all, there can be little more embarrassing than discovering not one but several Roman tombs under the house where the Virgin Mary allegedly grew up. How to explain this to the flood of pilgrims continually visiting the Church of the Annunciation? "Well," we can imagine the pious tour guide explaining, "here is where the Angel Gabriel announced to Mary, 'Blessed art thou amongst women,' and [walking a few steps in *any* direction] here are the remains of a tomb, and here the remains of another, and here a third'..." Naturally, this interesting scenario does not actually occur and one will find not the remotest mention of a tomb in any tourist literature. Even in his mammoth two-volume tome from 1969 Bagatti scarcely mentions tombs at all. Yet they definitely exist in the Venerated Area and have been known since the nineteenth century, as carefully documented in my first book. At least three tombs are directly under the Church of the Annunciation (CA), with several more close by.[22]

Of course, Jews were proscribed from living near tombs—a source of ritual impurity. Thus, the well-documented presence of *kokh* tombs under and around the CA is damning of traditional claims, for the alleged home of the Virgin Mary lies in a Jewish cemetery dating to Roman times.

Before the Second World War, the Catholic Church was able to ignored this conflict between the presence of tombs and its fanciful recreation of history. Amateur archeologists, imbued with Christian faith, took scant note of Jewish funerary prohibitions and gleefully described (even sketched) the various funerary installations under the CA, hoping one of them might be the tomb of, perhaps, St. Joseph himself.[23]

But the presence of tombs in the Venerated Area is fatal to the traditional view of Nazareth, both as regards the habitation of the Blessed Virgin and the location of the ancient village on the hillside in Roman times. The inconvenient funereal evidence has required a 'return to the drawing board,' as it were. To that uncomfortable evidence must be added the steep slope and the lack of domestic structural evidence on the hillside—all inimical to a tradition now scrambling to devise a scenario that will satisfy all this inimical data. As we have seen (Chapter 6), Dark proposes one solution: Jesus' Nazareth existed on the hillside—but *before* the tombs were constructed there. This view requires that Nazareth moved at some time in antiquity

---

22. See Chapter 13; also Salm 2008a: Figs. 5.3 and 5.4.
23. *E.g.* Viaud 1910:115.

to make way for tombs. The tradition is sympathetic to this option, and it now seems disposed to propose the following general sequence of events:

A. Mary and her future husband Joseph were neighbors living on the steep slope above Nazareth at the turn of the era;

B. Mary received a visitation from the Archangel Gabriel informing her that she would conceive a child;

C. Mary wed Joseph and gave birth to Jesus;

D. Jesus, Mary, and Joseph lived at Joseph's home (the Church of St. Joseph 100 m north of the CA);

E. Some generations later Nazareth 'moved' to the valley floor;

F. In the second century CE tombs were constructed where Mary and Joseph used to live on the hillside.

These steps are not precisely what Dark proposes—he would date all the above activity to the first century CE. Those who have read my first book will recognize this as a return to the "mobile Nazareth" hypothesis first broached by Fr. Clemens Kopp in the mid-20th century (Salm 2008a:65–70). Kopp attempted to reconcile the gospel version of Nazareth with the growing scientific evidence to the contrary. To do so, it was necessary to hypothesize that the settlement moved. In fact, Kopp proposed that it moved twice. In any case, the settlement's movement in antiquity is the only scenario which will accommodate both the exigencies of scripture and the scientific evidence brought to light in the last decade. The archeologists recognize this and propose (like Dark) a variation of the same 'moving settlement' theme. Ehrman, however, does not broach such a detailed solution and simply asserts the double negative alluded to above: tombs from a later time do *not* prove that there was *no* earlier village:

> It is hard to understand why tombs in Nazareth that can be dated to the days after Jesus indicate that there was no town there during the days of Jesus. That is to say, just because later habitation can be established in Nazareth, how does that show that the town was not inhabited earlier?
>
> (*DJE?* 194)

I have argued in the past that *the lack of recovered evidence from the hillside* does indeed show *the absence of a settlement both on the hillside and on the valley floor* at 'the time of Jesus' (Salm 2008a:290). This is quite clear when one acknowledges that the people living on the valley floor were certainly those who built and worked the installations on the nearby hillslope. We know that no one lived in the Nazareth basin in 'the time of Jesus' simply because no evidence of their presence has been found on the nearby hillslope, which all dates to CE times. This is, in fact, quite telling. The ample material found on the hillside (numbering hundreds of objects and 20+ tombs) is quite conclusive regarding the people living on the valley floor and *requires* us to date their settlement to CE times—and not before.

An analogy may be in order. Consider the high water mark left on embankments by a river, reservoir, or lake. In times of drought the hydrologist looks at the water mark and knows that the water once reached that level. He does not see any water nor does he need to. Similarly, the archeological profile on the hillside of Nazareth is a telling gauge for the inhabitants who lived on the valley floor nearby.

Ehrman points out that no one has dug on the valley floor, and therefore my thesis of a basin floor location for the settlement is unproven:

> This view [that archaeologists have never excavated the Nazareth valley floor] creates insurmountable problems for [Salm's] thesis. For one thing, there is the simple question of logic. If archaeologists have not dug where Salm thinks the village was located, what is his basis for saying that it did not exist in the days of Jesus? (*DJE?* 195)

This evinces some confusion on Ehrman's part, for he is here arguing (from silence) that a settlement may have existed *on the valley floor* in the time of Jesus. But no one has claimed this, least of all myself. The tradition has long maintained that the village was located *on the hillside* 'in the time of Jesus'—not on the valley floor. Hence, Ehrman's above argument is moot.

Simply put, what Ehrman needs to argue (if he wishes to support the traditional view) is that a village existed on the hillside 'in the time of Jesus.' However, my 2008 book clearly showed the evidence for *that* proposition to be nonexistent. After all, the evidence from the hillside is all post-Jesus. None dates to the turn of the era. To an impartial observer, this proves not only that no settlement existed on the hillside 'in the time of Jesus,' but also that *no settlement existed anywhere in the Nazareth basin at the turn of the era.*

It should be noted that I had already clarified this issue for Ehrman before he wrote his book, namely, in personal correspondence. Ehrman questioned me on this precise point in a 2011 email. I duly explained my position, and now find his 'unwillingness to hear' and his later feigning ignorance in print a tad deceitful:

> Bart,   July 13/2011
>
> Thanks for the email. To answer you... I take a scientific approach, looking at the evidence, and drawing conclusions therefrom. There is absolutely nothing in the material evidence to suggest habitation in the Nazareth basin at the turn of the era. I think my book makes that clear. Is there anything to suggest that Nazareth was NOT on the valley floor at the turn of the era? Well, yes—there is no evidence whatsoever on the hillsides of [its] presence at that time. What has been excavated at Nazareth is more than ample to infer a dating for the people who lived on

the valley floor, *for they of course are the ones who built the tombs and agricultural installations on the hillsides...* —René   [Emphasis added.]

Thus, I made it clear that there is good reason—from the recovered archeological evidence on the hillside—to conclude that there was no settlement anywhere in the basin at the turn of the era.

It is clear, however, that Ehrman's treatment of the entire Nazareth issue is superficial. This, unfortunately, conforms with the tenor of his entire book *DJE?*, a work lacking footnotes, Index, and patently written with the Christian layperson in mind. Ehrman does not bother to carry his logic through to any inevitable (and uncomfortable) conclusions. He expects similar laziness from his readers. For him—and for them—the absence of evidence is not particularly disconcerting. In the last analysis—since there *is* no evidence—Ehrman apparently expects his readers to simply *believe* in the earlier existence of a village. Traditionalists, of course, are happy to go along. For them, the absence of evidence has never stood in the way of faith. They even manifest a most curious pride in acknowledging this truth.

	Hillside habitations at time of "Jesus" Existence of / Evidence for		Habitations later moved (due to tombs)
B. Bagatti	Claimed	Claimed	(Ignores tombs)
B. Ehrman	Claimed	Claimed	(Ignores implications)
K. Dark	Claimed	(Sis. of Naz. Convent)	Claimed
R. Salm	Denied	Denied	Denied

In sum, Ehrman is satisfied to (falsely) impress upon his readers that: (1) Salm is *wrong*; (2) there is *no* proof that Nazareth was *not* on the valley floor in 'the time of Jesus' (a moot point, as we have seen); (3) the settlement in Jesus' time was on the hillside (though no evidence remains of it); and (4) the entire Nazareth issue is irrelevant (see below).

Ehrman's arguments are essentially rhetorical (ignoring what he finds inconvenient) and *ad hominem* (focussing on my lack of credentials). He appears to 'score points' based on authority, and he capitalizes on the average layperson's ignorance regarding these somewhat arcane matters.

Nevertheless—to those who care—the material evidence must speak, and it can only be a matter of time before Ehrman's unfounded arguments implode under their own weight, namely, under *a lack of evidence*.

Ehrman begins and ends his discussion with what appears to be a convenient (and perhaps desperate) ploy—that the entire Nazareth issue is 'irrelevant':

> ...I could dispose of this argument fairly easily by pointing out that it is irrelevant. If Jesus existed, as the evidence suggests, but Nazareth did not, as [Salm] claims, then [Jesus] merely came from somewhere else.
> (*DJE?* 191).

> Again I reiterate the main point of my chapter: even if Jesus did not come from Nazareth, so what? The historicity of Jesus does not depend on whether Nazareth existed. In fact, it is not even related to the question. The existence (or rather, nonexistence) of Nazareth is another Mythicist irrelevancy. (*DJE?* 197)

I call Ehrman's bluff and challenge the tradition (at this very late stage) to jettison its beloved epithet *Jesus of Nazareth*—perhaps in favor of "Jesus of Anywhere." Alternatively, it could introduce a blank in all the requisite places of the New Testament and in the vast quantity of Bibles and related literature, both scholarly and otherwise—thus: *Jesus of* _____. Far from being 'irrelevant,' I maintain that such a ploy would be tantamount to open heart surgery on a very sick and perhaps dying patient. Ehrman blusters that 'Nazareth' is inconsequential. I suggest, however, that we are dealing with a critical element at the very heart of Christianity—part of a revolution no less epochal than was the Reformation itself.

Chapter 10

THE "HOUSE FROM THE TIME OF JESUS"

On winter solstice, 2009, four days before Christmas and twenty months after publication of *The Myth of Nazareth*, IAA archeologist Yardenna Alexandre gave a massive press conference in Nazareth, Israel, at newly excavated ground just across the street from the Church of the Annunciation. All major news agencies from around the world were present, including AP, UPI, Reuters, and Agence France Presse. Enigmatic advance notices had already alerted both them and the general public that this news conference was of major religious significance and would contain unprecedented information.

When Alexandre stepped up to the microphone on that blustery morning of December 21, she announced the news: for the very first time, incontrovertible evidence of a village from "the time of Jesus" had been found. The evidence, she explained, was before their eyes: remains of a dwelling which—in all likelihood—Jesus himself had known as a child.

The assembled reporters looked about and saw a few holes in the ground, the remains of some low walls, and assorted rubble. But they received Alexandre's news well, responded with tremendous applause and, for the remainder of the day, were escorted on tours of the digging area and (of greatest interest to them) of the enormous International Marian Center—a Catholic megastructure then still very much under construction—which surrounded the excavation on three sides and would eventually cover it over like a giant goose brooding over her golden egg.

The headline immediately flashed around the globe: *A House from the Time of Jesus Has Been Discovered in Nazareth*. Why this would be newsworthy defies explanation, for the world has never doubted the existence of Nazareth in Jesus' time. On the other hand, if there were any doubt at all regarding the existence of the village at the turn of the era, then one might certainly understand some interest in the story. So, given the *enormous* interest in the story, I choose the only interpretation that seems reasonable: *great doubt* in fact exists at a fundamental level regarding the existence of a Jesus-era Nazareth, and *powerful forces have been mobilized to remove all doubt regarding this inflammatory question*—to nip it in the bud.

The pre-publication notices, the 'full house' at Alexandre's press conference, the flood of news stories *immediately* following—these betray the existence of a massive publicity campaign, one worthy of Madison Avenue's finest. The story dominated Catholic media during the 2009 Christmas season. The global news agencies also headlined it, as did Israeli media.[1] A relevant IAA article follows, one whose publication date betrays that it was written *before* Alexandre's news conference of the same day:

Residential building from the time of Jesus exposed in Nazareth

21 Dec 2009

The remains were discovered in an archaeological excavation of the Israel Antiquities Authority near the Church of the Annunciation.

(Communicated by the Israel Antiquities Authority)

An archaeological excavation the Israel Antiquities Authority recently conducted has revealed new information about ancient Nazareth from the time of Jesus. Remains of a dwelling that date to the Early Roman period were discovered for the first time in an excavation, which was carried out prior to the construction of the "International Marian Center of Nazareth" by the Association Mary of Nazareth, next to the Church of the Annunciation.

According to the New Testament, Mary, the mother of Jesus, lived in Nazareth together with her husband Joseph. It was there that she also received the revelation by the Angel Gabriel that she would conceive a child to be born the Son of God. The New Testament mentions that Jesus himself grew up in Nazareth.

In 1969 the Church of the Annunciation was erected in the spot that the Catholic faith identified with the house of Mary. It was built atop the remains of three earlier churches, the oldest of which is ascribed to the Byzantine period (the fourth century CE). In light of the plans to build there, the Israel Antiquities Authority recently undertook a small scale archaeological excavation close to the church, which resulted in the exposure of the structure.

---

1.   *http://www.mfa.gov.il/mfa/israelexperience/history/pages/residential_building_time_jesus_nazareth_21-dec-2009.aspx* (viewed Aug. 12, 2014). Also see above, pp. 122 *f.*

According to Yardenna Alexandre, excavation director on behalf of the Israel Antiquities Authority, "The discovery is of the utmost importance since it reveals for the very first time a house from the Jewish village of Nazareth and thereby sheds light on the way of life at the time of Jesus. The building that we found is small and modest and it is most likely typical of the dwellings in Nazareth in that period. From the few written sources that there are, we know that in the first century CE Nazareth was a small Jewish village, located inside a valley. Until now a number of tombs from the time of Jesus were found in Nazareth; however, no settlement remains have been discovered that are attributed to this period."

In the excavation a large broad wall that dates to the Mamluk period (the fifteenth century CE) was exposed that was constructed on top of and "utilized" the walls of an ancient building. This earlier building consisted of two rooms and a courtyard in which there was a rock-hewn cistern into which the rainwater was conveyed. The artifacts recovered from inside the building were few and mostly included fragments of pottery vessels from the Early Roman period (the first and second centuries CE). In addition, several fragments of chalk vessels were found, which were only used by Jews in this period because such vessels were not susceptible to becoming ritually unclean.

Another hewn pit, whose entrance was apparently camouflaged, was excavated and a few pottery sherds from the Early Roman period were found inside it. The excavator, Yardenna Alexandre, said, "Based on other excavations that I conducted in other villages in the region, this pit was probably hewn as part of the preparations by the Jews to protect themselves during the Great Revolt against the Romans in 67 CE".

In a few of the archaeological excavations that were carried out in this crowded city, a number of burial caves dating to the Early Roman period were exposed that are situated close to the inhabited area. The modern Church of the Annunciation was constructed in the heart of Nazareth, above the Crusader Church of the Annunciation and atop the ruins of a church from the Byzantine period. In the middle of these churches is a cave that was already ascribed in antiquity to the house of Jesus' family. Many storage pits and cisterns, some of which date to the Early Roman period, were found in the compound of the Church of the Annunciation.

The "Association Mary of Nazareth" intends on conserving and presenting the remains of the newly discovered house inside the building planned for the "International Marian Center of Nazareth"

To the casual reader the above article may seem straightforward. But problems emerge when one compares it with others also published on or in the days following December 21. In fact, a number of contradictions become apparent—some affecting rather fundamental issues.

One such issue is *the general size* of the excavated "house"—was it small or large? Alexandre stated (article above, fourth paragraph) that the dwelling was "small and modest." This indeed corresponds with another statement she made in a *FOX News* video of December 27, 2009: "So we can certainly say that this was a small house belonging to the Early Roman Jewish village."[2] But in a December 22, 2009 article[3] published online by NBC news we read: "It is not clear how big the dwelling is—Alexandre's team have uncovered about 900 square feet (85 square meters) of the house, but it may have been for an extended family and could be much larger, she said."[4] The NBC article goes on to state: "Alexandre said limited space and population density in Nazareth means it is unlikely that archaeologists can carry out any further excavations in the area..." So, it appears that we really do not know—nor does the archeologist—even such a basic parameter as the size of the alleged house (*cf.* discussion below, p. 201).

We also note a *discrepancy in chronology.* The second sentence in the above-cited IAA article reports that the excavation "was carried out *prior to* the construction of the 'International Marian Center of Nazareth.'" This seems clear enough and does not disagree with a formal communication (the short IAA report, see below) which reveals that the excavation actually took place between November 12 and December 7, 2009. Yet in an NPR article dated Dec. 21, 2009, Alexandre states that "workers uncovered the first signs of the dwelling *in the summer*, but it became clear only this month that it was a structure from the era of Jesus" (emphasis added).[5]

Now, if the official excavation took place in the Fall of 2009, and if construction of the IMC was *later*, then who was digging at the site *already* in the summer of 2009? And why? We surmise, then, that a dig was carried out *before* the official excavation. There must have been, accordingly, *two* excavations—the first one unofficial and, presumably, off the record.

In an attempt to reconstruct a timeline of the discoveries, we now revisit the second sentence of the above IAA article:

---

2. "A Christmas Discovery: House from time of Christ Unearthed in Israel." *FOX News* video #707 (3' 48"). Sunday, Dec. 27, 2009 (no longer available).

3. All the press announcements ultimately reflect (or are reflected in) the news conference delivered by Alexandre on Dec. 21, 2009.

4. *http://www.nbcnews.com/id/34511072/*, published 12/22/2009, viewed Aug. 13, 2014. The article was authored by Diaa Hadid for the Associated Press.

5. At the time of this writing the story is online at *www.npr.org/templates/story/story. php?storyId=121724812.*

Remains of a dwelling that date to the Early Roman period were discovered for the first time in an excavation, which was carried out prior to the construction of the "International Marian Center of Nazareth" by the *Association Marie de Nazareth*, next to the Church of the Annunciation.

The excavation described here was conducted by the *Association Marie de Nazareth*. It was not the one conducted *by the IAA* under the direction of Alexandre in November-December of 2009. This confirms the existence of *two excavations*, one in the "summer" of 2009 and one in the Fall. The former was conducted by the *Association Marie de Nazareth*, and the latter by the IAA. The first found signs of a "dwelling." The second determined that dwelling to be "from the time of Jesus."

According to a timeline provided by the *Association Marie de Nazareth*,[6] the IMC site already had a considerable relevant history before 2009. Construction of the future megastructure had begun with laying the cornerstone in March, 2007 (below, p. 192). This was a full four years before inauguration of the IMC and five years before its opening to the general public. Thus, the *Association Marie de Nazareth* had been busy for a long time, digging at the site for *years* before the official IAA excavation of Fall, 2009!

The relevant chronology now becomes clearer. Commercial digging began at the site in 2007. In later 2009 (the "summer" *pace* Alexandre, "October" *pace* the *Association Marie de Nazareth*) "archeological remains" were found, described by Alexandre as the "first signs of a dwelling." She made the sensational interpretation that this was a dwelling *"from the time of Jesus"* in December 2009 ("this month")—that is, at the termination of the official IAA excavation and not long before her solstice news conference.

That is the official story, mirrored by articles in the popular press. "In 2009, mechanical earthworks fortuitously exposed archaeological remains at the site of the new *Chemin Neuf* Mary of Nazareth International center," reports one article.[7] Another offers a little more information: "Workers preparing the centre were digging up an old courtyard when they uncovered the walls of an ancient house."[8] All this took place in the summer–fall of 2009, *before* the official IAA excavation of November–December.

Israeli law mandates that work must be suspended when ancient remains are found. This is clearly what occurred in October, 2009. The IAA then assumed responsibility for the excavation work and took over from the *Association Marie de Nazareth*, assigning Y. Alexandre to direct a formal exca-

---

6.   At the time of writing (February, 2015) the timeline is online at: *http://www.marie-denazareth.com/association/qui-sommes-nous/dates-principales.*

7.   Alexandre 2012b:32. The *Chemin Neuf* ("New Path") is a Catholic organization directed by O. Bonnassies, considered below (pp. 237 *f*).

8.   *http://www.seetheholyland.net/mary-of-nazareth-international-center/.* Accessed 7/4/2014.

vation beginning the following month. The transfer of responsibility surely included consultation with the Catholic interests involved, for henceforth the venture was a joint enterprise: (1) an IAA-controlled excavation under (2) a Catholic edifice, one for which planning was complete and construction *already* well underway. The history and circumstances of the IMC excavation reveal close cooperation between both Israeli and Catholic interests.

A nexus of anomalies

The *Centre Internationale Marie de Nazareth* (International Marian Center—hereafter: IMC), at 15A Casa Nova Street, is a mere fifty meters from the Church of the Annunciation when measured wall-to-wall. It is hemmed in by buildings on three sides. Seventy meters to the west is another emerging Catholic tourist destination: the Sisters of Nazareth Convent (Chapter 6). Thus, this entire region of the Nebi Sa'in hillside is undergoing an apparently inexorable transformation into an expanded "Venerated Area"—with the abundant blessings of the Municipality of Nazareth and the Israel Ministry of Tourism.[9] Before the early 2011 completion of the IMC, the following notice appeared online:[10]

> The International Centre Mary of Nazareth will be built facing the Basilica of the Annunciation in 5 large structures providentially acquired in the course of the last three years. They contain in excess of 4000 square meters to be placed at the disposal of the project. The diagrams, plans, and data presented here allow one to evaluate the arrangements as planned. [*Several diagrams follow.*]
> First floor: reception and initial rooms.
> Second floor: other rooms and auditorium.
> Third floor: Chapel and gardens.
> Fourth floor: Terraces with panoramic view.

It is, of course, most fortuitous that the structural remains under the new International Marian Center happen to date *precisely to the time of greatest interest* to Christian tourists who would be streaming there! Had those remains reflected, say, the Bronze or Iron ages—or the Late Roman, Byzantine or subsequent eras—the excavation would constitute something of a distraction. Certainly, it would add nothing to the visitor's experience, whose primary interest is the story of Jesus. One can imagine embarrassing questions which might arise daily: "Why is the International Marian Center built over *Iron Age* remains?" Or: "Why has a *Mamluk-era* house been

---

9. See "Christian-Jewish collaboration" pp. 242 *f* below. A map of the expanded Venerated Area is in Plate 1.

10. *http://pt.mariedenazareth.com/4092.0.html?&L=6%255C%255C%255C%255C%25 5C%255C%25255* (in French). Accessed Oct. 22, 2014.

memorialized by this center devoted to the Virgin Mary? But such questions are not posed. The remains date—so goes the official line—precisely to the turn of the era.

To this fortuitous coincidence we can add the unprecedented nature of the discovery: a dwelling from the time of Jesus! Despite the passage of almost two millennia during which the existence of Early Roman Nazareth was never doubted, *no Jesus-era dwelling had ever been claimed there before.*[11]

To coincidence and uniqueness, we must finally acknowledge the markedly sloping terrain (where, incidentally, no evidence of terracing has been found) as well as the pitted nature of the ground. These make the claims of ancient dwellings in the vicinity most counterintuitive.

The Myth of Nazareth demonstrated that the valley floor was indeed settled in the Bronze and Iron Ages and then abandoned following the devastating Assyrian invasions of the late eight century BCE. The basin remained uninhabited until after the First Jewish Revolt. In a century of digging, no remains have been recovered attesting to human presence in Hellenistic and Herodian times. Considered in the larger context and from an archeological point of view, then, the "house from the time of Jesus" precisely on the site of the new Marian Center is—besides being amazingly fortuitous—a radical departure from the panoply of evidence examined in my first book. Furthermore, when we consider that the site of the imposing four-storey IMC was determined in 2002[12]—long before the "first house from the time of Jesus" was discovered precisely there—then this case, by any calculation, constitutes a most astonishing stroke of good fortune.

Ancient remains are, of course, all over the hillside, including under a number of Christian venues—the Church of the Annunciation, the Church of St. Joseph, and the Sisters of Nazareth Convent (*cf.* Plate 1). However, in all these cases the structural remains are clearly *agricultural* and *funereal*—according to one scholar (Taylor 1993) and confirmed by my research. Yet the tradition has—at every one of the aforementioned venues—obstinately interpreted the remains as those of an habitation: the house of Mary, the house of her husband Joseph, and (latterly with the work of Prof. Dark) a 'model courtyard house' under the Sisters of Nazareth Con-

---

11. *Pace* Alexandre and the global press. About this time Ken Dark was also claiming discovery of the 'first' Jesus-era house only 75m to the west, under the Sisters of Nazareth Convent (Chapter 6)—which now Dark suggests may have been the home of Jesus himself (Dark 2015). To my knowledge, Alexandre has not explicitly acknowledged Dark's work. In 2012, she merely notes (in the bibliography to her monograph on Mary's Well) a two-page resumé of his work (Dark 2010b). Otherwise, Alexandre, the IAA, and the Catholic Church seem remarkably uninterested in Dark's work.
12. See the timeline below, p. 191.

vent—perhaps even the house of Jesus. Thus, the alleged dwelling under the IMC—though the first to be signaled in the press—is at least the fourth house to be *claimed* in the Venerated Area. Surely, more than coincidence is operative here—at the sites in Nazareth owned and managed by the Roman Catholic Church, *dwellings from the time of Jesus are the rule.*

Given the known existence of ancient structures on all sides, the religious and tourism-oriented planners of the IMC would have been fairly confident of uncovering *some sort* of ancient remains while digging the extensive foundations for the IMC—foundations which, after all, extend over a full city block. Yet, even before the first trench was dug and the first pylon placed in 2007, the planners were subject to certain preconceptions. According to Roman Catholic tradition, Mary lived next door and Joseph a little further uphill. Thus, the IMC site was the likely location of a 'neighbor's house' dating to the turn of the era—whatever the nature of the actual remains. That much is preordained. When the "first signs of a dwelling" were found in the Summer-Fall of 2009 (above p. 182), this must have been immensely satisfying to the planners—even if they were projecting their own interpretation on the remains. From that time on, the new megacomplex was accompanied by a house 'from the time of Jesus'— indeed, it was the house of his neighbor! This notoriety would help ensure an enduring stream of visitors to the site and could also be announced to the world for maximum *éclat* at Christmas, 2009.

No professional report

Generally, the IAA issues professional reports on excavations in a timely manner, that is, within a couple of years. If the findings are minimal or of little interest, the report may be small and consist merely of one or two paragraphs in the pages of *Hadashot Arkheologiyot* ("Archeological News"), a scholarly periodical of the IAA. The planning and budget of larger and more important excavations may include a substantial 'final report' in *'Atiqot* ("Antiquities," also from the IAA) or—in special cases—an entire book-length treatment. The IMC excavation was substantial. Figs. 10.1 and 10.2 (pp. 193–94) reveal the structural remains uncovered in late 2009 while—as we will see—(unofficial) later digging further expanded the area to include four 'rooms,' a cistern, triple silo, movable finds, *etc.*[13]

The smallest IAA excavations may last only one or two days, but the IAA excavation exceeded three weeks during November–December 2009, demonstrating that it was indeed substantial. The foregoing discussion has

---

13.   See Fig. 10.3 (p. 197) for the features in late 2009, including the outline of an allegedly modest 'house.' Alexandre would outline an expanded dwelling in her plan from 2012 (Fig. 10.12, p. 219).

also revealed that this IAA excavation was both preceded by and followed by unofficial digging related to construction of the surrounding IMC. Persuant to all this digging, then—and given the lack of a (routine) professional report—legitimate and fundamental questions abound. Where are photographs, diagrams, evaluations and discussions of the various structural features? What is the precise nature of the pottery found under the IMC? What other movable objects (*e.g.* coins) were discovered?

In the preceding section we saw that the claims made for this excavation are exceptional, unprecedented, and counterintuitive. Exceptional claims require exceptional evidence, yet the public has received only vague statements in the popular press, while the scholarly world has received nothing. *The claims are monumental, the substantiation nonexistent.*

Alexandre has authored many professional reports over the years—with illustrations, itemizations, discussion, evaluation, and conclusions. The IMC excavation probably marks the highpoint of her career as far as her public persona is concerned. Thus, the lack of a report five years on is notable—whether or not one is planned.

Though the absence or unusual delay of a scholarly report is not typical of the IAA's procedures, it is not new for Alexandre whose career has gravitated toward more 'sensitive' sites in and around Nazareth. Her report on Mary's Well (Chapter 11) appeared only after an astonishing thirteen years. That report conflicts with another IAA statement on the Mary's Well excavation. Interestingly, similar delay and conflict with an IAA document also attend the IMC excavation (*cf.* next section).

Admittedly, these high-profile excavations are not typical. Both the International Marian Center and Mary's Well are venues of great significance to Christians, drawing vast numbers of pilgrims—second only to the Church of the Annunciation itself. An onsite excavator's report, with its authoritative public revelations and interpretations, potentially carries considerable religious and commercial ramifications. Such a report would understandably receive extra scrutiny, possibly engendering delay. It must also be acknowledged that powerful and potentially conflicting interests are involved. Three can be noted here: (1) the *scientific* interests of archeologists, historians, and scholars; (2) the *religious* interests of Christian denominations (primarily Catholic); and (3) the *commercial* interests of the Nazareth Municipality (and, more broadly, of the Israeli State). One can well imagine simple questions leading quickly to complex and involved discussions, questions such as: "Must we report this?" "What should the world be told?" And perhaps most ominously: "How do we stand to gain the most?"

The long delay in reports following significant Nazareth excavations—and in the IMC case the continuing lack of *any* scholarly report—suggests that some of the above considerations may indeed be in play. Certainly, if the facts of this excavation did *not* validate what powerful secular and religious interests (Israeli and Christian) wished to conclude, then there would be considerable incentive *not* to release an objective (and effectively hostile) scholarly report. One could appreciate the temptation—if not the pressure—to affirm findings only which validates a traditionalist view of the site and to ignore (or reinterpret) all else. After all, *a great deal of money is at stake*—as well as the integrity of the Christian tradition itself.

Broadly speaking, powerful commercial and religious interests have, over the past two decades, gradually merged to marginalize the scientific interests of archeologists, historians, and scholars not only in Nazareth but all over the land of Israel. The IMC excavation is not exceptional in this regard. Shoddy and delayed reporting has been widespread for a long time, particularly at venues of importance to Christianity and/or Judaism. In such cases, 'quack archeology' is common. The visitor experience of the believing Christian and the believing Jew has emerged as the primary consideration (*cf.* Perdue 2005), often entailing the sacrifice of objectivity.

The lack of rigorous publication is a two-edged sword. Though much-touted claims may in the short run serve conservative religious and baldly commercial interests, inevitably they fuel suspicion which ultimately undermines these powerful forces. Without a rigorous and documented scientific basis, unfounded and speculative traditionalist claims are ultimately unpersuasive. Not surprisingly, this has led to the overriding crisis seen in modern biblical archeology—it is often simply *unbelievable*.

So with the IMC excavation. At the time of this writing, the assertion of a 'house from the time of Jesus' is scientifically baseless. It will remain so until supporting evidence is not merely claimed but published in a professional manner.

The IMC excavation presents us with unending fodder for surprise. In the last section we mentioned some anomalies. To these we may add sensational claims made precisely at Christmas; the lack of a professional report; and (demonstrated below) the stunning divergence of the professed interpretation and the material remains.

These anomalies and coincidences are mutually reinforcing. Yet they are ultimately of a circumstantial nature. The skeptic may *suspect* that the IMC excavation is largely an exercise in commercial gain and in theological expedience, that the authorities have employed shoddy methodology and scanty reporting to promote non-scholarly motives... But one cannot be *sure* until and unless the evidence is actually examined.

This presents us with a *Catch-22*, for *where is the evidence?* Without a professional report, does reliable evidence even exist?

Thankfully, the answer is affirmative. Even without a final IMC excavation report, a number of resources are at hand. These have been carefully gathered in compiling this chapter. Such resources include many photographs taken before, during, and after the excavation, two drawn plans of site, multiple disclosures by the archeologist who directed the excavation, and two releases by the IAA itself. While it can be freely admitted that the ensuing consideration of the material remains under the IMC is based on limited materials, it must nevertheless also be acknowledged that those materials are substantial and revealing. *They inexorably lead to the astonishing conclusion that the 'official' interpretation of the site is unambiguously at variance with the physical remains.* By examining the data that are available, we can easily glean enough knowledge to invalidate the major claim made regarding this excavation. It was no 'house' dating to the turn of the era. The remains prove to be clearly agricultural in nature. They *certainly* do not go back to 'the time of Jesus.'

The short IAA report

Though "Communicated by the Israel Antiquities Authority"and disseminated by the Israel Ministry of Foreign Affairs, the article cited at the beginning of this chapter is of course not a professional report. It was not authored by Ms. Alexandre, the excavation director, nor does it pretend to itemize, evaluate, or even discuss individual finds. On the other hand, it states as fact axioms of Christian belief, noting that (according to the New Testament) Jesus lived in Nazareth, that Mary received the Annunciation not far away, and so on. The article also stresses the religious significance of the site. "The discovery is of the utmost importance," Alexandre states in the fourth paragraph, "since it reveals for the very first time a house from the Jewish village of Nazareth and thereby sheds light on the way of life at the time of Jesus." The trained archeologist (and the skeptical reader) may wonder how a few walls can signify a "village," much less a "Jewish" village. They will inevitably also be curious regarding how those remains shed light "on the way of life" precisely *at the time of Jesus.*

In the above-cited article Alexandre gives no satisfaction in these matters beyond affirming that the house is "typical" of the dwellings in Nazareth in that period. But this too invites wonder, for in the preceding sentence she stated that this was the *first* and *only* such structure dating to the turn of the era. By definition, then, that structure cannot be "typical" of anything!

The above-cited IAA article is similar to many which appeared during Christmas week of 2009 and were directed at the general public. These press releases, in numerous languages, carried much the same information and were all based on Alexandre's apparently carefully scripted press conference of December 21.

However—virtually unknown and hardly noticed—a second and much shorter statement by the IAA relative to the IMC excavation appeared briefly online. I read it on the very day of Alexandre's news conference, printed it out, and noted with surprise that it was no longer on the Web one month later. Its content is here cited in full:[14]

Public Information

Nazareth, Church of the Annunciation
Institute: Israel Antiquities Authority
Permit: A-5740
Excavation dates: 12/11/2009 - 7/12/2009
Excavators: Alexandre Yardenna

The excavation in the Church of the Annunciation was expanded to include two squares. Remains of a building from the Roman period were exposed in which there were two rock-cuttings in the bedrock: one a silo and the other, in the excavator's opinion, a refuge pit. There were also the remains of a large building there that dates to the Mamluk period, of which a vault and a number of walls were exposed.

The excavation has ended.

This short notice reports on a substantial excavation lasting twenty-five days ("12/11/2009–7/12/2009," *i.e.*, November 12 to December 7, 2009). It was published on the Web probably merely for protocol and reference purposes, offering the public and the scholarly world the permit number, official dates of the excavation, and scant description. The final sentence "The excavation has ended" shows that the above notice originated after December 7, 2009.

This notice describes an excavation "in" the Church of the Annunciation (CA)—a translation inexactitude where the words "next to" are elsewhere used (above, p. 179). The IMC location is in fact across the street, fifty meters distant from the CA. That the above pertains to the IMC site, however, is confirmed by the excavation's dates, permit number, mention of a "refuge pit" (above, p. 180, third paragraph) and of "a large building there that dates to the Mamluk period"—clearly an interpretation of the "large broad wall that dates to the Mamluk period" (*cf.* p. 180 above, second paragraph, and Fig. 10.2, feature [t]).

Despite its brevity, this short IAA report is the closest to a professional archeological assessment of the IMC excavation that we possess. We will be referring to it as the "short IAA report" (or simply "short report"), in contrast to the longer article cited at the beginning of this chapter which we will refer to as the "long IAA report" (or "long report").

---

14. An actual copy of the printout with URL and timestamp is reproduced in Plate 4.

Though both reports originated with the IAA, the short report is much more restrained in its claims. One immediately notes an astonishing difference: the short report makes absolutely no mention of first-century remains, much less of evidence from the turn of the era ('time of Jesus'), while the long IAA report emphasizes this chronological element—which, of course, sensationalized the IMC excavation and caused it to 'go global.' Here once again is the beginning of the long report:

> An archaeological excavation the Israel Antiquities Authority recently conducted has revealed new information about ancient Nazareth from the time of Jesus. Remains of a dwelling that date to the Early Roman period were discovered for the first time in an excavation, which was carried out prior to the construction of the "International Marian Center of Nazareth" by the the Association Mary of Nazareth, next to the Church of the Annunciation.

In contrast, the short IAA report is anything but sensational. Its earliest dating is to the "Roman period." This is entirely benign, for the Roman period lasted into the fourth century CE and we already have considerable evidence from the Nazareth basin dating to the second, third, and fourth centuries of our era (Salm 2008a: Appendices 4, 5 and 6).

In the short report we read of "remains of a large building there that dates to the Mamluk period." But in the longer report those remains were "constructed on top of and 'utilized' the walls of an ancient building" dating to the Early Roman period (p. 180 above, second paragraph). It is clear that the longer report has made (in fact untenable) claims that are unknown to—or ignored by—the short report.

A difference in treatment of the "refuge pit" is also evident. This feature will be considered separately (pp. 225 f).

Thus, we have two IAA reports subsequent to the principal IMC excavation season, both dating to December, 2009. Yet, both reports offer *very different* interpretations of the finds! The long report claims both structural and movable (pottery) evidence from the 'time of Jesus,' while the short report reflects mundane archeological discoveries from "Roman" times, consistent with neighboring sites (including tombs) on the hillside.

Whatever the explanation for the differences in reports (*cf.* also below p. 258), the short notice is a solitary IAA communication completely out of step with the rest of the documentation regarding the IMC excavation. It is also inconsistent with the media deluge during Christmas, 2009.

To the anomalies mentioned in the previous section regarding the IMC excavation we must now add a fourth: *two* views concerning the material remains—one sensational and one benign—and *both* originating from the Israel Antiquities Authority.

In this chapter we will see that the short report is correct. Nothing in the IMC excavation merits sensational treatment at all. Careful examination of the extant evidence reveals the straightforward remains of agricultural installations dating well *after* the turn of the era.

The timeline

The IMC was carefully planned for many years. Its conception dates back to 1998, and purchase of the site (in three parcels) began in 2002, as the following timeline reveals.

Timeline of the International Marian Center (IMC)

1901: Creation of the Catholic *Association Marie de Nazareth.*

Oct. 1, 1998: Meeting between Edmond Fricoteaux, Olivier Bonnassies, Pierre Saurat, and the mayor of Nazareth regarding the creation of a "museum" in Nazareth dedicated to the Virgin Mary. *Notre Dame de France* finances the project and begins collecting donations.

Summer, 2000: Bonnassies visits all Christian denominations represented by at least one church in Jerusalem, with the purpose of gaining their support for the construction of a new *ecumenical* center in Nazareth dedicated to the Virgin Mary.

August–September, 2000: The bishops of Lourdes, Nazareth, and Lorette (Monseigneurs Perrier, Marcuzzo, and Comastri) commission Bonnassies to create a new organization to direct the *Marie de Nazareth* project.

May 18, 2001: Registration of the statutes of the organization and its legal creation, then called the "Association of Friends of the Museum Mary of Nazareth" (*Association des Amis du Musée Marie de Nazareth*).

March 19, 2002: Signing with the *Sisters of St. Joseph of the Apparition* to lease buildings once used for a school less than 100m from the Church of the Annunciation in Nazareth.

October 25, 2002: Purchase of the first building in Nazareth from the Sisters. (Purchase of the two remaining neighboring buildings followed in December 2003 and May 2006.)

April 2002: Founding of the periodical *Ave Maria* to publicize the Nazareth Center.

2003–2004: Concerts, films, and events in Europe to publicize the Nazareth Center.

2005: The *Communauté du Chemin Neuf*, a Catholic organization, takes over the Nazareth Center.

March 25, 2007: Official placing of the cornerstone for the *Centre International Marie de Nazareth* (IMC). Construction of the Center begins.

June 19, 2007: Creation of the *Fondation Marie de Nazareth*, which will henceforth run the Center.

October, 2009: Discovery of archeological remains at the planned entrance of the Nazareth Center (on its south side).

Nov. 12–Dec. 7, 2009: IAA excavation under the direction of Yardenna Alexandre.

Dec. 21, 2009: News conference by Alexandre, with presence of global media, announcing discovery for the first time in Nazareth of a "house from the time of Jesus," followed by appearance of numerous articles in the global press.

Dec. 2009–Jan. 2010: Short IAA report briefly online. (See p. 189.)

March 25, 2011: Grand inauguration of the IMC and dedication of the "Chapel of Adoration" (*Chapelle de l'Adoration*), with presence of the mayor of Nazareth, Catholic prelates, representatives of the Israeli government, and members of the press.

Jan. 1, 2012: Official opening of the IMC to the public.

THE MATERIAL EVIDENCE

On December 21, 2009, the sizable contingent of reporters present at Yardenna Alexandre's news conference toured the IMC site, pens, cameras, microphones, and video equipment in hand. The many articles, photographs, and film clips that resulted provide an important, even 'saturated,' record of the visual state of the excavation on that day.

Many more photographs would be taken in subsequent days, months, and years. The most important, however, turned out to be a few which predated the December 21 news conference. These precious witnesses to the actual state of the discoveries *as found* were recorded during the excavation and in its immediate aftermath. Hence, one of my first tasks in analyz-

Figure 10.1. Photo of the IMC excavation in early December, 2009.

For diagram and key, see following pages.
(Photo Assaf Peretz. Courtesy of the Israel Antiquities Authority.)

ing the evidence from the IMC site was to place all the visual media (and reports) in chronological sequence. Remarkably, it soon became clear that the site 'evolved' over time. Some features as later claimed did not exist in the earliest photos (particularly some walls of the alleged 'house'). Other features in the excavation photos seem to have been considerably altered over time. In other words, *the final presentation of the site to visitors after the opening of the IMC in January of 2012 does not match the state of the excavated remains in December of 2009.*

According to the short IAA report (above), the excavation terminated on Dec. 7—two weeks before the lion's share of media recorded the state of

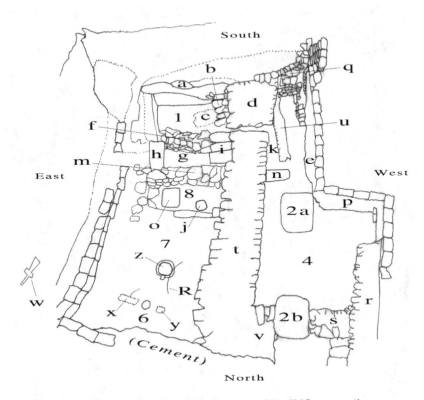

Figure 10.2. Comprehensive diagram of the IMC excavation in early December, 2009 (based on Fig. 10.1).

Key to Figure 10.2:

Areas

Area 1	Plastered wine collecting vat.
Area 2a	South treading floor segment.
Area 2b	North treading floor segment.
Area 4	Grape treading area.
Area/Locus 6	Socket possibly supporting the platform under the frails.
Area 7	Southern part of "courtyard."
Area 8	Depression with wine cellar (j).

Key to Figure 10.2 (cont.):

Loci

a. Edge of possible second wine collecting vat.

b. Steps inside wine collecting vat.

c. Sump in floor of vat.

d. Southern portion of central partition.

e. Excavation limit (wall) in Dec. 2009.

f. Northern border of wine collecting vat,
    or Mamluk addition.

g. Area for workman stopping jars.

h. Eastern shelf for working materials.

i. Western shelf for caps/sealants.

j. Mouth of small wine cellar.

k. Channel for grape juice.

m. Partition between wine vat and cellar area.

n. Extension of (m) marking southern extremity
    of grape treading Area 4

o. Standing area for worker.

p. Western excavation limit in Dec. 2009.

q. Southern partition.

r. Northwestern partition.

s. Northern partition.

t. Thick north-south partition (Mamluk).

u. Partition of channel for grape juice.

v. Northern extremity of partition (t).

w. Niche in vertical rock face (not in Fig. 10.1).

x. Possible locus of screw press.

y. Concave depression in rising bedrock.

z. Mouth of large wine cellar.

R. Overhanging ridge in the bedrock.

the excavation on winter solstice day. It became clear that, in those fourteen days, initial changes had been effected to the site in order to 'prepare' it for the global press. Thankfully, two important photographs were taken prior to Dec. 7, 2009. One depicts the entire site at the end of the excavation. It is presented in Fig. 10.1 above and shows the major structural features as they appeared during the first week of December, 2009.[15]

Fig. 10.2 is a master diagram based on that photograph. An extensive key accompanies the diagram and it will be referred to often in the (sometimes detailed) discussion which follows. The reader is urged to consult Figs. 10.1 and 10.2 as necessary. Labels of the various areas (numbers) and loci (letters) are maintained in subsequent figures and are consistent throughout this chapter.

Figs. 10.1 and 10.2 reveal a number of important divergences from the visual media, descriptions, and plan already recorded on December 21, 2009. Evidently, *artificial* changes had been effected to the excavation site in the two weeks prior to the winter solstice news conference. We will look at those and other changes below, but a theoretical point must first be acknowledged: where an alteration in some feature becomes evident through inspection of photographs, diagrams, plans, *etc.*—the *earlier* witness takes precedence, for it is closer to the original state of the remains.

The grand inauguration of the IMC (though not the opening of the excavation for public visitation) took place in March, 2011, at which time more photographs were taken. By comparing this evidence with that from sixteen months earlier, a second stage in alterations to the excavation site becomes evident.

The remains of the "house from the time of Jesus" were finally opened to public viewing on New Year's Day, 2012. After that time visitors have been able to take unlimited photographs of the excavation site from the viewing platforms (boardwalks) contructed a few feet above the ground. Thus, a photographic record of the site exists at various stages—excavation, news conference, inauguration, and public opening. It is often possible to determine, from internal evidence alone, at which stage a photograph of the excavation was taken.

The 2009 "house" plan. Two plans of the excavation exist, one drawn in December 2009 and the other in early 2012 (at the opening of the IMC to visitors). Surprisingly, the plans are very different. The earlier one was

---

15. At the time of this writing (Feb. 2015), the photo in question is online at *http://www.blog.standforisrael.org/articles/photos-and-details-about-nazareth-find-house-sheds-light-on-life-in-jesus-era#ixzz36thwW3eA*; see also *http://www.mfa.gov.il/mfa/israelexperience/history/pages/residential_building_time_jesus_nazareth_21-dec-2009.aspx#*.

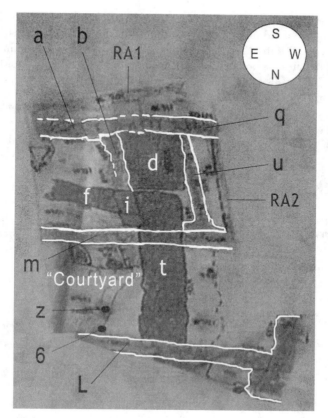

Figure 10.3. The plan of the alleged 'house from the time of Jesus,'
based on the plan shown to reporters Dec. 21, 2009 and published online.

White lines have been added to outline 'house walls' as conceived by Alexandre.
The plan has been rotated to conform to Figs. 10.1 & 10.2,
rendered B&W, and redrawn by the author.
Key: All labels conform to Fig. 10.2.
f - i - d - t = Mamluk features. RA 1 and RA2 = alleged 'Roman Additions.'

photographed on Dec. 21, 2009, after the news conference.[16] It is reproduced in Figure 10.3. On it, Alexandre used three colors to designate her
proposed eras of construction: (1) alleged walls of the "Late Hellenistic to
Early Roman" dwelling (originally yellow—outlined in white in Fig. 10.3);
(2) "Early-Middle Roman additions" (orange—RA1 and RA2); and (3) features (f, i, d, t—originally purple) from the Mamluk era (1250–1517 CE).

16. At the time of this writing, the 2009 plan can be seen in an online video at URL
https://www.youtube.com/watch?v=ITxd_qebujY#t=38, beginning 0' 37".

First of all, it can be noted that the dominating feature in the entire excavation is a broad north-south partition (t-d) with an extension (f-i) to the east. It is no less than 1.5 meters thick. Of course, such a feature immediately eliminates the possibility that we are dealing with a 'house,' for houses did not have walls 1.5 m thick! Recognizing this, Alexandre interprets the wide partition as a Mamluk addition and conveniently (and arbitrarily) supposes that an *earlier*, thinner wall once existed below and within it. However, *this supposition will prove entirely unfounded* (see pp. 202, 219).

The later "Roman Additions" (RA1) and (RA2) are located on the periphery of the site to the south and west. Remarkably, in Alexandre's later 2012 plan these two features have disappeared (*cf.* Fig. 10.11, p. 217). She was no doubt forced to change her mind regarding them pursuant to subsequent (undocumented) digging which photos and plans reveal took place *after* the Dec. 21, 2009 news conference (and thus well *after* the Dec. 7, 2009 official termination of the excavation, according to the short IAA report above). This extra-official digging was associated with construction of the immediately adjacent IMC. Quite unexpectedly, that construction exposed a very interesting *new* area on the southwest of the excavation site ("Room 3" in Fig. 10.11). It includes the discovery of a triple silo—a feature which, *nota bene*, is agricultural and of an emphatically communal nature. It has no obvious role in a "modest" dwelling. In any case, *after 2009 we do not hear anything more of (RA1) and (RA2) which, it seems, were simply 'best guesses' later superceded by the revelation of other finds.*

The proposed "Late Hellenistic to Early Roman" dwelling includes all the remaining letters in Fig. 10.3. The main part of the small 'house' is bounded by parallel 'walls' (a-q) and (m) running east-west. Its north-south 'walls' are (b) and (u). In Alexandre's conception these define one or possibly two small 'rooms.'

One soon notes that 'wall' (b) does not exist for half of its length. Inspection of Fig. 10.1 shows that this feature is actually no more than a series of four steps. In the discussion that follows we interpret it as a typical feature in a wine collecting vat—a type of installation that often possessed steps in one corner.

Thus, we gradually realize that the physical remains at the IMC site poorly reflect the 'house' Alexandre and the tradition propose—the presence of a triple silo, an *unattested* long wall 'under' a patent feature (t), steps curiously interpreted as another wall... Yet we are only beginning our analysis, and bigger surprises are in store!

The nonexistent 'wall' (L). On her 2009 plan, Alexandre notes a long east-west 'wall' at the northern extremity of the site (*cf.* Fig. 10.3). *Astonishingly, no sign of such a wall exists in the physical remains*—as an examination of the

Figure 10.4. The northern portion of the IMC excavation (from Fig. 10.1).

The 'wall' (L) noted on Alexandre's 2009 plan (Fig. 10.3) would be between the thick white lines. However, no such structure exists in the physical remains.

(Redrawn from photo by Assaf Peretz. Courtesy of the Israel Antiquities Authority.)

photograph in Fig. 1 shows. Above is a segment of that photograph, with white lines added to indicate where Alexandre has designated 'wall' (L) on her 2009 plan.[17] One notes the eastern half of the 'wall' (the left side of Fig. 10.4)—no structure at all is visible in this area, only bedrock around the man-made cavities (6) and (z).

It is a matter of the gravest concern when an archeologist (repeatedly) indicates the existence of a structural feature which simply does not exist in the physical remains. *This is pure invention.* I invite the reader to recheck Fig. 10.1. (At the time of this writing, the photograph is also online on numerous webpages.[18]) All this is disturbing enough, but additional ramifications relate to the fact that Alexandre is employed by the Israel Antiquities Authority. She is not merely a privately-hired expert offering an 'opinion.' She is the *only* professional granted a permit to excavate the premises, and her activity is an expression of the Israeli State. The non-existence of a substantial feature like (L) raises serious questions regarding trustworthiness and, unfortunately, places not only *all* that Alexandre writes under a cloud, but inevitably also casts suspicion upon her employer—the IAA.

But *why?* For what reason might an archeologist invent, as is now obvious, an entire ancient wall where none exists in the evidence? Feature (L) is not even part of the proposed "small and modest" dwelling. It is several meters south of the alleged house. Then why is this mythical wall (L) indicated at all on Alexandre's 2009 (and 2012) plan?

---

17. *Cf.* also Figs. 10.11 and 10.12, pp. 217 and 219 below. These show that the hypothetical wall (L) is a persistent feature.

18. *E.g.*, *http://www.welcometohosanna.com/LIFE_OF_JESUS/012_NazarethHiddenYears. htm*, and *http://www.dailymail.co.uk/news/article-1237532/Uncovered-days-Christmas-Remains-home-Nazareth-Jesus-known.html.*

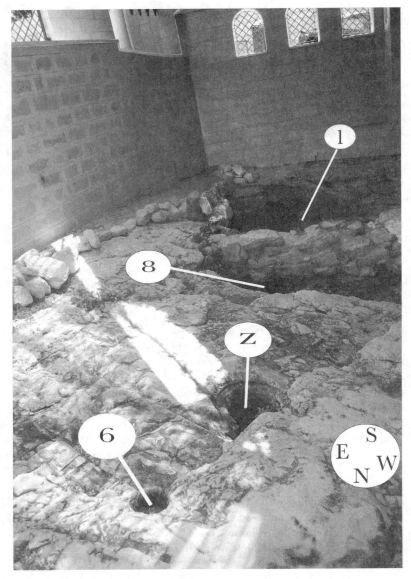

Figure 10.5. The eastern half of the IMC excavation viewed from the north.

The photo was taken in 2011. For key see pages 194–95.
(Photograph courtesy of E. Oserov and used with permission.)

Figure 10.6. The eastern half of the IMC excavation viewed from the SW.

On the modern wall in the background, each black line (artificially added) marks a new course of ashlar blocks—betraying the dramatic slope of the site from north to south. (L) is the location of the nonexistent 'wall' claimed by Alexandre (see text). The stones around the periphery help disguise a considerable amount of modern cement. Area 1 is a plastered basin cut into the bedrock (much altered over time), which this book argues was initially used as a wine collecting vat. Part of the mouth of cavity (j) is barely visible at bottom left (*cf.* Fig. 10.2).

(2014 photograph taken by E. Oserov and used with permission.)

An answer can be attempted. We have already noted a conflict in press reports regarding the size of the alleged Roman house. The long IAA report at the beginning of this chapter characterized the dwelling as "small and modest." But Alexandre also stated that "it may have been for an extended family and could be much larger" (p. 181, above). So, already in December of 2009 there was uncertainty regarding the size of the dwelling. We are left to wonder if this uncertainty could be related to the depiction of wall (L) on Alexandre's plans—a feature implying a *larger* 'house.' In any case, however, the unresolved question of *house* size is a moot point, for we will see that the structural features at the IMC site are not even domestic—they are *agricultural* in nature.

The question still remains: *Why?* What is the reason that the IAA might wish to propose the discovery of a *large* house to the public? One can only speculate in this regard, but it is not altogether out of the question that the enormous pressure to produce a *substantial* settlement of Nazareth at the turn of the era is gaining ground over the more traditional view that the settlement was too small to be noticed in antiquity. In this connection, we note the IMC 'house' is one of *several* now claimed by the tradition (*e.g.* by Dark—see Chapter 6). Following the implications of the gospel story, claims of at least four dwellings are currently being made in the Venerated Area: the houses of St. Joseph, of Mary, under the Sisters of Nazareth Convent, and under the IMC. Some conservative scholars also claim that a "bathhouse from the time of Jesus" existed near Mary's Well—though this has been thoroughly discredited.[19]

It is, therefore, undeniable that conflicting views presently exist regarding Nazareth, with astonishing consequences—*leading even to claims of evidence which does not exist.* It may be that the nonexistent 'wall' L is such a consequence.

We will see that wall L is also drawn on a later plan of the excavation (Fig. 10.11, p. 217), showing that in 2012 it had indeed evolved conceptually to become an integral part of a now-proposed larger "house." To anticipate for a moment, this alleged larger dwelling would require yet another major unverified structure—a long north-south "Early Roman" wall which Alexandre *presumes* exists entirely embedded within and under the broad Mamluk partition (t). *Yet no evidence exists for this thin wall either.*

Finally, we will see that the alleged *larger* dwelling incorporates Area 4 as its largest "room." However, we will also learn that *Area 4 was nothing other than the grape treading floor of a fairly typical wine-making installation.*

Other house "walls." Serious problems attend Alexandre's basic conception of a dwelling—even a small one in the southern half of the IMC site. One outstanding difficulty is that none of the alleged walls exceeds three to four feet in height. This obvious fact—immediately evident at first sight—would seem to categorically disqualify the IMC excavation as the venue of any ancient habitation. It could, perhaps, be argued that *all* the walls were once higher and that many of their stones were long ago pilfered for other constructions. Such was a frequent occurrence. However, if pilfering took place at the IMC site, one would expect a haphazard presentation of these walls (whether Mamluk, Byzantine, or Roman). There would be gaps and a jagged appearance, and in at least in a few places the walls would reach to their original height.

However, a glance at the photograph in Fig. 10.1 shows that the walls are uniform in height (rising to approximately one meter from the surface) and that they are remarkably level on top. These structures are clearly not the haphazard remainder after pilfering. Even the lower partition (u) slants evenly downwards, showing that it was designed as found.

---

19. Above pp. 166 *f*, and pp. 261 *f* below.

The walls of a dwelling would have attained a height of about eight feet—at least double what we encounter in the IMC excavation. Partition (m) is especially instructive in this regard (*cf.* Figs. 10.1 and 10.2). It is a precarious construction of large unworked field stones lacking any means of stabilization (*e.g.* interstitial mud filling). Such a construction could not have been much higher than its present height without falling of its own weight. Yet Alexandre considered this feature to be an outer wall of the 'house' (Fig. 10.3)—presumably strong enough to support a roof and *even a second storey* (see Fig. 10.13 below and discussion). Neither its height nor method of construction, however, support these far-fetched theories.

As for 'wall' (a), it follows the uneven bedrock and was supplemented by stones in its western portion, near steps (b). The feature was formed by digging *out* the Area 1 basin, of which it clearly constitutes the southern side. (a) rises to a height of three feet above the *sunken* floor of Area 1 and *does not rise above ground level.* How this bedrock feature could be construed as the southern "wall" of a house (plan Fig. 10.3) is a complete mystery.[20]

In fact, all of the features on the eastern side of the IMC excavation are *below* ground level. This may not be obvious to the casual observer, for partitions (m) and (f) indeed rise several feet in height. Their base, however, is not ground level but is *bedrock* (Fig. 10.1). The features associated with Areas 1 and 8 rise only *to* ground level, that is, to the level of Areas 6 and 7 immediately to the north.

Only in the western half of the excavated area do the partitions rise above ground level. This includes the broad Mamluk partition (d)-(t)-(v), as well as (u), (r), (p), and (s). These latter features also rest on bedrock, but the bedrock has obviously risen dramatically from east to west. This slope, in fact, allowed the ancient inhabitants to locate a wine producing installation at the site of the IMC excavation (as we will see), for the grape juice which was treaded in Area 4 flowed downslope into Area 1—that is, from west to east and from north to south (Plate 2).

A Dec. 2009 article[21] relates: "Alexandre's team found remains of a

---

20. Feature (b) itself is not the remains of a 'wall' after pilfering but simply a short series of four steps (p. 198 above). Nor can it be argued that the walls were once higher by virtue of originally extending deeper into the ground, for the IMC walling clearly rests on bedrock throughout.

21. Diaa Hadid, "First Jesus-era house found in Nazareth." Associated Press Dec. 22, 2009. Online at *http://www.nbcnews.com/id/34511072/ns/technology_and_science-science/t/first-jesus-era-house-found-nazareth/#.VM_N-8ZRcos* (accessed Feb. 2, 2015). It can be mentioned that only a solid roof would have produced runoff water. The simplest roofs in antiquity solid enough to produce runoff were "wooden beams woven with smaller branches and then covered with a thick layer of plaster" (Fiensy and Strange: 229; *cf.* p. 223 below). It is questionable whether the crude fieldstone walling evident

wall, a hideout, a courtyard and a water system that appeared to collect water from the roof and supply it to the home." But the low height of the walls, of course, makes the existence of a roof impossible—unless we are speaking of a dwelling for midgets!

The "water system" that collected "water from the roof" would have to refer to cavity (j)—interpreted as a cistern—for that is the only cavity in proximity to the alleged dwelling. We, however, will propose a very different use for this cavity.[22]

Another astonishing problem regarding the proposed reconstruction of the 'house' is that the various walls do not match. The reader is invited to examine Fig. 1 and compare walls (u), (q), and (m). Each clearly varies in material used and technique of construction. It would be a strange house indeed where each wall was differently constructed! Yet Alexandre considers these three walls to belong to one and the same "Late Hellenistic to Early Roman" habitation (Fig. 10.3). This is a most unflattering example of archeological creativity.

Finally, not all the claimed walls—as drawn on Alexandre's plan—are even extant in the documented remains (compare Figs. 10.1 and 10.3). We have already noted the problems with feature (L) and that the archeologist interprets (b) as a 'wall,' though it is merely a short flight of four steps *below* ground level.[23] The 2009 plan also misrepresents the length of this 'wall,' for the feature does not reach as far as (i), much less to (m) as depicted.

Also misrepresented on the 2009 plan is the short partition (u). Contrary to Alexandre's design on Fig. 10.3, it does not reach as far as wall (m). The physical remains show that it slants evenly downwards from a high point at (d). This was certainly never a domestic wall. In contrast, we will see that the feature was expertly designed to guide fluid from Area 4 downslope into Area 1 via channel (k). We will consider this portion of the wine-making installation below (p. 209).

To review, each of the "walls" conceived by Alexandre as part of a dwelling presents unique problems when attempting to interpret it in a domestic context: feature (a) is rock-cut, (b) is a short flight of steps, (u) slants evenly downwards, and (m) is a rather poor construction of large

---

at the IMC site would have supported such a roof (particularly the poorly-constructed [m]—an outer wall)—even were the walls high enough.

22. The 2009 plan of the IMC excavation (underlying Fig. 10.3) identifies the "cistern" at some remove from the dwelling, namely, at the large cavity (z) (see *https://www.youtube.com/watch?v=lTxd_qebujY#t=38*, beginning 0' 37"). Cavity (z) could not have received rainwater from the 'house' for it is *uphill* from Area 1. There is similarly some confusion in the various reports as to which of the cavities functioned as the 'refuge pit.' See below pp. 226 *f.*

23. Such steps were often found in wine collecting vats (below p. 207).

Figure 10.7. Another view of the eastern half of the IMC excavation, from the south.

Note the astonishing E-W slope of the "courtyard" where the two gentlemen are standing. The nonexistent 'wall' (L) *should* be between feature (6) and the "Modern cement" in the background. The photo was taken in late 2011 before the opening of the IMC to visitors. (Public domain.)

field stones. In addition, the walls do not match and are too low to have functioned as the walls of an habitation (or to have supported a roof), while other walls do not exist at all. In sum, it appears that Alexandre, in various and creative ways, has contrived to produce a dwelling (whether small or large) where none *remotely* exists in the material remains.[24]

Changes made to the site. In the figures accompanying this chapter one frequently encounters the words "Modern cement." Some was added to the nothern and southern borders (Figs. 10.1, 10.4, 10.6), and also on the east (Figs. 10.6, 10.7) where it appears to be a composite mixture approximating the color of the excavation bedrock. Thus, we use the word "cement" in this chapter in a generic, nontechnical sense. The purpose of all this cement is not entirely clear, but it was probably ancillary to construction of the modern ashlar walls, pylons, *etc.*, which now surround the excavation

---

24. Because the 'walls' do not attain the height required for a dwelling, we will oftern refer to them as *partitions* in the remainder of this chapter.

area. In any case, considerable effort has gone into disguising the cement, particularly through the placement of numerous stones, as seen in the various figures.

In Figure 10.1—the earliest comprehensive image we possess of the excavation—the first signs of added cement are already visible at the bottom of the photograph (enlarged in Fig. 10.4), which dates to early December, 2009. Comparison with Fig. 10.7, taken two years later, shows that the cement in the area to the west of the pylon had by then been greatly augmented, to produce an artificially horizontal surface contrasting with the remarkably sloping bedrock of the "courtyard" (where the two gentlemen are standing).

On the eastern side of the excavation up to one foot of cement was also added. This cement is visible in Fig. 10.7 but not in Fig. 10.1, showing that it, too, is a post-2009 addition. Presumably, it's purpose was to furnish an even (though sloping) foundation for the present ashlar wall to the east. On the southern side of the excavation, a thinner layer of cement was also added (Fig. 10.6—*cp.* Fig. 10.1).

All this cement, of course, gives a misleading impression of the site. It suggests flat or even surfaces where none existed in antiquity. It also falsely delineates the site, which in all likelihood extended to include *neighboring agricultural installations* that have not been excavated.

Changes have also taken place within the excavated area itself. Cement was added to Area 4, producing a flat surface for posts supporting the modern boardwalk (Plate 2). A more egregious change is evident in partition (m). This looks very different in Figs. 10.1 and 10.7—the underlying photographs being two years apart. In the preceding section we discussed partition (m) as "a precarious construction of large unworked field stones lacking any means of stabilization" (p. 203 above). That description corresponds to its original excavated form. In the figure on page 205 (from 2011), however, the partition is irregular, and *it appears that smaller stones have been substituted for the larger ones present in 2009.*

In these and other ways, it is clear that the IMC excavation site has been much reworked, so that the modern visitor cannot be at all confident he or she is viewing the ancient remains as they were actually found in the original excavation.

The slope. Figure 10.6 (above p. 201) is a photograph taken from one of the boardwalks after the IMC was opened to visitors on Jan. 1, 2012. It portrays the eastern half of the IMC excavation, and the modern wall in the background graphically reveals the lay of the land through its parallel courses of ashlar blocks. If one follows the base of that wall from north to south, one notes the emergence of no less than three courses over a distance of about ten meters. Since each course is roughly a foot high, it becomes clear that *the northern end of the IMC excavation is a full meter higher than its southern end!*

This steep N–S slope would alone appear to invalidate the proposition that a house of any "larger" dimensions (extending from [L] to [a] and including the "courtyard") once existed at the site. Such a house would have at least required stairs in the vicinity of partition (m)—none of which have been noted.

The alleged "courtyard" (Areas 6–7) is also astonishingly slanted from west to east, as Fig. 10.7 makes abundantly clear. On the other hand, the western half of the excavation area has only a mild incline from north to south and from west to east. This incline (from [2b] to [q] in Fig. 10.2) would have ensured that the juice of grapes treaded in Area 4 would have flowed easily through the channel (k) downslope into Area 1 (*cf.* discussion below and Plate 2).

The winemaking installation

Area 1: a wine collecting vat. The squarish structure taking up the southeast quadrant of the excavation is a large, sunken, rock-cut basin with sides three to four feet high (Area 1 in Fig. 10.2). In one corner of the basin are steps (b), next to which is a fairly shallow depression in the floor several inches deep (c). Unlike the rest of the site, photographs show that the floor of the basin and its walls are smooth. At one time they were thickly plastered, though some of the walling and plaster have disappeared over time. This rock-cut basin is located at the lowest point in the excavation area. Being plastered, it has all the earmarks of once having served to collect some sort of fluid. Channel (k) cuts through the thick partition (t) and links Areas 1 and 4. The physical layout of these contiguous installations strongly suggests that the upslope Area 4 once fed the rock-cut basin in Area 1 with fluid through the channel (k).

Though Area 1 is the heart of Alexandre's alleged 'house' (see Fig. 10.13, p. 223), it possesses all the characteristics of a typical wine collecting vat, one carved into the bedrock and lined with plaster:

> Harvesting was done by cutting clusters of grapes from the vine with pruning knives. Then the grapes were placed in baskets and carried to the winepress, ordinarily situated within the vineyard but sometimes in the city. Winepresses were hewn from bedrock to form a flat surface for treading. They consisted of a pair of square or circular vats (called *gat* and *yeqeb* in Hebrew) arranged at different levels and connected by a

channel. The grapes were treaded by bare feet in the treading platform (*gat*), which was higher and larger than the deeper *yeqeb*, the receptacle into which the new wine flowed from the press... After the grapes were treaded, the expressed juice ran into vats carved in the bedrock or constructed and lined with plaster. The juice collected in these vats was then set in a cool place for fermentation.   (King and Stager 2001:100–01.)

Area 1 is rock-cut, its sides and floor are heavily plastered, and it is connected by channel (k) to the upslope Area 4. All these are signs that we are dealing not with a house whose floor (for no obvious reason) was sunken and plastered, but with a wine collecting vat (*yeqeb*) which received grape juice via channel (k) from the grape treading floor (*gat*, Area 4). Alternative interpretations simply do not match the physical evidence—the rock-cut sides of Area 1 are not deep enough for a *miqve*, nor by any means high enough to have functioned as the 'walls' of a dwelling.

While the winemakers in antiquity attempted to hew as many sides of the *yeqeb* from the rock as the physical characteristics of the venue allowed, these were supplemented as necessary by sides made of earth and/or field stones. The entire installation was then plastered (often several times) to ensure watertightness and impermeability.[25] Rock-cut features required plastering, for no natural surface will retain liquid for long (Pritchard 1962:83). Unless mosaic was used, it was necessary to periodically reapply plaster—whether the feature was originally hewn out of the rock or constructed with field stones and then plastered.

The steps (b) in Area 1 further suggest that we are dealing with a wine installation, for such steps were often hewn in a corner of the collecting vat to aid workers entering and exiting while carrying large and heavy jars full of grape juice.[26] The transfer of juice from the collecting vat into the jars had to be accomplished expeditiously:

> After the juice of the grapes is expressed, natural fermentation begins immediately "by means of wild yeasts" which live on the skins of the grapes (Lukas 1934:14). In order to derive a wine of good quality, the juice had to be transferred for fermentation into wineskins or large jars, since juice remaining in the vat (*yekeb*) longer than six hours could develop too much yeast.[27]

---

25. On the plastering of wine collecting vats, see also Ayalon *et al.*: 35, 139; Walsh 157.

26. Ahlström 38 describes five wine vats with steps. At Hirbet Castra in Western Galilee, a dozen wine vats dating to Byzantine times *all* had steps in one corner. See Ayalon *et al.* 105, photograph p. 109, also pp. 24, 139. It is probable that the IMC wine installation dates to Later Roman, Byzantine, and subsequent eras.

27. Ahlström 41. The internal citation is to A. Lukas, *Ancient Egyptian Materials and Industries*, 2nd. Ed. London: Arnold, p. 14.

A small depression was often also found at the bottom of the collecting vat/*yeqeb*, as is the case with feature (c) in Area 1. This slight depression served as a settling area or sump to separate any remaining solid matter from the grape juice, thus functioning as a final stage of filtration.[28] Prior filtration had already taken place on the treading floor (Area 4) and in the channel (k)—the latter with a sharp bend (usually augmented by thorny twigs to catch solids and impurities—see next section).

The above features, taken together, convincingly show that the western and southern parts of the IMC excavation site were once dedicated to the production of wine. Indeed, the winemaking installation may have been larger. Often a single vat served two treading floors, or alternatively one treading floor could lead to more than a single collecting vat. Because of the limited area of the excavation, however, we cannot know if immediately adjacent (to the south or east) once existed ancillary winemaking installations. Today, a busy road abuts the south of the excavation area, while a residential building unrelated to the IMC is immediately to the east.

A nearby winemaking installation certainly existed under the Church of the Annunciation, less than 75m to the south.[29] The Sisters of Nazareth Convent (Chapter 6) is an equal distance to the west and sits atop a silo, cisterns, and filtration basins. *It is beyond doubt that this entire region of the Nebi Sa'in hillside was devoted to agricultural activities in antiquity.*

This has been known for a long time. Referring to the western hillside of Nazareth in Roman times, Bagatti wrote that during the time of Jesus the village (that is, the Venerated Area in his conception) was "an agricultural settlement with numerous winepresses, olive presses, caves for storing grain, and cisterns for water and wine" (Bagatti 1969:25).

Channel (k). This revealing feature slices through the wide partition (t), connecting the uphill Area 4 with the downslope Area 1. We have interpreted both those areas as a grape treading floor and wine collecting vat respectively. For the winemaking installation to function, a connecting channel would be necessary, enabling the flow of liquid downslope from one area to the other.

In antiquity, the channel between the treading floor and the collecting basin was often filled with thorny branches. This allowed the grape juice to pass into the vat, yet it impeded the movement of grape skins and other solid (and semi-solid) matter. The channel would be regularly cleaned and the thorny branches replaced as necessary.

A glance at Figs. 10.1 and 10.2 shows that channel (k) is shaped like an "L," with a hard, almost 90-degree bend. This design feature augmented

28. Ayalon *et al.* 45, 46, 139.
29. Salm 2008a:237.

the function of the thorny branches by enhancing the trapping mechanism. At the point of the bend fewer branches were necessary. The channel could also be easily cleaned by a person simply reaching over the partition (u) which slopes downwards—another clever and no doubt calculated design feature—for the worker could reach every part of the channel (especially the bend in the "L") from the other side of the partition.

This telling channel confirms that, together with Areas 1 and 4, a major part of the IMC excavation site was dedicated to the production of wine in antiquity.

Area 4: a grape treading floor. Treading the grapes is an ancient and efficient way of removing most of the juice while leaving the skins and the core of the grape (the *rape*) for secondary mechanical pressing and for the production of inferior wine. It was necessary that the treading floor be upslope from the wine vat, and the treading floor itself generally possessed a modest slope so that grape juice once expressed would naturally flow in the direction of the connecting channel (Plate 2). During the Fall winemaking season, the grapes were usually treaded by several people, thus the treading floor could be quite large. The one represented by Area 4 is average in size, but it must be noted that the treading area may well have originally extended beyond the limits of the excavation to the west, which is bounded in Fig. 10.2 by features (r) and (p). It is eminently possible that a second treading floor—perhaps contiguous with Area 4—served another wine collecting vat located south and west of the excavation area.

Plate 2, in the central section of this book, is a photograph of Area 4 taken after the opening of the IMC in 2012. It is important to discriminate a number of different surfaces there which are not at all evident to the casual visitor to the excavation. As is evident in the photograph, most of the area of the treading floor was excavated down to the hard bedrock— *a decision which effectively destroyed most of the flat treading floor.*

Above the hard rock layer (known as *nari*) is a softer layer which originally composed the treading floor. Alexandre wisely conserved two flat 'islands' of the soft layer (labeled [2a] and [2b] in Fig. 10.2 and in Plate 2). We recall her equivocation regarding a 'small' *vs.* a 'large' house (p. 181 above). If a larger dwelling were on the site, then the flat limestone in this area could be interpreted as parts of the floor of that dwelling. This may be why Alexandre did not excavate the entire area down to hard *nari* bedrock, but conserved the two islands of what was, in fact, not a dwelling but a grape treading floor. In antiquity the limestone was worked to a flat surface in order to furnish an even treading area. One notes that it slopes precisely in the direction (southeast) that would be required to guide the grape juice into channel (k).

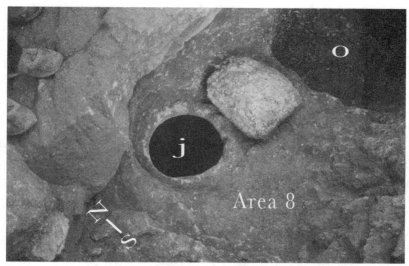

Figure 10.8a. Photograph of Area 8.

The workman at upper left stands on an overhanging rock shelf which hides cavity (j) in many photos. The stone next to the cavity may have been its actual capstone. Such wine cellars were capped to maintain temperature and humidity for optimal underground fermentation. (Public domain.)

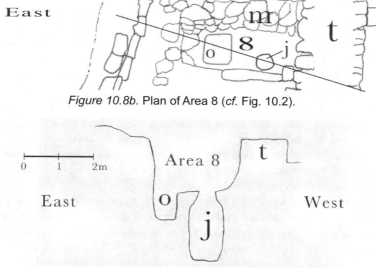

Figure 10.8b. Plan of Area 8 (*cf.* Fig. 10.2).

Figure 10.8c. Area 8 in section, seen from the north.

(Follows the line on the plan in Fig. 10.8b. Drawn by author.)

Grape treading areas could be plastered or not (Ahlström:23). It appears from the available photographs that Area 4 was not plastered. A ribbon of cement has been applied next to partition (t), providing a relatively horizontal base to secure the supports for the overhead boardwalk.

A wine making installation usually had facilities for several stages and qualities of wine. A holding area may lie under the unexcavated earth to the west of the site. Farmers would often initially place their loads of grapes in the holding area, which often itself contained a small vat for collection of the juice that seeped naturally from the grape loads before treading. This was the source of the finest wine. Workers would remove wooden stalks and debris from the grapes in the holding area and then place clusters on the treading floor as necessary to continually replenish supply.

After the grapes were treaded, the remaining rape (skins, seeds, stems) was not discarded but pressed by mechanical means—either by a beam and lever mechanism or by a screw press. It is thus certain that such a mechanical press existed in antiquity in the vicinity of the IMC excavation. When we come to discuss Area 6 and its features (pp. 230 f), we will consider the possibility that such a press may once have existed there. Each pressing of the same load required pithos collection or else a separate vat. In the latter case ancillary wine installations may well also have been nearby.

Locus (j): a wine storage cellar. In the diagram Fig. 10.2 above, the reader notes a depression in the center of the excavation, one located to the east of the grape treading foor (Area 4) and north of the wine collecting vat (Area 1). Figures 10.8 (a), (b), and (c) on the following page offer three views (photograph, plan, and section) of that depression, which we have labeled Area 8.

Area 8 can be divided into two halves, each on a different level. The eastern half contains a secondary depression (o) hewn out of the bedrock to a depth of approximately one meter. The bottom of (o) is a flat surface about two feet square—sufficient to allow one man to stand in the depression. In the western half of Area 8 we encounter cavity (j), discussed below.

Area 8 is immediately next to two large installations once devoted to viniculture—Areas 1 and 4. This is because the rock-cut Area 1—which we have interpreted above as a wine collecting vat—stretched from the region of locus (a) all the way to wall (m) in Fig. 10.2. We know this because the intervening partition (f) is a later Mamluk feature (above, p. 196 and Fig. 10.3). Next to two areas devoted to wine production, we should thus not be surprised to discover that Area 8 was in all likelihood also associated with viniculture. This places cavity (j) in a new light:

> Storage cellars were an integral part of wine making installations in antiquity. Such cellars needed to be close by, for the grape juice could not remain long in the vat lest the wine be ruined:

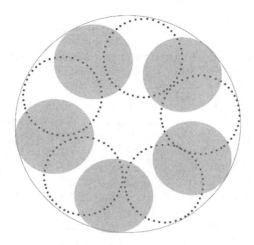

Figure 10.9a. Reconstructed plan of cellar (j) with wine jars in situ.

The large outer circle is the circumference of the cellar (*c.* 1m in diameter).
When full, the cellar accommodated ten jars (smaller circles), five in the bottom tier
and five on top. Each jar measures 35 cm. in diameter at its widest point.
(Drawn by author.)

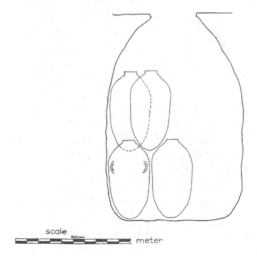

Figure 10.9b. Cellar (j) in section, with four wine jars depicted.

A worker within the cellar would receive jars from a coworker standing in the neighboring depression (o) and would place five jars around the circumference in the
bottom tier. He would then exit the cellar and place the top tier of jugs from above.
(Based on Pritchard 1964:Fig. 53. Redrawn by author.)

> After the juice of the grapes is expressed, natural fermentation be-
> gins immediately "by means of wild yeasts" which live on the skins of
> the grapes (Lukas 1934:14). In order to derive a wine of good quality,
> the juice had to be transferred for fermentation into wineskins or large
> jars, since juice remaining in the vat (yeqeb) longer than six hours could
> develop too much yeast...   (Pritchard 1964:24)

It was natural, then, that wine making installations would include underground cellars in the immediate vicinity of the collecting vats.

The plan and section of cavity (j) functioning as a wine cellar are diagrammed in Figs. 10.9a and 10.9b. This cavity would have been a relatively
small cellar—only one meter in diameter, as revealed in a published section
of the excavation (Fig. 10.13 below, p. 223). Most wine cellars were approximately twice as wide as (j)—very similar, in fact, to the nearby cavity
(z), which was very likely also a wine cellar (Fig. 10.14 below, p. 224).

A number of photographs taken during the excavation in late 2009
show a man standing within cavity (j) and peering out from below ground.[30]
He is upright and the top of his head is a few inches below the opening.
This gives an idea of the depth of cavity (j) from floor to mouth—about
six feet (Fig. 10.8c). The fact that the cavity would admit a man shows that
its mouth (about 18 inches in diameter) was large enough to permit an
adult to enter and exit. It is probable that the worker did so with his arms
raised over his head, for this decreases the shoulder-to-shoulder distance to
as little as 14–16 inches. "The openings [of wine storage cellars]," writes
James Pritchard, "were made large enough to admit a man but were kept
purposely small so that they might be covered easily by a flat slab of stone"
(Pritchard 1962:90). Indeed, the photograph Fig. 10.8a shows such a sealing stone, which would have functioned to keep out rain, rodents, and to
maintain optimal coolness in the cellar. Because no considerations were
given by Alexandre or the press to this cavity functioning as a wine cellar,
it appears that at least some people have falsely interpreted it as a small
'refuge pit'—an impossibility, as we will see (pp. 225 f).

Wine storage jars were of standard size and shape (about 35 cm. in
diameter at their widest) and specially designed to be amenable to stacking
as seen in Fig. 10.9b. Such underground cellars were about twenty degrees
cooler than the surface temperature, and the coolness aided fermentation.
When the cellar opening was covered with a stone slab or a bevelled stop-
per, the temperature within would be fairly constant throughout the fall and
winter months (Pritchard 1964:25–26, 84).

---

30. See for example the *Wall Street Photographjournal* of Dec. 21, 2009, *http://blogs.wsj.
com/photographjournal/2009/12/21/pictures-of-the-day-321/* (accessed July 22, 2014).

It would be possible for a man of average height, while standing on the floor of cavity (j) and without using a ladder, to lift a full wine jar from inside and hand it to a helper positioned above the mouth of the cellar. The reverse procedure would take place when filling the cellar with jars.

Being a relatively small wine cellar of approximately one meter in diameter, cavity (j) would have accommodated roughly ten jars when full—five on the bottom tier and five on top (Fig. 10.9a). An additional two jars could be placed in the center of the cellar after the workman exited.[31] Due to the constrained space inside the cellar, the workman would only have positioned the bottom tier of jars while inside the cavity. The jars in the top tier would be placed (and removed) from above by reaching into the cavity and using the handles on the shoulders of the jars.

Cavity (j) is perfectly proportioned to accommodate two tiers of wine jars (Fig. 10.9b). Each jar measured 0.7m from top to bottom, and the top tier would hence reach to about 1.3m from the bottom of the cavity (allowing some overlap between the two tiers). This distance perfectly corresponds to the parallel sides of cavity (j). Above the top of the upper tier of jars, the sides of the cavity begin to slope inwards towards the mouth.

We are also able to now appreciate the ergonomic relevance of the neighboring depression (o), seen in Fig. 10.8 (a), (b), and (c). Reaching into the cavity (j) to place and remove jars (especially heavy jars full of wine) would be awkward on a level surface, requiring the worker to continually kneel outside the cavity (j) and perhaps even to lie on his stomach. However, depression (o) is perfectly positioned next to the mouth of (j) to allow a worker standing inside that depression to hand each full jar to a coworker within (j)—or alternately (when fermentation was complete) to receive the full jar passed upwards from underground. It also helps the workman place and remove the top tier of jars within the cellar.

It is now possible to speculate regarding the purpose of the locus (g) with surrounding features (Fig. 10.2)—in fairly recent existence (only after construction of partition [f] in Mamluk times). This small area appears to have been a later refinement expressly devoted to sealing the wine jars.[32] This intermediate task was accomplished, of course, after the jars were filled in Area 1 and before being placed in a storage cellar. Thus, the function of area (g) reflects perfectly its intermediate location between the wine collecting area on the south and the storage cellars on the north.

Locus (g) offers enough standing room for two workmen receiving full jars passed to them over partition (f) from Area 1. Their job was to seal the

---

31. The bottom center jar would be lowered and raised with a rope fastened to the jar handles.
32. The jar stoppers were sealed with wax or *amurca* (a sticky olive oil remainder).

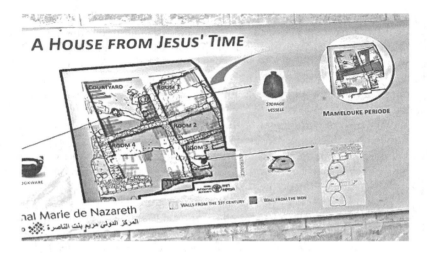

Figure 10.10. The 2012 excavation plan as posted on the wall of the IMC.
The area at bottom right of the plan was not yet excavated in 2009 (*cp.* Fig. 10.3).
Note the arrow linking the dark round circle in "Room 3" with the diagram of a triple
silo, at lower right. (Photograph by E. Oserov and used with permission.)

jars. For this they needed a provision of stoppers as well as sealing material. These would be at hand, to either side, on the flat surfaces (h) and (i)—one side for each worker (Fig. 10.1)—conveniently at waist height. When each jar was properly sealed, each workman in (g) then passed it over wall (m) to a coworker in the standing depression (o). The latter, in turn, passed the sealed jar to a man waiting underground in cellar (j)—or, if the first tier of jars had already been stacked in the cellar, the workman standing in (o) could himself reach the jar into the cellar and place it on the second tier from above. However, if the small cellar (j) were already full, then the jars would be routed to another cellar, such as (z).

In summary, the greater portion of the IMC excavation—Areas 1, 4, and 8, together with their associated loci—is a well-designed installation serving the production and storage of wine. Given the dimensions and form of cavity (j), the size of its mouth, its location near other winemaking installations, and the presence of an onsite sealing stone, we can now confidently conclude that it was a wine cellar in antiquity, one of modest size.

To review the specific stages involved in wine production at the IMC excavation site: the grapes were treaded in Area 4; the juice then passed through channel (k)[33] into the wine vat (Area 1); workmen expeditiously

---

33.   The fact that the Mamluks preserved channel (k) when they built partition (t) shows that Areas 1 and 4 were still being used for winemaking in their era. The IMC

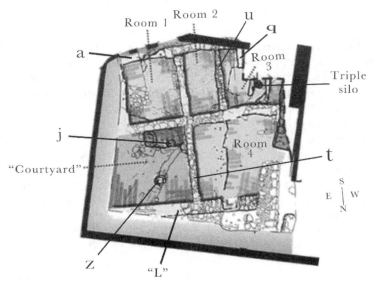

Figure 10.11. The 2012 excavation plan oriented north-south.

The 'house' is no longer "small and modest" but of considerable size (*cp.* Fig. 10.3, p. 197), with a long and now thin wall (t) forming its north-south backbone. (Photograph by E. Oserov and used with permission.)

collected the already-fermenting wine into jars; sealed the jars (in Mamluk and later times) in area (g); and finally stored them in an underground cellar such as (j). *Hence, at least half of the IMC excavation site* (Areas 1, 4, and 8) *was associated with the production of wine.*

The unauthorized excavation

The 'large house' of the 2012 plan. Thus far we have been referring to the excavation photographed in Fig. 10.1 and sensationally described in the global media in December 2009 as a "small and modest" house. Astonishingly, that conception (*and excavation!*) was soon obsolete. It corresponds neither to the material remains on view by visitors today nor to a *second* plan of the 'house' first posted in January, 2012 on the IMC wall for viewing by visitors (photograph, Fig. 10.10 above). This second plan differs considerably from the older one that we have considered in detail (Fig. 10.3). Thus, the reader is now presented with *two* plans of the same excavation, and with the fact that they, in fact, dramatically differ from one another.

---

site was evidently dedicated to wine production for a very long time.

The principal (but not sole) difference between the 2012 plan above and the plan from 2009 is a new area of the excavation in the southwest quadrant. This area was not yet excavated in 2009 (*cp.* Figs. 10.1 and 10.3), and thus is not reflected in any of the photographs and videos taken on December 21, 2009. The new area is located south of (p) and west of (e) in Fig. 10.2. On the 2012 plan above, it is labeled "Room 3" of the alleged dwelling. Surprisingly, a triple silo was found in that area (diagrammed at bottom right in Fig. 10.10). The feature was obviously intended for the storage of grain. It consists of three spacious chambers one on top of the other and is far too large to have served private purposes, especially those of a "small and modest" household. Also, *a triple silo certainly would not have been located in the middle of a room in a domestic dwelling—modest or otherwise.*

The 2012 plan has been rotated above (Fig. 10.11) to conform with other figures in this chapter (north at bottom and south at top). Besides the addition of "Room 3," we readily observe other obvious differences between the two plans, Figs. 10.3 and 10.11. In the latter, Alexandre dispenses entirely with the wide Mamluk partition (t)—which had been such a dominant feature of her 2009 plan. She replaces it with a long, fairly thin wall stretching all the way from (a) in the south to the (mythical)[34] 'wall' (L) in the north. This is most curious, for the Mamluk-era structure stands today untouched and entirely unexcavated—as all the photographs by recent visitors show. Thus, the 'thinner' north-south wall which Alexandre postulates is hypothetical. Nothing indicates that such a long, thin structure lies within and under the broad Mamluk partition. It appears to be yet another invention by the archeologist.

At the same time, the equally hypothetical partition (L) is now drawn on the 2012 plan with great clarity. It has become the northern wall of a respectably-sized dwelling of four rooms. Thus, between 2009 and 2012 Alexandre's conception of the house had clearly changed from a "small and modest" dwelling to one of substantial size (*cf.* discussion above, p. 181). However, this larger dwelling must be deemed totally speculative, and even contrary to the evidence, for both its northern 'walls'—the long, thin (t) and the immaterial (L)—are, as we have can now appreciate, *not* represented by the physical remains.

Furthermore, Alexandre has arbitrarily skewed the thin wall (t), apparently to make it parallel to (u) and (h), as well as perpendicular to (a), (g), and (L)—the other walls of the alleged dwelling. Since there is no evidence for the thin wall (t) to begin with, this 'off center' orientation is also untenable. In Figure 10.12 below, the stairs (b)—which we have argued were a typical feature of an ancient wine collecting vat—*have now mysteriously*

---

34. See pp. 198 *f.* above.

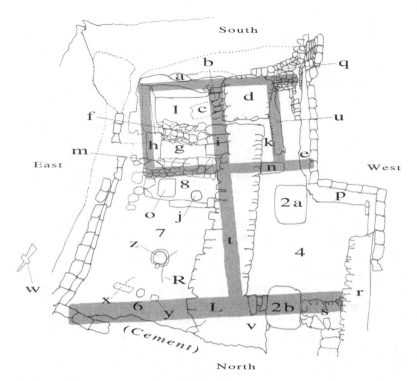

Figure 10.12. The 2012 'house' plan
superimposed on the physical remains (*cf.* Fig. 10.2).

None of the 'walls' of this proposed large dwelling reach higher than four feet from
the ground. All are at least partially hypothetical, and the two longest 'walls' (thin t)
and (L) have no basis in the physical remains at all.

transformed into the southern extremity of the equally mysterious narrow wall (t). The
result (preordained, as it were) is that a hypothetical narrow wall falsely
begins at (b) and arbitrarily migrates from the eastern side of the wide
Mamluk wall (t) to its western side, when progressing from south to north.
The only objective conclusion to be derived from all this is that *the greater
part of Alexandre's larger 2012 'house' is pure invention.*

Furthermore, *all* the 'walls' of the alleged dwelling are not extant, either in whole or in part. We find serious problems in *every* case. The problems can be summarized as follows:

(L) does not exist in the physical remains.

(t) in its thin reincarnation under the Mamluk structure is entirely
     hypothetical.

(a) is a rock-cut structure totally *below* ground level.

(u) is a short, slanting partition reaching no more than four feet in height which, we have argued, was one side of the channel (k) guiding grape juice into the wine collecting vat of Area 1.

(n) is a short feature which attains no height at all (see Fig. 10.1). It may have been part of the original grape treading floor of Area 4. In any case, it does not reach as far as (e), as Alexandre's 2012 design claims. It is is no wise the 'wall' imagined at that locus.

(m) is a low, poorly constructed partition of large fieldstones lacking interstitial matter (Fig. 10.1). It could not have attained the height required for a dwelling without falling of its own weight.

(h) is an earthen construction below ground level. It served as the (plastered) eastern side of a wine collecting vat in Area 1, and perhaps later its top served as a shelf for the stopping of jars.

Thus, every single wall of the alleged 'larger' dwelling is not reflected by the material remains. We have also remarked that these various structural elements do not complement one another in material used nor in construction method: (a) is rock-cut; (m) is constructed of large fieldstones without interstitial material; and (u) of small stones with interstitial material. These incompatibilities would be most unusual in a dwelling, but they are typical of an agricural installation where different functions are represented by differing structural elements (side of a collecting vat, of a channel, of storage Area 8, *etc*). Furthermore, the low height of *all* these features conforms with an agricultural installation—but not with a dwelling.

Room 3 and the triple silo. The most remarkable difference between Alexandre's 2009 and 2012 plans is the added area which suddenly appears in the southwest quadrant of the excavation. This is most clearly seen when comparing the location of feature (q). In Fig. 10.12 (the excavation as of December, 2009) feature (q) represents the southwest boundary of the excavated area. However, Fig. 10.11 shows that in 2012 this was no longer the case—an additional several square meters had been excavated in what Alexandre now labels "Room 3."

This is remarkable, for the excavation had already officially *terminated*. We recall the short IAA report (cited above, p. 189) which furnished the official dates: Nov. 11 to Dec. 7, 2009. It concluded pointedly: "The excavation has ended." Thus, on December 21, 2009, it was generally understood by everyone (the IAA as well as the media) that the excavation had terminated two weeks earlier. But now we see that important structures *later* came to light!

The new area opened up by later excavation is not particularly large—about eight square meters. Thus, remonstrations regarding its date and permit status may appear academic. However, those eight square meters held a signal surprise which—had anyone previously known of its existence—might have led not only to a cancellation of the December 21 news conference, but also to a reconsideration of the entire 'Jesus house' theory. For the surprise in store was nothing less than a triple silo—a manifestly *non-domestic* installation. Today it is diagrammed for all visitors to see, on the modern wall bordering the IMC excavation area (Fig. 10.10, lower right).

The triple silo consists of three fairly spacious underground grain storage cavities, one stacked on top of the other. The IMC wall display locates it in the middle of "Room 3," though such a feature is far too large to have served the needs of a single family—much less one living in a "small and modest" dwelling (long IAA report). Furthermore, had such a large feature been hewn intramurally within or under any dwelling, it would have been out of reach of the community it was manifestly designed to serve. For these reasons, the existence of the triple silo is strong evidence that no dwelling existed on this site in antiquity, and also that the IMC venue was plainly dedicated to communal agricultural activity. To the production of wine we must now add another: the storage of grain.

The steep slope of the terrain and the presence of various wine installations onsite—as well as the possible presence of a press in the 'courtyard' area (see below, pp. 230 f)—these are all indications that the IMC site in antiquity was clearly devoted not to habitation but to agricultural pursuits.

As mentioned above, this tallies with what we have learned regarding nearby sites on the hillside—this was a steep, rocky hillside area outside the boundaries of the ancient village. Seventy-five meters northeast of the IMC is a remarkable quadruple silo under the Church of St. Joseph.[35] An equal distance to the east are complex agricultural installations under the Church of the Annunciation (including more winemaking facilities). Evidently, the entire Venerated Area was devoted to agricultural use of a communal nature in antiquity.

In such superimposed cavities, each silo would be separately sealed with a fitted stone. The lower silos thus provided not only additional storage capacity, but also could serve as insurance in times of poor harvest and of famine. When the grain in an upper silo was consumed, its floor would become visible and the lower silo opened.

---

35. Unlike the triple silo, the St. Joseph complex has a network of radiating tunnels and a large room with the silo for provisions. M. Aviam considers it a "typical" hiding complex. See below pp. 225 f. On the other hand, the IMC triple silo, cavities (j) and (z), were clearly designed with agricultural purposes in mind (grain and wine storage). For a plan of the St. Joseph complex see Salm 2008a: Illus. 5.5; discussion p. 241.

It must have already been obvious during the 2009 excavation season that feature (q) continued to the west and that Area 4 was only partially excavated. One wonders, then, why the excavation was officially terminated on Dec. 7 and not continued at that time farther towards the west, where obvious features were yet to be excavated.

Given the date of the news conference only two weeks later, a cynical answer suggests itself: a *knowingly incomplete* excavation ended on December 7 simply in order to be able to break the news of a "house from the time of Jesus" at Christmastime, when public interest was at its peak. In other words, media considerations may have overruled archeology in determining developments at the IMC. Indeed, such media considerations will prove critical when we consider how the IMC fits into the broader Catholic media strategy.[36]

Another reason the excavation was not continued in the western direction is that the modern four-storey (commercial) IMC structure begins immediately west of (q). In other words, the present IMC excavation area was probably the sum total of terrain allotted for archeological (historical) considerations. There would thus be a conflict between scientific/historical considerations and those deemed commercial. The official Israeli injunction that all *commercial* digging must cease if historical remains are found is essentially pragmatic. Archeological and historical considerations are indeed served *when possible*. At the same time, accommodation to present commercial needs are made *when necessary*. In the IMC case, the terrain bordering on the west and north was designated 'commercial'—and thus the IMC excavation was limited in 2009 and again in 2011.

Thus, it appears that the triple silo was uncovered by commercial digging after December, 2009—digging unrelated to any archeological/historical excavation. Even so, this important find would have been immediately communicated to the IAA and subsequently to Yardenna Alexandre. As a result, it appears that the 'official' limit of the IAA excavation was simply extended by a couple of meters to the west in order to include the triple silo. This accommodation took place in 2010. Also in that year extensive construction of the International Marian Center occurred, with the official dedication taking place in March of 2011 (see timeline above, p. 192). When the IMC excavation area was finally opened to visitors at the beginning of 2012, an updated (second) 'house' plan was simply placed on the wall for public viewing—one which now included a *larger* 'house' with "Room 3," the triple silo, the hypothetical thin wall (t), and the mythical (L).

---

36. See "O. Bonnassies and the 'New Evangelization'" (below p. 237).

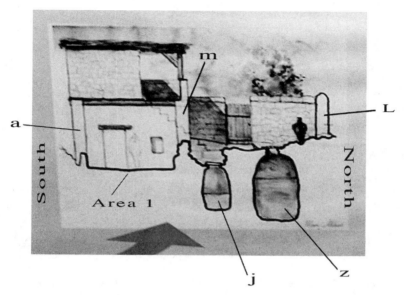

Figure 10.13. An artist's rendering of the 'house from the time of Jesus.'
The drawing is posted on the wall of the IMC excavation for viewing by visitors.
Labels added by author. (Photograph by E. Oserov and used with permission.)

The "courtyard"

We now turn our attention to Areas 6 and 7 of the IMC excavation (Fig. 10.2). These bedrock areas lie in the northeast quadrant, which is by far the steepest part of the excavation (as graphically shown in Fig. 10.7, p. 205). Obviously, this patch of bedrock was not part of any dwelling in antiquity—it is simply too steep. Even Alexandre grants as much, and she denominates this quadrant a "courtyard" *outside* the alleged house.

The wall banner which, since 2012, has been in full view of visitors to the IMC excavation site, includes an artist's rendering of the "house from the time of Jesus" (Fig. 10.13). The drawing is interesting in several respects. First of all, we observe that the dwelling is situated over Area 1 and conforms to Alexandre's earlier (2009) assessment of a "small and modest" habitation. However, it has an annex to the northeast (background right in the drawing).[37] Astonishingly, the 2012 house has not only a roof (which we have seen did not exist)[38] but now also a built up *second* floor with walls of

---

37. Another artist's rendition (online) depicts the annex as a stable for animals.
38. Above pp. 202 *f*, and note 18.

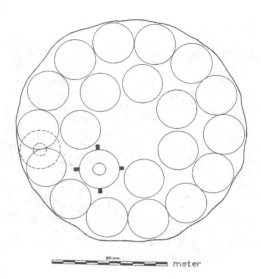

Figure 10.14a. Reconstructed plan of cellar (z) with wine jars *in situ.*
(Based on Pritchard 1964:Fig. 52. Redrawn by author.)

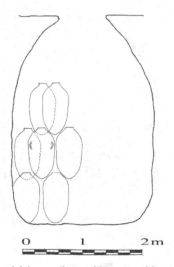

Figure 10.14b. Cellar (z) in section, with several jars stacked in three tiers.

A worker entered and exited the cellar via a knotted rope or ladder.
The capacity of cellar (z) is approximately sixty jars when full.
(Based on Pritchard 1964:Fig. 53. Redrawn by author.)

worked stones. *All this is pure fantasy, for we have seen that none of the alleged 'walls' of the IMC excavation reach more than four feet in height.* At least one (m) is so precarious—even at its present low height—as to be almost falling of its own weight (Fig. 10.1). Lacking interstitial filling, it could hardly rise beyond a few feet as found, much less support a second storey! Yet in the drawing above we observe that (m) is *a solidly built wall reaching up even beyond the level of one complete storey!* All this is breathtaking in its inventiveness.

From the drawing we see that cavity (j) is the intended receptacle for alleged rainwater from the roof. However, there was no roof, so the cavity must have served another use. We have argued above that it was a modest wine storage cellar with the capacity of 10–12 jars. This would not have sufficed to store all the wine produced in the collecting vat of Area 1 and additional storage cellars in the immediate vicinity would have been necessary. Indeed, it appears that cavity (z) may have served such a function. It is scarcely two meters to the north of (j) and, being larger, appears to have been the principal wine storage cellar in the IMC excavation area.

Cavity (z) is twice the diameter of (j) and also somewhat deeper. The mouths of both cavities are approximately the same size, with a beveled rim to take a fitted closing stone. The dimensions of (z) are those of a typical wine storage cellar in antiquity. This cellar could accommodate three tiers, and thus had a capacity of between sixty and seventy wine jars (Fig. 10.14).

Not a 'refuge pit.' The many reports following Alexandre's December 21, 2009 press conference included her interpretation that one of the cavities onsite was for refuge:

> Alexandre said her team also found a camouflaged entry way into a grotto, which she believes was used by Jews at the time to hide from Roman soldiers who were battling Jewish rebels at the time for control of the area.
>
> The grotto would have hid around six people for a few hours, she said.
>
> However, Roman soldiers did not end up battling Nazareth's Jews because the hamlet had little strategic value at the time. The Roman army was more interested in larger towns and strategic hilltop communities, she said.[39]

One would assume that Alexandre is referring to cavity (z)—the only pit large enough to contain "six people."[40] However, cavity (j) seems to also have attracted attention as the intended 'refuge pit.' Thus, a certain

---

39. Diaa Hadid, "First Jesus-era house found in Nazareth," Associated Press, Dec. 22, 2009, at *http://www.nbcnews.com/id/34511072/*, (accessed Aug. 13, 2014).

40. Another report mentions room for "five people." The large triple silo to the west of the 2009 excavation area is out of consideration for it had not yet been discovered. The short IAA report, written in the same month as Alexandre's news conference also knew of only two cavities in the ground: (j) and (z).

amount of confusion exists between the various reports. The mouth of (j) is below ground level—a characteristic which may have led some in the press to consider "camouflage." Also, a number of photographs of a man peering out of (j) also seem to have convinced some, at least, that this smaller cavity was the 'refuge pit' referred to by Alexandre. However, it is hardly possible that half a dozen people could have crammed into a space only one meter wide (Figs. 10.9, 10.13).

Some confusion in the various reports is also noted as to which cavity was a "cistern." We have noted that in one place Alexandre asserts that a cavity received rainwater from the "roof" of the dwelling. This could only indicate (j), for (z) is *upslope* from the alleged dwelling and several meters away. Nevertheless, in another article we read of "a courtyard that held a rock-hewn cistern that would have collected rainwater."[41] This indeed points to cavity (z). Thus, some confusion exists between the reports. Also, on the 2009 excavation plan, cavity (z) is denominated "Cistern/pit."[42] We should remind ourselves, however, that such conflicting information may have less to do with the physical remains than with their *interpretation*. After all, a 'cistern collecting rainwater from the roof' supports the existence of an onsite dwelling. A 'refuge pit' similarly supports the notion that Jews lived *onsite*. The latter thesis caught the popular imagination, and it also added an element of drama to the Christmas 2009 news conference.

The short IAA report (above p. 189) employed the words "in the excavator's opinion," thus entertaining some reservation regarding Alexandre's interpretation of the 'refuge pit.' In the polite and generally understated language of scholarship, such wording often conveys disagreement. In any case, the short IAA report signals that it is Alexandre (and perhaps she alone) who interprets *any* cavity at the IMC site as a 'refuge pit.'

We, of course, have arrived at a very different conclusion: both pits (j) and (z) functioned as wine storage cellars (among several other installations at the IMC site devoted to viniculture).

This interpretation is strongly supported by arguments that neither of the cavities in question could have been a 'refuge pit.' We will now consider some of those arguments.

First of all, the above citation mentions a "camouflaged entry way." This is hyperbole. Cavity (z) is at the surface of the ground and possesses no "entry way." As for cavity (j), the broad (and entirely open) depression of Area 8 cannot be readily construed as an "entry way" (*cf.* Fig. 10.1).

---

41.   *http://www.blog.standforisrael.org/articles/photos-and-details-about-nazareth-find-house-sheds-light-on-life-in-jesus-era*, accessed Feb. 24, 2015.

42.   Online at various sites, including *https://www.youtube.com/watch?v=ITxd_qebujY#t=38*, beginning 0' 37" (accessed Feb. 26, 2015). The label "Cistern/pit" is not included on Fig. 10.3 which is a redrawing by the author.

Secondly, the word 'camouflaged' also appears to be hyperbole. The only conceivable camouflage of cavities (j) and (z) is a single closing stone of modest weight, one similar to that seen in Fig. 10.8a. Of course, it is precious little protection from Roman soldiers who needed only to lift the stone (or push it aside) in order to discover the cavity below. It is not camouflage at all.

Thirdly, Jews are known to have hewn not simple 'pits' for hiding but underground *complexes*—a much more appropriate term. Underground refuges were designed to be extremely difficult to find. In his survey of "Secret Hideaway Complexes in the Galilee" M. Aviam writes of hidden warrens which "were clearly intended to discourage intruders by rendering movement very difficult and slow" (Aviam 2004:123). The difficulty of movement, of course, would not be of the people hiding underground (*e.g.,* of six persons crammed into either cavity [j] or [z]) but of those who might try to find them. Underground hideaways typically included thin tunnels which were (a) difficult to find, and (b) if found, difficult to navigate. They often required a single person to crawl for some distance underground *before* accessing the hiding chamber. That chamber, however, could be quite roomy—as we see under the Church of St. Joseph, only 100m northeast of the IMC.

To be successful, underground hiding complexes were necessarily sophisticated and well planned. It appears that many were hewn before the *Second* Jewish Revolt, when there was some warning of impending turmoil.[43] On the other hand, the First Jewish Revolt caught the land largely unawares. Alexandre maintains that the 'refuge pit' in the IMC excavation "was probably hewn as part of the preparations by the Jews to protect themselves during the Great Revolt against the Romans in 67 CE" (long IAA report cited at the beginning of this chapter).[44] However, Sepphoris did not side with the rebels in the First Jewish Revolt (provoking great animosity among partisan Jews).[45] This certainly diminishes the likelihood—even if Nazareth existed at the time—that hiding complexes (or even 'refuge pits') would have been hewn there during the First Jewish Revolt.

Typically, the entrance to a hiding complex was itself underground—off of a shaft, tunnel, unused silo, *etc.*[46] These complexes were secretive

---

43. Tepper and Shahar 1984; Shahar 2003. Aviam 2004:130–31 reports evidence of a few hideaway complexes hewn in the First Revolt and reused in the Second Revolt (and even later).

44. Alexandre also excavated what she claims was a 'hiding shaft' about 6 km NE of Nazareth (near Kafr Kanna) and dates it to the First Jewish Revolt. See *Hadashot Arkheologiyot* vol. 120 (2008): Karm er-Ras (online at *http://www.hadashot-esi.org.il/report_detail_eng.aspx?id=610&mag_id=114*, accessed Feb. 20, 2015).

45. Schürer, E. 1890/1998, II.1:139–40.

46. *Cf.* Kloner and Zissu 2003: Fig. 9, and their discussion of fourteen underground

refuges for both people and provisions, often multiple chambers with associated silos, cisterns, and tunnels, usually hewn for the possibility, *in extremis*, of a (hopefully short) stay underground. They were a last resort—cold, dark, cramped, and unpleasant. Under the Church of St. Joseph is a spacious grotto whose floor is six meters below the surface (diagram at Salm 2008a:242). The grotto is thirteen meters long and three meters high—ample room for a score of people. Narrow tunnels radiate in various directions, and a quadruple silo at one extremity of the grotto could provide ample provisions of food for a considerable period of time. Aviam describes the St. Joseph complex as "typical of underground hideaways."[47]

Obviously, none of the above is the case with the two IMC cavities excavated in 2009. These are single chambers with undisguised openings at ground level. Nothing recommends them as places of 'refuge.' On the other hand, we have seen that they admirably conform with what we know of wine storage cellars and, furthermore, that *they are right next to wine-producing installations where such cellars would have been needed.*

Ironically, the year after Alexandre claimed the discovery of a refuge pit at the IMC site, a much more elaborate cavity was indeed found there—the triple silo. Though this complex feature was certainly intended for communal grain storage, it *could* have secondarily functioned as a refuge pit of last resort, probably at the time of the Second Jewish Revolt. The main reason for inferring this is that two short walls (about two feet square and six inches thick) were excavated above ground, one on each side of the mouth of this cavity. It appears that their purpose is none other than to disguise the entrance to this silo. Astonishingly, Alexandre's identification of the 'hiding complex' passed from the other cavities to the triple silo after the latter's discovery (Alexandre 2012a:7). In any case, the triple silo is rather thinly disguised at the surface and would have made a poor hideout. But we should keep in mind that the sector we are considering was outside the village proper—in a hillside agricultural and funereal area. Presumably, it would have received less attention from Roman soldiers. So, disguising the entrance to larger agricultural silos for possible use *in extremis* as refuge pits would have made some sense at the time of the Bar Kokhba Revolt.

It can be remarked that, while diverting attention away from the patent agricultural nature of the site, the concept of a refuge pit supports a dramatic storyline of great interest to the modern Catholic tradition—namely, the potential involvement of 'proto-Christians.' Unstated but understood is that the alleged refuge pit hid (or was designed to hide) the

---

hideaway complexes with accompanying diagrams and photographs.
47.   Aviam 2004:130. An examination of the St. Joseph complex is found in Kloner and Tepper 1987:295–99 (Hebrew).

Figure 10.15. Linear alignment of features in Area 6.

These features point to the possible existence in antiquity of a beam (lever) press extending in a straight line from (w) to (y).

(w) Anchor of the wooden beam.
(6) Possible press point and location of stone press bed holding frails (flat bags).
(x) and (y) Ancillary bedrock features possibly associated with press.
Broken stones may be remains of the press bed.
(Photograph by Gil Cohen-Magen. Used with permission.)

inhabitants of the equally alleged house onsite. The Christian imagination is pleased to envision a dwelling under the IMC which was the home of Jewish-Christian rebels. Orthodox Roman Catholic tradition has long maintained that such early Christians populated the settlement of Nazareth from the time of Jesus.[48] If true, such a thesis would offer a chain of authentication—unbroken through the generations—back to the time of Jesus. It best substantiates the ancient holiness of the currently venerated sites. This logic has also proven popular with Christian and Israeli tourism interests, both of which are wont to find Jesus-related features at almost every turn and to memorialize them via the development of as many new pilgrim destinations as possible. However, *the work of Joan Taylor has shown this line to be unsupportable* (Taylor 1993). Furthermore, it is known that Late Roman and Byzantine Nazareth was very Jewish and not at all sympathetic to the Christian faith—inhabitants of the town even participated in massacring Christians in the early seventh century.[49]

The end result of all this pious confabulation is that the Jewish rebels who took refuge in cavity (z) under the IMC were none other than Jewish-Christian proto-martyrs struggling against the oppressive Roman yoke. Furthermore, those heroes were related by blood to the family of Jesus!

Area 6 and its features. A remark is in order regarding the small and enigmatic feature 6—the round, shallow depression located approximately one meter north of cavity (z). A drawing of the IMC site in section (dated December 7, 2009 and not reproduced in this book) reveals that cavity 6 is only 0.4m deep and 0.3m wide. Careful inspection of Fig. 10.1 shows that this modest cavity is accompanied by other features. Barely detectable in the bedrock is what seems to be a circle (diameter about 1m) having cavity 6 as its center. Immediately east of the cavity is an unmistakable man-made indentation in the bedrock, labeled (x) in Fig. 10.2. Examination of various photographs also reveals a slight working of the stone on the other side of the cavity (feature [y]). Finally—and perhaps most interestingly—the natural wall to the east of the entire excavation area displays what appears to be a man-made hollow in the form of a + sign. The southern horizontal arm widens, the northern horizontal arm is narrow.[50] At first, these observations appear meaningless. But when one notices that several features are surprisingly in a line—(y), cavity 6, (x), and the hollow (w) in the eastern wall (see Fig. 10.15)—then a possible interpretation related to viniculture emerges.

---

48.   Proto-Christian habitation of Nazareth is also integral to Dark's view. See Chp. 6.
49.   Salm 2008a:333; Kopp 1938:215.
50.   Feature (w) was walled off in 2010. *Cf.* Figs. 10.6 and 10.7.

Figure 10.16. A typical free-standing press bed.

The frails were stacked on the middle of the bed to be crushed by the beam press. The grape juice (or olive oil) would run into the circular groove and then out the lip into either a pithos or a collecting vat. (From Dar 1986: Fig. 97. Redrawn by author.)

Without entering into a detailed analysis, the foregoing characteristics are compatible with the onetime existence of a press installation in Area 6. Whether we are considering a grape press or an olive press is not clear, for the same installation often served both purposes (see below). As far as wine is concerned, after the grapes were treaded, the considerable semisolid residue of skins and seeds (the rape) was collected from the treading floor. The rape was then placed in flat bags (called *frails*) made either of thick thread loosely woven or of folded cloth (Frankel 1999:147). As many as ten frails were stacked on top of one another and then crushed in a press installation. Various forms of the mechanical press were devised, most predominant being the lever press and (later) the screw press. As the force on the frails increased through pressing, the liquid product was expelled and ran either into a collecting vat or into a strategically placed pithos. If a collecting vat was hewn into the ground, in southern Israel it was usually directly under the frails ("central collection"). In the Galilee, however, the collecting vat was most often to the side of the press point ("lateral collection").[51]

The lever type of press typically employed a long wooden beam (Fig. 10.17)—usually the trunk of a tree—to which were attached massive stone weights (or alternatively a secondary screw mechanism). The beam would exert downward force on the stack of frails, and the grape juice (or olive oil) would stream out, to be collected either in a vat dug in the ground or in a pithos. The existence of the niche hollowed out of the earthen wall at (w)— and perfectly aligned with the small cavity 6—suggests that (w) anchored one end of a press beam.

---

51. Ayalon *et al.*, 2009:9. For exceptions see Frankel 1999:84, 167.

The general shape of the hollowed out niche is also suggestive. Into the central (squarish) area would have been wedged one end of the wooden beam. It was important to minimize the play of the beam, that is, motion either vertically or horizontally. Thus, we see (barely visible in Fig. 10.15) a flat stone at the bottom of (w) possibly to stabilize the beam. The flared, hollowed out extension to the south is also telling. Such a device was commonly used at beam anchor points for the secondary insertion of fairly large objects (stone or wood) in order to prevent side-to-side motion during pressing. The flared shape of this feature allowed several sized stones to be jammed into the hollow as available.

Finally, we note a number of light-colored, broken stones in the background of Fig. 10.15, between the anchor point (w) and the press point 6. The stones are flattened and appear to be broken elements of the same larger artifact. In fact, they bear considerable resemblance to pieces of a broken press bed (Fig. 10.16).

The greatest variety of presses for both grapes and olives have been found in Palestine, using mechanisms involving a beam, weights, a screw (or double screw), *etc.* The ancients creatively adapted whatever mechanism was most appropriate to the physical characteristics of the terrain, to the space available, and to the resources at hand. If a press installation indeed existed at the IMC site, it is not possible to say with any confidence how it was organized. Though the anchor point would be clearly at (w), the press point (location of press bed and frails) might have been at locus 6 or perhaps more to the east. If at locus 6, then it is likely that the method of collection was in pithoi.

One notes the striking breakdown in the stone rim of cavity (z), seen in Fig. 10.1. This breakdown occurs precisely at the point where the rim is closest to locus 6, suggesting some relationship between the two cavities—as if the rim of (z) had disintegrated at that point through use. Given the foregoing discussion, two possibilities suggest themselves. The first is pithos collection involving an upslope press installation. In this case, a pithos rested sideways on the mouth of (z) to receive fluid from the neighboring press bed. This would have been an effective and very simple procedure. The weight of the pithos would lie entirely on the northern side of the rim of (z), thus understandably causing a breakdown in the rim due to years, decades, and perhaps even centuries of use.

A second alternative (and the two are not mutually exclusive) is that a knotted rope extended into cavity (z) from above. The rope would have facilitated the entry and exit of the worker stacking wine jars in the cellar (z). The rope would have been secured above ground, probably around whatever stood at cavity 6—a simple post or (as discussed above) the stone

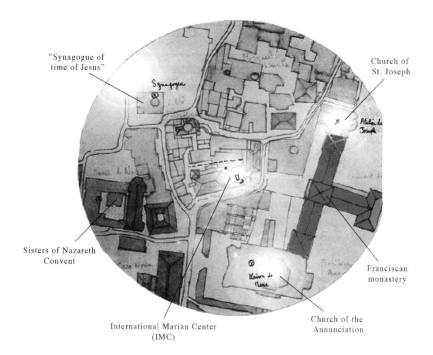

"Synagogue of time of Jesus"

Church of St. Joseph

Sisters of Nazareth Convent

Franciscan monastery

International Marian Center (IMC)

Church of the Annunciation

Plate 1. The 'expanded' Venerated Area as currently understood by the Roman Catholic Church (Chp. 10, p. 183).

This is the neighborhood in which Jesus 'would have grown up.' The four corners represent existing or emerging venerated sites: the "house of Mary" (Catholic Church of the Annunciation) at bottom right, the "Atelier of Joseph" (top right), the synagogue (top left), and the "Tomb of the Just One" (bottom left). In the middle is the recently-built International Marian Center.

[Diagram from *http://pl.mariedenazareth.com/15337.0.html*.
Redrawn from *http://pl.mariedenazareth.com/15337.0.html*,
accessed Oct. 22, 2014.]

Plate 2. Area 4 of the IMC site viewed from the northwest (Chp. 10, pp. 205 *f*).

Flat areas 2a and 2b are surviving remnants of the original grape treading floor, the rest of which was removed in excavating the area down to hard bedrock. The triangle at upper right indicates the direction of flow of the trodden grape juice, which continued downslope through channel (k) and into the collecting vat of Area 1 (see Chapter 10). [Photograph by E. Oserov. Used with permission.]

Labels within image: Modern cement / Downward slope of the grape treading floor / V / t / 2b / Downward slope of the bedrock / Remnants of treading floor / Area 4 (Bedrock) / 2a

Plate 3. The souvenir gift shop "Cactus" near Mary's Well (Chp. 11, p. 261).

Waterworks dating to Crusader times exist under the shop. The owners claim they are the remains of a bath house dating to the time of Jesus. The claim has been thoroughly discredited—even by Y. Alexandre and S. Pfann.

[Photo by Konstantin Hoshana. Used with permission.]

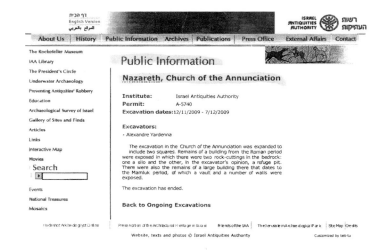

Within the figure the following text appears:

English Version
العرف بالعربي

About Us | History | Public Information | Archives | Publications | Press Office | External Affairs | Contact

The Rockefeller Museum
IAA Library
The President's Circle
Underwater Archaeology
Preventing Antiquities' Robbery
Education
Archaeological Survey of Israel
Gallery of Sites and Finds
Articles
Links
Interactive Map
Movies

Search

Events
National Treasures
Mosaics

Public Information

Nazareth, Church of the Annunciation

Institute: Israel Antiquities Authority
Permit: A-5740
Excavation dates: 12/11/2009 - 7/12/2009

Excavators:
- Alexandre Yardenna

The excavation in the Church of the Annunciation was expanded to include two squares. Remains of a building from the Roman period were exposed in which there were two rock-cuttings in the bedrock: one a silo and the other, in the excavator's opinion, a refuge pit. There were also the remains of a large building there that dates to the Mamluk period, of which a vault and a number of walls were exposed.

The excavation has ended.

Back to Ongoing Excavations

Hadashot Arkheologiyot Online | Preservation of the Architectural Heritage in Israel | Friends of the IAA | The Jerusalem Archaeological Park | Site Map | Credits

Website, texts and photos © Israel Antiquities Authority   Customized by teti-tu

Plate 4. The short IAA report relative to the IMC excavation
(Chapter 10, pp. 188 *f*).

The URL is at top right.
The date stamp of printing (Dec. 21, 2009) is at bottom right.

Plate 5. Mislabeled coins from Mary's Well (Chp. 11, p. 296).

Plate 6. Coin number 11 from Mary's Well (Chp. 11, p. 304).

These are the two sides of a coin which has been used as proof of Hellenistic activity at the site. It is one of ten similarly water-worn "Hasmonean" coins recovered from Mary's Well. The numismatist A. Berman claims that the obverse depicts an "anchor" and the reverse a "star with six rays." However, the coin is so pitted that it is not possible to discriminate any images, nor even to differentiate which side is the obverse ("anchor") and which the reverse ("star"). The face of the left side has been so worn away as to render it concave. The top photographs were professionally furnished to the author by the IAA, rendered from color to B&W. The bottom photographs are identical but have been enhanced with high exposure.

[Photographs taken by Dr. Robert Kool of the IAA. Used with permission.]

Plate 7. The large cave under the Greek Bishop's Residence (Chp. 13, pp. 381 *f*).

The view is of the two recesses opposite the entryway.
[Photograph taken by E. Oserov. Used with permission.]

Plate 8. The Church of the Annunciation in its modern architectural context. The church is alleged to stand over the house in which the Virgin Mary was visited by the angel Gabriel. The presence of tombs under the site would have rendered "The Annunciation" ritually impossible.

[Credit: *Fotosearch*. Used with permission.]

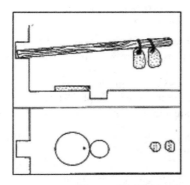 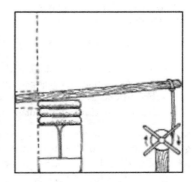

Figure 10.17. Two lever presses of antiquity.
Left: Lever and weights press (lateral collection) in section (top) and plan (below).
Right: Lever and drum press.
From Frankel 1999, List B: T201121101 and T0115. (Public domain.)

press bed anchored into cavity 6. In either case, the friction of the rope would have been on the rim of (z) in the northern direction. Over time, this would have caused breakdown in the rim of the cavity.

There is no proof, of course, that a press installation actually existed in Area 6. However, this possibility makes sense given the intersection of arguments in the foregoing discussion. The cavity (z) almost certainly functioned as a wine storage cellar, as described in the previous section. It is altogether too large to have served as a vat (lateral collection) for olive oil or grape juice. Thus, if a beam press indeed existed upslope, then a pithos could have been inserted into the mouth of (z) to collect the fluid product. The occasional use of the mouth of cavity (z) for pithos collection of fluid (during the two–three months per year when the upslope press was in active use) does not preclude the use of cavity (z) as a wine storage cellar for most of the year.

Many agricultural sites contained installations with dual and overlapping purposes. This was possible because the season for producing wine preceded the olive oil season. Wine production "lasted 6–8 weeks during which it was possible to carry out 10–12 pressing cycles," writes N. Feig.[52] Another scholar notes: "The olive harvest occurred one month (in October–November) after the grape harvest" (Ahlström 34). Each fall, then, a multipurpose installation could shift from wine to olive oil production. A mechanical press (whether a beam press or a screw press) could be used first for pressing the rape of grapes and later for the olive mash. Surrounding features would be creatively adapted as circumstances allowed.

---

52. N. Feig in Ayalon *et al.*, 46.

It is often difficult for the archeologist to determine whether a press crushed grapes, olives, or both at separate times:

> The production of olive oil and wine has much in common. Both involve extracting a liquid from a fruit. For this reason the installations are in some cases very similar and therefore it is not always clear whether installations from archaeological contexts were for producing wine, oil or another product. This is so particularly in the case of simple installations or when only parts of an installation are found.   (Ayalon *et al.*, 2009:1)

Given the existence of onsite wine producing installations, it is tempting to conclude that the northeastern quadrant of the IMC excavation once contained a lever (beam) press dedicated to the secondary crushing of grapes, and perhaps also of olives. The largest structures of such a press would have long since disappeared—the stone weights would have been carried off, the wooden beam would have disintegrated, and the press bed might well have broken up (*cf.* the pieces visible in Fig. 10.15).[53]

A lever and screw press at the IMC site would be compatible with agricultural work on the Nebi Sa'in hillside during Middle Roman through Mamluk times. This dating is compatible with the chronology presented in *The Myth of Nazareth* (pp. 205–07) and with settlement of the town between the two Jewish revolts.

Pottery and dating

Thus far we have considered the structural evidence in the IMC excavation—bedrock features and 'domestic walls.' The preceding discussion concludes that the built structures were in fact low partitions in a fully-developed winemaking installation, one which included a treading floor, collecting basin, two storage cellars, and possibly a press in the northeast quadrant. These features reflect two general eras of construction—Roman and Mamluk. To them must now be added evidence from the movable finds—pottery, tools, and coins. It must be borne in mind that no such artifacts have been itemized in the literature, since (as of this writing) no scholarly literature relative to the IMC excavation exists (above pp. 185 *f*).

In a *FOX News* video from December 2009 Alexandre states: "On the basis of the *pottery* [from the IMC excavation] we could understand that this building was, in fact, a house from the Early Roman Period. We're talking about the first century BC (Before the Common Era) and the first century

---

53.   Given the lay of the land and worked bedrock features at the IMC, one might venture that the most logical press installation in Area 6 is Frankel's so-called Type 2 ('lever and screw'). Such presses were introduced into Italy during the first century BCE. They appeared in Palestine during Middle Roman times (Frankel 1999:107).

CE, which is really the time of Jesus Christ"[54] (emphasis added). According to this statement, the pottery constitutes the *only* basis for dating the IMC excavation to "the time of Jesus Christ." We will now consider whether the pottery finds can support such a precise dating.

The long IAA report that began this chapter communicates a somewhat different dating:

> ...The artifacts recovered from inside the building were few and mostly included fragments of pottery vessels from the Early Roman period (the first and second centuries CE). In addition, several fragments of chalk vessels were found, which were only used by Jews in this period because such vessels were not susceptible to becoming ritually unclean.
>
> Another hewn pit, whose entrance was apparently camouflaged, was excavated and a few pottery sherds from the Early Roman period were found inside it...

This citation is based on Alexandre's remarks in the Dec. 21 news conference. A careful reading reveals two significant differences with her *FOX News* remarks above: (1) the archeologist makes no mention of the first century BC; and (2) she significantly defines the phrase "Early Roman period" as "the first and second centuries CE." The chronology between the different reports (*both* reflecting Alexandre's remarks!) has moved one century later—from the first century BC–first century CE, to "the first and second centuries CE." Of course, her dating in the longer IAA report is minimally compatible with "the time of Jesus," while the *FOX News* remarks reflect a more sensational dating carried by the mass media in December, 2009.

In 2010 I attempted to contact archeologists who had the opportunity to see the shards in question and requested their opinions regarding dating. In private correspondence with me, one well-placed archeologist in Israel (who wishes to remain anonymous) asserted that "the typology is first-second century CE."[55]

Alexandre also mentioned "fragments of chalk vessels." These are the fabled "stone vessels" used by Jews during the Early Roman Period for reasons of ritual purity, as the archeologist explains in the above citation. However, such vessels were produced as late as the Bar Kokhba Revolt.[56] *Thus, their discovery in the IMC excavation is by no means diagnostic of the turn of the era.* They could well date to the second century CE—and used later.

---

54. "A Christmas Discovery: House from time of Christ Unearthed in Israel." *FOX News* video #707 (3' 48"). Sunday, Dec. 27, 2009. (No longer available.)

55. The archeologist continues: "[T]he ceramic finds are so sparse and disjointed that it is still too early to rule out stratigraphic intrusion." However, we may rule out "stratigraphic intrusion" since no stratum at the IMC corresponds to the turn of the era.

56. See Salm 2008a:181*ff* for a discussion of stone vessels and pertinent bibliography.

Once the movable finds (pottery and stone vessel fragments) are put aside, an astonishing conclusion emerges with clarity: *nothing at all found in the IMC excavation demands a dating before the second century CE*. This is precisely the overarching conclusion arrived at in *The Myth of Nazareth*: "not a single post-Iron Age artifact, tomb or structure at Nazareth dates with certainty before 100 CE" (Salm 2008a:205, *cf* p. 165). Alexandre's remarks regarding chronology—when analyzed and compared—do *not* point to the "time of Jesus" at all. They extend in some cases as late as the Second Jewish Revolt, and in other cases as late as 200 CE!

This is familiar—even tiresome—territory. *Myriad* claims have been made over the last several decades, claims of evidence at Nazareth "from the time of Jesus." Under investigation, however, they inevitably prove to refer to periods as late as the second (or even the third) century CE.

It should be borne in mind that *the time of use is always later than the time of fabrication*. Some artifacts were (and are) used *long* after they were produced—as seen today in houses which possess some antiques. Thus, the fragment of a chalk vessel whose *production* is datable, say, to *c.* 100 CE, does not necessarily (or even probably) reflect an archeological context of *c.* 100 CE. The context "of use" could well be 150 CE, 200 CE—or even later.

We are now in a position to appreciate how weak the chronological claims are for "the time of Jesus." No pottery at the IMC has been itemized. Only vague statements have been offered which relate *without prejudice* to the second century CE. Furthermore, these are dates of production. The dates of use are later—perhaps centuries later. In other words, sensationalist remarks regarding "the time of Jesus" are entirely without merit and precisely as described—*sensationalist!*

This follows a familiar pattern in the Nazareth archeological literature. *Middle* Roman evidence is denominated "Early Roman"—typically by considering long timespans of production, and then *ignoring* the later part of those timespans—as we have seen with chalk (stone) vessels. The bow-spouted oil lamp too—a critical element in the earliest evidence from Nazareth[57]—continued in production until the time of Bar Kochba. Yet Christian scholars have persistently labeled those lamps "Herodian" and, furthermore, have falsely attached them to the time of Herod the Great— resulting in a chronology for such lamps which is too early by generations, if not by a century or more. Similarly with the *kokh* tomb—another critical aspect of the Nazareth evidence. One contemporary and prominent Christian scholar (Dark) supposes that this type of tomb ended *c.* 100 CE when, in fact, it continued in use through Late Roman times (above, pp. 84 *f*). All these examples conform to a long pattern of 'backdating' by a number of

---

57.   Salm 2008a:167 *f.*

scholars, now including Kopp, Bagatti, Strange, and Dark—all Christian archeologists. This is all very convenient for as regards the Christian tradition—but *it is a great disservice to science and to history*.

Unfortunately, this familiar pattern of backdating evidence now includes a Jewish archeologist working for the IAA—Y. Alexandre. Even the short IAA report given above (p. 189) corrected her "time of Jesus Christ" dating by noting only general "Roman" evidence at the IMC site. That short report makes no mention of pottery and other movable finds—the only rationale for Alexandre's dating to the turn of the era. Thus, the archeologist's findings at the IMC, when carefully examined, have no force as regards her chronological conclusion: "the time of Jesus Christ." Indeed—given the vastly later dating ranges which obtain in every case—that sensational conclusion must be deemed entirely irresponsible.

Conclusion

No rationale exists for dating any material evidence (whether structural or movable) in the IMC excavation to "Early" Roman times, much less to the "time of Jesus." Not only do we lack a final report with the requisite itemizations, descriptions, diagrams, and discussions, but we also have the archeologist's own admission that her dating applies to a period as late as the second century CE.

The steep slope of the terrain, the absence of several claimed 'walls,' the low partitions (which do not match, and some of which are very poorly constructed), and the multiple cavities in the ground (including a triple silo in the middle of one of the alleged domestic rooms) all show that no dwelling existed at the site of the International Marian Center in the past. In antiquity the area (as also several areas in the vicinity) was demonstrably used for agricultural purposes—primarily the production and storage of wine, and secondarily the storage of grain (the triple silo). The northern part of the IMC excavation (Area 6) may also have been involved in the production of olive oil.

In the foregoing, we have presented two arguments regarding the physical evidence—one positive and one negative. The positive argument finds that the remains are agricultural in nature, as noted in the preceding paragraph. This alone is sufficient to invalidate Alexandre's assessment of the site—for *no house could have existed over a winemaking installation*.

The negative argument is equally strong. It finds that the low 'walls' and other physical remains do *not* (and cannot) reflect an habitation. Thus, by proving what certainly *was* there (a winemaking installation) and what certainly was *not* there (a house), we have now—in two ways—invalidated the tradition's interpretation of this venue beyond doubt.

The fact that the IMC site is currently interpreted by the general public as the venue of an habitation is preposterous from a scientific point of view. However, the general public is not composed of scientists. Those who visit the IMC do so for validation and affirmation of their religious beliefs. The first thing they see from the boardwalk is the excavation, which is on their right as they approach the IMC ticket office. On the facing wall is a long banner explaining the 'house from the time of Jesus.' To doubt this would be to doubt everything that brought them to that place.

More egregiously, however, is the fact that the site has been interpreted as a "house from the time of Jesus" *by a working IAA archeologist*. Alexandre's interpretation flies in the face of the obvious evidence and is scientifically appalling. But that does not seem to matter for, due to high-powered promotion and the investment of a great deal of money onsite, her interpretation is simply a formality paving the way to commercial success. This is quack archeology at its finest.

The IMC and the Church

O. Bonnassies and the "New Evangelization"

What is the "Association Mary of Nazareth" that sponsors the International Marian Center, and that conducted the first "excavation" at the site already in the summer of 2009? *L'Association Marie de Nazareth* (MDN), its official title, is but one of a bewildering number of recent commercial, religious, and media entities belonging to (or closely linked to) the Roman Catholic Church. These entities are intertwined in myriad ways—by personnel, funding, and fealty to Rome. Together, they witness to a formidable across-the-board initiative, one which the Church describes as a "new evangelization." The words "initiative" and "evangelization" are far too sanitary to describe what is really involved—a public-relations *war* conducted on multiple levels, from a centralized Vatican bureaucracy down to the far-flung streets of an often brutish and religiously indifferent world.

The twenty-first century has witnessed some surprisingly inimical developments from the Church's point of view, developments necessitating immediate action. Perhaps it is too soon to affirm an outbreak of 'panic,' but emergency measures have been implemented, as witnessed for example by the strange abdication in 2013 of Pope Benedict XVI. His abdication merely coincides with a remarkable breakdown in *confidence* on multiple fronts, evidenced by dark sex abuse scandals, revelations of blood-curdling Vatican Bank corruption, and the exponential growth of a no-nonsense, take-no-prisoners international movement known as the "New Atheism."

The "new evangelization" is intended to repair the recent erosion in global public opinion, and to stem an alarming exodus of faithful from the Catholic Church—particularly in Europe and North America. The Vatican has decided to 'turn the page,' as it were, and to counter an inimical world not by attacking, but by inviting. Fire and brimstone have been replaced by the gentle Pope Francis and the soft image of Mary.

The International Marian Center in Nazareth is linked to this global sea change in the Catholic Church, one already in the making for some years. Indeed, the IMC is but a small cog in a very large machine promoting the "new evangelization." It is intimately linked to a virtually endless web of young, inter-related Catholic entities. Specifically, *SARL-MDN Productions* (headquartered in Paris) produces the films shown in the third-floor IMC theaters, besides creating television programs with Catholic content. *Jeunes Volontaires au Service du Monde* (JVSM) is dedicated to involving youth with the IMC and with other Catholic venues. *Hozana* attempts to extend the image and story of Mary to non-Catholics, both at the IMC and elsewhere.

Catholic Christianity has unapologetically found in Mary—*once again!*—the most powerful image with which to evangelize lands and peoples around the globe. One of the first encyclicals of the new Pope Francis—*Evangelii Gaudium* ("The Joy of the Gospel," issued November 2013)—ends with the following stirring call for Catholics everywhere to rediscover Mary:

> We ask the Mother of the living Gospel to intercede that this invitation to a new phase of evangelization will be accepted by the entire ecclesial community. Mary is the woman of faith, who lives and advances in faith, and "her exceptional pilgrimage of faith represents a constant point of reference for the Church." Mary let herself be guided by the Holy Spirit on a journey of faith towards a destiny of service and fruitfulness. Today we look to her and ask her to help us proclaim the message of salvation to all and to enable new disciples to become evangelizers in turn. Along this journey of evangelization we will have our moments of aridity, darkness and even fatigue. Mary herself experienced these things during the years of Jesus' childhood in Nazareth: "This is the beginning of the Gospel," the joyful good news. However, it is not difficult to see in that beginning a particular heaviness of heart, linked with a sort of night of faith – to use the words of Saint John of the Cross – a kind of 'veil' through which one has to draw near to the Invisible One and to live in intimacy with the mystery. And this is the way that Mary, for many years, lived in intimacy with the mystery of her Son, and went forward in her pilgrimage of faith.[58]

---

58. Online at *http://w2.vatican.va/content/francesco/en/apost_exhortations/documents/papa-francesco_esortazione-ap_20131124_evangelii-gaudium.html#Star_of_the_new_evangelization* (accessed Feb. 23, 2015).

Thus, at the very beginning of his papacy, the still largely unknown pope from Argentina invoked Mary as intercessor for "a new phase of evangelization." Here, Pope Francis was probably simply carrying forward a strategy already in place and now coming to fruition, a powerful strategy resulting in a transition to a milder image for the Catholic Church. And—following the rather severe papacy of Benedict XVI—who could object to the benign Francis presenting the world with the tender, wholesome, and quintessentially innocent Mary as the *new* face of a *renewed* Church for a *new* millennium? Of course, we are here only speaking of a change in *image*. No one doubts that, behind the scenes, a jaded Vatican curia still directs events with the same chillingly cold calculation learned in ages past.

Managing the new evangelization is a vast new media apparatus bearing the name *Aleteia* (from Gk. *aletheia*, "truth"). This huge umbrella organization has an impressive webportal (*www.aleteia.org*) modestly subtitled "Seekers of the Truth." *Aleteia* was launched in Rome in January 2013—and the timing carries some significance. A month later (28 February) Pope Benedict stunningly resigned his papacy, and two weeks later (March 13) Pope Francis assumed leadership of the world's largest religious organization.

Aleteia describes itself as an "aggregator of Catholic content" with goals to garner "30 million visitors within four years," to become the preferred source for religious information around the globe, and to rise to the top of the Google rankings. To attain these rather ambitious objectives, it considers "the cooperation and collaboration of Christian media indispensable." According to ts website, a the time of this writing *Aleteia* employs forty content editors, feeds 1,200 media outlets, and operates in fifteen nations and ten languages. It is parent to the Eternal Word Television Network (EWTN) in the Unites States, TV Cançao (Brazil), and Télé Lumière (the Arab world).

Aleteia also wishes to become the Roman Catholic alternative to Wikipedia, the universal and unabashedly *secular* source of information. It strives to produce "articles of quality... which will be an important contribution toward evangelization," in the words of Olivier Bonnassies, a media expert, Catholic activist, and French businessman. Bonnaissies (b. 1966) received a diploma from the Ecole Polytechnique in 1989 with a focus on media studies, and subsequently a License in Theological Studies from the Institut Catholique de Paris. He has founded a number of the aforementioned Catholic organizations involved with the IMC in Nazareth, and is on the boards of numerous others.

A remarkably busy and successful individual, Bonnassies has since 1993 directed a long list of agencies with various acronyms, including

METALOG (founder), STELLA, MEDIALOG, and PANAGHIA PRO-DUCTIONS—the last a cinematographic production company. He organized a program for start-up enterprises at the prestigious HEC School of Management (Paris) and in 1997 cofounded OPALE SMR (a management consulting company) with his brother, Axel Bonnassies, himself a graduate of Harvard Business School. The latter's estimated annual revenue alone is $2,833,000.

Olivier Bonnassies is intimately involved with the IMC in Nazareth. He was Executive Director of *Chemin Neuf* ("New Path") in 2011 when that organization managed construction of the five-storey IMC. As "Director of the Association Mary of Nazareth," Bonnassies has explained that the Nazareth complex is but the first of many projected Marian centers. "In a second phase," he states in an interview, "the Mary of Nazareth project will unfold throughout the whole world, via the creation of associate Marian Centers which will use the contents elaborated by the Nazareth Center. Three are already planned—in Lebanon, Brazil and Poland—with increasing local funding for the multiplication of multimedia productions distributed in these Marian Centers, for traditional means of communication, and for the display of web pages referring to the Virgin Mary and to the whole of the Christian faith in its association with other movements."[59]

Bonnassies has been described in the Catholic press as "President of the foundation for evangelizing via media." It is apparent that he is currently at the helm of the Church's New Evangelization inititative, which he explains simply as "how to find ways to present the faith to people today." As regards *Aleteia*, Bonnassies expounds on its mission: "Our societies are experiencing a rapid digital revolution in which it is necessary that the Church be a pioneer in evangelization. The Internet is a formidable means for the transmission of the faith. . . *Aleteia* has the mandate of choosing the best content and delivering the strongest Christian responses in two clicks." Bonnassies laments that "from an international standpoint one finds no contemporary Christian media with comprehensive presence on the Internet. Though Christian content is important, it is expressed at a local level, is poorly ranked on Google, and is limited in reach. It takes the websurfer much time to uncover quality Christian content."[60] Evidently, Bonnassies considers it his professional, religious, and moral task to right this perceived imbalance.

---

59. *Catholic Online* interview with J. Colina, Feb. 19, 2009 (*http://www.catholic.org/featured/headline.php?ID=6111*).

60. "Le projet Aleteia la cathédrale digitale," interview on *radionotredame.net* dated Sept. 26, 2012.

Christian-Jewish collaboration

A major aspect of the New Evangelization is outreach to non-Christian religions. Bonnassies has stated that the goal of the *Association Marie de Nazareth* is to "diffuse the knowledge of the personality and role of Mary of Nazareth, in order to contribute to the establishment of peace among communities… among people of all races, of every culture, and of every civilization."[61] Elsewhere he expands: "We wish to explain Mary, to explain the Christian faith via multimedia, in a way which is both original and which employs the modern technical means at our disposal today. We saw early on that this tool did not exist to disseminate the faith…"[62] This outreach pre-eminently includes Israel—the birthplace of Christianity and ground zero for Catholic ecumenism. In the same interview Bonnassies intimates that the Israeli establishment has been very supportive. This is not surprising, as Christian and Jewish commercial interests overlap so strongly. Bonnassies is not at a loss to find more uplifting reasons for such pragmatic cooperation: "From the Jewish perspective, we received immense support when it became clear that we are presenting Mary as as a Jewish woman, the daughter of Zion, as she existed in this culture and among this people. The entire multimedia production has been made with Jews working on the lighting, the sound, the footage…"

This ecumenism is no accident. The reality is that no Christian venture—Catholic or otherwise—materializes in Israel without the complete approval of the Jewish state. The IMC is a major Christian enterprise located on Israeli soil, and full cooperation between Christian and Jew must be cemented *before* such a venture goes forward. Presenting Mary as a "daughter of Zion" is one nicety of such cooperation. The commercial aspects, of course, are fundamental. The Israeli economy stands to benefit a great deal from Christian visitors in the country multiple days dispensing a good deal of money while visiting sites such as the IMC. Obviously, the only reason those visitors come to the IMC owes to its relevance regarding Jesus and his time. Israel recognizes this, and the IAA archeologist assigned to excavate the premises (herself an employee of the Israeli government) accordingly determined the site—contrary to all the material evidence—to be that of a "house from the time of Jesus."

A few decades ago this was not the case. Catholic interests in the time of Bagatti and De Vaux were in charge of major excavations, and Israeli concerns were more or less sidelined. Today, the Israeli government has emphatically assumed control of excavations on its own soil.[63]

---

61.   "Association MDN" homepage (*http://www.mariedenazareth.com/qui-est-marie/lassociation-mdn*), accessed June 18, 2014.
62.   Interview with E. Veillas on *Radio Notre Dame*, March 25, 2011.
63.   The debacle of the Dead Sea Scrolls—manuscripts under an embarrassing Catho-

Once cooperation between Christian and Jewish interests is satisfactorily established, projects go forward with unparalleled speed and efficiency. The IAA becomes a full partner. Alexandre has, for example, not only given a very 'Christian-friendly' interpretation to the venue, but the IAA has also agressively publicized her 'authoritative' interpretation—as witness the article at the beginning of this chapter as well as significant reports in *Am Haaretz* and other Israeli press outlets.

In sum, the International Marian Center in Nazareth attests to the closest cooperation between Christian and Israeli interests on multiple levels. That cooperation is ultimately commercial and based on the recognition that attracting Christian tourists to sites in the Holy Land greatly benefits both Israel and the Church.

Of course, commercial interests have no necessary nor obvious connection to the facts of history (nor even to religious dogma). Conflicts inevitably arise between what is historically provable and what is good for commerce, and science is inevitably the orphan left out in the cold. When inconvenient, the facts in the ground are simply ignored—or, if necessary, *actually repudiated*. This is not mere hyperbole. The IMC excavation examined in this chapter furnishes the perfect example, for the patently *obvious* onsite existence of a wine-producing complex in antiquity has been repudiated in favor of a (scientifically) preposterous "house from the time of Jesus." The reasons are ultimately pragmatic. The Israeli state, with the collusion of the Catholic Church, considers the 'facts' of history interesting only so long as they promote tourism to that fragile country.

Similarly, *many* other pilgrim venues are now under development in the land of Israel—places where Jesus walked or simply *may* have walked: Capernaum, Magdala, the River Jordan... The list is virtually endless. The gospel storyline is so full of possibilities that it is a dream for the Israel Ministry of Tourism. After all—according to the gospels—Jesus walked *throughout the Galilee and Samaria!* Hence, there is no theoretical limit to the number of pilgrim sites potentially awaiting construction. Who can say that Jesus did *not* walk—or bathe, or sit—at a certain place? This recognition is, in fact, very old. In the Middle Ages, the Jewish inhabitants of Nazareth were pleased to show Christian pilgrims a certain bench. As proof that Jesus had once *himself* sat on that very bench, they demonstrated with huffing and puffing (and for a certain amount of money) that, no matter how hard they tried, they could not move the bench even an inch—because they were *Jews*. Christian pilgrims, of course, could and did move the bench with ease. The Christian faith was thus vindicated, the locals were remunerated, and everyone was pleased.

---

lic embargo for more than a generation—was certainly a catalyst of the new Israeli attitude.

Today, new ways are devised to take advantage of gullible Christian pilgrims arriving to the Holy Land in search of uplifting spiritual experiences. The Israeli government now actively initiates outreach in the United States. A vital part of this outreach—ultimately promoting tourism—agressively courts the Conservative Christian establishment. This has been a matter of record for the past generation. A 2002 Washington Post article entitled "Israel's Evangelical Approach" (by Mark O'Keefe) is subtitled "U.S. Christian Zionists Nurtured as Political, Tourism Force." It attests to the growing strategic cooperation between Israel, on the one hand, and interests in the U.S. variously denominated as conservative Christian, evangelical, and Christian zionist, on the other. This cooperation has borne extraordinary fruit in Israel, including development of the Nazareth Village Farm—with a number of mega-donors in the U.S. (above, p. 63). O'Keefe writes:

> In an effort to solidify its relationship with American evangelicals, the government of Israel has launched initiatives that include expense-paid trips to the Holy Land and strategy sessions with the Christian Coalition and other conservative groups. The objectives: to revive Israel's sagging tourism industry and strengthen grass-roots support in the United States. The target audience is the estimated 98 million U.S. evangelicals, but especially a subset of that group, Christian Zionists.[64]

The author goes on to state that the Israeli government hired an American PR firm and approved a "multimillion-dollar marketing plan… with certain aspects dependent on funding by the Knesset, the Israeli parliament." The frenetic construction activity associated with numerous recent Christian sites in Israel shows that funding for these initiatives has the full support of the Israeli government.[65] The bottom line is encapsulated in one word: *commerce*.

---

64. *The Washington Post,* "Israel's Evangelical Approach," Jan. 6, 2002.
65. *Cf.* below "Controlling the story," pp. 396 *f.*

Chapter 11

QUACKERY AT MARY'S WELL

The background

In 1997–98 two excavations took place on the northern slope of the Nazareth basin, in the area of Mary's Well, also known as "The Virgin's Fountain" (*'Ain Miryam* in Arabic). Both excavations are included under the rubric "Mary's Well excavations," though they took place in successive seasons and included two non-contiguous areas separated from one another by approximately 70m (Fig. 11.1). The actual water source is deep within the mountain behind the Greek Orthodox Church of the Annunciation which, since its erection in Byzantine times, has been venerated by the Eastern Church as the spot of the Annunciation to the Blessed Virgin Mary.

Thus, there are *two* churches of the annunciation in Nazareth and *two* alternate traditions regarding the location of that allegedly cosmic event. Greek Orthodox Christians follow a non-canonical account, one extraordinarily popular in the early Christian centuries through Byzantine times. It can be found in the *Protevangelium of James*, a Christian text dating to the second century. In that account, Mary hears a voice from heaven as she goes to draw water from the local well. She immediately returns home. It is there and then that the Archangel Gabriel visits her (Salm 2008a:212 *f*).

The *Protevangelium* does not know Nazareth. In fact, it doesn't even mention the Galilee. This is certainly one reason it became 'non-canonical.' Another is that Mary is raised in a most astonishing place—the Jerusalem temple (PrJ 8:1–2). Joseph's home is nearby Bethlehem of Judea (PrJ 8:3, 17:1).[1] All this (which I have termed the 'southern' tradition) was studiously ignored after the time of Constantine when Nazareth in Galilee became

---

1. As Frank Zindler has pointed out in his writings, the Israeli archeologist Aviram Oshri has shown there is no evidence at all for the habitation of Bethlehem of Judea at the turn of the era (see *Archaeology*, Nov.–Dec. 2005, pp. 42–45). From this, we can be sure that the geography of the *Protevangelium* is entirely mythical—or perhaps a better word would be 'cosmic.'

the acknowledged domicile of the Holy Family, and when Christian pilgrims were henceforward directed *there*, eventually streaming in droves to 'the town where Jesus was brought up.'

In the *Protevangelium of James*, the village well (in Judea, we recall) plays a central role in the account of Mary's visitation by the angel. But after the venue was duly transferred to Nazareth in Lower Galilee, the Greek Orthodox Church of the Annunciation was constructed above the only place in the basin where water issues year around—Mary's Well.

That water source was in a cave, and Peter the Deacon, Arculf, and other Christian pilgrims of yore piously supposed that Mary actually lived in that very cave and that Jesus drew water daily for her. Presumably, he also drew water for the entire town of Nazareth, since this is the only reliable water source in the valley (Salm 2008a:216).[2] We can also conclude that Joseph (now wedded to Mary and the presumed father of Jesus) moved into the cave-house of Mary, rather than Mary moving into his house (as was the custom)—for how else could the boy Jesus draw water for the populace at the site of the Annunciation? Such irritating details, however—the result of discursive *reasoning*—apparently did not occur to pilgrims nor vex the early Church at all.

When the Greek Orthodox Church of the Annunciation (also known as the Church of St. Gabriel) was finally built in early Byzantine times, a 60 meter channel was simultaneously hewn so that locals could access the water they needed. From June to August 1997 a small excavation consisting of two probes was conducted there, specifically in the area fronting St. Gabriel's Church, known as "St. Gabriel's Church Square." It revealed a vaulted reservoir and movable finds from various eras.

In early times (discussed at the end of this chapter) separate channels were extended approximately 70 meters further downslope to the present "Mary's Well," where the townsfolk have long gone for water. This is the lower "Fountain Square" area, the site of the principal excavations which took place both in 1997 and from July to October 1998 (Alexandre 2012:vi).

---

2. Prof. Ken Dark has berated this writer in print for misunderstanding the hydrology of the Nazareth basin (Dark 2008d:142), but the shoe is probably on the other foot. Dark has recently proposed that "Ancient Nazareth was served by three to seven springs" (Dark 2015:57) and that it was quite large at the turn of the era. The British archeologist is alone in proposing such theories. Y. Alexandre has clarified the hydrology: "Spring waters were scarce in the ancient village. The only perennial source was located outside Nazareth, where it emerged from the rock slope about 150 m north of the site that would become Mary's Well. A significantly smaller spring, which became known as the Apostle's fountain, flowed seasonally down the western slope of the village" (Alexandre 2012a:2). This is the view known to Bagatti and also reflected in my first book (Salm 2008a:41).

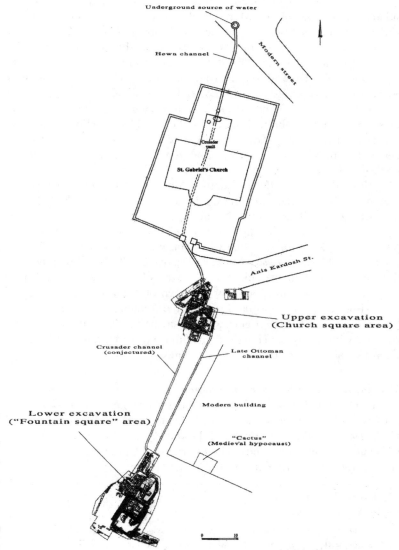

Figure 11.1. General plan of the Mary's Well excavations.

The main excavation took place in the summer of 1997 in the Fountain Square area ("lower") around Mary's Well. During that season, limited work was also carried out in the Church Square area to the north. In 1998 additional "small-scale probes" took place in the Fountain Square area adjacent to the work of the previous summer. (Redrawn by author based on Alexandre 2012a:4 and 10.)

Thus, two excavation seasons and two non-contiguous areas are considered under the rubric "Mary's Well excavations." For clarity, in this chapter I will sometimes use the references "upper" (Church Square area) and "lower" (Fountain Square area) to distinguish the two sites (Fig. 11.1)

Both excavations were directed by Israel Antiquities Authority (IAA) archeologist Yardenna Alexandre, who has worked for the IAA for decades. Alexandre has specialized in the Lower Galilee area, conducting routine salvage excavations and inspections, and authoring (or co-authoring) a host of shorter reports published in one of the two Hebrew/English periodicals of the Israel Antiquities Authority, *Hadashot Arkheologiyot* and *'Atiqot*, on generally little-known sites spanning all eras from the Bronze Age to the present.

Alexandre's 1997-98 excavations at Mary's Well mark her first work at a high-profile Christian site. She would go on to excavate at Kafr Kanna (five kilometers NE of central Nazareth), causing a stir four days before Christmas 2004 when she announced that it was probably the Cana where Jesus got his start (*cf.* Jn 2:1–12). Ever cognizant of commercial possibilities, Alexandre told *The Jerusalem Post*, "This is a real possible attraction, because there are a lot of Christian pilgrims who are looking to see the real context of Jesus's life." She suggested that the town of Cana was later occupied by Jewish Christians and that a synagogue probably existed there which has yet to be unearthed. It goes without saying that such theories do not conform with known data but do align admirably with traditional Christian interests—as also with Israeli tourism interests.

The Salm-Alexandre correspondence

In December 2005, while researching *The Myth of Nazareth*, I came across a short report on an excavation "next to the White Mosque in Nazareth" (*Hadashot Arkheologiyot* vol. 112 [2000] p. 118). What struck me was the claim of Hellenistic finds. The excavation was directed by Yardenna Alexandre and its pertinent passages are cited here:

Nazerat (Nazareth)
(Hebrew section: p. 148)

During May 1998 a salvage excavation was conducted in the poultry market next to the White Mosque in Nazareth (map ref. 1780/2340), following the discovery of Roman-period sherds during work in preparation of infrastructure improvements. The excavation was directed by Y. Alexandre on behalf of the Antiquities Authority.

Two squares were opened about five meters from the spot where the remains were discovered, due to the presence of pipelines. In Sq A, bedrock was exposed 0.3 m below the surface level and no building remains were discovered. Sherds from the Iron Age, Hellenistic, Roman, Byzantine, Mamluk and Ottoman periods were found on the bedrock... Pottery sherds from the Mamluk period were discovered on the floor, and sherds from the Ottoman period were found in the fill overlying it. The ceramic assemblage from both periods[3] includes domestic vessels characteristic of these periods, similar to those discovered in the excavations recently conducted at the Nazareth fountain[4] (forthcoming), located about half a kilometer east of the site.

Neither the English nor the Hebrew notice in the same issue is accompanied by itemizations, diagrams, *etc.* Comparing the two versions shows the English to be a faithful translation—the Hebrew notice also possesses the critical word "Hellenistic." This was sufficiently provocative to me that I decided to contact Ms. Alexandre via email to request further information on this particular point. It was my first communication with this IAA archeologist who would become the most active excavator in the Nazareth area in the ensuing years and—as developments witness—would play a critical role in the accounts recorded in this book.

My email to Alexandre has not survived,[5] but she soon replied to my inquiry:

From: Y. Alexandre
Jan. 1, 2006

Dear Mr. Salm,

I received your request via the IAA internet. Indeed I excavated a very small excavation at the site and published the results in HA 112: 118. The finds were minimal, due to the size of the excavation, and more exactly, as the result of the extensive infrastructures that must have severely damaged whatever there was once there. I have no more to say on the site than what I have published.

---

3. *I.e.*, Mamluk and Ottoman.
4. The "Nazareth Fountain" is Mary's Well, which Alexandre excavated almost a decade earlier. The word "forthcoming" signals her final report, a 2012 monograph which will become the main subject of this chapter.
5. Since 2006 I have gone through a succession of computers and culled my digital files more than once. Unfortunately, I no longer possess all the emails, and in some cases lack the complete headers. It should also be noted that in at least one place Ms. Alexandre appended a footer that her message is confidential. However, in the email citations which originate from her, I conclude that the rights of the public regarding access to this now published information outweigh her personal desire, stated or implied, for confidentiality.

On the other hand, I carried out an interesting and larger excavation at Mary's well, Nazareth, and I am in the process of working on this material.

Yours sincerely,
Yardenna Alexandre

I recall having specifically asked Alexandre to address the claim of "Hellenistic" pottery—indeed, that was the reason I initiated contact with her regarding this small excavation. Thus, I was a little surprised to receive the above, which pointedly ignored my request with (what appeared to me at least) an abrupt "no more to say." Her admissions that the "finds were minimal" and possibly "severely damaged" did not inspire my confidence. It would not be possible for me to use any of her information in my first book. The findings were *claimed*; there were no published descriptions, diagrams, *etc*.; the archeologist admitted the finds were "minimal" and possibly "severely damaged"; and no further information would be forthcoming.

However, Alexandre's closing mention of "an interesting and larger excavation at Mary's well" piqued my curiosity. I supposed those finds were either very old (pertaining to the Bronze-Iron Ages) or dated to the second century CE and later—consistent with the evidence that I had verified from the rest of the basin. So, I wrote her again:

From: R. Salm
Jan. 2, 2006

Dear Ms. Alexandre,

Thank you for your reply. My book reviews all the evidence from the Stone Age to the present at Nazareth. It goes to the publisher at mid-year and may be open for additions for a little while after that. If possible I would like to include the results of your excavations at Mary's Well in the text and bibliography. In return, I would be happy to mail you a free copy of the published book at my expense.

From other material in the Nazareth basin, I assume that the context of this excavation at Mary's Well is MB, LB, Iron (like your work at Har Yona), and/or Roman-Byzantine +.

Best wishes,

Rene Salm, esq.

As we see from this note, I anticipated that the text of my book would be finished by mid-2006. This was optimistic. As it happens, I was still writing in 2007, after which Frank (Zindler) edited the text, formulated an index, and his late wife (Ann) carried out the formatting. The book finally appeared in March, 2008.

At the time of this email correspondence Alexandre did not know the provocative title of the book I was so deeply immersed in writing—*The Myth of Nazareth: The Invented Town of Jesus*. Actually, Frank and I had not yet even finalized the title. But I was careful not to poison the well by cavalierly apprizing Alexandre of my basic thesis—that Nazareth did not exist at the turn of the era. Such knowledge would in all likelihood have summarily ended our communication. As far as she knew I was a scholar—no institutional affiliations divulged—probably with a background in history or religion who was writing a book on the evolution of Nazareth through the ages. However, her next email reveals that she wanted more information on my project and intentions:

> From: Y. Alexandre
> Jan. 11, 2006
>
> Shalom,
>
> The excavation at Mary's well was the result of the initiative of the Nazareth municipality, who decided to demolish the 1960 fountain house and rebuild according to the 1860s building. Following the demolition, we excavated the actual site of the fountain house as well as a limited excavation in the area in front of the Greek orthodox church. In the former area extensive remains of the Crusader and the Mamluk fountain houses with stone water channels were uncovered, as well as very limited wall and channel remains from the mid Roman period (1/2-3 centuries) and Hellenistic sherds. In the latter area, a vaulted Ottoman reservoir with 4 well holes in the roof was found, an ancient (at least Crusader on) water channel, as well as a few various damaged walls from the Hellenistic, Roman and Byzantine periods.
>
> No prehistoric evidence, but of course a very small area, and constantly disturbed by later building remains. Also the later periods were not removed as the idea was to exhibit the earlier remains under the present day well house. Unfortunately, the upkeep is catastrophic, as there are vandals around.
>
> That's it in a nutshell. I am working on the publication at present, but I'm afraid that there is no way that it will be ready in time for your book. It may be possible to give a short summary as it would be a shame not to include info on the finds.

Of course I'm very interested in your book. Is it an archaeological book, or does it cover other aspects?

I have read some material, including the early pilgrims and travellers. I am rather frustrated that I do not know enough German to read the articles by Kopp. Have you incorporated his data?

Yours,

Yardenna Alexandre

Again Alexandre was claiming "Hellenistic" finds. She used the word twice in the first paragraph—once in connection with "sherds" and a second time in connection with "damaged walls." She did not mention stratigraphy, and it appeared that she was dating the walls in question on the basis of associated "Hellenistic sherds."[6] In any case, her statement "I'm afraid that there is no way that [my final report] will be ready in time for your book" was decisive. Because there would be no itemization of discrete finds, diagrams, *etc.*, before the appearance of my book, I could not use her very general information which amounted to no more than email claims of Hellenistic evidence from Nazareth, as well as one *unsubstantiated* reference in *Hadashot Arkheologiyot*.

Of course, Alexandre's repeated claims of Hellenistic evidence were of the greatest interest to me. If *bona fide* they had the potential to derail my entire thesis. But this was not new. Her claims were still only that—*claims* lacking any authentication whatsoever. Already in 1999 I had become familiar with empty promises of unsettling forthcoming data from Nazareth. In the *CrossTalk* exchanges (Chapter 1) I had received advice to just "wait and see," perhaps for "this season's dig" which would surely produce incontrovertible evidence of Nazareth in the time of Jesus.[7] The next season's dig never did produce such evidence, and one might wait a long time—indeed, *forever.*

Nevertheless, even before publication of my first book, the leading archeologist in the field was on record (unknowingly) denying my basic thesis through claims of Hellenistic evidence. Yet both Frank and I were fully convinced of the value of proceeding on the basis of verifiable data, not on the basis of *claims* regarding what *has* been found, what *is* being found, or what

6. This inference ultimately proved correct. Alexandre also dated the "Hellenistic" walls and floors by structural cutting—an argument, however, which she later abandoned (see below p. 267).

7. *CrossTalk* post #6628, dated May 21, 1999.

may be found. This care regarding what constitutes 'evidence' has served us well. It has allowed my Nazareth research to evade the many pitfalls related to unsubstantiated claims of every conceivable nature—some very curious indeed. It has also allowed me to proceed despite the assurance (sometimes on high authority) of 'forthcoming' evidence which is hostile to my thesis. In *every* case, such hostile evidence—when/if it was eventually published and duly examined—has *never* measured up to much-inflated claims regarding the time of Jesus.[8]

It would be another six years (a full fourteen years after the actual excavation) before Alexandre's final report on Mary's Well was published in the form of her 2012 book: *Mary's Well, Nazareth: The Late Hellenistic to the Ottoman Periods*.[9] That book's appearance has, in turn, precipitated the writing of this chapter. As we will see, Alexandre's tome is riddled with not a few errors which belie her several Hellenistic claims relating to Mary's Well.[10] In addition, the book contains irreconcilable contradictions and what can only be characterized as instances of dissimulation.

In the penultimate paragraph of the last-cited email, Alexandre writes: "Of course I'm very interested in your book. Is it an archaeological book, or does it cover other aspects?" I answered her question in my next email (below). But I had the sneaking suspicion that our correspondence may no longer have been private. With email there is no way of knowing whether one's message will be forwarded—possibly to numerous recipients (caveats, warnings, and prolix e-signatures notwithstanding). And it was all too clear to me that colleagues of Alexandre's at the IAA would entertain some interest in my work...

I also found it interesting that she admitted to not being competent in German. Alexandre mentioned Fr. Clemens Kopp—an important author of the mid-twentieth century whose articles in German (particularly on the Nazareth *kokh* tombs) are essential.[11] Fortunately, I read German without difficulty.[12] Alexandre asked pointedly: "Have you incorporated his data?" Perhaps she was probing to see how deep was my acquaintance with the Nazareth archeological literature. If this was the case, my following reponse can have left her with little doubt:

---

8. On my views regarding verifiability and "diagnostic" evidence, see above p. 131 and Salm 2008a:272.
9. IAA Reports No. 49, "With Contributions by Guy Bar-Oz, Ariel Berman, and Noa Raban-Gerstel." Jerusalem: Israel Antiquities Authority.
10. The small excavation near the White Mosque (together with its claim of Hellenistic evidence) never received further documentation or attention by Alexandre.
11. On Kopp's Nazareth work, see the many index references under his name in *The Myth of Nazareth*.
12. I completed a B.A. in German in the 1970's.

From: R. Salm
Jan. 17, 2006

Shalom,

The fact that your article will not appear this year presents a problem for me. You see, I have a strict policy with regards to the book: I accept statements only based on artefacts that are actually itemized and diagrammed in the published literature (as in your Har Yona article). I must work in this way, because many claims have been made about the evidence at Nazareth that people cannot verify from the published artefacts themselves. So, until your article[13] appears I'm afraid I cannot give your results much weight. This is especially true when you write that you uncovered only "very limited" sherds at Mary's Well. Still, if you wish to make a statement on your work at Nazareth for my text, I would be very pleased to consider it, in a "provisional" manner.

You mention Kopp. I have read his reports in German. Unfortunately, some of his conclusions were doctrinal and not based on the evidence in the ground, and even Bagatti disagrees with Kopp on a number of points. So, you see, a proper history of the place should be written based on the material evidence. The first part of my book is a review of the archaeological evidence, and the second part considers implications for Christian studies. I have read Nurit Feit on Nazareth, and the reviews of tombs and pottery by various scholars. I have wanted to contact Zvi Gal,[14] but have been unable to locate him. In any case, I look forward to the eventual appearance of your published results from Nazareth, and will certainly consider any statements you may wish to make for my text.

Best wishes,

Rene Salm

I received no response to the above and assumed that the email exchange with Alexandre had ended. However, in early May I was surprised to receive a short email from her. It was Alexandre's belated response to my above offer to "consider any statements you may wish to make for my text." The email was accompanied by a totally unexpected summary of the Mary's Well excavations which would prove critical:

---

13. I expected an article from Alexandre, not a whole book dealing with Mary's Well.
14. The Israeli archeologist and historian Zvi Gal specializes in the Iron Age in the Galilee. I wished to contact him primarily regarding evidence for the depopulation of the Galilee following the Assyrian invasions of the late eighth century BCE. Alexandre did not furnish the contact information.

From Y. Alexandre
May 4, 2006

Dear Rene Salm,

Browsing through my Outlook Express, I came across our correspondence and I think that I never sent you a short summary. If it is not too late I am enclosing a few words, which I hope may be of use to you.

In my excavation report, I am considering whether I should include a chapter on the material from earlier excavations. In the light of your book in process (when scheduled?), I would like to ask you for more detail on your review of the archaeological evidence in your book in order to decide whether simply to refer the reader to your book, or to write my own summary. In my work I would only include the ancient area of the town itself and not sites like my Har Yona.

Yours,

Yardenna Alexandre

The above short email is interesting—even curious—in a number of ways. First of all, Alexandre writes: "I am considering whether I should include a chapter on the material from earlier excavations." Her wording (especially use of the word "chapter") signaled that in 2006—eight years after the excavation—a book-length final report on Mary's Well was in the process of being written. I had no idea that final report would take another six years to appear.

Secondly, the final sentences of the above email request explicit information on my projects and intentions: when is my book scheduled, and "more detail on your review of the archaeological evidence." However, Alexandre does not couch these requests in terms of mere curiosity or even of professional interest. She deems my views sufficiently significant as to influence *her* final report: she wants to know whether to "refer the reader to your book" or whether "to write my own summary" (of the archeological history of Nazareth). I was flattered but found this curious, for I had given her no details at all regarding my Nazareth views and only the briefest possible statement about my forthcoming book.

The reader can smile today at the prospect that Yardenna Alexandre once contemplated referring her readers to *The Myth of Nazareth*! Of course, she didn't know that would be the title of the book. (I didn't yet myself.) Nor did she know that it would challenge every traditional aspect of the town's archeology. However, that is precisely the sort of information she sought in 2006, as her email makes clear. She wanted to know *where I stood vis-a-vis the tradition.*

A final comment is in order regarding Alexandre's last sentence. Her use of the phrase "the ancient area of the town itself" reflected the received view: the ancient town was where Bagatti and the Christian tradition have located it since ancient times—on the hillside. Alexandre betrayed no recognition that this question is (or even could be) subject to discussion. This was simply one indication, already clear to me, that we were worlds apart.

As it happened, I did not send Alexandre the information she requested. Nor did I reply to her email. I found her somewhat evasive regarding the information I had specifically requested, namely, details regarding the all-important (to me) "Hellenistic" evidence that she was claiming. Also, given her obviously traditional position, I saw little productive to be gained by apprising her of my views—to which she would probably react with astonishment and perhaps even hostility.

ARCHAEOLOGICAL EXCAVATIONS AT MARY'S WELL, NAZARETH

Yardenna Alexandre, Israel Antiquities Authority

1st May 2006

Archaeological excavations were carried out in the Fountain Square and in the adjacent St. Gabriel's Square in 1997-1998 by the Israel Antiquities Authority under the direction of Yardenna Alexandre on the initiative of the Government Tourist Ministry and the Nazareth Municipality in the context of the Nazareth 2000 development programme.

The main excavations were carried out under the modern 1960s concrete Fountain House, which was demolished with the aim of reconstructing the ruined Ottoman stone Fountain House. The archaeological remains exposed dated from the Roman, the Crusader, the Mamluk and the Ottoman periods. From the Roman period part of a covered dressed stone channel was exposed, as well as some wall stubs and Middle Roman pottery. Major construction works carried out in the Crusader period produced finely-dressed stone pools paved with marble slabs, a fine plastered arched reservoir and large and small stone channels, the major of which may have carried water from the spring the the Church of the Annunciation. The evidence indicates that [sic] a clear Crusader presence at the site, including a variety of local and imported glazed wares and coins from Feodalic France. In the early Mamluk period the Fountain House continued in use, without destruction and in the fourteenth century the Mamluks built a new vaulted Fountain House, whilst the old Crusader pools served as a 'shop', or small storeroom for a local potter's wares. The activity around the Fountain House is reflected in considerable quantities of broken jars and other vessels, coloured glass bracelets, wire earrings and worn coins. A fifteenth century destruction of the shop seems to have been followed by a period of delapidation. A clean-up including the dredging of many 14-15th century small denomination coins, may date the Franciscan efforts in the early 17th century (known from the written records), but David Roberts drawing from the 1840s indicates that the Fountain House was in a bad state of repair. The vaulted Fountain House was rebuilt in the 1860s and stood until it was replaced in the 1960s.

The limited excavations in the St. Gabriel's Church Square were carried out as some ancient walls were exposed when the infrastructures were being renewed. The excavations revealed a complete underground vaulted reservoir with four well openings in a row, overlain by a stone-paved courtyard. This plastered reservoir or cistern was in use in the 18th-early 19th centuries. Two large stone channels were exposed here, the ancient of which seems to have been part of the Crusader channel that originally transported the water from the source, under and past the St. Gabriel's church and down to the water house. The vaulted reservoir, however, captured these waters and cut off the connection with the Fountain House. The second channel was built after the vaulted reservoir, to bypass this reservoir and again allow the waters to reach the Fountain House. Some fragmentary stone walls and floors were cut by the vaulted reservoir, thus indicating that there was some occupation here in the Hellenistic, Crusader and Mamluk periods.

The 2006 Mary's Well report

Appearance and reaction. Of course I was pleased to receive Alexandre's attachment on the Mary's Well excavations.[15] But that unbidden document raised a number of questions. According to its date, I received it only three days after its writing. Hence, the report was certainly not yet published anywhere. Given its entirely 'official' appearance, my natural inference was that it was destined for publication in the IAA's online journal *Hadashot Arkheologiyot* ("Archaeological News")[16] where excavation summaries are typically found. Apparently, I was priviledged to receive a pre-publication copy—with freedom of use in my forthcoming book, per Alexandre's declaration above: "If it is not too late I am enclosing a few words, *which I hope may be of use to you.*" She could even have written the above report *for me* and purely for consideration regarding my book, except that I later learned that Ken Dark had also seen the report when it was briefly online (below).

Once again the report did not meet the requirements of diagnostic evidence. It lacked itemizations and any description of discrete finds that would allow others to verify her claims. For a more detailed assessment, I would presumably have to wait for her promised final report on Mary's Well. It was unusual for a final report to be delayed so long (though, as it happens, not so unusual for Alexandre—*cf.* p. 186 above). In fact, I was not at all sanguine that a final report would *ever* appear. For all I knew, the short

15. Above and also cited pp. 161–62 *supra.*
16. *Hadashot Arkheologiyot* ceased hardbound publication in 2004, after which time it is found only online. See *http://www.hadashot-esi.org.il/reports_list_eng.aspx.*

report was the most definitive word I might ever have regarding the Mary's Well excavations.

In March, 2008, *The Myth of Nazareth* appeared. On pages 132–33 I commented on Alexandre's two excavations. Concerning the small White Mosque excavation (above, p. 249), I wrote: "Given the lack of even rudimentary information on the shards, we must consider this an unsubstantiated Hellenistic claim." On the Mary's Well excavations, I wrote:

> According to personal [*sic*] correspondence with the archaeologist, a short report on this excavation is scheduled for publication in *Hadashot Arkheologiyot*. Unfortunately, it again lacks specificity as regards description, itemization, or illustrations of discrete finds, which constitute the requirements of verification so important in this context...
>
> ...[O]nce again, this Hellenistic claim must be reckoned as unsubstantiated.

This citation shows that at the time I fully expected Alexandre's three-paragraph Mary's Well summary to appear in *Hadashot Arkheologiyot* (HA). Since 2006 I have periodically searched the IAA publication archives and have found no trace of it. However, in the summer of 2015 research revealed that Prof. Ken Dark had accessed the report online on "30 May 2006" (Dark 2012c:177). This shows that Alexandre's above paragraphs were in fact online—but apparently only for a short time. Why they were removed from public notice is not obvious, yet we will see that Alexandre's 2012 book on Mary's Well will contradict her 2006 report. Indeed, the earlier report will prove to be a revealing embarrassment. Perhaps this had something to do with its disappearance.

It also bears note that this is not the first time an IAA public notice on the Internet has disappeared. We recall the short HA notice regarding the IMC excavation (above, p. 189) which apparently also disappeared within a month of its posting online. That short notice similarly was contradicted by Alexandre's published statements.

For the purposes of the present writing, the above report from Alexandre represents an *authoritative* statement on Mary's Well. It is important for the ensuing argument that this be clearly acknowledged. The report is authoritative because its author directed the excavation and the byline indicates that the communication was from Alexandre in her official status as an employee of the Israel Antiquities Authority. We know that the report appeared briefly online. The fact that she was sending it for use as I saw fit in my forthcoming book (*cf.* her accompanying email) is further confirmation that Alexandre stood fully and officially behind the report. Of course, no IAA archeologist sends out a communication *with the prospect of its being published* if that communication is not deemed authoritative.

Therefore it is not possible to merely dismiss the above 2006 Mary's Well report as some sort of unintentional 'mistake' on the part of Alexandre, or perhaps as an ill-conceived anomaly. It was written as an official document, with albeit temporary publication online, and with a view towards potential publication in my first book.

Taking Alexandre's above 2006 report seriously will be important in the pages that follow, for we will see that it contradicts—in *critical* ways— her 2012 book on Mary's Well. Ironically, it may be that I am the last person to whom Alexandre should have personally transmitted the report, for I am among the few who are able to demonstrate those contradictions and to draw their inevitable conclusions. As will become clear, Alexandre's 2006 report opens the door to *indisputable evidence for the late introduction of "Hellenistic" and Jesus-era evidence into the material finds at Mary's Well.* The following pages will clarify this astonishing accusation.

"Hellenistic" in the 2006 report. As regards turn of the era evidence at Nazareth, Alexandre's May, 2006 excavation summary is entirely benign with the exception of the single word "Hellenistic" in the final sentence. Because *no information provided in the three preceding paragraphs substantiates that word,* its presence in the report is jarring.

In the main excavations which took place in the Fountain Square area (second paragraph), "archaeological remains exposed dated from the Roman, the Crusader, the Mamluk and the Ottoman periods." We read of a "dressed stone channel" from the Roman period and of "Middle Roman pottery." There is also a "clear Crusader presence at the site," as well as "many 14-15th century small denomination coins." So, in this paragraph nothing precedes the Roman period.

As for the final paragraph (secondary excavation in the St. Gabriel's Church Square area), we read of a "vaulted reservoir" in use in the 18th–early 19th centuries and of a "Crusader channel." A second channel was built *after* the vaulted reservoir. Thus we have the sequence: Crusader channel–vaulted reservoir–second channel. No material (structures or movable finds) are thus far claimed in the upper area before the Crusader period.

Then comes the final enigmatic sentence of the report. Within it is a complete argument: premise, reasoning, and conclusion. The premise is that "Some fragmentary stone walls and floors were cut by the vaulted reservoir." The reasoning is that this cutting implies *precedence*: because those walls and floors were cut by the vaulted reservoir, they were first. Alexandre describes the vaulted reservoir as a "plastered reservoir or cistern" (3rd paragraph, line 4). She dates its use to the "18th–19th centuries." Thus, according to her reasoning, the "walls and floors" date *before* the 18th century.

So far, nothing raises suspicion. But then we come to a completely incongruent conclusion: "thus indicating that there was some occupation here in the Hellenistic, Crusader and Mamluk periods." The reader is left to wonder how walls and floors dating *anytime* before the 18th century CE specifically indicate activity two millennia earlier in the Hellenistic period! Strictly speaking, those structures do not even indicate human activity in the Crusader or Mamluk periods—they merely show there was activity in the Church Square area *before the 18th century CE.*

Her argument from structural precedence cannot be forced. The walls and floors could have been constructed as late as the 17th century (in Alexandre's chronology, the Early Ottoman Period).[17] Unless the archeologist has some significant proprietary information which she has never communicated, the "walls and floors" in question cannot even be dated to the Mamluk period (which ended in the 1517 CE when Greater Syria passed into Turkish possession)—even less to Crusader times.

In short, using an 18th century cutting to establish activity in long bygone eras is an argument which no professional archeologist would freely make. It is obviously and stunningly false. Furthermore, its appearance in the final sentence is rather surprising, for *the report is otherwise altogether cogent.* The cutting appears contrived—perhaps a secondary imposition—merely a pretext to insinuate the word "Hellenistic" into the material remains.[18]

In any case, once the error of Alexandre's logic is exposed, it becomes patent that the one-time appearance of the word "Hellenistic" in her report is embarrassingly indefensible. There clearly is no Hellenistic evidence in her 2006 report.

Jesus' bathhouse and the 'larger' Nazareth

It seems that, sooner or later, every architectural and archeological feature in the Nazareth area is pressed into service as evidence for the fabled "time of Jesus"—regardless of how far-fetched such a dating may be. In recent years a small drama has been playing out next to Mary's Well, one involving the (overheated) claim that a fully developed Roman bathhouse once existed at the site—a bathhouse in which Jesus *himself* may have bathed! Today, the installation is under a souvenir-perfumery shop called

---

17.   According to Alexandre 2012a:46ii the Ottoman period lasted four centuries (15th–19th), the first two being the "Early Ottoman period" followed by two centuries of the "Late Ottoman period" The Ottoman period comprises Stratum I at Mary's Well. Stratum II is the Mamluk period.

18.   The reader may recall that this is not the first time that a suspicious structural "cutting" has been invoked at a critical juncture to justify habitation in earlier times. Ken Dark used a similarly indefensible argument from a "cutting" at the Sisters of Nazareth Convent site (above, pp. 97 *f*).

Cactus. (see Fig. 11.1 and Plate 2). The shop is about fifteen meters northeast of Mary's Well (the excavated Fountain Square area) where the Nazarenes have traditionally come to draw water. We will dedicate a few words to this brouhaha before continuing our investigation into the more significant material evidence from Alexandre's Mary's Well excavations nearby.

Undeniably, some sort of waterworks exist under *Cactus.* They were discovered by the owner Elias Shama shortly after he purchased the premises in 1993. He quickly noted a humidity problem and began digging in the basement of his premises. The digging proved more extensive than anticipated, one thing led to another, and Shama ultimately exposed "an extremely well-preserved hypocaust bathhouse, including a furnace and an elaborate terracotta piping system"—in the words of Alexandre who personally examined the installation in 1993 on behalf of the IAA. She writes about it in her Mary's Well book (pp. 156–57) and concluded that the waterworks were remnants of a *hammam* (Turkish bath) built no earlier than 1885. That is, of course, a far cry from what Shama was hoping to hear. In any case, she considered the installation of little historical value and concluded that, as far as the IAA was concerned, Elias was free to excavate under his premises as much as he pleased.[19]

Shama was convinced that the substantial waterworks under his shop dated back to Roman times—even to the time of Jesus. He apparently based this conclusion partly on the encouraging opinion of Christian tourists who were visiting Mary's Well across the street and who stopped in at *Cactus.* Some of those visitors probably drew parallels with ancient Roman installations they had seen elsewhere.

It wasn't long before these speculations reached their inevitable conclusion: Jesus (and/or members of his family—Mk 6:3) once bathed under Shama's very shop. Furthermore, Mary drew water only a few paces away.[20] The latter activity has great importance in the Christian Greek Orthodox tradition for, according to the *Protevangelium of James,* Mary's (first) visitation by the Archangel Gabriel took place when she went out to draw water. She immediately returned home to receive the (second) visitation and the Annunciation proper, that is, the news that she would bear "Emmanuel" (Heb. "God With Us"—Mt. 1:23).

19. See also *http://www.nazarethbathhouse.org/en/ExcavationHistory.htm* (accessed March 16, 2015). In my first book I briefly discuss the installation (Salm 2008a:133) based on Alexandre's (now obsolete) view of 1993.
20. In fact, the first channel connecting the present Mary's Well to the water source far up on the hillside was not yet in existence. That channel dates from Middle Roman times (see below, pp. 309 *f*).

All in all, then, Shama's shop was on—or at any rate *next to*—extraordinarily holy ground.

The idea of a Roman-era bathhouse in Nazareth also interested Dr. Richard Freund of the Center for Judaic Studies at Hartford University (Connecticut). Arguably, Freund has become the intellectual protagonist behind a "Roman" dating of the *Cactus* waterworks. Advocating a high-tech approach, he and his team have since 2002 conducted ultrasound studies, radar surveys, carbon dating studies, and ground-penetrating depth surveys of Shama's premises. Freund's conclusion: that an older bathhouse lies under the one excavated by Shama. "What we are looking at now is probably Roman," declares Freund. "But even if it proves to be from a later period, then the bath underneath certainly is Roman. Either way, we know that under the shop lies a huge new piece of evidence in understanding the life and times of Jesus."[21]

A *huge* new piece of evidence? This based upon the possibility that Jesus may have merely *bathed* there?

Actually, the waterworks under the *Cactus* shop are not insignificant, whatever their date, even though they do not justify Shama's assertion of "possibly the largest and most important Roman bath ever discovered in the Middle East." This is hyperbole, and it shows that the owner is apparently unfamiliar with the Roman baths of Jerusalem, not to mention those of Hammad Gader with their thirty-two marble fountains.[22] But he did expose a tunnel (later identified as a large water-furnace), piles of old stones, and arches—once the underfloor heating system for the bathhouse—as well as white marble tiles that constituted the actual floor of the bath.[23]

However, these features are quite typical of turkish baths of the sixteenth to nineteenth centuries. They would indeed have been remarkable in ancient times. If such an extensive installation existed in Lower Galilee at the turn of the era it would surely have been noted, as were Roman bathing complexes at Hammat Gader, Ptolemais (Akko), Callirrhoë (on the eastern shore of the Dead Sea), Livias, and Tiberias. These sites were much visited two thousand years ago and are amply documented. No such documentation, however, exists for a bathing installation in the Nazareth basin.

It is also curious how a small, poor, and insignificant village (as Jesus-era Nazareth is traditionally envisaged to have been) could have possessed such a massive bathhouse, a pagan installation only marginally tolerated by

---

21.   Jonathan Cook, "Is this where Jesus bathed?" *theguardian* (newspaper), Oct. 22, 2003. (Online at *http://www.theguardian.com/world/2003/oct/22/research.artsandhumanities*, accessed 3/16/2015.) For Freund's published writing on the Nazareth bathhouse, see Freund 2009:295–323.

22.   NEAEHL 2:572.

23.   *Nazareth Today,* June 2011:10.

Jews, and one which catered to the upper classes. Such a bathhouse could perhaps have existed in Sepphoris—but in *Nazareth?*

Such inferences are familiar to both Shama and Freund, who logically suggest that *perhaps Nazareth was not so small after all.* To Freund, the large scale of the bathhouse suggests that Nazareth, rather than Sepphoris, was the local hub of military control from Rome. He opines that such a giant bath would only have been built for a Roman city, or to service a significant garrison town.[24]

Thus, the tail wags the dog. Beginning from a false Early Roman dating for this large bathing complex, one is led to contemplate a settlement at the turn of the era, then a large town, then a "garrison" town... Of course, there is no historical attestation of a garrison at Nazareth in Roman times—the very idea seems preposterous. The headquarters of the second and sixth Roman legions was at Legio—situated at the foot of the ancient Mt. Megiddo twenty kilometers to the west. Legio was far more strategically located than the out-of-the-way Nazareth basin, being at the head of the Jezreel Valley and also at the mouth of the Wadi 'Ara (the narrow pass traversing the Carmel Range) on the critical north-south trade route known as the Via Maris.[25] These are the practical reasons why the Roman garrison was quartered *there* and not in the upland Nazareth basin.

Though a 'large Nazareth' in Roman times is astonishing historically and scientifically, it is a view which has recently gained some adherents in addition to Freund. Perhaps human psychology also comes into play, for asserting something *large* is far more impressive (and easier) than asserting the existence of something *small.*

To a rational person, however, the big lie is even less tenable than the small one. But to others, the big lie has the advantage of *presence*—it is easy to communicate and easy to grasp. In the writing of *history* (I use the term advisedly) the big lie has proven far more successful than the small one.

It may be, then, that doubt regarding the existence of Nazareth at the turn of the era has contributed to a recent interpretive shift by the tradition away from a small and insignificant 'village of Jesus.' Freund, Dark, and Alexandre have now all voiced interpretations consistent with the 'larger Nazareth' view: Freund at the *Cactus* waterworks; Dark at the Sisters of Nazareth Convent, where he claims to have found a substantial 'courtyard house'; and Alexandre at the International Marian Center, where she similarly claims to have found a house that may have been quite large.[26]

---

24. Cook 2003.
25. Salm 2008a:21.
26. Dark has especially argued for a large settlement of Nazareth in Jesus' day. *Cf.* p. 76 above, also p. 112 and Fig. 6.6. For Alexandre's 'larger house' views at the IMC, *cf.*

Alexandre, however, has not dated the waterworks under Shama's shop to the Roman era. In her 2012 book on Mary's Well (pp. 156–57) she took into account new information available since her initial assessment in 1993, including that brought forward by Richard Freund and an incidental remark by a sixteenth century traveler who mentioned the existence of warm baths in Nazareth. She accordingly moved the incipience of the "furnace and hypocaust-heated pools" under *Cactus* as far back as the Mamluk period. This dating nicely conforms to her chronology of the adjacent Mamluk period bathhouse (*hammam*) just behind Mary's Well. Once again, however, she concluded that there is no justification for dating the *Cactus* waterworks a millennium earlier to Roman times.[27]

THE MATERIAL EVIDENCE

Layout and chronology of the excavations. Yardenna Alexandre directed two excavations at Mary's Well, in two seasons, and in two locations separated by about sixty meters. The main work took place between June and August of 1997.[28] This was in the immediate vicinity of Mary's Well—the lower (southern) area in Figure 11.1. Alexandre calls this the "Fountain Square" (or sometimes "Fountain House") area, a terminology we will retain for uniformity. As mentioned in the last section, for several centuries a Turkish bath (*hammam*) existed immediately behind Mary's Well. Upon excavation, it yielded the most remains (structural and movable) from the Fountain Square area.

During the 1997 season Alexandre also excavated a "vaulted reservoir" about sixty meters farther to the north, in front of St. Gabriel's Church. This "upper" area is known in her parlance as "Church Square." It yielded far fewer remains than the Fountain Square area.

Between July and October of the following year Alexandre returned to the lower Fountain Square area to carry out small-scale probes next to the 1997 excavation.[29] These probes were secondary to the placement of urban infrastructure.

---

above pp. 216 *f.* Alexandre seems unsure in this regard. As we saw in Chapter 10, she has offered two interpretations (and two plans) of the 'house' at the IMC site—a small dwelling in 2009 and a large one in 2012 (above Figs. 10.3 and 10.10).

27. Dr. Tzvi Shacham (curator of Tel Aviv's Antiquities Museum) has recently voiced the opinion that the *Cactus* bath installation may date as far back as Crusader times (Shacham 2012 and *Nazareth Today*, June 2011 p. 11).

28. IAA permit no. A-2689/1997.

29. IAA permit no. A-2912/1998.

Thus, the lower Fountain Square area was excavated in both 1997 and 1998. It yielded the most remains, including all the recovered coins (below).

The Nazarenes have long come to draw water at the Mary's Well "Fountain." For centuries that water has been piped from the underground source located in the hillside over a handred meters to the north (*cf.* the top of Fig. 11.1).

The 2006 report and "Hellenistic" evidence. In Alexandre's short 2006 report (cited above pp. 256–57), the second paragraph contains a synopsis of the main excavation results from the Fountain Square area. That paragraph's second sentence neatly summarizes the findings there: "The archaeological remains exposed dated from the Roman, the Crusader, the Mamluk and the Ottoman periods." This statement is straightforward and encompasses both structural and movable finds. It can be noted that *the Hellenistic period is not mentioned.*

As regards the Church Square area (third paragraph of her 2006 report), Alexandre notes "some ancient walls," a vaulted reservoir "in use in the 18th–early 19th centuries," and a "Crusader channel." The only chronological vagueness pertains to the "ancient walls." The archeologist clarifies this with a problematic final sentence: "Some fragmentary stone walls and floors were cut by the vaulted reservoir, thus indicating that there was some occupation here in the Hellenistic, Crusader and Mamluk periods." We have already examined this statement and found that the cutting in question has no obvious relevance to the Hellenistic, Crusader, or Mamluk periods—it merely indicates that those walls and floors *preceded* the vaulted reservoir which was "in use in the 18th–early 19th centuries."

Alexandre did not signal any Hellenistic remains at all—structural or movable—in the Fountain Square area. Nor did she mention any Hellenistic *movable* artifacts from the upper area. The single Hellenistic claim made in the entire 2006 report has to do with "Some fragmentary stone walls and floors" excavated during the first season in the upper Church Square area. It bears emphasis that *nowhere in her 2006 report does Alexandre claim pottery, coins, or other movable artifacts from the Hellenistic period.*

Furthermore, we have seen that the single claim of Hellenistic structural evidence in her 2006 report is untenable. It is based on the 18th–19th century cutting of one feature into another. This very late evidence has no relevance to the Hellenistic period.

Once this is understood, then the entirety of Alexandre's Hellenistic evidence vanishes from her 2006 Mary's Well report. Her single use of the word "Hellenistic" in the final sentence is untenable and, furthermore, it does not cohere with the remainder of the report. In sum, the highly anomalous word "Hellenistic" appears contrived.

The "Hellenistic" Pottery

In her email to me dated January 11, 2006 (above, p. 248), Alexandre wrote:

> Following the demolition, we excavated the actual site of the fountain house as well as a limited excavation in the area in front of the Greek orthodox church. In the former [*i.e.* Fountain Square] area extensive remains of the Crusader and the Mamluk fountain houses with stone water channels were uncovered, as well as very limited wall and channel remains from the mid Roman period (1/2-3 centuries) and *Hellenistic sherds.* [Emphasis and bracketed note added.]

This statement that the archeologist discovered some "Hellenistic sherds" in the Fountain Square area clashes with an observation emphasized in the last section, namely, that *"nowhere in her 2006 report does Alexandre claim pottery, coins, or other movable artifacts from the Hellenistic period."* This contradiction between statements is a second curiosity regarding the alleged Hellenistic evidence from Mary's Well. The first was, we recall, the untenable interpretation of a structural 'cutting' by a modern feature—used as evidence for *Hellenistic* walling (above, p. 265). To this we now add the contradiction between statements by Alexandre regarding Hellenistic shards. Her 2006 report knows nothing of such shards. Thus, *both* the Hellenistic structural and the Hellenistic ceramic evidence from Mary's Well are subjected to contradictory claims by the archeologist.

We now turn to Alexandre's 2012 final report on the excavations, *Mary's Well Nazareth: The Late Hellenistic to the Ottoman Periods* (IAA Reports No. 49). In contrast to her 2006 report, several passages in the book assert the discovery of Hellenistic pottery. Thus, on page 11 (her "Table 1.2") we read that the Fountain Square area had "Accumulations with pottery and coins" dating to the "Late Hellenistic" era. Then on page 16 we read:

> No Hellenistic building remains were exposed in the Fountain Square area, but late Hellenistic sherds were discovered in accumulation or fill layers excavated to deep levels, including L125, L132, L146 and L156. A few Hellenistic sherds were also found on a small area of a crushed limestone floor (L219) and in the fill or accumulation layer (L221) beneath this floor (see Fig. 3.1). Most of these Hellenistic loci were located in the area exposed to the east of the Crusader and Mamluk constructions, where the later major earthworks had not completely removed the earlier strata.

Six loci mentioned in this citation divulged Hellenistic shards. Apparently, then, Hellenistic pottery was found all over the Fountain Square area (Fig. 11.3, p. 275). But how are we to reconcile this with Alexandre's 2006 report which knew no "Hellenistic sherds" from the Fountain Square area? In fact, that report mentions no Hellenistic pottery anywhere in the Mary's Well excavations. Departing from this astonishing lacuna, however, the 2012 book goes several *huge* steps: it not only knows of Hellenstic shards, it assigns their findspots to multiple loci and, finally, it itemizes the shards (Alexandre 2012a:57–59). We will examine all this information in due course—and will find the specifics also problematic and contradictory.

Turning our attention to the upper Church Square area, we recall that in 2006 Alexandre dated some "walls and floors" there to Hellenistic times based on an 18th–19th century "cutting." In her 2012 book, however, her argument has changed. The walls and floors in question[30] are still "Hellenistic," but now she has wisely jettisoned that entirely untenable argument for one far more respectable. She now ventures to date those structural elements to "Hellenistic" times on the basis of associated pottery:

> No associated floors were exposed in the small 1.5 sq m area excavated between these three walls, and *the dating of the walls is based on the worn late Hellenistic sherds in the accumulated earth layers* (L327, L330) they enclosed... A crushed limestone floor (L336) cut by a later Mamluk wall (W62) 2 m northwest of W72 and W69 *was also dated to the late Hellenistic period based on a few worn sherds.* (Alexandre 2012a:12, emphases added.)

To review, Alexandre's 2012 book presents a radically different interpretation of the findings than did her 2006 report. In the earlier document, no Hellenistic pottery is mooted—neither in the Church Square area nor in the Fountain Square area. In 2012, however, it is claimed that both areas divulged such pottery: the Fountain Square area has numerous loci with "Hellenistic sherds," while the Church Square area has "worn late Hellenistic sherds" now used to date the associated walling.

A review of the documentation shows that already in 2006 different presentations of the Hellenistic evidence existed. For in Alexandre's email to me dated January 11, 2006 (p. 251 above) she claims Hellenistic shards in the Fountain Square area. Yet in her summary report of only a few months later (p. 256 above) she makes no mention of Hellenistic shards anywhere in the Mary's Well excavations.

In fact, as far back as the year 2000 Alexandre claimed Hellenistic pottery evidence from a Nazareth excavation. We recall her notice in *Hadashot Arkheologiyot* of that year (above pp. 248–49) where she asserted the discovery of Hellenistic shards in the small excavation next to the White Mosque. However, she did not further characterize that assertion—despite my request. It is clear, then, that Alexandre's *claims* of Hellenistic pottery evidence in Nazareth go back many years—yet they are accompanied by a persistent *lack of* documentation and/or by *contradictory* documentation.

---

30. See p. 269, Fig. 11.2, features W69, W72, and W76.

Another example of such a contradiction occurs relative to a statement in Alexandre's 2012 book. In discussing the alleged Hellenistic pottery evidence from the Church Square area (p. 57), she writes: "Most of the Hellenistic sherds came from the very small area in between the three Hellenistic wall segments in Church Square (L327, 330, 334, 336)..." But two of these loci (L334 and 336) are not where the archeologist here specifies them (see Fig. 11.2). L334 is entirely at the other end of the excavation (in the southern probe), while L336 is some meters to the west of the walls in question. Perhaps this is mere sloppiness. But we recall that Alexandre is using these Hellenistic shards to date some precise "walls and floors" to Hellenistic times. Thus, *if the loci in which they were allegedly found are not even close to those walls, then her argument has no force.*

Furthermore, her argument has already *changed* once—it was originally the argument of Hellenistic dating from a structural "cutting." She abandoned that logic in 2012 to argue from associated Hellenistic pottery. But, as we will see, the data attendant to that pottery are also problematic.

As we proceed in our examination of the documentary trail left by Alexandre and the IAA, the Hellenistic evidence becomes ever weaker as questions mount and contradictions multiply. On several levels, the allegedly Hellenistic evidence simply *does not bear scrutiny.*

It can be noted that the propensity to 'create' Hellenistic evidence at Nazareth is very old. In *The Myth of Nazareth* I devoted an entire chapter ("The Hellenistic Renaissance Myth") to this problem, one which has a long and sordid history. Already in 1931 the Director of the Department of Antiquities of Palestine (precursor to the IAA) *himself* published a claim that six oil lamps from a Nazareth tomb were Hellenistic (Salm 2008a: 105 *f*). This claim was too early by as much as five hundred years (all the lamps are Roman), yet it was subsequently 'confirmed' by a Catholic scholar-priest who even claimed to have examined the lamps! A cursory examination of a photo of the lamps in question (even by a novice) shows them to *obviously* be Roman. In such cases (and examples are numerous), it is clear that we are not dealing with errant mistakes, incompetence, or sloppiness on the part of archeologists, scholars, and priests. We are dealing with something far more nefarious—with the tendentious, entrenched, and persistent creation of archeological 'data.' The inescapable result of all this pseudo-scholarship is that the history of Christian beginnings is an *invented* history.

What may be new—or relatively new—is the apparent wholesale collaboration of Jewish archeology (as a government sponsored entity) in the confabulation of Christian beginnings.[31] The motive is clear. Religious tourism is at stake—and a very great deal of money.

---

31. *Cf.* above, pp. 241 *f.*

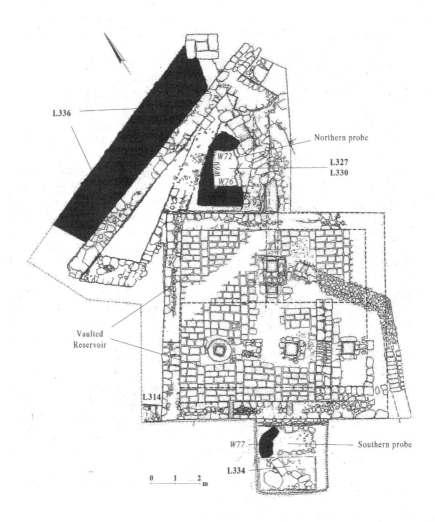

Figure 11.2. Plan of the Church Square (upper) excavation area
with loci containing alleged Hellenistic pottery.

Hellenistic structural features (walls, floors) are shaded gray. Marked in bold are
four loci in Alexandre's 2012 book where Hellenistic shards were allegedly found.
An additional locus (L333) has not been located. Alexandre also claimed Hellenistic
pottery (not itemized or diagrammed) from L334 and L336.
(Redrawn by author from Alexandre 2012a:Plans 2.1 and 2.3.)

There is now commercial and doctrinal pressure—as indeed there has always been—to support the traditional view of Christian beginnings and to suppress other views. It should come as no surprise, for example, that Alexandre's fairly benign May 1, 2006 report *was never published*, that similarly the short IAA report on the IMC excavation (above p. 189) was quickly pulled off the *Web*, and that fairly late claims of "Hellenistic" evidence (particularly in Alexandre's 2012 book) are encumbered with contradictions.

As regards the 2006 report on Mary's Well from Alexandre, I may be the only person (besides its author) who ever laid eyes upon it—that is, until I chose to publicize the report in my writings.[32] In hindsight, it appears that the report's communication to me was later regretted by Alexandre. This is understandable, for it demonstrably contradicts the archeologist's later book and thoroughly undermines her subsequent claims of Hellenistic evidence at Mary's Well. As we will see, the extent of the contradiction is breathtaking and goes far beyond the existence or non-existence of Hellenistic *pottery* in the Church Square and Fountain Square excavations. It includes an even more important parameter—the thoroughly bogus Hellenistic coin 'evidence.'

The late appearance of Hellenistic evidence

We have seen that Alexandre's 2006 Mary's Well report sent to this author made no mention of Hellenistic pottery either in the Fountain Square area or in the Church Square area. In contrast, her 2012 book itemizes Hellenistic pottery from both areas.

Of the nine chapters in Alexandre's 2012 book, Chapter 3 deals with the pottery (pp. 57–88). Most of those thirty-some pages are devoted to Crusader and Mamluk pottery—clearly the lion's share of ceramic evidence from Mary's Well. The pages of interest to us are merely five (57–61), half of which are taken up with diagrams.

There is in fact a limited and quite manageable repertoire of "Hellenistic" (eleven shards) and "Roman" (twenty shards) pottery from Mary's Well. The Hellenistic repertoire is itemized and diagrammed on page 58 of her book. Six of the shards allegedly came from the lower Fountain Square area, and five from the upper Church Square area.

We begin with a statement in Alexandre's book, page 16 (in her Chapter 2): "No pottery predating the Roman period was recovered from this channel or in its immediate vicinity." The channel in question is "CH138,"

---

32. This author's first public notice regarding Alexandre's unpublished 2006 Mary's Well report was in *The Myth of Nazareth* (pp. 132–33). Scholarship was also apprized of its existence in BAIAS 2008 (above p. 55), as well as in my contribution to Zindler 2012 (reprinted above pp. 161–62).

at the center of the Fountain Square excavation area (Fig. 11.3). Astonishingly, however, in her Chapter 3 (p. 58) Alexandre itemizes five "Hellenistic" shards *within five meters of CH138*! Furthermore, one of those allegedly Hellenistic fragments (her catalog number 8) was recovered from locus 142—which *abuts* Channel 138.

In the following paragraphs we consider more problems of a similar nature in Alexandre's 2012 presentation. But it is clear that the ceramic itemizations presented in her Chapter 3 ("The Pottery") contradict her Chapter 2 ("The Architecture and Stratigraphy"). It is as if the two chapters originated from different authors. It may be, however, that they owe their differing claims to varying *conceptions* of the evidence held at different times by the same author. This is not as unlikely as it may at first appear, for we have already seen (above p. 267) that Alexandre held two radically different views regarding dating certain "walls and floors" to Hellenistic times: in 2006 she espoused an argument by structural "cutting," while in 2012 she argued from associated "Hellenistic" pottery.

In her Chapter 2 (pp. 16–18) Alexandre discusses a small region of the lower Fountain Square area, namely, loci 223, 224 and wall W10. These loci straddle the critical Channel 138 discussed above (see Fig. 11.3).[33] The archeologist offers the following straightforward statement regarding the vicinity of that channel: "The stratigraphic evidence points to the Roman period." This is curious, because we saw (at the top of this page) that Channel 138 is precisely where she elsewhere (that is, in her Chapter 3) claims five *Hellenistic* shards. Even more curious is the archeologist's continuation: "*the ceramic evidence refines the date to the Middle to Late Roman horizon*" (emphasis added). Alexandre is still speaking of the vicinity of Channel 138, and thus we have here an astonishing contradiction between chapters. It is clear that in her Chapter 2 the archeologist has no knowledge of Hellenistic finds in the vicinity of Channel 138. She even writes that the ceramic evidence

---

33. The passage occurs in Alexandre's Mary's Well book, Chapter 2 ("The Architecture and Stratigraphy"), section "Stratum V: The Roman Period," and subsection "The Fountain Square Area." The entire paragraph reads as follows: [P. 16] "The topography dictated the water flow from north to south in Channel 138. In the area excavated immediately to the north of the channel, some Roman pottery was retrieved from accumulated deposits (L223 and L224), but no channel was found, and it seems that later building activities must have removed the earlier Roman structures. As the channel was blocked on the south by the later Stratum III–II fountain house wall (W10), it was not possible to discover whether the channel was still extant to its south or had been destroyed, as the floor of the later Mamluk fountain [P. 18] house (L114; see Plan 2.5) was not removed. The stratigraphic evidence points to the Roman period; the ceramic evidence refines the date to the Middle to Late Roman horizon." (Alexandre 2012a:16 and 18—her page 17 is taken up by a diagram.)

there dates from Middle to Late Roman times. But in her Chapter 3 she itemizes numerous "Hellenistic" shards from the vicinity of that very channel!

The inevitable implication is that Alexandre's conception regarding Channel 138 was not the same when she penned her Chapter 2 as when she penned her Chapter 3 with its pottery itemizations. In Chapter 2 the locus is clearly Roman—both stratigraphically and according to the recovered pottery. In her Chapter 3, however, Channel 138 has become *the* central locus for Hellenistic ceramic finds. Upon reflection, it becomes evident that the archeologist had a purely Roman view of Channel 138 *before* becoming cognizant of Hellenistic pottery there. The sequence will be of some importance. For now we simply note that her 2012 book's ceramic presentation (at least as regards the Hellenistic evidence) is a pastiche of two incompatible conceptions.

The pastiche is not merely between chapters, but also within chapters of Alexandre's book. There is not space here to give every example in that monograph of the contradiction between views regarding the Hellenistic evidence. One more, however, will be furnished. On p. 59 (her Chapter 3), the archeologist is considering the Roman pottery and writes:

> A concentration of worn water-eroded potsherds together with some plaster fragments found in the fill or accumulation layer (L142), adjacent to and possibly blocking Channel 138, date the channel to the Roman period.

Once again, Alexandre here explicitly dates Channel 138 *to the Roman period*—just as she had done on her pages 16–18 cited above. Furthermore, she does so here specifically on the basis of potsherds and plaster fragments from L142, which abuts (and possibly blocked) Channel 138. In contradiction to all this, however, on her immediately preceding page (p. 58) Alexandre has itemized *Hellenistic* pottery also from L142!

It is clear that Alexandre's 2012 book was not carefully edited. We will discover abundant and even more startling confirmation of this when we consider the numismatic evidence below. In sum, it appears to this author that Hellenistic material was introduced into Alexandre's book at a *later* stage in that monograph's evolution. It also appears that much of the pre-existing text was not properly edited to conform to the new material but was simply left alone. The result is what we see: two radically different conceptions of the Hellenistic evidence at Mary's Well. In the earlier conception, there simply *was no* Hellenistic evidence! In the later conception, not only does Hellenistic structural and ceramic evidence exist, but a confused attempt has apparently been made to itemize the pottery and locate reasonable findspots for it in the Mary's Well excavation areas. Since the earlier discussions regarding those findspots do not appear to have been subsequently edited, they still reflect an understanding of activity beginning there in *Roman* times and know nothing of the 'later' Hellenistic finds.

The documentary evidence we have now reviewed suggests that in 2006 the Hellenistic evidence from Mary's Well was still unclear. That year was a sort of turning point and reflects both views. We know this because Alexandre claimed Hellenistic shards in her email of January 11 (page 251 *supra*), yet she makes no mention of such shards in her May 1 report—only of Hellenistic "walls and floors" in the Church Square area (page 256 *supra*). As it happened, a number of scholars would thereafter attach varying Hellenistic claims to the Mary's Well excavations (already completed eight years before)—claims even including numerous Hasmonean coins.

During all those years, Alexandre was working on her Mary's Well book (she mentions adding a "chapter" to the book in her email of May 4, 2006; p. 255 *supra*). Now, it is very difficult—if not impossible—for an author to accommodate a *changing* view of the evidence while a book is in progress. After all, the revisions required would be continual, indeterminate, and probably both time-consuming and exhausting. It is no wonder, then, that her 2012 final report on Mary's Well is a 'pastiche' regarding the evidence—sometimes describing loci as Roman, sometimes as Hellenistic, and containing numerous conflicting statements in the text. In any case, conflicting views will never be satisfactory and can never *both* conform to the empirical reality of a site.

The two conceptions in tension with each other can be abbreviated as "a Roman inception of Nazareth" (pre-2006) and "a Hellenistic inception of Nazareth" (post-2006). Of the two, the pre-2006 conception—without the Hellenistic *additions*—is eminently reasonable and certainly correct. For example, a "Middle to Late Roman horizon" (above, p. 271) conforms well with the earliest post-Iron Age pottery already itemized in the Nazareth basin (Salm 2008a: Appendices 5 and 6). Similarly, Alexandre's assertion that "No pottery predating the Roman period" was found in the vicinity of Channel 138, and her assertion that the stratigraphy and ceramic profile of that channel were Roman—these are entirely as expected. Such statements also correspond to the major revelations in my first book, namely, that there is no demonstrably Hellenistic evidence from the basin, and that the settlement of Nazareth began during the sixty years between the First and the Second Jewish Revolts (70–130 CE).

Unfortunately, the documentary trail relative to Mary's Well reveals that this *former* view was superceded by a very problematic conception involving numerous bogus "Hellenistic" finds.

'Hellenistic' pottery itemization from the Fountain Square area. Six pottery shards, allegedly Hellenistic and with findspots in the lower Fountain Square area, are diagrammed and itemized by Alexandre on page 58 of her 2012 book (see Fig. 11.4). The archeologist admits that most of the shards were "rather eroded" (Alexandre 2012a:57). Her parallels are few. In fact, in three cases (nos. 5, 6, 7) she assigns the same parallel. Yet inspection shows that these three fragments clearly differ one from another, and thus her single parallel must be weak in at least two of the three cases.

• *Shard number 1* is the fragment of a fish plate allegedly from locus 218. Alexandre writes that this is "a local production" and dates it from the late fourth to the early first century BCE. It should be mentioned that *L218 is described in one passage as a Stratum II fill layer dating to Mamluk times* (Alexandre 2012a:57). Thus, the question arises as to how a "Hellenistic" shard could intrude into such a late context. The archeologist's parallels for this shard are not close. For example, all her parallels have slip while the claimed fragment does not. Alexandre also tentatively notes that "A bowl from Yodefat may be similar," but M. Aviam has observed that the *earliest* ceramic finds at Yodefat (Jotapata) date to the first century BCE.[34] In all, this writer finds Alexandre's "Hellenistic" interpretation of the shard weak.

• *Shards numbers 5, 6,* and *7* are parts of storage jar lips with rim diameters 10–12 cm. As mentioned above, Alexandre offers only one parallel (and the same parallel) for all three fragments. This superficial treatment must be deemed inadequate as the rims differ in form (*cf.* the diagrams in Fig. 11.4) and in description. The single chosen parallel (Guz-Zilberstein 1995:384, Fig. 6.35, type JR 1a) dates from the Persian to the Early Hellenistic periods, thus offering (at best) tangential 'Hellenistic' support—and none to Late Hellenistic times as implied by Alexandre's discussion.

Regarding shard no. 5, there is some question as to its provenance, L219. On page 16 of her book the archeologist characterizes that locus as part of a *"crushed limestone floor."* Yet on page 57 she describes it as a *"deep accumulation layer."*

As to shard no. 6, this author was able to quickly find a goodly number of similar Middle Roman vessels in the literature.

• *Shard number 8* is also part of the rim of a storage jar (diameter 8 cm). We have already discussed the astonishing contradictions attending this shard (above pp. 270–71). It was allegedly found in locus 142—a findspot that Alexandre elsewhere describes contained *no pottery older* than Roman times: "A considerable quantity of extremely worn Roman potsherds was found in an accumulation layer (L142) located adjacent to and directly above the top

---

34. *NEAEHL*, "Galilee" p. 454.

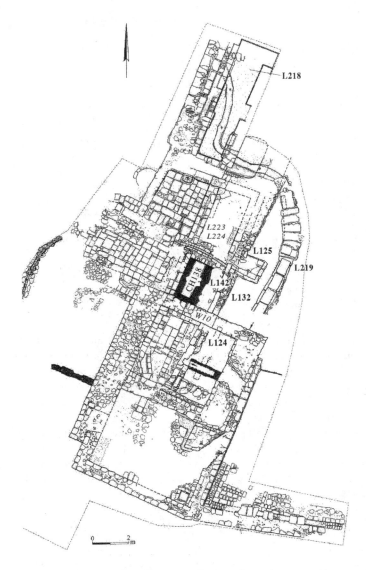

Figure 11.3. Plan of the Fountain Square (lower) excavation area with loci allegedly containing Hellenistic pottery.

Six loci in Alexandre's 2012 book where Hellenistic shards were allegedly found are marked in bold. All but one are within five meters of Channel 138. (Redrawn by author from Alexandre 2012a:Plans 2.2, 2.4, and 2.5.)

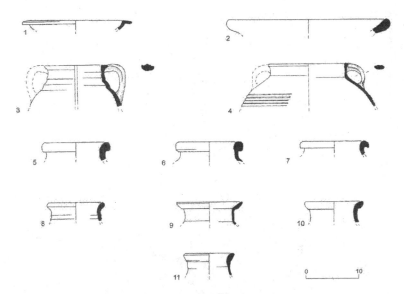

Figure 11.4. Diagrams of the alleged Hellenistic shards from Mary's Well.
(From Alexandre 2012a:58. Fair use.)

course of W 27. Although the sherds' water-eroded state rendered most of them unworthy of publication, the pottery clearly belonged to well-known Middle Roman-period pottery forms (see Fig. 3.2). *No pottery predating the Roman period was recovered from this channel or in its immediate vicinity*" (Alexandre 2012a:16). *This is one of the clearest contradictions in her pottery discussion.*

Alexandre offers one parallel for this shard—to Capernaum (Loffreda 2008:119, Type ANF 3). However, inspection shows this not to be a close parallel. In any case, Loffreda includes the Early Roman era (which ended about the time of the Bar Kochba revolt) as a possible dating for this shard, thus placing it within the purview of Nazareth emerging between the two Jewish Revolts.

• *Shard number 9* is also part of the rim of a storage jar (diameter *c.* 11 cm) allegedly found in locus 125. Alexandre offers one parallel—the same as for the preceding no. 8. Yet the two storage jars are obviously quite different in form (the wall of no. 9 is thin with a high neck, while no. 8 has virtually no neck and a thick wall). Of course, treating clearly different jar types with the same parallel is (once again) inadequate. And—yet again—the suggested parallel does not appear close. Finally, the parallel's dating range includes the second century CE—clearly weakening Alexandre's "Hellenistic" interpretation.

In summary, these six allegedly Hellenistic shards from the Fountain Square area are problematic as to condition ("eroded"), findspots, parallels, and dating. The fragments appear to be a potpourri from several periods. Two (5, 7) seem to date from Persian to Early Hellenistic times—somewhat earlier than even Alexandre proposes. No. 6 appears to come from a common Roman storage jar. It was found in L132—the same locus where several pre-Roman coins were allegedly found: "Four coins of the Hasmonean dynast Alexander Jannaeus were found *together with later Hellenistic sherds* in the deep Hellenistic period accumulation layer (L132) mentioned above, indicating that there may have been here a first-century BCE occupation layer" (Alexandre 2012a:16, emphasis added). We will consider the problematic coins later. But one difficulty with this passage is that Alexandre itemizes only one of those "later Hellenistic sherds" (no. 6) and—as we have seen—it appears by all accounts typically *Roman*. The case is instructive: (1) an apparently Roman shard has been (2) interpreted as belonging to the Hellenistic period, and (3) has then seemingly 'multiplied' into an unspecified number of "Hellenistic" fragments, to (4) finally support the notion that "there may have been here a first-century BCE occupation layer."

Other shards are also compatible with Middle Roman times, and *none* of those itemized by Alexandre seems to require the Late Hellenistic dating that she avers. Certainly, her presentation does not permit one to claim with any confidence that these shards are diagnostic of human presence during the Hellenistic period. While their re-examination by an independent ceramic expert would be useful, the underlying problems regarding the *late* appearance of these shards in the repertory of Mary's Well would still remain (discussion above pp. 270 *f*).

'Hellenistic' pottery from the Church Square area

In the 1997 season Alexandre conducted two small probes in the Church Square area, one to the north of the large Ottoman vaulted reservoir, and one to its south (Fig. 11.2). The northerly probe was where, in 2006, she had argued a 'cutting' as basis for dating some structural features to the Hellenistic period. This argument from structural features is detectable in two 2006 documents: her email to this author of January 11 ("a few various damaged walls from the Hellenistic" period), and the final line of her May 1 report (*cf.* pp. 251 and 256 above).

In 2012 Alexandre jettisons the above argument in favor of one from associated Hellenistic shards (above pp. 266–67). While her 2006 report mentioned no Hellenistic pottery at all, the 2012 book now itemizes five shards 'found' in the northern probe of the Church Square area—three shards specifically from the vicinity of walls W69, W72, and W76 (Fig. 11.2). These walls Alexandre accordingly dates to the Hellenistic period.

The archeologist's 2012 book also claims Hellenistic shards in several other sectors of the upper excavation. An overview of her claimed Hellenistic pottery from the Church Square area follows:

+ Northern probe, L327 and L330 (vicinity of W69, W72, and W76), three shards: catalog numbers 4, 10, and 11.
+ Southern probe, L314, one shard: catalog number 2 (a "mortarium" fragment).
+ Unknown locus, one shard: catalog number 3 (a "krater" fragment). The alleged findspot (L333) is not noted on any plan.
- Not diagnostic: Northern probe, L336: "a few worn [Hellenistic] sherds". *These artifacts are not itemized or further characterized but are used to date some walling specifically to the Late Hellenistic period* (see discussion below).

Thus, we find that in 2012 Alexandre was claiming Hellenistic shards in *all* the major sectors of the 1997–98 Mary's Well excavations: the Fountain Square area (various loci) as well as several sectors of the Church Square area. As previously remarked, the 2012 publication of profuse Hellenistic ceramic evidence at Mary's Well radically contrasts with its total absence in her 2006 IAA report and in her email communications to me of that year.

'Hellenistic' pottery itemization from the Church Square area. Five pottery shards, allegedly Hellenistic and allegedly found in the upper Church Square area, are diagrammed and itemized by Alexandre on page 58 of her 2012 book.

• *Shard number 2* (allegedly found in L314) is the fragment of a mortarium with a rim *c.* 30 cm in diameter, of sandy clay with many grits.[35] Alexandre offers two parallels—both to the second century BCE—which she characterizes as "similar" (2012a:58). In this writer's opinion the parallels are not close in form, as a comparison of diagrams reveals.[36]

• *Shard number 3* is the largest fragment of Alexandre's small "Hellenistic" pottery repertoire from Mary's Well, but it is an enigma for the archeolo-

---

35. Alexandre writes: "To the south of the Ottoman reservoir wall (W66), a row of a few stones (W77) and some worn late Hellenistic sherds were found in the lowest stony surface and overlying an accumulation layer (L334)..." (Alexandre 2012a:12). Cat. no. 2 was among these alleged Hellenistic shards. The mortarium was a sturdy and squat bowl with a wide mouth used primarily for mixing and grinding. It first appears in Persian and Early Hellenistic assemblages. (Leibner 1995:48).
36. The first Alexandre parallel (to Silberstein 441, Pl IX:3) has a protruding (not rounded) rim. Her other parallel is to Berlin 1997:126, Pl 38:PW 341-43—again, not close in form. On the other hand, this author has identified a number of parallels in the literature that date either to the Early Hellenistic Period (prior to *c.* 100 BCE) or to Late Roman times. Determination would require re-evaluation by an expert ceramicist.

gist. She writes "No exact parallels were found" and denominates it a "krater" though we are in all likelihood dealing with a globular cooking pot.[37]

The fragment was allegedly discovered in L333 (precise location unknown) of the Church Square area. It includes part of the rim (*c.* 10 cm diameter), neck, and shoulder of the artifact, giving a good idea of the form. The neck widens in a series of steps—not typical of Hellenistic ware: "In the Hellenistic era the neck of the pot is distinguished from the body by a sharp angle" (Silberstein 298). On the other hand, there are Roman examples of this form which Silberstein associates with cooking pots whose "chronological span is wide and relatively undefined," noting that similar pots have been dated to the time of Bar-Kokhba.[38]

• *Shard number 4* is a fragment of a cooking pot rim (15 cm diameter) which Alexandre once again (*cf.* above p. 270 no. 1) compares to "fairly similar" examples from Yodefat/Jotapata. We recall Aviam's observation that the *earliest* ceramic finds at Yodefat are from the first century BCE, suggesting this is in fact Roman ware. Alexandre's two other suggested parallels are to cooking pots with much smaller mouths.[39] Closer parallels date to early Roman times.[40]

• *Shard number 10.* This is a fragment of the rim of a bag shaped storage jar with a mouth diameter of *c.* 10 cm. Alexandre treats it along with nos. 5, 6, and 7 (from the lower area), writing: "The heavier thicker-walled jars have an earlier chronological range, in the early Hellenistic third and second centuries BCE" (Alexandre 2012a:59). This being the case, one wonders why she assigns the shard a parallel dating to the Late Hellenistic–Early

---

37.   Kraters were deep, wide-mouthed (generally 15–30 cm diameter) vessels used for serving food or drink, often for mixing wine and water into which a smaller vessel could be dipped for serving (for extensive treatment see A. Berlin 1997:133 *f*). They are generally incurving below the handles, whereas in the Alexandre example no. 3 the vessel is widening at this point (typical of cooking pots). Also, the mouth diameter of the artifact (*c.* 10 cm) is too small for a krater. Even the smallest krater from Dor (Guz-Zilberman, p. 362) has a mouth diameter of *c.* 13 cm. On the other hand, cooking pots often were of this size. A few had a carinated shoulder, as does this artifact no. 3.

38.   Silberstein 431, Pl V. 16, 17 and discussion pp. 430–31.

39.   Guz-Zilberstein (1995: 398-99 and Fig. 6.17:10) Type CP2. Dated III-II BCE. This parallel from Dor has an elaborate rim and a mouth only *c.* 10 cm in diameter. Another parallel given is to Berlin (1997:89-90, Pls. 22, 23), date: II BCE, with mouth *c.* 12 cm in diameter.

40.   Silberstein 2000, Pl. V:4–6 (esp. no. 6). Date 50 BCE–200 CE; Arav and Freund 1995:Pl. IV.1; Calderon 2000:94 (Pl. II:29): "The classic cooking pot commonly found in Israel," dating from the end of I BCE to II CE; Diez-Fernandez (an author who generally dates too early—see Salm 2008a:271–72) 1983, type 10.4 (#270) dating *c.* 50 CE–*c.* 150 CE, and type 10.6b (#309) dating *c.* 110 CE–*c.* 350 CE.

Roman periods and one not particularly close in form (Loffreda 2008:119, Type ANF 3). The shard indeed appears to this writer to be of a fairly common Persian–Early Hellenistic type.[41]

• *Shard number 11.* This is a fragment of yet another rim (diameter *c.* 8 cm) of a storage jar with thinner walls than the preceding. Alexandre assigns this shard the same parallel as no. 10, but such a cursory treatment is clearly unsatisfactory for the two shards differ in form. Regarding the thinner-walled jars, Alexandre writes that they "appear in the second half of the second century BCE" (Alexandre 2012a:59). They overlapped chronologically with the thicker-walled jars in the late second century BCE. A search of the literature reveals parallels to the Persian–Early Hellenistic eras. Other parallels suggest a Middle–Late Roman dating.[42]

Regarding the "worn" and allegedly Late Hellenistic pottery fragments from L336, the archeologist writes: "A crushed limestone floor (L336) cut by a later Mamluk wall (W62) 2 m northwest of W72 and W69 was also dated to the late Hellenistic period based on a few worn sherds" (Alexandre 2012a:12). Here we have an unverifiable affirmation of the archeologist, of a type familiar to those who have read my first book (Salm 2008a:272). The question arises: Why, if these shards are sufficiently recognizable to *use* in a diagnostic manner, are they not sufficiently recognizable to *describe?* It should be noted that Alexandre uses these uncharacterized (and indeterminate in number) "worn" pottery fragments as evidence for dating walls to a specific era: the *Late* Hellenistic period. *Such a definite and extraordinary conclusion requires at least* some *evidence*—which she does not furnish. As a result, her dating the large locus L336 (Fig. 11.2) to Late Hellenistic times is *evidently without* basis.

Summary of the pottery results

At the end of her book Alexandre summarizes the pottery finds from Mary's Well and draws the following untenable conclusions:

> The scanty architectural remains and potsherds in Church Square and the small areas of accumulation layers and fills deep-down in Fountain Square indicate that there was some occupation near the spring in the Hel-

---

41. Guz-Zilberstein Jar type JR 1b (p. 311); Fig. 6.48:15 (p.401) and Fig. 6.57:7 (p.414).

42. The most compelling parallels in form are to Guz-Zilberstein Fig. 6.57:10 (p. 414) Type JR1, and Fig. 6.64:15 (p.401), both "Persian-All Hellenistic." Silberstein dates a similar jar (Pl. 3:8, p. 427) to the end of II BCE. Similar jars were also common in later Roman times and many have been found in the Nazareth basin. *Cf.* Diez-Fernandez Type 1.8 #91 and Type 1.10 #121. No less than nine examples of such Roman jars have been published in the Nazareth literature (Diez-Fernandez pp. 109–10).

lenistic period. The earliest potsherds belong to the later half of the second century BCE, probably reflecting the founding of the new hamlet.
(Alexandre 2012a:153)

However, the scanty parallels, unconvincing datings, and generally perfunctory treatment by Alexandre of the eleven allegedly Hellenistic shards examined above do not support the above citation. Those shards appear to be a potpourri from numerous periods, including the Middle and Late Roman. They also include substantial affinities to Persian and Early Hellenistic types (nos. 5, 6, 7, 10, 11). This is something of a surprise, for *no one (not even Alexandre) has claimed habitation in the Nazareth basin preceding the second century BCE.*

From the information provided in her book, Alexandre's conclusion of a Late Hellenistic ("Hasmonean") dating for these shards appears weak to this author. Some shards point to Roman times, and there appears to be a high probability that at least a couple are Persian–Early Hellenistic.

The likely presence of a few such early shards, however, by no means signals human activity in the Nazareth basin between the fifth and second centuries BCE.[43] Given the conflicting and entirely suspicious documentation set forth in the preceding sections of this chapter, the small ceramic repertoire from Mary's Well spanning seven hundred years regrettably suggests to this author the presence of an artificial assemblage of little scientific value. While a re-examination of these fragments by an independent specialist would be useful, the underlying problems regarding their post-2006 appearance in the documentation would still remain (above pp. 266*f*). At the very least, the pottery repertoire from Mary's Well does *not* support the conclusion cited above that these shards are diagnostic of human presence during the generalized "Hellenistic" period. This becomes clearer when we realize that *several passages in Alexandre's writings contradict the existence of pre-Roman ceramic evidence at Mary's Well* (see next page).

A note is in order regarding the Roman pottery. Alexandre diagrams twenty Roman shards with accompanying discussion (pp. 59–61). *All the shards but one are from the lower Fountain Square area.* This provenance is of some moment due to the remarkable summary statement by the archeologist:

> The [Roman] pottery repertoire points to a chronological range for the activity in Fountain Square, presumably related to the functioning of the early water channels, from the end of the second or early third century to the first half of the fourth century CE, within the Middle and Late Roman periods.   (Alexandre 2012a:61)

---

43.   No scholar since Bagatti has claimed habitation in the Nazareth basin during Persian times. A review of the evidence shows a complete lack of archeological finds dating to the fourth and third centuries BCE (Salm 2008a:60–61).

According to this, the Roman pottery repertoire from Mary's Well witnesses to the timespan *c.* 200–*c.* 350 CE. In other words—by the archeologist's own admission—*no Roman pottery was found at Mary's Well dating to 'the time of Jesus'!* The earliest Roman pottery from Mary's Well (as *originally* analyzed) is *Middle* Roman.

A Middle Roman incipience of ceramic evidence is similarly detected in another passage from Alexandre's book:

> *Based on the ceramic evidence,* it seems that the construction, or at least the functioning of the two water channels, Channels 138 and 150 in Fountain Square, *should be dated to the Middle Roman period* (late second or third–fourth centuries CE).　　(Alexandre 2012a:154, emphasis added.)

This statement is very strange because Channel 138 was—as we have now seen (*above* p. 268)—the locus of no less than *five* allegedly "Hellenistic" shards! Thus, the "ceramic evidence" in and around Channel 138 points—in Alexandre's *present* text—not to the Middle Roman period but to the Hellenistic period.

It is clear that the above two citations are holdovers from the earlier view of Mary's Well—the view existing *before the invention of Hellenistic evidence.* These two citations agree not only with one another but also with numerous other statements in Alexandre's book (some cited above pp. 270–72), *e.g.,* that "the ceramic evidence [around Channel 138] refines the date to the Middle to Late Roman horizon," that "A concentration of worn water-eroded potsherds... adjacent to and possibly blocking Channel 138, date the channel to the Roman period" and, most egregiously, "No pottery predating the Roman period was recovered from this channel [CH138] or in its immediate vicinity."[44]

These 'early' passages all ignore—and even repudiate—the existence of pre-Roman ceramic evidence at Mary's Well. They also cohere with the view expressed in the 2006 report which Alexandre communicated to me (above p. 255). Its second paragraph begins:

> The main excavations were carried out under the modern 1960s concrete Fountain House, which was demolished with the aim of reconstructing the ruined Ottoman stone Fountain House. The archaeological remains exposed dated from the Roman, the Crusader, the Mamluk and the Ottoman periods. From the Roman period part of a covered dressed stone channel was exposed, as well as some wall stubs and *Middle* Roman pottery.
> (Emphasis added.)

It seems that, at the time Alexandre wrote all these passages, she was unaware of any Hellenistic ceramic evidence at Mary's Well. She espoused this 'non-Hellenistic' view as late as 2006. But then her conception appar-

---

44. Alexandre 2012a:16, 18, 59.

ently changed. It seems that a significant amount of Hellenistic (and some Early Roman) evidence was then artificially inserted into the Mary's Well results—whether by Alexandre or by some other hand. Put bluntly, it appears that this critical early evidence was *invented*.

When we come to discuss the coins at Mary's Well, we will be able to document further steps in this apparent invention. For now we simply acknowledge that, due apparently to sloppiness (or mere oversight), the above embarrassing citations were never edited out of Alexandre's 2012 book. Their presence—side-by-side with a good deal of contradictory "Hellenistic" evidence—has produced the pastiche effect obvious to anyone who reads her book with care. That tome will be incomprehensible to anyone who is blissfully unaware of the two opposing views described above. One view is empirically based, the other apparently invented.

Despite many references in Alexandre's book to pottery from *Middle* and *Late* Roman times, in only two instances does she mention *Early* Roman pottery. This is remarkable given how important the latter period is to Jesus-studies. Both references occur on p. 61. In one case, Alexandre refers to a high-necked jug which she admits, however, "is found in Early *to* Middle Roman contexts." This jug cannot be used as evidence for Early Roman times, as it may well date to the second (or even the third) century CE.[45]

In the second case, the archeologist writes: "A nozzle of a first-century CE knife-pared lamp (Fig 3.2.20) found in a fill above a Mamluk floor (L151) cannot be used for dating architectural elements, but does indicate an Early Roman presence." This is, however, incorrect. I extensively discuss such knife-pared oil lamps (often termed "Herodian") in my 2008 book.[46] In the Lower Galilee (per the work of lamp specialist V. Sussman) they date from *after* the time of Herod the Great *until the Bar Kochba Revolt*.[47] Thus, such lamps may have been produced in the early second century CE and, in any case, their presence is entirely compatible with Nazareth beginning *after* the First Jewish War.

Thus, Alexandre's meagre Early Roman pottery evidence evaporates under scrutiny. No pottery found at Mary's Well demonstrably dates to 'the time of Jesus.' To this conclusion we may also confidently add a second: no pottery found at Mary's Well certainly—*nor even probably*—dates to Hellenistic times.

---

45.   The jug is itemized at Alexandre 2012a:Fig. 3.2:19. Parallels given are to Diez Fernandez 1983:150, No. 212 and M. Balouka, "The Pottery From the House of Dionysos," in R. Talgam and Z. Weiss, *The Mosaics of the House of Dionysos at Sepphoris* (*Qedem* 44), Jerusalem:2004, p. 39, Fig. 1:10.
46.   The lamps are also termed "bow-spouted" after their form. See Salm 2008a:167 *f.*
47.   Salm 2008a:168.

The "Hellenistic" Coins from Mary's Well

Important as the alleged Hellenistic-Early Roman pottery is for an assessment of human activity at Mary's Well around the turn of the era, the claimed "Hellenistic" coins there have assumed a particularly critical place in the 'existence of Nazareth controversy.' Perhaps this is because coins are datable in ways that pottery is not, and/or because they are (at least in theory) extraordinarily durable. Whatever the reason(s), over the last several years numerous questionable claims have been made regarding some "Hellenistic" coins from Mary's Well. While the Mary's Well pottery merely presented contradictions within the writings of Alexandre and the IAA, the documentation regarding coins from the site includes extraordinary published statements by *other* scholars not affiliated with the excavation. At the same time, these scholars apparently did not know what each was saying nor exactly what Alexandre was saying, so that an instructive scholarly free-for-all has taken place full of innuendo and with very little basis in the evidence itself. In fact, the following saga regarding alleged Hellenistic coins offers—from beginning to end—one of the most stunning displays of scholarly ineptitude to be found in the entire realm of that dysfunctional enterprise commonly known as 'New Testament Archaeology.'

The Strange Documentary Trail

(A) Alexandre's January 11, 2006 personal communication

If Hellenistic coins were in fact found at Mary's Well, this 2006 email is the first instance when I would have *expected* them to be mentioned. After all, in that communication (see above, p. 251) Alexandre provided a snapshot of the main findings from the excavations ("That's it in a nutshell," she writes in the third paragraph). She mentioned "Hellenistic sherds" and a few "damaged walls" from the Hellenistic period—both claims we have now obviated in the previous section, concluding that the pottery in question is probably not Hellenistic and, hence, that neither are the walls (since she dates them by association to the shards, *cf.* above, p. 277).

The omission of Hellenistic coins from this review of the Mary's Well finds—if they existed—appears strange, given that Alexandre mentions Hellenistic "sherds" and "walls." The obvious question arises: if such early coins were known to Alexandre at the time, then why did she not mention them? Then again, however, she makes no mention of coins at all, though I would later learn that over 160 coins would be claimed from Mary's Well.

As the reader is aware, our preceding examination of the pottery has suggested that the "Hellenistic" evidence is a *later* phenomenon, an *addition to* the Mary's Well finds. 2006 appears to have been a 'swing' year in this regard (see above, p. 273), for in that year Alexandre composed reports reflecting both views: her January 11 email to me mentions "Hellenistic sherds" in a general way, but her more complete May 1 report (next section) still does not. There is no mention anywhere yet of Hellenistic coins, artifacts which assume an increasingly important role in subsequent years.

(B) The 2006 Mary's Well report

If Hellenistic coins actually existed in the Mary's Well finds, their omission from this report by Alexandre (above pp. 256–57) is even more surprising than their omission from her January 11 email. For her May 1 document actually *characterizes* the recovered coins. From the lower Fountain Square area (second paragraph) we have (1) "coins from Feodalic France" (Crusader); (2) "worn coins"; and (3) "many 14–15th century small denomination coins." Alexandre mentions no coins from the upper Church Square area.[48]

Patently, there is *no mention at all* of Hellenistic coins in this report. It is, one might venture, possible perhaps to claim that Alexandre intended such coins with her vague phrase "worn coins." The implication would then be that *she did not know at the time that some of those worn coins were Hellenistic*—for, if she did, she surely would have mentioned them!

Alexandre is no numismatist and she did not author the Chapter 5 in her book which deals with the coin evidence. She engaged Ariel Berman for that task. In 2012 Berman will claim no less than twelve pre-Roman (*i.e.* Hellenistic) coins from the Mary's Well repertoire (below, pp. 295 f). But it is difficult to imagine that *all* of these coins evaded Alexandre's earlier identification. After all, she is a trained archeologist with many years experience in the field. She certainly possesses more than passing acquaintence with the coins of Palestine from Hellenistic and Roman times. Every coin recovered from Mary's Well—worn or not—certainly passed through her hands and under her gaze in 1997–98. So, when in 2006 she twice omits any mention of pre-Crusader coins (January 11 and May 1), the conflict with Berman's later assessment is at least noteworthy.

For now, we need only be aware of the fact that the "Hellenistic" interpretation of coins from Mary's Well postdates 2006. As conveyed in italics two paragraphs above, in that year Alexandre was evidently not yet aware of such an interpretation. Hence—like the "Hellenistic" pottery—the "Hellenistic" coins belong to a *later* stage in the evidence. This strengthens our view that, in fact, *all* the "Hellenistic" evidence from Mary's Well is *late*.

---

48. A. Berman clarifies that only one coin (from the Ottoman period) was found in the upper Church Square area (Alexandre 2012a:107).

(C) The Myth of Nazareth

Publication of the book was in March, 2008, but research ended approximately one year earlier. Thus the book does not yet note the first astonishing claim of Hellenistic coins from Mary's Well. (The NVF report was published in December, 2007—see next section.) Regarding early coins, I wrote simply: "They are totally absent from the Nazareth basin even through Roman times. The earliest recovered coin is of the emperor Constantius, who ruled 337–361 CE" (Salm 2008a:146–47). This is still correct when we astutely discount Berman's later problematic claims.

(D) The Nazareth Village Farm report

In December 2007 the extensive report on the archeological finds from the NVF appeared.[49] On pages 39–40 it discusses coins finds at Mary's Well, over one kilometer away. This is of course curious, because the finds at Mary's Well have no obvious relevance to results at the Nazareth Village Farm. Nevertheless, those two NVF pages announce astonishing *new* information on Alexandre's finds at Mary's Well—information, we recall, ostensibly derived from an excavation carried out *a full decade earlier*. Pfann *et al.* write:

> In addition, 165 coins were uncovered by Yardenna Alexandre in the 1997–1998 excavations at Mary's Well, Nazareth. The coins were overwhelmingly Mamluk, but also included a few Hellenistic, Hasmonean, Early Roman, Byzantine, Umayyad and Crusader coins (Alexandre, forthcoming). (Pfann *et al.* 2007:40)

This is, of course, an entirely different assessment of the coins than that furnished by Alexandre in her May, 2006 report where she mentioned Crusader ("Feodalic"), Mamluk ("14th–15th century"), and "worn" coins. She made no mention of Hellenistic, Hasmonean, and Early Roman coins. Nor did she divulge the exact number: 165. That figure appears here in the literature for the first time, and it tallies perfectly with the number of coins in Berman's later Mary's Well catalog (to appear in Alexandre's 2012 book). It is clear that Pfann *et al.* were party to privileged information.

Such detailed knowledge *could only come from the IAA*. This is certain, for no agency other than the IAA had (and has) access to the actual evidence from the Mary's Well excavations. Alexandre, of course, is a member of the IAA, but her 2006 reports to me (points A and B above) together with the foregoing discussion suggest that this information did not come from her. (It appears she may have been among the *last* to know of Hellenistic coins!) The most obvious source, in fact, would be Dr. Ariel Berman himself, the IAA numismatist assigned to evaluate and report on the Mary's Well coins.

---

49. BAIAS vol 25:16–79; *cf.* discussion above pp. 160 *f.*

Evidently, then, sometime before the writing of the 2007 NVF report, comunications took place between Stephen Pfann and the IAA.[50] Those communications must have included specific information on the Mary's Well finds and a *new* twist: "The coins were overwhelmingly Mamluk, but also included a few Hellenistic, Hasmonean, Early Roman, Byzantine, Umayyad and Crusader coins."

Such communication between Pfann and the IAA would not be surprising and probably has been close and ongoing for many years. The NVF is a major commercial and religious venue—with some pretense to also being an archeological one. In all likelihood Pfann has regular and cordial working relationships with relevant agencies, including the Israel Ministry of Tourism, the Nazareth Municipality, and the IAA. This previously unpublished Mary's Well information was proprietary and within the purview of the IAA. It would only reach Pfann if the IAA made it available to him.

Nonetheless, Pfann had nothing to do with the Mary's Well excavation. It is remarkable that such sensitive numismatic information was not first published by Alexandre herself, the excavation director. This places Alexandre in an interesting light and indicates that she may not, in fact, be the 'moving force' behind revelations at Mary's Well. She appears to be the mouthpiece for broader—and more powerful—commercial and religious entities involved with Nazareth. In looking at the history of her various reports, public statements, and activities, it is clear that over the years her archeological work has taken place in tandem with another role—the sometimes high-profile spokesperson for tourist and commercial interests in the Nazareth area (including surrounding villages like Cana). She is a messenger, and her messages have frequently pertained to large commercial enterprises of a religious-commercial nature. As an archeologist, Alexandre appears in the first instance to be an authority on, and source of, new archeological information in Nazareth. But she may be more correctly viewed as the primary conduit of "information" carefully vetted at higher levels of the Israeli government.[51]

(E) The BAIAS responses (2008)

My strong critique of the lengthy NVF report was published in the subsequent issue of the *Bulletin of the Anglo-Israel Archaeological Society* (vol. 26, 2008, pp. 95–103). In that critique, I take Pfann *et al.* to task for all sorts of problems in their report—including multiple double-datings, a conflict be-

---

50. Though three scholars authored the NVF report, its discussion of coins at Mary's Well must go back principally to Pfann, the Director of the University of the Holy Land and the 'intellectual' force behind the NVF. Rapuano was responsible for the report's pottery analysis and Voss for the archeological survey of the NVF.

51. On Alexandre being 'co-opted' by broader considerations, see below p. 291.

tween surveys, and Rapuano's generally specious conclusions regarding the alleged Hellenistic pottery. I also mentioned the NVF report's remarkable attribution of "Hellenistic" coins to Alexandre, as discussed in the preceding section, noting that Alexandre's 'official' 2006 Mary's Well report—sent to me by email and unsolicited—"contains no mention of '165 coins' nor of coins from Hellenistic or Hasmonaean times" (BAIAS 2008:100). On the same page of my published critique I added:

> It may well be that the 'many 14–15th century small denomination coins' cited above total 165, a fact perhaps subsequently shared by Ms. Alexandre with the authors of the NVFR. But, once again, her report makes no mention of coins belonging to eras other than the '14–15th century.' Certainly, it is difficult to believe that such significant evidence as coins from the Hellenistic, Hasmonaean, and Early Roman periods (incidentally, not otherwise attested in the Nazareth basin) was subsequently divulged to the authors of the NVFR, but escaped the official IAA report.

Stephen Pfann responded in the same issue of BAIAS.[52] Not only did he assert that Alexandre had *personally* communicated to him the existence of Hellenistic coins, but he asserted that the claim as published in the NVF report (NVFR) was a verbatim statement provided by her "to quote in our report":

> *Pace* Salm, Dr. Alexandre herself provided the following text to quote in our report: 'In addition, 165 coins were uncovered by Yardenna Alexandre in the 1997–1998 excavations at Mary's Well, Nazareth. The coins were overwhelmingly Mamluk, but also included a few Hellenistic, Hasmonaean, Early Roman, Byzantine, Umayyad and Crusader coins.' A more detailed analysis by Ariel Berman will be included in the forthcoming report. (Alexandre, forthcoming). (BAIAS 2008:106)

In Chapter 9 I considered this citation (which was first printed on p. 40 of the 2007 BAIAS article). If it had originally been a verbatim quote from Alexandre, as *now* claimed, it would have been a very strange one—she refers to herself *in the third person*, and her quote was in 2007 embedded into Pfann's prose *without* the customary quotation marks and also *without* the customary footnote of attribution (see discussion above, pp. 160 *f*).

But there is another problem here, one larger than whether the critical information regarding "a few Hellenistic, Hasmonaean, Early Roman" coins was in fact a verbatim quotation from Alexandre herself. I am referring to the fact that *Alexandre still did not know that some of the Mary's Well coins were Hellenistic* (above p. 285). She did not know this in May, 2006, and *there are indications that she was still unaware of such "Hellenistic" coins until after 2010*

(point F below). This certainly places Pfann's assertion regarding Alexandre under suspicion. Additionally, we have noted that the IAA scholar whom Pfann would most likely contact in this matter would be the numismatist A. Berman. He is the most logical source of the above information, not Alexandre.[53]

On the other hand, if Pfann is to be believed, then the following rather incredible sequence of events presumably took place:

— Alexandre excavated 165 coins at Mary's Well but *omitted* critical information about Hellenistic and Roman coins in her 2006 IAA report which she shared with me;

— While withholding such early coin information from myself (and from the IAA?), Alexandre selectively shared it with Pfann *et al.* working at the other end of the Nazareth basin;

— Pfann *et al.* revealed that critical coin evidence for a 'Jesus-era Nazareth' in *their* 2007 report dealing with the NVF, while Alexandre was entirely silent on this point;

— After being critiqued by myself, Pfann *et al.* alleged that the two sentences under scrutiny were a verbatim quote from Alexandre, despite the fact that the original passage doesn't appear to be a quotation and that in substance their claim conflicts with Alexandre's own IAA report—one which I already had in my possession for two years.

One more observation can be made regarding the citation above. Pfann states that Alexandre would not be authoring the chapter on coins in her forthcoming book. That task would devolve to Ariel Berman. Once again, this is 'inside' information.

(F) The First International Conference, Nazareth (2010 / 2012)

2010 witnessed the incipience of a new "International Conference" series focussing on the archeology, history, and heritage of Nazareth. This first conference included presentations by S. Pfann and Y. Alexandre, subsequently published in the "Nazareth Academic Studies Series" (also new), whose first issue appeared in June of 2012.

---

53. This suspicious claim of having received detailed numismatic information from Alexandre herself brings to mind the casuistry of Fr. C. Kopp in the 1930s, as described in my first book pp. 107 *f*. As mentioned above (pp. 36, 142, 268), six oil lamps from a Nazareth tomb had been claimed as "Hellenistic," though they are obviously Roman. Kopp—who certainly knew better—instead of correcting the error wrote that he himself had consulted the photographs of the lamps and that they were "surely" Hellenistic. Thus, I observed in my book, "deception is heaped upon deception."

Pfann's paper[54] is essentially an abridged version of the 2007 NVF report (*cf.* Chapter 4 above) written with the layperson in mind. The NVF report had claimed Hellenistic pottery finds at the NVF, a claim I vehemently contested in a published *Response* (Salm 2008b). That *Response* in turn provoked an extensive *Amendment* appearing in the 2008 issue of BAIAS (Rapuano 2008). It is interesting that *Pfann's 2010 conference paper no longer claims Hellenistic pottery finds at the NVF. It also makes no mention of the controversial Hellenistic coins at Mary's Well*—something the 2007 NVF report surprisingly did (above, point D).

Alexandre's article[55] reviews the *traditional* history of Nazareth, essentially avoiding overt mention of my earlier book though admitting the existence of a hiatus following the Assyrian invasions of the eighth century BCE. She asserts:

> The earliest mention of a settlement by the name of "Nazareth" is in the 1st century CE, in the New Testament, where it is referred to as the site of the Annunciation to Mary of the birth of Jesus by the Angel Gabriel (Lk 1, 26), and as the village in which Jesus grew up (Matthew 2, 23). The identification of Nazareth is certain and unequivocal.
>
> (Alexandre 2012b: 32)

Right. Alexandre also conceives Nazareth as having been a "very small Jewish village, or hamlet" in the Early Roman period (p. 36). How she can be certain that this *particular* hamlet was "the village in which Jesus grew up" (above) remains enigmatic.

Alexandre then reviews her IMC excavation, cataloguing errors we have reviewed in the previous chapter, such as that "In the courtyard of the house a rock-hewn, bell-shaped cistern channeled run-off water from the roofs." We have seen, however, that the "courtyard" in question has a very steep slope (Fig. 10.7), that there were no "roofs" (the IMC partitions are altogether too low), and that the cistern (feature [z]) is *uphill* from the alleged house and thus could not have received its "run-off water."[56]

Reviewing a century of past excavations in the Venerated Area, Alexandre then draws "Roman" and even "Early Roman" conclusions based on the vaguest of bedrock features (which could be from any period):

> Many underground rock-hewn cavities were found [under the Church of the Annunciation] including dozens of silos, pits, water cisterns, quarries, olive presses and a wine press [Fig. 4]. While some of these underground

---

54.   S. Pfann, "The Nazareth of Jesus: The Excavations and Reconstruction at the Nazareth Village Farm" (Yazbak and Sharif 2012: 9–25).

55.   Y. Alexandre, "Uncovering Ancient Nazareth: Past and Present Archaeological Excavations" (Yazbak and Sharif 2012: 27–41).

56.   Above pp. 204 and 226.

elements were dated by the excavators to the Iron Age, most were in use in the Roman period. Negative line impressions in the bedrock indicated that there were once stone walls from *houses* dating to the *Early Roman* period overlying these underground basement chambers.
(Alexandre 2012b:34. Emphasis added.)

Alexandre's venturesome use of "Negative line impressions in the bedrock" to date *houses* to the *Early Roman period* entails multiple huge leaps in logic. It is well known that structural features in isolation are difficult to date and, furthermore, that stratigraphy is generally inapplicable to bedrock. Hence such line impressions are virtually undatable. In the absence of compelling ancillary information, dating bedrock line impressions specifically to the Early Roman period is breathtakingly wishful. In this case, it basically concludes what the tradition simply wishes to hear. Finally, that such line impressions indicate "houses" (rather than agricultural features, as betrayed by the surrounding context in every direction) is also wishful, particularly given that several tombs lie directly under the Church of the Annunciation—and Jews did not *live* in the vicinity of tombs!

It is important to note Alexandre's willingness to make such unfounded assertions in 2010 (the date of the conference, two years earlier than the publication). This prepares us for a consideration of her 2012 Mary's Well book. It is now clear that nothing is off the table where vindication of the Jesus story is concerned. If line impressions in bedrock can be made to signify a dwelling from the Early Roman period, then no assertion is *too* outlandish, no falsehood *too* great—regardless of the evidence at hand. Yet, as we have observed, Alexandre is not working in isolation. She is neither the author nor the motivator behind such quack archeology, but is its agent. Alexandre is an employee of the *Israel Antiquities Authority*, and broader considerations are at play (above, p. 287).

Conflicting coin statements. In our prior discussion of the alleged Hellenistic pottery, we detected two views in Alexandre's writings on Mary's Well: an earlier view which knows no Hellenistic evidence, and a later view which does. Thus, we characterized the archeologist's 2012 book as a "pastiche" of two incompatible views (pp. 282–83 above). Surprisingly, both views also appear in the 2012 Nazareth conference publication. This leads one to suspect that some 'editing' of Alexandre's original 2010 presentation has taken place.

Concerning the numismatic evidence, in the 2012 conference publication Alexandre is credited with two statements. One reflects the earlier view which does not make any reference to Hellenistic evidence from the site. It is found on pages 39–40 of the conference monograph:

> Over 160 worn low-denomination bronze Mamluk coins were found in piles that were dredged out of the water in the clean-up operation. Coins were commonly thrown into water sources to bring good luck. The coins also included a few Roman and Byzantine coins and four silver Crusader coins.   (Alexandre 2012b:39–40)

The first sentence of this passage echoes Alexandre's 2006 report which notes "the dredging of many 14–15th century small denomination coins" (above, p. 256). Other elements are new but not in conflict with the 2006 report: an approximate number of coins ("Over 160") and the second sentence with its details regarding "a few" Roman, Byzantine, and Crusader coins.

However, the total absence of Hellenistic coins—if a dozen were indeed present—is again jarring, particularly given the fact that Alexandre here actually details the coin finds (as she did in her May 1, 2006 report).

In a conflicting passage, also from the 2012 conference publication, Alexandre describes different finds:

> In the excavations at Mary's Well undertaken in 1997, Late Hellenistic pottery shards and ten coins of the Hasmonean King Alexander Jannaeus (103–73 BCE) were found in the earth fills below the fountain house.   (Alexandre 2012b:32.)

Here, *for the first time* since her 1997–98 excavations, Alexandre *herself* asserts the existence of Hellenistic coins at Mary's Well. It is difficult to reconcile the two passages in the same conference report. In order to do so, one has to presume sloppiness on Alexandre's part: in the former passage she simply 'overlooked' these ten Hasmonean coins. Because she had not mentioned such coins in her 2006 report nor in her correspondence with me (points A and B above), one would have to conclude that sloppiness is either endemic with Alexandre or she has a penchant for ignoring Hellenistic evidence.

On the other hand, the above passage reads very much like specialist information proceeding from the numismatist A. Berman. We know that he was assigned to the Mary's Well coin catalog already in 2007 (above, p. 288) and hence, by the time of the conference publication (2012), he would have already completed his work.[57] It is possible that this contradictory informa-

---

57. The ten Hasmonean coins come from "earth fills," while in the prior passage the coins "were found in piles that were dredged out of the water in the clean-up operation." The two descriptions are not necessarily in conflict. A "fill," archeologically speaking, is the earth (or other material) that has intruded into a previously existing structure, such as a ditch, channel, *etc.* The fill is later, the enclosing structure is earlier. Thus, it is possible—and altogether likely—that many (if not most) of the coins recovered from Mary's Well would have been found in fill, whereas they were once at the

tion was inserted into the 2012 printed transcript of Alexandre's presentation. Biblical scholars have a word for such activity—*interpolation.*

(G) Bart Ehrman's **Did Jesus Exist?** *(2012)*

Ehrman's book—written for the layperson, not the scholar—rather superficially addresses claims regarding the nonexistence of Jesus which "are seeping into the popular consciousness at an alarming rate" (*DJE?* 6–7). The author devotes several pages to my work (*DJE?* 193–97), pages in which he ignores vital elements of my case (*e.g.*, the Nazareth oil lamps, all of which date to the common era) and in which he appears unacquainted with the pertinent data. However, Ehrman is aware of Pfann's above assertion that Alexandre had uncovered Hellenistic, Hasmonean, and Early Roman coins at Mary's Well. He mirrors that claim and adds a new twist:

> There is an even bigger problem, however. Many compelling pieces of archeological evidence indicate that in fact Nazareth did exist in Jesus's day and that, like other villages and towns in that part of Galilee, it was built on the hillside, near where the later rock-cut kokh tombs were built. For one thing, *archaeologists have excavated a farm connected with the village*, and it dates to the time of Jesus. Salm disputes the finding of the archaeologists who did the excavation (remember that he himself is not an archaeologist but bases his views on what the real archaeologists—all of whom disagree with him—say). For one thing, when archaeologist *Yardena Alexandre indicated that 165 coins were found in this excavation*, she specified in the report that some of them were late, from the fourteenth or fifteenth century. This suits Salm's purposes just fine. But as it turns out, among the coins were some that date to the Hellenistic, Hasmonean, and early Roman period, that is, the days of Jesus. Salm objected that this was not stated in Alexandre's report, but Alexandre verbally confirmed that in fact it is the case: there were coins in the collection that date to the time prior to the Jewish uprising. (Ehrman 2012:195–96. Italics added.)

This passage betrays some confusion. Ehrman doesn't mention Mary's Well at all and writes about excavations that took place at "a farm con-

---

bottom of water. The clean-up operation to which Alexandre refers was not in modern times. In their long history, the channels and pools at Mary's Well were cleaned more than once. According to Berman, the last clean-up of the Mary's Well channels took place in the late fifteenth century (Alexandre 2012a:108). Each cleaning would remove the coins and deposit them nearby, probably in piles. Those piles could also be in one or more fills. Therefore, it is often not possible to infer the original placement of a coin from its ultimate findspot. If the coin was thrown into water, however, it would be reasonable that its findspot would be in the vicinity or downstream. It is also reasonable to infer that coins found in the Fountain Square area were originally thrown into the watery channels and associated pools. In fact, both Alexandre and Berman are on record as making this assumption—an assumption which will later prove critical.

nected with the village" (no doubt the NVF). Hence, the passage reads as if the "165 coins" were found at the NVF ("in this excavation"). Whether intentional or simply poor writing, the passage is most misleading. It reads as if Alexandre affirmed that the 165 coins were found at the NVF (italics above)! The contrary is in fact the case: Pfann *et al.* claimed that *Alexandre* found the coins *at Mary's Well*.

Once we unpack the confusing elements of Ehrman's prose—and make the necessary substitutions and additions—we realize that he is relying on statements culled from BAIAS 2008 (section E above). He is privy to no new information. Nor has he been in direct communication with Alexandre—despite a possible interpretation of his statement that "Alexandre verbally confirmed that in fact it is the case" (that Hellenistic/Hasmonean/Early Roman coins exist). Alexandre did not verbally confirm this *to Ehrman*. She verbally confirmed this to Pfann. Hence, such information is *according to Pfann!* (BAIAS 2008:106; see section E above.)

The upshot is that this "compelling" archeological evidence is hearsay at third hand. *Ehrman* relies on what *Pfann* claims that *Alexandre* found at Mary's Well. All this is ridiculously remote from anything that can be called rigorous scholarship. What happened to verifying the material evidence? That the James A. Gray Distinguished Professor of Religious Studies at the University of North Carolina, Chapel Hill, engages in such muddled sandbox archeology simply manifests the abysmal state of the field.

(H) Alexandre's monograph: Mary's Well, Nazareth (2012)

Our review of the "Hellenistic" coin passages in the literature concludes with Alexandre's 2012 book on the excavations. As mentioned above, the chapter specifically dealing with coins was contributed by Ariel Berman, a numismatist employed by the IAA. Berman, whose specialty is Arab-Mamluk-Ottoman coins, offers the following précis of the Hellenistic coin evidence found at Mary's Well:

> Ten Hellenistic coins (see Cat. Nos. 3–12) from the reign of Alexander Jannaeus (104–76 BCE) would seem to indicate that by the end of the second century BCE the village of Nazareth had been integrated into the expanded Hasmonean kingdom (Syon 2004:224–235). Four coins came from *a Hellenistic accumulation layer (L132) and another six coins, from adjacent L115, L136, L141, L142, and L156.* An earlier Seleucid coin (No. 1) may hint at a presence at the site in the first half of the second century BCE. A single Hellenistic coin minted at the autonomous mint at Tyre (No. 2) was recovered from the much later Mamluk coin pile, but may originally have been associated with the Hasmonean settlement.
>
> (A. Berman, "The Numismatic Evidence," from Alexandre 2012a:107; italics added.)

The remainder of the book contains only a single passage addressing the numismatic evidence. It is in Chapter 2, "The Architecture and Stratigraphy"—authored by Alexandre. In the following passage, Berman's influence is clearly evident in Alexandre's own writing, as we see by comparing the italicized words in the preceding and following citations:

> The discovery of several coins provided additional support for occupation in the Hellenistic period (see Chapter 5, Cat. Nos. 1-12). A Seleucid coin (175–165 BCE; Cat. No. 1) was recovered from a Mamluk floor (L182; see Plan 2.5), and a quasi-autonomous late second-century BCE coin (Cat. No. 2) was found in a mostly Mamluk coin pile (L166; see Plan 2.5). Four coins of the Hasmonean dynast Alexander Jannaeus were found together with later Hellenistic sherds *in the deep Hellenistic period accumulation layer* (L132) mentioned above, indicating that there may have been here a first-century BCE occupation layer. *Six other Alexander Jannaeus coins came from L115, L136, L141 (2 coins), L142 and L156* (Cat. Nos. 3, 8-12). These coins, together with the late Hellenistic pottery sherds, may reflect Jewish settlement of Nazareth in the context of the Hasmonean expansion from Judea into the Galilee at the turn of the second century BCE (Josephus, Jewish Antiquities 13:318–319, 332, 337–338; Freyne 1980:41–50; Chancey 2002:42–45 and bibliography therein). However, as the coins of Jannaeus continued to circulate, it is also possible that the coins arrived here in the Early Roman period.
>
> (Alexandre 2012a:16; italics added.)

A secondary clue that Alexandre is drawing upon Berman is that she elsewhere characterizes L132 not as an "accumulation layer" (Berman's description) but as a "deep fill" layer (Alexandre 2012a:164). How much of the above coin passage owes to Berman and how much to Alexandre is impossible to say—and perhaps inconsequential. The point merits note, however, because *in the same year* Alexandre is on record as *still* having acknowledged no Hellenistic coins at all from Mary's Well (p. 292 above, top citation).

The Berman coin chapter

Berman's Chapter 5, "The Numismatic Evidence," is full of errors. Perhaps the most noticeable is his Fig. 5.1 (Alexandre 2012a:107) which depicts five coins from the Mary's Well catalog, both obverse and reverse (see Plate 5). However, not a single coin in that figure is correctly referenced. That is, all the numbers accompanying the five coins in fact refer to other coins. This becomes evident if one takes the time to compare the coins in Berman's figure with his catalog information. For example, the first coin on the left displays *Arabic* writing on both sides and sports catalog number

"17." According to the catalog, however, coin no. 17 is *Roman* and dates to 108–09 CE (the reign of the emperor Trajan). Obviously, the depiction of this coin carries the wrong catalog number. It turns out that this coin with Arabic writing in fact dates to the mid-nineteenth century and is Catalog No. 159.

A similar problem exists with the other four coins depicted in Berman's Fig. 5.1. The numbers as printed are 17, 18, 23, 88, and 159, but the correct order should be 159, 17, 18, 23, and 88. It is clear that an erroneous 'shift' has taken place:

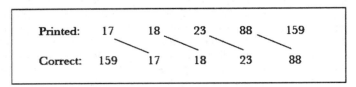

Perhaps the above shift—which will confuse any attentive reader—was not Berman's fault but merely a secretarial or typesetting error. Similar problems, however, occur in the actual coin catalog, to which we now turn.

The coin catalog

Berman's Coin Catalog (Alexandre 2012a:111–120) is a list arranged chronologically. Only 23 (14%) of the 165 coins date before 1173 CE. Of those 23 coins, the first sixteen are dated before the First Jewish Revolt. Those sixteen coins, naturally, are our primary concern for they represent *new* evidence which—if valid—would substantiate human activity in the Nazareth basin before *c.* 70 CE.

Or would they? A closer consideration shows that those sixteen earliest coins in the Mary's Well catalog may not present particularly strong evidence of pre-70 CE presence after all. The coins in question can be divided into three subgroups:

(a) two non-Jewish coins from pre-Hasmonean times (175 BCE to the end of the 2nd cent. BCE) [Cat. nos. 1–2]

(b) ten Hasmonean coins explicitly attributed to Alexander Janneus (103–76 BCE) [Cat. nos. 3–12]

(c) four coins attributed to Herodian times (37 BCE to 54 CE) [Cat. nos. 13–16]

It can be argued that the four Herodian coins in group (c) continued in circulation well after Nazareth was founded in the generations between the two Jewish Revolts. Their presence in the catalog would hardly be determinative of a pre-70 CE settlement.

As for group (b), coins of the Hasmonean Alexander Janneus also continued in circulation long into Roman times. Alexandre alluded to this at the final sentence of her prior citation (p. 295 above). The longevity of Janneus' coins is widely recognized:

> It must be noted that Jannaeus's coins remained in circulation for a long time. In general, Jannaeus coins are found more worn than, say, the coins of Hyrcanus I, suggesting a longer period of circulation (Meshorer 1981, 12). At Horvat Mazad, they were fund in Herodian archaeological strata (Gur 1998, 40). At Givat Hamatos in Jerusalem, they were found together with coins of Agrippa I and Roman procurators, indicating that they might have been in circulation until the first half of the first century C.E. (Bijovsky 2000, 97). At Khirbet Shema, Jannaeus coins were reportedly found together with Roman coins of the fourth century C.E., although it is really not possible to accept even the tentative suggestion that Jannaeus coins might have remained in circulation for as long as five centuries (Hanson and Bates 1976, 151; 169). Thus stray finds of Jannaeus Type 7 coins must be treated with care. The occasional coin may have been lost at the site by a chance visitor long after the place was abandoned, or after the site was resetttled. (Shachar 2004:11. *Cf.* Syon 2004:135)

This leaves us with the two non-Jewish coins in group (a)—the allegedly earliest coins in the entire Mary's Well catalog. However, they raise a number of separate issues which we will soon consider.

Unfortunately, not one of the allegedly Hellenistic coins is accompanied by a photograph. In each case, the reader is entirely dependent on Berman's *word* that the coin appears the way he states, was found where alleged, and that he is correct in drawing the parallels as given. Unfortunately, this places all the Hellenistic coin evidence *outside* the realm of verifiability. It is rather astonishing that such a situation obtains in the 2012 Mary's Well monograph—which is, after all, a 'final report.'

No other category of evidence receives such poor consideration in Alexandre's book. Even the pottery chapter contains numerous diagrams, as does also the chapter devoted to the glass finds. Yet the coin chapter is graced with only a single illustration—which, as we have seen, is very misleading. Of course, it would hardly be practical to illustrate all 165 coins from Mary's Well. But that is not the point. Representative coins could be illustrated, including at least one or two critical pre-Roman coins.

This author contacted the IAA in 2014 with a request for photographs of *all* the "Hellenistic" coins from Mary's Well. This proved impractical, for I was told that photographs of none of those coins exists.[58] They would have to be expressly made. After a considerable amount of negotiation

---

58. This was a surprise, for it was my understanding that all coins in IAA storage are routinely accompanied by both identifying data and a photograph.

effected through an intermediary in Israel, the IAA accepted my request to have photographs taken of four coins (both sides). The terms were as follows: I would be able to select the coins from Berman's catalog; the photographs would be professionally taken by the IAA (in color, with proper lighting, and in high digital resolution) without charge for my personal use; and if I wished to publish any of the prints, there would be a fee.

The results were nothing less than stunning. I expected to receive photographs of coins with at least some identifying characteristics. After all, Berman notes numerous Hellenistic-type designs in his catalog—wreath, cornucopia, palm tree, anchor surrounded by fillet, star with six rays... But the photographs I ultimately received were of four coins that had suffered *such severe water damage and pitting that seven of the eight sides displayed no discernible image at all.* On only one side (cat. no. 4, reverse) was part of a double cornucopia barely visible (all writing had been worn away). That design, however, is found on coins as late as Herod Archelaus (4 BCE–6 CE).[59] Hence, the double cornucopia does not necessarily signal a Hellenistic coin, nor even a Hasmonean coin, much less a coin of Janneus *as Berman avers.*

The other three coins were *completely* unidentifiable!

It was now manifestly evident to me why Berman's coin chapter contains no photographs of pre-Roman coins—public depiction of the evidence would constitute an embarrassment and surely provoke questioning from readers, for the coins are far too worn and pitted to ascertain even the crudest design feature. These bronze coins could be from *any* era.

I decided to purchase one coin for publication (Plate 6) simply in order to publicly expose the abysmally poor state of these coins. It is No. 11 of Berman's catalog—supposedly a Hasmonean *prutah* (bronze coin of lesser value) which the numismatist ascribes to the time of Alexander Janneus.[60] As a glance will show, however, the coin could be virtually *anything*—perhaps even an Ottoman coin of the nineteenth century!

On this particular coin Berman claims to see an "Anchor surrounded by fillet" on the obverse, and a "Star with six rays" on the reverse. The reader is challenged to gaze upon the pitted, unrecognizable Plate 6 in order to find those designs! (Perhaps a Rorschach test would be more applicable.) Let the reader duly note that the coin shown in Plate 6 is the *best* evidence for Hellenistic presence at Mary's Well. *This is the "Hellenistic" evidence ultimately proffered in multiple reports and echoed in hearsay by a string of scholars including Alexandre, Berman, Pfann, and Ehrman.* Of course, it is not evidence at all. Plate 6 graphically demonstrates, in fact, that *there is no Hellenistic coin evidence from Mary's Well.*

---

59. See TJC nos. 40, 67, *etc.*

60. The other photos I requested for personal use are Berman Cat. Nos. 2, 4, and 13.

Coin no. 1. This is allegedly the earliest numismatic evidence found at Mary's Well. Berman identifies it as a bronze dilepton from the reign of Antiochus IV (175–164 BCE), the Seleucid ruler who is largely credited with provoking the Maccabean revolt. The various inscriptions on his coins include *Antiochus Epiphanes* ("Manifest God") and *Nikephoros* ("Bringer of Victory"). We do not know what this coin looks like, for no photograph or drawing is available.

The coin was found in L182, along with another coin dating to 1528 CE (Cat. no. 158). The locus is described as portion of a "Mamluk floor" (Alexandre 2012a:16) and one can wonder how a coin dating to the second century BCE would be found in a *Mamluk* floor. Interestingly, elsewhere in her book Alexandre equates L182 with L155, a locus she now characterizes as the marble floor of a *pool* (Alexandre 2012a:165). However, L155 contains no Hellenistic evidence. We are left to wonder at this conflicting data and surmise that—like Plate 6 and the other photographs of 'early' coins sent to this author—this coin is similarly unreadable and falsely ascribed.

Coin no. 2. The second earliest coin in the Mary's Well catalog is allegedly from the late second century BCE. This is the first of four coins whose photographs I requested from the IAA "for personal use." As mentioned above, the photographs were professionally taken and are of good quality. They were supplied in high-resolution digital format and enlarge well on the computer. I have the two images (one of each side) of this coin no. 2 in front of me as I write and can assure the reader that the coin depicted is so greatly pitted (apparently from water erosion) that no certain man-made features are visible on either side. A considerable part of the reverse has been eroded away, forming a ridge which may (or may not) have originally been part of a design feature. One might hazard a ridge or two on the obverse also—but it is sheer guesswork. No writing, of course, nor any coherent image is discernible.

Yet Berman amazingly claims to see the goddess Tyche (Gk. "fortune") on the obverse and a palm tree on the reverse. He characterizes the coin as "Phoenicia, Autonomous," further specifies its mint as Tyre, and dates it to the "End of second century BCE."[61] Despite all this mysterious precision—clearly unjustified by the photo—Berman is unable to provide even the basic denomination for this coin (lepton, dilepton, *etc*). His single word catalog description for this coin is an admirable understatement: "Worn."

---

61.   Even if the Tyche/palm tree image combination were discernible on this coin, that would not be definitive of the second century BCE. Such a combination was common on Phoenician coins through the second century CE. (*Cf.* BMC 249–50, dating 108–64 BCE; BMC Pl 31:11–13, dating 18 BCE–115 CE; and BMC Pl. 32:2–3, dating 104–167 CE.)

There is another curiosity. Like no. 1 (above), no. 2 was also discovered in a *Mamluk* locus (L166), a coin pile located not far from channels 138 and 150 (Fig. 11.5). These Mamluk-era coin piles were a result of the last cleaning/dredging of the Mary's Well channels that took place in the late fifteenth century (Alexandre 2012a:107, 108). How did "Hellenistic" coins from almost two millennia earlier find their way into such late coin piles?

Given the amazingly worn state of this coin, Berman even ventures to offer a reference: "BMC Phoen: 253, No. 247."[62] I have consulted the reference and it is also an eye-opener, for the numismatist may have located the single most ambiguous coin in the entire thick manual he references. The obverse is described merely with the words "details very obscure," while the reverse lacks all description whatsoever. This is, of course, *not* a useful reference and appears almost a joke. In effect, *Berman is making an equivalence between one completely ambiguous coin (verifiable via the photos) and another completely ambiguous coin.* All this does not prevent him from proposing that this "Hellenistic coin minted at the autonomous mint at Tyre... may originally have been associated with the Hasmonean settlement" of Nazareth (Alexandre 2012a:107)! That is, of course, an impossibly grand conclusion derived ultimately from a *completely unidentifiable* coin.

Finally, there is a revealing problem with the catalog reference, a problem which prompted me to request photographs of this particular coin in the first place. It is that Berman also applies the same ambiguous reference in Hill's manual ("BMC Phoen: 253, No. 247" with "details very obscure") to *another* coin in his catalog, No. 18. Now, Hill dates the referenced coin "Towards end of Second Cent. B.C." Since both Berman's No. 2 and No. 18 carry the same reference, they must be identical and from *the same date*. However, Berman dates No. 2 to the "End of 2nd c. BCE" and No. 18 to "131/2 CE"! This is proof positive that we are in the realm of confabulation and quack archeology.

As it happens, coin no. 18 is one of the coins pictured (and also mislabeled) in Berman's Fig. 5.1 (*cf.* the center coin in Plate 5, and above, p. 296). Inspection shows that the coin depicted is indeed Roman and from *c.* 130 CE (the date stamp is on the coin itself). Thus, this coin has *nothing* to do with the reference in Hill's volume to an ambiguous Hellenistic-era coin.

To recap, coin no. 2 presents us with a very worn coin with no discernible design. It was found in a Mamluk coin pile and Berman assigns it a grotesquely vague Hellenistic reference in an old coin manual. Berman misapplies the same reference to a second century CE Roman coin. Furthermore, he mislabels these coins in his Fig. 5.1. In sum, we are clearly (or not so clearly) in the murky underworld of vague allusions and false associations.

---

62. The reference is to G. F. Hill, *Catalogue of the Greek Coins of Phoenicia* (London 1910), page 253, coin number 247.

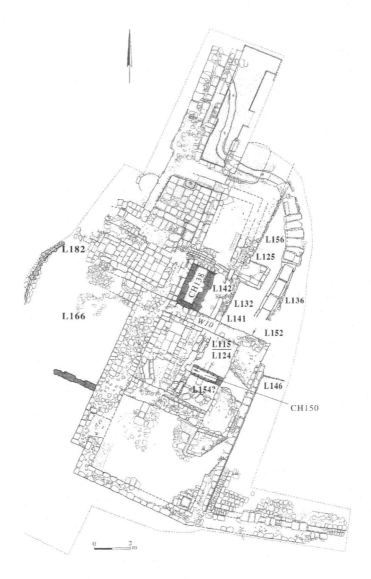

Figure 11.5. Plan of the Fountain Square (lower) excavation area
with loci allegedly containing Hellenistic–Early Roman coins.

Loci where the earliest 16 coins were allegedly found are marked in bold.
(Redrawn by author from Alexandre 2012a: Plans 2.2, 2.4, 2.5, and 2.7.)

The "Hasmonean" coins

The third section of the Berman catalog contains ten coins (cat. Nos. 3–12). The section bears the title "HASMONEANS" and on a separate line, "Alexander Jannaeus (103–76 BCE)." Photographs of two of those ten coins were requested by this author for examination (cat. nos. 4 and 11, the latter pictured in Plate 6). If the images received are any clue to the condition of the remaining eight, then Berman's claims regarding a Hasmonean dating of these ten coins is a travesty.

We will briefly consider the coins in turn. Regarding four of them (cat. Nos. 3, 4, 5, 8) Berman signals a design combination common to coins of Hasmonean and Early Roman times: the wreath surrounded by legend on the obverse, and the double cornucopia with pomegranate on the reverse. The double cornucopia (symbol of plenty imported from Greece) with pomegranate (indigenous symbol of fertility) was common throughout Hasmonean times. It is found to a lesser degree on the first century coins of the Herodian dynasty, as well as on coins of the First Jewish Revolt.[63]

From this group of coins I received photographs of coin No. 4. The obverse is entirely illegible on account of a great deal of pitting—no wreath or any other incused (*i.e.* stamped or hammered) feature is detectable, not even with magnification. On the reverse, however, the high ridges of a double cornucopia with pomegranate in the center are still visible, though all detail has been lost. This is, in fact, the single image at all detectable among the eight photographs I received of all these very worn coins.

Berman furnishes cat. No. 3 with the reference "Cf. TJC:203, No. D1 (ruler uncertain)." The reference is to Y. Meshorer's *A Treasury of Jewish Coins From the Persian Period to Bar Kokhba* (Jerusalem, 2001). The referenced page 203 deals with coins of Hyrcanus I, not Jannaeus. This is overlooked by Berman (followed by Alexandre)[64] who simply writes that ten Hellenistic coins "from the reign of Alexander Jannaeus" were found at Mary's Well (Alexandre 2012a:107). However, this quibble is purely academic. Given the poor state of the coins, it is impossible to tell whether they date to the time of Hyrcanus I, the time of Janneus, or even some other ruler.

Coins Nos. 4, 5, and 8 have no reference—a reasonable omission given the poor state of the coins. The main question is whether the *claimed* wreath on the obverse and *claimed* double cornucopia with pomegranate on the reverse are in fact present. The condition of the coins depicted in the

---

63. Romanoff 1944: 26 *f*, 51 *f*. See Meshorer 2001: P30 *et multi* (Janneus), 40 (Mattathias Antigonus), 67 (Herod Archelaus); Hill 1910a: XX 16–21; XXVI:8; XXVII:10, 12, 16, *etc.*

64. We have seen that the passage at the beginning of her Chapter 2 (above, p. 295) may be by Berman, not Alexandre, noting that "Berman's influence is clearly evident."

Cat. no.	Obverse	Reverse	Reference /Notes	IAA no.
1	Head r.	Female fig. standing l.	*Cf SNG* 1:156 nos. 1130–1138	88031
2	Head of Tyche r.	Palm tree	*BMC Phoen.* 253, No. 247 (worn)	88032
3	Wreath, oblit. legend	Double cornucopia w/pomegranate	*Cf. TJC*: 203, No. D1 (ruler uncertain)	88033
4	Same	Same		88034
5	Same	Same	Worn	88035
6	Obliterated	Obliterated	*TJC*:209–210, Nos. 9–17	88036
7	Same	Same	Same	88037
8	Wreath, oblit. legend	Double cornucopia w/pomegranate		88038
9	Anchor, fillet, obliterated legend	Star with six rays	*TJC*:209, Nos. 3–6	88039
10	Same	Same	Same	88040
11	Same	Same	Same	88041
12	Same	Same	Same	88042
13	HERΔ [ΒΑΣΙΛΕ] Anchor, legend	Double cornucopias	*TJC*:222, No. 59	88043
14	Same	Same	Same	88044
15	Prow of galley r. legend around: HPW	Within wreath: EΘN	Same	88045
16	[NEPW] KΛAY KAICAP; two crossed shields & spear	Palm tree, above legend: BPIT. In field date: [LI Δ /KAI] (54 CE)	*TJC*:259, No. 340	88046

Table 2. Berman's catalog listing of the alleged earliest 16 coins found at Mary's Well. (From Alexandre 2012a:112–13.)

photographs I received does not inspire confidence in this regard. However, because the designs noted were commonly minted on coins for about two centuries, Berman's assignment of these four coins specifically to the time of Janneus seems arbitrary, especially given that the legend (offering important identification information) *is obliterated in every case*. Nevertheless, such wreath-double corncopia coins—if actually present in the material remains—would not be surprising finds at Mary's Well. *Such coins could have been minted as late as 70 CE.* If Nazareth was settled between the two Jewish revolts (as argued in my first book) their presence in the catalog would not be notable.

With catalog Nos. 6 and 7 Berman reaches the acme of 'reading the tea leaves,' as it were, for both obverse and reverse of these two coins are by his own admission "Obliterated." There is thus absolutely no basis for hazarding a typology, much less a dating. Undaunted, however, he assigns them to the time of Janneus—an interpretation which must be deemed in conflict with the coin's condition and whose rationale is a complete mystery. Even more curious is the assignment of a reference—for how is it possible to setect a parallel for reference when both sides of the coin are too "Obliterated" to even *describe?*

Furthermore, the reference itself makes little sense. It is to Meshorer's *Treasury of Jewish Coins*, pages 209–210, "Nos. 9–17." But on the referenced page Meshorer does not employ simple numbers but the letter K + number, that is, K1, K2, *etc.* Perhaps this is another case of sloppiness (we recall the confusion involved with Berman's Fig. 5.1). Secondly, there is no obvious rationale for drawing a parallel to coins K9–K17, for in some cases these are simply *variants* of the preceding entries K1–K8. Why exclude them? Finally, the referenced coins represent a remarkable variety. For example, K11 is a coin with the star erroneously struck on *both* the obverse and the reverse. But K12 has the anchor on both sides but *no star.* So, when Berman draws a parallel between his catalog Nos. 6–7 and all these very different coins, what on earth can it mean?

We now come to the quartet of coins, catalog Nos. 9–12. These form a group in sharing the same description and reference. As discussed above, I received photographs of coin No. 11 from the IAA. Those images are reproduced in Plate 6. Of the four coins whose images were sent to me, No. 11 is arguably the most worn and pitted. It is not even possible to determine which side is the obverse and which the reverse. Once again, I invite the reader to scrutinize Plate 6 and divine where is an "Anchor surrounded by fillet" (border) on one side, and a "Star with six rays" on the other. The coin attests to nothing so much as Berman's ability to see what is *not* there. Indeed, no greater proof of that ability would be possible.

A note is in order regarding the designs themselves. The star may be related to the famous oracle in Numbers 24:17, "There shall come a star out of Jacob," in which case Janneus (on whose coins the symbol predominates) may have fancied he fulfilled that prophecy. However, the symbol has also been interpreted by various specialists as a wheel, and also as the sun.[65] The anchor symbol was probably borrowed from Seleucid coins. "It may also perhaps allude to the possession of the sea-ports which Alexander [Janneus] had gained and joined to his kingdom."[66] The anchor-star combination was the last of the Janneus coins and became extremely common. Though crudely fashioned, such coins were minted in vast quantities and perhaps also struck by the Hasmonean successors of Janneus.[67] Their (alleged) appearance on coins at Mary's Well does not at all suggest activity there in the time of Janneus, nor even in the first century BCE. One scholar writes: "It must be noted that Jannaeus's coins remained in circulation for a long time... At Khirbet Shema, Jannaeus coins were reportedly found together with Roman coins of the fourth century C.E." (Shachar 2004:11; *cf.* citation above p. 297). All this, however, is moot, because the coins—as far as we have been able to determine—do not even exhibit the designs which Berman 'sees' on them.

As a reference for coins Nos. 9–12 Berman signals page 209 of Meshorer's 2001 *Treasury of Jewish Coins.* This is the same page that the numismatist signaled for coins 6 and 7 above. This time Berman points to "Nos. 3–6" and, once again, the references begin with the letter "K." In a major oversight, however, the coins on that page in *TJC* do not have the "Star with six rays" at all—they have the much more common star with *eight* rays!

This discrepancy is really quite astonishing and shows yet again how unreliable is Berman's chapter on the coins from Mary's Well. There is a considerable difference between the two star designs (Fig. 11.6). The star with eight rays was customary on Janneus coins, but the six-rayed star—though not entirely unknown—is rare. Meshorer does not even mention the latter in the prose of his compendious and now standard *TJC.* When one consults the notes to Meshorer's various plates, however, one sees that a very few coins in his "Group L" had the star with six rays (*TJC* 210: L8–L11). These are underweight coins with an Aramaic instead of Hebrew inscription. The Group L coins are known to have been minted in 78 BCE, towards the end of Janneus' reign.

At a minimum, then, either Berman's reference for coin Nos. 9–12 is false, or his description "Star with six rays" is false. Most likely, however, both the reference *and* the description are in error. After all, *it would be most unusual for almost half (40%) of the Hasmonean coins found at a site to possess a very rare star design, while not one of them exhibits the standard design.* This can hardly be the case at Mary's Well, and we can be quite confident that the "Star

---

65. Madden 68; Rogers 26. The anchor symbol also occurs on coins of Herod the Great and Herod Archelaus.
66. Madden 1967:67; *cf.* Meshorer 2001:37.
67. Shachar 2004:9–10 ("Type 7").

Figure 11.6. The star symbol from the time of Janneus.

Left: The common 8-pointed star. Right: The much rarer six-pointed star.
(Redrawn from *TJC*:302, L8.)

with six rays" description is an error. Indeed, given the illegible faces of the coins as attested by the received photographs, it seems eminently probable that Berman himself saw *neither* star on *any* Mary's Well coin.

The "Early Roman" coins

Four post-Hasmonean coins predating the First Jewish Revolt are claimed by Berman from Mary's Well. Two are from the time of Herod the Great (cat. Nos. 13–14), one is from the time of his successor Herod Archelaus (4 BCE–6 CE, cat. No. 15), and one from the time of Nero (cat. No. 16). The presence of such Early Roman coins at Mary's Well is not surprising, even if the settlement of Nazareth began between the two Jewish revolts, as argued in *The Myth of Nazareth*.

However, it is certain that Berman's claim regarding these Early Roman coins is untenable. Photographs received by this author of cat. no. 13 reveal a chipped and thoroughly water-worn coin, one as illegible as that shown in Plate 6. Berman claims to see writing on the obverse (HERΔ) with anchor and surrounding legend. On the reverse he sees the "Double cornucopias." None of these elements, however, are remotely detectable on the photographs received, even with magnification.

Berman signals that cat. No. 14 *is another example of the same coin*. This being the case, one must entertain a similar lack of confidence in his claims regarding *this* coin.

As to the Archelaus coin (cat. No. 15), Berman's reference is "*TJC*:225, No. 72." The reference describes a coin with "Prow of galley l." Berman's catalog, however, has the description "Prow of galley r." It is a minor difference, but the coin photographed in Meshorer's *TJC* is clearly that of a galley pointing left. Once again we have reason to question Berman's data.

There is little to say regarding coin no. 16, for photographs of this 54 CE coin have not been made available. One minor quibble: the 'in field date' is "L IΔ" (year 14 of Claudius), not "LI Δ" as in Berman's catalog.

Coin summary

It is impossible to accord Berman's coin claims even a modicum of respect. The photographs sent to me—as a result of an express request and persuant to a special photographic session set up by the IAA—contradict Berman's claims absolutely and completely. Although photographs of only four early coins were received (25%), they constitute a random sampling and prove that Berman's data, conclusions, and interpretations do not tally at all with the empirical evidence from the field. The astonishingly pitted and waterworn coin no. 11 (Plate 6) speaks for itself. The other photographs received stand in confirmation that we are dealing here not with evidence but apparently with an edifice of dishonesty intended to *mask* the evidence. The most straightforward explanation is that some of the most waterworn coins found at Mary's Well were, for convenience, simply designated "Hasmonean" and "Early Roman."

Multiple catalog errors suggest that Berman himself imperfectly selected convenient types for these extremely defaced coins. The assignment of types and dates is sometimes clearly bogus. In some instrances references do not exist—at least not in the way that Berman signals them. Two cases (cat. Nos. 2 and 18) have the same reference—though the coins are dated over two centuries apart! Berman also confuses the star of six rays with the star of eight rays. In one case the prow of a ship points in the wrong direction. All these errors, mind you, deal with the first dozen coins. They reveal that Berman's coin catalog is a farrago of mistakes. Additionally, his Fig. 5.1 suggests that the entire coin chapter is incoherent.

Above all, the photographs received by this author from the IAA prove that Berman's catalog and conclusions do not reflect the material evidence. Persuant to an examination of the photographs, it can be stated quite that *no demonstrable Hellenistic or Early Roman coin evidence from Mary's Well exists at all*. I enjoin any numismatist to examine the coins in the IAA archives for himself or herself[68] in order to verify this conclusion.

The foregoing observations are remarkable, but we must now make an astonishing declaration: it makes little historical difference whether or not Hellenistic coins were found at Mary's Well. This remarkable assertion owes to the fact that *the water channels at the site were not constructed until Middle Roman times. Thus, whether or not Hellenistic coins were found, those coins were necessarily* deposited *at Mary's Well in Middle Roman times and later.*

---

68. The coins in Berman's catalog begin with IAA No. 88031 in sequential order.

The water channels at Mary's Well

All the allegedly Hellenistic and Early Roman coins found at Mary's Well were recovered from the (lower) Fountain Square area, a locus of channels, pools, and even cisterns built up and altered over the centuries.[69] (Only one coin out of the 165 in Berman's catalog was discovered in the upper Church Square area.) It is hence understandable that the coins bear signs of waterwear. Indeed, the images of the four coins sent to me by the IAA *all* exhibit pronounced water damage. I have also examined unpublished images of four other coins from Mary's Well.[70] All except one (IAA no. 88048) clearly show waterwear.

Neither Alexandre nor Berman question that the coins recovered from Mary's Well were associated with the waterworks in the lower Fountain Square area. Alexandre writes:

> Over 160 worn low-denomination bronze Mamluk coins were found *in piles that were dredged out of the water* in the clean-up operation. *Coins were commonly thrown into water sources* to bring good luck. The coins also included a few Roman and Byzantine coins and four silver Crusader coins.
> (Alexandre 2012b:39–40; *cf.* p. 292 above. Emphasis added.)

This important statement from the Excavation Director shows that—as late as 2012—she considered that *all* the coins ("Over 160") recovered from the Fountain Square area had once been in the water. The last dredging she refers to "in the clean-up operation" took place in Mamluk times.[71] Only seven coins postdate that dredging (Berman cat. nos. 158–65). The findspots for six of them are also certainly associated with water channels or pools, according to Alexandre's list of loci.[72]

It is also Berman's understanding that the recovered coins were once associated with water. Thus, he writes in his coin chapter:

> The presence of coins on the floors of the pools and the fountain house seems to be connected to the widespread custom among pilgrims and other visitors of throwing coins into springs and fountains as they wished for health, happiness, fertility and prosperity.
> (Alexandre 2012a:109)

---

69.   Figs. 11.3, 11.5 above; Alexandre 2012a:16 *f.*
70.   IAA nos. 88046, 88047, 88048, 88116. These photographs were already in the IAA databank. The first three are Roman coins, and the last from the 15th century CE.
71.   See above pp. 292–93, n. 57.
72.   Berman cat. no. 158 = L182/pool L155; cat. no. 159 = L130/pool L155; cat. nos. 160 and 163 = L113/"pool"); cat. no. 161 = L188/dredged; cat. no. 162 = L187/dredged; cat. no. 164 = L112/ "pool." *Cf.* Alexandre 2012a:163 *f.*

This wording by Berman—"the floors of the pools and the fountain house"—includes many loci where Hellenistic-Early Roman coins were found (Fig. 11.5).[73] The findspots of these early coins were 'fills' in the ancient channels and pools (*cf.* note 57 above), as well as nearby 'piles' after dredging. Ten of the sixteen earliest coins in Berman's catalog can be immediately associated with channels, pools, or dredged coin piles:

Coin cat. no. 1	L182	= Pool L155
Coin cat. no. 2	L166	Dredged Mamluk coin pile
Coin cat. no. 3	L115	In CH124A[74]
Coin cat. no. 11	L142	CH138 (*cf.* Plate 6)
Coin cat. nos. 8, 13	L136	Crusader CH26
Coin cat. no. 12	L156	Crusader CH26
Coin cat. no. 14	L152	Crusader CH26
Coin cat. no. 15	L154	Crusader CH26
Coin cat. no. 16	L146	Pool

The presence of no less than five allegedly 'early' coins in *Crusader* channel 26 should give pause. If that channel was not constructed until Crusader times, then how can *waterworn* 'Hellenistic' and 'Early Roman' coins have been found in it?

We recall that the 'lower' Fountain Square area of the Mary's Well excavations is over one hundred meters downslope from the ultimate source of water deep within the hillside (Fig. 11.1). In fact, water reached this area in antiquity only after the construction of two channels.

We now broach a remarkable fact: the two channels that brought water down to the Fountain Square area did *not yet exist* in Hellenistic times. They were constructed in the Roman period—more precisely, in the Middle to Late Roman periods (see below). Thus, *no water yet existed in the Fountain Square area in Hellenistic times.* This being the case, the "Over 160" coins "dredged out of the water" according to Alexandre (that is, virtually the *entire* Mary's Well catalog) could only have been deposited *into water* in Roman and post-Roman times. Critically, *the ten allegedly 'early' coins listed above—clearly associated with pools and channels—must also* postdate *the construction of those water installations.*

Alternative explanations soon become preposterous. Without channels in the area, one would have to propose (a) that *a large number* of Hasmonean

---

73. In fact, almost all of the 'earliest' coins were retrieved from within a few meters of CH138. The most remote location is L182 which was the floor of pool 155 (Alexandre 2012a:164, 165). L166 is a Mamluk coin pile that was produced from dredging the nearby channel in the fifteenth century (*cf.* above p. 300).

74. Alexandre 2012a:Plan 2.2 and p. 164.

and Early Roman coins were dropped onto dry ground in an empty, sloping vicinity with no known feature to recommend it; and (b) that *all* those
coins made their way into the water *by themselves* after the pools and water
channels were constructed in Middle Roman times.

Even if a few Hellenistic coins *might* authentically be present in the
Mary's Well catalog (a dubious proposition, in any case), it is clear that not
one of them could have been *deposited into water* before Roman times if no
channels yet existed in the Fountain Square area. Effectively, then, we have
a Roman *terminus post quem* for all the coins from Mary's Well which bear
signs of water wear—that is, for virtually all 165 coins in the catalog. This
point is so important that we will briefly review the genesis of the channels
which brought water down to the Fountain Square area.

The Roman incipience of the water channels

The structural history of Mary's Well—including the history of the
water channels—is presented in detail in Alexandre's 2012 book. Chapter
2, "The Architecture and Stratigraphy" (pp. 13–55) reviews the history of
Mary's Well stratum by stratum. Her analysis begins with "Stratum VI:
The Late Hellenistic Period." It is worth noting that she quickly disposes of
that era in a single page of prose.

The brevity of Alexandre's treatment is no surprise, for the foregoing
paragraphs suggest that no "Hellenistic" activity took place at Mary's Well
at all. Indeed, she writes: "*limited* evidence for occupation around the spring
in the late Hellenistic period [consisting] of fragmentary architectural remains, potsherds, and coins" (Alexandre 2012a:12).

These three categories of evidence—structural remains, pottery,
coins—are interdependent. We have already considered the pottery (above,
pp. 266–82), concluding that the dating of eleven shards to the Hellenistic
period is fraught with problems—not least being conflicting statements by
Alexandre which produce a 'pastiche' of views.

As for the "fragmentary architectural remains," Alexandre dates these
on the basis of the pottery. As goes the pottery, then, so goes the "Hellenistic"
structural evidence. Finally, regarding the coins: *if they were all deposited into*
Roman *water channels, then they do not constitute evidence for human activity there in*
pre-Roman times—whether Hellenistic coins exist in the catalog or not. Hellenistic coins had a long span of use, and older coins could well have been
deposited into the water channels long after their date of minting.

Hence the importance of determining the incipience of the earliest
water channels in the Fountain Square area, for if those channels were
constructed in Roman times, then all water-related pre-Roman activity in
the Fountain Square area can be immediately rejected. Alexandre is quite

clear on this matter. Her short treatment of the *Hellenistic* stratum makes no mention of the channels. Indeed, the archeologist states bluntly: "No Hellenistic building remains were exposed in the Fountain Square area" (p. 16). *This statement is decisive.*

It is in Alexandre's treatment of "The Roman Period" (Stratum V) that we first read of water channels at the lower Fountain Square area of Mary's Well. The pertinent sentences follow:

> In the Fountain Square area, a few incomplete but significant architectural elements underlying the Strata III–II Crusader and Mamluk structures were attributed to the Roman period. Segments of two different stone channels were unearthed from this stratum. First, a short segment of a southward-running channel (CH138...)... The floor of Channel 138 (elevation 48.84 m) was washed away, leaving no evidence of plaster. A considerable quantity of extremely worn Roman potsherds was found in an accumulation layer (L142)... Although the sherds' water-eroded state rendered most of them unworthy of publication, the pottery clearly belonged to well-known Middle Roman-period pottery forms (see Fig. 3.2). No pottery predating the Roman period was recovered from this channel or in its immediate vicinity...
>
> The topography dictated the water flow from north to south in Channel 138. In the area excavated immediately to the north of the channel, some Roman pottery was retrieved from accumulated deposits (L223 and L224)... The stratigraphic evidence points to the Roman period; the ceramic evidence refines the date to the Middle to Late Roman horizon.
>
> (Alexandre 2012a:16/18.)

Here, then, we have a clear incipience of the channels: *both stratigraphic and ceramic evidence point to "the Middle to Late Roman horizon."* Though only parts of the channels were excavated, it is clear from the above that Alexandre attributes those "incomplete but significant architectural elements... to the Roman period." Particularly significant are her assertions that "Segments of two different stone channels were unearthed from this [Roman] stratum," and that "No pottery predating the Roman period was recovered from this channel or in its immediate vicinity."

This recalls Alexandre's statement to me in her email of Jan. 11, 2006 (above p. 251) that "very limited wall and channel remains *from the mid Roman period (1/2-3 centuries)*" were found in the Fountain Square area. In general agreement is also her 2006 report, which states: "From the Roman period part of a covered dressed stone channel was exposed, as well as some wall stubs and Middle Roman pottery" (above p. 256, second paragraph).[75] "No Hellenistic building remains," she writes in 2012, "were exposed in the

---

75.   Dark has misinterpreted the hydrology in Alexandre's 2006 report, for he writes of "canalisation bringing water" no earlier than the 12th century (Dark 2012c:177).

Fountain Square area" (Alexandre 2012a:16). Thus, the stratigraphy of the channels in that area is no older than Roman and the context provided by the associated pottery is Middle Roman.

Alexandre even more explicitly associates the "early water channels" with the Middle–Later Roman periods in the following statement:

> The [Roman] pottery repertoire points to a chronological range for the activity in Fountain Square, presumably related to the functioning of the early water channels, from the end of the second or early third century to the first half of the fourth century CE, within the Middle and Late Roman periods.   (Alexandre 2012a:61; *cf.* above p. 281)

The recovered pottery was largely waterworn, an aspect which now takes on added significance. The archeologist writes:

> The limited pottery from the Hellenistic, Roman and Byzantine periods derived mostly from fills and tended to be very water worn. It's main contribution was to indicate that there had been some activity or occupation around the water source during these periods. (Alexandre 2012a:57)

We can now understand that this passage is correct save for one word: "Hellenistic." *The incipience of the water channels in the Roman period is decisive evidence that no* waterworn *Hellenistic pottery was recovered!* As we saw with Alexandre's 2006 report emailed to me, the single word "Hellenistic" appears here to be—once again—an *interpolation* (above, pp. 257, 293).

It is possible that Alexandre failed to connect the dots and to consider the ramifications of her own history of the structural evidence. An interpolation of the word "Hellenistic" by another hand, however, is more likely and fits the 'pastiche' or 'mosaic' aspect of her 2012 book, with its numerous conflicting statements—particularly regarding the early evidence.

The lack of claimed Hellenistic waterworn pottery now also places under suspicion the existence of *any* Hellenistic pottery in the Fountain Square area. Alexandre states that such pottery was "limited" and "tended to be very water worn." But without channels and water in the vicinity, we may wonder how pottery could become "very water worn." We may even wonder why people would have been there at all, for the Fountain Square area is over one hundred meters from the water source, essentially in the middle of a sloping hillside. No evidence has been recovered of a Hellenistic-era camp, whether including permanent or semi-permanent structural remains. We recall the excavator's assertion: "No Hellenistic building remains were exposed in the Fountain Square area" (Alexandre 2012a:16). Hence, we find no reason for human activity at the site in pre-Roman times. To this we now add the fact that the early evidence is largely, if not entirely, water worn.

Conclusion

Alexandre shows that the channels which first brought water to the Fountain Square area were constructed in Middle Roman times. A review of the material evidence has shown that the pottery, the coins, and the structures in that area were also heavily water-related. By combining these two conclusions, it becomes clear that the water-related finds at Mary's Well—that is, most if not all the pottery and coins—could not have been placed at the site before Middle Roman times.

Furthermore, we have found that the allegedly "Hellenistic" movable finds are fraught with problems. The so-called Hellenistic coins are frankly unrecognizable due to extreme water wear, while the pre-Roman pottery—also water worn—has been subject to a cursory treatment with conflicting statements, unlikely findspots, and unsatisfactory parallels.

Once we recognize that the history of the Fountain Square area begins in Middle Roman times, then all notions of human activity there in Hellenistic and Early Roman times completely lose force.

The lack of water in the lower Fountain Square area before the second century CE is fatal to the traditional view of Mary's Well and, in fact, weakens any claim that pre-Roman artifacts were actually found there. It is scarcely feasible that *waterworn* coins or pottery existed there in Hellenistic times. This alone immediately removes the lion's share of so-called "Hellenistic" evidence from consideration—and probably *all* of it.

Hasmonean coins had unusually long lifespans extending well into Roman times. It is possible that a few could have been thrown into the water of the Fountain Square area during the first period of the channels' existence in the Middle to Late Roman eras, that is, long after the Hasmonean period ended. However, this problem is no longer critical and perhaps not even pertinent. After all, what difference does it make if—in the second century CE—some Late Roman residents of Nazareth threw (or dropped) into the new water channels a few long-lasting coins minted in Hasmonean times? We are interested in dating *human activity*, and such coins (whose existence is highly dubious, in any case) would have been deposited into the channels and pools *no earlier than Middle Roman times*. Hence, despite all the efforts to insinuate Hellenistic evidence into the documentary record of Mary's Well—as reviewed exhaustively in the foregoing pages—in the final analysis it does not particularly matter if a few Hellenistic coins are represented in the panoply of evidence.

In sum, the extensive water related structures and waterworn movable finds from Mary's Well clearly indicate a beginning of human activity at the site in Middle Roman times. The evidence—numismatic, ceramic, and structural—shows that human activity at Mary's Well occurred neither in the Hellenistic nor in the Early Roman periods.

Chapter 12

THE FORGERY OF THE "CAESAREA INSCRIPTION"

The CER

In 1863 the French semitic scholar, philosopher, and author Ernest Renan penned an enormously popular and controversial book, the *Vie de Jésus*. It caused a furore because, for Renan, Jesus was a mere man. This is, in fact, an old idea going back to the Ebionites and early Jewish-Christians of the first century CE—as scholars are well aware. But in 19th century Catholic France it was thoroughly unacceptable. Renan denied the divinity, the miracles—and the Jewishness—of Jesus. A lesser scholar would have simply been ignored. But Renan was one of the most influential luminaries of his day, a *grand officier* of the *Légion d'Honneur*, member of the *Académie Française*, and professor at the College de France (though suspended from this position in 1864 for his sacrilegious views on Jesus Christ).

Renan's outspoken anti-clericalism survived his death in 1892 and led to the founding of a small confraternity in Paris dedicated "to the history of religions, biblical criticism, and research into Christian origins." The Cercle Ernest Renan, as it is called, was founded in 1949 by two intellectuals—Prosper Alfaric and Georges Ory. The former had abandoned the priesthood in 1909 to study the history of Christianity. After attaining a doctorate and securing a professorship at the University of Strassbourg, Alfaric penned *Le Problème de Jésus et les Origines du Christianisme* (1932), which argued against the historicity of Jesus of Nazareth and of his mother Mary. The book summarily led to the ex-priest's excommunication and punishment by "decree of degradation" of the Holy Office.

The other founder of the Cercle Ernest Renan (CER) was the astonishing Georges Ory, a writer whose works on Christian origins are as unknown today as they are insightful. While Ory denied the existence of Jesus, he asserted that of John the Baptist and, underneath the canonical accounts, perceived traditions associated with the Samaritan Simon Magus. Ory's views were too far ahead of his time to receive much attention. However, his co-founding of the CER gave his many works, and those of other independent thinkers, an enduring and reliable outlet for publication in France.

A 2010 issue of the *Cahiers du Cercle Ernest Renan* published an article concerning the "Caesarea Inscription." Marble fragments of a Byzantine-era[1] plaque sporting a list of the twenty-four priestly families ("courses") were discovered in Caesarea Maritima in 1962. The inscription mentions "Nazareth" as a place of residence for one of the courses and has been widely used to argue the village's existence as early as the first century CE. We will see that several assumptions underlying that conclusion are tenuous. Nevertheless, up until now, the Caesarea Inscription has been the *only* accepted non-Christian epigraphic witness to the existence of Nazareth dating to Roman times. It has, accordingly, assumed enormous significance (particularly in conservative Christian circles) as "proof" of the existence of the town at the turn of the era. After 1962, the inscription quickly entered the standard literature and its authenticity has never been doubted.

The article was by a certain Enrico Tuccinardi and entitled "*Nazareth, l'épigraphe de Césarée et la main de Dieu*" ("Nazareth, the Caesarea Inscription, and the Hand of God").[2] It pointed out some surprising coincidences—even anomalies—relating to both the discovery of the inscription and its nature. Tuccinardi maintained that the inscription could be a fraud. I found his article interesting but put it aside, for I already considered that the Caesarea Inscription had minimal relevance for the existence of Nazareth at the turn of the era. I argued in my first book that it could not have reflected events after the First Jewish Revolt (as commonly thought) but only after the Bar Kokhba Revolt (Salm 2008a:275–78).[3]

However, in 2013 Tuccinardi contacted me and directed my attention once again to his article. This was auspicious, for I was now in a better position to evaluate his "surprising coincidences." In rereading the article,

---

1. Avi-Yonah supposed that the plaque was originally part of a fourth–fifth century synagogue (below p. 357). These pages, however, will argue that view to be untenable: no synagogue existed in the area, and two of the fragments are modern creations. The remaining fragment (found in 1956), if authentic, certainly came from outside the area.

2. *Cahier du Cercle Ernest Renan* 252 (2010), pp. 35–64.

3. *Contra, e.g.,* R. Carrier who has asserted that a *c.* 300 CE inscription 'proves' that Nazareth existed in 70 CE (see *http://freethoughtblogs.com/carrier/archives/3522*). Already in his 1909 thesis S. Klein also argued that there was no northern movement of priests to the Galilee in second temple times, but that the priests migrated northwards after the Bar Kokhba Revolt in mid-II CE. It is now recognized, however, that no northern migration of priests may have occurred at all (below, n. 7).

I was astounded to encounter a name that had meant nothing to me a couple of years earlier: Dr. Jerry Vardaman. He was the conservative archeologist-scholar (d. 2000), mostly remembered for the notorious claim of having found microscopic lettering ("microletters") referring to Christianity on ancient Roman coins.[4] This claim has been completely discredited and Vardaman revealed as a fraud. His proven quackery regarding the microletters now presented a monumental red flag to me, for it was Vardaman himself who, in 1962, had discovered the critical marble fragment of the Caesarea Inscription—the one that bears the name 'Nazareth'! The fact that we would not have any "Caesarea Inscription" *at all* were it not for Vardaman's 1962 activity was just too suspicious to overlook. *Could fraud be involved here too?*

In the summer of 2013 I began to collect and carefully examine the documents regarding the 1962 excavation in Caesarea Maritima, focussing particularly on Vardaman's role in the discovery of the so-called "Caesarea Inscription."

The twenty-four priestly courses

In 1 Chr 24:7–18, King David allegedly ordered the twenty-four priestly "courses" (families) by the casting of lots. In that passage, only the family names are given, beginning with Jehoiarib (1) and ending with Ma'aziah (24). The priestly families thenceforth took turns ministering in the temple according to the predetermined Davidic order. Theoretically, this continued until the destruction of the temple in 70 CE. It is not known what became of the priestly families thereafter, but they would certainly have vacated Jerusalem after the Bar Kokhba Revolt, during which the city was totally destroyed and Jews were forbidden to reenter under pain of death.[5] The intellectual centers of Judaism then moved elsewhere—principally to the Galilee (where the Mishna was finalized c. 200 CE) and to Babylon.

History had moved against the priests and henceforth Judaism would be rabbinical, not sacerdotal. But the priests did not suddenly disappear. Their traditions reappear in the Galilee through the assignment of each priestly family to a different village in the northern province.[6] Recent research, however, has cast doubt on any general or organized migration of priests northward in late antiquity,[7] and priestly assignments were in all

---

4. On Vardaman and the microletters, see Carrier at *http://infidels.org/library/modern/richard_carrier/quirinius.html#Vardaman* (accessed May 2, 2015).

5. Schürer I.ii 314 *f.* The city was renamed Aelia Capitolina by Hadrian.

6. Rabbinical sources, too, contain passages in which places of habitation of priests in Galilee are mentioned (Vardaman and Garrett 1964:51).

7. As argued, *e.g.*, by Dalia Trifon (1989:84–86). The association of various priestly

likelihood symbolic and not historical.

Only a few stone fragments of the list of twenty-four priestly courses have been found in places both inside and outside of Israel—one as far afield as the Yemen. These fragments most likely belonged to plaques each affixed to (or leaning against) a wall in a synagogue. More complete lists have been found in manuscript form, generally in the form of medieval liturgical poems in Hebrew or Aramaic intended for singing (*piyyutim*).

In the early twentieth century, Dr. Samuel Klein (Professor of Palestinology at the Hebrew University) assembled the evidence available at that time and attempted a reconstruction of the entire list of twenty-four priestly courses together with their (alleged) places of residence in the Galilee.[8] The results of his lines 17–21 read as follows:

Seventeenth course Hezir MAMLIACH	משמרת שבע עשרה חזיר ממליח
Eighteenth course Hapitsets NATSRATH	משמרת שמונה עשרה הפיצץ נצרת
Nineteenth course Petachiah AKLAH ARAV	משמרת תשע עשרה פתחיה אכלה ערב
Twentieth course Ezekiel MIGDAL NUNIYA	משמרת עשרים יחזקאל מגדל נוניא

Here we see that the eighteenth course of priests, the family Hapises ("Hapitsets") was associated with the settlement of Nazareth ("Natsrath").[9]

After establishment of the state of Israel in 1948, Klein's reconstruction took on considerable importance in the search for ancient synagogues. The reason is that stone plaques of the list of priestly courses were affixed *only* to the walls of synagogues. Thus, discovery of such a plaque—even only a fragment—betrayed the former existence of a synagogue on site. Such presence was particularly meaningful to the first generation of Jewish archeologists, scholars keenly on the lookout for tangible evidence of

---

courses with specific residences in the Galilee appears to have been a retrojection by the Late Roman-Byzantine priesthood which wished to authenticate its earlier existence in the Galilee as far back as Hasmonean times. U. Leibner also notes that the list of twenty-four courses "does not reflect a historical reality of priestly families settling in the Galilee during the Mishnaic period" (Leibner 2012:410, *cf.* pp. 404 *f*). Vardaman's claims that priests were in the Galilee already in the second temple period and then moved northwards after the First Jewish Revolt are not tenable (Vardaman and Garrett 1964:52).

8.   Klein's 1909 doctoral dissertation dealt with the priestly courses: *Die Barajta der vierundzwanzig Priesterabteilungen: Beiträge zur Geographie und Geschichte Galiläas* (Klein 1909). His 1939 book, *Sefer ha-Yishouv*, attempts a reconstruction of each place of residence.

9.   The Hebrew tsade is conventionally transliterated "ts," the tav "th," and the heth "ch." The familiar voiced "z" of the Greek gospels (*cf.* Nazareth, Nazarene, Nazorean) does not correspond to the voiceless tsade (*e.g.* in "Natsrath") and represents an artificial linguistic anomaly.

ancient Jewish presence in the land. In a Zionist context, of course, such presence would go a long way toward validating the larger issues of Jewish return to Palestine and the 'right' of Jews to the ground under their feet.

The SRA and FEAS

Validating the Jewish right of return to the land of Palestine, noted above, has been a component of Zionism since its inception, one with particularly important responsibilities in the field of archeology. Already toward the end of the Ottoman period the Society for the Reclamation of Antiquities (SRA) was established in Palestine. This society was by Jews, for Jews, and was created as a counterweight to the many foreign excavations (American, French, British, Russian) taking place in the land. One recent source—a retrospective article in the Israeli newspaper *Haaretz*—has described the SRA as "an important part in formulating the central Zionist narrative of the return to the Land of the Patriarchs."[10] Yet, at the time, the society lacked any Jewish archeologist, and hence Eleazar Lipa Sukenik (one of the "fathers" of Israeli archeology) was sent to Berlin to study the discipline, at the society's expense. When Sukenik returned to Jerusalem in 1925 he joined the newly-established Hebrew University and was simultaneously nominated secretary of the SRA. Sukenik subsequently excavated and published on the sixth century synagogue of Beit Alpha—which yielded some famous mosaics. The title of his 1930 Schweich Lectures (in London) was "Ancient Synagogues in Palestine and Greece."

In 1930, Sukenik's colleague at the Hebrew University, Samuel Klein—the same scholar who had reconstructed the list of twenty-four priestly courses—discovered a stone capital inscribed with a menorah in Caesarea Maritima. This occurred in an area north of the Crusader wall and near the seashore, known as "area A" (in turn part of "Field O").[11] Klein immediately suspected the presence of an ancient synagogue. Two years later heavy rains exposed patches of mosaic in the vicinity. In 1942, 1945, and 1946, the Department of Antiquities investigated area A (under the direction of J. Ory) and uncovered yet another mosaic as well as Greek stone inscriptions.[12] The general impression among Jewish archeologists was that an ancient synagogue certainly existed in area A.

---

10.   N. Hasson, "Israel's archeological triumphs through the eyes of a man who was always there," *Haaretz*, March 29, 2013.

11.   Govaars 2009:5. In the 1950s and 60s Avi-Yonah excavated in the relatively small area A where Klein made his discovery. Later, this and other areas became known collectively as "Field O," as denominated by the Joint Expedition to Caesarea Maritima (JECM) in the 1980s (Fig.s 12.1 and 12.2).

12.   Goodenough I:263.

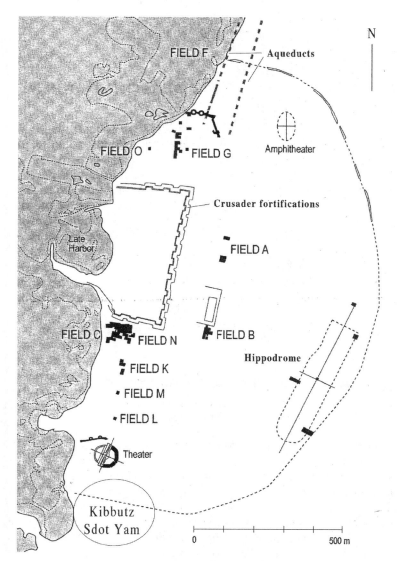

Figure 12.1. Major features of ancient Caesarea
and field sectors of the Joint Expedition.

Field O is located near the seashore and north of the Crusader fortifications.
The areas A to F (Fig. 12.2) within Field O and excavated in 1962 should not be
confused with Fields A, B, C *etc.* located elsewhere in ancient Caesarea (above)
and not pertinent to this chapter. (Redrawn from Govaars 2009: Fig. 62.)

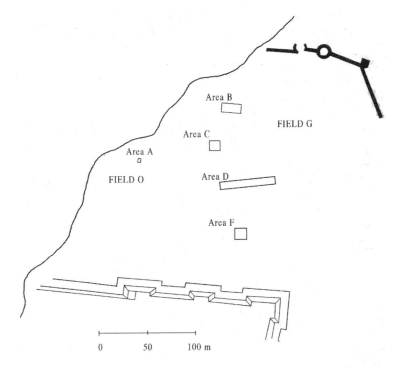

Figure 12.2. Areas within Field O excavated in 1956 and 1962.

For map location see Fig. 10.1.
(Redrawn from Govaars 2009:59.)

After the state of Israel was born in 1948, funding was sought to excavate possible synagogue sites in earnest. Thus, in the postwar years Sukenik founded the Fund for the Exploration of Ancient Synagogues (FEAS), a fund seeded by the American philanthropist Louis M. Rabinowitz and based in Cinncinnati. One of the major activities of FEAS was to finance an excavation in the area of Caesarea where the above-mentioned capital and mosaics had been found.[13] The excavation occurred after Sukenik's death in 1953, and the task devolved on a protégé and erstwhile colleague of Sukenik, the prominent Israeli archeologist Michael Avi-Yonah. The latter would direct two seasons of excavation in Caesarea for the Hebrew University and FEAS, the first in 1956 and the second in 1962.

---

13. There is ancient literary evidence for at least two synagogues in the city (Govaars *et al.* 2009:1). Josephus (*Wars* II, 14:4–5) reports that critical troubles relating to a "synagogue" in Caesarea actually led to the First Jewish War.

Another prominent Jewish scholar became involved with the Caesarea "synagogue" site. The epigrapher Dr. Moshe Schwabe analyzed the various finds from area A and wrote an article in 1950 entitled "The Caesarea Synagogue and its Inscriptions."[14] Schwabe taught at the Hebrew University from its founding in 1925. In 1939 he became head of its Institute for Classical Studies, and from 1950 to 1952 he was Rector of the University.

In this way, it appears that area A in Caesarea became something of a *cause célèbre* among the higher echelon of Israeli archeologists, from Klein, to Sukenik, to Schwabe, to Avi-Yonah. It was a test, as it were, of their ability over several decades to 'find' what their Jewish faith required.

However, a simple menorah on a capital and a few Greek inscriptions are far from proof of a synagogue, as the American scholar Marylinda Govaars would fully demonstrate in various writings. She reviewed the history of the Caesarea finds and devoted an extensive monograph to the history of area A (Govaars 2009). She concluded that there is no evidence for a synagogue:

> In 1930, the recovery of a capital with an inscribed menorah from the shore north of the Crusader fortifications at Caesarea was the first physical evidence for a possible location of Jewish associated site remains. As early as 1932, inspectors from the British Mandate Government's Antiquities Department recorded fragments of mosaic pavements near the find spot of the capital. In late 1945/early 1946, Antiquities Department Inspector Jacob Ory made several trips out to the location to record these mosaic pavement fragments, two that had Greek inscriptions, and to preserve them for later generations. In 1947 a small notice was published mentioning the possible find of a synagogue on the north side of Caesarea Maritima (Sukenik 1949:17). In a 1950 article boldly titled "The Caesarea Synagogue and its Inscriptions," Moshe Schwabe set forth the idea that because three levels of mosaic pavement fragments (two with Greek inscriptions) had been recorded by Ory, there were at least three levels of synagogue structure located at the site. However, no structural outlines were identified, and there were no plans or drawings of the proposed structures.   (Govaars 2009:2)

The last sentence of this citation hints at a major thesis of Govaars which we will be exploring later: that no structural evidence of a synagogue (or of any other building) was found in the vicinity of the Caesarea finds (below pp. 324 *f*, 353 *f*). This will have important implications for the discovery in Field O of the "Caesarea Inscription." After all, without a synagogue, how is it possible that a *synagogal* inscription could have been found there?

---

14. The priestly courses inscription from area A had not yet been "discovered." The first fragment would appear in a 1958 article (below pp. 327 *f*).

The professor and the kibbutznik

1950 was a notable year for professor Schwabe. In that year he assumed the prestigious position of Rector of the Hebrew University, as we have noted. That year also saw the publication of his article, "The Caesarea Synagogue and its Inscriptions." Less known to scholars, however, is that in 1950 Schwabe founded a small museum of antiquities in Caesarea Maritima. The museum was on the property of Sdot Yam, a kibbutz immediately to the south of the ancient town (Fig. 12.1). Schwabe established the museum in association with a certain Aaron Wegman, the man who founded the kibbutz in 1940. Wegman's name will appear often in this chapter, and his sometimes nebulous role in the strange developments to be recounted should not be underestimated.

From 1940 on, Wegman was well known to the archeologists who worked in Caesarea: Sukenik, Schwabe, Avi-Yonah—and Vardaman. He would be director the Caesarea Museum for several decades. Of course, the success of any museum depends on the quality of its holdings, and Wegman was a known and avid collector of antiquities—'chance finds' one scholar calls them (Holum 2014:185). His close connections to the highest stratum of Israeli archeology (as manifested by his co-founding of the museum with Schwabe) was no doubt a most useful asset. Indeed, the Caesarea Museum not only endured but flourished. Today it is "one of the finest local museums in Israel" (Holum, *ibid.*).

A survey of Schwabe's professional publications shows that the benefit was mutual. A 1951 article by Schwabe begins: "Some time ago a fragment of an inscription (Pl. xv, Fig. 1.1) was found in the grounds of Sdot-Yam, a collective settlement, situated south of Caesarea Palestinae outside the Herodian city wall..." A footnote alerts the reader: "My thanks are due to the Department of Antiquities of the Government of Israel, for permission to publish this inscription, and to Mr. Aron Wegmann [*sic*] of Sdot-Yam, who found and photographed it."[15]

Similarly, in a 1953 article Schwabe writes: "The first of these two new inscriptions was found in February 1952 in a sandy area south of Sdot Yam. The discoverer was a member of the youth group attached to the settlement." The footnote reads: "I have to thank my friend A. Wegman, Sdot Yam, for drawing my attention to this find; my thanks are also due to the Director, Department of Antiquities, for enabling me to study these inscriptions."[16]

---

15. M. Schwabe, "A Jewish Sepulchral Inscription from Caesarea Palestinae." IEJ 1.1 (1950–51):49–53.
16. M. Schwabe, "Two Jewish-Greek Inscriptions Recently Discovered at Caesarea." IEJ 3.2 (1953):127–30.

It must be emphasized that Wegman was himself neither an archeologist nor a scholar. As far as this writer has been able to ascertain, he never published anything in the field, nor did he engage in any (official) excavation work. Yet, in the above articles by Schwabe, Wegman is the acknowledged supplier of two important artifacts. Both happen to be inscriptions.

We have no precise find spots for these artifacts, only the vaguest generalities: "in the grounds of Sdot-Yam," and "in a sandy area south of Sdot Yam." Obviously, however, the inscriptions were accepted without reserve by both Schwabe and by the Israeli Department of Antiquities, and they had no difficulty entering both the official and the scholarly databases.

This sequence of events is quite amazing, for it diametrically conflicts with established practice in the field. Archeologists today may react with shock at such loose procedures, cognizant of the long-standing and rampant problems with forgery. Thus, Jo Ann Hackett of Harvard University: "because we have seen that there are forgers at work who are very sophisticated, we must make epigraphic (grammatical and palaeographic) conclusions based solely on inscriptions found *in situ* by trustworthy scholars and excavators." The archeologist Joseph Naveh also wrote—and he did so several decades ago—that "Forged inscriptions have frequently appeared on the antiquities market. These may be papyri, leather documents, seals, or inscriptions on stone and other material."[17] Such information is elementary and has been for a long time. Yet, clearly, Schwabe did not observe Hackett's and Naveh's stringent but basic *modus operandi.* Nor did Avi-Yonah after him, as we will soon see—for Wegman would also play a prominent role in the discovery of the "Caesarea Inscription."

Chaos in the field

Avi-Yonah dug in Caesarea twice: in 1956 and in 1962. The documentation relative to those two excavation seasons is scanty, contradictory, and even chaotic. It is often unclear who was in charge of what area and where certain important artifacts were found. Even the names of the areas excavated are not always certain. In addition, Avi-Yonah was absent for days at a time. It can honestly be said that these two excavation seasons were disorganized to the point of embarrassment.

Govaars made a valiant attempt to order the information and fill in the many lacunae, but her frustration is evident in the introduction to her 2009 monograph: "Unfortunately, no final report appeared and no photographs or plans showing the exact structural remains were published... [A] concerted effort was made to locate any drawings from the excavations. None were said to exist and none were found... The difficulty in assembling

---

17. Both the Hackett and Naveh citations are from Vaughn and Rollston 2005:63.

this information should not be underestimated."[18] Furthermore, internal problems emerged in Avi-Yonah's data. Govaars notes "contradictions and confusion... absence of stratigraphy and artifact analysis... paucity of photographs... [N]o site plans or drawings of any kind were published."[18]

Govaars' attempts to define the results of the 1962 excavation met with multiple challenges. Her following passage is typical:

> Also noted for the Stratum IV structure are "small square foundations (of shops?)," but one report places them on the southern side of the structure, while another report has them on the east side... Attempts to locate these constructions were blocked by the lack of more detailed information. Additionally, the numerous architectural fragments attributed to this stratum in the early reports are subsequently placed in the later Stratum V in later reports (Avi-Yonah 1956, 1963a:147; Avi-Yonah and Negev 1975:279; Appendix H). These architectural fragments include marble columns, marble capitals, smaller columns, a slab with a carved menorah, fragments of a chancel screen, marble inlays, and fragments of a decorated roof. The reason for this re-assignment is unclear... Also, the location of water channels with pottery pipes changes from being on the east and west sides of the broadhouse structure in Stratum IV to being on the east and west sides of the north-south structure in Stratum V... This is quite a significant change and accentuates the deep conflict over the strata indentification and artifact assignments.   (Govaars 2009:42)

The push to find a synagogue

Despite Govaars' assiduous attempts to find tangible evidence of a structure corresponding to a synagogue in area A, she ultimately failed. Even so, the locus has been known among Jewish archeologists as "the synagogue area" since the 1930s. In fact, Avi-Yonah would claim the discovery of *two* different synagogue structures in area A, "one dated to the fourth century AD and the other to the fifth/sixth century AD."[18]

The funding for the 1962 excavation season was also directed at finding a synagogue. We know this because—of the two principal funding sources (one Jewish, and one Christian)—the principal Jewish funder was none other than the Louis M. Rabinowitz Fund *for the Exploration of Ancient Synagogues*, founded in 1949. Besides the long tradition already firmly established that this was a synagogue site, Avi-Yonah certainly was motivated to show evidence of a synagogue to his Jewish funder. This seems the only reasonable explanation why so much material evidence of a Jewish nature (chancel screen with *lulab* and *ethrog*, marble capitals with menorah, fragments of a priestly courses inscription) is claimed by Avi-Yonah for the immediate "synagogue" area, yet (as we will see) has attested findspots either elsewhere (areas D, F) or "unknown." A cynical observer might suspect

---

18. Several brief citations in the following paragraphs are from Govaars 2009:2–4.

that Avi-Yonah was paid to produce a "synagogue" in area A and did just that—in some cases by "expropriating" material either unprovenanced or from places 50 to 150 meters away.

Avi-Yonah's claims of a synagogue in area A were sufficiently remarkable that in the 1980s an American endeavor—the Joint Expedition to Caesarea Maritima—mapped the area where digging had taken place and "made a serious effort to clear up the uncertainties of Avi-Yonah's excavation site."[18] Perhaps this American venture was perceived by the Israeli archeological establishment as an unwelcome challenge, for "Permission for the Joint Expedition to excavate or insert small test probes was denied" by the Israel Department of Antiquities (later the IAA).[18] That was in 1982. Two years later, "the Joint Expedition once again requested permission to excavate within the site to clarify stratigraphy and sort out the discrepancies in the reports of Avi-Yonah, but was again turned down."[18]

These denials are a symptom of enormous and long-standing tensions within Israeli archeology. The *Haaretz* article alluded to above[19] writes of the "wars of the archaeologists," namely, between "the biblical approach— those who find evidence for the Bible narrative in excavations—and the critical approach, which finds mainly contradictions between archaeological finds and the Scriptures."

The upshot is that, through the decades, a synagogue has been consistently imputed to an area of Caesarea where no such structure has ever been authenticated. Govaars politely concludes that "The results of the research challenge the preliminary [synagogue] identications by Klein, Schwabe, and Avi-Yonah." (On this critical question, see below pp. 353 *f.*)

As regards the first (1956) excavation season in Caesarea, its stated purpose was "to establish the character of these remains and their period."[20] The "remains" in question were those in the vicinity of area A brought to light over the previous decades (above, p. 318). The documentation for the first excavation season is very limited and consists principally of Avi-Yonah's two-page entry in the "Notes and News" section of the 1956 issue of the *Israel Excavation Journal* (pp. 260–61). To this 'preliminary report' (no final report ever appeared) can be added summary information in Bulletin 3 of the *Fund for the Exploration of Ancient Synagogues* (which, however, deals primarily with the 1962 excavation season),[21] as well as a number of unpublished photographs of the 1956 excavation site taken by Wegman.

Our main source of information for the 1956 season (Avi-Yonah's two-page IEJ report) is problematic for a number of reasons. Govaars writes:

---

19.   Above p. 318 n. 10.
20.   Avi-Yonah 1956:260.
21.   Govaars 2009:25. *Cf.* Govaars 2009: Appendices A and B.

Avi-Yonah's 1956 preliminary report has more than a few points of
confusion and discrepancy. For example, when reporting on the lowest
level of findings, Avi-Yonah states that "at the bottom of the excavation
Hellenistic and Persian foundations were found, belonging to the Tower
of Straton which preceded Caesarea on this site" (Avi-Yonah 1956: 260).
This is quite a profound statement based upon such limited findings;
subsequently, Avi-Yonah would claim finding Stratons' Tower over 100
m to the east. In another example, Avi-Yonah states, "this building was
destroyed by fire" (the mosaic was discolored and pieces of sulphur were
found on the pavement; Avi-Yonah 1956: 260). Just finding a fragment of
mosaic pavement that is discolored does not support the statement that
an entire building was destroyed, especially without further clarification.
One would look to see more evidence such as an extensive burn layer or
other signs of damage/burning. In this same report, Avi-Yonah states
that marble capitals, at least two different sizes, belonged ot the fourth-
century-AD public building, and then later observes, "in the eighth century an attempt was apparently made to re-use the sixth century capitals...."
It is difficult to reconcile the capitals moving from the fourth century, to
the sixth century and then to the eighth century without more details.
Avi-Yonah made some very broad statements, drawing conclusions to historical events, seemingly without presenting the confirming/solidifying
evidence. Unfortunately, this tendency was not overcome in later reports,
and without a final report publication these claims remain unsubstantiated.　　　　　　　　　　　　　　　　　　　　(Govaars 2009:27)

Among the finds claimed by Avi-Yonah from the 1956 excavation are
two marble Corinthian capitals incised with the menorah, "a slab carved
with a menorah, fragments of a chancel screen, fragments of marble inlays
and of a decorated roof, *etc.*" The vague "*etc.*" is unfortunately typical of
the poor documentation attending this excavation. While Avi-Yonah interpreted the claimed elements as those of a synagogue, Govaars found
them consistent with a public structure which "we cannot unequivocally
identify... as a synagogue at any level" (Govaars 2009:142).

Enter Jerry Vardaman

One year after Avi-Yonah's first Caesarea excavation, a young adjunct
professor at the Southwestern Baptist Theological Seminary (Fort Worth)
was in Israel to hone his archeological skills. Dr. Ephraim Jeremiah Vardaman (b. 1927, Dallas) signed on in the summer of 1957 as a junior participant in the Drew-McCormick excavations at Shechem, having just completed his Th.D from Southwestern.[22]

The ongoing Drew-McCormick excavations (1956–74) were directed
by G. Ernest Wright, professor at McCormick Seminary and later Presi-

---

22. Vardaman's dissertation was entitled "Hermeticism and the Fourth Gospel."

dent of the American Schools of Oriental Research (ASOR). In a remarkable 1972 letter to be cited in full later on (below pp. 346–48), President Wright depreciates Vardaman's character and abilities in scathing terms.[23] In fact, it would be difficult to imagine the stronger denunciation of a scholarly peer by another peer in authority:

> As you may know, way back in 1957 in our Shechem excavations, we were trying out a great many people because we had no trained scholarship to man our Jerusalem School at that time, and the Shechem dig was to be the training ground. Virtually all American work in Israel and Jordan since that time, with minor exceptions, has been carried out by people who were initially connected with the Shechem Expedition.
>
> While Joe Callaway came out strong as a brilliant field director and stratigrapher, Jerry Vardaman was an unmitigated disaster from start to finish. Hence, we could not invite him back for solid training. He does not have the judgment, the temperament, nor the essential honesty and solidity of personality that he could be trusted with any work in the Near East on his own...
>
> ... He simply cannot be trusted to do anything right, not even when he is watched every minute. He is as devious and as untrustworthy an ambassador in the Near East as any man could possibly be.

This uncompromisingly negative professional and character assessment will assume great significance when we take up Vardaman's intimate association with the 1962 'discovery' of the Caesarea Inscription fragment—the critical fragment bearing the name "Nazareth."

The lost fragment of the priestly courses inscription

About the time Vardaman was in Israel, the photograph of a stone fragment of a priestly courses inscription (Fig. 12.3) appeared in the scholarly literature. A footnote to the photograph (see below) mentioned Caesarea. One might therefore infer that the fragment was found in Avi-Yonah's 1956 Caesarea excavation—and that inference would indeed become widespread. But Avi-Yonah apparently knew nothing of it, for his 1956 report makes no mention of such a fragment nor of its discovery. In fact, *the provenance of the fragment is a complete mystery.*

The photograph appeared in an obscure scholarly volume recording the proceedings of a Dead Sea Scrolls conference. The conference took place in Strassbourg in 1957 and the volume appeared a year later. It is entitled *Aspects of the Dead Sea Scrolls*, edited by Chaim Rabin and Yigael Yadin (the son of Eleazar Sukenik). At the Strassbourg conference, a certain

---

23. The letter is addressed to Dr. William E. Hull, Dean, Southern Baptist Theological Seminary (Louisville), and is dated May 30, 1972. At the time of this writing (May 2015) it is online in the ASOR digital library.

Figure 12.3. Photograph of "Fragment of a Table of Priestly Courses from Caesarea" in S. Talmon's 1958 article on the Dead Sea Scrolls.

(Talmon 1958: 171.)

Shemaryahu Talmon presented a paper entitled "The Calendar Reckoning of the Sect from the Judaean Desert."[24] Talmon writes that the *Book of the Priestly Courses* from Qumran (only fragments of which survive) presents an expanded table of twenty-six priestly courses, rather than the twenty-four known from I Chronicles 24. The expanded number would allow each course to serve annually in the temple for two weeks, with no part of the year left over. In his article, Talmon then offered the following remarkable information:

> Tables of this sort were apparently used also in rabbinic circles. This can be inferred from a fragmentary inscription discovered not long ago at Caesarea, in which the priestly courses are listed in order. Unluckily, only that part of the inscription is preserved in which the serial numbers of the courses were inscribed:
>
> | | |
> |---|---|
> | The fif[teenth cour]se | [משמר]ת חמש ע[שרה] |
> | The sixtee[nth co]urse | [מש]מרת שש עש[רה] |
> | The seve[nteenth c]ourse [19] | [מ]שמרת שב[ע שרה] |
>
> (Talmon 1958:170–71)

Though the above was published in 1958, Talmon ostensibly presented it at the 1957 conference. Thus, his words "discovered not long ago" apparently refer to Avi-Yonah's Caesarea excavation, which took place in 1956.

---

24. Talmon 1958:162–99.

However, it is scarcely credible that, in 1956, Avi-Yonah would have overlooked a find that constitutes a virtual smoking gun for the existence of a synagogue. After all, plaques of the priestly courses are known only from synagogues in antiquity. Confirmation that Avi-Yonah was quite divorced from the genesis of this fragment is found in Talmon's footnote number "19" of the above citation. There Avi-Yonah's name does not appear:

> 19. The author's thanks are due to Dr. Y. Yadin for having directed his attention to this inscription, and to Mr. Y. Aviram of the Hebrew University for putting a photograph at his disposal. The photograph is published with the kind permission of Mr. A. Wagmann [*sic*] of Caesarea.

The "Mr. A. Wagmann" can only be the now familiar Aaron Wegman, resident of Kibbutz Sdot Yam, friend of Moshe Schwabe, and co-founder and director of the Caesarea Museum.

Talmon apparently saw only the photograph, not the fragment itself. *The photograph, in fact, represents the totality of our knowledge regarding this fragment whose provenance remains entirely unknown.* Talmon writes of "a fragmentary inscription discovered not long ago *at Caesarea*" (previous page), but naming Caesarea may simply be an inference from the fact that Wegman took/provided the photograph. Or Caesarea may only have been Wegman's *claim.* Caesarea may even have been simply a verbal claim of Y. Aviram (who put the photograph at Talmon's disposal), of Schwabe, or of another of Talmon's colleagues at the Hebrew University.

Of course, if Wegman indeed took the photograph, this does not mean that he also *found* the fragment (assuming it indeed exists).[25] It is always possible that someone gave it to him or merely showed it to him. We know, after all, that Wegman was in the business of collecting antiquities. The fact, however, that the fragment disappears and is never heard from again reveals that Wegman did not preserve it in his museum.

In other words, one can have no confidence regarding any parameters of this fragment. Based on a single photograph, it is not possible to hazard an opinion at all whether the fragment is authentic or forged, much less regarding its provenance.

It does appear, however, that Wegman was an intermediary in communicating this fragment to the Hebrew University. Unfortunately, we do not know what Wegman's standards were regarding authenticity—assuming he had any. In the case of this priestly courses fragment, we are completely at the mercy of an amateur collector and also entirely outside the parameters of accepted academic practice.

---

25.   In 1956 there were not yet personal computers and PhotoShop. The black and white photograph in Fig. 12.3 is sufficient evidence of an artifact bearing Hebrew writing. Nothing more can be supposed.

משמרת ראשונה יהויריב מסרביי מרון
משמרת שניה ידעיה עמוק צפורים
משמרת שלישית חרים מפשטה
משמרת רביעית שעורים עיתהלו
משמרת חמשית מלכיה בית לחם
משמרת תשישית בימין יודפת
משמרת שביעית הקוץ עילבו
משמרת שמינית אביה כפר עוזיה
משמרת תשיעית ישוע ערבל
משמרת עשירית שכניה חבודת כבול
משמרת אחת עשרה אלישיב כהן קנה
משמרת שתים עשרה יקים פשחור צפת
משמרת שלוש עשרה חופה בית מעון
משמרת ארבע עשרה ישבאב צפת עיתשיחין
משמרת חמש עשרה בילגה זונית
משמרת שש עשרה אימר כפר נמרה
משמרת שבע עשרה חזיר ממלית
משמרת שמונה עשרה הפיצץ נצרת
משמרת תשע עשרה פתחיה כפול ערב
משמרת עשרים יחזקאל ביר דומא
משמרת אחת ועשרים יכין כפר יוחנה
משמרת שתים ועשרים גמול בית חוביה
משמרת שלוש ועשרים דליהו גנתון צלמין
משמרת ארבע ועשרים מעזיהו חמת אריח

Figure 12.4. The reconstructed "Caesarea Inscription" of the twenty-four priestly courses with its three extant fragments.

The Hebrew is based on Klein's scholarship of the early 19th century. Uppermost is the "Talmon" fragment published in 1958. At left is the "Nazareth" fragment discovered by Vardaman in 1962. At right is the "mem" fragment allegedly discovered in the final week of the 1962 excavation season (Avi-Yonah 1962:138; *cf.* Fig. 12.12).

Nevertheless, the "Talmon fragment" (as it will be referred to hereafter) entered the academic literature without raising the slightest suspicion. Accompanied by two other (equally dubious) fragments to be discussed below, it would become an accepted part of the so-called "Caesarea Inscription" of the priestly courses (Fig. 12.4).

It is most revealing that—apparently with complete faith—Talmon included this unprovenanced and previously unpublished artifact in his 1958 article. From Talmon's footnote, we gather that both Yadin and Aviram also placed confidence in the artifact. Given the pervasive problems in the Middle East with forgeries and 'altered' finds, such confidence by the staff of the Hebrew University in this fragment is astonishing. But the find *does* suggest the existence of a synagogue—and therein may lie the key to its ready acceptance.

Equally remarkable is that the Talmon fragment was never heard from again. No one—other than Talmon in his cursory 1958 remarks—has independently written about the fragment in the six decades since its 'discovery.'[26] Apparently, no one knows where it is now. The fragment is 'lost.'

In his 1962 report Avi-Yonah will accept the Talmon fragment without reservation as *hard evidence* for the existence of a synagogue *in area A*.[27] The foregoing discussion shows this line to be ridiculously untenable. In any case, Kibbutz Sdot Yam—where Wegman ostensibly 'found' the fragment—is at the southern extremity of Caesarea, far from area A (Fig. 12.1). One cannot begin to describe the numerous problematic issues which should have undermined Avi-Yonah's acceptance—from the unknown findspot, to the extra-professional source (Wegman), to the lack of confirmation (no one has seen the fragment), to the lack of scholarly documentation and discussion.

An accurate description for this is *quack archeology*.

Since Avi-Yonah's 1962 endorsement, the Talmon fragment has gained acceptance in the scholarly world and beyond. It is now universally regarded as the first of three fragments making up the "Caesarea Inscription"—a marble plaque listing the twenty-four priestly courses, one believed to have been placed in a Caesarea synagogue in antiquity. According to numerous

---

26. A drawing of the fragment also exists in B. Mazar *et al.* (ed.), *Views of the Biblical World*, IV. Jerusalem, 1961, p. 257.

27. Avi-Yonah writes: "A third fragment, picked up on the surface at Caesarea, reads..." He then gives the Hebrew of the inscription and adds significantly: "It seems that the three fragments formed part of one and the same marble slab." (Avi-Yonah 1962:137–38.) This, of course, shows that the archeologist locates the origin of all three fragments within area A, and also that he supposed they belonged to the same artifact. He was wrong on both counts.

Jewish scholars, that synagogue was located in area A, precisely where evidence of a synagogue has been assiduously sought for decades.

Vardaman and the Talmon fragment

The above observations are testimony that the ubiquitous cant found in biblical archeology regarding evidence, rigorous method, and verfiability is sometimes mere bluster, for we have now seen how a perfectly unprovenanced, thoroughly unverified, and even lost artifact can achieve total scholarly acceptance if the 'right' authorities approve. As it happens, in this case all of those authorities were reputable Israeli archeologists.

Because we do not know the provenance of the Talmon fragment—nor what happened to it—we likewise do not know when Jerry Vardaman became aware of the fragment or, incredibly, if he might even have had something to do with its 'discovery.' The latter suspicion would ordinarily be entirely unjustified. But Vardaman's character, as described in Wright's letter above, and his undeniable subsequent involvement (in 1962) with yet other fragments of allegedly the *same* inscription—these astonishing facts impel us to carefully consider any possibility that the young Baptist professor *could* have also been involved with the Talmon fragment.

However, we have little to go on—only vague circumstances. For example, it is interesting that the appearance of the Talmon fragment coincided with Vardaman's first stay in Israel in the summer of 1957. This was the year that Talmon presented the fragment to the scholarly community in his conference paper in Strassbourg.

Or did he? For certain is only that the 1958 publication of Talmon's paper included the above photo we have dubbed "the Talmon fragment," as well as some discussion of the priestly courses inscription. It is possible that Talmon in fact made no mention of the fragment in his 1957 paper, and that the photograph and a brief comment were 'included' in the print edition only a year later.

It is also possible that Vardaman was in Israel one year earlier, that is, already in the summer of 1956—the first season of the Shechem excavations and the year that Avi-Yonah first excavated in Caesarea.

In any case, Vardaman's presence in Israel in 1957 coincides closely with these developments—it was after the fragment's (implied) 1956 discovery by Avi-Yonah, and before its publication in 1958. In 1957 Vardaman interacted on a daily basis with professional peers in Shechem and would have been immersed in the contemporary currents of biblical archeology. At the very least, he would have known about the Talmon fragment. Whether or not he had a hand in its recent (or concurrent) appearance we may never know.

The possibilities for mischief are, admittedly, entirely speculative—but they are endless. The discovery of the Talmon fragment figures significantly in future maneuvering and planning. Largely on the basis of its "discovery" (already associated with area A) Vardaman was able to later persuade his school (now the *Southern* Baptist Theological Seminary, Louisville),[28] *as well as Jewish interests*, to undertake a second round of excavations at Caesarea. Vardaman's remarkable trump card was that he was able to secure funding for that second excavation season (see next section).

The Talmon fragment chronologically marks the beginning of Vardaman's involvement with the Caesarea excavations. In the ensuing years he worked to arrange that the Southern Baptist Theological Seminary (henceforth SBTS) provide a large subsidy to help fund and staff a second Caesarea excavation season in 1962. In other words, *Vardaman himself had a deciding hand in ensuring that further excavations in Caesarea came about.* We will soon consider in detail how the young scholar was able to place himself in such a powerful position vis-a-vis the ongoing Caesarea excavations. Tuccinardi writes:

> The discovery of fragment 3 [the Talmon fragment] was crucial to the decision of the [SBTS] to underwrite the 1962 archeological excavations in Caesarea.
> The reasons are patent.
> Fragment 3 clearly demonstrates that a marble plaque—similar to what Klein had reconstructed—was in antiquity affixed to a synagogue wall in Caesarea. And if this was indeed the case, then it was possible to prove—once and for all—the existence of Nazareth from at least the second century of our era.   (Tuccinardi 2010:54–55)

The above is, however, tangential. After all, the Talmon fragment itself does not include the seminal word "Nazareth" but only a few banal words at the beginning of three lines ("The fifteenth course... sixteenth course... seventeeth course..."). Then, too, Klein's reconstruction is entirely *theoretical*—drawn from research into medieval Jewish liturgical poems. If one *really* wished to prove the existence of Nazareth in Middle Roman times, it would be necessary to show that Klein's reconstruction of *the eighteenth line* was correct: "The eighteenth course Hapises Nazareth." The only way to do this, of course, would be to find a fragment of the priestly courses inscription which includes the word "Nazareth."

---

28.   There are two institutions with very similar names. Vardaman secured his Th.D from the *Southwestern* Baptist Theological Seminary in Fort Worth, Texas. However, he later became professor at the *Southern* Baptist Theological Seminary in Louisville, Kentucky. The latter institution partially subsidized the 1962 Caesarea excavation.

As it transpired, Vardaman discovered that precise fragment in the second excavation season at Caesarea—a season he himself orchestrated.

Vardaman and the 1962 excavation funding

After receiving his doctorate Vardaman secured a teaching position at the Southern Baptist Theological Seminary in Louisville, Kentucky. No mere lecturer, he was soon forging powerful relationships which significantly impacted his institution and also enhanced his prestige. In 1961 Vardaman scored a coup—he secured the funding for a new museum at SBTS:

> Jerome Eisenberg, antiquarian, numismatist and director of the Royal-Athena Galleries in New York City, has a faith that knows no national boundaries.
>
> In June, 1961, Mr. Eisenberg established the Eisenberg Museum of Egyptian and Near Eastern Antiquities at the Southern Baptist Theological Seminary in Louisville. It was given in honor of his parents and dedicated to them because "I wanted to do something for them while they were still alive."
>
> This all came about through Mr. Eisenberg having an earlier chance meeting with Dr. E. J. Vardaman of the Seminary over a case of ancient coins in a museum in Jerusalem. Both being interested in Judeo-Christian antiquities, they formed a firm and lasting friendship. When Mr. Eisenberg decided to give the museum it was only natural that his friend Dr. Vardaman and the Southern Baptist Theological Seminary would be the recipient. The archaeological materials in the museum are invaluable to students and the general public interested in the everyday life of the Bible period.
>
> (W. Ishmael, "The Power of Faith," *AP Newsfeatures*, May 14, 1966)

Vardaman's success in securing the Eisenberg Museum for his employer gave him powerful leverage in his future dealings with the SBTS. From ASOR President Wright's letter of 1972, partially cited above, we learn that Vardaman himself imposed conditions on the Eisenberg funds, conditions which resulted in his receiving a goodly portion of money which should have helped the "whole school":

> [Vardaman] must not be allowed to represent any American interests, and least of all the reputation of Southern Baptist Theological Seminary, by his wild schemes for Near Eastern archaeology. No matter how much money he has, and Duke [McCall, President of SBTS] says that he got that money out from under the noses of the Seminary Planning Committee (which had other plans for this gentleman's funds to help the whole school rather than simply to help a man who can never he helped)...

This "gentleman's funds" can only refer to the money that Eisenberg bequeathed to the SBTS as a result of Vardaman's initiatives. That money

was earmarked for a museum and intended for "the whole school." Vardaman, however, successfully extracted "much money" from these funds for
his own ends. This, of course, constitutes a bribe: either the SBTS plays by
Vardaman's rules or it risks losing the entire Eisenberg bequest.

To what use did Vardaman put this 1961 money? The answer is clear
when we look at the funding of the second Caesarea excavation season:

> In July-August 1962 the Department of Archaeology of the Hebrew
> University resumed its excavations at the site north of the Crusader wall.
> The excavations were directed by Prof. M. Avi-Yonah, with the assistance
> of Mr. A. Negev and Prof. J. Vardaman of the Southern Baptist Theo-
> logical Seminary, Louisville, Kentucky; several students of archaeology
> also took part in the work. The funds for the season were supplied by
> the Department for the Improvement of Landscaping and Restoration
> of Historic Sites of the Prime Minister's Office *and the Southern Theological
> Seminary (Eisenberg Museum).*
>
> (Avi-Yonah and Negev 1963:146; emphasis added.)

It is evident, then, that at least part of the money that Vardaman extracted from the Eisenberg Museum funds went to support the second Caesarea excavation season. Vardaman was also able to leverage these funds to
secure a place on the elite archeological staff. From the extant excavation
notes, it appears that an undetermined number of SBTS student volunteers participated in the 1962 Caesarea excavation. Their expenses were
probably also defrayed by the Eisenberg Museum funds.

Thus, between July 15 and August 21, 1962, Avi-Yonah returned to
Caesarea for a second season of excavations. In contrast to the first 1956
season, this time the excavation funding was more ample—for the subsis-
tence was provided by both the SBTS and the state of Israel.

The area of excavation was also comparatively larger than in 1956,
including areas B, C, D, and F (Fig. 12.2). One report also notes an "area
E" in connection with the findspot of the third and last fragment of the
priestly courses inscription.[29] But in another report the findspot is "area
F."[30] This is but one aspect of the general confusion attending the 1962
excavation season.

In 1956 Avi-Yonah had excavated only the small quadrant area A. In
1930 Samuel Klein had found remains there suggestive of ancient Jewish
presence (above p. 318). However, Govaars concludes that the capital with

---

29. Three fragments were allegedly found in the same general area of ancient Caesarea, all claimed to derive from the same marble inscription of the twenty-four priestly
courses. We will see that this conclusion is untenable. The "Nazareth" fragment was
the second fragment, allegedly found in Area D by Vardaman on August 14, 1962.

30. See Govaars 1983:68 and below pp. 360 *f.*

inscribed menorah and other Jewish artifacts found in area A were probably brought in from elsewhere in antiquity and reused in a secular, not
synagogal, public building (Govaars 2009:142).

Avi-Yonah of course knew nothing of Govaars' later conclusions
which, in any case, would have been most uncongenial to him, to Sukenik,
and to the entire *raison d'être* of the Caesarea excavations whose original and
enduring purpose was precisely to find evidence of a synagogue.

With better funding and more manpower, in 1962 Avi-Yonah resumed
excavating in the large sector known as "Field O," now officially aided
by two assistants: Avraham Negev and Jerry Vardaman. Other personnel
of undetermined status also helped, such as Eliezer Oren (not yet a full-
fledged archeologist) who, according to a footnote, directed excavation of
the somewhat mysterious area E/F.[31] An unspecified number of volunteers
from both the United States and Israel also helped.

Despite the sparse and disjointed reports of the 1962 Caesarea excavation season, enough data is available to show that a number of unusual
occurrances took place. The data come principally from Vardaman's field
notes (published selectively at Govaars 2009:185–86), complemented by
notices subsequently written by Avi-Yonah and by Vardaman.

Chronology of the excavation

We have very few written records of the 1962 Caesarea excavation
season. Avi-Yonah and Negev did not keep field notes. However, Vardaman
did. At the excavation site, he often quickly jotted down a sentence in his
notebook when some artifact was unearthed. Thus, his field note for a day
might consist of five or six sentences, each added at different times. Sometimes a rough pencil sketch or diagram accompanies the notes.

The main resource for establishing a chronology of the 1962 Caesarea
excavation season is Vardaman's field notebook. It is also the best resource
for establishing Vardaman's whereabouts from day to day. In what follows,
dates are marked in bold type. The many *missing* days—including those
when Vardaman would be expected at the excavation site—are marked
with an asterisk.

Sunday, July 15, 1962. The excavation season begins in area A with
thirty-six workers. Remarkably, however, neither the excavation director
(Avi-Yonah) nor Negev are present—they are in Tel Aviv. Thus, Vardaman
is in charge during the first two days of the excavation.[32]

---

31. Avi-Yonah 1962:137, n. 3. Attempts to contact Dr. E. Oren by both this writer
and by M. Govaars have been unsuccessful (*cf.* below p. 364).
32. Govaars 2009:185.

Regardless of Avi-Yonah's and Negev's reason for absence, no circum-stance could be better calculated to express confidence in a co-worker and to set the tenor of a *loosely* controlled season. We are reminded that such great confidence in Vardaman dramatically contrasts with the extremely poor impression he made in the Shechem excavation a few years before (above, pp. 327–28). Such absence conveys, in effect: "You are in charge. Do as you see fit, for you have free rein. You are certainly not being watched."

Monday, July 16. Vardaman makes the first three entries in his field notebook. Parts of a storage jar, pottery bowl, and piece of dressed marble are found in area A.[33]

Tuesday, July 17. Avi-Yonah returns from Tel Aviv. Some post-Ro-man artifacts are found.

Wednesday, July 18. A single grave (undated) is found, as well as the fragment of a "synagogue chancel screen" (see below). As noted above, any synagogogal artifact found in this excavation is suspect, for Govaars found no structural evidence of a synagogue in the area. *If the burial were ancient, it would also constitute telling evidence against the contemporary existence of a Jewish house of assembly in the vicinity.*

Thursday, July 19. The immediate area of the grave is excavated. Fragments of Arabic artifacts are uncovered.

* Friday, July 20–Saturday July 21. A two-day lacuna in Vardaman's field notes ensues and the next entry (see below) surprisingly begins: "Back at Caesarea; somewhat late because only left Jerusalem at 2:00 a.m."

Thus Vardaman left Caesarea for Jerusalem after the day of digging on the 19th, or possibly early on the 20th. In any case, there would have been no excavation work on the sabbath (the 21st). He returns to work in Caesarea on Sunday the 22nd (the beginning of the Jewish week).

Vardaman's reason for going to Jerusalem is unknown. This is only the first of several possible trips to Jerusalem during his tenure in Caesarea.

Sunday, July 22. Vardaman writes:

> Back at Caesarea; somewhat late because only left Jerusalem at 2:00 a.m. arrived at Zetchron turnoff at 4:00 a.m.; drove on to Zilchron[34] in car at 5:00 a.m. overslept. Arrived in Caesarea by hitchhiking at 7:45 (only way I could negociate my travel). Told Negev about the camera opportunity (a Rolleflex for $95)[.] Wants to go on Tues and look at it.

---

33. The artifacts were found in "C7" and "D5." These designations are to units (each measuring one square meter) in area A, not to *areas* C and D which had not yet been opened. (For the diagram of area A, see Govaars 2009:44.)

34. Probably Zihron Ya'akov, north of Caesarea (on Highway 70).

Vardaman obviously had a very late Saturday night in Jerusalem, leaving the city at 2:00 a.m. His only sleep would have been en route and thus it is no wonder he "overslept." Was he partying in the city? Or did he have pressing business in Jerusalem that detained him half the night?

A day's work in what Vardaman calls the "Synagogue" area (area A) ensues. He uncovers some pottery fragments, as well as part of a short Greek inscription not elsewhere noted (redrawn at Govaars 2009:46).

Monday, July 23. A coin (no further description given) is found. Samuel Moskovits, Surveyor for the Israel Department of Antiquities arrives to survey area A. Vardaman writes:

> Since Hellenistic cut so large, moved with Eleazar to D. This is the new "cut" which has good likelihood of being "Strato's Tower" area.

The new Area D was opened by a bulldozer removing three feet of topsoil in a long trench.[35] Thus, on July 23 Vardaman and Oren left area A to begin work in Area D—the area where the critical Nazareth fragment of the priestly courses would be found three weeks later (below).

Wednesday, July 25. Avi-Yonah uncovers a hoard of coins in area A. Vardaman writes: "approximately 3,600 bronzes probably 4th cent. Roman coins. We worked from 11:30 a.m. until 2:10 p.m. clearing the hoard and counting the number of pieces."

* Thursday, July 26–Sunday, July 29. No entries have been found for these four days in Vardaman's field notebook. It is possible that he was again in Jerusalem for the second sabbath weekend in a row.

Monday, July 30–Friday, Aug. 3. By culling scattered passages in the reports, one can infer Vardaman's presence at the Caesarea excavation site on each of these days.

* Saturday, Aug. 4. Sabbath—no field note entry.

Sunday, Aug. 5. A short entry: "In area A pottery, another terra sigillata stamp (footsole)."

Monday, Aug. 6. Field note.

* Tuesday–Wednesday, Aug. 7–8. No field note entries.

Thursday–Friday, Aug. 9–10. Field notes.

* Saturday–Sunday, Aug. 11–12. No field note entries.

Monday–Tuesday, Aug. 13–14. Field notes. *Discovery of the "Nazareth" fragment. Vardaman is relieved of his duties in the excavation.*

---

35. Govaars 2009:53.

Tuesday Aug. 21.[36] Last day of the excavation.

Thus, it would appear that Vardaman was absent from the excavation site no less than eleven days out of thirty-one.[37] His absent days included seven *non*-sabbath days when one would expect to find a field note. During the first weekend (July 20–21) Vardaman was certainly in Jerusalem. We do not know his whereabouts during the other 'missing' days.

For unspecified reasons, Vardaman was expelled from the excavation on August 14—the same day as his 'discovery' of the Nazareth fragment and one week before the official termination of the 1962 excavation season (see n. 36 below).

The "chancel screen" fragment

The work began on Sunday, July 15, with all hands in area A—less the excavation director Avi-Yonah and his principal assistant, A. Negev. They were in Tel Aviv. Thus, Vardaman was in charge of the thirty-six workers.

Avi-Yonah and Negev returned on Tuesday, the 17th. The following day Vardaman found a "chancel screen" fragment measuring 19 x 14 cm. He offered a quick sketch of the fragment in his notebook, reproduced by Govaars (2009:46; Fig. 12.5 below). It shows what appears to be an *ethrog*[38] on one side and a "guilloche" (Vardaman's description) on the other.

To Avi-Yonah a chancel screen fragment was yet another sign of a synagogue, or at least of ancient Jewish presence in area A. Already in 1956 the archeologist had claimed the discovery of "fragments of a chancel screen" along with "small columns (of an ark?) in marble" and "a slab carved with a menorah."[39] Only the "menorah" had been objectively described, however, while the "chancel screen" and "ark" were venturesome interpretations *already* presupposing an on-site synagogue. In 1930, Klein

---

36. Govaars writes: "The notebook entry written [by Vardaman] about the discovery of the first ["Nazareth"] fragment of the Twenty-Four Priestly Courses occurred on 14 August 1962, just one week before the end of the field season" (Govaars 2009:55). Thus the season ended on Tuesday, August 21. Vardaman's leaving a week early is also stated in another passage: "Vardaman left the site in August with only one week remaining in the excavation" (Govaars 2009:247, n. 91). Thus Vardaman must have left immediately after the discovery of the "Nazareth" fragment (*cf.* below p. 350).

37. This is confirmed by Govaars who mentions the total of "twenty days of notes" by Vardaman (Govaars 2009:55). Since the entire excavation season had thirty-one days, this leaves eleven days without any field notes by Vardaman.

38. The autumn feast of Sukkot ("booths," "tabernacles") features the gathering of the "Four Species" (Leviticus 23:40). These include the *ethrog* (fruit of citron tree), the *lulab* (date palm frond), the *hadass* (bough of myrtle) and the *aravah* (branches of willow). The last three are bound together and traditionally waved with one hand.

39. Avi-Yonah 1956:261.

had found a Corinthian capital with the menorah in area A, and he also assumed the presence of a synagogue. Govaars, however, pointed out that it was impossible to identify the structural remains as those of a synagogue "at any level," while she also pointed out that Jewish secular buildings were frequently ornamented with the menorah and other religious symbols (Govaars 2009:142).

Ironically, it may be remarked that synagogues of Talmudic times were often ornamented with what we would today consider decidedly pagan symbols (such as the sun god Helios, the zodiac, *etc*). Thus, inferring a synagogue from a few fragmentary artifacts is most hazardous. This is one reason why synagogal *structural* remains are critical—yet no such remains have been found in the entire Field O, as Govaars insists.[40]

By characterizing one fragment as part of a "chancel screen" Vardaman was continuing in the spirit of his co-workers, finding 'synagogal' evidence when possible, even though such vague ornamentation could be from many things. The main curiosity relative to this fragment, however, is that it was never heard from again *in area A*. Yet the fragment popped up later in the excavation season *in area F,* located approximately 130 m to the southeast of area A (Fig. 12.2). This is altogether remarkable and we will return to the question of this fragment's 'migration' in due course (below, p. 368).

Avi-Yonah mentions the Area F "chancel screen" fragment in several places,[41] but never the earlier area A fragment—of which he does not seem to have been aware and which simply disappeared. Yet Vardaman's July 18 note and drawing of an area A "chancel screen" fragment is irrefutable. It would be most strange if Vardaman did not communicate the find to Avi-Yonah, for the latter was most interested in evidence of a synagogue. Govaars, too, notes with surprise that "This item is not reported or discussed elsewhere" (Govaars 2009:271, n.145).

Unfortunately, we do not have a drawing of the Area F fragment, or even any description beyond the information that on one side was an *ethrog* and on the other a *lulab*. A glance at Fig. 12.5 shows what appears to be an *ethrog* (citron) at the left. Perhaps what Vardaman characterized on July 18 as a "guilloche" in area A subsequently became for Avi-Yonah a *lulab* (date palm frond) in area F? Indeed, Avi-Yonah characterizes the find in Area F as "part of a synagogue chancel screen, showing an *ethrog* and a *lulab*" (Avi-Yonah 1962:137). If this is the case, however, it represents an additional liberty taken with the evidence, for in Fig. 12.5 the *ethrog* is obviously on one

---

40.   Govaars 2009:141–42.
41.   Avi-Yonah 1962:137; Avi-Yonah 1964:46; Avi-Yonah and Negev 1975:278; *cf.* Govaars 2009:56, 124, 232.

Figure 12.5. A notebook sketch of the "chancel screen" fragment from Area A, drawn by Vardaman on July 18, 1962.

The "Unit D7" refers to the square meter grid in area A, not to area D. (Redrawn by M. Govaars. From Govaars 2009:45 and used with permission.)

side of the fragment and the *lulab*/guilloche on the other. Thus, the two depictions are not in artistic relation. Instead of *ethrog + lulab*, we have an *ethrog* on one side and a guilloche on the other.

Avi-Yonah's persistent relating of chancel screen fragments to a possible synagogue is also questionable on chronological grounds. The archeologist's dating of the alleged synagogue receded with the passage of the years, from the fourth-fifth centuries (1962) to "the third century" (1975).[42] However, the chancel screen came into use only in Byzantine times:

> On the basis of archaeological and literary data, it has become clear that the synagogue sanctuary had no permanent internal division; the term "partition" (*mahitsah*) appears only rarely in relation to the synagogue. Partitions were erected for unusual occasions. . .
>
> The one kind of partition that appears with some frequency is the chancel screen separating the area of the apse or bima from the rest of the main hall. .. *The appearance of the chancel screen in the Byzantine synagogue seems to be a classic example of Christian influence.* In the Byzantine church, the chancel screen had a very definite and important purpose, *i.e.*, to separate the congregation from the clergy, which officiated primarily in the apse area, particularly around the altar.. .
>
> (L. Levine, *The Ancient Synagogue.* Yale: University Press, 2000, p. 341. Emphasis added.)

We have mentioned that the 1962 excavation was "apparently disorganized to the point of embarrassment" (above p. 323). The suspicious elements regarding the "chancel screen" fragment (chronology, description, findspot) are a manifestation of that disorganization. Unfortunately, such confusion offers numerous opportunities to a "devious" character who "simply cannot be trusted to do anything right." Those were Wright's

---

42.   Avi-Yonah 1963a:147; Avi-Yonah and Negev 1975:278. Govaars was well aware of Avi-Yonah's conflicting datings, which also underlie his confusion regarding strata. On his third century date for the synagogue, she curtly observes: "This appears to conflict with the preceding reference" (Govaars 2009:272 n. 12).

words in describing Vardaman (above p. 327). Such an unscrupulous person might well seek the opportunities inherent in a disorganized field excavation, opportunities to tamper with evidence, or even to 'introduce' evidence—whether he is watched or not.

Subsequent developments fully vindicate Wright's negative assessment. Vardaman was eventually expelled from the Caesarea excavation. Some years later he was arrested by the Jordanian police for bribery. Later still he asserted claims as astonishing as they are bogus, claims regarding microscopic lettering on Roman coins.[43] Only now, years after his death, is the full extent of Vardaman's astonishingly dishonest activity finally emerging into the light of day.

The discovery of the "Nazareth" fragment

The find
In the days following the discovery of the "chancel screen" fragment, areas B, C, D, and F (apparently first denominated "E") were opened in a rough north-south line about one hundred meters east of area A. The northernmost area B was later described by Avi-Yonah as a "Byzantine house paved with mosaics." Area C was the findspot for "a small deposit of coins, lamp fragments, and glass vessels."[44]

On July 23, 1962—approximately one week after the start of the excavation—a bulldozer removed three feet of topsoil to form the long 25-meter trench "area D." Avi-Yonah hoped to uncover some evidence of Strato's Tower (the pre-Herodian settlement) there. While Avi-Yonah stayed in area A, he placed Vardaman in charge of area D. The student Eliezer Oren moved to D with Vardaman.

Vardaman spent the afternoon of July 25 in area A helping to count a newly-discovered hoard of fourth century Roman bronze coins (numbering approximately 3,700). Avi-Yonah would interpret this as a cache hidden under or near the "synagogue."[45] The fact that hoards of coins are generally associated with secular governmental or banking structures apparently did not occur to him.

---

43. Vardaman's obtuse engagement with 'microletters' ultimately stemmed from his desire to rectify the Quirinius census error in the Lukan birth story (Lk 2:2), where the evangelist dates Jesus' birth to *c.* 6 CE—long after the death of Herod (hence a clear historical error). Vardaman proposed a second, earlier census of Quirinius and also an earlier birth year for Jesus of 12 BCE. The bogus microletters were his way of 'substantiating' that earlier chronology.

44. Avi-Yonah 1963a:146; Govaars 2009:53 (with photograph of area B, p. 51).

45. Avi-Yonah 1963a:148; Govaars 2009:231.

Figure 12.6. The "Nazareth" fragment of the priestly courses inscription discovered by Vardaman on August 14, 1962 in Caesarea.

The letters [nu]n-tsade-resh-tav ("[Na]tsrath") are visible in the second line.
(Ameling *et al.*, 2011, fig. 1145.1b.)

After Vardaman's notebook entry of July 23, the available data from all sources becomes very sparse for the remaining month of the excavation season. For example, Govaars (Appendix C, pp. 185–86) devotes two full pages in her 2009 volume to Vardaman's field notes. But those pages are taken up with his entries before the 23rd (that is, during the first week), except for two very short entries for the entire remaining month of the excavation (August 5 and August 10).[46]

Though Govaars published Vardaman's field notes pertaining to the first week of the excavation, a careful search of her 2009 book reveals that

46. Vardaman's entry for Aug. 5 reads: "In area A pottery, another terra sigillata stamp (footsole)." His entry for Aug. 10 reads: "Another terra sigallata [*sic*], footsole type (planta pedis) from synagogue (area A)."

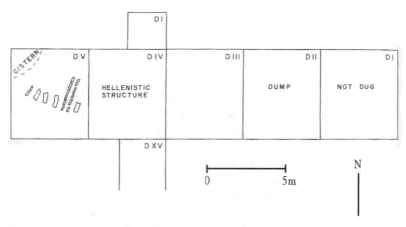

Figure 12.7. Area D where the "Nazareth" fragment of the priestly courses
inscription was found.

(Redrawn from Govaars 2009:53.)

Vardaman wrote field notes on many additional days, showing that he was
at the excavation site on those dates. We don't have those additional notes,
unfortunately—only mentions of them by Govaars in her discussions of
various areas/artifacts. All the days Vardaman was demonstrably present at
the excavation site have been duly noted in the section above, "Chronology
of the excavation." The result is that eleven days are totally unaccounted
for. That is a considerable amount of time. It includes the four-day stretch
July 26–29, as well as August 7–8 and 11–12.

On Tuesday, August 14, Vardaman was working in the area D trench.
On that day he made an unprecedented discovery which he later described
with the following words:

> This fragment of the inscription was found August, 14, 1962, at a
> depth of 90 cm. below the surface of the sands of Caesarea. It was reg-
> istered with pottery basket D.V.9. It was found near the end of the sea-
> son of excavation, and due to fatigue, the men who were working with
> picks and hoes were becoming careless about spotting some of the objects
> which were turning up in this area of work. For this reason, as the excava-
> tor I gave strict instructions to the workman on the wheelbarrow (whose
> name was Shalom Attiah) to pay close attention to the debris which was
> being emptied there by the basket men. This proved to be most fortunate,
> for the particular fragment mentioned above (no.1) was found by Mr.
> Attiah as he searched through his wheelbarrow before carting the debris
> away to the dump. The Fragment was quickly washed and at first proved
> difficult to read intelligibly. The second line I immediately read as N Ṣ R

> T ('Nazareth'), even though others read it as B Ṣ R T ('drought'). The first
> letter of line 2 was only partially preserved of course. It must be realized
> that Professor Avi Yonah has done a brilliant job of epigraphical inter-
> pretation, having as he did so few clues as to the nature of the documents
> which Eleazar Oren and I found and reconstructing the whole so master-
> fully. Full credit for recognizing the significance and relationship of the
> various fragments to each other and to older sources must be given to his
> ingenuity as an epigraphist.   (Vardaman and Garrett 1964:42)

This was the "Nazareth" fragment. It was immediately recognized as
part of the priestly courses inscription and, hence, was reflexively associated with the Talmon fragment ostensibly found in Caesarea some years
before. The discovery of this second fragment was greeted with great applause throughout the Christian world and quickly became the most tangible "proof" that Nazareth existed as early as 70 CE (the date after which
more conservative Christians suppose the priestly family of Hapises migrated from Jerusalem northwards to Nazareth). Henceforth, the "Caesarea Inscription" emerged as the earliest witness to the existence of the town
of Nazareth outside of Christian writings.

However, Vardaman's account presents several stunning irregularities
and even some frank impossibilities. We will now consider the many issues
attached to the discovery of this critical fragment.

The problems

Vardaman himself was directly responsible for the discovery of the
"Nazareth" fragment. This conclusion is at once inescapable and incriminating. It was, after all, Vardaman who directed the laborer Attiah to look
carefully though the refuse in his wheelbarrow. Had Attiah not undertaken
this *special* search, the "Nazareth" fragment—the most important find of
the 1962 excavation season—would not have been discovered.

Though Vardaman was responsible for Attiah's searching through his
wheelbarrow, one might still regard the fragment's discovery as a fortuitous
coincidence. But then another question presents: Why did the fragment
get as far as the wheelbarrow *unnoticed*? Vardaman's account requires that
an unnamed workman in charge of one of the baskets (variously numbered basket 9 or basket 10—see below) excavated a sizable object which
he thought was mere debris, and he placed that item in the debris wheelbarrow. However, we are talking about a *marble* fragment 2.4 cm thick, 15.3
cm high, and 12.4 cm wide. When caked with mud (as Vardaman's account
infers) the object would have easily weighed upwards of five pounds. Presumably, the laborer paid no mind to this substantial object—neither when
he dug it out of the ground nor when he placed it in his basket. It also did
not cause him pause when he placed (or dumped) it into Attiah's wheelbarrow.

Letter from Dr. G. Ernest Wright,
President, American Schools of Oriental Research
to Dr. William E. Hull, Dean, Southern Baptist Theological Seminary
(Louisville, Kentucky)[1]

30 May 1972

Dear Dean Hall: [2]

I am writing you about the proposed excavation of Jerry Vardaman at Machaerus in Jordan. I am determined that this excavation shall not take place and
I am willing to use every means at my disposal to prevent it.

As you may know, way back in 1957 in our Shechem excavations, we were
trying out a great many people because we had no trained scholarship to man
our Jerusalem School at that time, and the Shechem dig was to be the training
ground. Virtually all American work in Israel and Jordan since that time, with
minor exceptions, has been carried out by people who were initially connected with the Shechem Expedition.[3]

While Joe Callaway came out strong as a brilliant field director and stratigra-
pher, Jerry Vardaman was an unmitigated disaster from start to finish. Hence,
we could not invite him back for solid training. He does not have the judgment, the temperament, nor the essential honesty and solidity of personality that he could be trusted with any work in the Near East on his own. His
attempt to dig at Caesarea some years ago was quietly stopped when the word
was passed to the appropriate Israeli authorities.

Then, while the Director of Antiquities in Jordan, Awni Dajani, was on his
death bed, the current Department of Antiquities, as well as the University
of Jordan, believe it to be a fact that Jerry bribed Awni's cousin, Rafiq Dajani,
to get a permit to dig at Machaerus.[4] That expedition was, from every point
of view, a disaster. In any event, when Jerry came back into the country to
see about digging again, the Department of Antiquities issued orders to the
police to arrest him at the airport. The only way he was rescued from arrest
and having to stand trial was that the American ambassador went to bat for
him and asked that the matter be settled quietly to prevent the scandal from
appearing in the papers. Now, as though that were not enough, this man has
the continental gall to start it again. The Department of Antiquities and we,
ourselves, meaning John Marks, the President of the American Center of
Oriental Research [ACOR] in Amman, and myself as President of the ASOR,

1.   The letter is online in the ASOR archives (*digilibtest.bu.edu/asor/?p=digitallibrary/
getfile&id=8104*, PDF, pp. 16–20), accessed May 20, 2015.
2.   Name misspelled by the typist.
3.   The Drew-McCormick Archaeological Expedition to Shechem took place 1956-74.
4.   This excavation took place in 1968.

have quietly advised the personnel in the Department of Antiquities, and people higher up in government, that we most emphatically will not support this expedition, but publicly with Jerry we have not yet gone any further than simply to insist that he go along with the regulations for ACOR approval. This means that, according to the department rules, he must write a report of his first expedition before he can be given permission for the latter. Secondly, he must present a plan and a budget and a staff which can meet the approval of other archaeologists who want to maintain standards.

The ASOR is the only organization that has managed, by creating "daughter" institutions in Israel and Jordan, to bridge the Near Eastern "Iron Curtain." The negotiations have been delicate and we cannot allow anything to happen which would jeopardize those relationships.

At the moment, Jerry, instead of going through the proper channels as all other expeditions do—namely, submitting his plans and staff to the ACOR executive committee for approval, so that our Director in Amman would then apply for the permit with the support of ACOR—is sending his plans directly to the Department of Antiquities, trying to get their approval first, knowing we are going to be difficult. This ruse is not going to work.

In the spring before the first expedition went into the field, I had a long talk with Duke McCall about how Louisville could risk its reputation by having such a man represented in the Near East. He replied that as a result of the problems he had a few years earlier with the exodus of faculty members, that when a dean certifies a faculty member for a certain project, he, Duke, simply was not in a position to turn the project down. However, you are not in that position. Remember that the reputation of Southern Baptist Seminary with the work of Joe Callaway is very high. You stand to lose everything with this man Vardaman if he gets into the field. Furthermore, if he is permitted even to go ahead with his plans for this expedition I am going to have to write about him in public through the organs of the ASOR and speak about how this must not be allowed to happen.

Normally, my course has always been to push people ahead and see to it that they obtain objectives. I have raised, through my name as principal investigator, thousands of dollars for Joe Callaway and the Ai Expedition. I introduced Joe to Dunscomb Colt and the Colt Archaeological Publications Series so that Joe is getting his Ai volumes published in a beautiful fashion and at no cost to himself or to the Southern Baptist Seminary. The relationship between Southern Baptist and the American Schools, therefore, has been close and most satisfactory. But I do not propose to allow this man Vardaman to jeopardize our reputation in the Near East with his complete incompetence and irresponsibility. If it were sheer incompetence, we could approve his expedition, provided we put around him competent archaeologists. But that is only one part of his problem. The real problem is his personality. He simply cannot be trusted to do anything right, not even when he is watched every minute. He is as devious and as untrustworthy an ambassador in the Near East as any man could possibly be.

I do hope that this very strong letter will give you some ammunition so that this matter can go to the highest circles in Southern Baptist Seminary. I simply do not want our carefully built up balance in the Near East in any way to be disturbed. I am sure I am not the only one, but that there are many faculty members, including yourself, who can agree with this assessment of Vardaman as a person. If that is so, then he must not be allowed to represent any American interests, and least of all the reputation of Southern Baptist Theological Seminary, by his wild schemes for Near Eastern archaeology. No matter how much money he has, and Duke says that he got that money out from under the noses of the Seminary Planning Committee (which had other plans for this gentleman's funds to help the whole school rather than simply to help a man who can never he helped), this expedition cannot be permitted to go ahead!

Sincerely yours,

G. Ernest Wright

President

Finally, Attiah did not notice it until Vardaman told him to sift through the contents of his wheelbarrow once more. Only then ("as he searched through his wheelbarrow") was the "Nazareth" fragment found.

Thus, we have already two irregularities: multiple failures in the field to notice an artifact of considerable size and weight, combined with Vardaman's fortuitous injunction that Attiah look through his wheelbarrow one more time.

In a properly conducted excavation, of course, had the "Nazareth" fragment been in the earth then it would have been discovered *in the earth*. The fact that the fragment eluded discovery at that early stage *as well as several steps beyond* must raise suspicion that perhaps its first appearance was indeed in the wheelbarrow. In fact, everything in Vardaman's account is extraordinary *until the fragment is discovered in the wheelbarrow*. From that point on, all is normal: the fragment is taken aside, it is washed, it is examined.

The extrordinary circumstances preceding the fragment's discovery justify our consideration that it may have entered the wheelbarrow in an extraordinary way. Given Vardaman's character, as noted above in the letter by ASOR President Wright, the possibility that the "Nazareth" fragment was *planted* in the wheelbarrow cannot be overlooked.

This was August 14, the hottest time of the year when the temperature in Israel can easily exceed 100 degrees. We do not know the time of day when the fragment was discovered, but if it was in the afternoon then the laborers were certainly tired and ready to go home. These circumstances somewhat mitigate their repeated failures to spot the object in the field (a task which was not properly theirs, however—see below).

As director of area D, it would have been a comparatively simple task for Vardaman to find the right moment to surreptitiously place the fragment in a wheelbarrow. One might hypothesize that he had even 'prepared' the fragment beforehand, caking it with mud and perhaps concealing it in a bag until, on some hot afternoon, the opportune moment presented when a wheelbarrow stood unsupervised.

Conflicting claims also exist regarding the basket number. According to Govaars, Vardaman's field note for August 14, 1962 reports that the debris basket in which the fragment was found was "labeled as basket 10" (Govaars 2009:55). But in his 1964 account of the discovery (above p. 344) Vardaman writes that it was "registered with pottery basket D.V.9 (*i.e.*, "the ninth basket from sector D-five"). Furthermore, later in the same paragraph Vardaman writes of "debris which was being emptied" into the wheelbarrow (*i.e.* from the baskets) "by the basket men" and that "the particular fragment mentioned above (no.1) was found by Mr. Attiah *as he searched through his wheelbarrow.*" According to this last account, the baskets had already been emptied before the fragment was found. We thus have multiple contradictions regarding details of the discovery: basket no. 9 *vs.* basket no. 10, and the statement that the fragment was in the wheelbarrow after the baskets had been emptied and thus not in *any* basket.

These contradictions open the possibility that Vardaman may have changed his account regarding the discovery of the "Nazareth" fragment. Indeed, a close reading of the citation above (pp. 344–45) suggests this was indeed the case.

The shoddy field methods employed by Vardaman also merit examination. He writes that several laborers were working with "picks and hoes." That may be acceptable in digging a trench, but it is not a satisfactory way to conduct sensitive excavation work. Since the laborers were all dumping their debris into the *same* wheelbarrow ("the debris which was being emptied there by the basket men"), then the findspots for *all* items were immediately lost upon the emptying of the baskets!

Vardaman writes that the laborers "were becoming careless about spotting some of the objects which were turning up." But it has never been the task of untrained laborers to spot objects of archeological value. That task belongs to the archeologist and his trained assistants.

The foregoing observations reflect on the remarkably poor practices untilized in the 1962 Caesarea excavation.

The fact that the "Nazareth" fragment was not discovered *in situ* but in a wheelbarrow has ramifications beyond possible foul play. It quickly leads to contradictions regarding provenance. Thus Avi-Yonah writes that the fragment came from "sector D. IV" (Avi-Yonah 1962:137). But in his account of the discovery,[47] Vardaman writes that it came from D. V (read: "D-five"). Vardaman's field note for August 14 (which Govaars saw) also maintains that the fragment was found in debris "from the north side of area D. V" (Govaars 2009:55)—that is, from the vicinity of a cistern.[48]

The general impression of the activity in area D on August 14, 1962, is one of a very hot day combined with poor field methods and lax supervision. If the area director himself wished to secretly place a substantial marble artifact—hidden perhaps in a bag or even in his briefcase—into an unguarded wheelbarrow, the circumstances would have been quite favorable to execute such a maneuver.

The foregoing is circumstantial evidence. But we now come to the most astonishing anomaly associated with the discovery of the "Nazareth" fragment, one which is no inference but quite provable: Vardaman was expelled from the excavation *immediately* after the discovery of the "Nazareth" fragment! Though his expulsion is altogether shocking, its timing is most revealing.

We are able to date Vardaman's expulsion to August 14 from the data furnished by Govaars, in conjunction with Wright's 1972 letter regarding Vardaman.

At the end of his third paragraph, Wright recounts: "[Vardaman's] attempt to dig at Caesarea some years ago was quietly stopped *when the word was passed to the appropriate Israeli authorities*." This important information tells us that Vardaman not only left the excavation early, but that he was compelled to do so by the "Israeli authorities."

Govaars reports that Vardaman's last day on the Caesarea excavation was August 14—the *same day* as the discovery of the "Nazareth" fragment. This was one week before the official end of the excavation season.[49]

The simultaneity of the discovery of the "Nazareth" fragment and Vardaman's expulsion is certainly the crowning anomaly among all the ir-

47. Vardaman and Garrett 1964:42.
48. See Fig. 12.7 above. Sectors D. IV and D. V were next to each other but characterized by radically different material. Sector D. IV was the locus of a "Hellenistic structure" which Avi-Yonah hoped was Strato's Tower. Sector D. V, on the other hand, was 5m to the west and characterized by a plastered cistern.
49. Govaars 2009:55 and 247, n. 91. *Cf.* above, footnote no. 36.

regularities we have thus far encountered. It would be ludicrous to deny a connection between the discovery of the "Nazareth" fragment, the *immediate* intervention of the Israeli authorities, and Vardaman's sudden dismissal from the excavation—all on the same day.

This precipitous and remarkable series of events suggests that someone was 'on to' Vardaman and blew the whistle regarding the "Nazareth" fragment. Other explanations are possible but seem less likely (see below). Who the whistleblower might have been is not clear (Wright does not name him). We cannot assume that he went to the excavation director, Avi-Yonah, with the untoward news regarding Vardaman and the fragment's discovery, and that it was Avi-Yonah who then notified the authorities. Indeed, this is unlikely given Avi-Yonah's later championing of the "Nazareth" fragment and his subsequent warm relations with Vardaman. The data suggest, rather, that the informant complained about Vardaman's find without delay and did so either to an official in the Department of Antiquities or directly to the Israeli police.[50]

The whistleblower communicated information sufficiently serious and persuasive that Vardaman's participation in the Caesarea excavation was *immediately* suspended. Whatever Vardaman did that August 14 was sufficiently significant that action could not be delayed.

My point here is that no grey, uncertain, or 'possible' wrongdoing would have resulted in such immediate and draconian consequences. The informant, if there was one (and this is certainly the most likely scenario), must have either caught Vardaman red-handed or must have possessed information of an *unequivocally* incriminating nature. Nothing less would cause the Israeli authorities to disrupt an active excavation. The gravity of the situation is clear when we remind ourselves that Vardaman was no mere laborer who could be dismissed for some minor grievance. He was a senior member of the excavation staff, was largely responsible for subsidizing the 1962 excavation season, and had even brought over from the States a number of co-worker (student) volunteers. For him to have been summarily expelled from the field by the Israeli authorities is most astonishing and indicates that a serious allegation backed by compelling evidence had been levelled against him.

Vardaman's expulsion need not have been in the open. In the Middle East such potentially embarrassing situations are often dealt with behind the scenes. Wright says that Vardaman's digging was "quietly" stopped. A pretext may well have been employed, such as illness or indisposition.

---

50. Vardaman again became embroiled with the police in the late 1960s, in connection with the Machaerus excavation in Jordan. (See Wright's letter, fourth paragraph.)

Nevertheless, what *really* happened at Caesarea that day became known to some outside the excavation, for Wright eventually learned of it and was able to recall it in 1972 to the Dean of SBTS—Vardaman's then current employer. Indeed, as a result of Wright's letter to Dean Hull, Vardaman was sacked.[51]

It is possible, though unlikely, that the informant was someone in the field who actually witnessed the sleight of hand which resulted in the "Nazareth" fragment entering Attiah's wheelbarrow on August 14.[52] More likely, however, is that someone already acquainted with Vardaman's propensity for foul play (perhaps, like Wright, a co-participant in the Shechem excavations of the mid-50s) had some incriminating information on the "Nazareth" fragment that he promptly shared with the authorities. It is also possible that the incriminating information did not derive from the excavation site at all, but leaked out from Jerusalem where the fragment would in all likelihood have been forged. In this case, no informant in Caesarea would be required. The authorities could simply have been waiting to see if Vardaman actually produced the forgery (thus committing a crime). When he did, they pounced.

In any case, the bizzarre events of August 14, 1962 indubitably indicate foul play involving Vardaman and the "Nazareth" fragment. To contest this one would have to offer some other cogent reason why the authorities intervened *precisely on August 14* and compelled Vardaman to quit the excavation a week early. But no other explanation fits all the circumstances: (1) the discovery of the fragment away from its find spot, (2) Vardaman's responsibility in that discovery, (3) the instant intervention of the Israeli authorities, and (4) Vardaman's expulsion that same day.

---

51.   Dean Hull of SBTS replied to ASOR President Wright on Oct. 2, 1972: "This is to inform you that Dr. Vardaman is no longer connected with our institution, having resigned as Associate Professor of Biblical Archaeology effective July 31, 1972... In the light of this separation, our Seminary now has no involvement in any archaeological work which may be undertaken by Dr. Vardaman in the future. Present plans are to assign all archaeological responsibilities to Dr. Joseph A. Callaway... While I did not share your letter with Dr. Vardaman, or divulge to him the specific nature of its contents, I did indicate that you had raised very serious allegations regarding the feasibility of permitting him to undertake further archaeological work in the Middle East..." (ASOR archive)

52.   Besides Vardaman, Avi-Yonah was assisted by A. Negev "as an assistent director" who "did not have a license in his own name for an excavation of his own." There were also four "graduate students" from the Hebrew University of Jerusalem: Eleazar Oren (but see p. 362 below), Rachel Hakhlili, Mira Shpilberg, and A. Ovadiah. It is not known how many students accompanied Vardaman from the Unites States. (Govaars 2009:244, nn. 57 and 58; Avi-Yonah 1962:137, n. 1.).

The forgery of the "Nazareth" fragment

The circumstantial evidence of wrongdoing involving Vardaman and the "Nazareth" fragment, as reviewed above, is powerfully confirmed when we realize that the fragment almost certainly *had* to be forged.

How do we know this? After all, no signs of forgery are immediately detectable when one simply considers the physical properties of the fragment. The marble is well and appropriately chiseled. Nothing pertaining to the stone itself immediately betrays foul play—though it has not been tested for antiquity or chemical composition (and is not likely to be).

But the "Nazareth" fragment was forged for a simple reason: fragments of priestly courses inscriptions were placed only in synagogues. This fact is virtually fatal for the authenticity of *all three* "Caesarea Inscription" fragments,[53] because the exhaustive work of Govaars quite convincingly shows that *no synagogue has ever been found in Field O*. The person who claims that any of the "Caesarea Inscription" fragments is authentic thus has an additional burden, one entirely apart from the question of forgery—namely, to explain how the fragment came to be found in Field O. No convincing explanation for this has ever been proposed. And, indeed, none exists.

This issue is far more damning than may appear at first glance. We will see that the three fragments do not match (pp. 359–60 and Fig. 12:12 below). Thus, if they are authentic, then we are speaking not of one priestly courses inscription, but of *three* different priestly courses inscriptions all in Field O! Such inscriptions are very rare, and one can readily see how the argument for authenticity thus becomes exponentially more difficult. Furthermore, *three different priestly courses inscriptions require three different synagogues!* Govaars (see next section) has been unable to find the remains of even a single synagogue. In all, then, we can appreciate that the argument for authenticity rather quickly moves from the rational into the realm of the absurd.

No synagogue

Without question, Marylinda Govaars is the most informed scholar to have published on the site of the 1962 Caesarea excavations. Her master's thesis (1983) was an extensive treatment of that area.[54] Govaars followed

---

53.   The very uncertainty regarding the Talmon fragment's find spot (it could have come from anywhere) lends it the greatest claim to authenticity among the three fragments. Nevertheless, as a thoroughly unprovenanced artifact sporting a rare inscription, the chances of the Talmon fragment being a forgery are still high.

54.   Govaars, M. "A Reconsideration of the Synagogue Site at Caesarea Maritima, Israel." M.A. Thesis, Drew University. Madison, NJ, 1983 (unpublished).

משמרת ראשונה יהויריב מסרבי מרון
משמרת שניה ידעיה עמוק צפורים
משמרת שלישית חרים מפשטה
משמרת רביעת שערים עיתהלו
משמרת חמשית מלכיה בית לחם
משמרת ששית מימין יודפת
משמרת שביעת הקוץ עילבו
משמרת שמינת אביה כפר עוזיה
משמרת תשיעית ישוע ארבל
משמרת עשירית שכניה חבורת כבול
משמרת אחת עשרה אלישיב כדן קנה
משמרת שתים עשרה יקים פשחור צפת
משמרת שלוש עשרה חופה בית מעון
משמרת ארבע עשרה ישבאב ציפתישיחין
משמרת חמש עשרה בילגה היונית
משמרת שש עשרה אמר כפר פרנברה
משמרת שבע עשרה חזיר ___
משמרת שמונה עשרה הפיצץ עירן
משמרת תשע עשרה פתחיה ___ עב
משמרת עשרים יחזקאל בי ___ וא
משמרת אחת ועשרים יכין כפר יוחנה
משמרת שתים ועשרים גמול בית חוביה
משמרת שלוש ועשרים דליה גנתון צלמין
משמרת ארבע ועשרים מעזיה חמת אריח

Figure 12.8. Avi-Yonah's depiction of the "Caesarea Inscription"
based on Samuel Klein's early 20th century reconstruction of the twenty-four priestly courses and their places of residence. The three fragments allegedly found in Caesarea are positioned relative to the inscription. (Avi-Yonah 1962:138.)

Translation
(*cf.* 1. Chr. 24: 7–18)

The first priestly course, Yehoiarib [called] Messarbey, [at] Meron.
The second priestly course, Yedaiah [and] 'Amok, [at] Tsepphoris.
The third priestly course, Charim, [at] Mafshetah.
The fourth priestly course, Seorim, [at] 'Aithalu.
The fifth priestly course, Malchiah, [at] Beit Lehem.
The sixth priestly course, Meamin, [at] Yodefat.
The seventh priestly course, Hakkuts, [at] 'Ailabu.
The eighth priestly course, Abiah, [at] Kfar 'Uzziah.
The ninth priestly course, Yeshua, [at] Arbel.
The tenth priestly course, Shechaniah [called] Chaburat, [at] Kabul.
The eleventh priestly course, Eliashib, priest[s of] Cana.

Place	Name	Number	"Course"

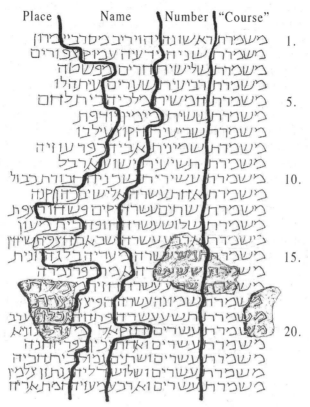

Figure 12.9. Hebrew syntactical divisions of the "Caesarea Inscription."

(cont.)

The twelfth priestly course, Yakim [and] Pashhur, [at] Tsafed.
The thirteenth priestly course, Chuppah, [at] Beit Ma'on.
The fourteenth priestly course, Yeshebeab [called] Chutsefit, [at] Shichin.
The fifteenth priestly course, Me'adiah [called] Bilgah, [at] Yevanit.
The sixteenth priestly course, Immer, [at] Kfar Nimrah.
The seventeenth priestly course, Chezir, [at] Mamliach.
The eighteenth priestly course, Hapitsets, [at] Natsrath.
The nineteenth priestly course, Pethahiah [called] Akhlah, [at] 'Arab.
The twentieth priestly course, Yechezqel, [at] Migdal Nunaiah.
The twenty-first priestly course, Yachin, [at] Kfar Yochannah.
The twenty-second priestly course, Gamul, [at] Beit Chobiah.
The twenty-third priestly course, Delaiah [and] Ginnaton, [at] Tselamin.
The twenty-fourth priestly course, Ma'aziah, [at] Chamat Ariach.

this up almost three decades later with an in-depth monograph, *Field O: The "Synagogue" Site*.[55] We note that the word "Synagogue" is in quotation marks—and for good reason. Arguably the main thesis of her book is that—contrary to almost a century of persistent Israeli claims—no synagogue existed there at all. In the next paragraphs we will consider Govaars' statements in this regard, but it is patent that if no synagogue existed in Field O then no *synagogue* inscription could have existed there either. We can go one step further: if no synagogue existed there in antiquity, then *all* three of the claimed fragments assigned to the alleged "Caesarea Inscription" must be bogus.[56] This is because inscriptions of the twenty four priestly courses were—as far as is known—placed only in synagogues. One could, perhaps, attempt to argue that one of the priestly courses fragments found its way to Field O through reuse in antiquity—a very slim possibility. But it would be ridiculous to argue that *all three* fragments of the "Caesarea Inscription" did so! In any case, other problems to be considered (such as the incompatibility of the fragments) nullify such strained rationalizations.

Avi-Yonah claimed that structural remains in area A (which he sometimes termed elements of a "broadhouse") belonged to a synagogue dating to "Stratum IV"—that is, to later Roman times. But Govaars ascerbically notes that "The Stratum IV structure is never described in the written reports in the same way twice" (Govaars 2009:77). Avi-Yonah's confusion regarding the structure is exemplified in the multiple conflicting elements found in the following passage:

> Also noted for the Stratum IV structure are "small square foundations (of shops?)," but one report places them on the southern side of the structure, while another report has them on the east side (Avi-Yonah 1963a:147; Avi-Yonah and Negev 1975:278). Attempts to locate these constructions were blocked by the lack of more detailed information. Additionally, the numerous architectural fragments attributed to this stratum in the early reports are subsequently placed in the later Stratum V in later reports (Avi-Yonah 1956, 1963a:147, Avi-Yonah and Negev 1975:279; Appendix H). These architectural fragments include marble columns, marble capitals, smaller columns, a slab with carved menorah, fragments of a chancel screen, marble inlays, and fragments of a decorated roof.

---

55. Govaars, M., M. Spiro, and L. White. *Field O: The "Synagogue" Site*. Vol. IX of *The Joint Expedition to Caesarea Maritima: Excavation Reports*. Boston: ASOR, 2009. Govaars is the principal author, with one chapter each contributed by Spiro (pavements) and White (inscriptions).

56. The question as to whether *authentic* priestly courses fragments (which are very rare, in any case) could have found their way to the Caesarea site—though no synagogue is in the vicinity—appears to be a very strained (perhaps absurd) argument. Nevertheless we will briefly consider it below.

The reason for this re-assignment is unclear. This is true, as well, for the re-assignment of the water channels and pottery pipes from Stratum IV to Stratum V. Also, the location of water channels with pottery pipes changes from being on the east and west sides of the broadhouse structure in Stratum IV to being on the east and west sides of the north-south structure in Stratum V (Yonah 1956:261, Avi-Yonah and Negev 1975:278). This is quite a significant change and accentuates the deep conflict over the strata identification and artifact assignments.

(Govaars 2009:42)

Furthermore, Avi-Yonah wrote that "fragments of... the inscription with the 'priestly courses' seem to belong to this building"[57]—though the "Nazareth" fragment was found 90m distant (area D; *cf.* Fig. 12.2), the "*mem*" fragment 120m distant (area F), and no find spot is known for the Talmon fragment at all.[58]

It is clear from the above that Avi-Yonah assimilated a good deal of material to his "synagogue" structure while, at the same time, having a very poor understanding of that structure. Govaars sums up the situation on the very first page of her 2009 book: "If one looks to consult written sources for references to locate an archaeologically recoverable Jewish structure, specifically a synagogue structure, it is a fruitless endeavor."

Elsewhere Govaars questions whether any "discernible structure" is even attested:

> Avi-Yonah places the fourth-century synagogue in this stratum [Stratum IV], but the mosaic pavement fragments do not help with determining an entrance, locations for niches, bema, seating, or orientation toward Jerusalem [all typical of a synagogue]... The lack of stratigraphy, associated artifacts, and architectural features hinders us. We are left with no real discernible structure. (Govaars 2009:109; brackets added.)

Even if a few artifacts were in some sort of building, Govaars argues, they "could be from structures other than a synagogue. We are left lacking, wanting, and wondering what to make of the remaining evidence for this to be a synagogue site" (Govaars 2009:115).

Avi-Yonah changed his mind regarding the outlines of the structure several times, while always maintaining that it was indeed a synagogue of the "broadhouse" type. In 1956 the building had internal walls with "one or two aisles" and dated to the fourth century. Two years later, Govaars writes, "with no additional excavation work," the building was of the "Hel-

---

57. Avi-Yonah 1963a:147.
58. Thus Govaars writes: "In at least two of these new areas, area D and area E or F, material was found that Avi-Yonah associated to area A" (Govaars 2009:41). For the Talmon fragment, see above pp. 327 *f.*

lenized type" but instead of walls had "columns" and pavement inscribed in Greek. Then in 1960 Avi-Yonah described "several lines of walls" and "the remains of two superimposed structures, one of the fifth and the other of the sixth to seventh centuries."[59]

On pages 135–36 of her book Govaars is particularly critical of Avi-Yonah's work and conclusions. We cite a few phrases and sentences (with emphases added): the evidence "*contradicts* Avi-Yonah's proposed north-south-axis building for Stratum V, which he interpreted as an apsidal synagogue with entrance on the north..." Govaars notes that Marie Spiro reconstructed all the mosaic fragments, "further *refuting* Avi-Yonah's contention of a narrow entry hall... Avi-Yonah's proposal falls short. He never presents his archaeological evidence for a hallway... no archaeological evidence for an apse on the south side of the site... *disquieting*... [A photograph] *contradicts* Avi-Yonah's assertion... he should have been aware... also he failed to discuss... Equally *inexplicable*..."

Govaars notes that Avi-Yonah's 1962 (*i.e.* final) outline of the broadhouse/synagogue structure patently does not match the onsite material evidence:

> Figure 123 shows the 1:50 scale plan for sketch outline "III, 500 A.C./400 A.C."[60] If we accept that this outline III is the interpretation of Avi-Yonah's Stratum IV (the blue-colored level, fig. 117), said to contain an 18 x 9 m broadhouse, then there are problems matching the sketch to the plan. First, the sketched structure outline does not measure 18 m (east-west) x 9 m (north-south). The strongest defined outline... does not fit with the excavated remains. The largest sketched structure... is less than precise because certain measurements are missing on the original sketch... [T]he structure outline sketch does not match with the on-the-ground evidence. There are not enough east-west walls. Also, the locations of the columns are questionable... (Govaars 2009:119)

In proposing a broadhouse synagogue, Avi-Yonah simply disregarded evidence clearly available to him from his own previous work at the site:

> Additionally, the sketch disregards Dunayevsky wall 103/JECM Wall 1057, as well as the various wall fragments used previously to tentatively indicate a hallway or entry vestibule in the center of the building outline. There is no evidence on the ground for a north entrance or for the entire north end of the structure as sketched. (Govaars 2009:121)

Reflecting her frustration over the myriad confusing aspects of the 1962 excavations, Govaars politely concludes: "Unfortunately, this site and the documented circumstances do not permit a clear identification of the

---

59. Govaars 2009:36–37.
60. I.e., fourth–fifth centuries CE.

remains. We have questions/concerns about the evidence. We have uneasiness about some of the data." She finally observes simply: "The more is learned from the research, the more questions are raised as to Avi-Yonah's conclusions."[61]

It is clear from the foregoing that no basis at all exists for postulating the onetime existence of a synagogue in area A. Govaars has shown that the evidence is not merely weak in this regard. *It is totally absent.*

Of course, the lack of a synagogue in the area immediately places the three 'recovered' fragments of the "Caesarea Inscription" under enormous suspicion, for that inscription is plainly synagogal in nature. Simply put, the lack of evidence for a synagogue strongly suggests that foul play was involved with *all three* of the fragments.

No "Caesarea Inscription"

Given the foregoing, the concept of a "Caesarea Inscription" is extraordinarily tenuous, if not impossible to uphold. For how can such an inscription have ever existed if it is made up of three fragments which themselves were introduced into Field O through foul play? After all, we now have convincing evidence that none of the three fragments originated in Field O, since no synagogue has been found there.

Of course, we already knew that the provenance of the three fragments was questionable. The Talmon fragment has no known find spot. The find spot of the "*mem*" fragment has never been divulged more precisely than simply "area F"—and this on the basis of a single short statement in Avi-Yonah's 1962 report. No date has even been given for that fragment's discovery, nor even who found it. By inference we have assumed that the discoverer was E. Oren—but that remains only an assumption.

As for the "Nazareth" fragment, we know that it was discovered by Vardaman in a wheelbarrow on August 14, 1962, immediately before the Israeli authorities removed him from the excavation.

The lack of any synagogue in Field O reveals that all three fragments came from *outside* the area. They cannot be the remains of any onsite structure that suffered the natural ravages of time. All three fragments were secondarily *placed* in Field O. Furthermore, we now know that those placements were effected *at different times* and *in non-contiguous areas*. With these facts, the concept that a single marble plaque ever contained all three fragments dissolves. Even as there never was a synagogue in the vicinity, so also there never was a "Caesarea Inscription."

A second strong argument against the existence of the "Caesarea Inscription" is evident by merely glancing at Fig. 12.12. There we see quite

---

61. Govaars 2009:142, 121.

plainly that the "Nazareth" fragment does not match the other two. *Its letters are much larger, while it's line spacing is much smaller.*

One would think this obvious observation would have immediately given pause to those who considered these fragments parts of the same physical artifact. But it did not. For half a century scholars have blithely assumed that the fragments belong together, when they obviously do not. That assumption—and the enduring presence of the "Caesarea Inscription" in mainline scholarship—constitute powerful testimony to the fabled ability of biblical scholars to see what they only wish to see.

The last week

The "mem" fragment

The lack of a synagogue in Field O—and hence the virtual certainty that the "Nazareth" fragment was forged—sheds new light on the appearance of the Israeli authorities towards the end of the Caesarea excavation season, on August 14, 1962. A ready explanation is now available for the removal of Vardaman: forgery. This is the only accusation which both fits the timing of Vardaman's arrest[62] and is of sufficient gravity that the authorities intervened in the field.[63] The accusation must have related to the Vardaman's stunning discovery made that very day—the appearance of the "Nazareth" fragment.

One week remained in the season. During that week, Vardaman's whereabouts are unknown. But strange events did not cease at the excavation site. A third[64] fragment of the priestly courses inscription—rather suspiciously chiseled—appeared within days of Vardaman's expulsion.[65] This is the "*mem*" fragment we have been discussing. Avi-Yonah writes:

---

62. "Arrest" may be the best term for what transpired, since Vardaman's activities were arrested by the authorities, though he was neither formally charged nor detained.
63. In fact, it would not be the last time suspicion befell Vardaman. See n. 50 above.
64. The numbering includes the "Talmon" fragment published in 1958, also linked to Caesarea and ultimately also part of the "Caesarea Inscription" along with the two fragments of the priestly courses inscription discovered in the 1962 excavation.
65. The appearance of the "*mem*" fragment after Vardaman's departure matches Oren's late presence in area F and is inferred by Govaars: "In Vardaman's notebook there is no mention of the finding of the second fragment [of the 1962 season, *i.e.* the "*mem*" fragment] of the Twenty-Four Priestly Courses or of the floor where it was reportedly found embedded. Vardaman left the excavation with about a week remaining in the season, so apparently the fragment was found after his departure" (Govaars 2009:55).

Fragment B.[66] Greyish marble, 145 by 140 mm., 24 mm. thick. Three beginnings of lines at the left, each 20 mm. high; margin 120 mm. wide to the right (Pl. 13B). The three lines begin with the same letters: ‏. . מש‎ ‏/. . מש‎ ‏/. . מ‎

Fragment B was found in area F,[3] 70 m. south of area D. It was found reused in the marble pavement of a Late Byzantine room; among the other paving stones was part of a synagogue chancel screen, showing an *ethrog* and a *lulab.*   (Avi-Yonah 1962:137.)

Avi-Yonah's footnote [3] reads: "Mr. E. Oren was in charge of area F." There is some confusion regarding the find spot of this fragment. Though Avi-Yonah notes "area F" (above), in his *IEJ* excavation report of a year later the archeologist writes that it was found in "area E":

> Area E—a Late Byzantine house paved with reused marble slabs; part of the Hebrew inscription already published[6] was found there.
>
> (Avi-Yonah 1963a:146)

Astonishingly, the location of "area E" is unknown. Govaars diplomatically observes:

> There is a slight discrepancy with the identification of the location where the second fragment was found. The excavation report, Avi-Yonah *IEJ* 13, p. 146–48, relates that it was in area E, while the other two articles, Avi-Yonah *IEJ* 12, pp. 137–39 and Idem, Teacher's Yoke, pp. 46–57, relate area F. Only 5 excavation areas are known from the 1962 work (A–E). If a consecutive numbering system was used in the 1962 excavations, then it may be argued that the location should be area E.
>
> (Govaars 1983:68, n. 22.)

One notes that the way Avi-Yonah describes "area F" is, however, similar to his description of "area E." This is clear when we place two passages side-by-side:

About 70 m. southwards of D, in Area F, the second fragment was found; it was reused in the pavement of a Byzantine room; the other marble pieces used in this pavement included also the fragment of a synagogue chancel screen, showing an *ethrog* and a *lulab.* (Avi-Yonah 1964:46; *cf.* Avi-Yonah 1962:137, cited on previous page.)	Area E—a Late Byzantine house paved with reused marble slabs; part of the Hebrew inscription already published[6] was found there. (Avi-Yonah 1963a:146)

The "Hebrew inscription already published" in area E (Avi-Yonah's note "6" above, right) can only be the "*mem*" fragment—not the "Naza-

---

66. That is, the second priestly courses ("*mem*") fragment found in the 1962 season.

reth" fragment—because later in the same article the archeologist refers to the "Nazareth" fragment in area D.[67] The fact that the location of area E is ambiguous strangely corresponds to the ambiguity regarding the provenance of the *"mem"* fragment (whose find spot is documented alternately as area F and area E). Avi-Yonah's contradictory reports regarding the find spot of the *"mem"* fragment suggest that he himself was not certain from whence the fragment came. It is almost as if area E is a nebulous, convenient—even invented?—locus for 'evidence' whose provenance is *unknown*.

Oren supervised area F and was credited later by Vardaman for the discovery of the *"mem"* fragment:

> It must be realized that Professor Avi Yonah has done a brilliant job of epigraphical interpretation, having as he did so few clues as to the nature of the documents which Eleazar Oren and I found and reconstructing the whole so masterfully.
> (Vardaman and Garrett 1964:42; *cf.* above p. 345.)

The "documents which Eleazar Oren and I found" refer to the "Nazareth" fragment (Vardaman) and the *"mem"* fragment (Oren).

Though Avi-Yonah (and after him Govaars) refer to Oren as a "graduate student" (see n. 52 above), in 1962 he was only about twenty years old and still in college. Oren graduated a year later (Archaeology and Ancient History, Hebrew University, 1963), went on to study at the University of Pennsylvania, and received his Ph.D in Archaeology (University of London, 1969) under Dame Kathleen Kenyon. Dr. Oren retired from Ben Gurion University (Beer-Sheva) in 2013 after a distinguished career.[68]

Oren seems to have worked fairly closely with Vardaman in Caesarea. Both left area A together to work in area D early in the season (above p. 338). It was in area D, we recall, that the "Nazareth" fragment was discovered in Attiah's wheelbarrow. Thus, Oren was apparently witness to the discovery of both the "Nazareth" and the *"mem"* fragments of the priestly courses inscription.

The role of Oren is not clear, and we cannot speculate regarding how much he did or did not know—with regards to any of the three fragments of the "Caesarea Inscription." He was too young at the time to have had

---

67. Avi-Yonah never confuses area D with another area. In that trench he ventured to locate Strato's Tower and writes: "In area D a trench 50 m. long and 10 m broad was made... The main fragment of the synagogue inscription was found in this area" (Avi-Yonah 1963a:148–49). The "main fragment" is of course the "Nazareth" fragment which has many more letters than the *"mem"* fragment. The trench was only about 25 m. long and 5 m. wide (see Fig. 12.7)—one more indication of Avi-Yonah's general lack of attention to detail.

68. See *http://in.bgu.ac.il/Pages/events/Eliezer-Oren.aspx* (accessed May 21, 2015).

Figure 12.10. The "*mem*" fragment of the Caesarea Inscription as found in the last week of the 1962 excavation season.

(Ameling Fig. 1145.2c. Labeling added.)

Figure 12.11. The possibly authentic state of the "*mem*" fragment

(Photoshop retouching of Ameling Fig. 1145.2 c.)

any leading role in the events that took place. On the other hand, his youth and ambition to please might have made him the ideal collaborator.

Over the years, Govaars, Tuccinardi, and myself have attempted to contact Dr. Oren. But our overtures received no satisfactory response (*cf.* note 31 above). Govaars writes: "Both email and regular posted letters to Dr. E. Oren were unsuccessful" (personal correspondence).

A glance at the "*mem*" fragment (Fig. 12.10) shows that the bottom two lines of text are very different from the top line, whose only preserved letter is a well-chiseled *mem*. The bottom two lines each contain a *mem* and the beginning of a *shin*. These are very poorly executed, certainly using inappropriate tools (perhaps nothing more than a pointed tool and hammer) and probably also inferior techniques. These characteristics may betray a hasty execution. The bottom *mem* is particularly revealing. Its short upper stroke is too big and extends almost to the neighboring *shin*, as if the worker used too much force and gouged the stone at this point. The fragment, then, reveals two very different hands in the composition of only a few Hebrew letters.

Most of the fragment is empty. The position of the top *mem* shows that it has a wide border to the right. Fig. 12.11 reveals that when the poorly-chiseled letters are removed, the borders to the right and bottom roughly correspond, and the well-chiseled *mem* emerges as the bottom right letter of an original inscription of indeterminate size.

Barely visible between the top two rows of letters in Fig. 12.10 is a straight horizontal line, probably not natural but man-made. Its significance (if any) is unclear, but it may have served as an aid to the original stone carver in aligning the letters. Or perhaps it marked the lower border of the original inscription.

Calcified deposits are visible to the upper right. Slightly darker bands in the lower part of Fig. 12.10 are either physical properties of the stone, the result of incomplete burnishing (perhaps from aggressive cleaning of the fragment), or discoloration due to lengthy burial in the ground.

How are we to interpret this curious fragment, one which exhibits two very different hands in the chiseling, which is accompanied by scant documentation, and which is of uncertain provenance (area E or F)?[69]

It is tempting to suggest that the bottom two lines were added in haste. It is simply not possible to credit the bottom two lines to an expert chiseler,

---

69. Avi-Yonah claimed that the "*mem*" fragment was found reused "in the marble pavement of a Late Byzantine room" (Avi-Yonah 1962:137, cited p 361 above). This is hardly convincing. Presumably, the inscribed face of the plaque was face down so that the Jewish frequenters of the room were not knowingly walking on the *mem*'s and *shin*'s of a one-time religious artifact.

Figure 12.12. The three fragments of the alleged "Caesarea Inscription." (No scale is available for the Talmon fragment.)

and thus it is most unlikely that an ancient stonecutter would have considered the fragment as found (Fig. 12.10) to be part of a finished piece.

The possibility must be considered that the "*mem*" fragment was hastily completed just before its discovery, that is, in the last few days of the excavation season.

If this were the case, then it could have served an important function to Vardaman. The discovery of yet another fragment of the *very same* inscription would support the authenticity of the "Nazareth" fragment. After all, now two fragments would have to be denied—indeed, *three* when we include the Talmon fragment from 1956/58. The quick succession of these linked discoveries in the final week of the season must have taken Avi-Yonah by surprise, and we can almost visibly see him caving into the inevitable: proof of a synagogue via a new priestly courses inscription, one composed of three fragments. Of course, what Avi-Yonah was really caving into was the cumulative force of Vardaman's machinations.

Convenient though this outcome may have been to Avi-Yonah and to the Fund for the Exploration of Ancient Synagogues, problems immediately arise. First of all, it is fairly obvious that the fragments do not go together (Fig. 12.12). Until now, apparently no one has bothered to look closely. The line spacing of the "*mem*" fragment is narrower than that of the "Nazareth" fragment.[70] Also, the size of the letters clearly do not match.

Then, too, we have noted that the "*mem*" fragment is not a finished piece. At the very least, it would have to be considered a 'work in progress'—very *unlike* the other two fragments. Again, until now apparently no one has recognized this.

Problems of provenance also interpose—none of the three fragments was found *in situ*, they were found at least fifty meters apart, and no synagogue has been verified in the vicinity.

All these anomalies seem to have been assiduously ignored by Avi-Yonah and the tradition.

On the other hand, we can propose a very different explanation of events. Vardaman possessed a marble fragment—or knew the location of one—that merely had an inscribed Hebrew letter *mem* at the upper left (Fig. 12.11). We can infer the fragment's original state from the fact that the top *mem* is professionally chiseled in the ancient style and also corresponds to the *mem* visible at the upper right of the "Nazareth" fragment (Figs. 12.6, 12.12).

---

70. The *lamed*'s in the "Nazareth" fragment are excluded from consideration in this regard, as they were conventionally written above the level of the other letters.

Vardaman then hastily executed the bottom two lines of the *"mem"* fragment during the final days of the Caesarea excavation season. He probably did this himself for—now suddenly under suspicion by the Israeli authorities—it would have been dangerous for him to go near forgers.

Vardaman was certainly very familiar with Klein's reconstruction of the priestly courses inscription. He knew that each line begins with *mem* (Fig. 12.4). He 'completed' this last fragment by quickly adding two lines of lettering in the large empty space below the top *mem*. This would simulate the beginning of three lines of the priestly courses inscription. It would only entail the addition of two or three characters for the fragment was chipped away at the left, which allowed for only one or two characters per line.[71] The entire project would not take much time—and Vardaman did not *have* much time.

The state of the *"mem"* inscription shows that time indeed appears to have run out on whomever was doing the work. If it was Vardaman, then he settled for a frankly unsatisfactory inscription which would not suffer scrutiny. Only Vardaman would perhaps have been able to get away with such a ploy, for he combined in his person an intimate knowledge of the Jewish quest for a synagogue, a vibrant desire to produce the "Caesarea Inscription" (with its history-changing "Nazareth" fragment), professional standing on the excavation staff, considerable clout as regards the excavation funding and, last but not least, enormous capacities for mischief.

Vardaman's production of the *"mem"* fragment in the last week of the Caesarea excavation appears to have been an act of desperation. But it was successful and may have saved the day for Vardaman. We do not hear again of the Israeli authorities in connection with the 1962 Caesarea excavation season. Furthermore, the authenticity of the *"mem"* fragment has never been questioned. Nor has that of the "Nazareth" fragment before it, nor of the Talmon fragment even earlier. These fragments have all received a free pass from the scholarly community. Despite their aforementioned problems both individually and collectively, the three fragments are now part of the celebrated "Caesarea Inscription."

The reason is clear. The area where Vardaman and Avi-Yonah worked had been dubbed the "synagogue" site for decades, yet no compelling evidence of a synagogue had been forthcoming. Such evidence was sorely needed if the august tradition of finding Jewish presence in the entire central coast region was to be vindicated. The "Caesarea Inscription" convincingly provides that evidence.

---

71. It is also possible that Vardaman chipped away some of the left side of the fragment in order to minimize the available surface for work.

Reappearance of the "chancel screen"

Together with the "*mem*" fragment, Avi-Yonah reports the discovery in area F of a "chancel screen" fragment which bears striking similarities to the one earlier found in area A by Vardaman—but apparently never reported.[72]

We have noted that the artifact may not have been part of a chancel screen at all, for such screens came into use only in Byzantine times (above, p. 341). The *lulab* of the area A artifact is actually a guilloche. Apparently, the guilloche became a *lulab* and the fragment became part of a chancel screen of uncertain and 'migrating' provenance.

It is clear that during and after the 1962 excavation season evidence of a potentially synagogal nature also migrated to area A, where Avi-Yonah sought to locate a synagogue. The "Nazareth" fragment was found in area D, and the "*mem*" fragment in area F (over 100 meters away)—yet Avi-Yonah would later write that both these artifacts were found "in the synagogue," clearly meaning area A. One scholar strenuously objects:

> *Three fragments of a large Hebrew inscription in grey marble.* In his later discussions of the synagogue, Avi-Yonah mentions the "Priestly Courses Inscription" (or *Mishmarot*) as if it clearly belonged to the same site [*i.e.* area A. Avi-Yonah writes that] "Mosaic floors were discovered in the synagogue, as were fragments of a Hebrew inscription giving the order of the 'priestly courses' and their places, as detailed in late liturgical hymns."[73]
>
> Presumably, as a result of this comment, it has regularly been assumed[74] that the inscription was actually found in the "synagogue site," but such is not the case. The first fragment of the inscription was found during the 1962 season of excavations but not in Avi-Yonah's area A (= JECM Field O). Rather, it was found some 70 meters to the east in his area D IV... The second fragment was found in the same year in Avi-Yonah's area F, some 70 meters farther to the south of area D. A third fragment [the "Talmon" fragment] was found "loose on the surface" some years earlier. Its precise find spot is not known.
>
> ...Other examples of this type of [priestly courses] inscription... date typically from the fourth to the seventh century AD. It is not possible to be certain that this one was in any way physically associated with the "synagogue site" of Field O [*i.e.* in area A] at any point in its history, since no fragments were found there. The same must be said of the supposed "chancel screen"...
>
> (L. Michael White in Govaars 2009:174.)

---

72. Above pp. 339 *f* and Fig. 12.5; citations p. 361.
73. Avi-Yonah 1993:279; Avi-Yonah and Negev 1975:278.
74. *E.g.*, Levine 1996:392, 399.

We note that the "chancel screen" fragment was first claimed in area A but was henceforth claimed in area F. We cannot suppose that Vardaman simply failed to tell Avi-Yonah about the area A "chancel screen" fragment during the first week of the excavation season—for such evidence is precisely what the latter wished to find.[75] Once we acknowledge, then, that Avi-Yonah must have known of the area A fragment early on in the excavation season, then he must be seen as an accomplice to its changed find spot, for it is Avi-Yonah who later reports its discovery in area F and who says nothing more about such a fragment from area A.

A detail now assumes some significance. Even though the "chancel screen" fragment is only a minor artifact in the panoply of evidence from the 1962 Caesarea excavation, its migration *in the opposite direction* (away from the 'synagogue') shows that powerful dynamics were operating in the field, dynamics strong enough to trump Avi-Yonah's basic premise for the whole excavation—that a synagogue was in area A.

Why Avi-Yonah engaged in such counter-intuitive behavior may have something to do with developments in the final week of the season, most particularly Oren's discovery of the "*mem*" fragment in area F. It was after the discovery of this last priestly courses fragment that Avi-Yonah seems to have quietly reassigned the "chancel screen" fragment from area A to area F. An obvious motive for this action now emerges: the reassignment of the "chancel screen" find spot lends support to the discovery of the "*mem*" fragment. Thus Avi-Yonah clearly emerges as an accomplice to multiple anomalies which ultimately trace back to Vardaman.

Avi-Yonah certainly had a good idea of what was going on around him. He was no simpleton and must have perceived Vardaman's motives at quite an early time. He no doubt had some awareness of the latter's propensity for mischief—but also of the American's ability to get things done (witness Vardaman's largely securing the excavation funding and personnel). But Avi-Yonah had his own ambitions and, in the 1962 Caesarea season, those ambitions dovetailed nicely with Vardaman's interests. Both Avi-Yonah and Vardaman would—scarcely a year later—sit together at a banquet in the Jerusalem King David Hotel when honors were bestowed upon "those who had recently made outstanding discoveries in Israel." On that occasion Avi-Yonah privately confided to Vardaman that "our joint discovery of this [priestly courses] inscription resulted in [my] recent promotion from associate professor to full professor at the Hebrew University."[76]

---

75. Given the numerous irregularities attending the 1962 excavation season, the area A "chancel screen" fragment could also have been a 'plant.' Nevertheless, Vardaman would certainly have apprized Avi-Yonah of the fragment's existence.

76. Vardaman 1998:15.

The choice

In the final days of the 1962 excavation season Avi-Yonah must have been faced with a stark choice. When the Israeli authorities surprisingly showed up on August 14 and removed Vardaman, Avi-Yonah could have turned against his co-worker and villified him in no uncertain terms: "This Vardaman is no more than a mischief-maker," he could have said. "He has insinuated evidence of a synagogal and of a Christian nature into this excavation. He is completely unworthy of confidence. In fact, the man probably should never wield the archeologist's spade again!"

Of course, Avi-Yonah uttered nothing of the sort. If he had, he would have had to to admit that the entire excavation had been ill-conceived and ill-conducted. He would have had to abandon the thesis that a synagogue once stood on the site, and would have had to tell his financial backers at the Fund for the Exploration of Ancient Synagogues that their money had been wasted. As a result, Avi-Yonah would surely forego any chance for promotion the following year. By turning on a colleague, the American archeologist might go to jail and there surely would be undesirable publicity in the newspapers. Finally, Avi-Yonah was an accomplice himself—arguably a tacit one—to Vardaman's disreputable activities in the field. It is thus altogether likely that Vardaman had some 'dirt' on Avi-Yonah and that the excavation director would have to face some questions.

Obviously, nothing positive is to be derived from the above litany of woes, which produces only a personal and professional nightmare for Avi-Yonah. On the other hand, though mutual recrimination was in no one's interest, the alternative was very promising. If Vardaman—and, by extension, Avi-Yonah—produced incontrovertible evidence of a synagogue in Caesarea, then the season would not only be a public success but fifty years of searching would be vindicated.

So, Avi-Yonah made the choice: he defended his colleague Jerry Vardaman. In so doing, he also defended his professional integrity and promoted his career. He apparently turned a blind eye where necessary and 'reassigned' evidence when opportune.

By maintaining a low profile, Avi-Yonah had everything to gain and little to lose. After all, he did not personally discover any priestly courses fragments. Vardaman discovered the "Nazareth" fragment and Oren the "*mem*" fragment. Thus by going along with his staff Avi-Yonah did not take any 'heat' but was conveying what others reported from the field.

It appears that Avi-Yonah rather masterfully provided himself with considerable distance from the controversial finds in his excavation. But he is clearly complicit in those anomalous finds by not questioning them and, most significantly, by providing minimal subsequent documentation for the excavation. That lack of documentation is largely responsible for the 'fast track' acceptance among scholars of the "Caesarea Inscription."

In the event, Avi-Yonah chose the only course that would make his Israeli backers happy. Indeed, the entire Jewish (and Christian) archeological establishment was pleased with both him and Vardaman.

In a sense, the die was cast even before the first day of the 1962 excavation season. From what we know of the archeologist's character, Vardaman's strong hand in the choice of personnel and in the excavation funding virtually guaranteed a skewed outcome. The surprising denoument, however, only arrived in the final week, with the appearance of two priestly courses fragments—and of the Israeli authorities.

We can now appreciate that one false turn led to another. The planting of the forged "Nazareth" fragment—the point of the excavation season, as far as Vardaman was concerned—led to the precipitous production and planting of the forged "*mem*" fragment. That in turn led to the reassignment of the "chancel screen" fragment. In this way, the entire 1962 excavation season imploded into a morass of falsehoods, abetted by competing interests, twisted hopes, and eventually high honor.

Conclusion

The 1962 Caesarea excavation's many disparate and confusing elements resulted from a combination of two powerful needs, each a reflection of deep societal desires. On the one hand was Avi-Yonah's pressing need to find a "synagogue." This led to shoddy working methods in the field, poor documentation, contradictory assertions, the ability to look the other way, and even the reassignment of artifacts.

On the other hand was Vardaman's need to rewrite Christian history. This would not be his last attempt in that overarching endeavor, one ultimately in defense of traditional Christianity.

Vardaman's great find of the excavation was the "Nazareth" fragment of the priestly courses inscription. We now conclude that no synagogue has ever been in the area, that the fragment is a forgery, and that Vardaman planted it in Attiah's wheelbarrow on August 14, 1962. We also note that it does not match the unprovenanced "*mem*" and Talmon fragments and, hence, that the "Caesarea Inscription" is bogus. Finally, we conclude that Vardaman himself in all likelihood forged the "*mem*" fragment in the last days of the excavation season.

Naysayers may object that a synagogue in the vicinity has not been found—*yet may be found in future*—and hence that the concept of a "Caesarea Inscription" remains valid. However, the problems reviewed in the foregoing pages are multi-faceted and will not be resolved by any such desperate argument from silence. We have three marble fragments *each* of which is problematic and for *differing* reasons. The fact that the fragments do not go together also presents an insurmountable problem for those who would include them in the same inscription. Finally, we have the astonishing fact that Vardaman was expelled from the excavation on the same day that the "Nazareth" fragment was discovered. All this is in addition to the fact that no synagogue has yet been found in the vicinity of the excavation.

The preceding are the main points of the argument made in this chapter. To them can be added Avi-Yonah's motive (to find a synagogue), Vardaman's (highly compromised) character, and anomalies such as the 'migration' of the "chancel screen" fragment and the contradiction between areas E and F. In sum, there are many smoking guns.

For obvious reasons, the focus of Christians is on the "Nazareth" fragment. The Talmon and *"mem"* fragments are of minor interest. The narrow objection might then be raised that nothing in the foregoing pages has actually shown the "Nazareth" fragment to be a forgery. After all, it is apparently well fashioned and could, for all intents and purposes, be the *only* extant fragment of an authentic priestly courses inscription, one whose provenance is as yet unknown. This minimalist view successfully jettisons large elements of the preceding arguments—including (1) the imperative to associate the "Nazareth" fragment with the other fragments, and (2) any (inconvenient) doubts regarding provenance.

Such a narrow construction, however, appears to be special pleading. It argues that an authentic synagogue fragment has been discovered while ignoring that no synagogue has itself been found—this despite many years of digging and the most careful review of the evidence by Govaars. It also ignores the fact of Vardaman's expulsion from the excavation on the same day that the "Nazareth" fragment was discovered. Finally, it ignores the discoverer's penchant for mischief, as expressed in ASOR President Wright's epistolary diatribe against Vardaman. Ultimately, even the most jaded Christian apologetic must admit that resting his case on a man of Vardaman's character and notoriety is like building a house on quicksand.

Rebuttals to such narrow, opportunistic rationalizations are also at hand. If the "Nazareth" and/or *"mem"* fragments were authentic, it is inexplicable that no *additional* fragments of the priestly courses inscription were found along with those finds. After all, we are supposedly dealing with a very long inscription, one of twenty-four lines. If the workmen were using picks and hoes, then one would expect other fragments of the inscription to have been broken off and found in the immediate contexts. None were.

Continuing in the same vein, it is not possible to contend that other fragments were not found because the excavation of areas D and F immediately ceased upon discovery of the priestly courses fragments. This is certainly not the case in area D for, according to Govaars, a plastered cistern was subsequently excavated underneath the locus where the "Nazareth" fragment was found (Govaars 2009:55). This detail, too, presents an additional problem for the traditional view, for *cisterns are not found in a synagogue.* What, then, was the "Nazareth" fragment doing there? More specifically, how did the fragment of a priestly courses inscription come to be above a cistern? But these are simply *more* find spot difficulties confronting the defenders of authenticity.[77]

Finally, we note a monumental coincidence that cannot have escaped the reader: the very fragment that Vardaman found on August 14 has the word "Nazareth" inscribed on it! For any archeologist to discover such a fragment is extraordinary (no other such fragment has *ever* been found). That a Southern Baptist with Vardaman's suspect character and reputation innocently stumbled upon such a potent witness to the Christian faith strains credulity. That Vardaman initiated the find (urging Attiah to check the debris one more time) further stretches that credulity to the limit. Finally, Vardaman himself moved mountains to make the 1962 Caesarea excavation season possible (above pp. 334 *f*). This must make one wonder whether some of the things that occurred he may have *intended* to occur.

Monumental coincidence also attaches to the writing of the "Nazareth" fragment itself. After all, the complete inscription (as reconstructed by S. Klein and Avi-Yonah) contains well over one hundred words and twenty-four place names, one toponym to each line. "Nazareth" is the only place of residence found complete (or virtually complete) on any of the three fragments.[78] The odds against this are twenty-four to one. Obviously, when Vardaman voluntarily urged Attiah to look through his wheelbarrow yet again, the archeologist was more than a little lucky!

According to the Occam's razor, the solution with the least number of assumptions is that Vardaman simply placed a forged "Nazareth" fragment in the wheelbarrow that August day. This view results from an intersection of the various extraordinary circumstances we have noted: the lack of a synagogue in the vicinity, Vardaman's penchant for foul play, the timing of

---

77. For any who might maintain that the "Nazareth" fragment is authentic, it would (of course) be ludicrous to suggest that Vardaman planted a *perfectly authentic* priestly courses fragment into Attiah's wheelbarrow. This line of reasoning would suppose that he found the "Nazareth" fragment somewhere else and brought it surreptitiously to Field O. But this approaches the limits of absurdity, for one does not *plant* authentic artifacts—one announces them!

78. The *nun* begins at the right hand break in the marble slab. Just enough of it exists to render the letter easily diagnosed upon examination.

the intervention of the Israeli authorities, the subsequent appearance of the "*mem*" fragment, and the internally contradictory nature of that fragment.

Thus, it is this author's confident conclusion that both the "Nazareth" and the "*mem*" fragments were forged with the complicity of Vardaman. The former fragment was expertly prepared, probably in Jerusalem during the first weeks of the 1962 excavation season. In contrast, the "*mem*" fragment shows signs of hasty execution and was probably chiseled by Vardaman himself during the last days of the excavation season. In short, Vardaman appears to have had a hand in forging two of the three fragments of the "Caesarea Inscription."

It is not impossible that Vardaman was also involved with the genesis of the Talmon fragment in the mid 1950s. We recall that the young archeologist was then in Israel participating in the Shechem excavations. Knowing what we now know about him—both from Wright's devastating letter and from our foregoing analysis of his suspicious activities in the Caesarea debacle—it cannot be ruled out that Vardaman himself secretly commissioned the Talmon fragment to be forged (*cf.* above p. 332). This would, in fact, agree with the altogether unusual history of that fragment, an artifact whose provenance is unknown and which has not actually been seen by anybody on record—all we have is a single photograph attributed to A. Wegman of Caesarea.

In this regard, it could be that in 1956–57 Vardaman made his first contact with Wegman who, as we have seen, was well connected to the highest stratum of Israeli archeology (*e.g.* to Schwabe at the Hebrew University). The mid-1950s, then, would have marked Vardaman's *entrée* into the underworld of biblical forgeries and into the antiquities black market. Indeed, he was apparently very adept in that underworld—a natural.

Vardaman returned to Israel in 1962. Perhaps during his multiple visits to the Holy Land the aspiring Baptist archeologist successfully forged no less than all three fragments of the "Caesarea Inscription."

BIBLIOGRAPHY TO CHAPTER 12
(For abbreviations please see p. 480.)

Albright, W.F.
  1946. "The names Nazareth and Nazoraean." JBL 65.2:397–401.
  1932. *The Archaeology of Palestine and the Bible.* New-York: F. Revell.
Ameling, W. *et al.* (eds). 2011. *Corpus Inscriptionum Iudaeae/Palaestinae, Vol. II: Caesarea and the Middle Coast.* Berlin: De Gruyter. Cols. 1121-2160.
Avi-Yonah, M.
  1956. "Caesarea." IEJ 6:260–61.
  1960. "The Synagogue of Caesarea, Preliminary Report." *Louis M. Rabinowitz Fund for the Exploration of Ancient Synagogues Bulletin* 3:44–48.
  1962. "List of Priestly Courses from Caesarea." IEJ 12:137–39.
  1963a. "Caesarea," in IEJ 13, "Notes and News," pp. 146–48.
  1963b. "Chronique Archeologique: Césarée." RB 70:582–85.
  1964. "The Caesarea Inscription of the Twenty-Four Priestly Courses," in Vardaman and Garrett 1964:46–57.
  1993. "The Excavation of the Synagogue" in NEAEHL I:278–79.
Avi-Yonah, M. and A. Negev.
  1963. "Caesarea." IEJ 13:146-48.
  1975. "Caesarea." EAEHL, pp. 270–85,
Burrell, B. 2010. "Field O: The 'Synagogue Site.'" (Review of the 2009 book by Govaars, Spiro, and White.) BASOR 2010:93-94.
Carrier, R.
  2002a. "Pseudohistory in Jerry Vardaman's Magic Coins: The Nonsense of Micrographic Letters." *Skeptical Inquirer* 26.2 (March-April 2002):39–41, 61.
  2002b. "More on Vardaman's Microletters." *Skeptical Inquirer* 26.4 (July–August 2002):60–61.
Govaars, M. 1983. *A Reconsideration of the Synagogue Site at Caesarea Maritima, Israel.* M.A. Thesis, Drew University. Madison, NJ (unpublished).
Govaars, M., M. Spiro, and L. White. 2009. *Field O: The "Synagogue" Site.* Vol. IX of *The Joint Expedition to Caesarea Maritima: Excavation Reports.* Boston: ASOR.
Govaars, M. and Vardaman, J. 2008. *Photographs of Caesarea Maritima, Israel.* Indianapolis: Dog Ear Publications.
Guignebert, C. 1933. *Jésus.* Paris: La Renaissance du Livre.
Holum, K. 2014. "The Archaeology of Caesarea Maritima," in *Archaeology in the 'Land of Tells and Ruins.'* Bart Wagemakers, ed. Havertown: Oxbow Books, pp. 183–200.
Klein, S.
  1909. *Die Barajta der vierundzwanzig Priesterabteilungen: Beiträge zur Geographie und Geschichte Galiläas.* Leipzig: R. Haupt.

1923. *Neue Beiträge zur Geographie und Geschichte Galiläas.* Vienna: Menorah.

1939. *Sefer ha-Yishouv.* Jerusalem: Mosad Bialik (Hebrew).

1945. *Erets ha Galil.* Jerusalem: Môsad ha-Rav Qûq (Hebrew).

Leibner, U. 2009. *Settlement and History in Hellenistic, Roman, and Byzantine Galilee.* Tübingen: Mohr Siebeck.

Meyers, E. (Ed. in Chief). 1997. "Synagogue inscriptions," in OEANE.

Perdue. C. 2005. *The Politics of Archaeology in Israel.* M.A. thesis, University of Oregon (unpublished).

Racy, R. 2007. *Nativity: The Christmas Story Which You Have Never Heard Before.* Bloomington: AuthorHouse.

Rigato, M. 2005. *Il titolo della Croce di Gesù.* Rome: Pontificia università gregoriana.

Robin, C. 2004. *Himyar et Israel.* Comptes-rendus des séances de l'Académie des Inscriptions et Belles-Lettres. Volume 148, Lyons: PERSEE.

Rosenberg, S. 2010. "Hershel Shanks: Jerusalem Forgery Conference, Special Report." (Review.) STRATA (formerly BAIAS) 2010:163-65.

Rosenblatt, S. 1976. *The days of my years: an autobiography.* New York: Ktav.

Storvick, O. and M. Govaars. 2014. "Excavations at Caesarea Maritima and the Vardaman Papers." BASOR 371:163–84.

Talmon, S. 1958. "The Calendar Reckoning of the Sect from the Judaean Desert." *Scripta Hierosolymitana, volume IV: Aspects of the Dead Sea Scrolls.* C. Rabin and Y. Yadin (eds.). Jerusalem: Magnes Press, pp. 162–99.

Taylor, J. 1993. *Christians and the Holy Places: The Myth of Jewish-Christian Origins.* Oxford: University Press.

Trifon, D. 1989. "Did the Priestly Courses (Mishmarot) Transfer from Judaea to the Galilee After the Bar-Kokhba Revolt?" *Tarbits* 59/1–2:77–93 (Hebrew).

Tuccinardi, E. 2010. "Nazareth, l'épigraphe de Césarée et la main de Dieu." *Cahiers du Cercle Ernest Renan* 252:35–64.

Schürer, E. 1890/1998. *A History of the Jewish People in the Time of Jesus Christ.* 5 vols. T. & T. Clark (1890), Hendrickson (1998).

Vardaman, J.
  1962. "A new inscription which mentions Pilate as 'Prefect.'" JBL 81.1:70-71.
  1965. *Archaeology and the Living Word.* Nashville: Broadman.
  1989. *Chronos Kairos Christos I.* Winona Lake: Eisenbrauns.
  1998. *Chronos Kairos Christos II.* Macon: Mercer University Press.

Vardaman, J. and J. Garrett, Jr. (eds.). *1964. The Teacher's Yoke: Studies in Memory of Henry Trantham.* Waco: Baylor University Press.

Vaughn, A. and C. Rollston. 2005. "The Antiquities Market, Sensationalized Textual Data, and Modern Forgeries." *Near Eastern Archaeology* 68:1-2:61-65.

Yardeni, Ada. 2002. *The Book of Hebrew Script: History, Palaeography, Script Styles, Calligraphy & Design.* London: The British Library.

Chapter 13

THE TOMBS UNDER THE HOUSE OF MARY

The enigma of the Nazareth tombs

Thus far, *kokh* tombs have been identified under many holy sites in Nazareth: the Church of the Annunciation, the Sisters of Nazareth Convent, and the Bishop's Residence (midway between the Venerated Area and Mary's Well), and possibly the Church of St. Joseph. All these sites are tourist venues or are presently under development for Christian pilgrims. This is really quite remarkable and we must ask ourselves: Why are so many *funerary* sites of interest to the Catholic Church—indeed, of such great interest that they are continually developed into pilgrim destinations?

One would think that charnel houses for the dead (in fact, several of the *kokh* tombs have remnants of ossuaries where bones were collected) would be particularly unedifying and among the venues *least* worthy of religious—or any other kind of—development. Tombs generally evoke emotions ranging from disinterest to repugnance. Yet, statistical data suggest that they hold some sort of fascination for the Church.

It may be, of course, that there are simply so many tombs on the hillside of the Nebi Sa'in (Fig. 8.5) that *wherever* the Catholic Church choses to build a shrine it will encounter a tomb—either directly at the site or in the immediate proximity. This argument has some force. For all that, the presence of tombs is minimized. As my 2008 book showed, at least three tombs lie under the Roman Catholic Church of the Annunciation (CA), with the possibility of several more.[1] Yet no guidebook mentions them. Even Bagatti, who wrote extensively on the site, takes no interest at all in the tombs there. He mentions only one in his long tome, and that merely in passing.[2] Of course, by his time the problematic implications of tombs within the precincts of an ancient Jewish village had become apparent. The explosive

---

1. See Fig. 8.5 and Salm 2008a:243 *f.*
2. *Exc.* 186, cited at Salm 2008a:253.

information that the houses of Mary and Joseph were actually *over* tombs was particularly unsettling, even appalling. That information needed to be kept secret—as it does even to this day.

In my prior book I discussed the changing views at mid-century regarding tombs (Salm 2008a:70 *f*). At the beginning of the twentieth century tombs in Nazareth were passionately sought out (Vlaminck, Viaud) as possibly belonging to the Holy Family. Then, towards mid-century, the presence of tombs was merely tolerated as the active search for habitations began in earnest. Kopp admitted the lack of domestic evidence and thus proposed a 'mobile Nazareth' hypothesis (Salm 2008a:65 *f*). Bagatti, on the other hand, interpreted manifestly agricultural structures as domestic or even as confessional—wine vats become *mikvaoth*, low partitions become walls of houses, *etc*. This would continue into the new millennium with the work of Alexandre and Dark, as shown in this volume. Bagatti's conclusion: Nazareth was on the hillside (of course). The explosive knowledge that tombs were precisely under the venerated sites as well as within the alleged town's precincts was ignored. That evidence simply disappeared. Since the 1960's an attitude of denial has reigned as regards tombs in and around the venerated areas.[3]

After the Second World War, the Jewish proscription against habitation in the vicinity of tombs became generally appreciated, with potentially threatening implications for Christians everywhere. Suddenly tombs were not a blessing to the tradition (as they had been before mid-century) but an embarassment and possibly even a curse. Their presence was now a smoking gun showing that the entire history of Nazareth, as popularly understood, was *false*.

One writer of the prewar decades who had no reservations describing tombs was Asad Mansur, a Protestant Arab minister living in Nazareth.[4] Mansur was traditional in his religious outlook and, like most of his Christian contemporaries, considered the New Testament a reliable (perhaps even *the* most reliable) guide to the archeology of ancient Nazareth—from its location on "the brow" of a hill (Lk 4:14 *f*), to the presence of an early Roman synagogue, to a town (Gk. *polis*) with enough residents to furnish a "crowd." One cannot blame Mansur for vastly misdating the *kokh* tombs, thinking they went back to Iron or even Bronze Age times. He lived at a

---

3.   Jack Finegan, in his influential 1969 book, *The Archaeology of the New Testament*, offers a map of the tombs of ancient Nazareth that ignores all the tombs within three hundred meters of the Church of the Annunciation (Finegan 1969:27; 1992:44; *cf.* Salm 2008a:260).

4.   On Mansur (also listed as Mansur al-Kass), see N. Matar, "Writing Back: As'ad Mansur and Tarikh al-Nasira, 1924," in Yazbak and Sharif 2013:155–169.

time before anything like a chronology of *kokh* tombs was available. Thus Mansur identified many such tombs within the Venerated Area, and he imagined no threat to Christianity in doing so.

Indeed, we owe Asad Mansur a debt of gratitude for signaling in print several *kokh* tombs under the Church of the Annunciation itself, as well as similar tombs under the Bishop's Residence (below), and apparently also under the Church of St. Joseph! Regarding the last named venue, the pertinent passage from his 1924 book is somewhat enigmatic.[5] But if he signaled a tomb there it has been completely ignored and the tomb itself is now probably lost forever, being either completely 'reworked' or destroyed. As for the Greek Bishop's Residence (see below), Mansur signals that he personally saw *kokhim* burials there. Today, overt signs of those cavities have disappeared. At the venerated sites today, a tomb is obvious only under the Sisters of Nazareth Convent. This is probably due to an impressive rolling stone *in situ*, one which for centuries has drawn attention to the site and rendered the tomb virtually *impossible* to ignore.

Under the four most venerated sites in Nazareth tombs of the *kokh* type once existed. This is remarkable. In every case the Christian tradition has seen fit to construct a monument above these installations and, indeed, to hallow these *funerary* venues with special veneration. The CA was constructed over several Roman-era *kokhim* tombs and is now the much-visited 'home of the Virgin Mary.' The Church of St. Joseph (about one hundred meters to the north) sits not only over a possible tomb but also over a quadruple silo and an elaborate hiding complex dating to Middle Roman times.[6] It was most *obviously* a non-residential venue in antiquity, yet it is now considered the ancient domicile of St. Joseph. As for the Sisters of Nazareth site, Prof. Dark proposes that this was the real house of Joseph, perhaps even the site of "the nutrition" (*i.e.*, where Jesus grew up), as well as being the first house from the turn of the era to be found in Nazareth. The

---

5. "Nazareth is older than the age of the Messiah, and it could be older than the age of the Hebrews as well due to the existence of tombs like this [*i.e.* of the *kokh* type] in the Church of the Annunciation and of Mar Yusuf" (Mansur 1924:33). As I showed in my first book, *kokh* tombs in fact postdate 50 CE in the Galilee (Salm 2008a:158*f*, based upon the work of H. Kuhnen). "Mar Yusuf" is St. Joseph, but no one besides Mansur has noted a tomb under the modest church which has born the name of St. Joseph since 1754 and was completely rebuilt in 1911. At mid-century, the German writer C. Kopp also concluded that Mansur had the Church of St. Joseph in mind (Salm 2008a:224). Nevertheless, an old tradition exists that St. Joseph was actually buried elsewhere, namely, under the Sisters of Nazareth Convent. Thus it is possible that Mansur has *that* venue in mind for the tomb of "Mar Yusuf." (Prof. Heather Sweetser has graciously translated all passages in this chapter from Mansur's Arabic writing.)
6. See above, p. 227, and Fig. 8.4 p. 135.

manifestly funereal rolling stone onsite and several surviving *kokhim* do not deter Dark who—through a complex scenario that we have discussed above (pp. 102 *ff*)—proposes that the tomb was constructed *after* abandonment of the house but before 100 CE. Both Dark and Alexandre currently vie for the laural of who was the *first* to discover a 'house from the time of Jesus.' Dark clearly bests Alexandre, for she claims merely to have discovered the first house from the turn of the era. The British archeologist, however, proposes that the 'dwelling' under the Sisters of Nazareth Convent was *the house of Jesus himself*![7]

However, neither the Dark nor the Alexandre venue was a house during *any* epoch (Chapters 6, 10). The Sisters of Nazareth Convent was the site of a Middle Roman *kokh* tomb and later adapted to agricultural use (above, pp. 114 *f*). As regards the International Marian Center, structural remains excavated there by Alexandre in late 2009 are clearly incompatible with an habitation and correspond to an elaborate winemaking installation (pp. 207 *f*).

The tradition has sedulously desired to find obvious evidence of habitations in the Venerated Area. This, to its continued dismay, has simply not been forthcoming. What we have chronicled in this volume is nothing less than a drive to *produce* habitations dating to the 'time of Jesus'—at the Sisters of Nazareth Convent, at the International Marian Center, and centuries ago at the Church of the Annunciation and at the Church of St. Joseph (the "Church of the Nutrition").

It is interesting that the four venerated sites in Nazareth, listed above, are located over particularly elaborate *non-domestic* structural remains. Consider: (a) Under the CA are three to five *kokh* tombs and numerous signs of agricultural activity (cisterns, silos, wine vats, *etc.* See Fig. 13.1). (b) Under the Church of St. Joseph is an impressive quadruple silo, as well as an elaborate hiding complex with many narrow passageways, together with a large underground chamber (Fig. 8.4). (c) Under the Sisters of Nazareth Convent are as many as two large *kokh* tombs, as well as a huge silo together with numerous other agricultural features (Fig. 6.5). (d) Under the Bishop's Residence is a large 'cave' as well as documentary evidence of *kokhim* (below).

At least the largest underground installations on the slope could be *managed*. It appears that the Church long ago made the decision to purchase, modify, build on, and sometimes even hide the most impressive ancient installations in the "Traditional Village" area of Nazareth—be they large tombs or complex agricultural structures—in order to best manage

---

7. Dark's imaginative views are treated *in extenso* in Chapter 6. On his recent thesis that Jesus himself may have grown up at the alleged house on the Sisters of Nazareth Convent site, see Dark 2012c:177 and especially Dark 2015.

untoward (and even contrary) evidence, and thus to ensure the continuing integrity of the tradition itself—that is, to control the 'story' (see below).

The end result, however, is entirely ironic. Because the Church has taken possession of the most embarrassing underground structures and venerated them as sacred dwellings from the time of Jesus, one finds under those claimed dwellings nothing other than evidence of tombs and of astonishingly complex agricultural installations!

While the Church of St. Joseph (also known as "Joseph's Carpentry Shop") sits above a tomb (per Mansur), as well as above an elaborate four-storey silo and also a hiding complex, the nearby Church of the Annunciation site must be deemed the quintessential manifestation of this karmic irony. It is so full of tombs, cisterns, wine presses, and ancillary structures as to present a veritable catalogue of *non-domestic* remains. Kopp wrote in 1938 that no less than 68 silos were filled in with cement during construction of the contiguous Franciscan monastery, lest the foundation of the edifice sag. In addition, under the CA itself are as many as six tombs (Fig. 13.1). That locus appears to be the very heart of the Late Roman necropolis. Perhaps already in Byzantine times this is why the house of Mary was sited precisely *there*—in order to cover up, convert, or perhaps destroy the most obvious non-domestic evidence from Jesus' Nazareth.

This was satisfactory until the mid-twentieth century. Since that time, however, huge advances in technology and computing have transformed the science of archeology, which now presents a formidable *threat* to the Church's pretensions. Furthermore, the ramifications of all the hillside tombs has resulted in the suppression of such evidence[8] and a redoubled quest for habitations dating to 'the time of Jesus.'

The Greek Bishop's Residence

The foregoing discussion alerts us that precisely under the venerated sites lies the evidence most incriminating to the traditional view of Nazareth. As noted above, this certainly is the case with the CA, the most celebrated and visited venue in Nazareth, the site of at least three unheralded *kokh* tombs and of numerous agricultural installations. According to Asad Mansur writing in 1924, the Church of St. Joseph was also above a tomb,[9] though all funerary evidence there has since apparently disappeared. Its large and remarkable four-tier silo was diagrammed by Viaud in 1910 (Fig.

---

8.   Indications exist at all four venerated sites listed above that underlying funereal evidence has been altered and in some cases destroyed. Though once documented, we no longer find obvious tomb features under the CA, under the Church of St. Joseph, and under the Bishop's Residence (*cf.* Salm 2008a:219 *f*, 236 *f*).

9.   Mansur 1924:33.

8.4). The associated hiding complex with numerous tunnels probably dates to the time of Bar Kokhba.[10] Thus, the Church of St. Joseph was built over an amazing array of underground installations which are very little known .

The CA, the Church of St. Joseph, and the Sisters of Nazareth Convent form a triangle delimiting the so-called Venerated Area, in the middle of which now exists the International Marian Center (Plate 1). The Venerated Area—largely owned by the Roman Catholic Church—has historically been the focus of excavation work in Nazareth.[11] However, we now turn our attention to a venue well outside that area, one purchased by the Greek Orthodox Church long ago and made the residence of its bishop as well as a monastery. The (Greek) Bishop's Residence is midway between the Venerated Area and Mary's Well, about 300m from each (Fig. 8.5, marked by a triangle).

No formal excavation work has taken place at the Bishop's Residence (BR) though, at the time of this writing, such work is planned.[12] Mansur visited the premises in the early 1920s and reported extensive installations there—a large "cave" (see Plate 7) and "tombs of the *kokh* kind." This is explosive news in at least one regard: the BR is located precisely *in the middle of the traditional ancient village* as proposed by Christian tradition and by Bagatti in his writings (Fig. 8.5). The presence of *kokhim* burials under the BR is incompatible with the existence of a Jewish village in that vicinity in Roman times!

Once again we find that Christian interests (in this case, Greek Orthodox) have purchased a decidedly non-domestic plot of land and have managed it for a long time. Admittedly, a hundred years ago the presence of tombs under the BR was not as alarming for the tradition as it is today.[13] We will see, however, that the large cave with a number of radiating "tunnels"—definitely not an habitation—had something to do with the Greek Orthodox interest in the site, for that cave has been venerated from very early times. In any case, the site soon became the venue of a church, a monastery, and of the archbishop's residence—a Greek Orthodox counterpoise to the Roman Catholic compound 300m to the south.

Mansur described the BR in the 1920s:

---

10.   Fig. 8.4 and discussion p. 227.
11.   We can now speak of an 'expanded' Venerated Area (Plate 1) much larger than that which existed in the 1960s (*cf.* Salm 2008a:229). The expanded VA includes not only additional venerated sites (the IMC and Sisters of Nazareth Convent) but also residences, shops, streets, and urban infrastructure in an area that the Church increasingly considers to be where the Holy Family once lived.
12.   BR map references: NIG 22831–36/73453–58; OIG 17831–36/23453–58.
13.   The dating of tombs was not clear, and the relevance of Jewish ritual uncleanliness was not fully appreciated.

On two sides are other rooms for the retinue of the bishop and on the higher floor is the [bishop's] residence. Bishop Nippon built this house in 1860 and, in 1863, the church which is a small house of worship. To the right [at the bottom of many steps] is a door that enters into a large cave that has an area that is just about the size of the entire house. In this area are three openings for light, and when you enter it you find two caves, one inside the other... The length [of the large cave] is about 20 meters and its width about 10 meters. Its roof is held up by supports in the middle. Bishop Nippon used it as a mill for *dabaka*. To your north is the small cave, and between the two [caves] is a wide door. The length [of the small cave] is about 6 meters and its width about 4 meters, and on the side of its ceiling to the southeast is a wide opening that is blocked now by construction. When you enter the large [cave], you see opposite yourself a recess [?];[14] *in it are tombs of the kokh kind.* Next to it on your left is another [recess] like it, but it passes through into the small cave.

—Mansur 1924:164. (Translated by H. Sweetser, emphasis added.)

The large cave must have drawn attention at an early time, and it appears that the BR site was *the first area in Nazareth* to be venerated. This is not surprising, for it is on the hillside (thus fulfilling the requirement of Lk 4:29) and—as would be logical for an ancient village—it is also not far from the only year-round source of water, Mary's Spring.

Some indications suggest that veneration in the cave may actually predate Christianity. Certainly, local lore holds that the cave is "one of the city's oldest historic sites" and "in use for more than two thousand years."[15] Though no formal excavation work has taken place at the site in modern times, one report claims that the Emperor Constantine built an enormous church there that does not survive.[16]

It is believed that the cave was secretly used before Constantine by the first Christians in Nazareth when they faced persecution from the Roman empire. This belief conforms with the cherished myth that Nazareth was a hotbed of Christianity before the religion received official recognition. In contrast, archeology and history show that the town was in fact very Jewish and even anti-Christian—its inhabitants aggressively participated in the persecution of Christians in the early seventh century.[17]

---

14.   Arabic: *mughbun.*

15.   *Nazareth Today,* Dec. 2011, "Christmas Market 2011," online at *http://www.nazarethtoday.com/en/* (accessed March 16, 2015).

16.   *Nazareth Today, op. cit.*

17.   J. Taylor's work dispels the notion of an early Christian Nazareth. The myth is favored by Christian institutions because it authenticates the antiquity of the various Nazareth shrines and the claimed historical foundations of the religion itself. See Taylor 1993; Salm 2008a:121, 333.

Christians, however, have been rewriting history as long as they have existed, embroidering their myths with an unending fund of colorful tales. Long ago, the spacious cave under the BR began to be venerated as the place where the Romans martyred forty Christian worshippers. Consequently, the church above is today known as the Forty Martyrs' Church.

Hollows lead off from different sides of the cave. They have been described on the Internet as the beginning of a network of tunnels. However, no scholarly documentation for this view exists and such a network of "tunnels" has neither been mapped nor studied. We will soon see that they cannot be part of a Bar-Kokhba era hiding complex, such as is found under the Church of St. Joseph,[18] and we will propose another interpretation.

In the passage cited above, Mansur notes that when he visited the cave about a century ago one area was blocked due to "construction." Indeed, a great deal of modern reworking of the underground structures is visible in a number of photographs, one reproduced in Plate 7. Those photographs betray much *secondary* masonry work that does not appear ancient. The flooring, too, is not ancient. It is clear that this cave has been subjected to a great deal of reworking up until recently. In the 2011 *Nazareth Today* article quoted above (note 15), a certain Father Yohanna frankly admits that "we had to make a lot of changes" to the cave.

We certainly cannot doubt that Mansur saw multiple *kokhim* under the Bishop's Residence when he visited the cave in the 1920s, for he writes (citation above) that "tombs of the *kokh* kind" were in the recess to the right in the photograph in Plate 7 ("First Recess"). That photograph, however, shows that *this recess has been sealed off by modern masonry*, clearly visible in the background. This would be one of the "tunnels" that has been sealed off. Other photos reveal that the First Recess has been transformed into a little cave with its sides reworked—as might be the case if there were multiple *kokhim* there whose mouths had been covered over with masonry. An altar has also been built in this little cave, a feature which is obviously secondary.

If it were not for Mansur's affirmation of *kokh* burials under the BR, we would have no inkling a tomb was once there, for no obvious funereal evidence has survived. One recent photograph, however, does show what appears to be a single *kokh*. Unfortunately, because the photo is a closeup, it has not been possible to place this *kokh* into its immediate material context under the BR.

Near the First Recess, Mansur notes another "next to it on your left." This Second Recess has similarly been sealed off by modern masonry, also visible in Plate 7. Scrutiny of that image shows what also looks like a 'bow'

---

18. On hiding complexes see above, pp. 225 f. On the St. Joseph complex, see Aviam 2004:130; Kloner and Tepper 1987:295–99 (Hebrew).

in the rock face to the left. This may have been an arcosolium or bench grave that has been filled in.

It appears from the documentary and photographic evidence that the cave under the Bishop's Residence did not have radiating tunnels but, rather, contained passageways that led to multiple *kokhim* chambers. The openings of two of the chambers are visible in Plate 7, but access has been blocked through secondary masonry work. Given the large size of the cave, it is probable that additional chambers with *kokhim* tombs also radiated in other directions. This was no hiding complex nor a secret meeting place. It was a *kokh* tomb complex. In fact, it may have been the largest funerary installation in all of Middle Roman–Early Byzantine Nazareth.

This need not cause surprise. Multi-chambered *kokh* tombs have been documented elsewhere in the basin. In fact, only 100m to the west of the BR and about 20m upslope is Tomb 77 (Fig. 8.5), a tomb with three chambers oriented in a straight line which once contained at least 24 *kokhim*.[19] Tomb K22 across the valley was larger still. It had no less than four chambers, a round blocking stone, and an undetermined number of *kokhim*. It is also highly probable that several of the *kokhim* documented under the CA (below) belonged to one and the same large tomb.

In sum, the impressive cave under the Bishop's Residence, together with its radiating chambers, belongs to a *kokh* tomb complex dating to later Roman times. It appears that the Greek Orthodox Church has effected massive changes to this large installation, sealing off the side chambers and filling in arcosolia to remove obvious evidence of burials. Much of this work may be recent, for before the mid-twentieth century tombs were not a great source of embarrassment. In any case, what remains is a large central "cave" that has been much reworked, as well as what may appear like radiating "tunnels" to anyone who has not explored the passageways. At least one writer has speculated that those tunnels were once very long and even led to far flung areas of the settlement (*Nazareth Today, op. cit.*). This view has no scholarly foundation.

Visitors, of course, are not told that burials once existed at the site, nor is that fact mentioned in the standard literature. Under the Greek Bishop's Residence, all are told, is the venerated site where early Christians secretly gathered. A large group of the faithful was discovered in Roman times and all its members paid with their lives—thus reaffirming how committed the ancient Nazarenes were to the emerging faith. Constantine subsequently built a great and beautiful church (none of which survives) over the spot, in commemoration of the "Forty Martyrs." All in all, it is a fascinating story.

It is simply not true.

---

19. See Kopp 1938:201 (his Tomb no. 13); Salm 2008a:259.

The tombs under the Church of the Annunciation

Potentially far more embarrassing to the tradition than the aforementioned tombs under the Greek Bishop's Residence (at the alleged *center* of ancient Nazareth) are the three to five documented tombs directly under the Roman Catholic Church of the Annunciation—under the very house of Mary! It is interesting to observe how the Church continues to deal with this absurd dilemma.

The Myth of Nazareth dealt with these tombs in detail.[20] In the intervening years no new archeological information regarding them has come forward. In fact, the site has been more or less archeologically 'closed' since Bagatti's excavations of 1955–56, the results of which were recorded in his 1967/69 book, *Excavations in Nazareth*. However, that tome completely ignores the tombs under the CA. This is the way the modern Church has chosen to deal (or not deal) with the tombs under the house of Mary.

This strategy is also adopted in the secondary literature. Either the tombs are totally ignored or substitute language is employed in the rare case that a guidebook actually notes sensitive remains. For example, Tomb 29 (Fig. 13.1) is called a "cave sanctuary"[21]—presumably a nook for prayer—though it is actually the *kokh* of a tomb where a body once lay and whose roof was long ago raised through digging. In another guide the same locus is a "Grotto containing various graffitti."[22] This echoes Bagatti's view, for he devoted no less than thirty-eight pages in his *Excavations* to the graffiti from T29, though he did not mention the tomb at all.[23]

My 2008 book made knowledge of the tombs under the CA generally available for the first time. As noted above, such knowledge has been suppressed since about mid-century when the Jewish prohibition against living in the vicinity of tombs began to be appreciated. Before then, Catholic researchers documented burials in the Venerated Area with enthusiasm, hoping one or more of them might be of members of the Holy Family. St. Joseph was the most frequent candidate. Through the ages his tomb has been mooted here and there—under the CA, under the Church of St. Joseph, and under the Sisters of Nazareth Convent. But after the War the

---

20.   Salm 2008a:243–259; also pp. 229–41 for the slope and general character of the area, p. 74 for Bagatti's excavation, pp. 76–77 for a description of the modern church.

21.   S. Doyle, *The Pilgrim's New Guide to the Holy Land*. Wilmington: Glazier, 1985 p. 120.

22.   G. Freeman-Grenville, *The Basilica of the Annunciation at Nazareth and Adjacent Shrines*. Jerusalem: Cana Carta 1994, p. 34.

23.   From Bagatti's book the only way the reader might infer that a tomb was *possibly* there is from a long citation which includes the information that this spot "in former times must have contained a tomb, judging, at least, by the remains of a recess still visible." (Salm 2008a:253.) Viaud, Kopp, and Bagatti were elsewhere more forthright in describing this tomb.

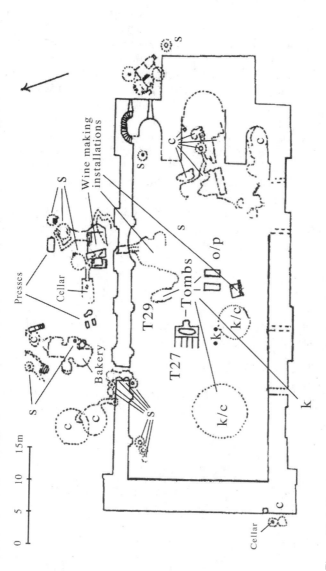

Figure 13.1. Roman-era tombs and selected agricultural installations under the Church of the Annunciation. The Crusader-era church is outlined. Several of the burials (T27, T29, o/p, •k•, k/c) may have been part of one kokh tomb in antiquity. Key: k = *kokh* burial identified by Meistermann, Viaud, and Mansur a century ago; k/c = tomb converted into cistern; •k• = burial identified by Bagatti (1969:49); c = cistern; s = silo. (After Bagatti 1969:27–70 and Plate XI. *Cf.* Salm 2008a:Illus. 5.4 and p. 244.)

Church has had to reverse its earlier course, basically burying any references to tombs in the Venerated Area.

It is undeniably macabre that three earlier documented burials under the CA actually surround the Chapel of the Angel—the spot where the Archangel Gabriel delivered the history-changing news to Mary that she would bear the "Son of God" (Lk 1:35).[24] T29 and *kokhim* o/p seem to be on opposite sides of a single *kokh* tomb chamber, while T27 to the west may represent a neighboring chamber. However, so much reworking (and removal) of stone has taken place that it is scarcely possible to re-create the original funerary installation.

According to tradition this is where Mary lived. Yet Bagatti never found structural remains in the vicinity dating before Middle Roman times.[25] The Church has long admitted that the 'house of Mary' is no longer in evidence at the site. In 1291 CE it produced the astonishing thesis that her house was transported to Tersatto in Dalmatia by angels on May 10 of that year—this by the grace of God in order to save it from infidel hands. But when the Moslems conquered Dalmatia three years later, the house disappeared from Tersatto and, according to some shepherds, was seen on December 10, 1294, being borne aloft by angels across the Adriatic Sea. The house came to rest near Recanati in Italy and soon became a place of pigrimage and the site of miracles. For the continuation of this pious saga I refer to a Catholic webpage:

> Bandits from the nearby wooded area began to plague the pilgrims, so the House was borne to a safer spot a short distance away. But the spot where the House was finally to rest was still not settled since the two brothers who owned the land were quarreling. The House was moved a third time to the site it now occupies [at Loreto]. The brothers became reconciled as soon as the House settled in its final location. Incidentally, wherever it landed, the Holy House rested miraculously on the ground, without a foundation.
>
> Once again miracles attended the presence of the House, and the townspeople sent a deputation of men to Tersatto and then to Nazareth to determine for certain the origin of the Holy House. Sixteen men, all reliable citizens, took with them measurements and full details of the House, and after several months arrived back with the report that in their opinion, the House had really come from Nazareth.[26]

---

24. In the Gospel of Matthew this surprising news comes to Joseph in a remarkable dream (Mt 1:18–25).

25. Salm 2008a:194. Bagatti's discussion of "The pre-Byzantine buildings" begins on p. 114 of his 1969 book. Taylor thoroughly re-evaluates the structural evidence under the CA and rejects an Early Roman presence (Taylor 1993: 231 *f*, 249 *f*, 265 *etc*).

26. *http://www.catholictradition.org/Mary/loreto1.htm* (accessed July 16, 2015).

Presumably, the sixteen "reliable citizens" who traveled to Nazareth visited the Church of the Annunciation site and duly studied the tombs underneath—T27, T29, and graves o/p—measuring the distances between the burials surrounding the Chapel of the Angel, the precise length and width of the *kokhim*, and noting the exact emplacement of bodies that must have been buried under the house of Mary in Roman times.

In any case, though Mary's house in Loreto betrays no signs of having ever been a simple Roman-period Galilean dwelling, today it continues to be readily available for visitation by the ultra-faithful.

Returning to our discussion of bedrock structures under the CA, a glance at Fig. 13.1 reveals the existence not only of *kokhim* burials but also of numerous agricultural installations. We find many cisterns and silos, a bakery ("oven"), cellars, presses, and installations associated with the production of wine. The slope is from north to south and from east to west. We particularly note the north-south alignment of the various wine making structures. At the north is a press,[27] and downslope from it a collecting vat, then a treading floor, and finally another vat (Fig. 13.1, "Wine making installations"). To the west are two cellars.

The great abundance and variety of these installations do not suggest the work of a single era. As demonstrated at the nearby Sisters of Nazareth site (above p. 104), the general chronology at the CA is also that of older tombs being intruded upon and partially or wholly converted to agricultural use over a long period of time.

Acknowledging the precedence of tombs disposes of alternate theories which propose that other structures came first. Wherever tombs and agricultural structures exist together on the Nebi Sa'in hillside, it is not possible to argue that the tombs came later (*e.g.* Dark, Chapter 6). Certainly, the ancient inhabitants would not have attempted to hew a tomb at a locus that was already full of cavities, some reaching deep into the ground (*e.g* double or triple silos). On the other hand, no maps existed of underground installations. Given the ubiquity of tombs, the inhabitants would certainly occasionally have intruded upon one while digging a cistern, silo, or cellar long after the *kokh* tomb was no longer active. Such tombs went out of use c. 500 CE, and it is clear from the ancillary movable finds that many of the agricultural installations postdate that time. It should also be noted that agricultural installations frequently intrude on funerary structures under the CA site—clear evidence of the funerary-agricultural sequence.[28]

---

27. Bagatti describes a second press nearby (his no. 39) as dedicated to the crushing of olives. Presses often had dual functions and it is indeed quite likely that olive oil was also produced at the site, in addition to wine. See above, p. 234.

28. Salm 2008a:247 (locus 52), 249 (T27), 253 (T29), 259 (o/p).

The correct sequence of use bears emphasis, for Prof. Dark has suggested that the convent site, the CA site, and other locations on the slope first had domestic installations and *then* tombs (above p. 76). Nothing recommends this view. It can also be noted that in dual-use chambers where light enters from above (such as at the convent site), agricultural use must have postdated funereal use, for the opening would have been effected to *admit* light for agricultural activities, not to *build* the tomb which requires a sealed space.

The *kokhim* T29 and o/p were probably on opposite sides of the same tomb chamber. T27 may well have belonged to a neighboring chamber which is incomplete (one easternmost *kokh* appears only to have been started). Several writers in the early twentieth century observed additional *kokhim* at nearby locations that were later converted into large cisterns (k/c in Fig. 13.1). Bagatti (1969:49) also notes a "burial" at L26 ("•k•" in Fig. 13.1). Unfortunately, he does not describe it. The burial is located directly to the south of T27 and is contiguous to a tomb that Meistermann and others noted long ago ("k/c").

When one counts the burials in the immediate vicinity of the Chapel of the Angel, there are no less than five, with two others a few meters farther to the south and west. Bagatti does not mention four of these funereal loci. He comments on only one installation, T27—being virtually forced to do so by Kopp's forthright assessment that this is *"eine typische Kokimanlage"* (Kopp 1938:137). Perhaps in desperation, in 1967/69 Bagatti attempted to redate it to Crusader times. But the macabre custom of Crusaders burying their dead under the house of Mary is unknown (see Salm 2008a:250). Bagatti also writes that the Crusaders had "the usual system of placing the bodies between small stone walls." Yet this can equally well describe a *kokhim* installation. Finally, it should be noted that the Italian contradicts himself, writing that T27 contains "tombs constructed by the Crusaders" but a few line later that the locus is "not funerary" (Bagatti 1969:50). In the aggregate it matters little, for if Bagatti were able to dispose of this installation, he would still have six more nearby to deal with.

As pointed out in my first book, the *kokh* type of burial did not arrive in the Galilee until after *c.* 50 CE. (Salm 2008a:158 *f*). From the associated pottery, we can date the *kokh* tombs thus far excavated at Nazareth to Middle-Late Roman times. All the burials under the CA considerably postdate the 'time of Jesus.' In one sense, the tradition is correct: Mary was indeed *not* surrounded by tombs. The reason, however, is not because the *kokh* tombs are a myth, but because Mary is a myth. She was not surrounded by *anything* at the turn of the era simply because she obviously did not exist. No habitation of hers under the CA has been found dating to the turn of the era.

This fact can also be readily extrapolated to the rest of the basin: *not a single post-Iron Age artifact, tomb or structure at Nazareth dates with certainty before 100 CE* (Salm 2008a:165, 205). This over-arching conclusion, emphasized in my 2008 book, holds as strongly today as it did seven years ago.

Dark revisited

In recent years professor Ken Dark of the University of Reading has emerged as the most assertive voice in proposing radically *new* interpretations of Nazareth archeology. IAA archeologist Yardena Alexandre's work, in contrast, has essentially supported the tradition. While her interpretation of a dwelling at the IMC site is certainly erroneous (Chapter 10), and her conclusion of Hellenistic–Early Roman presence at Mary's Well is also untenable (Chapter 11), nothing in Alexandre's work radically challenges long-standing tradition.

The same cannot be said for Dark. The British archeologist has lately published theories that recast Nazareth archeology in both specific and general ways. These venturesome theories include (a) the transferring of both "Mary's Well" and the "house of the nutrition" (where Jesus was raised) from their traditional locations to the Sisters of Nazareth Convent; and (b) proposing that Early Roman Nazareth was much larger than commonly thought. We now consider these in turn.

Water, water everywhere. All writers on Nazareth—past and present—are agreed that Mary's Spring is the principal water source of the basin. However, at several points in his writings Dark asserts the existence of a second major source in the traditional 'center' of the ancient village. Though contradicted by expert opinion (see below), this ideosyncratic and even curious position is of critical importance to Dark's theories. Already in 2008 he berated this author regarding the hydrology of the basin, though my view has always been thoroughly orthodox:

> [Salm] seems to believe that the only significant natural water source is St. Mary's Well (p. 21) and has apparently not seen any of the evidence—the relevant publications are absent from the discussion and the bibliography—showing this to be incorrect. In fact, at least three natural springs are known in Nazareth. Another plentiful water source in the centre of the Byzantine settlement (*i.e.* near the Church of the Annunciation) could be surmised from Adomnán of Iona's *De Locis Sanctis*, supported by archaeological evidence published in 2006, so probably too late for inclusion in Salm's book.   —Dark 2008d:142

It should be stated without further ado that Dark's view of the basin's hydrology is untenable. In 2012 Alexandre carefully reviewed the subject and concluded:

Spring waters were scarce in the ancient village. The only perennial source was located outside Nazareth, where it emerged from the rock slope about 150 m north of the site that would become Mary's Well. A significantly smaller spring, which became known as the Apostle's fountain, flowed seasonally down the western slope of the village (Bagatti 2001:30–32).   —Alexandre 2012a:2.

This is certainly the generally accepted view, as also reflected in my 2008 book: "There is one year-round spring in the Nazareth valley, known as Mary's Spring (*'Ain Maryam*)." I also noted "a seasonal water source with low volume located near the Mensa Christi church."[29] This modest second source has been alternatively known as the "New Spring" (*'Ain ed-Jedide*). It has not flowed in recent years.

A century ago Mansur commented on the basin's hydrology and the difficulty of the residents in finding sufficient water:

> There are some springs in Nazareth and its surroundings, but they are not enough for the residents. It is probable that this has been the case since ancient times, according to the evidence of the number of receptacles and old cisterns that collect rainwater on the mountains and mountain slopes, as well as in the valley... It is rare now to encounter a house with no receptacle or cistern for rainwater. Many efforts were exerted to find new springs or to increase the water from the old springs, but most of these [efforts] were in vain and the city rarely benefited from them.
>   —Mansur 1924:16

Thus, Dark's proposal of a "plentiful water source in the centre of the Byzantine settlement (*i.e.* near the Church of the Annunciation)" is simply not corroborated by the physical characteristics of the basin and, to my knowledge, is not espoused by anyone else. The root of his theory appears to be an attempt to locate the secondary water source under the Sisters of Nazareth Convent (see below). By doing this, *and* by presenting that secondary spring as a "plentiful water source," Dark proposes something quite astonishing: that Jesus himself was raised at the Sisters of Nazareth Convent site! This juggling of venues amounts to a relocation of the "house of the nutrition" which has been traditionally venerated at the Church of St. Joseph (about 150m to the northeast of the convent).

Dark bases this relocation on a unique passage in a seventh century work. It describes the place where Jesus was raised as both "in the middle of the city" and over "a very clear spring":

> [Nazareth.] An unfortified town on a hill with two large stone-built churches. One church, *in the middle of the city*, is built over two vaults, on the spot where there once stood the house in which our Lord the Savior was

---

29. Salm 2008a:21, 222.

brought up. Among the mounds [*tumuli*] below this church, which, as has been said, is supported upon two mounds and intervening arches, there is a very clear spring, frequented by all the citizens, who draw water from it, and from the same spring water is raised in vessels to the church above by means of wheels. —ELS translation. Emphasis added.[30]

The above passage is by a certain Adomnan of Iona, a late seventh century Irish abbot whose *De Locis Sanctis* describes holy sites in the Levant. While Adomnan explicitly states that the spring is in the *middle* of the city, Alexandre (2012a:141) points out that an error has taken place:

> [T]he association of the church inside the village with the "very clear" or "clearest spring, frequented by all the citizens" is inaccurate and it is almost certain that the spring here referred to in superlative terms is the source lying outside the town near Mary's Well. The mistake may be a copier's error that transpired when first transmitted to Adomnan, but it is quite probable that it was a later editing gloss resulting from the divergent Annunciation traditions of the Western and Eastern churches.
> —Alexandre 2012a:141.

The "divergent Annunciation traditions" apparently long ago led to some tampering of manuscripts, and—in the Adomnan case—to a literary relocation of the single major spring to within the village. This relocation had nothing to do with the spring *per se*, but with relocating all the sites important to Jesus from Greek Orthodox loci to the interior of the village— where the Roman Catholics owned terrain.

Though many ancient sources identify the major water source with the home of Mary,[31] except for the Adomnan passage they all locate that source *outside* the village, as in the following passage from the twelfth century pilgrim Peter the Deacon:

> The cave in which [Mary] lived is large and most luminous, where an altar has been placed, and there inside the cave itself is the place from which she drew water. Inside the city, where the synagogue was where the Lord read the book of Isaiah, there is now a church. *But the spring from which Mary used to take water is outside the village.*
> —Geyer 1898:112 (emphasis added).

Dark's apparent attempt to relocate Jesus' dwelling to the convent site requires that a major spring not only be located within the village proper, but also that it be sited precisely under the Sisters of Nazareth Convent. This rather ambitious *programme* takes the Adomnan passage literally and

---

30. D. Baldi (ed.), *Enchiridion Locorum Sanctorum* (ELS). No. 6: *Documenta S. Evangelii* Jerusalem: Palestine Pilgrims' Text Society III, 1955, p. 45.

31. Arculf, Adomnan, (VII CE), Peter the Deacon (XII CE). This tradition loosely follows the *Protevangelium of James*. For discussion see Salm 2008a:214 *f*.

also ignores the actual hydrology of the basin, as noted by Alexandre, Mansur, and others. All indications are that the seasonal water source of *'Ain ed-Jedide*/New Spring was never plentiful. Furthermore, that intermittent source has been universally located at the Mensa Christi—a full 250m to the northwest of the convent.[32]

Dark is apparently encouraged that under the Sisters of Nazareth Convent exist several elements identified in pilgrim accounts—most notably (1) a "luminous cave," (2) an ancient altar (betraying pre-Crusader veneration at the site), and (3) *some* presence of water. The "luminous cave" can (without too much difficulty) be identified with the *Grotte Eclairée*, an area of Tomb 2 in which light was introduced from above by making a hole in the original tomb roof. As for the altar, one is located at the far north of the convent site (Fig. 6.5) and may date to Byzantine times.

Only the presence of plentiful water is fatal to Dark's reinterpretation of the convent site. Thus, he is apparently led to grossly exaggerate the hydrology of the Sisters of Nazareth compound, generally finding the site compatible with "complex water systems" (Dark 2007:11–12), interpreting the filtration basins (above, p. 115) as water-related, finding particular significance in the multiple cisterns for "the storage and drawing of water on more than a household scale," considering the "seasonal" spring of *'Ain ed-Jedide* as having once been far more productive than documentation attests, and—most egregiously—locating that secondary spring beneath the Sisters of Nazareth Convent itself and far from its well-known location. All this is breathtaking in its novelty, as well as in its disregard for what other scholars have written and for what the basin's terrain actually reveals. Most revealing is the following passage by Dark:

> The church was, Adomnán tells us, a large building in the centre of Nazareth above a vaulted crypt containing two tombs (*tumuli* in Adomnán's Insular Latin) and between them a 'house', with a well nearby from which water was raised by means of a bucket and rope. Thus... the similarity between this description and the archaeologically-identified features of the [convent] site is striking. It seems inescapable that the surface-level church and cave-church together comprised the church to which Adomnán refers, that is, the Church of the Nutrition. —Dark 2009:16–17

The archeologist's logic is clearly forced, and the above words do not at all correspond with what Adomnan wrote. Perhaps most astonishing is Dark's translation of *tumuli* by "tombs" (invoking "Insular Latin"). We recall that the standard ELS translation (above, p. 393) translates *tumuli* by "mounds." But mounds are not found under the convent—*tombs* are! Dark's translation appears to be an arbitrary accommodation to the *kokhim*

---

32. For map, see Fig. 8.5, "New Spring." For discussion, *cf.* Bagatti 2001:30 *f.*

burials under the Sisters of Nazareth Convent. This would be the logical inference for, in drawing parallels with the Adomnan passage, *kokhim* are the only "tombs" found under the convent.

Then, too, we wonder how Dark can write of two tombs with a house *between* them, for the tombs under the convent are *below* ground while the alleged dwelling is entirely *above* ground. In sum, Dark's conception is a complete non-starter and certainly does not correspond to the "archaeo-logically-identified features" at the convent site.

Despite all these incongruities, Dark finds the Adomnan passage "strik-ing" in its "inescapable" application to the Sisters of Nazareth site! I leave the reader to judge if the least merit is to be accorded Dark's conclusions.

In Chapter 6 we discovered that no 'house' existed at the convent. That fundamental point seems fairly minor, however, when dealing with scholarship that relocates Mary's Well from the well-known site outside of town to the Sisters of Nazareth Convent, that relocates the Church of the Nutrition from St. Joseph to the convent, that relocates the "New Spring" from the Mensa Christi to the convent (250m to the south), that locates the domicile of Jesus over *kokh* tombs, and that proposes a plentiful water source where none has ever existed.[33]

The 'larger Nazareth' question. In contrast to Alexandre, Dark has to this writ-er's knowledge never *excavated* in or around Nazareth. He has repeatedly visited the Sisters of Nazareth Convent site, which is under Roman Catho-lic ownership, has studied the visible remains there at length, and has stud-ied the literature regarding that venue. Dark has also conducted surface surveys of the area between Nazareth and Sepphoris.

The result of all this attention is, unfortunately, a number of untenable new theories regarding both the convent and the upland valley between Nazareth and Sepphoris. Most important, certainly, is the latter. Stem-ming from his surveys, Dark argues the remarkable view that Nazareth was a *large*—or at least a substantial—settlement at the turn of the era.[34] Of course, this represents a radical departure from age-old Christian tradition. Jerome (*fl. c.* 400 CE) wrote that Nazareth was merely a tiny village (a *viculus* rather than an *oppidum*). In modern times scholars have been impressed by the lack of mention of the settlement in ancient sources. They have sup-posed that Nazareth was a "small village" (J. Strange), a "hamlet" (J. D.

---

33. It can be pointed out that Dark has also apparently misread Alexandre's 2006 report regarding the incipience of the water channels at Mary's Well. He infers that the channels there date to the twelfth century whereas, in fact, they date to Middle Roman times. (Dark 2012c:177; *cf.* above pp. 309 *f.* and p. 311 n. 75.)

34. See above p. 263 n. 26.

Crossan), and generally too insignificant to receive any notice at the turn of the era.[35] The thrust of Dark's writings, however, leads altogether in another direction.

Indeed, several of the installations found in the Venerated Area are clearly communal in nature. Triple and quadruple silos, the extensive hiding complex under the Church of St. Joseph, the elaborate wine making installation under the IMC—these were not made by and for any modest family in antiquity. They represent a settlement of some size, one which the pottery and other evidence shows clearly existed *in Middle to Late Roman times*. It is also clear from the waterworks at Mary's Well (Chapter 11) that by the third–fourth centuries the settlement was large enough to construct channels bringing water over one hundred meters downslope to the Fountain Square area.

Though the foregoing does not correspond with a small and modest hamlet, the problems for anyone who would postulate a large Nazareth at the turn of the era are two. The first is chronology: the evidence (most emphatically tombs and pottery) points to the founding of the village in *Middle Roman* times, a village which reached a considerable size in Late Roman and Byzantine times. The second problem is *location*: habitations still have not been found *on the hillside*. This was the area where the Late Roman village buried its dead, stored its grain, and processed its oil and wine. But the people manifestly did not *live* on the slope, as the tradition insists.

The Christian tradition has long had its hands full parrying the information continually brought in by science. Over the last decade a good deal of new information has become available. The longstanding endorsement of a 'small and modest Nazareth' (contrary to scripture) was a necessary reaction to the general lack of evidence for a town of *any* size. Recently, however, Alexandre and others have uncovered installations of considerable dimensions. Thus the tradition is noticeably modifying its view and now tentatively exploring a 'larger Nazareth' hypothesis. Unfortunately, it has not yet negociated the chronological and location problems noted above.

Our analysis in Chapter 6 concluded that Dark has not identified an habitation under the Sisters of Nazareth Convent. He also did not excavate nor uncover any domiciles in his survey area between ancient Nazareth and Sepphoris, but simply quantities of pottery fragments which he describes as the "ubiquitous presence of Roman-period and Byzantine cooking-pot and storage-vessel sherds."[36] Of course, the Roman period lasted into the fourth century, hence this evidence is hardly probative for turn-of-the era human

---

35. J. Strange, ABD (1992), "Nazareth," col. 1051; J. D. Crossan, *The Historical Jesus*, New York: HarperCollins, p. 18.
36. Dark 2008b:95.

presence in the survey area. Nevertheless, on the basis of that pottery Dark soon writes not of one but of multiple settlements in the valley south of Sepphoris. He also insinuates claims regarding the Early Roman period, for example: "The settlements to the south of the study area also *seem* to have been established at the start of the Roman period..." (Dark 2008b:95, emphasis added). As we have noted, all this is based on the recovered surface pottery. Dark's logic could not be more tentative:

> This pottery (much of it found as small abraded body sherds) probably covers the entire Roman period and it is, therefore, possible to argue— on the basis of the ceramic evidence alone—that the settlement-pattern recorded here may have originated very early in the Roman period (perhaps in the late first century BC), or just possibly (in view of the few Hellenitic sherds) at the end of the Hellenistic period.
> —Dark 2008b:96 (emphasis added)

Taking the archeologist at his word, it is indeed *probably possible* to argue that settlement *may* have originated *perhaps* in the late first century BCE—or *just possibly* at the end of the Hellenistic period! The presence of all these qualifying words, however, renders this essentially an argument from silence. In any case, the very first 'probably' in the above citation nullifies the entire argument. It is not possible to conclude anything based on the alleged *probability* that pottery covers the "entire Roman period"!

In any case, a few shards—even if they are Hellenistic—hardly suggest a settlement in that era. As Dark is no doubt aware, the valleys on both sides of Sepphoris (which was located on a hill) were well traveled in many periods. To the north was the Trunk Road (*Darb el-Hawwarnah* in Arabic) connecting the Via Maris with the Damascus road (Fig. 1.1). A Roman road also connected Sepphoris with Tiberias.

To the south of Sepphoris a route connected Jokneam/Shim'on in the west to Gath Hepher, Jabneel, and the Sea of Galilee in the east. It is not surprising that Dark's surface surveys uncovered quantities of pottery there. Indeed it is likely, in this author's opinion, that if he looks further he will uncover pottery of virtually every era. But that hardly leads to the manifestly over-the-top conclusion that one or more settlements existed in Early Roman times *in that well-traveled vicinity.* Much less does it support the notion of a 'larger Nazareth.'

The Synagogue Church site. A comment is in order regarding a small excavation about one hundred meters north of the Sisters of Nazareth Convent (Plate 1, top left). Today this is known as the Synagogue Church, piously believed to be where Jesus preached in Luke 4. Most scholars doubt the account: the existence of dedicated brick and mortar synagogues in Lower

Galilee at such an early period is unlikely, and Nazareth was too 'small and insignificant' to possess such an establishment. However, Dark and a colleague, E. Ribak, came across a small 1945 excavation report by Roland de Vaux relative to the Synagogue Church site.[37] While de Vaux concluded that "the building does not appear to be of any great antiquity," Dark and Ribak hold that it might yet go back to antiquity. They couch this verdict with numerous qualifiers, as familir from the citation above:

> The discovery of a layer with 'pre-Crusader' (*perhaps* either Roman-period or Byzantine) pottery beneath that underlying the church walls *suggests* that this area of the present city was *perhaps* occupied prior to the existing structure, and the limited scale of the test-pit allows the *possibility* that one or more undiscovered earlier building(s) *could have stood* on the site.   —Dark and Ribak 95 (emphases added).

Once again we have an argument from silence, for Dark and Ribak here simply speculate regarding the existence of an early structure *outside* the excavated area. Besides the fact that no empirical evidence has been forthcoming for such a structure, one can point out that all the proposed sites for the ancient synagogue (there are three)[38] are in the immediate vicinity of *kokh* tombs. This uncomfortable fact is thoroughly overlooked by the tradition but is of considerable relevance.

Prof. Dark apparently has a pronounced penchant for writing what he *wishes* to see. Thus, he observes regarding the IMC site that it was the locus of "another first-century courtyard house" which "was built on relatively flat ground."[39] A glance at Figs. 10.6 and 10.7 quickly reveals the dramatic slope of the IMC terrain, while our discussion in Chapter 10 has demonstrated that no house ("courtyard" or otherwise) existed at the site.

It is not possible to expand at length on every misstatement by Dark—a goodly number of which misrepresent other scholars (above pp. 94 *f*). From inferences by vegetable matter, to imaginary settlements on a caravan route, to arguments from complete silence, the British archeologist's novel views and unusual methodologies currently grace the pages of well-read

---

37. De Vaux's French report *in toto* is part of Dark and Ribak's article, p. 99.

38. Dark and Ribak seem to conflate two synagogue locations (b and c below) into one. The present Synagogue Church site does not apparently correspond with James of Verona's (fourteenth century) observation that the synagogue was located "two stone throws" south of the Church of the Annunciation, for no CA is known north of the site. The three historically proposed sites of the CA yield (per Verona) the following locations for a synagogue, all near Roman tombs: (a) in the vicinity of Kopp's tomb K5 (see Salm 2008a:Illus. 5.2); (b) in the vicinity of the Bishop's Residence (where Mansur saw *kokhim* in 1924) or the nearby T79; and (c) in the vicinity of the Sisters of Nazareth Convent, which is located directly over *kokhim* burials.

39. Dark 2015:58–59.

journals such as the *Palestine Exploration Quarterly* and the *Biblical Archaeology Review*. This is an unfortunate indication of how greatly the field of New Testament archeology stands in need of the most rigorous scientific methodology.

Nazareth between two books

In 2008 the general public learned that the venerated ancient village of Nazareth was barren at the turn of the era. *The Myth of Nazareth: The Invented Town of Jesus* revealed that no evidence of human habitation has been found there from 'the time of Jesus' and, indeed, that not even a solitary pottery shard from the rocky hillside can be dated with certainty before 100 CE.

The book also showed, for the first time, that numerous tombs surprisingly exist where the mythical village of Nazareth *should have been*. Those tombs are of the *kokh* type, a form of interment dating in the Galilee to no earlier than Middle Roman times. This information is incontrovertible, as is the fact that no habitations have been found where Jesus, Mary, and Joseph reputedly lived.

Shortly after publication of *The Myth of Nazareth*, highly publicized discoveries of Jesus-era dwellings began to take place in Nazareth. The first occurred in December, 2009 at the newly constructed International Marian Center (Chapter 10). "The discovery is of the utmost importance," announced the archeologist Y. Alexandre to global media, "since it reveals for the very first time a house from the Jewish village of Nazareth and thereby sheds light on the way of life at the time of Jesus."

The British archeologist Ken Dark also signaled the discovery of the 'first' house from the time of Jesus at the nearby Sisters of Nazareth Convent (Chapter 6). At the same time, he proposed that the dwelling came first and the on-site tomb succeeded it, thus inferring a new multi-stage model for the ancient village: habitations existed on the hillside at the turn of the era, but they were abandoned as residents moved onto the valley floor (this in the first century CE), and those same residents then built *kokh* tombs on the slope of the Nebi Sa'in and under their former dwellings (above, p. 74).

This book has disposed of that model. Careful review of the documentation reveals multiple contradictions and that a dwelling from the turn of the era could have existed neither at the IMC site nor at the convent site. No evidence of human habitation at Nazareth from 'the time of Jesus' remains, in 2015, the only credible assessment of the data and is not likely to change any time in the future.

As reflected in documents spanning over a hundred years, the history of Nazareth archeology is thoroughly unsatisfactory from the traditional point of view. Indeed, those documents have permitted the conclusion that "not a single post-Iron Age artifact dates with certainty before 100 CE" (Salm 2008a:165, 205). In consequence, the tradition has in the last few years attempted to 'right' the record by augmenting it with what prove to be thoroughly embarrassing and untenable claims. In so doing it has jumped from the frying pan into the fire, for now the world possesses a new documentary record even less defensible than the old. *NazarethGate* is the recognition of a dual reality doubly damning: that the settlement not exist in the 'time of Jesus' *and* that the tradition recognizes no limit to deceit. The mythical existence of Nazareth at the turn of the era has now provoked the mythical invention of walls, roofs, hiding places, Hellenistic coins, and courtyard houses over tombs. From any sensible point of view, the archeology of Nazareth in the last decade has become exponentially more ridiculous. That *bona-fide* archeologists are responsible for this situation simply shows that the entire field is now corrupt beyond redemption.

I would like to present one further example of systemic corruption in the field. In 1999 the Rashidiya School in Nazareth was demolished, prior to developing the area for the papal visit of 2000. In the demolition several ancient structures were exposed. In 2003 the IAA conducted a small excavation at the site. It published a report in *Hadashot Arkheologiyot* in 2009 (online).[40] In researching this book, I noted that the report mentions "a ceramic assortment from the Hellenistic to the Mamluk periods." The itemization gave only one artifact: "a jar (Fig. 4:1) from the Hellenistic period." The accompanying figure was minimally instructive, and I determined to contact the archeologist and question him on this Hellenstic evidence. I did so by email, noting that "The early dating surprises me greatly, because my research has verified no other Hellenistic material from Nazareth." I added: "Unfortunately, the *Hadashot* article does not give very much information on 'Figure 4:1.' There is no description. For example, is this a small piece, or is it the entire jar?" The archeologist soon replied as follows in broken English:

> Dear Rene Salm
>   Thanks for your letter. The Hellenistic shard showing in the publication is a small one and not a complete Jar. We brought it because we don't have a Hellenistic finds at the site. Anyhow, its just one shard.... You can't make from that so much. Best and good lack
>   [Name withheld.]

I was certainly not expecting this most unusual explanation: "We brought it because we don't have a Hellenistic finds at the site." What

---

40.   *http://www.hadashot-esi.org.il/report_detail_eng.asp?id=1132&mag_id=115* (accessed July 12, 2015).

does this mean? I leave the reader to decide, and only remark that we have here—once again—a *published* claim of "Hellenistic" ceramic evidence from the IAA, and yet an assertion by the excavator himself that "we don't have a Hellenistic finds at the site."

In this book we have seen how the IAA has repeatedly withdrawn reports from the Internet, how it has published material evidence that is at variance with statements by the excavator (*e.g.*, above), how it has shared privy information with traditionalist scholars but not with the excavator herself (*cf.* above p. 286), and how it has even produced diametrically opposing reports (*cp.* above pp. 179 and 189; pp. 256 and 291). More egregious than any number of anomalies, however, is the apparent liberty enjoyed by archeologists in the field to interpret data according to doctrinal, commercial, and political agenda which often have nothing to do with the material evidence in the ground. The most reasonable conclusion to be drawn from these pages is that the IAA seems to have an over-arching role in fostering this unsatisfactory state of affairs.

The Myth of Nazareth made the scientific argument that Jesus' hometown did not exist. The settlement was founded about one hundred years after his alleged birth, along with the establishment of other Lower Galilean villages following the debacle of the First Jewish Revolt.

As a sequel, *NazarethGate* strengthens the argument of its predecessor, but in this book we have placed the focus equally on the lack of ancient evidence and on modern behavior. That behavior is irresponsible and, indeed, inexcusable. In defending a collection of myths with sham strategems, those in high places—academic, religious, commercial, and governmental—debase themselves and thereby not only betray the trust they *demand* from society, but forfeit any claim to represent the aspirations of upright and rational human beings everywhere.

Chapter 14

IN SEARCH OF THE REJECTED SEER

Controlling the story

For the last half century Christianity has adopted a defensive posture as regards the archeology of Nazareth. It has been engaged in an extended rearguard action in defence of an iconic story—a protracted attempt to manage the ever rising flood of incoming data, most of it uncongenial. The maturation of the Internet and the general democratization of knowledge are breaking down ancient monopolies over information—from communication, to research, to publication. Demographically, Atheism, humanism, and "free thinking" is on the ascendant in the West. At the same time, the Roman Catholic Church continues to stumble. Pedophile scandals, Vatican Bank irregularities, and a thoroughly opaque administrative mechanism continue to confront an increasingly progressive world. Meanwhile, the Church drags its feet on women's rights, birth control, celibacy, the right to die, and a host of issues which could—if handled differently—actually make it relevant.

Of course, the Roman Catholic Church wields enormous clout. Without an army, it is in a sense still the largest and most powerful state, for it claims the allegiance of more people than any sovereign nation. The Church is also a significant actor in world affairs. Only a few weeks before this writing the Vatican mediated a historic thaw between Cuba and the United States. It still functions as a seasoned (indeed, the *most* seasoned) and valuable political ally behind the scenes.

But the Church's grip on power is not firm. Even at rest its hands shake like those of a doddering old man. He receives deference—sometimes begrudgingly—but the honors to which he was once accustomed are no longer proffered. In many places he is now merely tolerated—and eyed with suspicion (if at all) by those children of the modern world who are much more rational and nimble. Some look on him with burning hostility, knowing his sordid past and how he lorded it over all others when he was in his prime. They may forgive, but they refuse to forget.

The Church lives on tradition. Its survival rests on the ability to control the past, and thereby to control the present. Without the power to monopolize learning, to burn books, to even burn heretics, it now is in the uncomfortable position of depending entirely on people *voluntarily* embracing the faith. That faith is based on a story enshrined in the New Testament, a story in which magic is the principal means of persuasion. The story is now old—and, indeed, it increasingly *seems* old. The wonder-working Son of Man may still inspire awe and veneration among more naïve folk. To many, however, his (alleged) virgin birth, forgiving of sins, walking on water, and resurrection from the grave are simply absurd.

Christianity claims to derive authority, definition, and sustenance from the crucified savior, Jesus Christ. In fact, however, it derives these from a mythology carefully crafted long ago. The Christian religion was born out of parables, paper, and power. It is no accident, no product of some fortuitous constellation of circumstances two thousand years ago. On the contrary. The religion owes its origins—its very success—to the calculation of the bank heist, to the deliberation of the palace coup. Christianity may be many things, but *innocent* is certainly not one of them.

The story *enshrined in scripture* is Christianity's sole remaining weapon. This is not unique, and parallels with Judaism's attempts to control the present through an invented narrative of origins are notable. To attack these narratives—and even to discuss them in terms of myth rather than history—is to attack the underpinnings of both religions. The existence of the Israeli state today is largely a result of the perceived Jewish claim to the land—itself the product of a shared (though far from universal, or even defensible) view of history. At stake is much that is hardly abstract. Israeli tourism garnered $11 billion in 2014, some 4.5% of the country's nominal GDP. Tourism employs 100,000 workers, two-thirds of them in the hotel industry. In short, controlling the story is, in the case of Israel, a simple matter of survival. No patriarchs, no Israel.

Nazareth is ground zero in the Christian narrative of origins. The settlement is more important to the Jesus story than Bethlehem, Capernaum, or even Jerusalem. If Nazareth did not exist at the turn of the era, then the character 'Jesus of Nazareth' immediately falls from the august level of man-god to that of puppet—entirely bypassing the intermediate human (historical) level. With that precipitous fall—the recognition of Jesus' *unreality*—the religion based upon *him* must deflate like a punctured balloon.

Let there be no doubt that Christianity is based upon a unique claim—that God entered history not in an abstract or mystical way familiar to religions in general, but by being *incarnated* in Jesus of Nazareth. Hans Küng has observed that the success of Christianity lies precisely in the historical *reality* of its quintessentially awesome (even miraculous) origins.[1] To deny the historical reality of those origins is to deny Christianity itself:

> It cannot be stated too strongly that Christianity is an historical religion, and that it is so intimately tied to history that if the historical credibility of its sources were to be proven false, it would at once collapse as a possible claimant for our loyalty.   —C. Anderson[2]

Questioning the historical origins of Christianity—as well as of Judaism—depends on access to recondite information now available in primary and secondary source materials, and also on the freedom to investigate. Neither the source materials nor such freedom existed in the past. Questioning the foundations of the Christian faith (including its historical underpinnings) could—and generally did—result in ostracism, imprisonment, excommunication, torture, or even death.

It is no surprise that doubts regarding the historicity of the Nazarene ("Jesus mythicism") are today multiplying precisely when the widespread freedom to investigate intersects with the equally widespread availability of information. This auspicious state of affairs is not merely unprecedented in history—it is a signal triumph of civilization.

During the Dark Ages the Catholic Church was the sole repository of knowledge in Western Europe. For long centuries Christianity carefully fashioned the worldview we have inherited, weeding out what it despised and simply making up what it desired. As a result, the West has inherited a fabricated worldview centered on a carefully constructed myth thoroughly unworthy of the modern mind: Jesus of Nazareth. Monks collected manuscripts, preserved them, and wrote 'history' according to the wishes of their superiors. They copied some few texts, changed more, and destroyed most. Learning was modest and monopolized. It can be no surprise that with the onset of the Dark Ages previous and competing religions fell into the shade—as if nothing else mattered and the world was simply waiting for the arrival of Jesus Christ! In fact, this is still what many Christians believe.

Regrettably, censorship is not reversible. Once books are burned, once the slate is erased, precious knowledge is *gone*, in some cases forever—or at least until reason and science laboriously *re-invent* the wheel.

The enormous wealth of ancient civilizations has been lost, and the loss is not at all limited to the sciences. The so-called "mystery religions"

---

1. I am indebted to H. Detering (2011:185) for this reference.
2. Anderson 1972:55.

are today little more than an enigma. Two thousand years ago the goal of every aspiring Roman was to become initiated into secret knowledge—to become *transformed* through gnosis. Such transformation was freely available to all but actually claimed (or accomplished) by few, in various forms, rites, and places. It carried the promise and potential of becoming *divine*. This view—so bizzarre to us moderns—is in fact as old as civilization. People *were* divine until materialism cheapened man's noble *spiritual* worldview. After all, what is there to live for, if metal and clay are all there is?

In the Sumerian epic of *Atrahasis* ("Ultra-Wise") we read of the transformation of man into God. Atrahasis seeks as a mere mortal. He finds, transforms into a divinity, and forevermore inhabits the lofty heights of Mt. Hermon. In another recension Gilgamesh seeks the wisdom of immortality at the distant "Cedar Mountain"—which was also successively Baal's abode (Mount Zaphon), the place where the Watchers came down to earth (1 Enoch 6:6), and the mount where Jesus was transfigured (Mk 9:2–8).

The rite of transformation enacted at Dan—located at the foot of Mt. Hermon—was a symbolic *water* ritual: the initiate entered the sacred water and there mingled with the gods, emerging purified (Lucian, *De Dea Syria*, 46–47). Water has been a symbol for gnosis since earliest times—another lost concept. Long ago, immersion in gnosis was the prerequisite for transformation. The symbolism vaguely survives in the Christian rite of baptism—deracinated, of course, of its gnostic essence. It is no coincidence that John baptized in the River Jordan—the sacred river emerging from Mt. Hermon itself.

Sooner or later, those who enquire into the origins of Christianity uncover unfamiliar, even unknown roots. This was originally a mystery religion concerned with formidable seeking, with life-changing gnosis, with self-transformation as the reward of extreme effort. *That* severe religion can still be detected in a few sayings of Jesus and in certain parables. Finding through seeking, giving one's all, and loving one's enemies are teachings that cannot have begun with an *invented* figure. They must have predated Jesus of Nazareth.

Christianity as we know it is no longer about seeking and finding, loving one's enemies, and giving one's all, but is about belief in the savior from Galilee. Thus, we venerate the finger that points—an invented finger at that. The new religion retained a few older rites, known from the mystery religions, but those rites were now geared to propagating the faith. Baptism no longer consecrated the symbolic descent into *gnosis* but marked initiation into a fellowship. The old spirituality of transformation became a new code of allegiance:

In the name of the Christian community I *claim* you for Christ our Savior
by the sign of his cross.

The above words lie at the heart of the modern Christian baptismal
rite. They are the *public* acknowledgment of ownership, belonging, and allegiance. Spiritual transformation has disappeared. As the emphasis moved
from *transformation* to *belonging* the ancient world quietly passed away, to
be replaced by a much colder materialism. Accomplishment gave way to
membership, as the 'proclamation' (*kerygma*) of 'good news' echoed from
village to village: those who believe are saved by the atoning death of Jesus
Christ, *and no other salvation exists, ever did, and ever will.* This proclamation,
first enunciated by Paul, became the backbone of a New World Order still
regent today.

But the proclamation is false. In this book we have brought forward
one proof: Nazareth did not exist 'in the time of Jesus.' Additional proofs
for the non-existence of the Prophet from Galilee also exist, and we will
explore some of them in the remaining pages of this chapter.

We have compared Jesus of Nazareth to a great puppet. Those who
pull the strings—as they have through the ages—are the liliputian priests,
prelates, and pastors of myriad churches. In their hands the puppet teaches, he heals, he raises from the dead, he rises from the dead, and he warns
(pre-mortem and post-mortem) that only *he* has the authority and power to
judge *our* souls in the end times. Fear and awe cow us into worshipping the
Great Puppet from Nazareth.

And maybe that's the whole point.

An early gnostic prophet

We have described two stages in the religion: (1) a gnostic pre-Christian
stage in which salvation is the product of man's effort; and (2) a subsequent
proclamation in which salvation is produced by faith in the Son of God,
Jesus. The former stage is man-centered, the latter God-centered. The former is a religion of achievement, the latter of redemption. The former
requires effort ('works'), the other allegiance ('faith'). Both preach salvation,
but they define the concept very differently.

Issuing from the same root, these two distinct religious systems have
opposed one another through the centuries. The orthodox view—salvation
by faith in Jesus Christ—gained the upper hand in Late Roman times and
soon branded its gnostic parent 'heresy.'

Signs of the earlier stage exist. Some are controversial, such as the
view that the gnostic system now called Mandeism preceded Christianity
(Lidzbarski, Bultmann), even as John the Baptist (the 'light-bringer' of the
Mandeans) preceded Jesus (ironically, the 'anti-Christ' of the Mandeans).

Even in the earliest stratum of the New Testament we encounter signs of an earlier view. Thus, for example, in the Letter to the Philippians (attributed to Paul but in fact a second century Marcionite work), we find an old gnostic hymn in which a spiritual entity descends into the world of matter, experiences humility and death, and then returns to the godhead (Phil 2:6–11).[3] That entity is named *Jesus* ("Salvation") *after* its successful mission is accomplished. The name is an honorific, the reward for a job well done. The naming could hardly have occurred post-mortem if "Jesus" had already possessed the name when a human being and *before* his task was accomplished. Robert M. Price observes:

> As P. L. Couchoud recognized, the hymn predates the process of re-conceiving the god Jesus as a historical figure since "Jesus" becomes his name *only after his earthly mission is complete*. Those who first sang this hymn never thought of a man named Jesus traveling the roads of Galilee, teaching and casting out demons, much less getting crucified on earth at a Roman governor's order.[4]

We may grant that the writer of this gnostic hymn had no knowledge of the Galilean prophet, Jesus of Nazareth. However, if "Jesus" was a received name "only after his earthly mission" was complete, does this not imply an earthly existence at some point in time? And if so, then *who* was the man thus *renamed*?

Of course, we don't know. It is little appreciated, however, that this complete ignorance may have been carefully abetted—even fostered—from the start. If another prophet actually existed, *his* authentic biography would serve to *undermine* the false biography of Jesus of Nazareth—point for point. Those who knew the prophet of history (and there would certainly have been many) would be on hand to give the lie: "I knew him and he wasn't at all like *Jesus of Nazareth*!" (Or: "My grandfather knew him..." *etc.*) Memories last a long time, and memories of unique people longer still. Hence, the Gospel of Mark adopts what we call the 'Messianic Secret'—

---

3. All that is required for this to become the adoptionist view of Christology is that the spirit 'adopts' a human being in order to sojourn on earth. According to Paul, such adoption is open to all those in the flesh who are predestined and "called" to enjoy the status of "many brothers" in Christ (Rom 8:28–29). This early view—which admits a creator God but knows no unique savior figure in human form, and which is "the end and vocation of all men" (Conybeare, *The Key of Truth*, Oxford 1898:vii)—would spawn numerous 'heresies' such as the Paulicians, whose name cannot be entirely coincidental. Already the evangelist Mark repudiates this semi-universalist view, however: Jesus is indeed adopted, but he is now unique, and thus the way to self-perfection (through gnosis or any other path) is forever closed.

4. Price 2012:460. The internal reference is to P. L. Couchoud, "The Historicity of Jesus: A Reply to Alfred Loisy," *Hibbert Journal*, vol, 37, no. 2 (1938):193–214.

those who knew Jesus in his lifetime (the apostles) *didn't understand* him at all. As the Fourth Gospel puts it, Jesus *really* came for "those who have not seen and yet believe" (Jn 20:29). The Church Fathers, too, will combat the mythicist view that Jesus of Nazareth was a fiction, that is, that he didn't exist in the flesh—a view among the ancients that scholars today ignore by conveniently stuffing it into the category 'docetism' (see below).

Paul did not yet know Jesus of Nazareth, as we will now argue. His view of the savior characterized an earlier and fairly universal stage in the religion, namely, that 'Jesus' was a purely *spiritual* entity.

Jesus of Nazareth was unknown to "Paul"

Pauline studies are presently in a state of considerable flux. Even traditionalist scholars admit that some of the epistles are pseudepigraphic. Scholars also generally consider that the Pauline corpus of thirteen New Testament letters represents a pastiche of views from different people, times, and places. The most radical view is that *none* of the attributed letters is by Paul, and even that Paul himself did not exist as a historical figure (H. Detering, R. Price, the Dutch Radical School). As Price writes:

> Prostestantism is based on Martin Luther, and Luther's theology is based on Paul, but Paul stands based on nothing at all. Paul does not have a unitary voice, is not a single author whose implied opinions might be synthesized and parroted. He is not even a single historical figure. He is certainly not a divine apostle who received his gospel, not from man nor through men, but directly from God one climactic day on his way to Damascus. That story, as we saw, is pure fiction, based on 2 Maccabees and Euripides's *Bacchae*.[5]

I am inclined to agree with this assessment. But even if Paul (I use the name for convenience) did not exist as a "single historical figure," and even if none of the epistles were written by the Apostle to the Gentiles, the Pauline corpus still manifestly *exists*. It dates from Middle Roman times (probably produced by Marcionites in the second century—*cf.* below p. 437), and from it we can extract a good deal of information.

First of all, it can be noted that the Pauline epistles do not know "Jesus of Nazareth." The words *Nazara, Nazareth, Nazarene,* or *Nazorean* do not appear even once in the entire corpus. Such silence can now be partially explained: Nazareth did not come into existence until *c.* 100 CE.

Secondly, there are many indications in the Pauline corpus that "Jesus" is not a man but a spirit. Admittedly, a few probably late Catholicizing amendments (*e.g.* Col 2:9; Phil 2:7; 1 Cor 15: 3 *f*) seem to have countered the predominant docetist conception of "Jesus" in Paul's writings. Hence,

5. Price 2012:535.

a blanket statement is not possible. This once again brings up the pronounced *pastiche* aspect of the corpus—Paul's epistles are all things to all people, and "Paul" himself is apparently all people to all Christians.

The predominant view described in Paul's writings is that "Jesus" is a *spiritual entity* that has the ability to *spiritually* save. Paul indeed learned from "Jesus," yet what he learned was "not of *human* origin" (Gal 1:11). This is an indication (whether or not the Damascus conversion actually occurred) that Paul's "Jesus" was not human.

Paul enthuses in his epistles about the spiritual entity he calls singly and severally the "Lord," "Jesus," and "Christ." The entity grants grace, peace, comfort, authority (2 Cor 10:8), will slay the "lawless one" at the Last Judgment, and will save those who "love the truth" (2 Thess 2:10). Most importantly, the entity has the power to overcome death (see below).

In Paul's conception, the spiritual "Christ Jesus" has an intimate relation to the godhead (Col 3:1). It is pre-existent and eternal just like God. Indeed, it is ever-present, for Paul himself preaches at any moment "through the Lord Jesus" (1 Thess 4:2). At the same time, Christ is in Paul and in every saint (Col 1:27). This correspondence between saints and Christ Jesus results in the conception that the body of Jesus is, in fact, none other than the Church.[6] In fact, when Christ comes in glory, those who are a part of his body "will appear with him in glory" (Col 3:4).

In sum, the Lord Jesus Christ is a great, expansive spiritual being which merges with the lives of the saints so that they are absorbed into it. It is our job to "rise up" to that spirit (Phil 3:12 *f*) and to partake in its being—that is, to be "saved." For Paul, only the spirit Jesus can *resurrect* from death. This is the true victory, and by uniting with that spirit we also can overcome death. Thus, baptism for Paul is a passage *through* death—a transformation. Incidentally, this conception is very close to that which obtained in the mystery religions of the age—it would not have been at all foreign to a Greek or a Roman of the time.

The efficacy of the spirit of Jesus is precisely that it is able to resurrect from death (1 Cor 15:12)—that is, it is able to render physical death *of no account* (1 Cor 15:51 *f*). Let us pause to consider this logic, for here is the Pauline conception of resurrection. To render death of no account is (effectively) not to "die" at all. Because the spirit of Jesus lives on with God *after* death, it automatically overcomes death—*if one unites with it*. This is the Pauline view of salvation. Either unite with the spirit Jesus—or perish.

---

6. 1 Cor 12:27; Eph 1:22–23, 4:12; Col 1:18, 24. The evangelist Mark will emphatically repudiate this universalist Pauline position. In a revolutionary leap, Mark reassigns "Jesus" to a single man from Galilee who is both "Son of Man" and "Son of God." Those (Paulines) who continued to view Jesus as a purely cosmic spiritual entity were now "false Christs" (Mk 13:6, 22) of a gnostic ilk. *Cf.* Weeden 1971:86–100.

This is why, in Paul's conception, one can be walking about in the body and yet have already "died" inwardly (that is, spiritually—Col 2:20). Thus,one is already "raised" (Col 3:1). All this takes place in the flesh if one has united spiritually with Jesus.

This concept is referred to as "realized eschatology": the resurrection is not at the end times, but has already taken place within the gnostic, and during this very life. Consequently, many gnostic texts from late antiquity report on events that occur in the time between the resurrection and the as-cension. This does not refer to a time after the bodily resurrection of Jesus from the grave (as *secondarily* depicted in the canonical gospels). It refers to a time after the resurrection of 'the Jesus' *within oneself*—and while the gnos-tic is still walking on the earth. Thus, the post-resurrection "era" depends upon the situation of each individual gnostic. It is relative.

If, as is generally suspected, a Jewish Christian stage preceded the for-mation of the Hellenist Christian church, then one could expect this early belief in an immaterial Jesus to also have existed among Jewish Christians. This is precisely what we find:

> For certain Jewish Christians, the word *Jesus* would not have been the name of an earthly person, but rather the title of a ce-lestial being. The Greek 'ΙΗΣΟΥΣ [*Jesus*] is the equivalent of the Aramaic or Hebrew ישוע (*Yeshuaʿ*), which means *savior*. Thus, it was not Jesus of Nazareth in whom they believed, but a heavenly Sav-ior. It is likely that gnostic treatises such as *Dialogue of the Savior* bear witness to communities that did not interpret either the Greek *Iesous* or the Aramaic *Yeshuaʿ* as the name of a man, but rather as a title—*The Savior.*   —Zindler 2003:85 (note)

The foregoing must seem strange to Christians today because it is not at all what one reads in the canonical gospels. This shows that the religion as we know it is not based on pre-canonical traditions, including Paul. Cen-tral to normative Christianity is Jesus of Nazareth—*a figure Paul did not yet know.* In the canonical gospels one reads of the adventures (for lack of a better term) of Jesus of Nazareth, of *his* death, and of *his* (bodily!) resurrec-tion from the grave. This does not at all cohere with Pauline theology. The canonical gospels represent a *subsequent* stage, one centered not around the spiritual Jesus but around a manufactured hybrid, the divine man (Gk. *theios anêr*) Jesus of Nazareth—the only-*begotten* Son of God.

The insight that the New Testament epistles had no knowledge of Je-sus of Nazareth—apparently broached here for the first time—will, if true, require a wholesale reassessment of the 'Pauline' writings. Much that has heretofore seemed strange, or even mysterious, gains clarity. One example is the frequent Pauline use of *kata sarka*, a phrase which both E. Doherty and R. Carrier have pointed out is odd as commonly translated: "according to the flesh." For, as Carrier writes:[7]

> The preposition *kata* with the accusative literally means "down" or "down to" and implies motion, usually over or through its object, hence it literally reads "down through flesh" or "down to flesh" or even "towards flesh." It very frequently, by extension, means "at" or "in the regions of," and this is how Doherty reads it... The word *kata* can also have a comparative meaning, "corresponding with, after the fashion of," in other words "like flesh."

This perfectly describes the foregoing discussion of a great spirit Jesus that *descends* (figuratively or literally) to merge with the saints and 'absorb' them, not *becoming* flesh so much as abiding for a time "in the regions of" flesh—which now appears something like a curtain separating man from god. The Pauline writings portray the spirit as withdrawing (resurrecting) again back to the godhead *with* the spirits of the saints who, as a result, have been 'raised.' Essentially, this stratagem of the spirit describes a species of robbery in reverse: giving life by coming down and *taking* it.

While Doherty has perceived the spiritual aspect of Jesus, he argues that the suffering and crucifixion were entirely in the spiritual realm. However, this chapter will present a somewhat different view: a man indeed suffered and died *on earth*—a man first thought to have been *possessed by Jesus*.

Quite apart from questions regarding the evolving nature of 'Jesus' in New Testament scripture is the critical observation that the Pauline writings betray no knowledge of Jesus of Nazareth. If this be admitted—as it must—then a theological chasm emerges dividing the earlier epistles from the later gospels. With the existence of that chasm comes an astonishing recognition: the 'Pauline' epistles are not *Christian* in any commonly accepted sense of the term today. This can be rephrased as a question: Is it possible to be a Christian without faith in Jesus of Nazareth, *the* Son of God?

The chronological implications are also great. If the Pauline writings date from the early to mid-second century CE—as is increasingly suspected—then the canonical gospels, being *later*, date at the earliest to *c.* 150 CE. Thus the *Gospel of Mark*—the first canonical presentation of Jesus of Nazareth[8]—dates an entire century later than traditionally thought, shifting from *c.* 65 CE to *c.* 165 CE. Such a shift, if valid, would have revolutionary implications for Jesus studies.

---

7. Carrier's discussion is found online and in Doherty 2009:162.

8. J. Crossan has identified possible precursors to the Gospel of Mark in the Jesus tradition. These include the "Cross Gospel" (embedded in the Gospel of Peter) and some surviving fragments of lost gospels. See Crossan, *The Historical Jesus: The Life of a Mediterranean Jewish Peasant*. New York: HarperCollins 1991:Appendix 1.

A human being

The Epistle to the Hebrews. It was stated above that "the Lord Jesus Christ is a great, expansive spiritual being which merges with the lives of the saints so that they are absorbed into it." This merging requires not only a divine spirit but also human saints. It is the human aspect of this merging which allows the authors of the New Testament epistles to write of the "blood of Christ," the "suffering of Jesus," and so on.

The pattern for this fusion of divine and human was evidently perceived as historical. The author of the *Epistle to the Hebrews* (certainly not the same person who authored the other epistles) knows of a man "made perfect," one who was "heard" because of his devotion (*eulabeias*) to suffering (5:7–9). That saintly man belonged to the tribe of Judah (7:14), was tempted, found to be without sin, crucified (6:6), and thus became (now in heaven) "a high priest according to the order of Melchizedek." He "passed through the heavens" to be henceforth "Jesus, the Son of God" (4:14–15, 5:10; 8:1b). It is evident in this multi-stage conception that we begin with (1) a man exemplary in holiness, who (2) suffers, and (3) is "heard," who (4) is spiritually elevated to the status of "High Priest" in heaven, and (5) is subsequently known as "Jesus, the Son of God."[9]

A human being is clearly intended by the words, "In the days of his flesh, he offered up prayers and supplication, with loud cries and tears..." (5:7). We learn further that the prophet (as he will be called here) "shed his own blood, thus obtaining eternal redemption" (Heb 9:12). Hence his high priesthood is superior to the Temple cult where only "goats and calves" are sacrificed. The prophet offered himself "through the eternal spirit" (9:14) and thus became the mediator who enables others to be saved. The actual mechanism of salvation is spelled out at 9:15:

> [H]e is the mediator of a new covenant, so that those who are called may receive the promised eternal inheritance, because a death has occurred that redeems them from the transgressions under the first covenant.

Thus, the *Epistle to the Hebrews* portrays a redeemed redeemer. Perhaps the most astonishing element—and what separates it irrevocably from Judaism—is that the prophet *fuses* with his redeemer. He *becomes* part of Jesus, the spiritual savior, and thus part of the godhead. More correctly, he is subsumed into the godhead. Absorbed. The man is not important, for everything human seems to disappear (including his earthly biography). In the *Epistle to the Hebrews* he is called the "Christ"—a fusion of the spiritual

---

9. The critical aspect that separates this theology from the gnostic outlook is that the agency is with God, not man. That is, man unaided does not save himself (Heb 8:2b). He must be "heard" and thus saved.

Jesus with the holy man of god. Evidently, the theology of the author of Hebrews was sufficiently advanced that even when the prophet was in the flesh he could be referred to as "Jesus"—for he had already been completely co-opted by the spiritual Jesus. In fact, only in this way could the spiritual Jesus have been the "pioneer and perfecter of our faith" who "endured the cross" (12:2), who "suffered outside the city gate" (13:12), and who was "brought back from the dead" (13:20).

The redeemed is assimilated to the redeemer. The holy one is "heard" from on high (5:7) and is able to conquer death. That conquest is then vicariously transferred to others who believe in this mechanism of salvation. They also become redeemed and assimilated to the great redeemer, Jesus.

J. Painter detects a very similar view in the *First Apocalypse of James*, a gnostic text discovered at Nag Hammadi:

> In the opening set of dialogues the Lord foretells his passion and the suffering and death of James. This is the gnostic assimilation of the motif of the redeemer and the redeemed. In 24.19–24 the Lord identifies himself with the unnameable One Who Is in the beginning, and James is told that, through casting away the bond of flesh and ascending to Him Who Is, he will no longer be James but the One Who Is (27.1–10). James thus returns to the place from when he came. The crucifixion of Jesus and the death of James are treated as complementary...[10]

The spirit Jesus lowered itself "for a little while" (Heb 2:9) by fusing with a particularly holy man. It will become apparent that the holy man in question may well have been known to history. For now, however, we merely observe that the spirit Jesus "shared the same things [that is, a corporeal body], so that through death it might destroy the one who has the power of death, that is, the devil, and free those who all their lives were held in slavery by the fear of death" (2:14–15).

We read that Christ ("anointed") "gave his own blood, thus obtaining eternal redemption" (9:12), and that Christ "sat down at the right hand of God" (10:12). Thus, it appears that "Christ" and "Jesus" are synonymous in *Hebrews*, though an original distinction may well have obtained between the two terms. Christ "through the eternal spirit offered himself without blemish" (9:14). Is "the eternal spirit" here *Jesus*?

The impression, then, is that Jesus Christ and the earthly prophet were for a brief time one and the same, in the sense that the spirit of God took on human attributes. Referring to that short time, the writer of *Hebrews* can speak of the "*blood* of Jesus" and "his *flesh*" as if those physical, human properties are somehow light and insubstantial, like the Temple "curtain" (10:19–20).

---

10. Painter 2004:171.

The original sacrificial act of the spiritual Jesus alone is efficacious. That spirit 'came down' and fused with the holy man of God. It is the energy of the spiritual Jesus which *raised* the man to the status of Christ the High Priest (5:5) and which enabled him to overcome death. The spiritual Jesus *perfected* the man (5:9).[11]

In the same way, the spiritual Jesus Christ can raise others. We can all become High Priests, as implied in the statement "*Every* High Priest *chosen from among mortals is put in charge...*" (5:1). Here God once again is the agent. We can become High Priests and join the eternal High Priest (7:24). We can even become divine—if we are "chosen" (or "predestined").[12]

The other New Testament epistles. The remaining epistles also contain references to a human prophet. The reader is reminded that we are not primarily concerned here with "authenticity." As mentioned above, even if some of the passages are interpolations, Catholicizing glosses, *etc.*, their content still merits scrutiny as first–second century CE writings. *Any* echo of a human prophet in these epistles is of considerable interest to us, for we have already established that such a prophet was *not* Jesus of Nazareth.[13]

(1) Rom 1:1–4:

> Paul, a servant of Jesus Christ, called to be an apostle, set apart for the gospel of God which he promised beforehand through his prophets in the holy scriptures, the gospel concerning his son, who was descended from David *according to the flesh* and designated Son of God in power *according to the spirit of holiness* by his resurrection from the dead, Jesus Christ our lord...

(2) Rom 8:1–4:

> There is therefore now no condemnation for those who are in Christ Jesus. For the law of the spirit of life in Christ Jesus has set me free from the law of sin and death. For God has done what the law, weakened by the flesh, could not do: *sending his own son in the likeness of sinful flesh* and for sin, he condemned sin in the flesh, in order that the just requirement of the law might be fulfilled in us, who walk not according to the flesh but according to the spirit.

---

11. Even the most scholarly English translations of the epistles (*e.g.* the NRSV) are, unfortunately, not faithful to the Greek text. Often, "Jesus" or "Christ" is supplied where "he" is written. Thus critical distinctions found in the underlying Greek are often lost in translations.

12. The un-gnostic view of predestination is also familiar from the Dead Sea Scriptures (see below, p. 463).

13. Above, pp. 406 *f.* In the following passages, all emphases (in italics) are added.

(3) Rom 9:3–5:

> For I could wish that I myself were accursed and cut off from Christ for the sake of my brethren, my kinsmen by race. They are Israelites, and to them belong the sonship, the glory, the covenants, the giving of the law, the worship, and the promises; to them belong the patriarchs, *and of their race, according to the flesh, is the Christ.*

(4) Gal 4:4–5:

> Then in the fullness of time, god sent his son, *born of woman, born under the law*, in order that he might purchase freedom for the subjects of the law, so that we might attain the status of sons.

(5) Eph 2:13–16:

> But now in Christ Jesus you who once were far off have been brought near in *the blood of Christ.* For he is our peace, who has made us both one, and has broken down the dividing wall of hostility, by abolishing *in his flesh* the law of commandments and ordinances, that he might create in himself one new man in place of the two, so making peace, and might reconcile us both to God in one body *through the cross*, thereby bringing the hostility to an end.

(6) Phil 2:5–8:

> Have this in mind among yourselves, which is yours in Christ Jesus, who, though he was in the form of God, did not count equality with god a thing to be grasped, but emptied himself, taking the form of a servant, *being born in the likeness of men. And being found in human form he humbled himself and became obedient unto death, even death on a cross.*

(7) Col 1:21–22:

> And you, who once were estranged and hostile in mind, doing evil deeds, he has now reconciled *in his body of flesh by his death*, in order to present you holy and blameless and irreproachable before him...

(8) 1 Tim 3:16:

> Without any doubt, the mystery of our religion is great: He was *revealed in flesh*, vindicated in spirit, seen by angels, proclaimed among Gentiles, believed in throughout the world, taken up in glory.

(9) 1 Pet 2:23–24:

> When he was abused, he did not return abuse; when he suffered, he did not threaten; but he entrusted himself to the one who judges justly. *He himself bore our sins in his body on the tree*, so that, free from sins, we might live for righteousness; by his bruise you have been healed.

(10) 1 Pet 3:18:

> For Christ also suffered for sins once for all, the righteous for the unrighteous, in order to bring you to God. *He was put to death in the flesh*, but made alive in the spirit...

(11) 1 Pet 4:1–2:

> *Since therefore Christ suffered in the flesh*, arm yourselves also with the same intention (for whoever has suffered in the flesh has finished with sin), so as to live for the rest of your time in the flesh no longer by human desires but by the will of God.

In summary, the New Testament epistles know a redemptive act in *history*, one brought about by the godhead. A *great, expansive spiritual being*—part of God and known variously as the Lord/Jesus/Christ but also as God's son (Rom 1:4, 9, 8:3, etc.)—merged at some point in history with a 'saint'— *a human being of exemplary character*. This merging (or fusion, or indwelling of the godhead), which occurred in the past, will serve as a perpetual model for the rest of us. It is our job to likewise "rise up" to the spirit (Phil 3:12 *f*) and to partake in its being—that is, to be "saved."

At the same time, none of the above passages betrays any specific knowledge of this 'suffering redeemer.' No details of his earthly life survived—not even in antiquity. The writer(s) of the Pauline epistles had access to virtually no information regarding his earthly life. It is also eminently possible that the facts of the prophet's biography were (somewhere along the line) actively suppressed. This would certainly have been the case if his teachings were somehow execrable to his *Jewish* milieu.

We are thus inexorably led to a view mooted by some scholars, namely, that the prophet in question lived in the distant past for those writing in antiquity. He was not a recent figure, not even someone whom 'oral tradition' could recall. A century ago Arthur Drews signaled this possibility:

> Either the Pauline Epistles are genuine, and in that case Jesus is not an historical personality; or he is an historical personality, and in that case the Pauline Epistles are not genuine, but written at a much later period. This later period would have no difficulty in raising to the sphere of deity a man of former times who was known to it only by a vague tradition.[14]

Robert Price notes that "Robertson is especially close to Drews when he defines the alternatives this way":

> It does not indeed follow that Paul's period was what the tradition represents. The reasonable inference from his doctrine is that his Jesus was either a mythic construction or a mere tradition, a remote figure said to have been crucified, but no longer historically traceable. If Paul's

---

14. Drews 1912:117.

Jesus, as is conceivable, be merely a nominal memory of the slain Jesus ben Pandira of the Talmud (about 100 B.C.), Paul himself may belong to an earlier period than that traditionally assigned to him... The only conclusion open is that the teaching of Jesus of the gospels is wholly a construction of the propagandists of the cult, even as is [Jesus] the wonder-working God.[15]

Docetism

Our deliberations regarding the fleshly existence (and non-existence) of Jesus inevitably raises issues modern scholarship has labeled "docetist." The word derives from the Greek *dokein*, "to seem." However, the category is strictly modern, and—it is here suggested—is misleading. *Docetism* is defined as the belief "that Christ had not come in the flesh," and that he only "seemed to have a physical body."[16] Contemporary mythicists also use the term this way: docetism is "the position that Jesus only *seemed* to be an actual man" (Doherty), and "the belief that Jesus did not have a physical body" (Price).[17] The problem is that a clear distinction is not made in these definitions between "Jesus" and "Jesus of Nazareth." Mainline scholarship admits no distinction, but the foregoing pages have shown that a great distinction indeed exists. Until the invention of the prophet from Nazareth, "Jesus" was a purely spiritual entity—one originally associated with gnosis. In a transitional stage, gnosis was ascribed not to man but to God, requiring its descent and merging with a particular saint, as seems to be described in the Pauline epistles. That saint is a human exemplar. *He* is not inimitable, but his role as lynchpin of history may be. That saintly "forerunner" (Heb 6:20) could also (rather imprecisely) be referred to as "Jesus."

Those who invented Jesus of Nazareth in the second century modified this transitional view. They transferred "the saint" to Jesus of Nazareth, retaining his uniqueness as lynchpin of history. But now Jesus *is* inimitable—only he has seen the Father, he is the "door," and no one comes to the Father except through him (Jn 6:46, 10:7, 14:6). As such, Jesus of Nazareth breaks direct communication between man and God. Only Jesus can confer salvation ("the Jesus").

Unfortunately, the word "docetic" does not discriminate between the above stages. There were those (stage 1) who believed that the 'savior' (Jesus/Ieshua) had no body. To simply call them "docetists" is insufficient, because it confuses them with others, including with ancient mythicists who denied that *Jesus of Nazareth* existed and/or that he was some other figure (Celsus supposed that Jesus' father was a Roman soldier named Pantera).

---

15. Robertson 1911:237. Cited at Price 2011:372.
16. IDB I.860.
17. Doherty 2009:210; Price 2012:146.

The various stages of docetism can be summarized as follows:

Stage 1: The 'savior' (Jesus/Ieshua) is the abstract gnosis. It has no material body. (This is 'Primary Gnosticism' and requires neither God nor a redeemer.)   [Until *c.* 50 BCE]

Stage 2: The savior/gnosis is associated with "God." It comes down and merges with one or more saints. The savior has no material body except what it "puts on" while *temporarily* inhabiting the saint(s) below. (This stage describes the Dead Sea Scrolls, Jamesian theology, and the 'Pauline' epistles.) [*C.* 50 BCE–*c.* 150 CE]

Stage 3: The savior, now associated with God, is divorced from gnosis. It assumes the material body of Jesus the Nazarene (Gospel of Mark)[18] and Jesus of Nazareth (Gospels of Matthew, Luke, John). This is the basis of normative Christianity. Ancient Jesus mythicists who affirmed the *invention* of Jesus of Nazareth would have used docetic-like terms in rejecting this stage: "He didn't walk on earth," *etc.* [Mid-second century CE.]

Stage 4: Later gnostics assimilated the Catholic figure of Jesus while retaining gnostic theology: Jesus of Nazareth was a 'phantom,' without a material body, *etc.* This is a fusion of Stages 2 and 3 above.[19]   [Later second century CE.]

Unfortunately, scholarship uses the term "docetic" only for stage 4. It does not recognize the preceding three stages. To broaden the discussion and include those other stages, of course, very much threatens the traditional view. Such a broadening admits the possibility that there were people in the first Christian centuries who actually denied the existence of Jesus of Nazareth altogether (stage 3). I would suggest, in fact, that the vast majority of references in the Church Fathers to "those who deny the existence of Jesus" are to ancient Jesus mythicists (not references to those who maintained he was a phantom). Such mythicists certainly existed. Memories are long— particularly memories of unique people. Those in Palestine would have had cause to object that neither they, nor their parents, nor their grandparents had recollections of a figure strutting about the Galilean-Judean countryside performing miracles, gathering followers, and generally awing the entire world. Roman records also betray no evidence of such a prophet. At the same time, the educated would immediately have been skeptical. Common sense would have told them that the astounding claims regarding the Christian Jesus were preposterous.

---

18.   In the "adoptionist" Gospel of Mark this fusion occurs at Jesus' baptism.

19.   R. Price devotes an entire chapter to the widespread ancient view that the divine sometimes took on human form but not materiality. (Price 2012:131–71.)

Clues to a lost teacher

It was mentioned above (p. 407) that the false biography of Jesus of Nazareth came with the necessity to obliterate all competing biographies. That necessity would be particularly pressing if a biography enjoyed the high ground of truth—that is, if another story *actually took place*. Any reference to such a biography would automatically include a severe indictment: Jesus of Nazareth is an invention. Psychology teaches that guilt breeds fear, aggression, and sometimes neurotic defensiveness. If Jesus of Nazareth was an invented figure, we can surmise that *all* traces pointing to the historical teacher/prophet were expunged from the record as soon as possible.

But clues remain. They are garbled almost beyond recognition, now scattered among disparate and very little known texts. Unfortunately (as they presently survive) it cannot be supposed that the clues are compatible one with another or point to a single well-defined figure of history. Nevertheless, they may have done so at some time in the past.

The paths leading to these texts are themselves largely hidden—especially to New Testament academics who all too often don blinders of orthodoxy and summarily equate what is off the beaten path with 'error.' They cannot go where we must now proceed.

Yeshu in Jewish writings

The reader perhaps may say "But, if Jesus Christ was born in the first year of our era, and Jeshu was born ninety years before, how can they have been one and the same person?" To which we reply, that there is no proof of Jesus Christ having been born in the first year of our era, and many indications to the contrary. Christian chronology has been arbitrarily established. There was great uncertainty among the early Christians, who reckoned like all Roman subjects from the reign of the Caesars, not only as to the birth, but also as to the age of their savior. Irenaeus, the first Christian father who mentions the four gospels, maintains that Jesus was fifty years old at his death, and the chronology of Luke is absolutely inconsistent with Roman history, as well as being at variance with that of Matthew.

—G. W. Foote and J. Wheeler, *The Jewish Life of Christ: Being the Sepher Toldoth Jeshu*. London: Progressive Publ. Co., 1885, "Preface." (Republished in Zindler 2003, Appendix A.)

The most accessible clues pointing to a prophet behind Christianity who is *not* Jesus of Nazareth are found in Rabbinic writings. The Mishna and Talmud preserve numerous (understandably antagonistic) references to the founder of Christianity. As Frank Zindler has shown,[20] none of these

---

20. Zindler 2003 is the most comprehensive treatment of the subject. For bibliography, see his pp. 469–77.

preserve historical value regarding a Jesus of Nazareth. He writes that the "only clear references to the Jesus of Christianity" are those relating to a certain Yeshu ha-Notsri (Zindler 2003:248). But this Yeshu lived in the time of Alexander Janneus (early first century BCE) and obviously has nothing at all to do with the New Testament Jesus.[21] In fact, we will see that Jewish writings are surprisingly uniform in dating "Jesus" to this earlier time.

The most remarkable passage may be Sanhedrin 107b (partly cited below). There we read of the Pharisaic head (nasi) of the Sanhedrin, Joshua ben Perachiah who, during an unsuccessful Pharisaic uprising against Janneus fled to Alexandria with a number of disciples. We know that the uprising began in 94 BCE and lasted six years. It culminated in the infamous mass execution (by crucifixion) of 800 Pharisees by Janneus.[22] The king then placed Sadducees in positions of power.

One of the pupils/protégés of Perachiah was Yeshu ha-Notsri.[23] On the return trip to Israel Yeshu was excommunicated by Perachiah on the grounds of lasciviousness (for interpreting an equivocal remark in a sexual way). We can surmise that the return trip took place *after* the death of Janneus, when his wife and the Pharisee-friendly Salome Alexandra began her reign. There is very good reason Alexandra was friendly to the Pharisees: her own brother, Simon ben Shetach, was a leading Pharisee. He had been in hiding during the persecution but, on the death of Janneus, sent for Perachiah to return from Alexandria. A glorious few years ensued for the Pharisees—remembered by them as a golden age. On the death of Perachiah, Shetach became *nasi*.

The Talmud records the figurative but joyous words with which ben Shetach advised Perachiah to return to Jerusalem:

> What of R. Jehoshua ben Perachiah? When Jannai the king killed our rabbis, R. Jehoshua ben Perachiah fled to Alexandria of Egypt. When there was peace, Shimon ben Shetach sent to him, "From me the city of holiness, to thee Alexandria of Egypt. My husband stays in thy midst and I sit forsaken." —b. Sanh. 107b.[24]

The return of Perachiah to Jerusalem would have been *c.* 75 BCE. Thus, it would appear that Yeshu spent as many as twenty years in Alexandria (*c.* 94–*c.* 75 BCE).

As is well known, at the time Alexandria was the intellectual center of the western world. Not even Rome or Athens compared with it. The

---

21. Interestingly, the fourth century church father Epiphanius of Salamis also dates Jesus to the time of Janneus (Pan 29.3.3). *Cf.* Allegro 1979:38.

22. Josephus, *Antiquities* 13:14:2.

23. *Cf.* the flight to Egypt by Jesus and the Holy Family (Mt 2:13–15, par. Hos 11:1)

24. Cited more fully and discussed at Zindler 2003:249–50.

city was the crossroads of East and West, continually trading with faraway India and (by proxy) even with China. Buddhist monks had been in Alexandria since about 250 BCE, when the Emperor Asoka sent them, together no doubt with a goodly number of sutras written on palm leaves.[25]

If Yeshu ha-Notsri were of an inquiring mind—and indications suggest as much—he could not have avoided being exposed in Alexandria to the most vital and diverse intellectual currents of the age. An open, well-educated young Jewish scholar in the great city would have been challenged to acquaint himself with the most far-reaching and provocative insights of the era.

The literary record attests that two decades in Alexandria witnessed a sea change in the young man's thought, for—according to the Talmud—he was excommunicated by his master (under the pretext of a sexual impropriety) upon their return to Israel. The above citation b. Sanh. 107b continues:

> [Rabbi Perachiah] came, and found himself at a certain inn; they showed him great honor. He said, "How beautiful is this Acsania!"[26]
> [Yeshu] said to him, "Rabbi, she has narrow eyes." [R. Perachiah] said, "Wretch, do you employ yourself thus?" He sent out four hundred trumpets and excommunicated him.
>
> [Yeshu] came before him many times and said to him, "Receive me." But he would not notice him. One day when [R. Perachiah] was reciting the Shema, [Yeshu] came before him. [R. Perachiah] was minded to receive him and made a sign to him. But [Yeshu] thought that he repelled him. [Yeshu] went and hung up a brick and worshipped it.
>
> [R. Perachiah] said to him, "Return." [Yeshu] replied, "Thus have I received from you, that every one who sins *and causes the multitude to sin*, they give him not the chance to repent."
>
> And a teacher has said, "Yeshu ha-Notsri practiced magic and led astray and deceived Israel."
>
> [Herford 51. Formatting and emphasis added.]

Obviously, a major change took place in Yeshu's thinking during his time in the Egyptian capital—*a change which led to his excommunication from Judaism.*

---

25. This is memorialized in Asoka's rock edict no. 13. See Dhammika 1993. The king of Egypt who received Buddhist missionaries and their texts would have been the extravagant and cosmopolitan Ptolemy II Philadelphus (d. 246 BCE) who is known to have sent embassies to Asoka in India. Philadelphus founded the Alexandria library and, according to legend, mandated that no ship could dock without bringing texts for its library. Interestingly, Dositheus reputedly wrote on palm leaves (below p. 454).

26. "Acsania" denotes both inn and innkeeper. Perachiah used it in the first sense; the answering remark implies the second meaning, "hostess."

The now middle-aged[27] Yeshu did not simply disappear. He garnered a following in Israel, and this indicates his subsequent activity there as a prophet and teacher. In the words of the Talmud, he caused "the multitude to sin," and "practiced magic and led astray and deceived Israel." Evidently, Yeshu was *very* successful—to the dismay of the now-ascendant Pharisees.

In the above passage we note that Perachiah apparently reached out to Yeshu several times after the excommunication and even suggested a reconciliation ("Return"). But Yeshu refused, using the rabbi's own teaching against him. This may echo subsequent events after Yeshu had met with initial success in his homeland.

Rabbinic literature also preserves some clues regarding the theology of the rebellious prophet. One is in the Palestinian Talmud, Taanith 65b. Though it does not mention Yeshu, "That it refers to Jesus there can be no possibility of doubt" (Herford):

> R. Abahu said: If a man says to you 'I am God,' he is a liar; if [he says, 'I am] the son of man,' in the end people will laugh at him; if [he says] 'I will go up to heaven,' he says, but will not perform it.[28]

These claims are vaguely familiar from the New Testament. The last, however, is especially significant—it reveals the view that man is in command of his own salvation and can ascend to heaven by himself—implicitly *without God's help* (or even without a God at all). This view we will term "Primary Gnosticism." Such views, of course, contrast with normative Judaism and Christianity. Jewish mystical traditions of late antiquity, together with the *Hechalot* literature, struggle with the desire—eternally suppressed—to cross the chasm separating man and God. Evidently, Yeshu ha-Notsri dared cross that chasm. This appears to have been the cause for his excommunication. Yeshu embraced the gnostic quest, and for that he was anathematized by those highly placed in Judaism.

A second Rabbinic passage does not mention Yeshu but "Balaam." Zindler has shown that none of the Balaam passages in Rabbinic literature refers to a historical Jesus of Nazareth. At the same time, it is clear that Balaam and Yeshu ha-Notsri refer to one and the same person:

> R. El'azar ha-Qappar says, God gave strength to his voice, so that it went from one end of the world to the other, because he looked forth

---

27.   Irenaeus of Lyon (d. *c.* 202 CE) writes: "Now that the first stage of early life embraces thirty years, and that this extends onwards to the fortieth year, every one will admit; but from the fortieth and fiftieth year a man begins to decline towards old age, which our Lord possessed while He still fulfilled the office of a teacher..." Irenaeus, *Against Heresies*, Chp. 5. Passage cited in full and discussed at Zindler 2003:127 *f.*

28.   Herford 1903:62.

and beheld the peoples that bow down to the sun and moon and stars and to wood and stone, and he looked forth and beheld that there was a man, son of a woman, who should rise up and seek to make himself God, and to cause the whole world to go astray. Therefore God gave power to his voice that all the peoples of the world might hear, and thus he spoke, "Give heed that you go not astray after that man, for it is written, *God is not a human being that he should lie* [Num 23:19], and if he *says that he is God* he is a liar, and he will deceive and say that he departs and comes again in the end, he says and he will not perform. See what is written: *And he uttered his oracle, saying, Alas, who will live when God does this* [Num 24:23]? Balaam said, "Alas, who will live of that nation which hears that man who has made himself God." —m. Jalqut Shimoni 766

This remarkable passage confirms the basic 'sin' of Balaam/Yeshu: he, a mere "man, son of a woman" rose up and sought "to make himself God." Apparently, he even claimed divinity, as the above passage accuses: the prophet "says that he is God."

Furthermore, we note that the prophet caused "the whole world to go astray." This of course means that he had great success in *drawing people away from the Jewish religion.*[29] The observation that Balaam "looked forth and beheld the peoples that bow down to the sun and moon and stars and to wood and stone" echoes the accusation against Yeshu ha-Notsri, that the latter was an idol worshipper (bowed down to a "brick," above p. 421).

The second embedded citation from the book of Numbers is used as justification for the execution of the prophet: "who will live when God does this?" Interestingly, the extended biblical passage began with an allusion to the gnostic quest: "he who hears the words of God, and *knows the knowledge of the Most High*" (Num 23:15). Yet the same passage ends ominously with the words "he also will perish forever" (v. 24b).

It is possible to interpret Balaam's astonishing closing words above in multiple ways. One is as a declaration of defiance: "Alas, *who will live* of that nation" which rejects his very message? The verb "live" here cannot carry a literal meaning—Balaam uses it *spiritually.* This spiritual definition of "life," in turn, has remarkable echoes in the New Testament and particularly in gnostic and quasi-gnostic texts such as the Gospels of Thomas and John.[30]

A less agressive interpretation of Yeshu's closing (final?) words sums up his ministry as a heartfelt effort to spread the truth, the inner 'gnosis' that yields spiritual life. Yeshu asks his brothers and sisters with sincere concern and compassion: "Alas, who will *live* (spiritually)?" The implied answer is not reassuring: *exceedingly few.*

---

29. Interestingly, there is also an allusion to the Second Coming: "he departs and comes again in the end." This is probably a rabbinic echo of New Testament theology.
30. *Cf.* Mk 8:37; Mt 10:39; Lk 9:60, 17:33; Jn 1:4–5, 12:25, *etc.* Th 1, 11, 52, 59.

It can be noted that the *upward* gnostic journey (of the self to enlightenment) is thought to represent an earlier stage ("Primary Gnosticism") than the mythological *descent* of a redeemer figure, so familiar from the florid Gnosticism of the early Christian centuries. As W. Schmithals observed, "At the beginning of Gnosticism stands no redeemer myth, but rather the redeeming Gnosis as such."[31] In another passage he cogently notes that "Gnosis is not oriented to the figure of a redeemer."[32] In fact, the Gnostic systems of late antiquity may have assimilated the redeemer myth from Christianity itself. They are replete with the redeemer myth—but are also very *Christian*. Even the spiritual Jesus communicated in the Pauline epistles (above, pp. 408 f) is essentially redemptive. It does not reflect the earliest stage of the religion.

* * *

While definite theological affinities are detectable between the words of Balaam and Christian scripture, the biography of Yeshu as outlined above is of an entirely different cast than the story of Jesus of Nazareth presented in the gospels. The renegade Yeshu is from Jerusalem, not the Galilee. He is obviously well educated and, furthermore, is connected to *the highest echelon of the Jewish establishment*—this, several generations before the turn of the era. Far from being a backcountry schismatic, Yeshu is very much an insider. He is apparently a well connected Jewish legalist, with a promising future in Jerusalem Pharisaic circles. Despite all this, *he turns against his entire religious heritage*.

But Yeshu comes to an unhappy end. His demise displays remarkable elements in common with the passion of Jesus in the New Testament. According to several passages in the Talmud, Yeshu is *hung on a tree* (or cabbage stalk). Moreover, this occurs *on the eve of Passover*.[33] Of course, there is also the virtual identity of names: Yeshu/Jesus (*cf.* Joshua/*Iesous*).

An important Talmudic passage reads:

> *And a herald precedes him, etc.*
> This implies, only immediately before the execution, but not previous thereto. In contradiction to this it was taught: On the eve of the sabbath and the eve of the Passover Yeshu ha-Notsri was hanged. For forty days before the execution took place, a herald went forth and cried, "Yeshu ha-Notsri is going forth to be stoned because he has practiced sorcery and enticed Israel to apostasy. Anyone who can say anything in his

---

31. This is, in fact, pure Buddhism.

32. W. Schmithals 1969:121, 126. *Cf.* also his pp. 118, 122, 132, 133.

33. Zindler 2003:237, 238, 241, 255. Incidentally, Honi the Circle-Drawer (*c.* 65 BCE) was also executed at Passover (*Ant.* 14.2.1.21).

favor, let him come forward and plead on his behalf." But since nothing was brought forward in his favor he was hanged on the eve of the sabbath and the eve of the Passover.

'Ulla retorted: Do you suppose that Yeshu ha-Notsri was one for whom a defense could be made? Was he not an enticer, concerning whom scripture says, *Neither shalt thou spare, neither shalt thou conceal him?*

With Yeshu, however, it was different, for he was connected with the government [or royalty, *i.e.*, influential].

—b. Sanh. 43a. (Brackets original. Formatting and emphases added.)[34]

Here we learn that the death of Yeshu was entirely in the hands of Jews—no Roman involvement is noted. Yeshu was killed by stoning—the religious penalty for sorcery and apostasy—and then he was "hanged." The forty day wait and public invitation for an 'ally' depict a measured effort to fulfill Jewish legal requirements. This is not at all the speedy, overnight trial portrayed in the gospels.

We now consider the astonishing final words of the above citation: *for he was connected with the government.*[35] This is the Schachter-Freedman translation and fully confirms our above observation that Yeshu was "connected to the highest echelon of the Jewish establishment." In fact, the pertinent words have secular meanings in Talmudic Hebrew. Thus the translation clarifies the word *government* with the bracketed phrase: "or royalty, *i.e.*, influential." Jastrow's Talmudic dictionary translates *malkuth* in this context as "court," and adds in parentheses: "influential."

Yeshu's return to Israel was ostensibly after the death of Janneus, and thus his trial would probably have been by a Pharisaic court in the time of Salome Alexandra. Yeshu is depicted as an important man connected to the affairs of state. Use of the word "government" (*malkuth*) shows that Yeshu's ties were secular. Nevertheless, the charges were fundamentally religious: "because he has practiced sorcery and enticed Israel to apostasy."

Before his departure for Egypt it appears that Yeshu was a member of the highest circles of the Pharisees in Israel. Yet at that time—during the reign of Janneus—the Pharisees did not have much power. Indeed, they were largely underground. Nevertheless, Yeshu's teacher and mentor Perachiah may have been the head of the Sanhedrin. Simon ben Shetach would have been a *very* close associate, probably of Yeshu's generation and

---

34. The 1994 Schachter-Freedman (I. Epstein, ed.) uncensored translation is cited and discussed at Zindler 2003:238 *f.* The translation given here adds a few words from older uncensored Hebrew editions as noted by Herford 1903:406. Those editions are the codices *Mon., Monac.,* and *Flor.* The variant readings are in Rabbinowicz 1967–97: vol. 9. See also Rabbinowicz:1877.

35. Heb: דקרוב למלכות. M. Jastrow (p. 791) translates the phrase, "connected with the court (influential)."

perhaps also a protégé of Perachiah. The reason Simon did not flee to Egypt was surely because he enjoyed the queen's personal protection—he was her *brother*! Simon merely went into hiding.[36]

Not only the Talmud, but later Jewish lore also records that Yeshu lived in the time of Janneus. Both The *Sepher Toldoth Yeshu* ("The Jewish Life of Christ") and "A Jewish Life of Jesus"[37] record Yeshu as involved with Jerusalem's aristocratic circles in the time of Janneus' successor, Salome Alexandra. These two works appear to be variants of one another. They demonstrate clear evidence of reliance on much later Christian traditions, yet at the same time show no intimate familiarity with the canonical gospels. They may themselves be described as "anti-gospels," perhaps originally deriving from the hostile and ill-informed pen of a Rabbi in post-Roman times.[38] These two texts betray particular acquaintence with Syrian traditions, which may be a clue to their provenance. They emphasize the bastardy of Yeshu[39] and depict his magical powers as deriving from the theft of the *ha-Shem* (name of the Lord) from the Jerusalem Temple. The latter, of course, is itself a curious form of magic. It seems to be a desperate pretext to explain Yeshu's phenomenal success while at the same time relieving it of all validity.

The *Jewish Life of Jesus* offers a remarkable passion narrative. It recounts that "When the wise saw that so very many believed on [Yeshu]

---

36. A famous Rabbinic story survives regarding the wary interaction between ben Shetach and Janneus. When Parthian envoys visited the king's court, they remarked the absence of the queen's brother at banquet. Upon the king's assurance that he would do the fugitive no harm, Salome Alexandra summoned her brother from hiding. Upon his appearance Simon took his place *between* the royal couple (a most presumptuous gamble, no doubt at the invitation of the queen). This greatly surprised the king, whereupon the confident Simon remarked, "The wisdom which I serve grants me equal rank with kings." (Recorded in the *Yerushalmi Nazir*, 54b; *Berakhot*, 48a.)

37. Both works are in full English translations at Zindler 2003, Appendices A and B.

38. As regards dating, the *Toldoth* writes "And this is the reason why now the hair of a monk is shaved off in the middle of the head" (3:81). It also knows of St. Simon Stylites (early fifth century CE—4:44). The work is familiar in garbled form with the claimed virgin birth, raising the dead, Yeshu in Upper Galilee, the betrayal by Judas, and Simeon Kepha (Simon Peter). H. Schonfield has observed that both lives of Yeshu probably were abridged forms of what we have today, lacking the latest additions (Zindler 2003:446, note).

39. Yeshu's mother Miriam is portrayed as having been seduced by a Roman soldier, Pandera. If anything of the kind were in fact the case, Yeshu would of course never have enjoyed the status of protégé of the Sanhedrin *nasi*, Perachiah. The illegitimacy accusation (persistent throughout Jewish depictions of Jesus in his various guises) is a fairly obvious attempt to dishonor the prophet's memory and ridicule the claim of a virgin birth.

they seized him and brought him before Queen Helene, in whose hand the land of Israel was. They said to her: This man uses sorcery and seduces the world" (Zindler 2003:431). No Queen "Helene" ever ruled over Israel, and this is in all likelihood a reference to Salome Alexandra.[40]

In both the *Toldoth* and *Jewish Life of Jesus* Simon ben Shetach is the principal antagonist. It is Simon who exposes Yeshu's illegitimacy. This is obviously a malicious expansion on the Christian claim that Jesus had no physical father. Nevertheless, it may also reflect the vague recollection that upon Yeshu's return to Israel—that is, after his excommunication—his major antagonist was indeed the future head of the Sanhedrin. This adds some irony, and even drama, to the story, for Yeshu and Simon may well have been close friends in youth but bitter enemies in adulthood. Furthermore, if Yeshu were brought before the Sanhedrin for trial, as appears to have been the case, he would have come before none other than his childhood friend, Simon—now sitting at the head of the Sanhedrin, with power over life and death.

Though Yeshu was raised a Pharisee, it would be entirely incorrect to characterise him as such. Yeshu *broke away* from the Pharisees, as he did even from Judaism.[41] The break was sufficiently complete and grave that Yeshu was charged with apostasy and paid with his life. At the same time, he took with him the secrets of the Pharisaic guild and inside knowledge of Jerusalem's highest religious establishment. One can imagine that a former insider like Yeshu would have engendered bitter gall among that Jerusalem establishment to which he himself once belonged. An informed, educated rebel like Yeshu could do both Phariseeism and Judaism enormous harm. And, apparently, Yeshu did precisely that.

He founded a breakaway sect, one with gnostic roots that would not secure a home within Phariseeism nor even within Judaism. Acrimonious interactions between Yeshu and Pharisees, as well as between Yeshu and members of other Jewish sects (Sadducees, "scribes") probably characterized the prophet's career. However, if our reconstruction of the state of affairs is near the mark, no one would have been able to best Yeshu in theological argument. Echoes of Yeshu's skill in such argumentation may still survive in the canonical gospels.

---

40. Zindler (2003:428, *cf.* 380–81) notes "the well-known phonological shift of *s* > *h* in Greek," whereby Selene becomes Helene. "Selene" (Gk. "moon"), in turn, may be a rough approximation in Greek of the Queen's actual Hebrew name, *Shalom-Tsion* ("Peace to Zion")—also often shortened to "Salome," i.e., Salome Alexandra. In addition, the medieval Jewish text may preserve echoes of the first century CE Queen Helen of Adiabene.

41. This curious pattern is interestingly found also with Paul—a Pharisee (Phil 3:5) "advanced in Judaism" (Gal 1:14) who completely abandoned his religious heritage.

James "the Just"

The theft of the "name of the Lord" from the inner sanctum of the Jerusalem Temple, noted above, implies that Yeshu possessed either the office or the prerogatives of the *High Priest*, for only that august personage enjoyed access to the Holy of Holies of the Temple.[42] The "name of the Lord," however, is obviously metaphorical and the story (composed in hindsight long after the fact) cannot be taken literally. The Talmudic account signifies that (1) Yeshu was remembered as having commanded great religious stature, and (2) he was remembered as having had access to the innermost secrets of Judaism.

Nevertheless, even metaphorical stories can reflect valid historical *interpretations*. We know of two other figures—living about the turn of the era—who claimed the prerogatives of High Priest but were not the *official* High Priest of the Jews. One is the so-called Teacher of Righteousness of the Dead Sea Scrolls. The text known as 4QMMT even deigns to instruct the Jerusalem priesthood on correct practice. We will return to the Teacher of Righteousness later.

A second figure is James the Just—known to Christians as an eminently righteous man who (according to the second century Church Father Hegesippus) had access to the Holy of Holies in the Jerusalem temple:

> James, the Lord's brother, succeeds to the government of the Church, in conjunction with the apostles. He has been universally called the Just, from the days of the Lord down to the present time. For many bore the name of James; but this one was holy from his mother's womb. He drank no wine or other intoxicating liquor, nor did he eat flesh; no razor came upon his head; he did not anoint himself with oil, nor make use of the bath. *He alone was permitted to enter the holy place*: for he did not wear any woollen garment, but fine linen only. *He alone, I say, was wont to go into the temple*: and he used to be found kneeling on his knees, begging forgiveness for the people—so that the skin of his knees became horny like that of a camel's, by reason of his constantly bending the knee in adoration to God, and begging forgiveness for the people. Therefore, in consequence of his pre-eminent justice, he was called the Just, and *Oblias*, which signifies in Greek "Defense of the People," and Justice, in accordance with what the prophets declare concerning him.
>
> —Hegesippus, *Commentaries*, Bk. V (emphases added).

---

42. A second temple existed in Egypt since the mid-second century BCE, at Leontopolis in the Nile delta, not far from Alexandria. The (ostensibly legitimate line of) High Priests there were of the Oniad family and styled themselves "Zadokites." Some scholars have posited links between the Oniads and the anti-Pharisaic sect of the Sadducees (*Zeddukim*).

This is, of course, extremely high praise—sufficiently extravagant to be offensive to Christian ears (and eyes) today. After all, the clause "in accordance with what the prophets declare concerning him" *should* apply to Jesus (Mk 1:2, 23; Mt 1:22; 2:15, 17, *etc*). The above recalls the similarly extravagant estimation of James encountered in the gnostic Gospel of Thomas:

> The disciples said to Jesus, "We know that you will depart from us. Who is to be our leader?"
>
> Jesus said to them, "Wherever you are, you are to go to *James the Just, for whose sake heaven and earth came into existence*."
>
> —Gospel of Thomas 12 (emphasis added).

For whose sake "heaven and earth came into existence"? That personnage should not be James—but *Jesus*!

Clarity is gained, however, when we recall the foregoing discussion of "Jesus" as a *purely spiritual being*.[43] No competition exists between James and Jesus—the former is the fleshly vessel, the latter the spirit of holiness. The former rises up in order to capture (or be captured by) the spirit of Jesus.[44] Thus, at the beginning of the *First Apocalypse of James*, the Lord (Jesus) explains to James: "you are not my brother *materially*." As J. Painter observes, "What is denied is the material being of the Lord."[45] This entire theology, however, is denied by the tradition, which since Roman times has seen fit to consider James as the *blood* brother of Jesus!

In the developed gnosticism of later Roman times, however, James himself is the quintessential recipient of revelation. He is the example— evident to history—that others are to follow:

> ...I am he who received revelation from the Pleroma [of] imperishability. (I am) he who was first summoned by him who is great, and who obeyed the [Lord]—he who passed [through] the [worlds...]
>
> —*Second Apocalypse of James* 46.6–14

In texts bearing his name, James is often portrayed as the "gate" or "door" through which others are enabled to find the spiritual Jesus.[46] Of

---

43. On the spirit of Jesus, *cf.* discussion above p. 409.

44. This lends itself to figurative depiction as a meeting in the sky. Such aerial meetings are found in multiple literary traditions, Jewish and Christian.

45. Painter 2004:171. Price 2011:336–43 also considers the possibility that "James was understood, like Thomas, to be the earthly, physical counterpart to a heavenly Jesus."

46. Eusebius reports: Some people asked James: "'What was the gate to Jesus?' and he answered, 'that he was the savior'" (H.E. 2.23). The "gate" is a key concept in texts bearing the name of James—*cf. The First* and *Second Apocalypse of James* (Nag Hammadi Library V.3, V.4), *etc.* For gate/door symbolism see also *Second Apocalypse* 55.5–14 and Eusebius *Hist. Eccl.* 2.23.8, 12–13. On parallels with Dositheanism, *cf.* below p. 460.

course, the Gospel of John has co-opted this theology and made a now *physical* Jesus the "gate" (John 14:6.) Thus, we can trace the deformation of an original gnostic religion in stages:

(a) gnosis saves (= Primary gnosticism)
(b) gnosis is objectified as "Jesus" (= "Savior")
(c) gnosis descends to earth and is figuratively met by the saint half-way (figuratively: 'in the air')
(d) the savior Jesus is divorced from gnosis and thus placed *out of reach* of man (= the necessity of a redeemer)
(e) the savior Jesus is conceived as part of the godhead
(f) the savior Jesus is anthropomorphized as *Jesus of Nazareth*, the only-begotten Son of God.

Several trajectories are indicated by the above: (1) "Jesus" transforms from spiritual to material; (2) man no longer saves himself (Primary Gnosticism) but now requires *redemption*; and (3) gnosis is (entirely) rejected.

Jamesian and Pauline theology correspond to stage (c) above.[47] It is probable that this stage continued into the late second century CE, that is, until the first canonical gospel (Mark) became current (*cf.* p. 418 above).

In Jamesian theology (that remained outside orthodoxy and would have been lost to us except for the Nag Hammadi finds), James enables others to "reign, and to become kings" (*Second Apocalypse* 56.4–5). James is the great middle term between man and gnosis. He is nothing less than the lynchpin of history. These gnostic texts depict James as the transmitter ("door") of hidden wisdom. The saving gnosis symbolically issues from his *mouth* (also a gateway/door symbol)—*e.g.*, via a "kiss" (NHL V.4.56:15).

An entire catalogue of symbols was developed in gnostic theology, symbols often using intimate sexual language to convey equally intimate *gnostic* meaning. In the encratite milieu of gnosticism, however, sexuality itself was categorically rejected. Thus, we have texts which are replete with sexual symbolism but have nothing to do with sexuality—a pitfall for outsiders.[48]

---

47.   The overlap between the theologies of James and Paul indicate an original unity. The emerging gentile church needed a mouthpiece, and "Paul" was the answer—an invented figure whose missives reflect an evolving theology—but still no knowledge of Jesus of Nazareth (above pp. 408 *f*). Paul was the anti-gnostic voice of the Church, a new voice that required separation from James (also an invented figure). Thus literary figures were created (or 're-written') according to the demands of evolving/competing theologies, eventually yielding an alphabet soup of invented characters.
48.   The Church Fathers were all too willing to portray the gnostics as licentious, not understanding the symbols nor being amenable to gnostic theology.

The passage known today as Secret Mark fits perfectly into a gnostic, Jamesian, and encratite milieu (*cf.* NTA I.108). It portrays Jesus raising a young man (*neaniskos,* symbolic of the person before enlightenment) from the dead, then "remaining" with him overnight clothed only in a linen cloth (*sindon*)[49] and "teaching" him "the mysteries of the kingdom of god."

Thus, Secret Mark portrays the sacred transmission of gnosis. That transmission (or, rather, *acquisition*) is the gnostic salvation, the high point of all life and, indeed, the beginning and seed of *true* life. It is equivalent to the marriage bed in the profane world—the beginning and seed of the fleshly life. This encratite-gnostic symbolism seeps into the canonical gospels, where we find imagery regarding the "bridal chamber," but there the underlying gnostic meaning has been quite obscured.[50]

One of the few surviving passages from the (lamentably) lost *Gospel of the Hebrews* is preserved in the writings of Jerome. It reads:

> The Gospel called according to the Hebrews which was recently translated by me into Greek and Latin, which Origen frequently uses, records after the resurrection of the Savior:
>
> And when the Lord had given the linen cloth [*sindon*] to the servant of the priest, he went to James and appeared to him. For James had sworn that he would not eat bread from that hour in which he had drunk the cup of the Lord until he should see him risen from among them that sleep. And shortly thereafter the Lord said: Bring a table and bread! And immediately it is added: he took the bread, blessed it and broke it and gave it to James the Just and said to him: My brother, eat your bread, for the Son of man is risen from among them that sleep.[51]

This is a proof-text for the doctrine of realized eschatology. The *sindon* is the thin linen cloth worn (according to gnostic-encratite symbolism) *before* the resurrection/enlightenment. The "Lord" (Jesus) *gives* the linen cloth to the "servant of the priest" (presumably, he donates ignorance/the physical world to an underling of the Jerusalem temple!) and then he presents himself to James the Just, who has sworn that he will not eat food until he sees the resurrection of Jesus (= gnosis). "Bring a table and bread" is a somewhat humorous way of emphasizing that *no waiting is necessary.* James has already seen the resurrected Jesus within his own heart/mind.[52]

---

49. The *sindon* ("linen garment") is the thin tissue symbolic of the flesh (alternately: ignorance) *before* the resurrection (*cf.* Mk 14:52; 15:46 and pars.). It is exchanged for the more substantial *stolē* ("robe") worn *after* the resurrection and upon receipt of "the mysteries of the kingdom of god" (*cf.* Mk 16:5; Rev 6:11; 7:13 *f*; 22:14). The possession (and lack thereof) of the requisite garment is the *krisis* in the parable at Mt 22.11 *f.*

50. Mt 22:1 *f*; 25:1 *f*; Lk 12:35 *f*; and parallels.

51. NTA I (1990–91):178.

52. In considering this *Gospel of the Hebrews* passage (together with 1 Cor 15:7, discussed above) one influential scholar supposed that "Like Paul, James was converted

From all this, James the Just emerges as *the* prophet, the one who possessed (or, rather, was possessed *by*) the spirit of Jesus, even as Paul taught. James then passed on the gnosis—*the Jesus* ("salvation"). James is the lynchpin of history, and *Jesus* is the treasure of gnosis that is passed on—an eternal attribute of the godhead.[53] This is the earliest theology detectable in Christian scriptures, the theology of the first and early second centuries of our era.

The role of James as intermediary was well known:

> The Lord imparted the gift of gnosis to James the Just, to John and Peter after his resurrection, these delivered it to the rest of the apostles, and they to the seventy, of whom Barnabas was one.

These are words of Clement of Alexandria (*Institutions*, Book 7) as reported by Eusebius (*Eccl. Hist.* II.1). While John and Peter shared primacy with James in orthodoxy (*cf.* Gal 2:9; Mk 9:2), the Nag Hammadi gnostic texts accord James alone stunningly high estimation.[54] "James is the heavenly guide of those who pass through the heavenly 'door' and are his (and the Lord's). He is the 'illuminator and redeemer.'"[55] Of James it is said:

---

by a vision" *after* Jesus' bodily resurrection (H. Betz, 1979:78). This is the traditional view, but it quickly leads to absurdities. For example, Jesus' inability while in the flesh to effect conversion of any members of his family (Mk 3:21) vindicates nothing so much as the old adage "familiarity breeds contempt"—even more remarkable since his parents had been informed by *angels* that their son was conceived *by the Holy Spirit* and was *the Son of God* (Mt 1:20; Lk 1:35). Jesus was similarly unable to convert his disciples (according to the Gospel of Mark) and his neighbors in Nazareth (Lk 4:16–30)—that is, essentially *everyone who knew him*! On the other hand, the gospels relate that Jesus enjoyed stunning success (in effecting prompt belief and other drastic changes) with people *not familiar* with him. It would seem that the more one knew Jesus, the more unsavory he became!

53.   James is also a potential candidate for the "Beloved Disciple" of the Fourth Gospel, the most gnostic-leaning of the canonical gospels. Uniformly in the Jamesian tradition Peter yields to James in authority. Painter writes: "Inasmuch as Peter is also named in the *Apocryphon of James*, it is to assert the superiority of James and of the revelation made to him. We are reminded of the subservient role played by Peter in relation to the Beloved Disciple in the Fourth Gospel" (Painter 2004:177).

54.   *Cf.* Doresse 1986:236. In the Great Church, the primary role of James in the transmission devolves to Peter (Mt 16:18). No doubt under the influence of orthodoxy, the *Apocryphon of James* includes Peter as co-equal in the reception of secret teaching (1.10; 15.7), but only James appears to understand what Jesus says.

55.   Painter 2004:174. Despite discovery of the Nag Hammadi texts and existence of the Letter of James, some scholars still maintain the fiction that "Nothing is known about James' theology" (Betz 1979:78).

You are he whom the heavens bless...
For your sake they will be told [these things], and will come to rest.
For your sake they will reign [and will] become kings.
For [your] sake they will have pity on whomever they pity.
—*Second Apocalypse of James* (55.24–25; 56.2–6)

Already in the *Second Apocalypse* we see some overlap between James and Jesus, for the words in the above citation could equally well characterize gnosis/Jesus. Thus, the prophet and the treasure become *inseparable*. Yet there is a major difference: James dies, but 'the Jesus' is undying. A reflection of this distinction survives in the *Epistle of James*:

> James makes no *obvious* use of any of the narrative traditions concerning Jesus. Most notably, he makes no mention of the death of Jesus. Those seeking allusion to Jesus' death in 5:6 and 5:11 must strain both the text and their eyesight. Neither is there any clear statement of Jesus' resurrection[56]... If "Christian" means "Christocentric," James fails the test.[57]

The *Second Apocalypse of James* from the Nag Hammadi corpus preserves with great clarity the exalted position of James *later* taken over by Jesus of Nazareth.[58] The tractate begins: "This is the discourse that James the Just spoke in Jerusalem... He said..." Thus, we are dealing with a *gospel* ("good news") of James. And what does James go on say? *That* is altogether astonishing and includes the following:

> I [am the] first [son] who was begotten...
> I am the beloved.
> I am the righteous one.
> I am the son of [the Father].
> I speak even as [I] heard.
> I command even as I [received] the order.
> I show you (pl.) even as I have [found].
> —*Second Apocalypse of James* 49.5–16.

The *ego eimi* sayings of the first lines show that James is essentially 'in heaven with God.' He is the 'beloved,' the 'righteous one,' and the 'son of the Father.' *He* commands and shows, demonstrating that he is able to stand *in the place of God*—that is, in heaven. The *Second Apocalypse* reveals that

---

56. In Jamesian theology, it was James who was resurrected, not Jesus. "Jesus" is the eternal power that *accomplishes* the resurrection in the saints.

57. Johnson 1995:49. Elsewhere Johnson states that "James makes no use of the standard elements of the kerygma: the death, burial, resurrection of the Messiah, and the sending of the Holy Spirit" (p. 55).

58. The *Second Apocalypse* has been tentatively dated *c.* 100–*c.* 150 CE (NTA I:328). It is thus roughly contemporary with the first Pauline/Marcionite epistles and *precedes* the Gospel of Mark/invention of Jesus of Nazareth.

James has risen up to heaven and shares that high place with God.[59] We recall that *this was precisely the accusation leveled against Yeshu.*

Rabbinic sources remember Yeshu as the prophet at the source of Christianity—a prophet who made himself into God, gathered followers, and was executed in Jerusalem. On the other hand, Christian *gnostic* traditions laud the prophet James the Just who stood in heaven, who said "I am the son of [the Father]" and "I command even as I [received] the order." Like Yeshu, James similarly gathered followers and was killed in Jerusalem by the religious establishment . Thus, Rabbinic and Christian gnostic traditions—differing from each other in so many ways—ultimately converge and point us toward a stunning and ineluctable conclusion: Yeshu ha-Notsri and James the Just are *identical.*

A chronology corrected

An obvious objection to the above astonishing conclusion will be immediately noted by traditionalist[60] scholars: Yeshu and James lived in different centuries. However, I suggest that the discrepancy is only *apparent.* To understand this we must first review the evidence for dating "James" to the first century CE. That evidence ultimately rests on two chronological indicators in the ancient texts, both of which are contrived. One is in the *Antiquities* of Josephus. The other is in Paul's *Epistle to the Galatians* (1:19).

James and the beginning of the Jewish War. We begin with the single surviving mention of James "the brother of Jesus" in the writings of Josephus (Ant. 20.200–03). A long-standing and enduring division exists in scholarship regarding the authenticity of the passage, and it appears that disagreement will continue no matter how compelling are the reasons brought forward that the passage is an interpolation.[61] This situation exists—and is even predictable—when a passage is "too big to fail," that is, when it is so critical to the tradition that it must be defended at any cost.

---

59. Parallels with the Qumran Teacher of Righteousness, as well as with the Samaritan prophets Simon Magus and Dositheus are equally compelling. Like James, however, it can be argued that these figures are also reflections of Yeshu ha-Notsri.

60. I use the word "traditionalist" to encompass the 99% of academics in the field who do not even admit the possibility that Jesus and/or Paul may be *ahistorical.* There is still a line in the sand that virtually no teaching professor dares cross. On the other side of that line are recent works of R. Eisenman, F. Zindler, T. Brodie, E. Doherty, R. Price, D. MacDonald, H. Detering, and a few others. Essentially revisionist (as is this work), they point the way to the future.

61. Those in favor of authenticity include Feldman, Bauckham, Painter, as well as more conservative scholarship. Those opposed include F.C. Baur, Schürer, Brandon, G. Wells, Rajak, Zindler, Detering, Price, and the present writer.

F. Zindler and H. Detering have considered the lengthy passage *in extenso.*[62] We cite only one sentence from Josephus: "Festus was now dead [*i.e.*, in 62 CE] and Albinus was but upon the road; so [Ananus] assembled the Sanhedrin of the judges, and brought before them the brother of Jesus, *who was called Christ,* whose name was James, and some others, and when he had formed an accusation against them as breakers of the law, he delivered them to be stoned..." (emphasis added).

Detering concludes that the italicized words—a single short clause—must be an interpolation. His principal reason is that Josephus would have taken pains to avoid the title "Christ," which was highly inflammatory in Roman eyes. After all, "Christ" denotes one who is "anointed" to bring about the freedom of the Jews—both religiously *and* politically. The Jewish historiographer avoids mentioning the title in relation to other messianic pretenders (Simon of Gamla, Menahem, John of Gischala).

Detering's argument is well taken, but even more decisive in my view is something numerous scholars have noted: the entire passage in Josephus is about Jesus, *the son of Damneus.* In other words, the phrase "who was called Christ" simply does not belong—Josephus had neither the Christian James nor the Christian Jesus in mind.

Zindler concludes that Josephus *may* have made some brief mention of James, but—

> More likely, however, the reconstructed text was an interpolation by a Jewish proto-Christian—a Jacobite who revered James the Just and did not know of any historical Jesus. The received text, then, would have been the result of further doctoring by a member of the Great Church.
> —Zindler 2003:85

An early believer "who revered James the Just and did not know of any historical Jesus" is precisely the sort of person we have described above—an early follower who believed in the *spiritual* Jesus (pp. 406 *f*).

Zindler finds persuasive reasons to doubt the authenticity of the larger context in which the passage is couched (Zindler 2003:86–88). The Josephus specialist Tessa Rajak concurs:

> I discount the conflicting verdict on Ananus appearing at AJ 20.199–203, where he is said to be bold and heartless, and held responsible for engineering the death of James, brother of Jesus, through the Sanhedrin. The case for the whole account of James being a Christian interpolation is very strong: not so much, as Schürer argued, because Origen had a different recollection of what Josephus had said on the subject, but simply because of its startling divergence from the previous assessment (in a case where Josephus is not transcribing a source), and its harsh criticism of the

---

62. Zindler 2003:75–88; Detering 2011:22–27.

Sadducees, and of the Sanhedrin. Furthermore, the James passage seems to suppose in the reader some knowledge of the man 'who was called the Christ,' so that anyone who takes the view, as many do, that Josephus' reference to Jesus (the *'testimonium flavianum'*) is completely an interpolation, should find difficulty in accepting the account of his brother. Yet it has been unfashionable, of late, to doubt the James passage; but *cf.* Schürer-Vermes-Millar, vol. 1, p. 430, n.1.[63]

We now turn our attention briefly to passages mentioning James the Just that have been *attributed to Josephus* by the ancients. It can only arouse suspicion that not one of these passages appears in any surviving manuscript of Josephus. Nevertheless, many scholars have defended the authenticity of the alleged passages—which attest not only to the existence of "James the brother of Jesus" but (and this factor is equally important for the present argument) also *date* him to the first century CE.

As Detering (2011:23) points out, Origen claimed in no less than three different places that Josephus explicitly specified a link between the death of James *and the beginning of the First Jewish War.* Yet no such passage survives in the prolix writings of the first century Jew. Here is one example from Origen's hand:

> Flavius Josephus, who wrote the *Antiquities of the Jews* in twenty books, when wishing to exhibit the cause why the people suffered so great misfortunes that even the temple was razed to the ground, said, that these things happened to them in consequence of the things which they had dared to do against James the brother of Jesus who is called Christ.
> —Origen, *Commentary on Matthew* 17

Though these words of Origen are clearly a paraphrase, it is inexplicable that the underlying passage does not exist in any extant manuscript of Josephus' *Antiquities,* for—if it existed—the passage would have been highly advantageous to the emerging Church. Why? Because dating "the *brother* of Jesus" to the first century CE validates the *invented* figure Jesus of Nazareth!

The fact that 'some people supposed that the murder of James was the cause of the First Jewish War' is of little obvious importance, yet it is assiduously transmitted by multiple Church Fathers. We can now appreciate why: the information serves the critical function *of anchoring James in history.*

Eusebius, two centuries after Origen, is the first to cite the *exact words* that Origen paraphrased above. According to Eusebius, Josephus wrote:

> These things [*i.e.,* the siege of Jerusalem] happened to the Jews to avenge James the Just, who was the brother of him that is called Christ, and whom the Jews had slain, notwithstanding his pre-eminent justice.
> —Eusebius, *Hist. Eccl.* II.23

---

63. Rajak 1983:131. *Cf.* Price 2011:350–351.

It is thoroughly unlikely that Josephus ever penned such words. The only way he could have used the term "Christ" would have been in disparagement (see above). Yet, in this citation—according to Eusebius—Josephus allegedly wrote (in the very same sentence) that the brother "of him that is called Christ" possessed "pre-eminent justice." While this lauds the brother, it constitutes (by association) a very positive reflection on the Christ—and this is unimaginable from the pen of Josephus.

On the other hand, Eusebius' citation clearly fulfills the *Christian* purpose at hand: it dates James (and by proxy, Jesus) to the first century CE.

Paul and "the brother of the Lord." The Pauline epistles mention James four times, once with the descriptive "brother of the Lord" (Gal 1:19, discussed below). If—as H. Detering and (before him) the Dutch Radical School have argued—the entire Pauline corpus is a product of the second century and possibly of Marcion and his followers, then of course all four of these references to James are historically suspect.

Here we will not argue the role of Marcion and his school in the authorship of the Pauline epistles. We are concerned more narrowly with the passages in the Pauline corpus which 'locate' James chronologically to the first century CE. As it happens, cogent reasons have been brought forward to reject the authenticity of all four Pauline passages that specifically mention James. We briefly consider each passage in turn, basing our observations principally on the arguments of Dr. Robert Price.

[1] **1 Cor 15**   3 For I delivered to you as of first importance what I also received, that Christ died for our sins in accordance with the scriptures, 4 that he was buried, that he was raised on the third day in accordance with the scriptures, 5 and that he appeared to Cephas, then to the twelve. 6 Then he appeared to more than five hundred brethren at one time, most of whom are still alive, though some have fallen asleep. 7 *Then he appeared to James,* then to all the apostles. 8 Last of all, as to one untimely born, he appeared also to me.

(Emphasis added.)

The list of scholars maintaining that these verses "constitute an interpolated piece of apologetics for the resurrection" is long (Price 2006:362 note *f*). Price observes that the "five hundred brethren" post-dates the gospels and is "even later than the rest of the list of appearances." As regards the italicized words above specifically regarding James, Price remarks:

The notion of James as a believer in Jesus already at the time of Easter is a second-century product, occurring also in the Gospel of Luke and the Gospel of the Hebrews. Earlier sources (Mark and even John) had him indifferent or hostile to Jesus. No New Testament source has him first hostile, *then* converted by a resurrection appearance; that is a post-biblical harmonization.[64]

The second Pauline passage that ostensibly places James in the mid-first century CE relates to Paul's first trip to Jerusalem, as reported in the *Epistle to the Galatians*. Together with the the single surviving mention of James "the brother of Jesus" in the writings of Josephus (discussed above), the following is the most important witness to James' existence in the first century CE, for Paul here not only describes James as "the brother of the Lord" but also claims to have actually met the man:

[2] **Gal 1** [15] But when he who had set me apart before I was born, and had called me through his grace, [16] was pleased to reveal his Son to me, in order that I might preach him among the Gentiles, I did not confer with flesh and blood, [17] nor did I go up to Jerusalem to those who were apostles before me, but I went away into Arabia; and again I returned to Damascus.

[18] *Then after three years I went up to Jerusalem to visit Cephas, and remained with him fifteen days.* [19] *But I saw none of the other apostles except James the brother of the Lord.* [20] (In what I am writing to you, before God, I do not lie!) [21] Then I went into the regions of Syria and Cilicia. [22] And I was still not known by sight to the churches of Christ in Judea; [23] they only heard it said, "He who once persecuted us is now preaching the faith he once tried to destroy." [24] And they glorified God because of me.

(Emphasis added.)

Price cogently argues that the italicized verses above are a post-Marcionite interpolation:

> In Tertullian's teatise *Against Marcion*, he does not mention the visit to Jerusalem (Galatians 1:18–20), which implies that probably Marcion had not mentioned it either, again marking it as an interpolation. Someone must have inserted the passage precisely to abet the notion rejected here, that Paul went to Jerusalem to submit himself to the twelve as soon as he was able to go. Had these verses been available to Tertullian, who was arguing against Pauline independence, there is no way he would have skipped an opportunity to appeal to them; they cannot yet have formed part of the Galatians text.[65]

In other words, there was no first visit to Jerusalem. With that knowledge we must now conclude that *Paul never met James in the flesh.*[66]

---

64. Price 2006:362 note f. *Cf.* Price 2012:361.

65. Price 2012:415. *Cf.* Price 2006:317–18.

66. Zindler (2003:88) also notes that "Apart from the prolem that we can't be sure if 'Paul' was a single individual or a school of theologians, there is the jarring 'I am not lying'—which makes me think, 'Methinks he doth protest *too* much!'"

Tertullian (*c.* 155–*c.* 240 CE) was active at the beginning of the *third* century CE. Thus, if the above passage was *still* not available to him, we can understand how late are some of these Pauline interpolations! A third century dating for the above interpolation, in turn, critically affects the phrase "James the brother of the Lord." This is the *only place* that the phrase occurs in the Pauline writings. We must now jettison that phrase, too, recognizing it as a very late interpolation. In short, *Paul never referred to James as the brother of the Lord*! Robert Price concurs:

> ...[E]arly Christian tradition seized upon the figure of James the Just, the head of his own sect (perhaps that of the Dead Sea Scrolls), and made him the "brother of the Lord" (long after the fact) in order to absorb and yet honor both the sect and its figurehead, while maintaining the centrality of Jesus (who by this late date had already been historicized).[67]

[3] **Gal 2** ¹ Then after fourteen years I went up again to Jerusalem with Barnabas, taking Titus along with me. ² I went up in response to a revelation. Then I laid before them (though only in a private meeting with the acknowledged leaders) the gospel that I proclaim among the Gentiles, in order to make sure that I was not running, or had not run, in vain. ³ But even Titus, who was with me, was not compelled to be circumcised, though he was a Greek. ⁴ But because of false brothers secretly brought in, who slipped in to spy on the freedom we have in Christ Jesus, so that they might enslave us— ⁵ we did not submit to them even for a moment, so that the truth of the gospel might always remain with you. ⁶ And from those who were supposed to be acknowledged leaders (what they actually were makes no difference to me; God shows no partiality)—those leaders contributed nothing to me. ⁷ *On the contrary, when they saw that I had been entrusted with the gospel for the uncircumcised, just as Peter had been entrusted with the gospel for the circumcised* ⁸ *(for he who worked through Peter making him an apostle to the circumcised also worked through me in sending me to the Gentiles),* ⁹ *and when James and Cephas and John, who were acknowledged pillars, recognized the grace that had been given to me, they gave to Barnabas and me the right hand of fellowship, agreeing that we should go to the Gentiles and they to the circumcised.* ¹⁰ They asked only one thing, that we remember the poor, which was actually what I was eager to do.

(Emphasis added.)

Price points out that verses 7–9 "must be an interpolation since they rudely interrupt the sequence of 6 and 10."[68] He explains: "This proviso [in v. 10], representing tribute money to be paid the Jerusalem Church as the price of recognition of Paulinism, obviously should follow verse 6."

---

67.   Price 2011:349.
68.   Price 2006:319, following William R. Walker Jr., "Galatians 2:7b–8 as a Non-Pauline Interpolation." *Catholic Biblical Quarterly*, vol. 65, no. 4 (Oct. 2003):568–87.

Marcion famously made a large financial donation to the Roman Church (*c.* 125 CE?). It was returned to him—a clear parallel both to Simon Magus' attempt to purchase the power of the Holy Spirit, and to Paul's attempt above to purchase the recognition of Paulinism. In his 2012 book Price makes the real *Sitz im Leben* of the Galatians passage clear:

> How far Paul's esteem for the Jerusalem leaders, or shall we say Marcion's esteem for the Roman leaders, has fallen! In Galatians 2:6 they are merely said to be supposedly something great, pretty much the same disdainful phrase that characterizes Simon Magus in Acts 8:9—not coincidentally, since in Acts we see the other side of this very argument.
>
> ... Note that the interpolator slips and calls Cephas "Peter," his more familiar name, whereas in the rest of the discussion he is Cephas. The interpolated passage partakes of the Catholic remodeling of Peter to make him just like Paul, a missionary to the gentiles....
>
> The stipulated collection of alms for the Jerusalem poor (*ebionim*, 2:10), which is to say the Jerusalem saints generally, for whom Paul is depicted in the epistles as having raised money in his churches, is a fictive version of Marcion's own initial gift of a large sum to the Roman church, which they refunded after deciding he was a heretic (Price 2012:418–19).

[4]　**Gal 2**　　　11 But when Cephas came to Antioch, I opposed him to his face, because he stood self-condemned; 12 *for until certain people came from James*, he used to eat with the Gentiles. But after they came, he drew back and kept himself separate for fear of those of the circumcision. 13 And the other Jews joined him in this hypocrisy, so that even Barnabas was led astray by their hypocrisy. 14 But when I saw that they were not acting consistently with the truth of the gospel, I said to Cephas before them all, "If you, though a Jew, live like a Gentile and not like a Jew, how can you compel the Gentiles to live like Jews?"

(Emphasis added.)

As Price (2012:419) writes, "It is not that any of this actually happened, of course." We have already concluded that the events narrated in the preceding verses (no. 3, above) relate to a second century *Sitz im Leben*, and that "Paul" may well be a cipher for none other than Marcion. In this light, is it possible to accord any historicity at all to the 'incident at Antioch' between Paul and Peter? The short answer is: *no.*

The longer answer will require more digging in the scholarly literature. I focus in what follows on the italicized phrase in v. 12, "for until people came from James." If one were to take the entire incident at Antioch literally— as does the tradition—that phrase becomes problematic. For example, Betz wonders if those "people from James" are to be associated with the "false brothers" of v. 4. He concludes: "Their actions are indeed parallel, but they must not be identical" (Betz 1979:108). *Parallel* but not *identical?*

H. Schlier opined that though James may indeed have sent the emissaries to Antioch, they were not "James' adherents."[69]

Of course, one can understand Betz and Schlier's quandary, for identifying the "false brothers" with James would impugn the entire Jerusalem Church—a conclusion simply not acceptable to Christian tradition.

W. Schmithals also wondered greatly, writing: "It is surely impossible that Peter could be afraid of the party of James."[70] Schmithals noted that the Jerusalem Church was a rag-tag association with little authority in Jerusalem itself, much less in Antioch. He finally observed that "those of the circumcision" (*tous ek peritomês*) manifestly included Peter—leading to the absurdity that Schmitals is forced to exclaim on p. 55: "Peter cannot after all be afraid of himself!"

Well, you never know... Nothing can be ruled out with people who *did not exist.*

The account in Galatians was commented upon already in the third century CE. In the so-called *Letter of Peter to James* (*Epistula Petri*), Paul is "the man who is my enemy" and Peter is a torah-observant Jewish Christian:

> For some from among the Gentiles have rejected my lawful preaching and have preferred a lawless and absurd doctine of *the man who is my enemy*. And indeed some have attempted, whilst I am still alive, to distort my words by interpretations of many sorts, as if I taught the dissolution of the law and, although I was of this opinion, did not express it openly. But that may God forbid! For to do such a thing means to act contrary to the law of God which as made known by Moses and was confirmed by our Lord in its everlasting continuance.[71]   (Emphasis added.)

In conclusion, we return to the view of Robert Price, who sees much of *Galatians* in a Marcionite light.[72] Despite a variety of views, the basic issue underlying the Antioch incident is the relevance of Jewish law (and, in turn, the authority of *torah*) to Jesus-followers. Table fellowship, permitted food, and circumcision were wedge issues of great sensitivity precisely in Marcion's time, for he essentially pulled Christianity out of a Jewish milieu. These issues were not relevant in the first century—that is, *before* the Jesus religion significantly moved into Gentile lands.

These pages present a chronology based on documents *redated* by liberal scholarship to the second or even the third century. It is clear that such late documents can have little—if any—historical value. They are propaganda texts of factions which have already developed. In turn, the

---

69. H. Schlier, *Der Brief an die Galater*. Göttingen: Vandenhoeck & Ruprecht, 1971:83.
70. Schmithals 1965:53–54.
71. NTA (1992) 2.494.
72. Price 2012:420.

NAZARETHGATE

figures encountered—Peter, James, Paul, *etc.*—are effigies. They conform not to history but to the exigencies of each faction. And the figures are malleable—as are all literary constructs. Hence we have different depictions of these 'personae' and conflicting assertions by them.

The entire 'Antioch incident' dramatizes the practical—and potentially very divisive—relevance of *torah* observance for Jesus-followers in the second century. It does so using the figures of Peter, James, and Paul. Composition of the scene can date no earlier than the time of Marcion.

In sum, the "James" of 1 Cor 15:7, Gal 1:19, 2:9, and 2:12 is a literary construct with no demonstrable historical value.[73] Like so many figures in the New Testament, he is made to serve functions and purposes of a later generation. He is as fictional as the events which surround him in the texts.

The acknowledgment of Marcionite involvement with the "Pauline" epistles must be considered one aspect of a major redating taking place in our generation—*a redating of virtually the entire New Testament from the first to the second century CE.* The implications for the historicity of the canonical gospels—and particular that of Jesus of Nazareth—are fatal. As research grapples with the realization that the gospels reflect second century forces and realities, many elements will become more understandable, such as the presence of Pharisees in the Galilee, of synagogues—and of Nazareth.

The later gospel chronology can also reveal much that was hitherto not suspected. For example, in the third century citation above from the *Epistula Petri,* Peter is presented as describing Paul (implicitly) as "the man who is my enemy." From the Jewish Christian point of view, Paul's activity was that of sowing tares among the wheat. We may wonder if Jesus' parable of the wheat and tares (Mt 13:24–30) might not itself be a product of Hellenist Christian activity among the Gentiles in the second century. In that parable we read:

> Mt 13 27 And the servants of the householder came and said to him, "Sir, did you not sow good seed in your field? How then has it weeds?" 28 He said to them, "An enemy has done this." The servants said to him, "Then do you want us to go and gather them?" 29 But he said, "No, lest in gathering the weeds you root up the wheat along with them. 30 Let both grow together until the harvest...

---

73. The Jamesian literature has assimilated the Catholic chronology of Gal. 1:19 (that Paul met with James in Jerusalem). Jamesian literature consists of (from Nag Hammadi) the *Apocryphon of James,* the *First* and *Second Apocalypse of James,* the *Gospel of Thomas,* and the *Gospel of the Egyptians.* Outside of the Nag Hammadi library are the canonical *Epistle of James,* the *Protevangelium of James,* the *Ascents of James,* and the *Kerygmata Petrou* of the Pseudo-Clementine writings. We also note the prominence of James in the writings of Hegesippus, Clement of Alexandria, Eusebius of Caesarea, and Epiphanius (Painter 2004:167).

If the "enemy" above is "Paul," then the parable must date to a post-Marcion era.

* * *

In the foregoing pages we have argued that "James the Just," the "brother of the Lord," is a literary figure with no demonstrable historical anchor in the first century CE. The surprisingly few passages which have been used by the tradition to locate James in history are late interpolations with no historical value. One is from Josephus and four from the Pauline epistles. In the last case (Gal 2:12) the entire story is apocryphal and without historical substance. It serves a theological purpose of importance in the second century when a branch of Jesus-followers (Marcionites) were in the process of separating from Judaism altogether.

There are, of course, rich traditions surrounding the figure of James the Just in the writings of the Church Fathers, in Jewish Christian literature, and in Gnostic texts. All these, however, depend upon the false chronology interpolated into Josephus and insinuated in the Pauline epistles.

Jewish and Christian traditions locate Yeshu ha-Notsri and James the Just in different centuries. We have noted affinities both in historical circumstances (particularly their mutual association with the Jerusalem hierarchy) and theology (emphasizing the gnostic ascent to the 'divine'). But if these two figures ultimately derive from the same prophet (above p. 430), then one of the chronological and historical settings is false. Which one?

The answer is clear: the *later* figure of James the Just is not attested in the literature—as we have now seen. The seminal passages placing him in the first century CE are interpolations. They are *all* late propaganda of the Church.

On the other hand Yeshu is quite well located in history, even though relatively few passages directly attest to him. Yeshu is a protégé of the head of the Sanhedrin, Joshua ben Perachiah, who was a high-ranking Pharisee *known* through rabbinic records. The circumstances of Yeshu's flight to Egypt in the time of Janneus make sense. Yeshu was excommunicated upon his return, gathered disciples, was eventually tried before the Sanhedrin, and was executed on the eve of Passover. All these elements of his biography are believable. There is no obvious reason to doubt any of them.

Similar passion accounts. Many descriptions survive regarding the death of James. Space does not permit us to compare them with the canonical passion accounts, nor with the various reports of the death of Yeshu found in Jewish literature. But some common characteristics between the various passages can be noted.

First of all, the death of Yeshu, James, and Jesus all took place in Jerusalem.

Secondly, the temple authorities—that is, the Jewish religious elite—were involved in each case.

Indeed, our above analysis has suggested that Yeshu himself once belonged to that elite. James the Just (*Jacob ha-Tsaddik*), too, seems to have enjoyed privileged religious status, for tradition portrays him as possessing access to the more sacred areas of the temple. Only Jesus of Nazareth is out of step here—perhaps an indication of the astonishing liberty that went into creating *him*. Jesus is portrayed strictly as an outsider—as a presumptuous Galilean merely 'visiting' Jerusalem.

Both Yeshu and Jesus are tried before the Sanhedrin and then executed. With the death of James there are conflicting traditions. The Pseudo-Clementine literature presents a gang murder in the temple precincts. But the *Second Apocalypse of James* "emphasizes the Jewish legal elements of the trial, making use of traditions now known to us in Mishnah tractate Sanhedrin" (Painter 2004:177). Of these two accounts only the *Second Apocalypse* echoes the formal trial and death of Yeshu considered above. It is no doubt the more correct.

Some accounts preserve a lengthy speech ('manifesto') by James preceding his death (Hegesippus; *Recognitions* 1.68.3–1.70.8). In this connection, the image of Stephen in Acts 6–7 also comes into play, for H. Schoeps and others have suggested that Stephen is a cipher for James the Just. *Acts* places Paul at the death of Stephen, but the Pseudo-Clementines have him (under a pseudonym) at the death of James. Stephen is "brought before the council," he gives a lengthy pre-mortem speech, accuses the religious authorities of being "stiff-necked, uncircumcised in heart and ears, forever opposing the holy spirit, just as your ancestors used to do" (Acts 7:51), and he is then stoned. However, since James the Just was himself an echo of Yeshu, then even less historical credence can be accorded the figure of Stephen.

The invention of the Christian Jesus

The foregoing pages have presented the view that the 'savior' was originally a pure abstraction—*gnosis* itself (above, pp. 418, 430). Secondly, at the Pauline stage, the gnosis became magnified into a great, eternal, and redeeming *spiritual* entity, Jesus (the "savior"), one that indwells the saints. Finally the savior Jesus took on the body—*once and only once*—of a single human being. This third stage was presented to the world via a radical new text—*The Gospel of Mark*. The astonishing new conception also required an astonishing God-man—Jesus 'the Nazarene.'[74]

---

74. The *Gospel of Mark* did not know Nazareth, which was not yet in existence. See

We can be quite confident that the miracle-working Jesus of the gospels *postdates* the epistles of Paul. The epistles do not know anything of the Nazarene's biography—they couldn't, because that biography had not yet been invented. As discussed above, the Pauline epistles know only a spiritual Jesus.

This is not the place to expand on the meaning of "Nazarene"—a critical consideration in its own right. However, *Iêsous* is the Greek rendering for "Joshua," in Hebrew *Yehoshua*. The New Testament name "Jesus" is thus closely related to the name *Yeshu* of the Talmud.[75] The link becomes even closer when we consider both names together with their descriptives: *Iêsou Nazarêne* and *Yeshu ha-Notsri*.[76]

It might be argued by some that the Talmudic Yeshu ha-Notsri is secondary—a very late echo of the New Testament Jesus of Nazareth. Yet this line is thoroughly untenable, for Yeshu has a completely different biography from Jesus. He even lives in a different century. It is not merely a question of the rabbis having gotten all the particulars of Jesus *very* wrong. One would additionally have to explain how (and why) they gave Yeshu a credible biography in the time of Janneus, one linking him to attested figures.

Leading to our identification of *James the Just* with Yeshu ha-Notsri above, we uncovered common elements in theology and biography, similarities which link the two figures despite their very different historical settings. Those common elements led to the conclusion that James was invented.

In now comparing *Jesus of Nazareth* with Yeshu ha-Notsri, the resonances are rarely specific—as might indeed be the case if the biographical details of the earlier figure were largely forgotten (or suppressed). However, a few potential echoes are unmistakable: years spent in Egypt; activity in Jerusalem; conflict with the Pharisees; involvement of Jewish religious authorities in the execution; death at Passover. Though not conclusive, these resonances are nevertheless remarkable. After all, how many prophets went to Egypt and then returned to Israel? How many prophets had deep conflicts with the Pharisees? How many prophets were executed at Passover?

Though we have precious little information regarding the teaching of Yeshu, we know that he was accused of making himself into God and leading Israel astray (above, pp. 422 *f*). These accusations perfectly fit Jesus of

---

Salm 2008:299 *f.*

75. *Yeshu* and *Yehoshua* (Joshua) are not precisely equivalent. The former (*yodh-shin-vav*) is probably an abbreviated form of *Yeshu'a* ("salvation," BDB 447). The other has the *heh* and incorporates the *nomen domini*: *Yeho-shu'a*, "Yahweh is salvation."

76. As has long been noted, the voiced Greek *zeta* in *Nazareth, Nazarenos, Nazôraios*. does not linguistically correspond to the voiceless *tsade* of the Hebrew. This demonstrates that the Greek terms are artificial. The Semitic languages (Hebrew, Aramaic, Mandaic, Arabic) universally present the *tsade*—not one has the voiced sibilant (*zain*).

Nazareth. If we interpret "making himself into God" in a gnostic sense—
that is, raising oneself up to perfection through gnosis ("Primary Gnosticism")—then a body of teaching attributed to Jesus (most obviously expressed in the *Gospel of Thomas*) would also resonate with Yeshu's teaching.

The surprising results of these pages, then, is that *both* James the Just
and his "brother" Jesus of Nazareth are echoes of none other than Yeshu
ha-Notsri, a prophet who lived in the time of Alexander Janneus.

Jesus of Nazareth does not enjoy equivalent historical attestation to Yeshu ha-Notsri. We can briefly review the reasons here: (a) The town where
Jesus was born (Bethlehem) did not exist at the turn of the era (per the
work of A. Oshri); (b) the town where he was raised (Nazareth) similarly
did not exist (Salm); (c) no pagan contemporary notes Jesus' existence; (d)
the slaughter of the babes of Bethlehem, the opening of the graves at Jesus' execution, and many other historical impossibilities (and errors such
as the false dating for the census of Quirinius) inform the New Testament
accounts; and (e) the presence of stand-alone synagogues and Pharisees in
the Galilee reflect a later time, showing that the *Sitz im Leben* of the gospel
accounts is the second century CE.

As for James the Just, once we reject the Josephan account of his death
(above pp. 435 *f*), no other independent witnesses exist and James vanishes entirely from history. Traditions regarding his death at the Jerusalem
temple generally conform to what we know of the death of Yeshu, while
his theology—as transmitted by the later gnostic Jamesian literature—also
conforms with Yeshu's gnostic theology as discussed above.

Once it is established that only one person of history can be involved
with these three figures (Yeshu, Jesus, and James), it becomes clear that two
of the three literary settings are also invented—with all the implications for
false biographies in the cases of Jesus, James, *as well as all their companions and
associates*. Indeed, the only literary setting that actually corresponds to history is that of Yeshu ha-Notsri, as we have seen.

It appears, then, that the New Testament gospels are little more than
fairy tales.

Simon Magus

It may be that other figures in early Christian literature—including
Simon Magus, Dositheus, and John the Baptist—are also to a greater or
lesser extent 'overlapping reflections' of a defining prophet who lived in
the early first century BCE. According to the *Pseudo-Clementines* (Hom. II.24)
Simon and Dositheus were in conflict for the mantle of the Baptist. Yet it
is little appreciated that the principal appellation of Simon Magus—the
"Standing One"—is based on the Semitic *'amad* (עמד)—which in Hebrew

means "stand" *but in Aramaic carries the primary meanings "baptize," "plunge."*[77] Christian Syriac writings—as well as Manichaean literature—employ the root *'mad* with strong gnostic overtones (*cf.* above p. 405). Thus, all three figures—John, Simon, and Dositheus—had a claim to the epithet "Standing/Baptizing One." A gnostic thrust underlies these figures.

Unfortunately, there is not space here to delve into the many colorful and conflicting stories regarding the "Magus," which is a title. "Simon" was a name shared with his nemesis, Peter—a sharing we will find significant. The animosity regarding Simon is patent, and this implies that the message he embodied was eminently threatening to the tradition at an early time. That message has been virtually obliterated from history, though we know that Simon is closely linked to the epithets "Standing/Baptizing One" and "Great Power" (*megalê dunamis*). His many reported conflicts also witness to a vital message that was continually rejected by the tradition.

Simon was clearly a gnostic figure, and he is thus remembered by the tradition. His consort "Helena" was originally simply a philosophical abstraction, *Ennoia* ("the faculty of thought"—Liddell), alternately *Sophia* or *Sapientia*.[78] But under the pens of the Church Fathers "she" descended to the rank of a prostitute whom Simon captivated. He was the author of all heresy (Eusebius), and Simon's assumption of the entire catalogue of evils suggests that "he" was (like his consort) also a personification, in his case of a much more troubling abstraction, namely, of *gnosis* itself. Thus the invention and rapid demonization of Simon "Magus" represent early stages in the devolution of the Christian religion away from the gnosticism of Yeshu.

Simon Magus was reputedly born in Gitta (Gath, presently Ramlah—Justin, *Apol.* I.26, 56), a town in Samaria approximately 40 km NW of Jerusalem. Archeologically the settlement has been identified with Lydda (Lod). Now, Lod was where a certain Ben Stada was crucified on the eve of Passover according to Rabbinic writings.[79] This link between Simon Magus and Ben Stada takes on more force when we realize that "Ben Stada" is probably another corruption for [the] 'Standing One'"[80]—a favorite euphemism of Simon Magus. Finally, Ben Stada clearly refers to Yeshu.[81] Jesus of Nazareth, of course, was also crucified on the eve of Passover.

---

77. Payne-Smith 1999/1902:416; *cf.* Allegro 1979:181. The root *'amad* in Jewish scripture also requires revisiting in light of this meaning. The term was particularly associated with the sect of the Rechabites (Jer 35:19)—a sect also linked to James the Just (Eusebius, *Eccl. Hist.* II.23.17) and which R. Eisenman has asserted "really does provide a good description of James as he has come down to us" (Eisenman 2006:167).
78. *Cf.* Allegro 1979:173.
79. Tosefta *Sanh.* X.11; Bab. Talmud *Sanh.* 67a. See Zindler 2003:237 *f*; Herford 78 *f*.
80. Eisenman 1997:1018, n. 53.
81. Herford 1975:37.

John the Baptist

The tradition is "unanimous in its declaration that the actual events proclaimed as 'gospel' by the church had begun with John."[82] Indeed, once we realize that Jesus of Nazareth did not exist, the figure of John must be re-evaluated independently, that is, not as a precursor *to anyone* but as a prophet in his own right. Only the Mandeans have preserved this view.

Yet John the Baptist is probably also a cipher. The evangelists are most interested in his birth (Luke 1), his status as precursor and subordinate to Jesus (Luke 3:4, 16 and pars.), and his death (Mark 6). When John's theology *is* presented, it is the same as that of Jesus (Lk 3:7–14). The distinction between John's baptism (with water) and Jesus' baptism (with fire) is artificial—"water" being symbolic of power over the spirit (*i.e.* gnosis), and "fire" symbolic of power over the body (*i.e.* Jesus' office to "burn with unquenchable fire" those who are unworthy, presumably at the Last Judgment—Mt 3:12).

John's status as precursor is strong acknowledgement that an important prophet *did* precede Jesus. If we describe Yeshu ha-Notsri as the lightning illuminating the sky, John the Baptist was the preliminary echo. Jesus of Nazareth was the great echo, the great thunderclap—arriving with most impressive sound, but no substance.

In its closing pages, *The Myth of Nazareth* argued that Nazara (Mt 4:13; Lk 4:16) was "the field of activity of John the Baptist" (Salm 2008a:307). Nazara is the earliest of the toponyms, and the *Gospel of Philip* defines it as "truth."[83] An argument can be made that the original "field of activity" of John and Jesus was simply *gnosis.*

My earlier book also pointed out the Galilean setting for Jesus' activity was late. Clues remain that the original setting was not Galilee but Judea (Salm 2008a:304). This also conforms with what we know of Yeshu ha-Notsri's activities.

Robert Price provocatively entitles a chapter from one of his books, "Was Jesus John the Baptist Raised from the Dead?"[84] He writes:

> ... Let us for a brief moment think the unthinkable.
> Suppose the figure of the pre-Easter Jesus is to be found under the alias of John the Baptist. When we impose this outlandish paradigm onto the gospels, we get some interesting results. A number of things make new sense.   —Price 2007:78

Price shows that the transition from "John" to "Jesus" occurred at the *baptism* of Jesus. In gnostic terms, baptism is *the* enlightenment experience. The operative symbolism is water = gnosis (above, p. 405). This symbol-

---

82. IDB Suppl. p. 487.
83. G. Philip 66.14; 62.8, 15; 56.12.
84. Price 2007: Chp. 7 (pp. 75–90).

ism occurs across traditions, from Mandaism to Dositheanism (below)—to Christianity. Price notes that the end of John's ministry = the beginning of Jesus' ministry. This makes perfect sense *only* if one interprets "Jesus" *spiritually*—as argued above.

Familiar terms necessarily assume unfamiliar *gnostic* meanings: the acquisition of 'the Jesus' is the 'enlightenment moment' of 'baptism' (Aramaic: '*amad*). That is the moment when the saintly John 'fused' with the Jesus (above p. 414). In a sense, he 'became' Jesus—they are *inseparable*.

This fusion with 'the Jesus' also describes Pauline theology, as well as James the Just's presentation in gnostic texts (above pp. 411, 433).

Price is not the only scholar to suspect that John 'became' Jesus at the baptism. Ross S. Kraemer has concluded that the gospel narratives about the death of John are a defensive response "to early 'Christian' concerns about the vexing relationship between John and Jesus, most particularly the unnerving possibility that *Jesus might have been John raised from the dead*."[85]

Like James the Just, John the Baptist has been 'fixed' to the first century CE by the writings of Josephus—in fact, via a single critical passage at Ant. 18:109 *ff*. Majority opinion holds the passage to be authentic, but such a view raises serious problems. Kraemer observes simply: "It is not impossible that this passage represents a Christian interpolation into the text of Josephus, since Josephus is transmitted by Christians, not Jews."[86] One problem that has drawn much scholarly ink is the obvious conflict between the dating of the activity of John in Josephus (*c.* 34 CE) and in the Gospel of Luke (28 CE, *cf.* Lk 3:1).[87] Both datings cannot be correct, and majority opinion has sided with Josephus on this question. But Frank Zindler has questioned the authenticity of the Josephan passage entirely, pointing out that elsewhere the historiographer gives a different account of why "god punished Herodias and Herod":

> A second non-contextual reason for concluding paragraph 2 [of the Josephan passage] is an interpolation is that in it Josephus cites—without indicating he believes otherwise—the supposed Jewish view that Herod came to a bad end because of his execution of the Baptist. Elsewhere [18:7:1; 18:255], however, Josephus gives his own—differing—view of why his god punished Herodias and Herod: "And so God visited this punishment on Herodias for her envy of her brother and on Herod for listening to a woman's frivolous chatter."   —Zindler 2003:98

In my view this is decisive, for Josephus would not present two very different explanations of the same event. Zindler offers additional reasons

---

to suspect a Christian interpolation, one being that the Baptist passage is intrusive—the preceding and following paragraphs dovetail perfectly when it is removed.[88] In all, it appears that the Josephan paragraph regarding John the Baptist is an inexpert Christian interpolation, one that does not even cohere with the dating provided by Luke, and that also conflicts with another passage in Josephus.

Once the Josephan witness for John is rejected, no independent historical attestation for the Baptist's existence in the first century CE remains.

Luke 3:15 reports that there were some who "wondered in their hearts whether John himself were perhaps the Christ." This view is even more explicit in the little known *Hebrew Gospel of Matthew,* a medieval manuscript that its editor, George Howard, claims preserves early Christian readings of that gospel. The *Hebrew Gospel* states at HebMt 3:10: "And all the people were thinking and reckoning in their circumcised heart: *John is Jesus.*"

This is astonishing. There, in black and white, a document explicitly states that *John is Jesus!* To be inferred from this statement is that *Jesus was a spiritual entity.* Only in this way could a person (John) also be 'the Jesus.' Was this the belief of very early followers—reflecting a gnostic stage in the religion predating the *invention* of Jesus of Nazareth? All avenues appear to lead in this direction. At an early stage of the religion, then, John is gnosis. He is enlightened, and he has merged with 'the Jesus' (= gnosis). Subsequently John stands as a human example for the rest of us—as a guide for emulation, not *worship* (*i.e.,* in the guise of Jesus of Nazareth).

The figure of Apollos in *Acts* enters into consideration. As Price notes, Apollos is confusingly said to have preached accurately *the things concerning Jesus,* yet he knows only the baptism of *John!* Priscilla and Aquila set Apollos straight in unspecified ways (Acts 18:24–28), but the passage is obviously window-dressing to steer the reader *away from* John and *to* Jesus. Price concludes with a question: "[W]hat if Luke's source preserves the fossil recollection that to know accurately the things about Jesus was precisely to know the baptism of John, since 'Jesus' was none other than the resurrected John?"[89] We might paraphrase by saying that 'John' is the imperfect *body,* while 'Jesus' is the perfect *spirit.*

It can be noted that, strictly speaking, the Greek *Iwannês* corresponds to the Hebrew *Yochanan,* "Yahweh has been gracious." This is the more obvious etymology. However, an ancient and quintessentially gnostic link exists to the Mesopotamian fish-man Oan/Oannês. Robert Eisler noted in 1931:

> As early as the end of the eighteenth century C. F. Dupuis put forth the conjecture, since revived by Drews, that the Baptist's name *'Iwannês* may

88.   Zindler 2003:97.
89.   Price 2007:85.

be no other than that of the strange Babylonian god of revelation who emerges from the water, according to the account of Berossus... Such a possibility is quite conceivable. For not only does the form *Joannes*, attested by Chaeremon in the time of Nero, exactly coincide with the New Testament name for the Baptist, but according to the view expressed in the *Fourth Book of Esdras* (xii.25; xiii.51 *sq.*) the Messiah is thought of as concealed in the deepest ocean, from which he is to emerge in the end. Similarly, according to Berossus, under the first dynasty of the antediluvian kings of Babylon, the *'Oannês*, (J)oannes, being the first of a series of such antediluvian 'sages,' emerged from the sea to teach the people all manner of wisdom, including politics and law.   —Eisler 1931:241

The "deepest ocean" home of Oannês is the Babylonian *abzu*, the realm of gnosis, *i.e.* "truth," and the dwelling place of the god Ea/Enki. We are now far anterior to New Testament times—indeed, in the Bronze Age. It would appear that John 'the Baptist,' the gnostic revealer, is none other than a reincarnation of Oannês, the Sumero-Babylonian demigod.[90] At a very rudimentary level this seems to have been transferred to Jesus of Nazareth for, as we have noted, "Nazara" in the earliest tradition is the field of activity of both the Baptist and of Jesus, a region that the *Gospel of Philip* interprets as "truth."

John Mark

A very obscure Greek work called the *Acts of Mark* has been extant for half a century, yet to this day no translation exists in any modern language.[91] The manuscript was discovered at Mt. Athos. The text contains astonishing declarations, including that Mark was a disciple of John the Baptist (5.1), was a Levite, was baptized by Peter, and went "to the West, to the Gauls."[92] Also remarkable is the statement that "Now at first this blessed apostle [i.e. Mark] was called *John*" (4.1)!

This author commissioned a scholarly translation of the *Acta Marci* in 2012, but as of this writing only the first 5 chapters (of 35) have been professionally rendered into English.[93] Thus, the comments that follow restrict themselves to those few initial chapters.

---

90.   In this writer's opinion, the "Jonathan" of Judg 18:30 who founds the gnostic priesthood at Dan is also an echo of Oannês.

91.   The Greek text is found in Halkin 1969. A note on the work is at NTA (1989) II:464–65.

92.   *Cf.* the ultra-heretical Marcosians of Southern Gaul (Acts of Barnabas 5; Acts of Andrew 2.293:25–27). The natural inference is that the apostle Mark = the heretic Marcus—a figure generally dated to the *second* century CE.

93.   At the time of this writing, the first five chapters are available in English on the author's website at *http://www.mythicistpapers.com/2012/10/02/translation/*

Space does not permit us to untangle all the novel threads the *Acta Marci* presents. Already, however, we note the equivalence John = Mark. The two names are indeed combined in the canonical *Acts*, where we read of "John whose other name was Mark" (Acts 12:12, 25; 15:37). It must come as a surprise, however, that this Mark is now reported to have been a disciple of the *Baptist* before becoming a disciple of Jesus (*cf.* Jn 3:26).

We also note in passing that John Mark's mother bore the same name as Jesus' mother: Mary (Acts 12:12). In the *Acts of Mark*, Mary's role is curiously evocative of the mother of Jesus: she is "truly blessed and honored" when she receives the "only-begotten son and word of god" (Jesus Christ) into her house—an uncanny echo of the Annunciation (AcMk 4.7).

The status of Mark as a Levite also merits note. The Levites are little understood, but it is clear that they were eclipsed when the priestly Aaronides arrogated power to themselves with the finalization of the Pentateuch.[94] This revolution in the Israelite religion involved the categorical subordination of the earlier Levitical priesthood—a subordination emphatically written (by the Aaronides themselves) into the Pentateuch.

The Levites predated the Jerusalem Aaronides. Nielsen has shown that Moses, a *Levite* (Ex 2:1–2), was a devotee of the gnostic moon religion indigenous to North Arabia, which he learned from the *kâhin* (priest) Jethro in Midian.[95] There are some suggestions (in Jewish scripture and elsewhere) that the Levites continued to perpetuate proto-gnostic traditions in an underground fashion after the Aaronides took power. For example, in Judges 17–18 a Levite priest from Bethlehem of Judah is responsible for nothing less than founding the (odious) gnostic priesthood at Dan in the north. On the surface the story is nonsense—the sanctuary at Dan had been long established and was famous already in the Bronze Age, attracting even Gilgamesh to the fabled "Cedar Mountain." But the story does reveal a gnostic-Levite link. Perhaps more interesting for our present purposes is that the name of the priest who went northwards to Dan from *Bethlehem* was none other than *Jonathan* (Judg 18:30), son of Gershom, son of Moses.

Gnostic vocabulary pervades the *Acts of Mark*. The apostle brings "the light of the knowledge of god", "hidden and obscure meanings", "divine illumination", and "perfection." Mark is known as a "speaker of mysteries" (*mystolektês*). He is "clear-sighted," and has reached "the highest degree" of excellence/perfection (*cf.* James the Just). In short, he appears to be a holy and "enlightened" herald of gnosis.

The *Acts of Mark* shows the strong presence of a southern (Judean) tradition. It quite ignores Galilee, mentioned only once in chapters 1-5. Jesus

---

94. E. Rivkin, "Aaron, Aaronides" in IDB (Suppl.) pp. 1–3.
95. Nielsen 1904:139–142.

performs miracles "many years" in and around Jerusalem. Then he journeys "from Jerusalem into Galilee"—a reversal of the canonical trajectory.

The *Acts of Mark* is violently anti-Semitic. It mentions "the baseless and lie-plastered betrayal of the all-brazen Jews," and "the accursed Jews" (Chp. 5). This surely betrays a time when the religion was moving out of the Jewish ambit—*i.e.*, the second century CE—also the time of Marcionite activity and of the composition of the New Testament (above p. 442).

Dositheus

While the Greek *Iwannês* in the New Testament transcribes the Hebrew *Yochanan* ("John"), it also loosely corresponds to *Yehonathan/Yonathan* ("Jonathan") with meaning "Yahweh gives" or "Gift of Yahweh." Synonyms include "Matthew" (*Mattanya*, "Gift of Yahweh"), *Nathanael* ("Gift of God"), and *Dositheus* (Gk. "Gift of God").[96]

Dositheus does not appear in the New Testament. Scholars are aware of him primarily from the Pseudo-Clementine writings, the Church Fathers, and obscure Samaritan texts—all hostile sources. "Dositheos" is also the eponymous author of an intensely gnostic tractate discovered at Nag Hammadi and entitled *The Three Steles of Seth* (NHL VII.5).

The first section of *The Three Steles of Seth* (that is, the 'first stele') is a meditation on the meaning of stand/*'amad*—a term generally associated with Simon Magus, not Dositheus. This 'borrowed attribution' is our first hint that the Magus and Dositheus may be reflections of one another—neither one a real person of history. We learn from the Nag Hammadi text that "stand" signifies the unchanging and the perfect. That which is created does *not* stand—only that which is self-begotten ("unconceived") stands. Enigmatically, however, only that which is unconceived is also *eternal*.

In the second section of *The Three Steles of Seth* we learn that perfection entails the gaining of gnosis (understanding, wisdom, knowledge).

The third section is a paean to "the unconceived"—that is, to the perfected one(s). Knowledge of the unconceived is salvation, and it is self-taught. No external savior exists (*cf.* "Primary Gnosticism").

Turning our attention now to the Pseudo-Clementine literature, we read (Hom II.24) that both Dositheus and Simon Magus are disciples of John the Baptist. On the death of John the two disciples vie for leadership of the sect, and the Magus wins. John thus is effectively the precursor to the "father of all heresy" (Simon Magus). This is truly ironic since in the gospels John is the precursor to none other than *Jesus of Nazareth*!

---

96. A resumé of ancient sources mentioning Dositheus is at Isser 1975:168 *f.* An important treatment of the conflation of personalities (including John the Baptist, Simon Magus, and the Teacher of Righteousness) with Dositheus is at Allegro 1979:185–89.

The issue at stake in the Simon-Dositheus conflict was the question of who is the Standing One—known to be one of the major epithets of Simon Magus. We have discussed the meaning of "stand" and its Semitic form '*amad*, which primarily means "baptize" in the Aramaic/Syriac language of the early Christian centuries. In a gnostic context, then, the issue between Simon and Dositheus was: Who is the baptized one? Figuratively one can rephrase the question: Who has thoroughly plunged into gnosis ("water")? In other words: Which of the two could claim to be *enlightened*?

The only text to preserve an extended account of Dositheus is a little known, garbled, medieval Samaritan work entitled the *Chronicle* of Abu'l Fath (fourteenth century).[97] "Simon the wizard" appears only in passing.[98] The *Chronicle* relates that Dositheus (Dusis) was an educated prophet, an author of "sinful books" who "altered much of the law."[99] His writings were on palm leaves,[100] and his followers "baptized in" or "plunged into" ('*amad*) water. They also prayed "in water," confirming that "water" is here a symbol of *gnosis* (above p. 405).

Furthermore, the books of Dositheus were smeared with "blood"— another symbol, this time probably of self-sacrifice/suffering. It is unclear from Abu'l Fath's account whether the baptizing/plunging was metaphorically into water/gnosis, into blood/self-sacrifice, or intellectually into the 'texts' Dositheus had written—or perhaps it was a combination of all these.

Abu'l Fath relates that the Samaritan High Priest ("Akbon") sent a number of influential people (including his nephew Levi) to apprehend Dositheus "who deserves to be killed." However, they encountered some of the prophet's writings and read them. This represented "taking the plunge" and they were converted on the spot—that is, they were baptized/rendered 'enlightened.' Of course, this surprising turn of events represented a great embarrassment to Akbon who had sent them on a rather different mission, for they were now openly exclaiming to everyone: "My faith is in you, Yahweh, and in *Dositheus* your prophet" (Bowman 165)!

While one might dismiss such a late and clearly embellished account as worthless, it may yet preserve a historical kernel. We have here an account of a *schism* among the Samaritans. Indeed, 'Dositheanism' was apparently a powerful but *heterodox* Samaritan sect. Bowman writes that "The chief opponents of orthodox Samaritans were the Dositheans."[101] By "orthodox"

---

97. Text at Bowman 1977:162–72.
98. Bowman 1977:168.
99. Bowman 1977:166, 167. Altering the scriptures was a major complaint of the Church against the Ebionites, as also against the Samaritans.
100. This is a curious medium for writing in the Levant. Palm leaves were, however, the standard medium of written communication in India until Late Roman times.
101. Bowman 1975:26.

is meant the Samaritan priestly hierarchy centered at Mt. Gerizim—also self-styled "Zadokite."[102] The Dositheans were a lay and anti-clerical movement. The two factions had opposing messiahs, each differently interpreting the *Taheb* (the "star that will come" of Num 24:17—*cf.* below, p. 458). The priestly faction anticipated and venerated the messiah son of Joseph of the tribe of Ephraim (the northern province including Samaria), a warrior who would fight, conquer gloriously, but succumb in the end and be killed.[103] The lay faction, however, venerated Joshua ("Jesus"), the messiah son of David of the tribe of Judah (southern province). He would come in the end times, and none is greater.

We must now make two critical observations. The first is that Dositheanism, though eventually dubbed "heterodox," in all likelihood *preceded* the priestly faction in Samaritan history. A. Crown writes: "[T]he priestly tradition as a whole is secondary and is based on an alternative to an older heterodoxy."[104] Crown then notes that the heterodoxy in question was probably founded by Dositheus. Elsewhere he writes that "Jewish sources place the Dositheans at the earliest level of Samaritanism."[105] Bowman considers that "the Dusis heresy was *the* formative force in Samaritanism."[106] Finally, K. Kohler dates Dositheus as the *founder of the Samaritans* to the time of Janneus/Simon ben Shetach.[107] If these scholars are correct, then Dositheus was none other than the founder of the Samaritans (*shamerim*)[108]—the "keepers" (*cf. notsri*, "keepers, watchers").

The second observation is theological. It appears that Dositheus/Dositheanism interpreted the messiah *spiritually*. This was not a person of flesh at all—and here we probably have the great revolution in thinking

---

102. Though Zadok was King David's priest (1 Kgs 1:32 *etc*), he impugned David for having many wives and not observing the law. The Samaritan Zadokite priesthood was inveterately anti-Davidic/anti-Judahite. *Cf.* Kohler 1911:410 *f*—now dated but still useful. The equivalence Zadokites = Sadducees bears reevaluation.

103. Torrey 1947:270. The following is drawn particularly from the first–century CE work *Second Esdras* ("*IV Esra*") 7:28–31, as analysed by C. Torry 1947:259 *f.*

104. Crown 1968:197.

105. Crown 1967:81.

106. Bowman 1975:187. The irony of an original *anti-priestly* view becoming heterodox (heresy) at the hands of later priests is not uncommon in religion. We will encounter a similar development at Qumran, where the gnostic view (and the founder) was apparently rejected in a conservative retrenchment (below).

107. Kohler 1911:406–07. This scholar also proposes that Dositheus "had some relationship to the mythical founder of Sadduceeism." *Zodokites* were in fact one self-reference of the priestly branch of Dositheans.

108. This is the preferred name of the Samaritans, as opposed to *shomeronim*, *i.e.* "inhabitants of Samaria" (IDB 4:191).

that "Dositheus" brought[109]—a view we have argued characterized Pauline thought and gnostic Jamesian literature. Indications of this view are scant but clear enough also in Samaritanism. In its oldest tradition, "The Taheb is a vague figure, at times similar to the preexistent Son of Man; he is *not* a human prophet at first"[110] (emphasis in original). It was only in the fourth century that the Samaritan priesthood (Marqah) first associated the Taheb with a *human* (Moses)—an association made "in order to undermine the position of Dositheus" (Isser 1975:173).

In Samaritan eschatology the Taheb was to be a prophet *like* Moses (Deut 18:15, 18). It is important to note, however, that Moses was conceived as *the fullness of divine light* (a gnostic concept) and his son Seth as "a special transmitter of the Light Image from Adam."[111] Indeed, "the Samaritans alone are the children of light" (Bowman 1975:188). One could be forgiven for thinking we are speaking here of florid "Sethian" gnosticism. We are in fact describing *original Samaritan theology*. That theology was apparently much obscured by the later Samaritan priesthood. We thus can infer the revolutionary origin of Samaritanism as a *gnostic* breakaway from Judaism.

According to T. H. Gaster, the Samaritans view Moses as

> ...an utterly unique being. He is a distillation of the primordial light, it-self none other than the holy light of God which illumines the saints. As such, he is the "light of the world," and all other lights derive from his. He therefore existed from the dawn of creation, and was only later in-carnated as the offspring of Amram and Jochebed. The whole world was created for his sake[112] (Marqah 67b). He intercedes for the deserving and leads the prayers of the celestial congregation. He is the future prophet foretold in Deut 18:18...   —IDB 4:193

All this implies that at the very beginning of Samaritanism a (gnostic) rewriting of the Pentateuch must have taken place. Dositheus was accused *of precisely such rewriting.*[113] The followers of Dositheus justified this for they

---

109. As we are learning in these pages, personal names are misleading and almost interchangeable. "Dositheus" probably is a reflection of some other prophet. "Simon Magus" had a similar claim—he was the *Megalê Dunamis* ("Great Power") which "clearly does not denote a personal being" (M. Edwards 1997:72). This observation could equally well be applied to Dositheus' conception of the messiah. In fact, the Simonian concept of *Megalê Dunamis* has long been known to be rooted in *Samaritan* theology (Kippenberg 1971:328 f.; cf. Fossum 1985:59)..

110. Isser 1975:172.

111. Fossum 1985:59, n. 109. Seth himself "built the city of Damascus," with clear implications for the interpretation of "Damascus" in the DSS..

112. Remarkably, this precise view is reported concerning James the Just in the Gospel of Thomas, logion 12.

113. Isser 1975:177.

considered him the 'second Moses' as predicted in Deut 18.[114] A revisionist Samaritan priesthood, however, later rejected this view.

We recall Abu'l Fath's description regarding the sending of a highly-placed contingent (including the High Priest Akbon's nephew Levi)—but instead of arresting Dositheus they converted to his religion. This describes a secession at a high level and is reminiscent of Yeshu's secession from the Pharisees in the time of Janneus, for Yeshu was also highly placed in religious circles. We will shortly see that a similar religious secession also may have occurred in the Dead Sea Sect as well.

If one draws blunt comparisons between the accounts of Yeshu and Dositheus, then Yeshu would fulfill the role of Levi in the Samaritan account, while "Dositheus" = gnosis. Indeed, one possible description of gnosis is "Gift of God"—*Dositheus*. It is possible, then, that what we have been considering a person of history may to a certain extent be viewed simply as a hypostasis of *gnosis*.

The tendency to hypostatize in the ancient texts bears note. For example, was Simon Magus a person or was he "the Standing One," that is, a hypostasis of *that which stands* (is eternal, *etc*). Was he a person or the "Great Power" of God (*Megalê Dunamis*)? Was his consort Helena a person or "wisdom"? Was Peter/Cephas a person or the "rock" upon which Jesus would build his church? When viewed in this way, the texts can be seen as not dealing with people at all, even though they may explicitly appear to do so. They are—at least partly—dealing with abstractions, perhaps mingled with some echoes of one or another historical person or event.

"Dositheus" may represent such a mixture of a reified abstraction ("gnosis") and a human being. Some biographical details have been transmitted which indeed point to a man of flesh and blood—though the person's actual name is lost to us. For example, the Samaritan *Tolidah* writes that Dositheus was "the son of Falfuli; he was not of the Samaritans but of the mixed rabble which came out of Egypt."[115] This echoes Yeshu's sojourn in Egypt and suggests a real person.

The twelfth century Arab historiographer Shahrastani dates Dositheus to "the century preceding Christ."[116] This was suspected already a century ago by K. Kohler who implicated Simon ben Shetach in the life of Dositheus. Kohler even thought the latter "had some relationship to the mythical founder of Sadduceeism."[117] It would appear, then—if we look closely enough—that Dositheus is implicated in many heterodox move-

---

114. Isser 1975:173.
115. Bowman 1977:204 n. 228.
116. Kohler 1911:413.
117. Kohler 1911:406–07.

ments of the late Second Temple Period (often negatively). Whether this is owing to his activities during his lifetime or owing to his eventual position as "gnosis" hypostatized is uncertain. It could be both.

Dositheus/Dusis was known in hostile Samaritan (priestly) texts as Ibn Falfuli, Fufali, Pilpuli, Palti, and Pilpul. Shahrastani wrote that he bore the name *Ilfan* ("teacher, master"—Payne-Smith 278) which makes it all but certain that the above variants are corruptions of the Aramaic *ilfan*. Evidently Dositheus was a teacher and a learned man.

Interestingly, the Samaritans substitute "Pilti" for the biblical Balaam character (whom we have also identified as a cipher for Yeshu ha-Notsri, above p. 422). They describe Pilti as "an Egyptian sorcerer, diviner, magician, and prophet." Zindler notes that on the birth of a great prophet, Pilti declares, "A star showed his glory in the heavens, and the Egyptians were astonished at this appearance."[118] Thus, we see striking allusions in Samaritan texts between traditions surrounding Yeshu ha-Notsri, Jesus of Nazareth, and Dositheus (also known as "the Star").

The star was associated by the Samaritans with their *Taheb*—the prophet like Moses who will return (Deut 18:15, 18). He is the prophesied "star [that] will come out of Jacob" (Num 24:17). The star (Heb. *kochav*) assumed strong messianic connotations towards the turn of the era and thereafter (*e.g.*, Bar Kochba = "Son of [the] Star"). It is hardly surprising that the evangelist Matthew has a star at Jesus' birth (2:1 *f*). The Dead Sea Sect also makes explicit use of the star prophecy (below).

A Rabbinic source reports that "Rabbi Dositai was born in a town named Kochaba."[119] Interestingly, Julius Africanus locates the relatives of Jesus in the "Jewish villages of Nazara and Cochaba."[120] According to Epiphanius, however, "Cochaba" near "Damascus" was where the Ebionites were centered (*Pan* 29.7.7; 30.2.7).

Epiphanius also tells us that Dositheus had "excessive desire for wisdom," was vegetarian, abstained from marriage, enjoined celibacy, and "detested every man."[121] He was "originally from the Jews" where "he sought to be among the foremost, but failed." After the Jews rejected Dositheus "he went over to the Samaritan people." Epiphanius adds that Dositheus eventually starved himself to death in a cave. Abu'l Fath's later account mirrors many of these elements.

---

118. Zindler 2003:211. See also Bowman 1977:285–90. The same Samaritan account has a version of the slaughter of the innocent children, but instead of Herod killing the babes of Bethlehem, the Pharoah drowns the children of the Israelites in the Nile.

119. *Pesikta rabbati* 16 (see Taylor 1993:38). In South Arabia *Kaukabta* was the morning star (Venus), worshipped as the Son of God (Haussig 1965:476; *cf.* 497 *f*, "Attar").

120. Eusebius, *Eccl. Hist.* 1.7.14.

121. *Panarion* 13.9 *f*. Cited in Isser 1975:168–69.

One more element can be gleaned from the relatively few reports regarding Dositheus. Isser writes: "He wrote books dealing with the Pentateuch, in which he made alterations of the text; *i.e.*, he possessed the authority to do so."[122] The "authority" referred to here must be that of Moses, and shows that Dositheus considered himself (and/or was considered to be) of equal stature—a *Moses redivivus*. This recalls Deut 18:18—"I will raise up for them a prophet like you from among their own people; I will put my words in the mouth of the prophet, who will speak to them everything that I command."

We can surmise that Dositheus' (gnostic) ideas and alterations to scripture were unacceptable in Jerusalem ("to the Jews"). He thus went elsewhere. Changing the text of the Pentateuch is, of course, a major accusation leveled by Jews against the Samaritans. We recall, however, that this accusation was also leveled against the Ebionites, who "do not accept the entire Pentateuch of Moses; some passages they reject."[123] Epiphanius further tells us that the Ebionites were similarly vegetarian and encratite.[124] *Ebion* means "poor one," and we have now, quite innocently, thus strayed from Dositheus directly into the world of James the Just—a vegetarian, encratite,[125] and leader of "the poor ones" in Jerusalem (Gal 2:10).[126] Epiphanius dubbed the leader of the Ebionites "Ebion," considered him a "teacher" and even that he wished to "become like God"—descriptions with which we are now quite familiar:

> But if you want to be like the master, Ebion—that is, if you want to be like the teacher—you are very wrong... You cannot become like God, for you are a mortal man, and under a delusion... —*Panarion* 30.34.3-4

The Dositheans considered the biblical Joshua ("Savior") to be a cipher for Dositheus himself. After all, Joshua *succeeded* Moses and entered (indeed, conquered) the land of Israel. The list of positive Dosithean figures includes Joshua, Judah, and David. On the other hand, the anti-Dosithean

---

122.   Isser 1975:177.

123.   Epiphanius, *Pan.* 30.18.7.

124.   What Epiphanius reports regarding the Ebionites conforms closely with what he also writes about the sect of the Nasarenes "who existed before Christ and did not know him (*Pan* 29.6.1). *Cf. Panarion* 18, *Anacephalaeosis* I. The name *Nasaraioi* (with sigma) is the only Greek cognate that reflects the Semitic *tsade*, e.g., Mandaic *Natsuraia*, "guardian of mysteries" or priest (Drower and Macuch 285).

125.   "In the past [the Ebionites] boasted of virginity because of James the brother of the Lord" (Epiph. *Pan.* 30.2.6).

126.   J. Crossan observes: "Why would the Christian poor of Jerusalem be in any worse straits than the Christian poor of any other city? I am inclined, therefore, to consider that the collection [of Paul] was primarily for the Jerusalem community itself and that they called themselves 'the poor ones'" (J. Crossan, *The Historical Jesus*).

Samaritan priesthood deprecated these while endorsing Joseph, Ephraim, and Zadok.

The Dositheans conceived of their prophet as the great gate: *Baba Rabba*.[127] Only through that gate does one find salvation. This immediately recalls Jn 14:6—"I am the way, and the truth, and the life. No one comes to the Father except through me" (*cf.* Jn 10:7). In Dositheanism the gate is *gnosis* and it is directly accessible to all. This bears striking resemblance to Jamesian gnostic theology (above pp. 429–30).

Of course, the Samaritan priesthood rejected this Dosithean view— one which renders them (and all priesthoods) entirely superfluous. When the Christian Church began to organize it likewise rejected gnosticism, and we can surmise for the very same reason.[128] The reader may take note of an essential law operative in all religions and in all eras: *organized religions* exist in opposition to *individual empowerment*. The one simply negates the other.

It would appear that the Dositheans were an enduring sect that found a home—of all places—in Alexandria. Could this have anything to do with Yeshu ha-Notsri's extended stay there in the early first century BCE? The Dositheans were a significant presence in that city for many centuries. Kohler observes: "According to Photius, the Dositheans in about 600 CE held a dispute with the Alexandrian bishop Eulogius, with the result that they were expelled from Egypt.[129] We wonder what that "dispute" involved. From the foregoing, we can be sure it concerned the nature of "Jesus." The Dositheans would have insisted that Jesus was not a human but a spiritual being. He was *gnosis* and the "great gate"—immediately accessible to anyone and everyone without any priesthood, church, or religion. Jesus was "Light"—and a prophet had brought them this great lesson towards the turn of the era.

The foregoing presentation of the Samaritans will perhaps strike many readers as unprecedented, perhaps even willful. However, few realize how little is actually known of Samaritan origins. One specialist admits:

> [T]here has been no certain statement in modern [scholarship] as to the number of Samaritan sects, their nature, or even a reasonable determination of whether sects listed as Samaritan were, in fact, Samaritan, Jewish, Christian or Gnostic. It is probable that differences between even the

---

127.   Crown 1968:198. Baba Rabba (alternately translated "Great Father") was apparently also a noted Samaritan High Priest of the third–fourth century.

128.   If Baba Rabba ("Great Gate") was associated with gnosis, it was rejected by the Great Church in favor of salvation through Jesus Christ. Perhaps this has something to do with the exhange of Barabbas (= Baba Rabba?) for Jesus in canonical accounts of the Passion (Mk 15:15 and parallels).

129.   Kohler 1911:433.

broader religious divisions of Jew, Christian and Samaritan, were, at various stages of their parallel development, minimal.[130]

A. Crown goes on to note that Samaritan Gnostics were among the numerous sects rife in the early second century CE, *before* the time of Valentinus and Marcion. He then notes that Origen associated the *Dositheans* with the *Simonians*,[131] and on the same page observes "there is an apparent contact with the Covenanters of *Qumran*."

The *Clementine Recognitions* (I:54) note that the Samaritans rightly "expect the one true prophet, but by the wickedness of Dositheus they were hindered from believing that Jesus is He whom they were expecting." Here we witness an early statement acknowledging that some people (the Dositheans) refused to accept Jesus of Nazareth—they preferred the *older* theology that Jesus = gnosis.

Modern readers should not allow the aribrary (and irresponsible) assignment of (varying) names in antiquity to obscure the fundamental issue: theology. Each ancient author had a special agenda, and no two agendas matched. The writers invented characters, changed names, and assigned motives and outcomes according to their *own* theologies. Thus, each text represents an independent view of the contemporary religious landscape from the author's vantage point. The result has little to do with what we would call history.

Our previous observations regarding Yeshu leaving high pharisaic position in Jerusalem to form a new religion parallels what Epiphanius tells us of Dositheus: he was "a leading Jew who had failed to make a mark amongst his own people but had gone over to the Samaritans among whom he had founded his sect, eventually retiring into hermit-like seclusion and dying in a cave" (Crown 1967:75–76, *cf.* above p. 358). Some traditions mooted that the body of Dositheus was never found. The view became extant that he was still alive—presumably as an eternal spiritual entity (*cf.* a spiritual Moses/Jesus/gnosis ever available). This recalls Paul's view of a the ever-present spiritual "Jesus" (above p. 409).

Qumran

Two theologies. Famously, some sectarian texts in the Dead Sea Scrolls (DSS) use a number of monikers to identify individuals: the "Teacher of Righteousness" (or "Just Teacher," *moreh ha-tsedek*), the "Man of the Lie," the "Wicked Priest," *etc.* Scholars have varying theories regarding the identities of these figures, yet no consensus exists today, more than fifty years after

---

130. Crown 1967:70.
131. Crown 1967:72.

discovery of the scrolls. This may owe to the fact that over-riding issues have not yet been solved: the date(s) the scrolls were written, who authored, them, their purpose, provenance, *etc.* Because numerous fundamental issues in DSS research remain unresolved, historical identities do as well.

No attempt will be made here to match the above monikers with people of history. It can be noted, however, that majority opinion increasingly dates events surrounding the Teacher of Righteousness to the early first century BCE. Michael Wise, for example, places the Teacher's death precisely in 72 BCE.[132] This would align with what we have surmised regarding Yeshu ha-Notsri, for according to our calculations he returned to Israel about 76–75 BCE (above p. 420).

Yeshu was active in Judea in the 70s BCE and seems to have had significant interactions with the temple priesthood. The same can be said for the Dead Sea Sect. Furthermore, Yeshu was charged, tried, convicted, and executed "because he has practiced sorcery and enticed Israel to apostasy" (above p. 422). If Wise is correct, a similar succession of unfortunate events may have befallen the Dead Sea Sect's leader. Wise proposes that the sentence was commuted and the prophet sent into exile. This agrees with what Josephus tells us:

> But the principal of those that were in danger [from the Pharisees] fled to Aristobulus, who persuaded his mother [Salome Alexandra] to spare the men on account of their dignity, but to expel them out of the city, unless she took them to be innocent; so they were suffered to go unpunished, and were dispersed all over the country. —Josephus, Wars I.5.3

This may have been the time the founding prophet fled to Qumran and there instituted a new community. Evidently he had considerable initial success. Eventually, however, the Jerusalem authorities came after him, found him, and executed him.

The prominent pharisee Simon ben Shetach was active during Yeshu's career. It was Simon who recalled Yeshu's master, Perachiah, from Alexandria (above p. 420). Wise identifies Simon with 'the man of the lie'—so often noted in the Dead Sea Scrolls.[133] Ben Shetach, as brother of Queen Alexandra, was probably the most powerful man in the land, the head of the Sanhedrin, and perhaps the man ultimately responsible for the execution of Yeshu ha-Notsri (above p. 427).

The foregoing are some historical elements that suggest a link between Yeshu and the founding prophet of the DSS. Theology also offers clues. Our particular interest is in elements of the DSS that reflect the gnostic path to the divine—thus echoing the accusation leveled against Yeshu ha-

---

132. Wise 1999:213–19. Allegro (1957:99; 1979:196) dates the death to 88 BCE.
133. Wise 1999:72, 172; Wise, Abegg, & Cook 1996:31.

Notsri. As we have seen, a similar accusation can be extended to the figures of Simon Magus ("the Standing One," "the Great Power"), James the Just (the "gate"), and Dositheus ("plunging into" whose writings confers enlightenment).

The DSS contain pronounced gnostic tendencies. This is denied by no one. Such tendencies are particularly detectable in the *Thanksgiving Hymns* (*Hodayoth*), the *Songs of the Sabbath Sacrifice*, and in a number of sapiential (quasi-gnostic) writings.

It is generally admitted that gnosticism lies *outside* the normative Jewish worldview which insists upon a chasm between man and God. Such a chasm permits *worship*. Gnosticism, on the other hand, places the quest for understanding above the need for worship. In doing so it rejects the chasm or attempts to 'cross' it. This is impossible and abhorrent in normative Judaism and is tantamount to the arrogance (a key accusation) of wishing to make oneself divine. This was precisely the accusation leveled against Yeshu as well as against Dositheus. It is also the attitude reflected in some gnostic Jamesian works (above, p. 433).

Thus, two theological poles can be identified—not merely in Judaism but in virtually every organized religion. One pole is gnostic and places happiness and ultimate fulfillment in the hands of man himself. This can be described as the 'ultra-liberal' end of religion, wherein the freedom of man is maximized.

At the other extreme is the conservative worldview in which man is *entirely* dependent upon an external power—generally called "God." This pole is characterized by obedience, scrupulous adherence to rite and ritual, and—in its ultimate form—the belief in predestination (determinism), that is, the view that man has no say whatsoever in his fate.

One can summarize the two contrasting worldviews in a word: *agency*. In gnosticism, the agency is *with man*. Indeed, extreme forms of gnosticism ("Primary Gnosticism") do not even require a God (nor, *nota bene*, a priesthood). What saves is *gnosis*/understanding. That is enough.

On the other hand, in the ultra-orthodoxy of conservative religions agency is *with God*. God decrees, commands, and receives (indeed, he insists upon) worship. It is no coincidence that this worldview requires a strong priesthood, one that not only worships God but also considers it necessary to *interpret* him for the masses.

In Judaism, a small 'grey area' has historically existed between the two poles, an area at the limits of what is permissible—one that is approached with great trepidation (even as is God). This intermediary area is traditionally known as 'Jewish mysticism' and includes the so-called *hechalot* and ascent literature.

The DSS are rife with ascent theology. Furthermore, we will see that they contain unmistakable clues of an even more extreme gnosticism.

Curiously, the opposite pole also exists in the scrolls—and in no small measure. The presence of these two contrasting theologies side-by-side has not yet been appreciated in Qumran scholarship. *Two major and very different theologies influenced the Yahad.* Furthermore, the theologies are fundamentally incompatible. The DSS may be viewed as a struggle to reconcile these two opposing worldviews—one traditionally Jewish, the other outlandishly heretical. This is revealed by internal evidence (that is, the expressed content of the writings themselves) which, as Eisenman has insisted, trumps external considerations such as carbon dating and paleographic theories.[134]

Of the two theological poles, the conservative is *by far* the better represented in the DSS. In fact, signs suggest a later conservative editing-out of originally gnostic material. We cannot detail the evidence for such editing, an important task that may devolve to another book. A historical framework to explain the resulting complex presentation of the texts can, however, be suggested.

Two hymns. Much attention has been focussed on the identity of the Teacher of Righteousness, whose name immediately brings to mind James "the Just." The identity between the two has, in fact, been made by at least one contemporary scholar—Robert Eisenman (and, before him, Robert Eisler).[135] In a previous section (pp. 428–34), however, it was argued above that James the Just is not a figure of history but the reflection of a prophet who lived in the early first century BCE—the prophet Rabbinic writings refer to as Yeshu ha-Notsri. Accordingly we would date the Teacher of Righteousness and associated figures to the first century BCE.

It cannot be automatically assumed that the Teacher of Righteousness—as described in sectarian texts—was the founder of the Qumran sect. The *Damascus Document* mentions a twenty year period of groping *prior* to God's raising up a Teacher.[136] We must defer more specific data relative to the Teacher, but regardless of who he was there appears to be room in the chronology for a founding prophet who may be virtually lost to history. The scrolls indeed champion the Righteous Teacher, but there are signs that he led a conservative retrenchment *against a prior gnostic theology*. The next few pages will attempt to clarify this surprising view.

The principal accusation against Yeshu, we recall, was that he 'made himself God' (above pp. 419–20). The discovery of this very element in the

---

134. Eisenman 2006:484–85.
135. Eisenman 2006:712.
136. 4Q266, 2.13 (DJD 18, p. 35); 4Q268, 1.16 (DJD 18, p. 120).

DSS constitutes one of the most astonishing revelations in the texts. Here is the well-known "Self-Glorification Hymn" from the *Hodayoth*:

> I am reckoned with the angels
>> my dwelling place is in in the holy council.
> Who has been regarded with scorn like me,
>> and who has borne oppression like me?
> Who is like me, lacking evil,
>> so that he can compare to me?
> I have never been instructed,
>> yet no teaching compares to my teaching.
> I sit on [high, exalted in heave]n...
> Who is like me among the angels?...
> The utterance of my lips, who can endure?
> Who can challenge me in speech
>> and so compare with my judgment?
> [I] am beloved of the King, a companion of the Holy Ones,
>> and none can oppose me.
> [To my majesty and my glory] can none compare,
>> for my station is with the angels.
> Neither glory [nor majes]ty have I laid up as treas[ure]
>> at the price of gold, neither of fine gold.
> None can compare with me,
>> and no [iniquity] has been reckoned against me.
>> > —1QH26:2–10 (formatting added).[137]

Contrary to so much Jewish scripture, the writer of this hymn is center stage. The first person pronoun is frequent. God is not even mentioned. Indeed, there are oblique jabs at Yahweh: Who "can compare to me?" asks the writer. "Who can challenge me in speech and so compare with my judgment?" He supplies the astonishing answer: "To my majesty and my glory can *none* compare." This view is thoroughly *humanist*.

This hymn presents no external power. Only the clause "I am beloved of the King" may echo a more traditional theistic mindset. At the same time, the hymn hints at a *personal*, familial relationship with that King—a relationship familiar from the New Testament. The writer is in the same *family* as the King. He is of the same *nature*.

The hymn also presents no redeemer figure. The writer has done all the work necessary for his own salvation. This shows in his self-characterization. After all, he is "lacking evil," and "no iniquity has been reckoned against me"—implying that he has thoroughly purified himself spiritually.

---

137. Wise 1999:223. "The translation is of the reconstructed 1QH 26:2–10, with lacunae filled in where possible from the other witnesses. Brackets indicate only reconstructions attested in none of the witnesses" (Wise 1999:323, n.5).

The fact that he has done this spiritual work *himself* is implied by another line: he has "never been instructed." At the same time the writer is peerless in knowledge: Who can "compare with my judgment?" he asks. "Who can challenge me in speech?" He concludes simply: "none can oppose me."

We recall (above p. 421) that both the *ascent of man* to gnosis and the *descent of a redeemer figure* are portrayed in the ancient texts. Of the two, it was suggested that the *ascent* trajectory is primary. It requires no redeemer or mythology—only gnosis. It does not even require a god. We have termed this Primary Gnosticism. Its most familiar surviving form today may be the Theravada school of Buddhism. The ascent trajectory has probably been in existence, in one form or another, since the very dawn of civilization. Primary Gnosticism is fundamentally humanist.

The developed systems of gnosticism familiar to scholars of early Christianity have a redeemer figure who descends from on high (or is sent from a king in a far country—*cf.* the *Hymn of the Pearl*).[138] The figure reveals gnosis (the "pearl") or helps the gnostic initiate rise up to gnosis/salvation, often by negotiating fearful obstacles or powers. The *descent and return* to gnosis were often presented in the form of complex mythologies which characterize "Secondary Gnosticism," in that the aspirant has the aide of an external or unknown power (which could also simply be one's *original* nature) to attain truth, gnosis, the godhead, or 'unity.' Christian scholarship has studied Secondary Gnosticism at length, but it has virtually ignored the possibility that gnosticism can thrive *without any mythology at all*.

The *Self-Glorification Hymn* is an outlier text among the DSS. Yet, four incomplete copies of the hymn were discovered in the caves, according to Israel Knohl. He notes that one copy was found in a condition that clearly betrayed deliberate mutilation in antiquity. This copy was separate from the rest of the *Thanksgiving Psalms*, was ripped to shreds, and the pieces then crumpled into a ball.[139] No other DSS scroll was discovered in such an obviously abused condition.

All four copies of the *Self-Glorification Hymn* were accompanied and immediately followed by another hymn, suggesting that the two texts were paired. Knohl labels them Hymn 1 and Hymn 2. We note that the theology of the second hymn is entirely contrary to that of the first, as if it was intended to 'cancel out' the former. For example, Hymn 2 explicitly defines the "King" as *God*: "ascribe greatness to our God and glory to our King" (line 15). Though Hymn 1 enjoins reliance on the *self*, Hymn 2 describes worship of God who *alone* acts, reveals, and lifts up:

---

138. The Acts of Thomas 108–13 (NTA II.380–85). In the Hermetic and Orphic literature one "remembers" his true nature and calling.

139. Knohl 2000:13. A photograph of the crumpled mass *in situ* is at Knohl 2000:14.

> ...worship in the common assembly. Bless the one who wonderfully does majestic deeds and makes known his strong hand, sealing mysteries and revealing hidden things, raising up those who stumble and those among them who fall by restoring the step of those who wait for knowledge, but casting down the lofty assemblies of the eternally proud...
>
> —4QHab frg. 7, col. 1, lines 18–20 (Knohl 2003:78).

Here, agency is entirely *with God*. The aspersions of casting down the "lofty" and the eternally "proud" are standard anti-Gnostic canards, for the Gnostic has the arrogance to think agency is *with him*, that he can venture across the aforementioned chasm separating man and God. Hymn 2 also declares: "Proclaim and say: Great is God who acts wonderfully, for he *casts down the haughty* spirit so that there is no remnant" (col. 2, line 7). Such writing is pointedly anti-gnostic.

Hymn 2 also threatens. It reaffirms the age-old fear of God: "Bless the one who judges *with destructive wrath*" (line 21); "Blessed is God *who works mighty marvels*, acting mightily to make *his* power appear" (col 2, line 12).

How could two such contrasting hymns have existed side-by-side?

Numerous texts in the DSS are wisdom-oriented. They consider the "secrets" of God, his "mystery" (or "mysterious ways"), and they laud the *"understanding one* who rejoices in the inheritance of *truth.*"[140] These texts are 'gnostic-leaning.' While they enjoin the gnostic quest, they (quite un-gnostically) also ascribe all agency *to God. He* is the "God of knowledge." *He* alone is "the foundation of truth... He expounded for *their* understanding every deed so that man could walk in the inclination of *his* understanding. And *He will expound for man...*"[141] Many more examples could be cited of this incompatible fusion between (a) man's unaided journey to gnosis and (b) God's indispensibility (*i.e.* his absolute pre-eminence as creator, ruler, and source of knowledge). *Herein resides the basic theological conflict between gnosticism and theism.*

A revolt in the community. The *Thanksgiving Hymns* preserve curious passages in which the writer—in a very personal style—accuses members *of his own community* of having turned against him. He feels like a "bird banished from its nest." The fact that a bird makes its own nest is but one clue that the writer of those words is the founder of the Yahad. Yet he has been made *persona non grata* by that very community. Furthermore, the writer is extraordinarily accusatory towards his one-time "friends and acquaintances." He accuses them of having "plotted wickedness against me," of being "mediators of a lie and seers of deceit," and of being "pretenders":

---

140. 4Q416, frg. 4:3. For the DSS sapiential texts, see Parry and Tov 2004, vol. IV.
141. 4Q417, frg. 1, col. 1:8–11. Emphases added.

6. *[T]hese Your people go astray...*

7. For they flatter themselves with words, and mediators of deceit lead them astray, so that they are ruined *without knowledge,*

8. For their works are deceitful, for *good works were rejected by them. Neither did they esteem me; even when You displayed Your might through me. Instead, they drove me out from my land as a bird from its nes*t.

9. *And all my friends and acquaintances have been driven away from me; they esteem me as a ruined vessel.*

10. But they are mediators of a lie and seers of deceit. *They have plotted wickedness against me,* so as to exchange Your law, which You spoke distinctly in my heart, for flattering words directed to Your people.

11. They hold back the drink of knowledge from those that thirst, and for their thirst they give them vinegar to drink, that they might observe their error,

12. behaving madly at their festivals and getting caught in their nets.

13. But You, O God, reject every plan of Belial, and Your counsel alone will stand, and the plan of Your heart will remain forever.

14. They are pretenders; they hatch the plots of Belial, they seek You with a double heart, and are not founded in Your truth. A root producing poison and wormwood is in their scheming.

15. With a wilful heart they look about and *seek you in idols*. They have set the stumbling block of their iniquity before themselves, and they come

16. to seek You through the words of *lying prophets corrupted by error*. With mocking lips and a strange tongue they speak to Your people

17. so as to make a mockery of all their works by deceit. For they did not choose the way of Your heart nor attend to Your word,

18. *but they said concerning the vision of knowledge, "It is not sure."*

  —1QHab, col. XII:6b–18a. (Formatting and emphases added.)

We do not have space here to explore all the facets of this revealing passage. We take note, however, that it is *Your people* who have gone astray (v. 6). These are the same people who saw God's might *displayed through me*. They drove *me* out from *my* land, and all *my* friends and acquantances... *esteem me as a ruined vessel* (vss. 8–9; on sectarian renegades *cf.* Allegro 1957:137).

The meaning is clear: the head of the community has himself been exiled *by his own people*. He is no longer their leader. He has been deposed.

For what reason? The answer is also plainly supplied above: they drove "me" into exile "*so as to exchange Your law*, which You spoke distinctly in my heart, for flattering words directed to Your people" (v. 10). In other words, the rift was over the "law" [*torah*]. But this is not the Mosaic law. It is a private law, a revelation, an *insight* "which You spoke distinctly *in my heart.*" Perhaps it could even be termed an 'enlightenment.'

For whatever reason, the Yahad was no longer receptive to the theological message of its leader. Concerning *his* vision of knowledge, they now said: "It is not sure" (v. 18). The implication is that the speaker was not only leader of the community but also its founder, for how else could *they* "exhange Your law, which You spoke distinctly in *my* heart"? It is evident that the speaker originally gathered a community around him, led it for a time, and was then rejected.

It would appear from the evidence that the founder of the community penned the *Self-Glorification Hymn* and inspired many of the surviving sapiential and gnostic-leaning texts of the DSS. However, his thoroughly humanist approach was later rejected. The contrary doctrine of predestination was adopted (perhaps for the first time in a Jewish milieu) and all power ('agency') was emphatically *returned* to God. The writings of the founder were then revised, rewritten, and some possibly destroyed. This successful conservative rebellion indicates that strong opposition to the founder arose from within the community itself. Wisdom/gnosis could still be the royal road to salvation, but God would henceforth be the *determining* role in that salvation. The result is works such as the *Thanksgiving Hymns*, the *Songs of the Sabbath Sacrifice*, and many sapiential writings which present an uncomfortable fusion of the two theological poles described above.

Thus, the DSS are somewhat schizophrenic. They present a mixing of traditional and non-traditional elements. The vast bulk of the sectarian texts portray Yahweh as in command and with full control of what happens here below—even to the point of his having predestined success and failure. Yahweh alone *provides* and *chooses*, even in the numerous sapiential texts. Yet those texts also preserve unmistakable signs of a gnostic mindset: they exalt the acquisition of wisdom/understanding, members of the community who acquire such understanding are similar to "angels," and the community is *already* in heaven.

The citation on the facing page betrays evidence of revision. Obvious markers that would identify the "mediators of a lie and seers of deceit" *within the community itself* have been removed. At the same time, elements have been added that emphasize the agency of God, *e.g.*: "But You, O God, reject every plan of Belial, and Your counsel alone will stand, and the plan of Your heart will remain forever" (v. 13).

It is important to note that the Teacher of Righteousness may *not* have been the founder of the sect, nor even a single person. He may have been the leader (perhaps in an elected position) of the *later* conservative faction. We cannot affirm categorically that the Teacher was also known by the titles "Interpreter of the Law" and "the Star," but such infererences are possible when considering passages such as the following:

> And the star is the Interpreter of the Law who came to the land of Damascus, as it is written, "A star will come forth from Jacob and a scepter

from Israel." The staff is the prince of the whole congregation, and when
he arises "he will smite all the sons of Seth."   —*Dam. Doc.* (4Q 269:2–4)

"Sons of Seth" definitely refers to gnostics. The above appears to be
part of a hostile and agressive retrenchment—one that emphatically rejected the original founder of the sect and his gnostic ideas.

Links between Samaritanism and Qumran are patent, for in Samaritan tradition (*Asatir* II.3) Seth founded "Damascus"—the metaphorical locale of the Yahad. Seth was known as a special transmitter of the light
(secret gnosis) from Adam. The DSS invite us to view "Damascus" as the
place of light (= heaven). Ironically, while the Yahad retained the toponym
"Damascus" for their spiritual locale, they apparently eventually rejected
the gnostic worldview that toponym originally designated.

The radical view that has been here presented—of a rebellion and
complete about-face in the Qumran community—is of course provisional
and even tentative. It betrays two stong personalities fighting for control of
the Yahad. This is not entirely without precedent, and we detect remarkable allusions to such high-level feuding elsewhere in the early records—*e.g.*,
Simon Magus and Dositheus feuding for the mantle of John the Baptist:

> ...[Simon], on meeting Dositheus, did not demand of him his post, much
> as he desired it for himself, for he knew quite well that the man who
> had forestalled him in this office could not be removed against his will.
> For this reason [Simon] made a pretence of friendship and for a while
> rested content with the second place after Dositheus. When, however,
> after a time he met his thirty fellow-disciples, he began to circulate slan-
> ders against Dositheus. This man, he asserted, hands down the doctrines
> incorrectly, and does so less because of an evil intent and more out of
> ignorance. Dositheus observed that Simon's well-calculated slanders
> were shaking his own standing among the great multitude so that they
> no longer regarded him as the Standing One; then on one occasion when
> Simon arrived for the ordinary meeting, [Dositheus] struck out at him
> with indignation. The stick seemed to go through Simon's body as if it
> were smoke. Affrighted at this, Dositheus shouted at him, "If you are the
> Standing One, I also will pay homage to you." As Simon answered in the
> affirmative, Dositheus—knowing that he himself was not the Standing
> One—fell down and did homage to Simon and, associating himself with
> the twenty-nine others, set [Simon] in his own place. Then Dositheus
> died a few days after Simon had attained to standing but he himself had
> suffered downfall.   —Ps. Cl. Hom II.24 (NTA 1992 II:513).

The above may be an echo of what took place at Qumran, in that the
founder of the Yahad was apparently deposed by his own community. According to the present thesis, he lost control of the community and went
into exile, perhaps because his views were simply too radical. Thenceforth,

the writing of the Dead Sea Sect are rigidly conservative. Indeed, this would not be the first nor last example of a 'palace coup' that produces a sharp change in the theology of a religious sect.

The canonical gospels may themselves preserve echoes of such developments. After all, Judas (an insider) betrays Jesus—who then loses not only control of his movement but even his own life.

* * *

We have now seen that Jesus of Nazareth was an invention. It is quite likely that Paul of Tarsus was also, for the New Testament epistles ascribed to him are in large part—if not wholly—products of the second century. John the Baptist, Simon Magus, Dositheus—they may also be literary constructs. James the Just, Simon Peter, John, Judas, Mark, Thomas, Barnabas—the whole cast of New Testament characters populate not history, but literature *deceptively written as history*.

The word "deceptively" is apposite, despite predictable objections of Christian apologists that the ancients did not have modern concepts of history, that factual accuracy was never the point, and that the gospels were conveying a message, 'and the message is *true*.'

In such a sense, however, *mythology* is also true. Perhaps, then, all will agree that "mythology" better characterizes the New Testament than the grossly inaccurate term "history." After all, mythology constructs a story using metaphor, parable, fantasy, and figurative language in order to convey some universal truth that transcends the mere events of history.

However, even "mythology" is an inaccurate term for the New Testament, because the term does not include the undeniable element of deception. In mythology the narrative events are not constructed in such a way as to deceive the reader/hearer into thinking the events actually took place in history. The myth of Jason and the Argonauts has gods, a golden fleece, and a cyclops. No one (except children) ever thought these were historical, or supposed that Jason and the Argonauts actually existed. On the other hand, the gospels populate their narratives with people and places *known* to history. For example, Luke writes:

> In the fifteenth year of the reign of Tiberius Caesar, Pontius Pilate being governor of Judea, and Herod being tetrarch of Galilee, and his brother Philip tetrarch of the region of Ituraea and Trachonitis, and Lysanias tetrarch of Abilene, in the high-priesthood of Annas and Caiaphas, the word of God came to John...   (Lk 3:1–2)

Obviously, the evangelist wants the reader to believe this is history. But it is *not* history, for Nazareth did not exist and the acts of Jesus of Nazareth were invented. But neither is Luke's writing mythology. The evangelist might readily have found the above factual particulars in the writings of Josephus. However, though the events described by Josephus are generally known to history, the events described in the canonical gospels are *not*.

Deception is at the heart of Christianity because the evangelists confabulate events, people, and even places, and at the same time they attempt to convince the reader that what is written *actually took place*. Thus the Christian scriptures are neither mythology nor history but simply a hoax.

The essential to Christians has always been that God *miraculously* entered into history. Believers accept the miraculous—indeed, they insist upon it. Faith affirms: Because the events *really happened*, Christianity is valid—regardles of how incredible those events might seem. Reason, however, points out: Because the events *never happened*, Christianity is invalid whether it seems incredible or not. Thus, each position hinges on whether the events *really happened*. Faith *does* depend upon the gospels being historically valid documents!

It is useless to contest claims of the miraculous, for no one can disprove a miracle. At the same time, however, it is often quite possible to prove that a miracle never occurred *in history*.

And therein lies the problem with the miracle known as Jesus of Nazareth—he never existed *in history*. That much is now proven beyond any reasonable doubt. The non-existence of Nazareth at the turn of the era—amply confirmed in these pages—is but one of myriad details witnessing to the colossal deception that informed the figure of Jesus and simultaneously gave wings to the Christian message. As mentioned before, Jesus is an effigy. His marvelous feats are as fictive as those recounted in a James Bond novel. With this deflating recognition, Christianity's long-held pretensions emerge into the light of day as being stunningly vacuous.

Nevertheless, this author maintains that a thread of truth is to be found woven among the innumerable false strands of Christianity. In this chapter we have detected signs of another teacher—*not* Jesus of Nazareth. This does not replace one false religion with another. Far from it! All signs point to a teacher who believed not in God but in the *man's supreme capability for happiness* emphatically based on correct reasoning and good will. What might best be termed good philosophy thus replaces false religion.

We are thus speaking of a very human teacher and a very human philosophy—of *humanism*, not religion.

We have argued that the teacher in question lived in the early part of the first century BCE, was probably a learned Pharisee, spent time in Egypt, and then repudiated his entire Jewish heritage in favor of a thoroughly heretical gnostic worldview. He evidently returned to his native land, began teaching, and became a formidable adversary to his former Pharisaic colleagues as well as to every established form of religion. This was not a *religious* man but a supremely *practical* man.

The rabbis remember this figure under the name Yeshu ha-Notsri. But that is probably only a cipher—*Yeshu* signifying "savior" and ha-Notsri "the watcher/keeper/guardian" (alternately: the "branch").[142]

Kernels of the teacher's view survive—ironically, principally in the canonical gospels themselves. More revealing heretical texts have been systematically destroyed by the Church through many long centuries. Nevertheless, a number of disparate logia and parables in the canonical gospels, when viewed together, witness to a coherent gnostic philosophy, one that is profound and meaningful, and one that also cannot be merely accidental.[143] They witness to a remarkable spiritual figure who taught the possibility of complete happiness in this life, a happiness not to be gained from riches and things either material or transitory.

Thus Christianity is, in the final accounting, a mixture of much falsehood with a little truth. We may wonder why it came into existence at all. The explanation is clear if we simply ask an obvious question: Who has *gained* through the centuries from the existence of the religion? The answer is not far to seek: an extraordinarily wealthy and powerful religious elite has benefitted, together with a sprawling establishment composed of thousands of clerics, all more or less insulated from the insecurities of ordinary life. Let no one suppose this is mere hyperbole. In the present era the most reprehensible conduct on the part of priests and prelates goes largely unpunished and even unacknowledged, simply because the perpetrators are functionaries of the Church and still largely 'outside the law.'

One could say that—as with other organized religions—Christianity is ultimately a self-serving special interest. It thrives through membership and donations—which, at one time, were coerced at the point of the sword. Priesthoods, of course, claim to derive authority from God, and some who call themselves religious claim the right from God to coerce and even to

---

142. Scholarship is divided as to whether the Christian term "Nazarene" and its cognates derive from the Hebrew verb *natsar* ("watch, guard, keep") or from the Hebrew noun *netser* ("sprout, shoot, branch"). Arguments can be advanced for either derivation.

143. The author has collected the sayings and refers the reader to the following, as numbered in J. D. Crossan's *Sayings Parallels* (1986): 9, 3-7, 13, 15–21, 25, 27, 33, 36-41, 45, 52–57, 59–68, 70, 74, 76, 78, 81, 85, 87, 103, 121-23, 140, 134, 152, 155, 159, 170, 172, 176-89, 203, 205-07, 209, 217-22, 225, 227–29, 235, 236, 250, 254, 272, 276, 281, 286, 287, 291, 292, 293, 313, 318, 319, 328, 348–50, 352, 357, 361, 364, 429, 430, 454, 482, 486; Jn 4:24; 6:63; 8:23b, POxy 840. All these sayings and parables have Buddhist parallels.

break every commandment in the holy books. They claim to be the ultimate and indispensible intermediary of *our* salvation. Yet, if there is one lesson to be taken from these pages, it is that priesthoods everywhere are both
self-servig and hostile to the free search for truth, a search that tolerates *no
intermediary*. Gnosticism, in essence, requires no intermediary.

In both Samaritanism and Qumran we have argued that a conservative
priestly rebellion took place, one which annulled and (almost) eradicated an
original gnostic message. Christianity did similarly. In all three cases an
original gnostic message apparently can be traced back to a single teacher.
It is also probable, in this author's view, that Mandaism, Manicheism, and
other (now forgotten) sects similarly trace their roots to one and the same
teacher. In each case, however, a self-appointed priestly organization co-
alesced in order to assume control, eventually declaring some variation of
this basic message: "If you wish to know the truth, I will explain it to you.
You cannot find it on your own. You *need* me."

At the beginning of this third Christian millennium we are able to scientifically evaluate the genesis of Christianity, bringing to bear the results
of two centuries of scholarship. The religion now emerges as principally a
literary development (Brodie, MacDonald) with manifest manipulative intent (Zindler, Salm, Ehrman). Once the Gospel of Mark is seen as a second
century text (Detering, Price)—as scholarship is increasingly admitting—it
becomes clear that the evangelists had access to the first century writings of
Josephus as well as to the legends surrounding the peripatetic philosopher-
magus Apollonius of Tyana, famous already in his lifetime (*c.* 15–*c.* 100
CE). Drawing from Josephus' prolix *oeuvre*, it would have been easy to place
the birth of Jesus in the time of Herod the Great and his death in the time
of Pontius Pilate, borrowing, changing, and adapting historical names and
details as necessary. At the same time, the evangelists used subtle techniques
of mimesis to draw from the Old Testament as well as from the Homeric
epics.

However, the evangelists had a unique agenda not shared by the Old
Testament, Homer, or Josephus. Their overriding goal was to create a God-
man able to command awe and allegiance from ordinary people. In pursuit
of this goal they often overstepped the bounds of credulity, as we see (for
example) in reports of the slaughter of the babes of Bethlehem, the daytime
darkness before Jesus' death (Mk 15:33), the opening of the graves immediately after (Mt 27:52), and the astonishing miracles of Jesus—besides his
virgin birth and bodily resurrection. In addition to all these obvious signs
that the New Testament is fictive, historical inaccuracies also intrude, such
as Luke's misdating of the census of Quirinius, the placement of Pharisees
and synagogues in first century Galilee, and the premature existence of the
town of Nazareth.[144]

---

144. Frank Zindler has also cogently argued that many other New Testament towns

Multiple lines of scientific inquiry are now powerfully converging on one conclusion: Jesus of Nazareth is a fiction. To any sensible person, this intersection of archeology, literary criticism, and historical analysis is persuasive.

Yet, for the greater part of society, fact still yields to faith. This is, unfortunately, unlikely to end soon, for humans appear more readily disposed to *hope* rather than to reason. And, from the very beginnings of Christianity, the figure of Jesus gave great scope to man's propensity to hope. Jesus Christ our savior may defy credulity, but the miraculous aspects attached to him are (and have ever been) welcome confirmation to the pious that God simply suspended the laws of nature precisely in order to effect *their* salvation. That is hope indeed, amply validated in holy writ. So, what matters to the pious, in the final analysis, are not the scientifically demonstrable facts of this life but the *promise* of an eternal life with Jesus in the beyond.

As is now becoming increasingly clear, however, Jesus Christ—the "savior" who made that remarkable promise—never existed.

Many have placed their final hope in Jesus Christ and in the empty promise of eternal life in return for faith in *him*. Often, little else remains. Christianity has always appealed to those of us who *need* to be saved, who look one day in the mirror with disillusionment and see only the wreckage of lives gone very much awry. *Then* we turn to Jesus. Such is the typical model of Christian conversion. First comes the admission of powerlessness, then conversion.

Who would wish to take away the hope of a better life? Is that not like taking candy away from a desperate, irascible, and unreasoning child? The predictable outcome is a tantrum. Far better is another course, one taught by the gnostic sage detectable behind so many ciphers discussed in this chapter—John the Baptist, James the Just, Dositheus, even Jesus Christ. That course is the exhortation to live a better life *now*, so that we can unburden ourselves of the desperate need to hope in a better life to come. This is ultimately a philosophy of empowerment, of raising ourselves to our full potential, of seizing the day, and of seizing the moment. In so doing we will find no need at all of a savior, of a redeemer, of a future life, or even of a god.

"We are the world," intones the chorus of a 1985 song. "We are the children. *We* are the ones who make a brighter day." To make that day brighter, however, we can no longer be dependent, guilt-ridden children, but must grow into reasoning, empowered, and *content* adults.

---

are fiction (Zindler 1997). In addition, the archeologist A. Oshri has determined that Bethlehem of Judea did not exist at the turn of the era (*Archaeology*, Nov.–Dec. 2005, pp. 42–45).

BIBLIOGRAPHY TO CHAPTER 14
(For abbreviations please see p. 480.)

Allegro, J.
—1957. *The Dead Sea Scrolls and the Origins of Christianity*. New York: Criterion.
—1979. *The Dead Sea Scrolls and the Christian Myth*. Devon (UK): Westbridge Books.
Anderson, C. 1972. *The Historical Jesus: A Continuing Quest*. Grand Rapids: Eerdmans.
Betz, H. D. 1979. *Galatians: A Commentary on Paul's Letter to the Churches in Galatia*. Philadelphia: Fortress Press.
Bowman, J.
—1957. "Contact between Samaritan Sects and Qumran?" *Vetus Testamentum*, Vol. 7, Fasc. 2 (Apr., 1957), pp. 184-189.
—1975. *The Samaritan Problem: Studies in the Relationships of Samaritanism, Judaism, and Early Christianity*. Pittsburgh: Pickwick Press.
—1977. *Samaritan Documents Relating to Their History, Religion and Life*. Pittsburgh: Pickwick Press.
Crossan, J. D. 1986. *Sayings Parallels: A Workbook for the Jesus Tradition*. Philadelphia: Fortress Press.
Crown, A. D.
—1967. "Dositheans, Resurrection and a Messianic Joshua." *Antichthon* vol. 1, pp. 70–85.
—1968. "Some Traces of Heterodox Theology in the Samaritan Book of Joshua." *Bulletin of the John Rylands Library*, vol. 50, pp. 178–98.
Detering, H. 2011. *Falsche Zeugen*. Aschaffenburg: Alibri.
Dhammika, S. 1993. *The Edicts of King Asoka: An English Rendering*. The Wheel Publication No. 386/387. Kandy, Sri Lanka: Buddhist Publication Society (ISBN 955-24-0104-6).
Doherty, E. 2009. *Jesus Neither God Nor Man: The Case for a Mythical Jesus*. Ottowa: Age of Reason Publications.
Doresse, J. 1986. *The Secret Books of the Egyptian Gnostics*. Rochester, VT: Inner Traditions.
Drews, A. 1912. *The Witnesses to the Historicity of Jesus*. New York: Arno Press.
Drower, E. and R. Macuch. 1963. *A Mandaic Dictionary*. Oxford: Clarendon Press.
Eisenman, R.
—1997. *James the Brother of Jesus*. New York: Penguin..
—2006. *The New Testament Code*. London: Watkins.
Eisler, R. 1931. *The Messiah Jesus*. London: Methuen.
Fossum, J. 1985. *The Name of God and the Angel of the Lord: Samaritan and Jewish Concepts of Intermediation and the Origin of Gnosticism*.Tübingen: Mohr Siebeck.

Halkin, F. 1969. "Actes Inedits de S. Marc." *Analecta Bollandiana* 87: 346-371. (Greek text, preceded by discussion.)

Haussig, H. 1965. *Götter und Mythen im Vorderen Orient. Band I.* Stuttgart: E. Klett.

Herford, R. 1903. *Christianity in Talmud and Midrash.* Rpt. 1975. New York: Ktav.

Howard, G. 1995. *Hebrew Gospel of Matthew.* Macon: Mercer University Press.

Isser, S. 1975. "Dositheus, Jesus, and a Moses Aretalogy." In *Christianity, Judaism and Other Greco-Roman Cults.* J. Neusner, ed. Leiden: Brill, pp. 167–89.

Jastrow, M. *A Dictionary of the Targumim, the Talmud Babli and Yerushalmi, and the Midrashic Literature.* Jerusalem [?]. N.d.

Johnson, L. T. 1995. *The Letter of James: A New Translation with Introduction and Commentary.* (The Anchor Bible.) New York: Doubleday.

Kippenberg, H. 1971. *Garizim und Synagoge: Traditionsgeschichtliche Untersuchungen zur samaritanischen Religion der aramäischen Periode.* Berlin: De Gruyter.

Knohl, I. 2000. *The Messiah before Jesus: The Suffering Servant of the Dead Sea Scrolls.* Berkeley: Univ. of California Pr.

Kohler, K. 1911. "Dositheus, the Samaritan Heresiarch, and his Relations to Jewish and Christian Doctrines and Sects." *American Journal of Theology,* vol. XV, 404–35.

Kraemer, R. 2006. "Implicating Herodias and Her Daughter in the Death of John the Baptizer: A (Christian) Theological Strategy?" JBL vol. 125(2):321–49.

Nielsen, D. 1904. *Die altarabische Mondreligion und die mosaische Ueberlieferung.* Strassburg: Trübner.

Painter, J. 2004. *Just James: The Brother of Jesus in History and Tradition.* Second Edition. Columbia: Univ. of S. Carolina Pr.

Payne-Smith, R. 1902/1999. *Compendious Syriac Dictionary.* Eugene: Wipf & Stock.

Price, R. M.

—2006. *The Pre-Nicene New Testament: Fifty-four Formative Texts.* Salt Lake City: Signature Books.

—2007. *Jesus is Dead.* Cranford: American Atheist Press.

—2011. *The Christ Myth Theory and Its Problems.* Cranford: American Atheist Press.

—2012. *The Amazing Colossal Apostle.* Salt Lake City: Signature Books.

Rabbinowicz, R.

—1867–97. *Diqduqe Soferim.* 16 vols. Munich [No. publ. given.]

—1877. *Kritische Übersicht der Gesammt- und Einzelausgaben des Babylonischen Talmuds seit 1484.* E. Huber: Munich. (OCLC 162478274).

Rajak, T. 1983. *Josephus: The Historian and His Society.* London: Duckworth.

Robertson, J. M. 1911. *Pagan Christs: Studies in Comparative Mythology.* London: Watts, 2nd rev. ed.

Schmithals, W.

—1965. *Paul and James.* Series: Studies in Biblical Theology, 46. London: SCM Press.

—1969. *The Office of Apostle in the Early Church*. Nashville: Abingdon.

Taylor, J. 1993. *Christians and the Holy Places: The Myth of Jewish-Christian Origins*. Oxford: Clarendon Press.

Torrey, C. 1947. "The Messiah Son of Ephraim." *JBL* 66:3, pp. 353–77.

Tromp, J. 2008. "John the Baptist According to Flavius Josephus, and his Incorporation in the Christian Tradition." In *Empsychoi logoi—Religious Innovations in Antiquity: Studies in Honour of Pieter Willem van der Horst*. Leiden: Brill.

Weeden, T. 1971. *Mark: Traditions in Conflict*. Philadelphia: Fortress.

Wise, M. 1999. *The First Messiah: Investigating the Savior Before Christ*. San Francisco: HarperCollins.

Zindler, F.

—1997. "Where Jesus Never Walked," *American Atheist*, vol. 36, Winter 1996:22–29.

— 2003. *The Jesus the Jews Never Knew: Sepher Toldoth Yeshu and the Quest of the Historical Jesus in Jewish Sources*. Cranford: American Atheist Press.

COMPREHENSIVE NAZARETH BIBLIOGRAPHY

Comprehensive Nazareth Bibliography

Note: This bibliography contains pertinent material listed in *The Myth of Nazareth* (2008) as well as more recent publications. Bibliographic material pertaining to the Caesarea inscription is at the end of Chapter 12. Sources in the text unrelated to Nazareth are not included below but are cited in full in footnotes of the various chapters.

Abbreviations and multi-volume reference works

ABD   1992. Freedman, D., editor in chief. *The Anchor Bible Dictionary*. New York: Doubleday.

AEHL   2001. *The Archaeological Encyclopedia of the Holy Land*. A. Negev and S. Gibson, eds. New York: Continuum.

AJA   *American Journal of Archaeology.*

APHL   Amiran, R. *Ancient Pottery of the Holy Land: From its Beginnings in the Neolithic Period to the End of the Iron Age*. Rutgers Univ. Press, 1970.

Arch.   1992. Ben-Tor, A., ed. *The Archaeology of Ancient Israel*. New Haven: Yale University Press.

BAIAS   *Bulletin of the Anglo-Israel Archaeological Society*. (Renamed STRATA.)

BAR   *Biblical Archaeology Review.*

BASOR   *Bulletin of the American Schools of Oriental Research.*

BDB   1906/2003. Brown, F., S. Driver, and C. Briggs. *The Brown-Driver-Briggs Hebrew and English Lexicon*. Peabody: Hendrickson.

CAH   1970–. *The Cambridge Ancient History*. Cambridge; New York: Cambridge University Press.

CCSL   1953–. *Corpus Christianorum Series Latina*. Ed. P. Geyer. Turnhout-Leipzig: G. Freytag.

CE   1911. Herberman, C., ed. *The Catholic Encyclopedia*. New York: Rbt. Appleton. (1967 edition. Washington D.C. The 2003 article "Nazareth" is a reprint of the 1967 edition).

CHJ   1984. Davies, W. and L. Finkelstein, eds. *The Cambridge History of Judaism*. 3 vols. Cambridge: University Press.

DACL   1935. Cabrol, F. and H. Leclercq, eds. *Dictionnaire D'Archaeologie Chretienne et de Liturgie*. Paris: Letouzey et Ané. Pt. CXXX, cols. 1021–1054.

DB   1960. Bagatti, B. *Dictionnaire de la Bible. Supplément VI*. "Nazareth," cols. 318-329.

DJBP   1996. *Dictionary of Judaism in the Biblical Period: 450 B.C.E. to 600 C.E.* 2 vols. J. Neusner, ed. in chief. New York: Macmillan Library Reference.

EAEHL 1977. Avi-Yonah, M. and E. Stern, editors, English edition. *Encyclopedia of Archaeological Excavations in the Holy Land.* Jerusalem and Englewood Cliffs, NJ: Oxford University Press.

EB   1899-1903. Cheyne, T. and J. Black, eds. *Encyclopaedia Biblica: a critical dictionary of the literary political and religious history, the archaeology, geography, and natural history of the Bible.* London: Adam and Charles Black.

EJ   1972. *Encyclopaedia Judaica.* Jerusalem, New York: Macmillan.

ESI   *Excavations and Surveys in Israel. (Hadashot Arkheologiyot.)* Jerusalem: Israel Dept. of Antiquities and Museums, 1984-

Exc.   1969. Bagatti, B. *Excavations in Nazareth,* vol. 1.

IAA   *Israel Antiquities Authority.*

IDB   1962/1973. Buttrick, G. et al. (eds.) *The Interpreter's Dictionary of the Bible: An Illustrated Encyclopedia.* 4 vols. + Supplement. Nashville: Abingdon Press.

IEJ   *Israel Exploration Journal.*

LA   *Liber Annuus.* Jerusalem: Franciscan Printing Press.

LTK   1998. *Lexikon für Theologie und Kirche,* Band 7, "Nazaret." Herder: Freiburg.

NEAEHL 1993. Stern, E., ed. *The New Encyclopedia of Archaeological Excavations in the Holy Land.* New York: Simon and Schuster.

NGP   1985. *New Gospel Parallels.* R. Funk, ed. 2 vols. Philadelphia: Fortress Press.

NHL   1977. *The Nag Hammadi Library in English.* New York: Harper & Row, 1977.

NIDBA 1983. *The New International Dictionary of Biblical Archaeology.* E. Blaiklock et al. (eds.). Grand Rapids: Zondervan Publishing House.

NSH   1910. *The New Schaff-Herzog Encyclopedia of Religious Knowledge.* New York: Funk and Wagnalls.

NTA   1991. *New Testament Apocrypha.* W. Schneemelcher, ed. 2 vols. Louisville: John Knox Press.

OEANE 1997. Meyers, E., ed. in chief. *The Oxford Encyclopedia of Archaeology in the Near East.* New York: Oxford Univ. Pr.

OTP   1985. Charlesworth, J. (ed.) *The Old Testament Pseudepigrapha.* 2 vols. New York: Doubleday.

PEFQS *Palestine Exploration Fund Quarterly Statement.*

PEQ   *Palestine Exploration Quarterly.*

QDAP   *The Quarterly of the Department of Antiquities in Palestine.*
        Jerusalem and London: Oxford Univ. Press.
RB   1915–. *Revue Biblique.* Paris : Librairie V. Lecoffre.
RPTK   1903. Hauck, D., ed. *Realencyklopädie für protestantische Theologie und
        Kirche.* Leipzig: J. C. Hinrichs.
TDNT   1964. Kittel, G. and G. Friedrich. *Theological Dictionary of the New
        Testament.* Tr. by G. Bromiley. 9 vols. Grand Rapids: Eerd-
        mans Publ. Co.

Adan-Bayewitz, D.
  1993.   *Common Pottery in Roman Galilee: A Study of Local Trade.* Ramat Gan.
  2003.   "On the Chronology of the Common Pottery of Northern Ro-
          man Judaea/Palestine." Pp. 5–23 in G. C. Bottini, L. Di
          Segni, and L. D. Chrupcala (eds.), *One Land – Many Cultures:
          Archaeological Studies in Honour of Stanislao Loffreda OFM* (Jeru-
          salem).
Adan-Bayewitz, D. and M. Wieder. 1992. "Ceramics from Roman Galilee:
          A Comparison of Several Techniques for Fabric Characteriza-
          tion." *Journal of Field Archaeology*, Vol. 19:189-205.
Ahlström, G. "Wine Presses and Cup-Marks of the Henin-Megiddo Sur-
          vey." BASOR 231 (Oct. 1978):19–49.
Alexandre, Y.
  2000.   "Nazerat (Nazareth)." ESI 112:118. Jerusalem: Israel Antiquities
          Authority. [Unsigned.]
  2003.   "An Iron Age IB/IIA Burial Cave at Har Yona, Upper
          Nazareth." *'Atiqot* 44:183-89.
  2005.   "Elut" (report date 11/4/2005). ESI 117. Jerusalem: Israel An-
          tiquities Authority.
  2006.   "Archaeological Excavations at Mary's Well, Nazareth." Israel
          Antiquities Authority report. Dated "1st May 2006." (Un-
          published personal correspondence.)
  2012a. *Mary's Well, Nazareth: The Late Hellenistic to the Ottoman Periods.*
          Jerusalem: Israel Antiquities Authority.
  2012b. "Uncovering Ancient Nazareth: Past and Present Archaeo-
          logical Excavations." In M. Yazbak and S. Sharif (eds.)
          2012:27–42. Nazareth: Nazareth Municipality.
  2012c   "Yafi'a." ESI 124.
In preparation. *An Early Roman House in Nazareth.* Jerusalem: IAA (*'Atiqot*).

Alexandre, Y., Covello-Paran K. and Gal Z. 2003. "Excavations at Tel Gat Hefer in the Lower Galilee, Areas A and B." *'Atiqot* 44.

Amiran, R. 1970. *Ancient Pottery of the Holy Land: From its Beginnings in the Neolithic Period to the End of the Iron Age.* Rutgers Univ. Press. [APHL]

[Anonymous.]
1963. "Nazareth." RB 70:563. [Virtually identical to RB 72:547 (1965).]
1999. "Resurrecting Nazareth: $60 Million Plan to Recreate Jesus' Hometown Underway." BAR vol. 25 (May–June 1999), p. 16.

Arav, R. 1989. *Hellenistic Palestine: Settlement Patterns and City Planning, 337-31 B.C.E.* Oxford: BAR International Series 485.

Arav, R. and R. Freund, eds. 1995. *Bethsaida: A City by the North Shore of the Sea of Galilee.* Vol. 1: Bethsaida Excavations Project. Kirksville: Thomas Jefferson University Press.

Avi-Yonah, M. 1962. "A List of Priestly Courses from Caesarea." IEJ 12:137-39.

Aviam, M.
2004a. "First century Jewish Galilee: an archaeological perspective." in D. R. Edwards (ed.), *Religion and Society in Roman Palestine. Old Questions, New Approaches.* New York and London, pp. 7-27.
2004b *Jews, Pagans and Christians in the Galilee: 25 Years of Archaeological Excavations and Surveys – Hellenistic to Byzantine Periods.* First part of the series "Land of Galilee." Institute for Galilean Archaeology. Rochester: University Press.

Aviam, M. and D. Syon, 2002. "Jewish ossilegium in Galilee," in G. Foerster and L. Rutgers, eds. *What Has Athens to do With Jerusalem: Essays on Classical, Jewish, and Early Christian Art and Archaeology in Honor of Gideon Foerster.* Louven: Peeters, pp. 151–87.

Ayalon, E., R. Frankel, and A. Kloner. 2009. *Oil and Wine Presses in Israel from the Hellenistic, Roman and Byzantine Periods.* BAR International Series 1972. Oxford: Archaeopress.

Bagatti, B.
1937. "B. Note Archeologische. I – Gli Scavi Presso Le Dame Di Nazaret." *Studi Francescani* 4, pp. 253-58.
1955. "Ritrovamenti nella Nazaret evangelica." LA 5:5-44.
1960. "Nazareth," DB, Supplement VI. Paris: Letouzey et Ané, 1960.
1967. "I Vetri del Museo Francescano di Nazaret." LA 17:222-240, figs. 1-7.
1969. *Excavations in Nazareth.* Vol I: From the Beginning till the XII Century. (Publications of the Studium Biblicum Franciscanum 17). Jerusalem: Franciscan Printing House, xi + 320 pp., 240 figures, 11 plates, index. Translation by E. Hoade of the 1967 Italian work.

1971a. "Scavo Presso la Chiesa di S. Giuseppe a Nazaret (Agosto 1970)." LA 21:5-32.

1971b. "Communication du P. B. Bagatti: Nazareth: Église S. Joseph." RB 78:587 (resumé of 1971a).

2001. *Ancient Christian Villages of Galilee*. Jerusalem: Franciscan Printing Press.

Bagatti, B. and J. Milik. 1958. *Gli Scavi del "Dominus Flevit." Parte I: La Necropoli del Periodo Romano*. Jerusalem: Tipografia dei PP. Francescani.

Bailey, D. M. 1975. *A Catalogue of the Lamps in the British Museum: I. Greek, Hellenistic, and Early Roman Pottery Lamps*. London: The Trustees of the British Museum.

Baldi, D. and B. Bagatti. 1937. "Il Santuario della Nutrizione a Nazaret." *Studi Francescani*, IX, No. 4:225-264.

Barkay, R.
1995. "Coins." Chapter 2 in E. Stern 1995 (pp. 88–90).
2000. "The Coins of Horvat 'Eleq." Chapter 11 in Y. Hirschfeld 2000 (pp. 377–419).

Batey, R.
1992. "Sepphoris: An Urban Portrait of Jesus." BAR, May–June 1992:52-62.
2001. "Sepphoris and the Jesus Movement." *New Testament Studies* 46:402-409.

Ben Tor, A., ed. 1992. *The Archaeology of Ancient Israel*. New Haven: Yale University Press.

Ben Tor A. and Portugali Y. 1987. "Tell Qiri: A Village in the Jezreel Valley." Jerusalem: *Qedem* 24.

Benzinger, I. 1910. Article "Burial" in NSH.

Berlin, A. 1997. *The Plain Wares*. In S. Herbert 1997:84–244.

Berlin. A. and J. Overman (eds.). 2002. *The First Jewish Revolt: Archaeology, history, and ideology*. London and New York: Routledge.

Berman, A.
1988-89. "Kafr Kanna," in ESI 7-8:107-08.
2012. "The Numismatic Evidnece." Chapter 5 in Alexandre 2012 (pp.107–120).

Burrage, C. 2001. *Nazareth and the Beginnings of Christianity*. (Reprint of 1914 edition.) Santa Clara: Church History Publishing.

Calderon, R. 2000. "Roman and Byzantine Pottery." Chapter 3 in Hirschfeld 2000 (pp. 91–165).

Carrier, R. 2014. "The Nazareth Inscription." In *Hitler Homer Bible Christ*. Richmond, California: Philosophy Press, pp. 315–26.

Chancey, M. 2004. *The Myth of a Gentile Galilee*. Cambridge: University Press.

Cook, Jonathan. 2003. "Is this where Jesus bathed?" *theguardian* (newspaper), London: Oct. 22.

Covello-Paran K. 1999. "Migdal Ha-'Emeq." ESI 19:19-20.

Crossan, J. and Reed, J. 2002. *Excavating Jesus: Beneath the Stones, Behind the Texts.* San Francisco: HarperCollins.

Dalman, G. 1935. *Sacred Sites and Ways: Studies in the Topography of the Gospels.* New York: The Macmillan Co.

Daniel the Abbot. *Zhitie I knozhenie Danila rus'kyya zemli igumena 1106-1108.* Ed. M. Venevitinov. St. Petersburg: Palestinskiy prvoslavnyy sbornik 3, 9. 1883-5. (Russian.)

Dar, S. 1986. *Landscape and Pattern: An Archaeological Survey of Samaria 800 B.C.E.–636 C.E.* (2 vols.) Oxford: BAR International Series 308.

Dark, K.

2005. *A preliminary report on the first season of work regarding the Sepphoris-Nazareth survey.* London: Late Antiquity Research Group. 23 pp. (OCLC 60963349.)

2007. *Archaeological Recording at the Sisters of Nazareth Convent in Nazareth, 2006.* London: Late Antiquity Research Group.

2008a. *Nazareth Archaeological Project: a preliminary report on the fourth season in 2007.* London: Late Antiquity Research Group.

2008b. "Roman-period and Byzantine landscapes between Sepphoris and Nazareth." PEQ 140 (2), 87–102.

2008c. "Nazareth Village Farm: A Reply to Salm." BAIAS 26:109-11.

2008d. "The Myth of Nazareth. The Invented Town of Jesus. Scholar's Edition." (Review.) BAIAS 2008:140-46.

2009. *Nazareth Archaeological Project: a preliminary report on the fifth season in 2008.* London: Late Antiquity Research Group.

2010a. *Nazareth Archaeological Project: a preliminary report on archaeological work at the Sisters of Nazareth convent in 2009.* London: Late Antiquity Research Group.

2010b. "Nazareth Archaeological Project 2009, Nazareth, Israel." PEQ 142, 144–45.

2012a. *Nazareth Archaeological Project: a preliminary report on archaeological work at the Sisters of Nazareth convent in 2010.* London: Late Antiquity Research Group.

2012b. [AJ] "Early Roman-Period Nazareth and the Sisters of Nazareth Convent." *The Antiquaries Journal* 92 (Sept. 2012):37-64.

2012c. "The Byzantine Church of the Nutrition in Nazareth Rediscovered." PEQ 144:3, 164–184.

2015. "Has Jesus' Nazareth House been Found?" BAR 41/2 (March/April 2015), pp. 54–63, 72.

Dark, K., and E. Ribak. 2009. "A report on the unpublished excavation by Roland de Vaux at the 'Synagogue Church' in Nazareth, Israel." In *Reading Medieval Studies* 35:93–100.

Deines, R. 1993. *Jüdische Steingefässe und pharisäische Frömmigkeit. Wissenschaftliche Untersuchungen zum Neuen Testament.* 2 Reihe 52. Tübingen: J.B. Mohr.

Desmarais, R. 1966. *Un lieu de culte 'Au Saint De Nazareth.'* University of Ottowa Faculty of Arts (unpublished thesis).

Dessel, J. 1999. "Tell 'Ein Zippori and the Lower Galilee in the Late Bronze and Iron Ages: A Village Perspective," in Meyers 1999:1–37.

Dothan M. 1956. "Excavations at 'Afula." *'Atiqot* 1:18-63.

Edwards, D. and C. McCullough (eds). 1997. *Archaeology and the Galilee: Texts and Contexts in the Graeco-Roman and Byzantine periods.* Atlanta: Scholars Press.

Ehrman, B. 2012. *Did Jesus Exist? The Historical Argument for Jesus of Nazareth.* New York: HarperOne.

Engberg, R., and G. Shipton. 1934. *Notes on the Chalcolithic and Early Bronze Age Pottery of Megiddo.* Chicago: University Press.

Eshel, H. 2000. "CD 12:15-17 and the Stone Vessels Found at Qumran," in *The Damascus Document: A Centennial of Discovery.* J. Baumgarten, *et al.* (eds.) Leiden: Brill.

Evans, C.
   2004. "Archaeology and the Historical Jesus: Recent Developments." SBL Forum #335 (online).
   2012. *Jesus and His World: The Archaeological Evidence.* Louisville: Westminster John Knox Press.

Feig, N.
   1983. "Nazareth 'Ilit.' Communication by the archaeologist." IEJ 33, no. 1-2:116-117.
   1990. "Burial Caves in Nazareth." *'Atiqot* 10:67-79 (Hebrew).

Fernandez, F. Diez. 1983. *Ceramica Comun Romana de la Galilea.* Madrid: Ed. Biblia y Fe Escuela Biblica.

Fiensy, D. and J. R. Strange, eds. 2014. *Galilee in the Late Second Temple and Mishnaic Periods.* Vol. 1: Life, Culture, and Society. Minneapolis: Fortress Press.

Fine, S. (ed.) 1996. *Sacred realm: The Emergence of the Synagogue in the Ancient World.* New York: Oxford University Press: Yeshiva University Museum.

Finegan, J. 1969, 1992. *The Archaeology of the New Testament.* Princeton: University Press.

Folda, J. 1986. *The Nazareth capitals and the Crusader Shrine of the Annunciation.* University Park [Pa.]: Pennsylvania State University Press.

Frankel, R. 1999. *Wine and Oil Production in Antiquity in Israel and Other Mediterranean Countries.* Sheffield: Academic Press.

Frescobaldi, Gucci, and Sigoli. *Visit to the Holy Places of Egypt, Sinai, Palestine, and Syria in 1384.* 1948. Jerusalem: Franciscan Press.

Freund, R. 2009. *Digging Through the Bible: Understanding Biblical People, Places and Controversies through Archaeology.* Lamham (MD): Rowman & Littlefield.

Frey, J.B. 1952. *Corpus Inscriptionum Iudicarum.* Vol II. Rome: Pontificio Istituto di Archeologia Christiana 988:173. [CII]

Freyne, S.

1980. *Galilee, from Alexander the Great to Hadrian, 323 B.C.E. to 135 C.E.: a study of second Temple Judaism.* Wilmington: University of Notre Dame Press.

1988. *Galilee, Jesus, and the Gospels : literary approaches and historical investigations.* Philadelphia: Fortress Press.

1997. "Archaeology and the Historical Jesus." In J. Bartlett (ed.), *Archaeology and Biblical Interpretation.* London: Routledge, pp. 117-138.

2002. *Galilee and Gospel: Collected Essays.* Leiden: Brill.

2004. *Jesus, a Jewish Galilean: a new reading of the Jesus story.* London: T & T Clark.

Gal, Zvi.

1988. "The Late Bronze Age in Galilee: A Reassessment." BASOR 272:79-84.

1991. "A stone vessel manufacturing site in the Lower Galilee." *'Atiqot* 20:25-26 (Hebrew). English summary, pp. 179–80.

1992. *Lower Galilee during the Iron Age.* Eisenbrauns: Winona Lake, Ind.

1994a. "Iron I in Lower Galilee and the Margins of the Jezreel Valley," in *From Nomadism to Monarchy,* ed. I. Finkelstein & N. Na'aman. Washington: Biblical Archaeology Society, 1994.

1994b. "Tel Gat Hefer." ESI 14:54.

1998. "Israel in Exile." BAR 24:3.

Galor, K.

2000. "The Roman-Byzantine dwelling in the Galilee and the Golan: 'house' or 'apartment'?" in *Miscellanea Mediterranea* (ed. R. Holloway): 109–24.

2003a. "Wohnkultur im römisch-byzantinishen Palästina," in *Zeichen aus Text und Stein. Studien auf dem Weg zu einer Archäologie des Neuen Testaments* (eds. S. Alkier and J. Zangenberg), pp. 183–208. Tübingen and Basel: Tanz.

2003b. "Domestic architecture in Roman and Byzantine Galilee and Golan." *Near Eastern Archaeology* 66 (1–2):44–57.

Geyer, P. 1898. *Itinera Hierosolymitana saeculi IIII-VIII.* In *Corpus Christianorum Series Latina*, vol. 39. Leipzig: G. Freytag.

Gibson, S. 1983. "The Stone Vessel Industry at Hizma." IEJ 33, Nos. 3-4:176-188.

Gonen, R. 1987. *Biblical Holy Places: An illustrated guide.* London: A. & C Black.

Goodenough, E.R. 1953-. "Jewish Tombs of Palestine," in *Jewish Symbols in the Greco-Roman Period.* Vol 1 of 13. New York: Pantheon Books, pp. 61-102.

Goranson, S. 1999. "Joseph of Tiberias Revisited: Orthodoxies and Heresies in Fourth-Century Galilee," in E. Meyers 1999:335-343.

Grässer, E. 1961. "Jesus in Nazareth (Mark VI.1-6a)." *New Testament Studies* 16:1-23.

Gray, M. 2011. *Jewish Priests and the Social History of Post-70 Palestine.* Ph.D dissertation. Chapel Hill.

Guy, P. and R. Engberg. 1938. *Megiddo Tombs.* Chicago.

Guz-Zilberstein, B. 1995. "The Typology of the Hellenistic Coarse Ware and Selected Loci of the Hellenistic and Roman Periods." in Stern 1995:289-433.

Hachlili, R.
1992. "Burials." ABD 1:785-94.
2005. *Jewish Funerary Customs, Practices and Rites in the Second Temple Period.* Leiden: Brill.

Hachlili, R. and A. Killebrew. 1983. "Jewish Funerary Customs During the Second Temple Period, in the Light of the Excavations at the Jericho Necropolis." PEQ 7-12:109-132.

Haiman, M. 1999. "Nazerat (Nazareth) Area, Survey." ESI 110:90.

Halevy, M. 2012. "Between Faith and Science: Franciscan Archaeology in the Service of the Holy Places." *Middle Eastern Studies* 48.2:249-67.

Hamidovic, D. 2004. "Nazareth avant Jésus: Un nouvel examen historique." *Ancient Near Eastern Studies* 41:95-197.

Hays, J.W.
1980. *Ancient Lamps in the Toyal Ontario Museum: A Catalogue.* Royal Ontario Museum.
1997. *Handbook of Mediterranean Roman Pottery.* Norman: Univ. of Oklahoma Press.

Hélène, M. 1936. *Histoire des Découvertes faites chez les Dames de Nazareth, à Nazareth.* Beirut.

Herbert, S. (ed.) 1997. *Tel Anafa II, i. The Hellenistic and Roman Pottery.* Ann Arbor: Kelsey Museum of the University of Michigan.

Hill, G.
   1910a. *Catalogue of the Greek Coins of Palestine.* Reprint: Bologna, Arnoldo
      Forni 1965.
   1910b. *Catalogue of the Greek Coins of Phoenicia.* Reprint: Bologna, Arnoldo
      Forni 1965.
Hirschfeld, Y.
   1995. *The Palestinian Dwelling in The Roman-Byzantine Period.* Jerusalem:
      Franciscan Printing Press.
   2000. *Ramat Hanadiv Excavations: Final Report of the 1984–1998 Seasons.*
      Chapter 1: "Architecture and Stratigraphy." Jerusalem: The
      Israel Exploration Society.
Holum, K., R. Hohlfelder, *et al.* 1988. *King Herod's Dream: Caesarea on the Sea.*
      New York: W.W. Norton & Co.
Horsley, R.
   1995. *Galilee: History, Politics, People.* Valley Forge, Pa: Trinity Press Inter-
      national, 1995.
   1996. *Archaeology, History and Society in Galilee: the social context of Jesus and the
      rabbis.* Valley Forge, Pa: Trinity Press International.
Kahane, P. 1961. "Rock-cut Tombs at Huqoq. Note on the Finds." *'Atiqot*
      III, pp. 126–47 (English Series).
King, P. and L. Stager. 2001. *Life in Biblical Israel.* Louisville: John Knox
      Press.
Klijn, A. and Reinink, G. 1973. *Patristic Evidence for Jewish-Christian Sects.*
      Leiden: Brill.
Kloner, A.
   1980. *The Necropolis of Jerusalem in the Second Temple Period.* Ph.D. diss.
      Jerusalem: Hebrew University. (Hebrew; English summary,
      pp. I–XIX).
   1999. "Did a Rolling Stone Close Jesus' Tomb?" BAR, Sept.-Oct.
      1999:23-29, 76.
Kloner, A. and B. Zissu. 2007. *The Necropolis of Jerusalem in the Second Temple
      Period.* Leuven and Dudley: Peeters.
Kloner, A. and Y. Tepper. 1987. *The Hiding Complex in the Judean Shefela.* Tel
      Aviv (Hebrew).
Koester, H. 1982. *History, culture, and Religion of the Hellenistic Age. Introduction
      to the New Testament, Vol. One.* Philadelphia: Fortress Press.
Kopp, C.
   1938. "Beiträge zur Geschichte Nazareths." JPOS, Jerusalem, vol.
      18:187-228.
   1939. "Beiträge zur Geschichte Nazareths." JPOS, Jerusalem, vol.
      19:82-119, 253-285.

1940. "Beiträge zur Geschichte Nazareths." JPOS, Jerusalem, vol. 20:29-42.

1948. "Beiträge zur Geschichte Nazareths." JPOS, Jerusalem, vol. 21:148-164.

1963. *The Holy Places of the Gospels.* "Nazareth," pp. 49-86. Herder and Herder.

Köppel, R. 1935. "Das Alter der neuentdeckten Schädel von Nazareth." *Biblica* 16:58-73.

Kuhnen, H-P.

1986. *Nordwest-Palästina in hellenistisch-römischer Zeit. Bauten und Gräber im Karmelgebiet.* Weinheim: VCH Verlag.

1989. *Studien zur Chronologie und Siedlungsarchäologie des Karmel (Israel) zwischen Hellenismus und Spätantike.* (Tübinger Atlas zum Vorderen Orient. Beiheft B 72.) Wiesbaden.

1990. *Palästina in griechisch-römischer Zeit.* (*Handbuch der Archäologie. Vorderasien II,2.*) München: C. H. Beck.

1994. *Mit Thora und Todesmut: Judäa im Widerstand gegen die Römer von Herodes bis Bar Kochba.* (*Führer und Bestandskataloge III.*) Stuttgart: Württ. Landesmuseum .

2002. "Bestattungswesen Palästinas im Hellenismus." In: *Die Religion in Geschichte und Gegenwart* (Göttingen), pp. 211 f.

2007. "Grabbau und Bestattungssitten in Palästina zwischen Herodes und den Severern." In: A. Faber, P. Fasold, M. Struck, M. Witteyer (Eds.), *Körpergräber des 1.–3. Jh. in der römischen Welt. Kolloquium Frankfurt am Main 2004.* Frankfurt: Schriften des Archäologischen Museums Frankfurt am Main, 57–76.

2009. (with W. Zwickel): *Archäologie und Politik im Land der Bibel: 60 Jahre Gründung des Staates Israel.* (*Kleine Arbeiten zum Alten und Neuen Testament*). Mainz: Spenner.

Lapp, N. 1964. "Pottery from some Hellenistic loci at Balatah (Shechem)," in BASOR 75 (October 1964), pp. 14–26.

Lapp, P. 1961. *Palestinian Ceramic Chronology: 200 B.C.–A.D. 70.* New Haven: ASOR.

Leibner, U. 2012. *Settlement and History in Hellenistic, Roman, and Byzantine Galilee: An Archaeological Survey of the Eastern Galilee.* Mohr Siebeck.

Levine, L. (ed.). 1992. *The Galilee in Late Antiquity.* New York and Jerusalem: The Jewish Theological Seminary of America.

Levy, T. (ed.). 1995. *The Archaeology of Society in the Holy Land.* London and Washington: Leicester University Press.

Livio, J-B. 1980. "Les fouilles chez les religieuses de Nazareth." *Le Monde de la Bible* 16:26–34.

Loffreda, S.
1977. "Ceramica del Ferro I trovata a Nazaret." LA 27:135-144, figs. 13–18.
2008. *Cafarnao VI: Tipologie e contesti stratigrafici della ceramica (1968-2003)*. Publications of the Studium biblicum franciscanum 48. Jerusalem: Edizioni Terra Santa.

Madden, F. 1967. *History of Jewish Coinage*. Chicago: Argonaut.

Mansur, A.
1913. "The Virgin Fountain, Nazareth." PEFQS 46:149-153.
1923. "An interesting discovery in Nazareth." PEFQS pp. 89-91.
1924. *Tarikh al-Nasirah min aqdam azmaniha ilá ayyamina al-hadirah* ("History of Nazareth: From its Remotest Times to the Present Days"). Cairo: Al Hillal (Arabic).

Mazar, B. 1973-76. *Beth She'arim*. 3 vols. New Brunswick, N.J.: Rutgers University Press on behalf of the Israel Exploration Society and the Institute of Archaeology, Hebrew University.

Meistermann, B. 1923. *Guide to the Holy Land*. London: Burns & Oates.

Meshorer, Y.
1967. *Jewish Coins of the Second Temple Period*. Tr. I. Levine. Chicago: Argonaut.
1995a. "The Coins of the Mint of Dora," Chapter Ten in Stern 1995a, pp. 355–65.
1995b. "Coins from Areas A and C." Chapter Eight in Stern 1995b, pp. 461–72.
2001. *A Treasury of Jewish Coins From the Persian Period to Bar Kokhba*. Nyack, NY: Amphora. Jerusalem: Yad Ben-Zvi Press.

Metzger, B. and R. Murphy (eds.). 1991. *The New Oxford Annotated Bible with the Apocryphal/Deuterocanonical Books*. (NRSV) New York: Oxford University Press.

Meyers, E.
1992. "Roman Sepphoris in Light of New Archeological Evidence and Recent Research." In Levine 1992, pp. 321 *f.*
1999 (ed.) *Galilee Through the Centuries: Confluence of Cultures*. Winona Lake: Eisenbrauns.
2002. "Aspects of everyday life in Roman Palestine with special reference to private domiciles and ritual baths." In J. Bartlett (ed.), *Jews in the Hellenistic and Roman Cities*. London, pp. 193-219.

Meyers, E., E. Netzer, and C. Meyers. 1992. *Sepphoris*. Winona Lake: Eisenbrauns.

Meyers, E. and J. Strange. 1981. *Archaeology, the Rabbis, & Early Christianity*. Nashville: Abingdon.

Mimouni, S. 1998. "Les nazoréens. Recherche étymologique et historique." RB vol. 105 no. 2:208-262.

Molinier, A. and C. Kohler. 1879. *Itinerum Hierosolymitanorum et descriptionum Terrae Sanctae series chronologica.* Geneva.

Najjar, A. and N. Najjar. 1997. "Nazareth." ESI 16:49. Jerusalem: Israel Antiquities Authority.

Nazareth, Soeur Marie de. 1956. "La Maison de Saint Joseph à Nazareth." *Cahiers de Joséphologie* IV.2: 243–71.

Nazareth Today (quarterly periodical). 2010–. Online at *http://www.nazareth-today.com/en/* (accessed March 16, 2015).

Neidinger, W. 1982. "A typology of oil lamps from the mercantile quarter of Antipatris." *Tel Aviv* vol. 9, pp. 157–169.

Orni, E. and E. Efrat. 1964. *Geography of Israel.* Jerusalem: Israel Program for Scientific Translations.

Perdue, C. 2005. *The Politics of Archaeology in Israel.* University of Oregon M.A. Thesis, Interdisciplinary Studies. (Unpublished.)

Pfann, S., R. Voss, Y. Rapuano. 2007. "Surveys and Excavations at the Nazareth Village Farm (1997-2002): Final Report." BAIAS 25:16-79.

Porat, L. 2005. "En Zippori" (report date 8/5/2005). ESI 117.

Pritchard, J.
    1962. Gibeon: *Where the Sun Stood Still.* Princeton: University Press.
    1964. *Winery, Defenses, and Sounding at Gibeon.* Philadelphia: University of Pennsylvania Museum.

Pritz, R. 1985. "Joseph of Tiberias: The Legend of a 4th Century Jewish Christian," in *Mishkan* No. 2:38-43.

Raban, A. 1993-94. "Nazareth and 'Afula Maps, Survey." ESI 12:19.

Rahmani, L. 1994. *A Catalogue of Jewish Ossuaries in the Collections of the State of Israel.* Jerusalem: IAA.

Rapuano, Y. 2008. "The Nazareth Village Farm Project Pottery (1997–2002): Amendment." BAIAS 26 (2008):113–35.

Rast W. 1978. *Ta'anach I: Studies in the Iron Age Pottery.* Cambridge, MA: ASOR.

Reed, J. 2000 & 2002. *Archaeology and the Galilean Jesus: A Re-examination of the Evidence.* Harrisburg: Trinity Press International.

Richardson, P.
    2004. *Building Jewish in the Roman East.* Supplements to the Journal for the Study of Judaism, 92. Leiden: Brill.
    2006. "Khirbet Qana (and Other Villages) as a Context for Jesus." In J. H. Charlesworth (ed.), *Jesus and Archaeology.* Grand Rapids: Eerdmans.

Richmond, E.T. 1931. "A Rock-cut Tomb at Nazareth." QDAP 1, No. 2. Page 53 and plates xxxiii-xxxiv. Jerusalem. Published for the Government of Palestine by Humphrey Milford. London: Oxford University Press.

Roberts, D., C. Croly, and W. Brockedon. 1855. *The Holy Land, Syria, Idumea, Arabia, Egypt & Nubia. After Lithographs by Louis Haghe From Drawings Made on the Spot By David Roberts, R.A.* London: Day & Son.

Robinson, E. and E. Smith. 1841. *Biblical Researches in Palestine, Mount Sinai and Arabia Petraea.* Vol. III. Boston: Crocker & Brewster.

Rogers, E. 1914. *A Handy Guide to Jewish Coins.* London: Spink & Son.

Romanoff, P. 1944. *Jewish Symbols on Ancient Jewish Coins.* Philadelphia: Dropsie College.

Rosenthal, R. and R. Sivan. 1978. *Ancient Lamps in the Schloessinger Collection.* Qedem 8. Monographs of the Institute of Archaeology. Jerusalem: The Hebrew University of Jerusalem.

Salm, R.
  2006. "Why the Truth About Nazareth is Important" (Introduction by Frank Zindler). *American Atheist*, Nov.–Dec. 2006:14–19.
  2007. "The Myth of Nazareth: The Invented Town of Jesus—Does it really matter?" *American Atheist*, March 2007:13–15.
  2008a. *The Myth of Nazareth: The Invented Town of Jesus.* Cranford: American Atheist Press.
  2008b. "A Response to 'Surveys and Excavations at the Nazareth Village Farm (1997–2002): Final Report.'" BAIAS 26:95–103.
  2009. "Nazareth, Faith, and the Dark Option." *American Atheist*, Jan. 2009:11–13.
  2010. "Christianity at the crossroads—Nazareth in the crosshairs." *American Atheist*, July–Aug. 2010:8–12.
  2012. "The archaeology of Nazareth: An example of pious fraud?" Paper delivered at the SBL convention, Chicago, November 2012 (*http://www.nazarethmyth.info/SBL_2012_Salm_(Nazareth).pdf*, accessed 3/23/15).
  2013. "Archaeology, Bart Ehrman, and the Nazareth of 'Jesus.'" In *Bart Ehrman and the Quest of the Historical Jesus of Nazareth: An Evaluation of Ehrman's 'Did Jesus Exist?'* Cranford: American Atheist Press, pp. 327–68.

Schumacher, G. 1889. "Recent discoveries in Galilee." PEFQS pp. 68–78 (with plates).

Schürer, E. 1890/1998. *A History of the Jewish People in the Time of Jesus Christ.* 5 vols. T. & T. Clark (1890), Hendrickson (1998).

Scranton, P. and J. Davidson, eds. 2007. *The Business of Tourism: Place, Faith, and History.* Philadelphia: Univ. Of Pennsylvania.

Sellers, O. and D. Baramki. 1953. "A Roman-Byzantine Burial Cave in Northern Palestine." BASOR Supplementary Studies Nos. 15-16. New Haven: Yale Station.

Shacham, T. 2012. "Bathhouse from the Crusader Period in Nazareth." In R. Keiner and W. Letzner eds. *SPA: Samitas per aquam. Tagungsband des internationalen Frontinus-Symposiums zur Technik- und Kulturgeschichte der antiken Thermen, Aachen 18–22 Marz 2009.* (Babesch Supplement 21.) Leuven: Peeters. Pp. 319–326.

Shachar, I. 2004. "The Historical and Numismatic Significance of Alexander Jannaeus's Later Coinage as Found in Archaeological Excavations." PEQ 136, 1:5–33.

Shahar, Y. 2003. "The Underground Hideouts in Galilee and Their Historical Meaning," in Peter Schafer, ed., *The Bar Kokhba War Reconsidered* (Tubingen 2003), 217–40.

Silberstein, N. 2000. "Hellenistic and Roman Pottery." Chapter 3 in Hirschfeld 2000, pp. 420–69.

Smith, R.
   1961. "The 'Herodian' Lamp of Palestine: Types and Dates." *Berytus* 14:53–65.
   1964a. "The Household Lamps of Palestine in Old Testament Times." *The Biblical Archaeologist* XXVII:1, 2–31.
   1964b. "The Household Lamps of Palestine in Intertestamental Times." *The Biblical Archaeologist* XXVII:1, 101–124.
   1966. "The Household Lamps of Palestine in New Testament Times." *The Biblical Archaeologist* XXIX:1, 2–27.

Steen, E.J. 2005. "The Sanctuaries of Early Bronze IB Megiddo: Evidence of a Tribal Polity?" *American Journal of Archaeology,* Volume 109, No. 1:1–20.

Stern, E.
   1982. *Material Culture of the Land of the Bible in the Persian Period, 538–332 B.C.* Jerusalem: Israel Exploration Society.
   1995a. *Excavations at Dor, Final Report Volume I A, Areas A and C: Introduction and Stratigraphy.* Jerusalem: Institute of Archaeology. Qedem Reports 1.
   1995b. *Excavations at Dor, Final Report Volume I B, Areas A and C: The Finds.* Jerusalem: Institute of Archaeology. Qedem Reports 2.

Strange, J.
   1975. "Late Hellenistic and Herodian Ossuary Tombs at French Hill, Jerusalem." BASOR 219 (Oct. 1975), 39-68.
   1983. "Diversity in Early Palestinian Christianity: Some Archaeological Evidences," *Anglican Theological Review* LXV:14–24;

1992a. "Nazareth." ABD vol. IV, pp. 1050–51.

1992b. "Some implications of archaeology for New Testament studies," in *What has Archaeology to do with Faith?* pp. 23–59. Harrisburg: Trinity Press International.

1993. "Archaeology and the New Testament," *Biblical Archaeologist*:56 (Sept. 1993):153–157.

1997. "First century Galilee from archaeology and from the texts," in *Archaeology and the Galilee*, pp. 39–48. Atlanta: Scholars Press.

1999. "Ancient texts, archaeology as text, and the problem of the first-century synagogue," in *Evolution of the Synagogue*, pp. 27–45. Harrisburg: Trinity Press International.

[See also articles by Strange entitled "Nazareth" in the *Encyclopedia of Archaeology in the Biblical World* (1991), ABD (1992), the *Macmillan Dict. of Judaism in the Biblical Period* (1996), and the *Oxford Encyclopedia of Near Eastern Excavations* (1997).]

Sukenik, E. 1947. "The Earliest Records of Christianity." AJA, vol. LI, pp. 351–365.

Suriano, Fra Francesco. 1385. *Treatise on the Holy Land*. Printed by the Franciscan Press, Jerusalem 1949.

Sussman, V.

1982. *Ornamented Jewish Oil-Lamps*. Israel Exploration Society: Aris & Phillips.

1985. "The Changing Shape of Ancient Oil Lamps: A Chronological Guide." BAR Mar–Apr 1985:44–56.

1990. "The Lamp," in S. Wachsmann, *The Excavations of an Ancient Boat in the Sea of Galilee (Lake Kinneret)*. *'Atiqot* 19. Jerusalem: The Israel Antiquities Authority.

Syon, D. 2004. *Tyre and Gamla: A Study in the Monetary Influence of Southern Phoenicia on Galilee and the Golan in the Hellenistic and Roman Periods*. Diss., Hebrew Univ.

Szentleleky, T. 1969. *Ancient Lamps*. Amsterdam: Adolf M. Hakkert

Tatcher, A. and Z. Gal. 2009. "The Ancient Cemetery at Migdal Ha'Emeq (el-Mujeidil)." *'Atiqot* 61:1–47 (Hebrew) +131–32 (English).

Taylor, J. 1993. *Christians and the Holy Places: The Myth of Jewish-Christian Origins*. Oxford: Clarendon Press.

Tepper, Y. and U. Shahar. 1984. *Jewish Settlements in the Galilee and their Hideaway Systems*. Tel Aviv. (Hebrew).

Testa, E. 1967. "Due frammenti di Targum sull'Incarnazione scoperti a Nazaret." *La Terra Santa*, 99–104.

Tobler, T. 1974. *Descriptiones Terrae Sanctae ex saeculo VIII.IX.XII. et XV.* Hildesheim: Georg Olms.

Trifon, D.

    1985. *The Jewish Priests from the Destruction of the Second Temple to the Rise of Christianity*. Ph.D dissertation. Tel Aviv: University. (Hebrew)

    1989. "Did the Priestly Courses Transfer from Judaea to Galilee after the Bar Kokhba Revolt?" *Tarbiz* 59:77–93 (Hebrew).

Viaud, P. 1910. *Nazareth et ses deux églises de L'Annonciation et de Saint-Joseph d'après les fouilles récentes*. Paris: Librarie A. Picard et Fils.

Vitto, F.

    2000. "Burial caves from the Second Temple Period in Jerusalem." *'Atiqot* XL. Jerusalem: IAA.

    2001. "An Iron Age Burial Cave in Nazareth." *'Atiqot* XLII:159–167.

Vlaminck, B. 1900. *A Report of the Recent Excavations and Explorations conducted at the Sanctuary of Nazareth*. Washington, D.C.: Commissariat of the Holy Land. (5 pages text + 3 pages diagrams).

Wachsmann, S. 1990. *The Excavations of an Ancient Boat in the Sea of Galilee (Lake Kinneret)*. *'Atiqot* 19. Jerusalem: IAA.

Walsh, C. 2000. *The Fruit of the Vine: Viticulture in Ancient Israel*. Winona Lake: Eisenbrauns.

Watzinger, C. 1935. *Denkmäler Palästinas*. Vol. II. Leipzig.

Wexler, L. and G. Gilboa. 1996. "Oil lamps of the Roman Period from Apollonia-Arsuf." *Tel Aviv*, vol. 23, pp. 115–131.

Wilkinson, J. 1981. *Egeria's Travels*. Warminster: Aris & Phillips.

Wood, B. 1990. *The Sociology of Pottery in Ancient Palestine*. (*Journal for the Study of the Old Testament: Supplementary Series*, 103.) Sheffield: JSOT.

Yavor, Z. 1998. "Nazareth." ESI 18:32.

Yazbak, M. and S. Sharif, eds.

    2012. *Nazareth: Archaeology, History and Cultural Heritage. Proceedings of the 1st International Conference Nazareth, November 22–24, 2010*. Nazareth Academic Studies Series No. 1. Nazareth: Nazareth Municipality.

    2013. *Nazareth: History and Cultural Heritage. Proceedings of the 2nd International Conference Nazareth, July 2–5, 2012*. Nazareth Academic Studies Series No. 2. Nazareth: Nazareth Municipality.

Yeivin, Z. 1963. "Notes and News: Nazareth." IEJ 13:145.

Zindler, F.

    1997. "Where Jesus Never Walked," *American Atheist*, vol 36, Winter 1996–97:33–42.

    1999. "Loud Arguments From Silence," *American Atheist*, vol 38, Autumn 1999:22–29.

    2003. *The Jesus the Jews Never Knew: Sepher Toldoth Yeshu and the Quest of the Historical Jesus in Jewish Sources*. Cranford: American Atheist Press.

2011. *Through Atheist Eyes: Scenes From a World That Won't Reason. —Vol. 1: Religions and Scriptures.* Cranford: American Atheist Press.

2012. (Ed. and contributing author.) *Bart Ehrman and the Quest of the Historical Jesus of Nazareth.* Cranford: American Atheist Press.

INDEX

INDEX

Aaronides (priests): —451–52
Abraham (patriarch): —34
Abu'l Fath: —453, 454, 457
abzu: —451
Acharya S: —146, 153
Acts of Mark: —451–52
Acts of Thomas: —466
Adam: —470
Adan-Bayewitz: —57, 58
Adomnan: —393 *f*
adoptionism: —418 n.
Africanus, Julius: —458
'agency': —463, 467
agriculture installation(s): Vener-
  ated Area —46, 104, 389
'Ain ed-Jedide: See "New Spring"
'Ain Maryam: See "Mary's Spring"
Akbon: —454, 457
Albright, W. F.: etymology of "Naz-
  areth" —6; W. F. Albright Insti-
  tute —127
Aleteia: —239 *f*
Alexandre, Y.: —18, 23, 26, 73, 139,
  154, 160, 393; 2006 report —67,
  125, 378; "Hellenistic" evidence
  —125; IMC —25, 59, 110, 124 *f,*
  158, **178** *f,* 242, Chapter 10; lack
  of documentation —159; Mary's
  Well —125, 159, 166, 248, Chap-
  ter 11; Nazareth International
  Conference —26
Alexandria: —420, 460, 462
Alfaric, P.: —314
Allegro, J.: —420, 447, 453, 462,
  468
Amarna letters: —33
'amateur': —147–48
Amendment: to NVF report by

Rapuano —58–59, 64, 290
American Schools of Oriental Research (ASOR): —327
American Atheist Magazine: —2
  n.3, 24, 44, 62; articles by Salm
  republished from —Chapters 2,
  3, 5, 7
Anchor Bible Dictionary: article
  "Nazareth" —6, 36
Annunciation, the: —47, 123, 137,
  174
Annunciation, (Greek Orthodox)
  Church of: —245, 251, 393
Annunciation, (Roman Catholic) Church of: —32, 43, 290;
  on steep slope —43; Chapel of
  the Angel —386; tombs under
  —42–43, 46, 61, 65, 77, 173 *f,*
  386 *f* (see also "Tombs").
'Antioch incident' the: —441–42
Antiquaries Journal, The: publish
  Dark's 2012 article on the Sisters
  of Nazareth Convent —27
Apollonius of Tyana: —474
Apollos: —450
Apostles' Fountain: See "New
  Spring"
archeology: "biblical" —22, 187;
  development as a science —22,
  36
archeology of Nazareth: Assyrian destruction —19; errors in
  —15–16; evidence, recent rush
  to find —23; Jesus myth theory —23; Jesus mythicism and
  —12–13, 44; "Nazarene" and
  —13; Roman settlement, beginning of —19. See "hiatus"

Index

501

argument from silence: —60, 69, 169 *f*

Asoka: —421

ASOR (*see* 'American Schools of Oriental Research')

Association Marie de Nazareth: —182, 191, 238

Assyria: conquers Israel in 8th cent. BCE —33, 36, 46

Atrahasis: —405

Atheism: 128, 399

'Atiqot (Heb. journal "Antiquities"): —160, 185, 248

Attiah, S.: —345 *f*, 357, 373

Avalos, Hector: —26

Aviam, M.: —85, 87, 89, 90, 94–95, 274, 279

Aviram, Y.: —329

Avi-Yonah, M.: —320 *f*, 329, 335, 339, 351, 356, 367, 369

Baba Rabba: —460

Babylonia: —450

Babylonian Period: lack of settlement in Nazareth basin during —34

Bagatti, B.: —6, 7, 15–16, 36, 41, 49, 69, 105, 116, 132, 142, 154, 208, 236, 242, 254, 256; chronology of *kokh* tombs false—17; continuous habitation, doctrine and —34; Crusader dating of Roman tombs —43; pottery misdated by—37–38; tombs under Church of the Annunciation —43, 61, 378, 390; trench dug by —35. See also "*Excavations in Nazareth*"

BAIAS: —24, 59; Chapter 4, 62

Balaam: Rabbinic cipher for Yeshu ha-Notsri —422–23

baptism: —405–06, 409, 418, 448, 452

Barabbas: —460

Bar Kokhba Revolt (*see* "Second Jewish Revolt")

Barnabas: 432. 439, 440

bathhouse: —166 *f*, 260 *f*

Bauckham, R.: —434

Bauer, B.: 19th century German mythicist —12, 22

Baur, F. C.: —434

bedrock: —291

Beer-Sheva: —362

Ben Stada: —447

Ben Tor, A.: — 138

Berossus: —450

Berman, A.: —286, 292 *f*

Beth Alpha (Beit Apha): —318

Beth Shearim: —86, 114

Bethlehem of Judea: —403, 475; birthplace of "Jesus" —4, 45, 245, 400; home of priest Jonathan —452

Betz, H.: —432, 440–41

Bishop's Residence: See "Greek Bishop's Residence"

Blavatsky, H.: —149

blood: —454

Bonnassies O.: —191, 238 *f*

Borg, M.: and founding of *Cross-Talk* forum — 1

Bowman, J.: —454, 455, 458

Brandon, F.: —434

Brodie, Thomas: mythicist author of *Beyond the Quest for the Historical Jesus* —11–12; 434, 474

Bronze Age habitation in the Nazareth basin: —37, 54, 131, 155–56, 184

Brown, D.: *The DaVinci Code*—145

bow-spouted oil lamp(s): —39–41; dating —46

Buddhism: —2, 473; gnosticizing influence on Christianity 2 (and n.2); missionaries sent by Asoka —421

Bulletin of the Anglo-Israel Archaeological Society: See "BAIAS"

Bultmann, R.: argued that Mandeans were "pre-Christian" gnostic disciples of John the Baptist —6, 406

burden of proof: —169 *f*

Byzantine: —342

Cactus **(shop):** —261

Caesarea excavations: area A —336–37, 342; area B —342; area C —342; area D —335, 338, 342, 361, 368; area E —335, 342, 360–62; area F —335, 340, 342, 360, 367; chancel screen —337, 339 *f*, 360, 367 *f*; cistern —372; coins —338, 342; confusion in— 323, 326, 335, 342, 356; Field "O" —336; forgery —373; "*mem*" fragment —359 f , 373; "Nazareth" fragment — 344 *f*, 373; synagogue not represented in the finds —353; Talmon fragment: 328 *f*, 345, 353, 374

"Caesarea Inscription": 358–59, Chapter 12; forgery of —28; Jerry Vardaman and —28; "Nazareth" fragment —338–39, 351

Caeasarea Museum: —322–23

Capernaum: —20, 78, 111, 276, 400, 403; and provenance of "Jesus" —4, 6 (and n.5)

Carrier, R.: —148, 315 n.2, 411

Carter, Jimmy (former U.S. President): 63

Casey, M.: —144; on the upsurge in the Jesus myth theory—23

Catholic Church: See "Roman Catholic Church"

cave: under Bishop's Residence —382; Sisters of Nazareth Convent —394

Celsus: —417

cemetery: Roman, in Venerated Area —46, 47, 104

census: Gospel of Luke —45

Center for the Study of Early Christianity (CSEC): —49

Cephas: See "Peter (apostle)"

Cercle Ernest Renan: —314

Charlesworth, J.: —123-24

Chemin Neuf, Communauté de: —191, 240

Cheyne, T. K.: —4, 69

Chicago: racial tension of —27–28

China: —421

Chrestos: —146, 152–53

Christ: —150 *f*; Paul and —409

Christianity: contemporary problems —402; end of —47, 399 *f*; mythology —400; U.S. —244

chronology: New Testament —441

Church of the Annunciation: See "Annunciation, (Roman Catholic) Church of"

Crusaders: —390

cistern(s): Caesarea excavation —372; Sisters of Nazareth site —104, 113

Clement of Alexandria: —432

Clementine Recognitions: See "*Pseudo-Clementines*"

cliff: none in Nazareth basin —70, 136

Cochaba: —458

coin(s): 139, 162, 295 *f*; Caesarea —338, 342; "Hellenistic" —67, 162–63, 302 *f*; Mary's Well —

160 *f*, 295 *f*, 304; NVF discussion of —55; star design —304–05

commercial aspects:—242

Conybeare: —407

Constantine (Emperor): —383

continuous habitation, doctrine of: —34, 36, 132

Couchoud, P.:— 407

Crossan, J. D.: —1, 396, 411, 459, 473

CrossTalk (1998–99 Internet forum): —1–8; and non-existence of Nazareth 2 (and n.2); demise of —8

Crown, A.: —455, 460, 461

crucifixion: —424

Crusader era: —113, 161–62, 309

Custodia di Terra Santa: manages, buys Nazareth holy sites —31

Damascus: —456, 470

Damascus Document: —464

Dan (biblical town): —405, 452

Dark, Ken: —23, 29, 64, 77 *f*, 137 n.5, 154, 174, 236, 378; at Sisters of Nazareth Convent —25, 29, 72, 74 (overall thesis), 379, Chp. 6; archeological conclusions indefensible —27; argument from structural "cutting" —97 *f*, 260; claims discovery of first house from I CE —75; conservative idiosyncrasies —78; errors in Hebrew —78; hostile "Reply to Salm" —59; ignores published work of Kuhnen —61, 78, 85, 87; Jerusalem evidence applied to Nazareth —85; misrepresentation of sources —94 *f*; misunderstanding of kokh tomb typology —90, 96; misunderstanding of Nazareth hydrology —246 n.2,

391 *f*; proposes larger Nazareth —395 *f*; proposes tombs under former dwellings —65, 75, 390; review of *The Myth of Nazareth* —24, 59–61, 64–65, 68–69, 86; violates accepted chronologies —27, 72, 88, 90

Dark Ages: —401, 404

David (King): —316, 459

Davies, S.: —3

Dead Sea Scrolls: —10, 418, 428, 461 *f*

De Dea Syria (Lucian) —405

deception: —471–72

Deines, R.: work ignored by Dark —79, 156

De Locis Sanctis: —391

Department of Antiquities: —322, 325, 338

Detering, Hermann: —400, 408, 434–37, 474

de Vaux, R.:—242, 398

Did Jesus Exist? (Book by Ehrman): —Chp. 9

docetist, docetism: —408, 417–18

Doherty, Earl: —30, 146, 148, 410, 417, 434; and *CrossTalk* —2; author of *The Jesus Puzzle* —2, 9

door: See "gate"

Dositheus (Dusis), Dositheans: —434, 446, 447, 448, 452, 453 *f*, 463, 470; disciple of John the Baptist —453; hypostatization of gnosis —457; invention —471; rewrites Pentateuch —456; schism —454

Drew-McCormick excavations (Shechem): —326–27

Drews, A.: —416, 450

Dupuis, C. F.: —450

Dutch Radical School: —437

Dykstra, Tom: 12

Ea/Enki: —451

Ebionites: altered scripture —454, 459; identified with the pre-Christian Nasarenes —4; possible links with the Mandeans —6

ecumenism:—242

Edwards, M.: —456

Ehrman, B.: —474; confusion regarding venues —165–66, 293; coins —160, 166, 293–94; *Did Jesus Exist?* —12, 23, 139, 293; irritated at Salm's invitation to 2012 SBL convention —26; See Chapter 9.

Eisenberg Museum: —334–35

Eisenman, Robert: —10, 434, 437, 464

Eisler, R.: —450, 464

Ellegård, A.: author of *Jesus–One Hundred Years Before Christ* —9

encratism: —430, 458, 459

end times: —455

Ephraim: —455, 459

Epiphanius of Salamis: Cochaba —458; —dates Jesus to time of Janneus —420; Dositheus —458, 461; Nasarene sect —4; Nazorean sect —13 n.12; See also *Panarion*.

Epistula Petri: —442

ethrog: —340–41

Eusebius of Caesarea: —429

Excavations in Nazareth (book by B. Bagatti): —6, 15, 36–38, 49, 386

evidence: absence of —22, 128, 135, 170, 176; backdating—17, 46, 75, 84 *f*, 236; diagnostic —253, 254, 258, 297; Hellenistic claims —160 *f*, 258; history

of — 131 *f*; invention of —265, 268, 272, 307; pressure to discover Jesus-era finds —66, 156, *cf.* 236; vs. authority —157; vs. faith —22, 67–68

faith: —472

Fakr ed-Din, Emir: —31

Falfuli: —458

farming: terrace —50

FEAS (see 'Fund for the Exploration of Ancient Synagogues')

Feig, N.: —254; and dating of bow-spouted oil lamp —39–41

Fernandez, F. Diaz-: —41

filtration basins: Sisters of Nazareth —105, 115

Finnegan, J.: —116

First Apocalypse of James: —429

First Jewish Revolt: —33, 128, 227, 315

Forty Martyrs: —384

Fossum, J.: —456

FOX NEWS: —123-24, 234

Franciscan monastery: —32

Freke, T.: co-author of *The Jesus Mysteries: Was the "Original Jesus" a Pagan God?* —9, 153

Freund, R: —262–64

Fund for the Exploration of Ancient Synagogues (FEAS): —320, 324–25

Gabriel (archangel): —245, 261

Gal, Z.: —34, 95, 254

Galatians, Epistle to the: —438 *f*

Galilee: 45, 316, 426, 448, 452

Gandhi, Mohandas: —146, 148

Gandy, P.: co-author of *The Jesus Mysteries: Was the "Original Jesus" a Pagan God?* —9, 153

Gaster, T.: —456

gate: —460

Gaza: —34

Gerasa: —34

Gerizim (Mt.): —455

Gezer: —34

Gilgamesh: —405, 452

Gitta/Gath: home of Simon Magus, equivalent to Lod/Lydda —447

Goodenough, E.: —86

Google: —240–41

gospel: —433; fairy tale —446

Govaars, M.: —321 *f*, 336, 353

gnosis, gnosticism: —401, 431, 444, 463, 470, 474; docetism and —418; DSS —462; hypostasis —457; Paul and —413; pre-Christian —2 n.2, 14; water and —454; Yeshu ha-Notsri and —422

graffitti: —386

Greek Bishop's Residence: —381 *f.*

Greek Orthodox Church of the Annunciation: See "Annunciation, (Greek Orthodox) Church of"

Grey, T.: —81

Haaretz: —318 n. 10, 325

Hachlili, R.: —60, 84, 89, 92; misunderstood by Dark —90

Hackett, J. A.: —323

Hadashot Arkheologiyot (Heb. "Archeological News"): —185, 248, 253, 257; Mary's Well—18; NVF —51

Haiman, M.: directs NVF survey —51

Halkin, F.: —451

Hapises (Hapizzez): —317, 345

Harper San Francisco (book publisher): and founding of *Cross-Talk* forum—1

Haussig: —458

Hebrew Gospel of Matthew: —350

Hebrew University of Jerusalem: —317, 318, 321–22, 329, 335, 374

Hebrews (Epistle to the): 412 *f*; redeemed redeemer: —412

Hebron: —34

Hechalot literature: —422

Hegesippus: —428, 444

Helen(e), Helena: —427, 457

Helen of Adiabene (Queen): —427

Hellenistic evidence (alleged): —66, 125, 161, 249; coins —67, 125, 139, 284 *f*; contradictory documentation —267; Hasmonean coins (alleged) —302 *f*; late appearance in the literature —266 *f*, 282 *f*, 285; Mary's Well —259 *f*, 265; Nazareth evidence misrepresented as —6–8, 15–16, 36–38; none from the Nazareth basin —36–38, 132; pottery —250, 266 *f*; structures —251, 259–60

"Hellenistic renaissance" hypothesis: —36, 132

Hermes, Hermeticism: —466

Hermon, Mt.: —401 *f.*, 405

Herod: Antipas —46; Archelaus —298, 306; "the Great" —306

Herodian: misnomer for the bow spouted oil lamp —6, 16–17, 39, 133 *f*, 236; misnomer for the kokh-type tomb —16, 236; See "bow-spouted oil lamp", "kokh tomb(s)"

hiatus: "Great Hiatus" —34, 131, 156; in settlement of Nazareth —19, 36, 39, 46

'hiding pit': See 'refuge pit'

hiding complex: —227, 382

Hirschfeld Y.: "model courtyard house" —73, 112

Hidayoth: See *"Thanksgiving Hymns"*

history: —471

Hoffmann, R. Joseph: —144; "mythtic" —23

Homer: —474

house: alleged "from the time of Jesus": — 122 *f*, Chps. 6, 10; "model courtyard house" —73, 107 *f*

Howard, G.: —350

Hutchesson, I. (*CrossTalk* participant): —3

hydrology: —167

hypostasis, hypostatize: —457

IEJ (see 'Israel Exploration Journal')

Ilfan: —458

India: —421

inerrancy of scripture: Nazareth and —14, 31, 43, 45, 46

inscription(s): —8

International Marian Center (IMC): —23, 126, 290; excavation —25, Chapter 10; Area 1—198, 202, 206 *f*; Area 4— 201, 209–10; Areas 6 & 7—222 *f*, 230 *f*; cement—204; feature (a)—202 feature (b)—198, 204; feature (g)—215; feature (j)—210 *f*, 223; feature (k)—209; feature (L)—198 *f*, 218; feature (m)—205, 223; feature (o)—212, 214; feature (t)—201, 218 *f*; feature (u)—202, 204, 209; feature (w)—230–31; feature (z)—223, 225 *f*, 232, 290; no habitation—380; plan of 2009—196 *f*; plan of 2012—216 *f*; plaster—207; pottery—234 *f*; press—231; 'refuge pit'—225 *f*; "Room 3"—198, 220;

slope—206; triple silo—198, 217, 220, 228; "walls"—218–19; news conference —122; short IAA report —127, 159, 226. See Chapter 10

"Interpreter of the Law": —469

Irenaeus: —419, 421

Iron Age: —37, 131, 155–56, 184, 290

Israel (modern state of): —36, 400; tourism and —403

Israel Antiquities Authority (IAA): —59, 122, 124, 158, 161; Mary's Well coins —286; short IMC report —127, **189**, 258

Israel Exploration Journal: —325

Isser, S.: —453, 456, 458

James (the Just): —10, 413, 428 *f*, 430, 452, 456, 463; fusion with 'the Jesus' —433, 448; gnostic —456; identified with Yeshu ha-Notsri —434, 444, 446, 464; invented literary figure with no historical value —443, 445–46, 471; Rechabites and —447 n. 77; virginity —459

James, Epistle of: —433, 442

Jamesian literature: —442 n. 73.

Janneus, Alexander: —297, 305, 420, 455, 457

Japhia: —20, 54, 156; located in Nazareth basin during Bronze-Iron Ages —33–34, 46, 131

JECM (see 'Joint Expedition to Caesarea Maritima')

Jericho: —34, 89

Jerome: —395, 431

Jerusalem: —34, 41, 337–38, 355, 400, 403, 420; King David Hotel —369. See also "Hebrew University of Jerusalem"

Jesus: name —407, 445; as gnosis/'light'—460; invention —471–72, 475; Paul and —409; "Joshua" —455; spiritual entity —408 *f*, 416, 444, 460, 461. See also "Yeshu ha-Notsri."

Jesus mythicism: —30, 401; ancient adherents —418; contemporary world, and —10–12, 14, 23–24, 404; Earl Doherty and —2; history of —2, 9, 12; Nazareth and —29, 44; "mythicist" and cognates —23; Renan and —314; "semi-mythicists" and —10

Jesus of Nazareth: —8; an invented figure —14, 43, 45; incarnation —404; postdates Pauline epistles —445; puppet —403 *f*.; reflection of Yeshu ha-Notsri —446

Jethro: —452

Jewish-Christians: belief in spiritual Jesus —410; not at Nazareth —41

John (apostle): —432, 439

John, Gospel of: —430

John Mark: —450–51

John (name): —452–53

John the Baptist: —146, 314, 446 *f* ; 450, 470; baptism —402; invention —471; John is Jesus —449–50; "pre-Christian" Mandeans and —6, 406; precursor to Jesus and Simon Magus —453

Johnson, L.: —433

Joint Expedition to Caesarea Maritima (JECM): —318 n. 11, 325

Jonathan: —452–53

Joseph: father of Jesus —174; son of Jacob —459

Josephus: evangelists use of —472, 474; Nazareth not mentioned —4; synagogues in Caesarea —320

Joshua: —150 *f*, 455

Johnson, L. T.: and founding of *CrossTalk* forum —1

Jordan River: —402

Josephus: —462

Joshua: —459. *Cf.* "Jesus."

Jotapata (Yodefat): —274, 279

Judea, Judah: —448, 459

Julius Africanus: See "Africanus"

Kafr Kanna: —86, 87

Karnis, J.: —51

Kenyon, K.: —362

kerygma: —10, 402, 433

Kevalin Press: pre-publication of *The Myth of Nazareth* in chapbooks —19 (and n.20)

Kfar Hananya: —81–83

Kfar Kanna: —248

Kippenberg, H,: —456

Klein, S.: —317, 318, 325, 333, 336, 355

Kloner, A.: ignored by Dark —79, 92

Knohl, I.: —466

Kohler, K.: —455, 457, 460

kokh tomb(s): appear in Galilee *c.* 50 CE —16, 46, 73, 169, 170; chronology —86, 133; Dark's false dating —75; dated too early —17; Ehrman and—168–69; etymology —16 n.15; in Venerated area —46, 137; in the Nazareth basin —17; mislabeled "Herodian" —16; ritual impurity and —46; Sisters of Nazareth Convent —84 *f*, 105; *terminus ante quem* —75, 84 *f*, 89; *terminus post quem* —88 *f*, 89; typology —90

Kopp, C.: —69, 105, 236, 253, 254, 381; misrepresents oil lamps as "Hellenistic" —36, 142, 268, 289 n. 53; mobile Nazareth hypothesis —174, 378; tombs —61, 379, 390

Kraemer, R.: —449

Kuhnen, H.-P.: and kokh tomb chronology—16, 17, 20, 60, 85, 86, 88–89, 130, 133; ignored by Dark —61, 78, 85, 87, 90

Kung, H.: —400; 404

lamp: See "Oil lamp"

Lapp, P.: —39 n.8, 135

Late Antiquities Research Group (LARG): —79

Levite(s): —451–52; gnosticism and —452; Mark as —451 *f*

Levi: —453, 454

Lidzbarski, M.: argued that Mandeans were "pre-Christian" gnostic disciples of John the Baptist —6, 406

light: —456

Loffreda, S.: —276

Lucian: —405

Lüdemann, G.: author of *The Great Deception and What Jesus Really Said and Did* —9

Luke (Gospel of): 4:16–30 and Nazareth —6, 49, 69–70, 76, 133, 383, 397. See also Index of Scriptural Passages.

lulab: —340–41

MacDonald, D.: —434, 474

Magdala: alleged hometown of "Jesus" —3

Mamluk: —127, 161, 260, 264

Mandaism, Mandeans: —406, 448, 474; and "Natsuraiia" —2; and "Nazorean" 4; possible link with

Ebionites and Nasarenes —6; and "Nazarene" —13

Manichaeism: —447, 474

Mansur, A.: —61, 377–79, 381 *f*, 392

Marcion, Marcionites: —407, 437, 440, 443, 452, 462

Marcus, Marcosians: —451

Marisa: —86, 89

Mark (evangelist): —451 *f*; ; baptized by Peter —451; Levite —451

Mark (Gospel of): —407, 444; 1:9 as interpolation —3; definition of "Nazarene" —4; Nazareth not known by —444; second century date —411, 474. See also Index of Scriptural Passages.

Marqah: —456

Mary: —173–74, 261; alleged house of —388; did not exist —390; mother of John Mark and Jesus —451; welcoming 'face' of the Church —239

Mary's Well: —Chapter 11, 186; 2006 report — 18, 55–56, 67, 161–62, 166, 256 *f*, 270; 2012 book — "pastiche" 271 *f*; channels built in Roman times —251, 256, 259, 282, 308 *f*, 311, Chapter 11; Church Square area —259, 268; coins found at —18, 55, 139, 160 *f*, 259; "cutting" (structural) —259–60, 265; Crusader —265; excavation at —18, 264; Final Report —18; Fountain Square area —259, 264, 308 *f*; "Hellenistic" documentation contrived —265, 293, 312; "Hellenistic" pottery —251, 266 *f*, 274 *f*, 310, 312; Roman pottery

—281 *f*; spring —383, 392
Matthew: —452
Matthew (Gospel of): —2:23 and artificial link between "Nazareth" and Nazarene" —6; 3:13 as parallel to Mk 1:9 —3. See also Index of Scriptural Passages.
Megalê Dunamis: —455, 457
Megiddo: —263; in existence for 3,000 years —34
Meistermann: —390
Mensa Christi: —392, 394
Mesopotamia: —450
messiah: son of David —455; son of Joseph —455
messianic secret: —407
Migdal ha-Emeq: —94
Middle Ages: —404
Midian: —452
mikveh: —114, 378
Milik, J.T.: —85
miracle(s): —472
misdating of evidence: —7, 8, 36
Mishna: —86, 419
misrepresentation of evidence: —29; as Hellenistic —37
moon: —452. See "Selene."
moral turpitude: of Christian tradition —7
Moses: —458; Levite —452, 456
Mount Athos: —451
mystery religions: —401, 405, 409
mysticism (Jewish): —463
Myth of Nazareth, The (book): —1, 7, 10, 130, 251, 268, 286; and 'quack' archeology —22; conclusions of —52–53, 154; pre-publication in chapbooks —19
mythicism: See "Jesus mythicism"
Mythicist Papers: website —28
mythology: —400, 471

Nag Hammadi: —453
Nasarenes: a pre-Christian sect —4, 13 n.11, 14, 459; Ebionites —4; Mandeans —6
nasi: —420, 426
Nathanael: —452
Natsrani (modern Arabic name for Christians): —2
Natsuraiia: Mandaic term for their priests, those skilled in esoteric knowledge —2, 13
Naveh, J.: —323
Nazara: —6, 448, 451, 458
Nazarene(s): 47, 445; cognates —2 (and n.2); definition of term by Markan evangelist —4; in *Gospel of Philip* —13; etymology of —6, 473; first Christians and —13; "Nazareth" not related linguistically —6; Pre-Pauline sect —47
Nazareth: archeology of —4, 154; basin —21, Fig. 1.4, 33, 49; Bronze-Iron Age settlement —33; chronology —396; cliff, alleged of —6; etymology of name —41; false conclusions regarding —6; first settled *c.* 100 CE —41, 46, 53, 57; evidence, earliest —39, 67; hiatus of settlement *c.* 700–*c.* 100 CE —7; history of —33, 43, 46 ; hydrology: —391 *f*; inerrancy of scripture and —14, 45; importance of —400, 403; International Conference —25 *f* ; 'irrelevant' —176; Japhia, not a necropolis of —20; Jesus mythicism and —30–31; Jewish scripture, absence of mention of town's name in —33; Jewish village, as —41, 46; larger settlement theory —263, 395 *f*;

location of —173 f, 396; 'moved' —174 f; Municipality of —161, 251; name —2, 6, 13, 445, 459 n.124; *Natsrath* (semitic form of the toponym) —2, 41; Paul did not know the settlement —409; turn of the era, doubt regarding the settlement's existence at —1, 2 (and n.2), 4 (Salm), 29; valley floor —174–75

Nazareth Village Farm (NVF): —23, 49, 62; pottery —26, 50, 52–53, 63, 90, 157–58; report —18, 24, 157. See Chapter 4.

Nazareth Village Farm Report **(NVFR):** —18; 157, 162, 290; 'Amendment' to —24, 290; 'double dating' and —24; coins and —286; "Hellenistic" evidence —125; "Response" by Salm — Chapter 4, 157, 290

Nazir, Nazirite: —4, 78

Nazorean: —47; cognates —2, 445; followers of Jesus —2; Epiphanius writes about —13 n.12

Negev, A.: —336, 339

netzer **(Heb.):** —3

New Spring ('Ain ed-Jedide): —392, Fig. 8.5

New Testament: Gospels as fiction —14

Nicene Creed: —172

Nielsen, D.: —452

Nippon (bishop): —383

Notsri **(Hebrew term for Christians):** —2

Oan/Oannês: —450–51

Occam's razor: —373

oil lamp(s): 39; alleged "Hellenistic" at Nazareth —6, 7, 16, 36–38; bow spouted (mislabeled "Herodian") —17, 39, 133 f, 168; as earliest Nazareth evidence in first cent. CE–39, 46, 168; ignored —153–54; nozzle misdated as "Hellenistic" —38; ornamentation, absence of —41; six "Richmond" lamps misdated as "Hellenistic"—36. See also "Herodian"

Oniad(s): —428

Oren, E.: —336, 338, 342, 352, 360 f

Origen: —20, 431, 435, 436, 461

Orpheus, Orphism: —466

Ory, Georges: —146, 150, 314

Ory, J.: —318, 321

Oshri, A.: —245, 475

ossuary: —87, 90–91

Ottoman: —161, 260

Painter, J.: —413, 429, 434, 444

Palestine Exploration Quarterly **(PEQ):** rejects article by Salm —120

palm leaf (manuscript): —421, 452, 454

Panarion **(by Epiphanius of Salamis):** on Nasarene sect —4; on Nazorean sect 13 n.12

Pandera (Pantera): —426

Passover: —447

Paul: —171–72, 408, 430, 434, 461; epistles —409 f; knew 'Christ' —150; knew spiritual Jesus —408 f, 455; "ringleader" of Nazorean sect —4; 'Spouter of Lies' —10. See "*kerygma*".

Pentateuch: —459

Perachiah, Joshua ben: —420, 462

perfect, perfection: —453

Persian Period: lack of settlement in Nazareth basin —34, 281

Peter (apostle): —426, 430, 432,

438–40; ; baptizes Mark —450; hypostasis —457

Peter, Gospel of: —411

Peter the Deacon: —393

Pfann, C.: —26

Pfann, S.: —29, 49, 140, 141, 154, 158, 290; co-author of NVF report —24, 26, 48, 162; espouses 1st cent. BCE refounding of Nazareth —26; Mary's Well "Hellenistic" coin claim —18, 125 n. 4, 286 *f*, 293–94; Nazareth International Conference —26; NVF pottery —52 n.8

Pharisee(s): —45, 420, 457

Philip, Gospel of: defines "Nazarene" —13, 451

Philippians: —407

"pious fraud": — 138

piyyut(im): —317

plastering: —115; IMC—207, 210

Pliny: —152

"polis" (Gk.): —76

Pope Benedict XVI: —238

Pope Francis: —238 *f*

pottery: NVF —50, 51*f*, 156–57, 165; in *kokhim* tombs —66; IMC —126, 234 *f* ; Kfar Hananya —81–82; north of Nazareth (Dark) —396 *f*; Sikhnin —82; Sisters of Nazareth Convent —74, 80 *f*

Price, Robert M.: —146, 147, 407, 408, 416, 417, 434, 437 *f*, 448 *f*, 474; author of *The Incredible Shrinking Son of Man* —10, 26

priests: —316; priestly courses —328; Samaritan —456

"Primary Gnosticism": —422, 424, 446, 453, 463, 466

Protestant scholarship: —36

Protevangelium of James: —123, 245 *f*, 261 , 393

Pseudo-Clementines: —442, 444, 446, 453, 461

Ptolemy II "Philadelphus": —421

puppet: —406

'quack' archeology: —7, 17, 237

Qumran: —89, 455, 461 *f*, 474

Rabin, C.: —328

Rabinowitz, L. M.: —320, 324

Rajak, T.: —434, 435

rape of grapes: see 'viniculture'

Rapuano, Y.: 57–58, 63, 90, 140, 165, 288; co-author of NVF report—48, 49–50, 157, 164; guilty of double-attributions of pottery —53–54, 63–64, 157

realized eschatology: —410, 431

Rechabite(s): —447

redeemed redeemer: —412

redeemer: —465

'refuge pit': —127–28, 190

Regenstein Library (Univ. of Chicago): —80

Renan, E.: —314

"Reply to Salm": —164

Research Centre for Late Antique and Byzantine Studies (University of Reading): published Ken Dark's reports —27

resurrection: —409, 431

revelation: —468

Richmond, E. T.: misrepresentation of oil lamps as Hellenistic —7–8, 16, 36, 140, 142, 268

Rivkin, E.:—451

Roberts, D.: —161

Robertson, J.: —416–17

"rolling stone": 85, 88, 92 *f*

Roman Catholic Church: censorship —401; pedophile scandal —121–22, 128, 399; power —399

Roman legions: —263

Sadducee(s): —420, 427, 428, 455, 457

Saint Gabriel, Church of: —161

Saint Joseph, Church of: —32, 379, 381, 392

Salm René: —69, 474; and archeology of Nazareth —15; and *CrossTalk* Internet forum 1–8; and modern Hebrew —17; and Society of Biblical Literature —26; as a Jesus mythicist —8–9, 12–13; first publicly argues the non-existence of Nazareth —4; Response to the NVFR —64; spurns credentials —19, 147

Salome Alexandra (Queen): —420, 462

Samaria: —455

Samaritan(s): —470, 474

Sammer, J.: —3

Samaritan(s): —434, 459, 460

Sanhedrin: —420, 444

Santa Claus: —68

Schlier, H.: —**441**

Schmithals, W.: —424, 441

Schoeps, H.: —444

scholarly opposition to 'no-Nazareth' thesis: —7

scholarship (modern biblical): —419, 434

Schonfield, H.: —426

Schürer, E.: —434

Schwabe, M.: —321–23, 325, 374

Schweitzer, A.: —146

Sdot Yam (Kibbutz): —322–23, 329, 331

Second Apocalypse of James: —429, 444

Second Jewish Revolt: —128, 171, 227, 235, 315, 382

Secret Mark: —430–31

Selene: —427. See "moon."

"Self-Glorification Hymn": —465

Sepphoris: —86, 87, 227, 262, 395 *f*

Senès, H.: box of pottery—81–84, 112

Sepher Toldoth Yeshu: 426

Septuagint: —150

Seth: —470

"settlement shift": Dark's thesis for Nazareth —76

Shahrastani: —457, 458

Shama, E.: "Roman bathhouse" —166 *f*, 260 *f*

Shechem: —34, 326–27, 333, 337, 346, 351, 374

Shetach, Simon ben: —420, 425 *f*, 455, 457, 462

silo(s): Sisters of Nazareth convent —105, 113; triple silo—see IMC; Venerated Area —137

Simms, T. (*CrossTalk* participant): —3

Simon Magus: —315, 434, 440, 455–47, 463, 470; invention —471; "Standing One" —446–47, 453; disciple of John the Baptist —453

sindon (linen cloth): —431

Sisters of Nazareth Convent: —23, 25, 27, 59, 379, Chp. 6; agricultural use —114 *f*; alleged dwelling ("Structure 1") —107 *f*; "Chambre Obscure" —109; cistern(s) — 104, 112; "courtyard" —110–11; "cutting" into —99; false application of Judean chronology —89 *f*, 117; filtration basins —115; "Model Courtyard House" —110, 112, 117; "Phase 1–Phase 2" —97 *f*, 111; roof (alleged) — 113, 115; silo —105, 113; squint —113; Tomb 2 —105; vegetable matter —101; Wall 1 —109, 112–13; Wall 2 —109–10

slope: Venerated Area, steepness of —43, 49, 11, 136

Smith, R.: —85

Society for the Reclamation of Antiquities (SRA): —318

Society of Biblical Literature: —26

Songs of the Sabbath Sacrifice: —463

Southern Baptist Theological Seminary (SBTS, Louisville): —327, 332, 346–48, 354

Southwestern Baptist Theological Seminary (Fort Worth): —326, 332

"stand" (*'amad*): —446–47, 453 *f* ; "baptize" —447, 454, 457

star: —458, 469

Stephen: —444

stolé (**robe**): —431

Stone vessels: at Nazareth —41, 156, 171, 235

Strange, James: —6, 7, 16, 69, 116, 236, 395

stratigraphy: —252, 291

Stylites, St. Simon: —426

Suetonius: —153

Sukenik, E.L.: —318, 320–22, 328, 336

survey(s): NVF —51

Sussman, V.: 79, 135, 283

Synagogue: Caesarea —317, 331, 332, 341, 356; Nazareth —6, 397 *f*; no Early Roman remains found —70

Syon, D.: —87

Syria: —426

Tabor, J.: —124

Tacitus: —153

Taheb: —455, 456, 458

Talmon fragment: See "Cesarea excavations"

Talmon, S.: — 328

Talmud: —419

Taylor, J.: —24, 41 n.10, 116, 383 n.17, 388 n.25, 458 n.119

teacher: Dositheus —457; Ebion —459. Cf. *"ilfan."*

Teacher of Righteousness: 10, 428, 434, 461 *f*, 469

temple (Jerusalem): —428

terminology: used tendentiously to backdate material evidence —17. See also "Herodian."

terrace farming: 50, 59, 136

Tertullian: —438–39

Thanksgiving Hymns: —463, 465, 467

Thomas, Gospel of: —2, 429, 446; parallels with the synoptic gospels —2 (and n.2)

Three Steles of Seth: —453

Tiberias: —397

tomb(s): —394, Fig. 8.5; Ehrman's view —168–69; impurity and— 42, 173; NVF —49; map of —49 n.2; Nazareth basin —49; Church of the Annunciation —28–29, 42–43, 61, 65, 102, 104, 137, 173 *f*, 386 *f*; Jewish prohibition —386; numerous —378; K22 —385; o/p —390; T27 —388, 390; T29 —386 *f*, 390; T77 —385; under former habitations (Dark) —59, 101–02. See *kokh* tomb

Torrey, C.: —455

tourism: —403

transformation: —405–06, 410

trench: stratigraphic dug by Bagatti —35

triple silo: See "IMC excavation"

Trunk Road: —397

Tuccinardi, E.: —315, 333

tunnels: allegedly under Bishop's Residence —384–85

University of Chicago: —27

University of Oregon: library of —15

University of Reading (U.K.): published Ken Dark's writings —27

University of the Holy Land: —24, 49, 158

Valentinus: —461

Vardaman, J.: 315, 322, 326 *f*, 336; absences from Caesarea excavation —339; character — 316, 327–28, 342, 346–47, 367, 373; expulsion from excavation —339, 350 *f*, 360; field notebook —336 *f* , 343–44, 360; fired by SBTS —351; forgery of the Caesarea inscription —28, 366–67; microletters —342; Talmon fragment —332. See Chapter 12.

Vegetarianism: —458, 459

Venus: —459

Venerated Area: 136; history and description of —31–32; primary venue of Catholic excavations —32; stratigraphic trench of —35; tombs in —173; used for agriculture and burial —43

Viaud, P.: —61, 69, 378, 381

viniculture: holding area: 210; rape of grapes: 209, 210, 231; Church of the Annunciation —389;

treading area, see "IMC—Area 4"; wine cellar, see IMC—features (j) and (z)

Vlaminck, B.: —378

Voss, R.: co-author of NVF report—48, 49, 162

Walker, W.: —439

water: gnosis and —405, 448, 454; See "Nazareth: hydrology"

Weeden, T.: —409

Wegman, A.: —322–23, 325, 329, 331, 374

Wells, George: —434

White Mosque: —248, 258

wine making (see "viniculture")

Wells, G..: British author of *The Jesus Myth* —9, 146

"Where Jesus Never Walked" (article by F. Zindler): —2

Wikipedia:—240

Wise, M.: —462

Wright, G. E.: —327, 332, 334, 352; letter concerning Vardaman —346–47, 372

www.nazarethmyth.info: Salm's website —19, 24–25

Yadin Y.: —328–29

Yemen: —317

Yeshu ha-Notsri: —419 *f*, 428, 443, 445, 457, 462; Alexandria: —460; humanist —472; identified with James the Just —434; parallels with Dositheus —457

Zadokite(s): —428, 455, 459

Zindler, Ann: 21, 251

Zindler, Frank: —30, 69, 252, 434–35, 438, 458, 474–75; *American Atheist* magazine —24; author of *The Jesus the Jews Never Knew* —10; author of "Where Jesus Never Walked" (article) —20;

Bethlehem, fictive existence of —245 n.1; John the Baptist —449; *The Myth of Nazareth* —20, 21, 251; Nazareth, fictive existence of —2 (and n.2); Yeshu ha-Notsri —419 *f. Editor's Notes:* —69–70, 152–53, 166–67.

Index of Ancient Passages

Jewish sources:
Ex 2:1–2 —452
Num 23:15, 19, 23, 24 —423
  24:17 —455, 458
Deut 18:15—458
  18:18 —458, 459
Josh 19:12 —33
Judg 17–18: —452
Hos 11.1 —420
1 Chr 24 —328
1 Enoch 6:6 —405
IV Esdras 12:25, 13:51 —450

Dead Sea Scrolls:
1QHab, col. XII—468
4QHab frg. 7—467
4Q416, frgs. 1, 4:3—467
4QMMT —428
Dam. Doc. (4Q 269:2–4)—470

Josephus:
Antiquities
  13:14.2 —420
  18:109 *ff* —449
  20.200–03 —434
Wars
  1.5.3 —462

Mishna:
  Bava Bathra 2:9 —42, 137
  Jalqut Shimoni 766 —422–23

Pal. Talmud:
  Nazir 54b —426
  Taanith 65b —422

Bab. Talmud:
  Sanh. 107b —420–21

New Testament:
Gospel of Matthew
  1:18–25 —388
  1:22 —429
  2:15, 17 —429
  2:13-15 —420
  2:23 —6
  3:10 —450
  3:12 —448
  3:13 —3
  4:13 —448
  10:39 —423
  13:24–30 —442
  22:1 *f* —41
  22:11 *f* —431
  25:1 *f* —431
  27:52 —474

Gospel of Mark
  1:2 —429
  1:9 —3
  1:10 —418
  1:23 —429
  1:24 —4, 13
  6:1 *ff* — 6 n.5
  8:37 —423
  9:2–8 —405
  13:6, 22 —409
  14:52 —431
  15:15 —460
  15:33 —474
  15:46 —431
  16:5 —431

Gospel of Luke
  1:35 —388
  3:1–2 —449, 471
  3:4, 16 —447
  3:7–14 —448

3:15 —350
4:16–30 and Nazareth —6, 49, 69–70, 76, 133, 383, 397, 448
9:60 —423
12:35 *f* —431
17:33 —423

Gospel of John
1:4–5 —423
3:26 —451
6:46 —417
10:7 —417, 460
12:25 —423
14:6 —417, 430, 460
20:29 —408

Acts of the Apostles
7:51 —444
12:12, 25 —451
15:37 —451
18:24–28 —450
24:5 —2, 47

Romans
1:1–4 —414
8:1–4 —414
8:28–29 —407
9:3–5 —415

1 Corinthians
1:18–25: —171–72
12:27 —409
15:3–8 —408, 437
15:7 —442
15:12, 15:51*f* —409

2 Corinthians
10:8 —409

Galatians
1:11 —409
1:14 —427
1:15–24 —438
1:19 —434, 442
2:1–10 —439

2:9 —442
2:10 —459
2:11–14 —440
2:12 —442–43
4:4–5 —415

Ephesians
1:22–23
2:13–16 —415
4:12 —409

Philippians
2:5–8 —415
2:6–11 —407
2:7 —408
3:5 —427
3:12 *f* —409, 416

Colossians
1:18 —409
1:21–22 —415
1:24, 27 —409
2:9 —408
2:20 —410
3:1—410
3:4 —409

1 Thessalonians
4:2 —409

2 Thessalonians
2:10 —409

Hebrews
2:9 —413
2:14–15 —413
4:14–15 —412
5:1 —414
5:5 —414
5:7 —413
5:7–9 —412
5:9 —414
5:10 —412
6:6 —412
6:20 —417

7:14 —412
7:24 —414
8:1, 2 —412
9:12, 14, 15 —412, 413
10:12 —413
10:19–20 —413
12:2 —413
13:12 —413
13:20 —413

1 Timothy
3:16 —415

1 Peter
2:23–24 —415
3:18 —416
4:1–2 —416

Revelation
6:11; 7:13; 22:14 —431

Christian apocrypha:

Acts of Andrew
2.293:25–27

Acts of Barnabas
Chp. 5 —450

Acts of Mark: —451 *f*
4:7 —451

First Apocalypse of James:
24.19–24 —413
27.1–10 —413

Second Apocalypse of James
49.5–16 —433
55.24–25 —433
56.2–6 —433

Gospel of the Hebrews: —431, 450

Gospel of Philip
56.12 —448
62.8: —13, 448
66.14 —448

Gospel of Thomas
1, 11, 52, 59 —423
12 —429, 456

Pseudo-Clementines
Hom II.24—470

Church Fathers:

Hegesippus:
Recognitions 1.68.3–1.70.8 —444

Origen:
Commentary on Matthew 17
—436

Eusebius:
Hist. Eccl. II.23 —436

Epiphanius:
Anacephalaeosis —459
Panarion 29.3.3 —420
30.18.7 —459

Samaritan sources:
Asatir II.3—470

Pagan sources:

Lucian, *De Dea Syria* 46–47—402